D1127283

The International
Banking Handbook

The International Banking Handbook

Edited by

WILLIAM H. BAUGHN
Dean, Graduate School of Business Administration
University of Colorado
Boulder, Colorado

and

DONALD R. MANDICH
Chairman
Comerica, Incorporated
Detroit, Michigan

DOW JONES-IRWIN
Homewood, Illinois   60430

ISBN 0-87094-303-0

Library of Congress Catalog Card No. 82–73620

Printed in the United States of America

2 3 4 5 6 7 8 9 0 K 0 9 8 7 6

Preface

During the last several decades, international banking has undergone continuous and substantive change. Until 1960 most of the international banking functions in the United States were performed by relatively few money center banks, and a large part of that business was carried on through correspondent bank relationships abroad. The rapid expansion of U.S. corporations into the multinational arena and the corresponding growth in the market for international financial services further impacted the international banking activities of U.S. banks. Beginning in the mid-1960s there was a stampede by money center, as well as regional, banks to establish a presence abroad. And although all of those moves were not productive, the nature of the international banking scene and the manner in which U.S. banks participated were drastically altered.

While American banks were rapidly expanding internationally, they were in fact participating in a much larger worldwide movement in which world-class banks evolved in many of the world's money centers. Head-on competition resulted in major American banks establishing a presence in a number of the major financial centers of the world. Larger banks of other nations competed for a significant share of the banking business of American multinational corporations. In addition, foreign banks followed their customers into U.S. domestic markets and today are actively engaged in expanding their banking business into the retail markets of this country.

The U.S. commercial banking system used a wide variety of approaches to world markets and developed variations in the way it delivers international banking services. Intense competition also led to a continuing pattern of change in the organizational patterns of banks. Hence, it is difficult to generalize on the many aspects of the international banking business.

This first publication of an international banking handbook demonstrates that the series of events which created a radically new international banking market have crystallized and matured to the point where the components can be reasonably described. Since the prepara-

v

tion of the bulk of the material within this text, prolonged worldwide recession and high oil prices have placed heavy strains on the capacity of a number of countries to service their external indebtedness. Although this does not alter the techniques and principles involved in international banking, it suggests that the industry will have some aspects that will differ from the patterns of the last few decades.

We have attempted to organize the book around the major issues and functions involved in international banking. The authors of the various chapters have been selected because of their extensive personal experiences in their subject areas and the perspectives that each can offer on the given topic. We are grateful to all of the authors for taking time from very demanding schedules to make their contributions to this handbook.

William H. Baughn
Donald R. Mandich

Contributing Authors

Lester D. Anderson, Jr. Vice President, Chemical Bank, New York, New York.

H. G. Ashton Director, J. Henry Schroder Wagg & Co. Limited, London, England.

Paul H. Austin Senior Vice President, Citibank, N.A., New York, New York.

Leonard A. Back Vice President, Citibank, N.A., New York, New York.

Robert R. Bench Deputy Comptroller of the Currency for International Banking, Washington, D.C.

Milton E. Berglund, Jr. Vice President, Mellon Bank, N.A., Pittsburgh, Pennsylvania.

David E. Bodner President, Baer American Bank Corporation, New York, New York.

John Patrick Casey Partner, Peat, Marwick, Mitchell & Company, New York, New York.

John M. Chalk Vice President, Wachovia Bank and Trust Company, N.A., Winston-Salem, North Carolina.

Joseph A. Colleran Vice President, Irving Trust Company, New York, New York.

Horst Duseberg Executive Vice President, European American Bank, New York, New York.

Jose D. Epstein Manager, Plans and Programs Department, Inter-American Development Bank, Washington, D.C.

Stephen C. Eyre Senior Vice President–Secretary, Citibank, N.A., New York, New York.

James R. Greene President, American Express International Banking Corporation, New York, New York.

John C. Haley Executive Vice President, The Chase Manhattan Bank, N.A., New York, New York.

William F. Hamlet Vice President, Wachovia Bank and Trust Company, N.A., Winston-Salem, North Carolina.

Aidan H. F. Harland Darien Consulting Group, Darien, Connecticut.

C. Keefe Hurley, Jr. Vice President and General Counsel, Shawmut Corporation, Boston, Massachusetts.

Clark H. Hutton Simpson, Thacher & Bartlett, New York, New York.

Daniel T. Jacobsen Chief Auditor, Citibank, N.A., New York, New York.

Earl I. Johnson   Assistant Vice President, Harris Trust and Savings Bank, Chicago, Illinois.

James L. Kammert   Executive Vice President, Equibank, Pittsburgh, Pennsylvania.

Robert Keenan   President, Foreign Credit Insurance Association, New York, New York.

William J. Korsvik   Senior Vice President (Retired), The First National Bank of Chicago, Chicago, Illinois.

Christopher M. Korth   Associate Professor of International Business, University of South Carolina, Columbia, South Carolina.

Leonard A. Lipson   Senior Manager, Peat, Marwick, Mitchell & Company, New York, New York.

Donald R. Mandich   Chairman, Comerica, Incorporated, Detroit, Michigan.

Donald R. Marsh   Senior Vice President, Rainier National Bank, Seattle, Washington.

Arthur H. Meehan   Executive Vice President, Bank of New England, N.A. Boston, Massachusetts.

Alfred F. Miossi   Executive Vice President, Continental Illinois National Bank and Trust Company, Chicago, Illinois.

Phillip G. Moon   Senior Vice President, National Bank of Detroit, Detroit, Michigan.

Albert F. Naveja   Vice President, Harris Trust and Savings Bank, Chicago, Illinois.

Frank W. Nee   Senior Executive Vice President, Private Export Funding Corporation, New York, New York.

M. C. Nelson   Partner, Ernst and Whinney, Cleveland, Ohio.

Denis Newman   Managing Director, The First Boston Corporation, New York, New York.

A. D. Orsich   General Manager, Treasury Division, Standard Chartered Bank Limited, London, England.

Karl M. Parrish   Chairman, Manufacturers Hanover Leasing Corporation, New York, New York.

David L. Pflug, Jr.   Vice President and Regional Manager, Manufacturers Hanover Corporation, New York, New York.

Don A. Resler   Vice President, First National Bank of Chicago, Chicago, Illinois.

David H. Riley   Joint Managing Director, Tullett and Riley International Limited, London, England.

David Rockefeller   Chairman (Retired), The Chase Manhattan Bank, N.A., New York, New York.

Louis G. Schirano   Vice President, Bankers Trust Company, New York, New York.

Barnard Seligman   Lubin Graduate School of Business, Pace University, New York, New York.

James B. Sommers   Executive Vice President, North Carolina National Bank, Charlotte, North Carolina.

E. C. Stone   Executive Vice President, First American Bank, N.A., Nashville, Tennessee.

Stewart E. Sutin Vice President, The First National Bank of Boston, Boston, Massachusetts.

Keigo Tatsumi Deputy President, The Sanwa Bank Limited, Tokyo, Japan.

Harry Taylor President, Manufacturers Hanover Corporation, New York, New York.

Turhan Tirana General Manager, Pittsburgh International Bank, Pittsburgh, Pennsylvania.

Sheila Trifari Senior Vice President and General Manager, International Division, Southeast Bank, N.A., Miami, Florida.

Charles F. Turner Senior Vice President, Comerica Bank, Detroit, Michigan.

J. Antonio Villamil Vice President and Chief International Economist, Southeast Bank, N.A., Miami, Florida.

Johann Wendt Vice President, Comerica Bank, Detroit, Michigan.

Allen S. Whiting Professor of Political Science, University of Arizona, Tucson, Arizona.

Contents

SECTION 1
The International Financial System

1. **International Financial Markets**   3
   Christopher M. Korth

   The Major Markets: *The London Markets. The U.S. Markets. Other Major Financial Markets.* The Structure and Size of International Financial Markets: *The Foreign Sector of Domestic Markets. The Euromarkets. The Eurobond Market. Other Euromarkets.*

2. **The Eurocurrency Market**   16
   Christopher M. Korth

   The Essence of Eurocurrencies: *Time Deposits. Eurocurrency. Informal Markets. Eurobanks. Transfer of Eurocurrencies.* Eurocurrency Deposits: *The Size of the Euromarkets. Depositors.* Attractions of Eurocurrency Markets: *Freedom from Controls. Attractions to Borrowers. Attractions to Banks.* Euro-Investments: *The Currency of Investment. Types of Investments. Lending Rates. Destruction of Eurocurrencies.*

3. **The Development of International Banking by the United States**   35
   John C. Haley and Barnard Seligman

   A Brief History of International Banking. Reasons for Growth. Forms of International Banking. The Impact of U.S. International Banking.

4. **The Role of Foreign Banks in International Banking**   47
   Johann Wendt

   Brazil. Canada. COMECON Countries. Germany. Hong Kong. Italy. Japan. Korea. Kuwait. Mexico. Singapore. Spain. Switzerland. United Kingdom. Venezuela.

SECTION 2
International Credits

5. **The Overall Role of the International Banker and Key Considerations in Lending**   73
   Harry Taylor and David L. Pflug, Jr.

   Introduction. International Banking Today. Key Considerations in Lending: *The Borrower. Cross-National Risk. Purpose. Foreign Currency Lending. Other Considerations.*

6. **Country Risk Analysis—Noneconomic Factors**   85
   Allen S. Whiting

   Introduction: Internal Factors: *The Political System. National Cohesion. Political Geography. Traditional Values. External Threat and Leadership Ability.* External Factors: *Political Geography. Traditional Relations.* Internal-External Interaction.

7. **Country Risk Analysis—Economic Considerations**   102
   Sheila Trifari and J. Antonio Villamil

   The Basic Premises of Economic Risk Analysis: An Offshore Lender's Perspective. Analyzing Key Economic Risk Factors: *Adequacy of the Resource Base. Quality and Effectiveness of the Economic and Financial Management Process. Indicators of External Financial Position.*

8. **Bank-to-Bank Lending**   117
   Phillip G. Moon

   Assessing and Managing Risks: *Country Analysis. Knowledge of a Country's Banking System. Analyzing Individual Banks. Financial Statements. Marketplace Reputation. Officer Visits.* Credit Facilities. Risks and Rewards.

9. **Government Borrowing in the International Financial Markets**   129
   James R. Greene

   Introduction. Dimensions of Euromarket Borrowing. Sovereign Lending: *Purposes of Government Borrowing. Recent Trends with Particular Reference to U.S. Banks.* Risks in Lending to Governments: *Country Risk. Differentiating between Government Borrowers. Direct Political Considerations.* Credit Availability: *Creditworthiness Indicators. Market Conditions.* The Default Record: *Historical Experience. Recent Experience. Sovereign Immunity. Protection. Problems of Successful Protection.*

10. **Project Financing**   161
    Louis G. Schirano

    Defining Project Financing. The Nature of a Project. Evaluation of the Project. Risk Analysis and Financing. The Role of the Project Advisor.

11. **International Leasing**   173
    Karl M. Parrish

    International Leasing. Bank-Affiliated Leasing Companies. Considerations in Establishing a Foreign Operations Network. International Leasing-Product Profile. Future Prospects.

12. **Tanker and Shipping Loans**   183
    Lester D. Anderson, Jr.

    Introduction: *Definition of Breadth. Specialization.* The Tanker Market: *Operations. Economics. Employment.* The Analysis: *Introduction. The "3 X 5 Card." Company Analysis. Project Analysis. Summary and Recommendation.* Structuring the Loan: *The Outline of Terms.* Documentation. Appendix I. Appendix II.

13. **Security Underwriting and Syndicated Loans**   204
    Denis Newman

    The International Bond Market. Foreign Bond Markets: *The Foreign Dollar (Yankee) Bond Market.* Syndicated Eurocurrency Credits.

14. **Foreign Currency Loans and Eurocurrency Markets**   223
    Horst Duseberg

    Introduction. Interest-Rate Structure of the Eurocurrency Market. Funding a Foreign Currency Loan. Uses of the Eurocurrency Market. Eurocurrency Loan Agreement. Prepayment of Foreign Currency Loans. Long-Term Loans. Operations. Appendix.

SECTION 3
International Banking Services

15. **Commercial Letters of Credit**   239
    Joseph A. Colleran

    Functions of Letters of Credit. Import Letters of Credit. Export Letters of Credit. Amendments. Discrepancies in Documents. Foreign Currency Letters of Credit.

16. **Bankers' Acceptances**   252
    John M. Chalk and William F. Hamlet

    Eligibility. Import and Export Transactions. Transactions Involving Goods in Transit. Transactions Involving Goods in Storage. Transactions for Dollar Exchange. Elements of Cost for the Borrower. Advantages/Disadvantages for the Borrower. Acceptances Provide Opportunity for Banks. Benefits to Banks. Bank Organization and Marketing. Conclusion: *Transaction.*

17. International Collections   **270**
Leonard A. Back

Exporters' Options for Payment: *Cash Advance Terms. Letter-of-Credit Terms. Open Account Terms. Collection Terms.* Collection Drafts: *Sight or Usance Drafts. Understanding Draft Terms. Checks for Collection. Clean and Documentary Drafts.* Collection Instructions for the Bank: *In Case of Dishonor. Remittance of Proceeds. Who Pays Bank Fee. Protest Instructions. Hold for Arrival of Merchandise. Provisional Deposit. Discount or Interest. In Case of Need. Legal Action. Principal/Agent Relationship.* Shipping Documents: *Commercial Invoice. Bill of Lading. Insurance Certificate or Policy. Consular Invoice or Customs Invoice. Inspection Certificate.* Collection Process for Exporters: *Agree on Terms. Effect Shipment. Dispatch Collection to the Bank. Receive Advices/Give Instructions. Receive Payment.* Drafts for Negotiation or Purchase: *Uniform Rules for Collections. Collections for Importers. Appendix.*

18. Funds Transfer and Corporate Cash Management   **290**
Don A. Resler

Introduction. Cross-Border Transfers. Corporate Cash Management Considerations.

19. Merchant Banking   **299**
H. G. Ashton

Introduction. Commercial Banking. Corporate Finance Services: *New Issues. Mergers and Acquisitions. General Financial Advice.* Investment Management. Project Finance: *Commercial Project Finance. Export Credit. Advisory Work.* Other Services: *Currency Management.* The Future.

SECTION 4
Foreign Exchange

20. A General Description of Foreign Exchange Transactions and Functions   **319**
Arthur H. Meehan

Why Foreign Exchange? What Is Foreign Exchange? Foreign Exchange as Money. Foreign Exchange as a Commodity: *The Cash Transaction. The Commodity Transaction. The Import-Export Transaction. The Corporate Transaction. The Financial Transaction. The Professional Arbitrage Transaction. The Speculative Transaction.*

21. The Major Foreign Exchange Markets   **331**
David E. Bodner

Market Participants. Mechanics of Foreign Exchange Trading. Currencies Traded. The Where and When of Foreign Exchange Markets. The Operation of the Major Markets.

22. Exchange of Minor Currencies and Special Exchange Systems   348
Earl I. Johnson

Introduction. Characteristics of Minor Currency Markets. Exchange
Rate Arrangements and Policies. Special Drawing Right (SDR). Eu-
ropean Secondary Currencies: *Scandinavian Currencies. Spanish
Peseta. Greek Drachma. Portuguese Escudo. Austrian Schilling.
Irish Pound.* Mideast and African Currencies: *Saudi Arabian Riyal.
Kuwaiti Dinar. South African Rand.* Asian Currencies: *Hong Kong
Dollar. Singapore Dollar. Australian Dollar. New Zealand Dollar.
Malaysian Ringgit. Indian Rupee.* Latin American Currencies: *Mex-
ican Peso. Brazilian Cruzeiro. Argentine Peso. Venezuela Bolivar.*

23. Foreign Exchange and International Money Broking   362
David H. Riley

A Backward Glance. How Do Brokers Operate in the Foreign Ex-
change and International Currency Deposit Markets? How Does
the Bank Dealer Operate? Dealer-Broker Interaction. Settlement
Procedures for Errors. Control and Supervision in London. The
Broker as an Individual. Composition of a Broker's Office: *London.
Overseas. Continental Brokers.* Introducing New Banks to the Inter-
national Market. Long-Term Prospects for Brokers. Market Custom,
Practice, and Ethics. Possibilities for the Future: *Direct Dealing.
Central Clearing Houses. Reuters Proposed System.*

24. Managing the Exchange Risk   373
Donald R. Mandich

Policies. Procedures and Controls. Special Problems.

25. Multicurrency Reserve Assets   379
A. D. Orsich

Introduction: The Evolution of Currency Baskets. Special Drawing
Rights. A European Counterpart: The ECU. The Performance of
the SDR and the ECU. Marketability. The Mechanics of Multicurrency Business. Other Currency Baskets.

SECTION 5
Special Institutions and Programs

26. The Export-Import Bank of the United States   393
Turhan Tirana

Introduction. Exposure. History. Congressional and Public Relations. Competition. Eximbank Programs: *Direct Credits. Supplier
Credits. Medium-Term Guarantees. Discount Loans. The Future.*

27. **Foreign Credit Insurance Association**   410
     Robert Keenan

     FCIA—History and Organization. Benefits of FCIA Coverage: *Insurance Protection. Financing Assets. Marketing Tool. Benefits to Commercial Banks.* Coverage: *Products Covered and Terms Extended.* Overview of Policies. Multibuyer Policies: *The Master Policy. Short-Term Comprehensive. Buyer Credits. Supplier Credits. Agricultural Commodities Program. Procedure for Approval of Limits. Prequalified Foreign Banks. Premium. Small Business Policy. The Services Policy.* Single Buyer Policies: *Medium-Term Single Sales (MTS). Medium-Term Repetitive (MTR). Short-Term-Medium-Term Combination Policy (MSC).* Political Only Policies. Special Coverages: *Nonacceptance. Preshipment Coverage. Consignment Coverage. Assignments.* Claims.

28. **Private Export Funding Corporation**   428
     Frank W. Nee

     Introduction and Summary. Origin and Relationship with Eximbank. Lending Operations: *General Characteristics. PEFCO's Fixed Interest Rate. Deferred Pricing. Commitment Fee. When and How to Approach PEFCO for an Offer. Loan Agreements and Other Documents. Disbursement Procedures.* PEFCO's Loan Purchase Program (LPP). How PEFCO Funds Itself. DISCs And PEFCO's Debt Obligations.

29. **Overseas Private Investment Corporation**   436
     James L. Kammert

     Purpose and Background. Operations and Resources. Organization and Policies. Basic Insurance Definitions. Basic Insurance Coverage. Basic and Special Program Costs. Special Insurance Coverages. Insurance Application Procedure. Finance Programs. Contacting OPIC. Future Trends.

30. **The World Bank Group**   462
     James L. Kammert

     Introduction. History and Purpose. Organization. Operating Method. International Relations and Coordination. Co-Financing Program. Research and Information Services. Treasury Functions and Future Trends.

31. **International Finance Corporation**   486
     James L. Kammert

     Introduction. Financial Resources and Operational Scope. Organization, Management, and Staff. Investment Policies. IFC's Catalytic Role. Technical Assistance and Financial Services. Future Trends. Contacting IFC.

32.   Inter-American Development Bank   503
      Jose D. Epstein

      Introduction. Origins: *A Multipurpose Approach. A Bank for Inter-
      American Development.* Membership, Purpose, and Organization:
      *Membership. Purpose and Functions. Levels of Authority. Institu-
      tional Features. Development Role. Latin America's Economic Inte-
      gration.* Resources: *The Capital Resources. The Fund for Special
      Operations. Other Funds. Mobilization of Other Resources. Two-
      Way Benefits.* The Bank's Lending: *Project Supervision. Procure-
      ment. Achievements.* Outlook for the 1980s.

33.   Regional Development Agencies   522
      Keigo Tatsumi

      Asian Development Bank—ADB Manila, The Philippines: *History.
      Membership. Sources of Funds. Activities. Record of Accomplish-
      ments.* African Development Bank—AfDB Abidjan, Ivory Coast:
      *History. Membership. Sources of Funds. Activities. Record of Accom-
      plishments.* African Development Fund—AfDF Abidjan, Ivory
      Coast: *History. Membership. Sources of Funds. Activities. Record
      of Accomplishments.* European Investment Bank—EIB Luxem-
      bourg: *History. Membership. Sources of Funds. Activities. Record
      of Accomplishments.* European Development Fund—EDF Brus-
      sels, Belgium: *History. Membership. Sources of Funds. Activities.*
      Islamic Development Bank—Jedda, Saudi Arabia: *History. Member-
      ship. Sources of Funds. Activities. Record of Accomplishments.* Pri-
      vate Investment Company for Asia (PICA) S. A. Registered Head
      Office—Panama City, Panama Operating Headquarters: Singapore:
      *History. Shareholders. Sources of Funds. Activities. Record of Ac-
      complishments.* Export-Import Bank of Japan—Tokyo, Japan: *His-
      tory. Sources of Funds. Activities. Record of Accomplishments.* Ex-
      port Development Corporation—EDC Ottawa, Canada: *History.
      Sources of Funds. Activities. Record of Accomplishments.* Export
      Credits Guarantee Department—ECGD London, United Kingdom:
      History. Sources of Funds. Activities. Record of Accomplishment.

SECTION 6
Approaches to World Financial Markets

34.   Correspondent Banking   547
      Albert F. Naveja

      Reimbursement Banks. Credit Related Correspondent Relation-
      ships: *Letters of Credit. Acceptances. Money Market Credits. Special-
      Purpose Letters of Credit.* Noncredit Services: *Payments. Clearings.
      Collection. Foreign Exchange Services. Documentation of the Cor-
      respondent Relationship.* Trade Development and Business Refer-
      rals.

35. **Foreign Branches**   557
Donald R. Marsh

Introduction. Reasons for Establishing Branches. Activities of Foreign Branches. Problems. The Future.

36. **Foreign Affiliates and Subsidiaries**   580
Stewart E. Sutin

Pre-Investment Considerations: *Strategic Planning. Feasibility
Study. Equity Investment Options.* Managing Foreign Investment
Vehicles.

37. **Representative Offices**   594
Milton E. Berglund, Jr.

Definition. Basic Rationale. Conditions Precedent to Opening. Setting Out a Defined Business Strategy. Normal Activities and Responsibilities of the Representative. Variation—A Regional Representative Office. Selection of the Representative Office Personnel.
Representative Offices—An Interpretive Evaluation.

38. **Edge Act and Agreement Corporations**   603
E. C. Stone

SECTION 7
Managing International Banking Activities

39. **Internal Organization and Personnel**   615
Charles F. Turner

Introduction. Traditional Structure. Functionally Integrated Structure. Choosing the Appropriate Structure. Staffing the International
Function.

40. **Marketing International Services**   624
Aidan H. F. Harland

Developing Marketing Plans. Developing Account Plans. Trip Organization. Selling Techniques—Personal Level. Withholding Tax Policy. Direct Mail and Advertising Assistance. Sales Training. Appendix.

41. **Managing International Funding and Liquidity**   644
Paul H. Austin

International Flow of Funds. Multicurrency Funding. Domestic and
Offshore Markets. Liquidity. Risks Associated with Gapping. Managing the Interest-Rate Risk under Gapping. Managing Liquidity Risk
under Gapping.

42. Accounting and Internal Controls   656
M. C. Nelson

International Banking Operations. Internal Control. Cash and Due
from Banks. Lending. Foreign Exchange Trading. Foreign Currency
Translation. Income Taxes. Foreign Corrupt Practices Act of 1977.
Other Reference.

43. Fundamental U.S. Taxation of International Banking Operations   674
John Patrick Casey and Leonard A. Lipson

Overview. The Foreign Tax Credit: *Direct Foreign Tax Credit. Indirect Foreign Tax Credit. Creditable Foreign Income Taxes. "In Lieu"
Foreign Taxes. Limitations on Use.* Source of Income: *Interest Income. Dividends. Personal-Services Income. Rental and Royalty Income. Gain from the Disposition of a U.S. Real Property Interest.
Gains from the Sale or Exchange of Personal Property. Underwriting Income. Other.* Allocation and Apportionment of Deductions:
*General Concepts. Interest Expense. Research and Experimental Ex-
penditures. Stewardship and Other Service Expenses. Legal and
Accounting Fees. Income Taxes. Net Operating Loss Deduction.
Losses from Property Transactions. Other Deductions.* Blocked For-
eign Income. Foreign Branch Translations. Controlled Foreign Cor-
porations: *Taxation of Operations. Dispositions.* Minimum Tax for
Tax Preferences. U.S. Employees Working Abroad. Transactions in
Foreign Currency: *General Rules.*

44. Audits and Examinations   710
Stephen C. Eyre and Daniel T. Jacobsen

Internal Audits: *Independence. Monitoring Controls. Reporting. Organization and Staffing. Credit Review. External Auditors. Supervisory Examinations.* Auditing International Banking Activities: *Scope
of Overseas Business. Regulation and Accounting Practices. Host-
Country Cultures. Investment Banking. Automation.* Organization
of Overseas Auditing. External Auditing and Examination Overseas:
Outside Auditors. Regulatory Examinations.

SECTION 8
Legal and Regulatory Framework for International Banking

45. Legal Constraints within the United States   723
Clark H. Hutton

Introduction. Legal Constraints Affecting Costs to Banks. Legal Constraints Affecting the Activities of Banks.

46. Legal and Regulatory Constraints within Other Countries   734
William J. Korsvik

Introduction. Classification of Restrictions. Entry Restrictions: *Other
Effective Barriers.* Operating Restraints.

47. **The Federal Reserve System and Regulation of International Banking**   751

C. Keefe Hurley, Jr.

Member Banks: *Foreign Branches. Bankers' Acceptances. Investments in Foreign Banks.* Edge and Agreement Corporations. Domestic and Foreign Bank Holding Companies: *Foreign Activities of U.S. Banking Organizations. Foreign Banks and Foreign Bank Holding Companies.* International Banking Facilities.

48. **The Prudential Framework for International Banking**   764

Robert H. Bench

Introduction. Purposes of Bank Supervision: *Supervisory Framework for International Activities of U.S. Banks. Examination of U.S. Banks' International Activities. The U.S. Supervisory Approaches for Evaluating Country Risk and Banks' Country Exposure Management Systems. Funds Management. Foreign Exchange and Interbank Deposit Activity.* Multilateral Supervision of International Banking: *Multilateral Coordination and Cooperation among Bank Supervisors. The International Supervisory Agenda.*

SECTION 9
The Future of International Banking

49. **Expansion of Foreign Banks in the United States**   785

James B. Sommers

Early History. Postwar History. Expansion. Form and Structure. Foreign Bank Operations in the United States. International Banking Act of 1978 and Competition. Future.

50. **The Future Role of U.S. Banks in the World Economy**   800

Alfred F. Miossi

Introduction. Setting the Stage: An Overview of Growth. The Scene Begins to Shift. Rising Energy Costs: Today's Situation. Foreign Exchange Volatility. Increased Economic Conflict. Evolving Position of the United States. Slower Overseas Growth and New International Opportunities. Internationalization: Achievement and Challenge. Competition and Capital. Where to Compete: U.S. Opportunities. Foreign Banks in the United States. Regulatory Change in the United States: Options Multiply. The International Banking Act. The Omnibus Banking Bill. The Changing Shape of Banking: The Financial Supermarket. Changing Approaches. Petrodollar Recycling: A Changing Issue.

51. **International Banking: The Achievement and the Challenge**   817

David Rockefeller

Global Convalescence. The Third World: First in Trade. Faith in Trade. A Surplus of Debt. Political Quarrels, Economic Needs. Government Intervention.

Index   827

SECTION 1
The International Financial System

1
International Financial Markets

CHRISTOPHER M. KORTH
Associate Professor of International Business
University of South Carolina

International financial markets comprise all of those markets where either the placer or taker of funds is from a country outside of the market being utilized. For example, for almost two centuries London was the site of the major market for foreign borrowers either to obtain bank loans or to sell their bonds; such funds were provided in pounds sterling. Much of the early industrial development in the United States, including a major share of American railroads, was financed with funds from London. Even the governments of individual states and the U.S. government itself utilized the British markets.

Correspondingly, international financial markets exist for the investors when they elect to *invest* their funds in a financial market outside of their home country. The Egyptian exporter who chooses to deposit his U.S. dollar receipts in New York or London is a participant in such a market.

Not too surprisingly, the markets which tend to attract deposits from abroad also tend to be markets which provide funds abroad—rather a symmetrical relationship. This will be seen to be true for most of the markets which will be examined here, whether *local* funds are used for financing *foreign* needs (as was commonly true of the aforementioned British financing in the 19th century) or whether the funds "flow through" from one country to another (as is generally the case with entrepot financial centers such as Singapore).

International financial markets can develop anywhere—so long as the local government permits such activity and so long as the potential users are attracted to the market. Many governments discourage such activity. Other governments favor the internationalization of their markets but are unable to attract the business. For example, political unrest or poor communications facilities (e.g., Egypt) can prevent the develop-

3

ment of international money and capital markets in those countries or even (as in the case of Lebanon) destroy existing markets.

THE MAJOR MARKETS

International financial markets have existed for hundreds of years. Even foreign markets which will accept the deposit and lending of foreign currencies have a very long history.

The London Markets

For centuries prior to the 1930s London maintained its preeminence as an international financial center. It does not matter that Britain no longer has the economic, political, and military preeminence that it once had. London still is unparalleled in the variety of services and the degree of financial expertise that it possesses, and London continues, despite all of the weaknesses of the British economy, to be a very dynamic and powerful financial market. Especially important is its role as an "offshore" financial center.

The U.S. Markets

In the aftermath of the Second World War, there was absolutely no doubt as to where the financial leadership of the world had moved. The dollar had become the preferred currency for international trade and investment (supplanting the pound sterling for the first time in history). The U.S. economy was the only major economy that had survived the war not only in good condition but in far stronger condition than it had been at the start of the war. The United States was the only country which could supply much of the goods that reconstruction demanded. The U.S. financial markets were the only markets that had the needed financial resources. Thus, for many years the domestic U.S. financial markets were avidly used by foreign, corporate, and governmental borrowers to help finance their reconstruction and expansionary needs.

The U.S. dollar was, at the same time, the only major freely convertible currency. Until 1958 even the major Western European currencies were inconvertible to various extents. Coupled with this was a wide range of laws which restricted foreign access to most of those markets. The domestic U.S. markets were the obvious alternative.

Other Major Financial Markets

The American and British financial markets are in a class by themselves. Other important markets exist, but they are much smaller. Major financial markets exist both in the principal industrial countries and also in a number of small countries which have carved out for themselves successful niches as financial centers.

Major Financial Markets in Other Industrialized Countries.   All major industrial countries have important domestic financial markets. For example, among the top 25 banks in the world, 7 are Japanese and 6 are French. Only four are American. Three are British and three are German. The Japanese and the German markets, because of the size and strength of their economies, are especially likely to continue to grow in significance. On a much smaller scale, Belgium, the Netherlands, and Canada have become important Euromarkets as well.

Entrepot Markets.   Some countries which are not major industrial powers have become important financial centers. In these countries the domestic markets are relatively unimportant. However, their offshore or Euromarkets, where foreign currencies are invested, have become very highly developed. Those markets thus serve as financial entrepots—that is, collection and processing centers that help to facilitate the financial intermediation between providers of funds *from outside* of those countries *to* users of funds *outside* of those countries.

Some of these entrepot markets benefit from their proximity to major industrialized countries. Switzerland and Luxembourg are examples of this in Europe.

Other entrepot centers do not have the advantage of proximity to major industrial markets. However, this has not proven to be a major barrier. The Bahamas are second only to the United Kingdom in the volume of Euromarket transactions.

In the Orient, Singapore and Hong Kong are important financial markets. In the Middle East, Bahrain has replaced Lebanon as the major financial center; Bahrain's development as a financial center has obviously been aided by its proximity to major Middle-Eastern petroleum-exporting countries.

THE STRUCTURE AND SIZE OF INTERNATIONAL FINANCIAL MARKETS

The Foreign Sector of Domestic Markets

Many countries make it virtually impossible for foreigners to participate in the local financial markets. Even foreign companies with local operations (e.g., a branch or a subsidiary) are sometimes constrained from the use of the local financial markets. However, in many other countries the markets are open enough that foreigners can borrow or invest—although often subject to special constraints that are not imposed upon domestic participants in those markets.

There are, of course, many different degrees of openness. Some countries will only allow foreigners to tap the local markets for use on local investments. We are interested in those countries that allow the tapping of their markets by foreigners for either local or foreign use: foreigners can sell common stock in the Dutch capital markets or bonds in New York; they can borrow from banks in London. In each of these cases the funds may be used where the taker of the funds chooses to use them: use is not restricted to the local economy.

The primary use by foreigners of domestic money and capital markets involves either bank loans or the negotiable debt market (e.g., commerical paper, bonds, etc.). Either can participate in these markets. Furthermore, participation can be either as a supplier of funds or as a taker.

In an open market, a domestic commercial bank can extend loans to most borrowers (whether local companies or foreign) with a minimum of legal limitations. This has generally been the case for the United States and the United Kingdom. However, even the U.S. government imposed extensive controls on capital *outflows* between 1963 and 1973. The "Voluntary" Foreign Credit Restraint Program (FCRP), which later became mandatory, greatly limited the flexibility of banks in the United States for extending loans to foreign borrowers or even to U.S. companies for foreign purposes. Switzerland and Germany are two other countries where foreign companies and governments have been generally free to tap the local markets (although at various times each country has discouraged the *inflow* of funds).

In a similar vein, foreigners can tap into domestic money and capital markets to float debt issues. As with bank loans, the U.S. record has generally been free of controls. However, in the same restrictive period that saw the creation of the FCRP, the Interest Equalization Tax (IET) was created. This was a tax which had the effects of raising the cost to many foreign borrowers of floating U.S. debt issues and very effectively driving them out of the U.S. market. This was, of course, exactly what the U.S. government had intended. The U.S. balance of payments had been in serious deficit, and it was hoped that such controls would buy a little extra time for adjustment which, it was further hoped, would once again increase the strength of the U.S. dollar. (That was at a time when the sanctity of the immutable value of the dollar was generally accepted by governmental officials, bankers, and other businessmen.)

The Foreign Bond Markets. An important part of the international financial markets is the so-called foreign bond market. This is simply that portion of a domestic bond market that represents issues of foreign companies and foreign governments.

Foreign bonds are subject to local laws and must be issued in the local currency. They will be floated by a local syndicate of investment bankers. Foreign bonds thus differ from domestic bonds only by the nature of the *issuer*.

The major foreign bond markets are in the United States, Germany, and Switzerland. (The U.S. portion of the market is often known as the Yankee bond market.) Exhibit 1 shows the total of all international bond issues—Eurobonds[1] and foreign bonds.

The foreign-bond portion is subdivided into its major components. The Yankee bond share dominated the market throughout most of the period, but in 1979 and 1980 both the German and Swiss portions exceeded that of the U.S. By the end of the decade the share of *each* of the three countries was as large or larger than the *entire* foreign bond market prior to 1974!

Exhibit 2 is a graph of the growth of new issues of the total international bond market and its two components, the foreign bonds and the Eurobonds. Neither part is predominant; they have alternated as the most significant sector in different years. The shaded areas indicate years of foreign bond dominance.

The most significant feature of Exhibit 2 is the very rapid growth and the extremely large size of the total market after 1974. The new issues of both Eurobonds and foreign bonds assumed a very major role in international markets beginning with the mid-1970s.

The Foreign Equity Market. Most of the major equity markets allow foreign companies to sell issues of their stock locally. Such listings must satisfy all requirements of the local markets. In the United States that means satisfying the requirements of the Securities Exchange Commission (SEC). Because SEC rules are much stricter than in most domestic markets abroad, foreign companies wishing to be listed in the United States must often release much more information than they are accustomed to doing at home. This has discouraged many companies from issuing their stock in the United States. (Among the foreign securities that have chosen to list on the New York Stock Exchange are Shell Oil and Sony.)

Some of the major foreign exchanges list large numbers of foreign stocks. For example, there are more than 200 foreign stocks listed on the German exchanges; among these are such American companies as Union Carbide, Black and Decker, Caterpillar, and General Motors. More than 500 foreign stocks are listed on the British stock exchanges. Included among these are ITT, Hoover, and Woolworth.

The Foreign Banking Market. Banks in some of the major industrialized countries are freely permitted to lend to foreign borrowers for use abroad. This is especially true in countries whose currencies are

---

[1] To be examined in more detail below.

Exhibit 1
New International Bond Issues (dollars in billions)

	1970	1971	1972	1973	1974	1975	1976	1977	1978	1979	1980
Eurobonds	3.0	3.6	6.3	4.2	2.1	8.6	14.3	17.8	14.1	18.7	24.0
Foreign bonds	1.6	2.7	3.4	3.6	4.8	11.3	18.2	14.5	20.2	22.3	17.9
In the U.S.	1.2	1.1	1.4	1.0	3.3	6.5	10.6	7.3	5.8	4.5	3.4
In Germany	0.1	0.3	0.5	0.4	0.3	1.1	1.3	2.1	3.8	5.4	4.8
In Switzerland	0.2	0.7	0.8	1.5	0.9	3.3	5.4	3.5	5.7	9.8	7.6
Elsewhere	0.1	0.6	0.7	0.7	0.3	0.5	0.9	1.6	4.9	2.6	2.1
Total	4.6	6.3	9.7	7.8	6.9	19.9	32.5	32.2	34.3	41.0	41.9

Source: *World Financial Markets*, Morgan Guaranty Trust Company.

Exhibit 2
New International Bond Issues

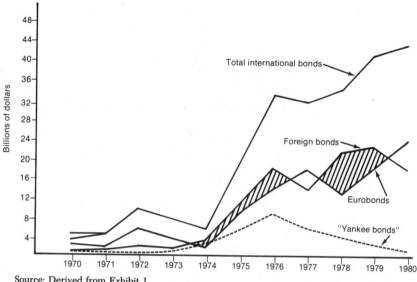

Source: Derived from Exhibit 1.

major international currencies, such as the United States, Germany, and the United Kingdom.

When access to such markets exists, they can provide attractive alternative sources of financing to a variety of borrowers. However, the development of the Eurocurrency markets has greatly reduced the relative attractiveness of the domestic banking markets for most borrowers.

The Euromarkets

The Uniqueness of Euromarkets. The Euromarkets are the other major sector of the international financial markets. The basis of their appeal is exactly that which lessens the appeal of the domestic markets—namely, the extent of governmental controls. *Euromarkets are almost totally free of control* by either individual governments, collective governments, or even a self-policing association of the participants. The laissez-faire nature of these markets is very unusual in today's world. Small wonder that there have been periodic calls by governments for controls to be imposed upon the markets. In the late 1970s a coalition of governments headed by the United States and Germany was leading the call for controls. The opposition was led by the United Kingdom. The effort to impose controls was repulsed, and it appears that barring any truly monumental tragedy in the Euromarkets, controls will continue to be rejected.

There are three basic parts to the Euromarkets: the Eurocurrency market, the Eurobond market, and the Euro-commercial paper market.

Eurocurrencies are deposits made in banks outside of the country whose currency is being deposited (for example, dollars deposited in London or pounds sterling deposited in Paris). They are not regulated by the banking authorities. The next chapter examines the Eurocurrency markets in detail.

Eurobonds are long-term debt instruments which are issued and sold outside of the country of the currency in which they are denominated. *Euro-commercial paper* is likewise issued outside of the country whose currency is used to denominate the issue. Neither Eurobonds nor Euro-commercial paper are regulated by authorities. Both types of issues will be examined below.

The Location of Euromarkets.   Euromarkets can develop anywhere that local laws will permit. The United States banned such activity for 25 years after the first appearance of the Euromarkets; not until late 1981 were Euromarkets permitted to develop in the United States.

In contrast, the Bank of England has been encouraging the development of the Euromarkets in London. This has been a major factor in maintaining the significance of the London markets in international financial affairs. Indeed, London has been by far the most important Euromarket. France and Luxembourg are the other two major Euromarket centers in Europe with further centers of strength in Belgium, the Netherlands, Germany, Italy, and Switzerland.

The term *Euromarkets* suggests that Europe is the location of the entire market. At one time this was basically true, but it has not been true for many years. For example, among the industrialized countries, both Japan and Canada have evolved as significant Euromarkets.

In addition to these countries which (except for Luxembourg) have large domestic financial markets upon whose infrastructure the Euromarkets could build, there are certain financial centers which have developed despite the lack of any significant domestic base for those markets. These developed solely as international (as opposed to domestic) financial centers. They are the entrepots which were mentioned earlier: for example, the Bahamas, the Cayman Islands, Singapore, Hong Kong, and Bahrain.

The Origin of the Euromarkets.   The genesis of the modern-day Euromarkets is somewhat clouded. They did not come into existence at one particular point in time as the result of some common agreement. Rather, like Topsy, they "just growed."

The first Euromarket to develop was the Eurocurrency market. One of the strongest early influences on its development was, curiously enough, the government of the Soviet Union. In the mid-1950s, at the height of the Cold War, when the U.S. dollar was the only universally acceptable currency, the Russians wished to maintain their international reserves in dollars, but not at American banks—for fear that the funds might be frozen or sequestered by the U.S. government. Therefore, the Russians found British, French, and German banks that would accept deposits in dollars. From this modest capitalist-cum-Communist beginning has grown a market with a gross size in excess of $1 trillon.

Growth of the Euromarkets. The return to convertibility of major European currencies in 1958 and the recovery and increased opening up of their economies and financial markets, expanded the horizons of their domestic financial markets. Nevertheless, the Eurocurrency market continued to grow steadily. Then, in the mid-1960s the rapidly mounting U.S. trade deficits led the U.S. government to impose the aforementioned series of three harsh capital controls: the Interest Equalization Tax, the Foreign Credit Restraint Program, and the Foreign Direct Investment Regulations. These controls greatly reduced the accessibility of the domestic American financial markets to most developed countries. This set of barriers acted as a second strong catalyst for the expansion of the internationalization of some of the major European financial markets and, most significantly, for the Eurocurrency market. These barriers were the basic cause for the development of the *Eurobond* market.

The trio of U.S. domestic capital controls was dismantled on January 1, 1974. There had been widespread speculation that the renewed access to the domestic American markets would lead to a sharp contraction of the Euromarkets. This not only did not occur but the Euromarkets grew very rapidly throughout the 1970s.

The Euromarkets had matured. The mechanisms were in place. Market participants were familiar with them. They had proved to be very valuable in aiding the integration of world financial markets. They were efficient and profitable.

A third major impetus to the development of the Euromarkets came with the oil crisis of the 1970s. The ensuing petrodollar crisis and the sharply increased borrowing needs, which soaring oil prices brought to many governments, illustrated the critically important role for the Euromarkets in the recycling of the petrodollar funds to the borrowing country from the oil exporting countries.

Corporate treasurers have also become major users of the Euromarkets and foreign domestic markets. As the world financial markets have become more closely integrated, and as corporate treasurers have become more sophisticated, the treasurers have become much more adept at using these markets not only for funding but also for investing purposes.

The Eurobond Market

Characteristics of Eurobonds.   The Eurobond market is an international market for bonds which are not registered in any country. Unlike a normal domestic bond (whether issued by a domestic or foreign entity), which must be registered with the appropriate local authorities (e.g., the Securities and Exchange Commission in the United States), issued in the local currency, and floated by a group of locally licensed investment bankers, a Eurobond requires no registration. Indeed, there is no international authority with whom to register. Eurobonds can be brought to market by investment bankers from any country or countries. Also, a Eurobond would be in a different currency than the domestic currency of the country in which the bond is sold.

The Eurobond market provides an alternative for the borrower who wishes to reach new sources of funds and avoid the regulation and expense of floating the bond in a domestic market. Eurobonds are negotiable, long-term debt instruments issued by borrowers with high credit ratings.

Because the borrower is able to raise the funds so quickly, flexibly, and with a minimum of noninterest expenses, the borrower will generally pay a higher interest rate than in the comparable domestic market. The investor will, of course, demand the higher return since there are fewer safeguards in the unregulated Eurobond market. The investor is generally able to avoid withholding taxes and the reporting of income to the tax authorities of his home country.

Eurobonds also have some other general characteristics: they are usually bearer bonds (another advantage for the investor who wishes to remain anonymous), and they are generally debentures. Some of them are fixed-rate obligations; others are floating-rate bonds with a changing interest rate every six months depending upon market conditions.

The Eurobond market has adopted several special formats from domestic U.S. markets which have helped to broaden the appeal of the market. Important among these sweeteners are convertibility and stock warrants which are sometimes provided with Eurobonds.

There is a secondary market for Eurobonds in the international markets—although, of course, a dollar-denominated Eurobond could not be sold in the United States, and a deutsche mark-denominated Eurobond could not be sold in Germany. (The vast majority of Eurobonds are dollar denominated or deutsche mark denominated.)

As with the Eurocurrency markets, the Eurobond market can be located in any country willing to permit the issuing of bonds denominated in a foreign currency. In general, the same countries predominate in both Eurocurrencies and in Eurobonds: the U.S. dollar and German deutsche mark.

The Size of the Eurobond Market. The Eurobond market has grown very rapidly. As Exhibit 3 indicates, the total market grew from $3 billion in 1970 to $24 billion in 1980. Most of the growth occurred after 1974.

The dollar-denominated portion of the market predominates—ranging from a low of 43 percent to a high of 68 percent of the total (Exhibits 3 and 4). The DM-denominated portion of the market is a distant, but respectable second.

Not Eurodollar Bonds. Note that the terms which were used above were *dollar-denominated Eurobond* and *DM-denominated Euro-bond—not* Eurodollar or Euro-DM bonds! Eurocurrencies are bank deposits and bank loans. Eurobonds are negotiable, long-term debt instruments. The Eurocurrency and Eurobond markets are as different as are the domestic bank and bond markets.

Other Euromarkets

The *Euro-commercial paper market* is not nearly as significant as are the Eurocurrency and Eurobond markets. Nevertheless, it has great potential and could grow rapidly in the future.

Sometimes reference is made to the *Euro-equity market.* This is a complete misnomer. There is no such thing! Publicly traded stocks must be registered with the appropriate governmental authorities and are subject to the regulations of the secondary markets. The thing to which writers who use the term are actually referring is the listing of foreign stocks in the stock markets in places such as Amsterdam, London, or New York. Those securities are merely domestic stocks which have been issued by foreigners—not Euro-equities. To be a Euro-equity, a stock would have to be free of governmental controls and sold in a country other than the one whose currency has been used to denominate the stock. No such equities exist!

SUMMARY

Modern techniques of communication, transportation, and financial control have helped to greatly enhance the integration of money and capital markets of the major industrialized countries of the world. At the same time, political factors, governmental controls, and demands for economic efficiency have led to the evolution of a truly international financial market: the Euromarket. These two groups of financial markets, the foreign portion of the major domestic markets coupled with the Euromarkets, comprise the international money and capital markets.

These markets have become very important to bankers' major commercial, industrial, and even governmental customers. More and more financial officers of such institutions have become much more sophisti-

Exhibit 3
Eurobonds: New Issues (U.S. dollars in billions)

	1970	1971	1972	1973	1974	1975	1976	1977	1978	1979	1980
U.S. dollars—denominated	1.8	2.2	3.9	2.4	1.0	3.7	9.1	11.6	7.3	12.6	16.4
DM—denominated	0.7	0.8	1.1	1.0	0.3	2.3	2.7	4.1	5.3	3.6	3.6
Other	0.5	0.6	1.3	0.8	0.8	2.6	2.5	2.1	1.6	2.5	3.9
Total	3.0	3.6	6.3	4.2	2.1	8.6	14.3	17.8	14.2	18.7	23.9
U.S. dollars—denominated as percentage of total	60%	52%	62%	57%	48%	43%	64%	65%	52%	67%	68%

Source: *World Financial Markets*, Morgan Guaranty Trust Company, various issues.

Exhibit 4
The Eurobond Market

Source: Derived from Exhibit 3.

cated than in the past with the use of such international markets for everything from capital financing to cash management. As a result, more and more companies will seek their funds from the most advantageous source wherever that source is located. They also will invest their excess funds wherever the return is the most attractive. Companies which only a few years ago would rely entirely upon domestic banks, domestic money, and capital markets are now active placers and takers of funds in the Euromarkets and in foreign domestic markets.

The domestic bank which is not familiar with these international money and capital markets, and prepared to utilize them itself, may well find its ability to compete even for its major domestic customers seriously impaired. As interstate banking competition in the United States heats up and as the penetration of foreign banks increases, these problems will only get worse for the uninitiated banker.

This chapter has examined the origin, location, structure, and size of the major components of international money and capital markets: the foreign markets and the Euromarkets (primarily the Eurobond markets). The next chapter focuses upon the principal Euromarket: the Eurocurrency market.

2

The Eurocurrency Markets

CHRISTOPHER M. KORTH
Associate Professor of International Business
University of South Carolina

In Chapter 1 the nature of international markets was examined. As was seen, the international financial markets include both the so-called foreign markets and the Euromarkets. The foreign markets comprise that portion of the domestic markets which encompasses issues of debt and equity of foreign entities—debt in the case of governmental agencies and international intergovernmental agencies, such as the World Bank, and both debt and equity for private-sector issuers. The Euromarkets are comprised of Eurobonds, Euro-commercial paper, and Eurocurrencies. Eurobonds and Euro-commercial paper were discussed in the first chapter. The discussion of Eurocurrencies was reserved for this chapter.

The Eurocurrency market is the oldest and by far the most important element of the Euromarkets. Indeed, the Eurocurrency market has grown to rival the largest national financial market—that of the United States.

THE ESSENCE OF EUROCURRENCIES

Time Deposits

The Eurocurrency market is made up of bank *time deposits* which are denominated in a currency foreign to the local market. They are created when a deposit is made in a commercial bank in a country other than the country that issued the currency. The bank thus acquires a foreign-currency obligation which must be repaid, along with interest earned, in the same currency as the deposit. The deposit is always a time deposit—either a standard time deposit or negotiable certificate of deposit. An active secondary market exists for Eurocurrency CDs.

16

If a corporation or government or individual deposits U.S. dollars with a bank in London instead of in the United States, then a Eurodollar deposit has been created. Similarly, if a deposit of pounds sterling is made in a bank in France, then a Eurosterling deposit has been created. However, since a Eurocurrency can only be created when a currency has been deposited in a country other than the country that issued the currency, if the depositor chose to make deposits of the above-mentioned dollars in the United States or the pounds sterling in the United Kingdom, then Eurodollars and Eurosterling would *not* have been created: the deposit would instead represent a standard domestic time deposit. Demand deposits do not exist in the Euromarkets: however, Eurodeposits can be made for as short as overnight. There is no maximum period of deposit. Periods of three and six months are the most common "medium-term" periods. All Eurodeposits are interest bearing.

This bank-deposit nature of Eurocurrencies clearly distinguishes them from Eurobonds. Yet, as was seen in Chapter 1, many observers confuse the two markets. Those who invest in Eurobonds have chosen not to make a Eurocurrency deposit. If Eurocurrency funds are withdrawn to buy a Eurobond, then the Eurocurrency ceases to exist. Of course, a bank may choose to buy Eurobonds with funds from Eurocurrency deposits; however, the enormous disparity in maturities between the deposit and the bond makes such investments generally unattractive to Eurobanks.

Eurocurrency

The term *Eurocurrency* is misleading. It is the U.S. dollar, not a European currency, which is the major element of the market. The term *Eurocurrency* refers to the origin of the market, but the market has grown well beyond its European origins; it is now worldwide. Therefore, the "Euro" in the title is inappropriate except for its historical connotations.

Reference is commonly made to the "Asia dollar" market and occasionally to the "Latin dollar" market. These are nothing more than the Asian and Latin American portions of the Eurocurrency market.

Many significant Euromarkets have evolved in a wide variety of locations in the world. Exhibit 1 shows that many of these are in traditional financial centers: for example, London, Paris, Tokyo, Brussels, Amsterdam, and Ottawa; these Euromarkets thus developed as adjuncts to significant domestic markets. Because the Euromarkets are parallel to the domestic markets and are actually part of an integrated worldwide market, they are often called "offshore" markets—even though markets such as Paris are not actually offshore from anything.

Many other Euromarket centers developed in locations where there

Exhibit 1
The Largest Eurocenters (dollars in billions)

		1970	1975	1980
1.	United Kingdom	$50	$172	$485
2.	Bahamas	7	55	126
3.	France	10	39	124
4.	Japan	6	32	100
5.	Luxembourg	3	27	84
6.	Belgium	5	17	62
7.	Netherlands	4	17	55
8.	Singapore	0	13	54
9.	Canada	9	17	54
10.	Italy	10	16	46
11.	Bahrain	0	2	38
12.	Switzerland	6	14	35
13.	Panama	0	9	35
14.	Cayman Islands	0	7	33
15.	Hong Kong	0	4	32
16.	Germany	3	10	25
17.	Austria	0	0	23
18.	Spain	1	6	21

Source: *World Financial Markets,* Morgan Guaranty Trust Company.

are very minor domestic financial markets: for example, the Bahamas and Cayman Islands in the Caribbean; Luxembourg; Singapore and Hong Kong in the Orient; and Bahrain (which replaced Lebanon as the Middle Eastern Eurocenter in the 1970s as a results of the Lebanese civil war). Collectively and individually these markets are very important. Indeed, Italy, Switzerland, and even Germany do not play as large a role in the Eurocurrency markets as do most of these small countries.

As Exhibit 1 illustrates, the United Kingdom with $485 billion of Eurocurrency deposits is by far the most important of all of these Eurocurrency centers. Exhibit 2 shows this relative significance graphically.

The Rise of Eurocenters.   Why do some traditional financial centers such as London and Paris rise to a major role in the Eurocurrency markets while other major economic powers such as Germany do not? How are such small islands as the Bahamas and Cayman able to play a major role? Why is the United States not even among the countries listed?

Euromarkets only arise where local governments permit them to develop and prosper. Some governments of countries with major economies encouraged, or at least did not discourage, such developments. The British government was very favorably inclined to attract the Eurocurrency markets to London so as to maintain the prominence of "The City" in international finance. The German government dis-

Exhibit 2
The Major Eurocenters (estimates)

	1970	1971	1972	1973	1974	1975	1976	1977	1978	1979	1980
United Kingdom	43%	41	39	40	39	35	34	31	34	32	32
Bank havens*	6%	10	10	12	16	19	22	23	22	22	21
All others	50%	49	50	48	46	46	44	46	44	47	47

* Bahamas, Cayman Islands, Panama, Netherlands Antilles, Bahrain, Singapore, Hong Kong.
Source: *International Financial Markets,* Morgan Guaranty Trust Company.

couraged such development while the U.S. government banned it altogether prior to 1981.[1]

Markets in banking havens are of a totally different character. Some
of them, such as Luxembourg, Singapore, Hong Kong, and Bahrain
attract enough operational business that Eurobanks in such markets
generally operate active branches. In locations such as Nassau and
Cayman, however, the attraction is basically favorable banking and
taxation laws. Relatively little of actual operations occur there. They
are havens of few regulations and low or no taxes. Yet, Nassau has
attracted $126 billion of Eurocurrency deposits—smaller than the

---

[1] The advent in 1981 of international banking facilities will be discussed in a later
chapter.

mammoth London market but on a par with the next largest markets: Paris and Tokyo.

The operational presence of most banks in Nassau and the Cayman Islands, which exist primarily to satisfy local laws, is typically via the services of a local lawyer or bank. The affiliation with the foreign bank is identified commonly with a brass plate on the door of the local agent's office (often along with the plates of many other foreign banks on the same door). Thus, these financial centers are often called "brass plate" banks. They are also often referred to as "shells" since they have no substance—just appearance. They are, in effect, legal fictions—ports of convenience.

Eurocurrency

The use of the term *Eurocurrency* is confusing to many people. Eurocurrencies are bank deposits—not currencies. Thus, *there is no issue of paper money known as the Eurodollar.* There is a bank deposit denominated in a foreign currency but no currency as such. Thus, Eurocurrencies are not legal tender. However, in all other respects they are identical to domestic bank deposits in that currency.

Eurocurrencies have the same value in foreign exchange markets, suffer the same ravages of inflation, and can be used to pay the same bills as do their domestic counterparts. A Eurocurrency is simply domestic money which is "living" abroad.

Informal Markets

Thus, unfortunately, not only is the *Euro* connotation of Eurocurrency misleading but so also is the *currency* implication. To confuse the issue slightly more, reference is commonly made (as was done above) to the Eurocurrency *market.* Here also the reader must bear in mind that this should not be envisioned as a market which involves face-to-face meetings of buyers and sellers. It is a market of telephone calls, telex messages, and electronic transfers of funds. The participants generally do not meet directly. In this respect the Eurocurrency market is analogous to over-the-counter stock markets and foreign exchange markets.

Eurobanks

The banks which can accept the deposit of a foreign currency may be of any nationality. Thus in London, British banks can be Eurobanks. However, German, French, Japanese, Brazilian, Russian, and even American banks can also be Eurobanks in London.

There is a distinct bias on the part of Eurocurrency depositors in favor of placing their funds with a bank from the country whose currency has been deposited. Thus, the American banks dominate the Eurodollar market and German banks dominate the Eurodeutsche mark market. This reflects the belief that, if the Eurocurrency market should seriously falter, the central banks of the countries whose currencies were on deposit would provide more protection to banks from that country than to other banks. (There is no deposit insurance on Eurocurrency deposits.)

Transfer of Eurocurrencies

As a practical matter, *currency* is seldom withdrawn. Transfer of funds is typically done electronically or by cable. The actual transfer does not even occur in the Eurocurrency market. The funds which are deposited, loaned, and withdrawn are all actually in the form of demand deposits in the domestic market of the country which issued the currency (for example, domestic U.S. dollars in the case of Eurodollars).

When the original deposit is made into a Eurocurrency account, it must generally be made in the form of a claim upon a demand deposit in a bank in the country whose currency is being deposited. Thus, a French exporter (FE) which has received a claim against an American bank (e.g., a maturing time draft drawn against Chase Manhattan) could deposit the funds at any bank in the United States. The initial impacts are shown on the following T-accounts (assume that the funds deposited were drawn on the account of an American Company (AC) at the same bank. (See Illustration 1.)

Illustration 1

American Bank (AB)		French Exporter (FE)	
DD_{AC}	$-\$100$	Receivable	$-\$100$
DD_{FE}	$+\$100$	DD_{AB}	$+\$100$

The French exporter, wishing to earn interest on the funds, could then direct that the U.S. dollar funds be transferred to Barclay's Bank, First Chicago, Paribas, or some other bank in London, Paris, or elsewhere. The Eurobank (EB) acquires a Eurodollar liability to the depositor together with a corresponding claim on the domestic American bank. The Eurobank would commonly hold such funds at its own U.S. affiliates: headquarters, subsidiary, or branch. (See Illustration 2.)

Illustration 2

American Bank (AB)		French Exporter (FE)		Eurobank (EB)	
DD_{FE} $-\$100$		DD_{AB} $-\$100$		DD_{AB} $+\$100$	TD_{FE} $+\$100$
DD_{EB} $+\$100$		TD_{EB} $+\$100$			

The American bank still has a demand deposit liability. For that bank the only change is a shift of the liability from the French exporter to the Eurobank.

Since the Eurobank is paying interest on the Eurodeposit, it will quickly invest the funds. When it does so, it will request the transfer of the funds out of its demand deposit at the American bank. Assume that the funds are loaned to a British importer (BI).[2] (See Illustration 3.)

Illustration 3

American Bank (AB)		Eurobank (EB)		British Importer (BI)	
	DD_{EB} −$100	DD_{AB} −$100		DD_{AB} +$100	$Loan_{EB}$ +$100
	DD_{BI} +$100	$Loan_{BI}$ +$100			

Again, the transaction has involved the transfer of the American bank's demand deposit liability—from the Eurobank to the British importer. Thus, throughout this series of transactions the basis for the entire process has been demand deposit liabilities in a bank located in the country whose currency is being used (that is, a bank in the United States in the case of Eurodollars). The summary T-account for the American Bank is as follows:

American Bank

DD_{AC}	−$100
DD_{FE}	+$100
DD_{FE}	−$100
DD_{EB}	+$100
DD_{EB}	−$100
DD_{BI}	+$100
DD_{AC}	−$100
DD_{BI}	+$100

As can be seen, for the American bank all of the impacts have been shifts in its demand deposit liabilities. Since the transactions with the French exporter (DD_{FE}) and the Eurobank (DD_{EB}) cancel out, the summary result is simply a shift of DD liability from the American Company (DD_{AC}) to the British importer (DD_{BI}).

This type of transaction underlies all transfers of Eurocurrency deposits and loans. The Eurobank does not issue direct claims against itself, but rather transfers its claim on a bank in another country— the country whose currency has been used.

In the above example it was assumed that all of the demand deposit transfers occurred at the same American bank. The impact would have been exactly the same if several different banks were involved.

---

[2] Note that there are no reserve requirements on Eurobanks; precautionary reserves would be maintained principally in the form of liquid interest-earning investments— e.g., call deposits with other Eurobanks.

EUROCURRENCY DEPOSITS

The Size of the Euromarkets

The size of the Eurocurrency markets is measured by the scale of the *deposits* which are made in Eurobanks. Exhibit 3 shows the pace of growth of the market since 1970. In 1970 the Eurocurrency market had grown to a *net size* of $65 billion. This includes deposits from such sources as corporations, governments, international agencies, and banks outside of the Eurocurrency markets. When interbank deposits within the Eurocurrency market itself are included, as is frequently done, the *gross* size of the market was $115 billion. However, these interbank deposits are actually interbank loans and, as such, do not really reflect the scale of the primary deposits from outside of the Eurocurrency market system.

In the decade of the 1970s, the growth of the Euromarkets was extremely rapid. By 1980 the net size of the market had soared to $755 billion (a 1,000 percent increase) while the gross size of the market had risen an even more impressive 1,200 percent to $1.5 trillion. Exhibit 4 illustrates this phenomenal growth. The total size of the Euromarkets dwarfs the size of all domestic financial markets in the world except that of the United States.

The totals in Exhibits 3 include all Eurocurrencies. Line 3 indicates the share of the total which is in U.S. dollars. The dollar share has been very stable at approximately 74 percent for the entire period with a range of 72 percent to 81 percent. In 1980 it represented 76 percent or $1,120 billion of the total gross Eurocurrency liabilities.

Theoretically, any currency could become a Eurocurrency. Indeed, Euro-Saudi rials, Euro-Kuwaiti dinars, and Euro-Singaporean dollars do exist. However, as a practical matter only a small handful of currencies actually comprise the bulk of the Eurocurrency market. This reflects the fact that only a small handful of currencies are actually used for the bulk of international trade and financial transactions. The currencies which are deposited in Eurocurrency accounts are the same currencies which are generally used in international trade and investments—the "vehicle currencies" of international trade and investment flows: primarily U.S. dollars, deutsche marks, Swiss francs, Japanese yen, and pounds sterling.

Depositors

Eurobanks will accept deposits from virtually anyone: individuals, companies, governments, international agencies, or other banks. In general, there is a deposit minimum of at least $100,000 or its equivalent in other Eurocurrencies. This would naturally exclude most individuals from the market. Indeed, the Eurocurrency market is basically

Exhibit 3
Size of the Eurocurrency Markets*

	1970	1971	1972	1973	1974	1975	1976	1977	1978	1979	1980
1. Gross deposit liabilities ($ billions)	$115	$150	$210	$315	$395	$485	$595	$740	$950	$1220	$1515
2. Net deposit liabilities ($ billions)†	65	85	110	160	220	255	320	390	495	615	755
3. Eurodollars	81%	77%	78%	74%	76%	78%	80%	76%	74%	72%	74%

* Based upon foreign currency liabilities and claims of banks in major European countries plus the Bahamas, Bahrain, Panama, Singapore, Hong Kong, Canada, Japan, the Cayman Islands, the Netherlands Antilles and Luxembourg.
† Net of interbank claims within Eurocurrency market.
Source: *World Financial Markets*, Morgan Guaranty Trust Company.

Exhibit 4
Size of Eurocurrency Markets

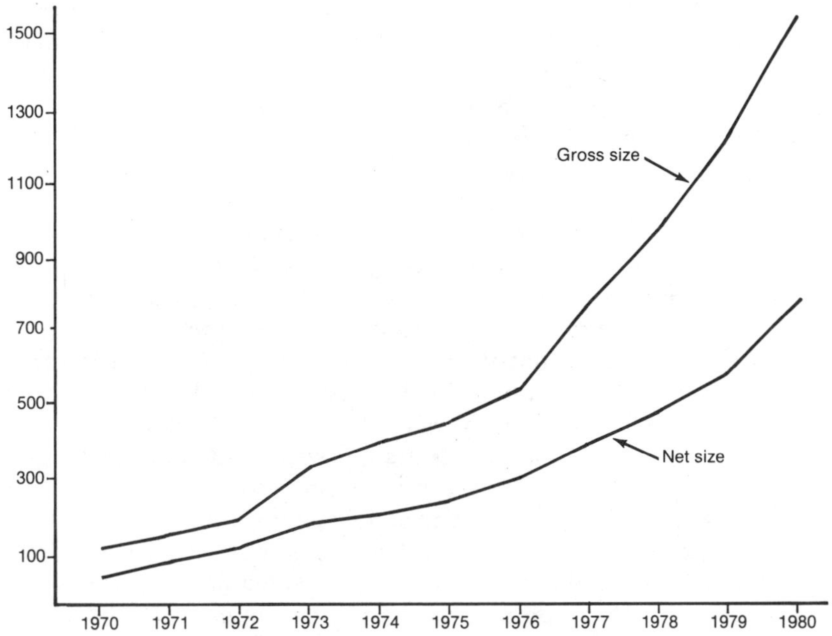

Source: Derived from Exhibit 3.

a wholesale market. However, the market is intensely competitive. As a result, some banks do accept deposits of as little as $10,000.

ATTRACTIONS OF EUROCURRENCY MARKETS

With a gross size of almost $1.5 trillion there is obviously a strong appeal of the Eurocurrency markets for depositors, banks, and borrowers. However, since large domestic markets do exist for most of the Eurocurrencies, why is there such a strong interest in these offshore markets?

Freedom from Controls

The key to the attractiveness of the Eurocurrency markets is their *lack of governmental controls*. Unlike domestic money and capital markets which are typically tightly regulated, Eurocurrency markets are essentially free from controls from *any* governing body. They are not regulated by their host government—which is one of the major reasons why the markets developed in those particular locations. The Eurocurrency markets also are not regulated by the governments which issued the currencies that have become Eurodeposits. Those governments could try to regulate the Eurocurrency activities of their banks' operations overseas. However, if this were to be done, (for example, control by the Federal Reserve System of the Eurobank activities of American banks and control by the Bank of England of such activity by British banks), then the Eurodeposits would easily and quickly move to banks of other countries.

Any effective control of the Eurocurrency markets would need to be multilateral. The banks themselves have not found it necessary to impose such discipline. Efforts have also been made by governments, especially those of the United States and Germany, to develop a multinational governmental system for controlling the market. However, the countries with the greatest share of the markets (e.g., the United Kingdom) have not shared in the opinion of the desirability of such mechanisms. They know only too well that if the host countries impose controls, it could easily cause the market to flow to other financial centers such as Bahrain, Nassau, Cayman, and Singapore. These countries have little or no incentive to impose comparable controls.

Freedom from Exchange and Capital Controls. The Eurocurrency markets have strong appeal for depositors from countries with exchange or capital controls, or those which fear the imposition of such controls. For example, the initial development of the Eurocurrency markets occurred because of fears of East European countries that the U.S. government might in the future impose such controls on deposits in the United States or even on foreign offices of U.S. banks.

At the same time in the mid-1950s the major European currencies were subject to many exchange controls which was an inducement for depositors to keep funds out of the domestic markets.

Most of these controls were removed in 1958. Nevertheless, the period of controls coupled with the Russian reluctance to deposit funds in the United States provided a strong initial thrust to the development and growth of the Eurocurrency markets.

In the period from 1963 to 1973 the U.S. government imposed a series of money and capital controls in order to reduce the flow of funds from the United States.[3] This deflected a substantial amount of borrowing demand to the young Eurodollar market. It also deflected short-term investment funds and even dividends and interests from abroad which would otherwise have gone into investments in the United States (for instance, into Treasury bills and bank deposits). This was the second major growth impetus to the Eurocurrency markets.

The third major growth period for the Eurocurrency markets began as the U.S. controls were removed on January 1, 1974. This action

---

[3] The Interest Equalization Tax, the Foreign Credit Restraint Program, and the Foreign Direct Investment Regulations are referred to here.

coincided with the oil embargo and the quadrupling of oil prices. Because of the embargo, some of the major oil exporting countries were fearful of depositing their petro funds in the United States (although their favorite choices were with American banks' offices abroad).

At the same time most governments found themselves faced with sharp increases in their oil-import bills. Many turned anxiously to the Eurobanks for loans. Thus, the banks became the major vehicle for recycling the petro-dollars from exporter to importer.

No Limits on Deposit Interest Rates.   There have never been limitations on the interest rates which Eurobanks can pay on deposits. This is in sharp contrast to domestic controls such as Regulation Q of the Federal Reserve System in the United States.

Also, although there are no demand deposits as such in the Eurocurrency markets, overnight time deposits are offerred. This is also in sharp contrast to the Regulation Q ban on interest being paid on demand deposits or short-term time deposits. The phasing out of such controls will lessen the advantages of the Eurodollar market but is unlikely to reduce its overall attractiveness.

No Reserve Requirements, Taxes, or Deposit Insurance.   The freedom from constraints on Eurocurrency deposits extends to the absence of reserve requirements, taxes, and deposit insurance upon deposits. This freedom greatly reduces the effective cost of deposits to Eurobanks. As a result, those banks are able to pay higher interest on deposits and charge lower interest on loans than can domestic banks in the same currency. Thus, the nominal spread between funding and lending costs is generally less than in the corresponding domestic markets of the same currency.

No Credit Allocations.   Eurobanks are also free from any requirements to allocate any of their loans to preferred borrowers, such as farmers, home buyers, and so forth. Such requirements in domestic markets, which typically involve forced inherent subsidies of such borrowers, can both reduce bank earnings and force interest rates on other loans to increase. Without such controls, Eurobanks once again enjoy lower costs.

Attractions to Borrowers

As on the deposit side, the Eurocurrency markets offer borrowers advantages which stem both directly from the freedom from controls and indirectly from factors which derive from the absence of controls.

The Absence of Regulations.   Lower funding costs give Eurobanks the opportunity to be much more flexible than in the corresponding domestic markets. One aspect of this flexibility is the ability to offer lower interest rates than in the corresponding domestic market. Since many or most of the borrowers could as readily borrow domestically, arbitrage keeps the Eurorate lower than but close to the domestic rates.

Because banks in their domestic operations have heavy expenses other than funding costs, they must operate at wider spreads domestically than in the Eurocurrency market.

Other Attractions.   As with the deposit side of the Eurocurrency market, the borrowing side of the market serves as a supplement to small or weak domestic markets. This is not limited to the short-term markets alone: the Euromarkets provide extensive amounts of term loans (to 10 or 12 years or even more—although this varies greatly according to prevailing credit conditions). The Euromarkets also provide, via the mechanism of syndicated Eurocredits, the potential for loans on a scale that cannot be matched in any domestic market; "jumbo" loan syndications in excess of $1 billion are not uncommon.

Access to the Eurocurrency markets broadens the funding base of a borrower. This diversification of sources can obviously reduce a company's financing costs. Such contact can also provide access, perhaps for the first time, to the possibility of borrowing in foreign currencies. Also, since the Eurocurrency market is perceived as a rather "prime" market, the ability to borrow there can lead to access to other markets such as Eurobonds and domestic markets in other countries.

Attractions to Banks

The ability to avoid reserve requirements and deposit insurance is a strong appeal of the Eurocurrency markets for most large banks. Participation in the market is also relatively low cost: it is a wholesale market, involving primarily prime-quality customers. Expensive retail facilities are avoided. Even in expensive financial centers such as London or Tokyo, the Eurobranches are commonly cost justifiable. If not, then the Eurobanks can utilize brass-plate branches as they do in Nassau.

Participation in the Eurocurrency markets provides diversification to a bank and gives it greater flexibility. It widens the bank's deposit base. It also broadens its borrowing base via the interbank market. This funding combination allows the bank to offer loans on more favorable terms to its customers. As a result of all of these factors, Eurobanks enjoy favorable economies of scale and, if managed carefully, increased profitability.

EURO-INVESTMENTS

The Currency of Investment

The Eurobank has assumed a foreign currency obligation (i.e., foreign to the local market in which the bank is accepting Eurodeposits—

although it either may or may not be the bank's own home currency). Banks generally protect themselves from the risk of loss from currency depreciation or devaluation by avoiding the issuance of cross-currency loans. Thus, the vast majority of all Euro-investments are in the same currency as the deposit. However, Eurobanks will sometimes make cross-currency loans if an increase in the value of the other currency is anticipated or if the cross-currency risk can be covered by selling the other currency in the forward market.

Types of Investments

There are a variety of common investment opportunities available to the Eurobank:

1. Interbank Euroloans.
2. Loans to corporations and governments.
3. Loans to its own affiliate in the country whose currency was deposited (most often to its headquarters).
4. Investment in negotiable securities.

Interbank Euroloans. A very major portion of the funds which are deposited in the major Eurobanks is reloaned to other, typically smaller, banks in the interbank market. This is especially true of deposits in banks from the same country as the currency (for example, Eurodollars deposited at American banks and Eurodeutsche marks deposited at German banks, etc.).

As can be seen in Exhibit 5 (line *a*), there is a very active interbank market within the Eurocurrency markets. Interbank loans represent approximately one half of the entire market.

Eurobanks have specific rates at which they are prepared either to borrow or lend Eurofunds—similar to the buy and sell quotes in the FX markets. In the Euromarkets in London these rates are known as the London Interbank bid and offer rates. Note that these rates, though set by the individual banks, are market rates—not administered rates such as a bank's prime rate or a central bank's discount rate. The market is highly competitive. The rates can change daily or even several times per day.

The lending or offer quote in the interbank market is of special significance in the Eurocurrency markets. It is not only the rate at which interbank deposits will be made but also the basis for pricing most Euroloans. The most important of these rates is the London interbank offer rate (LIBOR).

There are, of course, many LIBORs which a Eurobank might quote to other banks: a Eurodollar LIBOR, a Eurodeutsche mark LIBOR, and so forth. However, even in a single currency a bank may well quote a variety of LIBORs. A bank's quote naturally reflects its percep-

Exhibit 5
Estimates of Euro-Investments* (dollars in billions rounded to nearest $5 billion; end of year)

	1970	1971	1972	1973	1974	1975	1976	1977	1978	1979	1980
Gross claims	115	150	210	315	395	485	595	740	950	1220	1515
a. Claims on Eurobanks	50	65	100	155	175	230	275	350	455	605	760
b. Claims on nonbanks	25	35	45	70	105	130	165	210	265	315	390
c. Claims on central banks and commercial banks outside of Euromarket area	30	35	45	70	95	105	130	150	185	240	290
d. Conversion of Eurofunds into domestic funds by Eurobanks	10	15	20	20	20	20	25	30	45	60	75

* Based upon foreign currency claims of banks in European countries plus Japan, Canada, the Bahamas, Cayman Islands, Netherlands Antilles, Panama, Hong Kong, Singapore, and Bahrain.
Source: *World Financial Markets*, Morgan Guaranty Trust Company.

tion of both the quality of the borrowing bank and the extent of the existing loans from the lending bank to that particular borrowing bank. The most creditworthy banks, especially those which have not previously accumulated large debts to the lending bank, are offered more favorable LIBORs than are less attractive borrowers or banks which have already borrowed heavily from that particular lender.

The London interbank rates dominate the Eurocurrency markets. The rates in other European Euromarkets will generally match the London rate. The same is also true of the Caribbean rates in both Nassau and the Cayman Islands. However, in some other Euromarket centers slightly higher rates exist. For example, in the Asia-dollar market the Singapore interbank offer rate (SIBOR) has traditionally been slightly higher than LIBOR. However, as the size, sophistication, and perceived safety of this market have increased, the SIBOR has very closely matched the London rate. In centers of greater perceived risk, such as Panama, a premium rate over LIBOR continues to exist.

Corporate and Governmental Loans. The Eurocurrency market, including the interbank market, is basically an intermediary market: the ultimate user of the funds will usually be outside of the borrowing bank. Corporations with high credit ratings, governments (even those without high credit ratings), and banks outside of the Eurocurrency market are all aggressive borrowers of Eurofunds. Exhibit 5, line *b* shows Eurobank claims on nonbanks. Such investments grew more than 1,300 percent between 1970 and 1980. Claims on central banks and commercial banks which are outside of the Euromarket area are shown in line *c;* they grew almost 900 percent over the same period.

The existence of the Euromarket provides corporate treasurers, governments, and banks with a major adjunct to their domestic markets. Just as with commercial banks, the international markets can be a very appealing alternative when domestic credit conditions get very tight.

Loans to Affiliates. Another major use of Eurofunds is for loans within the same banking organization. This could be either to the parent company or to some other affiliate. (If the intrabank borrower was within the Euromarket area, such loans would be listed in line *a* or line *d* of Exhibit 5. If the borrower is outside of the Euromarkets, for example, a Eurobranch of an American bank lending to its U.S. headquarters, then the transactions would appear in line *c.*) The most common target would be to the affiliate in the country whose currency has been deposited or borrowed. For example, the London office of an American bank could be used to funnel dollars back to its home office in the United States—either because the Eurodollars were cheaper or because of domestic credit stringency in the U.S. Non-American banks can finance some of their U.S. operations in the same fashion, but the flows are larger for American banks.

Investment in Negotiable Securities.   Loans are not the only channel for the investment of Eurofunds. Eurobanks can also employ their funds in investments in marketable securities. Such investments, which will typically be short term in order to maintain liquidity, have the advantage (unlike loans) of being readily marketable before maturity. Of course, banks also attempt to balance the maturity structure of their *loan* portfolio carefully as well—so that there is a steady inflow of funds from maturing credits. However, investments in marketable securities can provide not only attractive investments but also, by providing ready marketability for some of the bank's investments, insurance against a possible short fall in funds. Such investments will appear in line *c* of Exhibit 5.

Lending Rates

As was indicated above, one Eurobank will lend to another at the former's LIBOR. Other borrowers would be charged a higher rate. In order to make a satisfactory return, the Eurobanks typically price such nonbank loans at LIBOR plus some prevailing *spread*. If a loan is made at LIBOR plus 1 percent, then when LIBOR is 15 percent the loan would be at 16 percent. The spread can vary from a fraction of a point (e.g., as low as ¼ percent to an attractive borrower in a borrower's market) to several points. The spread will often be *stepped up* for longer-term loans. For example, in the first three years of a loan, the lending rate may be LIBOR + ½ percent. The spread may then increase to LIBOR + ⅝ percent for the rest of the loan.

Eurocurrency lending rates generally move parallel to comparable domestic rates. Because of competition from the domestic market and because of lower costs in the Eurocurrency markets, the lending rates in the latter will generally be lower than the effective lending rates in the former. This is the normal pattern; it can be violated if capital or exchange controls, such as the Foreign Credit Restraint Program of the United States during the latter two thirds of the 1960s and the first third of the 1970s, are in effect.

Profitability of Euroloans.   Lending spreads of less than ½ percent over LIBOR are often too narrow to justify the lender's risks. Nevertheless, many Eurobanks will participate in what may in effect be loss leaders. For other banks the funding cost may be well below LIBOR; this is especially true of the large primary deposit banks (since quotes on nonbank deposits would generally be less than on interbank deposits). Alternatively, the lender may be short funding, using short-term funds to finance longer-term loans, with the expectation that funding costs will decline in the near future.

Lending fees, which are mostly paid front end, also play a critically important role in the Eurocurrency markets. Such fees can readily tip the balance between loss or profit. They are, of course, primarily the property of the lead managers (if the loan is syndicated). However, for longer-term loans the amortized value of the fees decreases significantly.

Roll-overs. Euroloans can be for any maturity from overnight to 15 or more years. If the loan is for longer than six months, the loan is generally made at a *floating rate*—that is, every three or six months the loan is rolled over and the LIBOR base is changed to reflect credit conditions at that time. This practice protects the lender. Banks can normally fund their Euroloans readily in the interbank market at LIBOR for three- or six-month periods. Therefore, by simply rolling over the loans each six months the banks will be lending at rates which reasonably approximate their funding costs. For example, the LIBOR + 1 percent loan mentioned above was initiated at 16 percent (i.e., when LIBOR was 15 percent). Six months later if LIBOR had risen to 18 percent, then the roll-over will be at 19 percent. Naturally, however, the pricing system can also work to the borrower's advantage. If LIBOR falls to 10 percent, then the roll-over will be at 11 percent— substantially less than when the loan was first drawn down.

Destruction of Eurocurrencies

As was seen above, the creation of Eurocurrencies occurs only when a foreign currency is deposited in a bank. The subsequent lending or investing of such deposits does not increase the net size of the Euromarkets. Similarly, the repayment of loans by borrowers or the sale of negotiable securities by a Eurobank does not reduce the size of the market. *Only the withdrawal of the original deposit will cause a reduction or destruction of Eurocurrencies.* Thus, if a depositor withdraws DM 1 million from a Euro DM account with a bank in London and repatriates them to Germany, then the size of the Eurodeutsche mark market has declined.

However, if the deposit had not been removed, but instead a DM 1 million loan was repaid to the Eurobank, the size of the Euro-DM market would be unchanged. The basic reason is, of course, that the underlying demand deposit in a domestic German bank is still there.

SUMMARY

Eurocurrencies are deposits at banks outside of the country that issued the currency deposited. Thus, the Eurocurrencies are not actually currencies at all.

Despite the term *Euro*currency, these deposits are not limited to European currencies; indeed, the U.S. dollar accounts for three quarters of the entire market. The markets themselves are not even limited to Europe: both the Caribbean and the Orient are major Eurocenters. The Asian portion of the Eurocurrency market is commonly referred to as the Asia-dollar market.

Eurocurrency deposits can be either standard time deposits or negotiable CDs. There are no demand deposits in the Eurocurrency markets. Deposits can come from governments, corporations, international agencies, or individuals.

The basic appeal of the Eurocurrency markets is that they are free from governmental controls. There are no reserve requirements, no interest-rate ceilings, no deposit insurance, and no credit allocations. This freedom and flexibility have proven to be popular not only with banks but also to depositors and borrowers. By the end of 1980 the gross size of the Eurocurrency markets had reached $1.5 trillion—and was continuing to grow rapidly!

Eurobanks invest most of their deposits outside of the country whose currency was deposited. However, since the funds plus interest must be repaid in the same currency, the banks also generally avoid cross-currency loans. There is, however, strong demand for loans in Eurocurrencies. These loans go to other banks or to corporations, governments, or international agencies.

Because of the freedom from expensive controls, for example, reserve requirements and deposit insurance, Eurobanks can generally offer higher interest on deposits than they can in the corresponding domestic market. They can also charge less for loans. Thus, Eurobanks generally operate on a smaller interest spread than they do domestically.

The Eurocurrency markets are a dynamic and important part of banking in the 1980s. The size of the markets and the importance of their role in the world economy are likely to continue to grow rapidly.

3

The Development of International Banking by the United States

JOHN C. HALEY
Executive Vice President
The Chase Manhattan Bank, N.A.
and
BARNARD SELIGMAN
Lubin Graduate School of Business
Pace University

A BRIEF HISTORY OF INTERNATIONAL BANKING

International banking has a long history. Although American banks have become a significant force in international banking only fairly recently, European financial institutions have operated across national boundaries for centuries. In the 12th through 16th centuries, Italian banks were important in international finance. Later, as their colonial empires grew, with the concomitant increase in international trade and the need for banking services, British, Dutch, and Belgian banks expanded all over the world. French and German financial institutions also built up worldwide banking systems, but British international banking was dominant until after World War II.

Before World War I, banks in the United States were preoccupied with financing the economic development of their own country—there was not much interest in overseas banking. Furthermore, there were legal restraints against offshore banking. National banks were prohibited from owning foreign branches and could not accept bills of exchange resulting from foreign trade. Some state banking codes, though, did permit international banking activity. Consequently, overseas expansion was limited to state chartered banks, most of whom were small, or to unincorporated institutions.

A few bankers did go overseas. J. P. Morgan was the first. Lazard, Freres, Seligman, Morton, Bliss and Company also went abroad and set up branches in Europe, and in the late 1800s, Jarvis-Conklin Trust Company opened an office in London.[1] These were exceptions—for the most part, American banks concentrated on domestic business, and only a small number had accounts with foreign correspondents or maintained foreign departments. The volume of international banking business was insignificant.

The economic-political environment in the United States began to change around World War I as the country became more involved in foreign affairs. This involvement was reflected in the Federal Reserve Act, passed in 1913. The Act permitted banks to establish foreign branches and to accept bills of exchange derived from exports and imports. Despite this new legal power, though, American banks were not enthusiastic about using it.

Citibank, however, did take advantage of the new law. It opened a branch in Buenos Aires, and shortly afterward it bought a controlling interest in the International Banking Corporation which had a network of 21 branches in 13 countries. But when war broke out in 1914, European banks, who had 2,000 branches outside their national borders compared to 26 American foreign branches, clearly controlled international banking.[2]

A few years after the Federal Reserve Act became law, in an attempt to stimulate American participation in international lending, the Act was amended in 1916. The amendment allowed member banks to invest in a subsidiary who could engage in international banking. A bank forming such a subsidiary had to enter into an "agreement" with the Federal Reserve authorities in which it described its activities, hence the name "Agreement Corporation." They were not popular, and only three were formed in the two years following the amendment.[3]

World War I and its aftermath gave an impetus to the development of American international banking. Because of the war, European countries could not export, and U.S. exports rose to fill some of the gap. After the war, American foreign trade continued to grow as did America's involvement in international finance. The dollar began to replace sterling as a key currency, and New York emerged as an international finance center. In response to these forces, U.S. international banking facilities gradually expanded.

In 1919, too, the so-called Edge Act (actually an amendment to

---

[1] Sarkis J. Khoury, *Dynamics of International Banking* (New York: Praeger Special Studies, 1980), p. 38.

[2] F. John Mathis, ed., *Offshore Lending by U.S. Banks* (Philadelphia: Robert Morris Associates, 1981), pp. 2–3.

[3] Neil Pinsky, "Edge Act and Agreement Corporations: Mediums for International Banking," *Economic Perspective, Federal Reserve Bank of Chicago,* September–October 1978, p. 28.

the Federal Reserve Act) was passed. Its aim was to stimulate foreign trade by authorizing the Board of Governors of the Federal Reserve System to charter corporations engaged either directly or indirectly in international banking operations. The potential in this legislation, however, was not realized until many years later, when Edge Act banks became widespread.

Unfortunately, after the war, credit was wildly overextended in the 1920s. In the Great Depression of the 1930s there was an epidemic of failures that brought international banking to a halt. Exchange controls, currency devaluations, quotas, and other government controls, plus the underlying threat of war made international credit hazardous. World War II was a further shock to the international banking system, and by the time it ended, U.S. banks had less than half as many foreign branches as they had had in 1920.[4]

In the period after the war, international banking was constrained by the "dollar shortage," as countries ravaged by war were short of foreign exchange reserves—the U.S. dollar had clearly become the international currency. In order to protect their reserves, these countries discouraged their banks from taking dollar deposits and lending them overseas. Dollar exchange was mostly supplied by the American government. The atmosphere of the Cold War also inhibited the growth of global banking.

In the 1950s international trade began to recover from the war. The Marshall Plan helped to restore the economies of the war-torn areas. The Export-Import Bank, rechartered in 1945 became more active in supporting commercial bank export debt obligations and participations in direct lending, and the World Bank Group, a creation of the Breton Woods Conference of 1944, contributed to economic growth in many countries. In addition, the colonial system of European countries became unsustainable, and large business corporations in the United States and in the Western countries began to internationalize as exports and imports grew. The stage was set for American banking's most dramatic movement into international banking.

Table 1 gives an indication of the growth of American international banking. In 1950 there were only seven banks with 95 overseas branches. Twenty years later, in 1970, there were 79 banks with 536 foreign offices, and although the rush overseas slowed down in the latter half of the 1970s, by the end of the 1970s, there were 139 banks with 796 foreign branches. The assets of overseas branches show a similar growth configuration, and now approach the $400 billion mark. Furthermore, there are now many banks that provide various levels of international banking services. It is difficult to get an exact tally of them, but a recent count by the authors showed that 238 banks

[4] Mathis, *Offshore Lending*, p. 4.

Table 1
Foreign Branches and Assets of U.S. Commercial Banks

	1950	1960	1970	1979
Number of banks with overseas branches	7	8	79	139
Number of overseas branches	95	124	536	796
Assets of overseas branches	n.a.	n.a.	$46.5B	$364.2B

n.a. = not available.
Source: Christopher M. Korth, "The Evolving Rate of U.S. Banks in International Finance," *The Bankers Magazine*, July–August 1980, p. 69.

offered international banking facilities of some kind.[5] There were a number of reasons for this growth.

REASONS FOR GROWTH

In the early post-World War II days, there were two forces that resulted in a greater presence of offshore American banks. First, at the urging of the government, overseas branches were set up simply to service military personnel who were stationed abroad. Second, Public Law 480, which authorized the disposal of surplus agriculture commodities for local currency, and other government assistance programs that required offsetting funds, led to deposits in foreign branches. These factors, however, were short-lived and minor compared to other events.

As previously mentioned, in the 1950s, world trade recovered, but over time it grew at increasing rates. In the 1950s, the annual volume of world exports and imports rose at an 8.4 percent rate. In the following decade it went up to 10 percent a year. The 1970s were unprecedented. World exports and imports grew at an annual rate of 20 percent—double the rate of the 1960s.[6] The United States shared in this movement. By the 1970s foreign trade was up about five times compared to the 1950s. This big rise in international trade automatically caused a need for more financing and international banking services. Government regulations, however, also played a major role in creating an incentive to internationalize banking.

In the 1950s, because of chronic deficits in its balance of payments, the U.S. government initiated three control programs—the Foreign Direct Investment Program (FDIP), the Interest Equalization Tax (IET), and the Voluntary Foreign Credit Restraint (VFCR) program. The objective of these restraints was to discourage the outflow of capi-

---

[5] *International Activities of U.S. Banks* (New York: American Banker, 1978).

[6] Some of this big jump is attributed to the price increases imposed by OPEC.

tal. Probably these laws and restrictions were ineffective in reducing the deficits of the balance of payments, but they generated a strong impetus for American banks to expand their foreign operations.

Originally, in 1964, the FDIP was voluntary, but it became mandatory in 1968. Under the FDIP, corporations were restricted in the amount of funds they could transfer to their foreign affiliates. Similarly, the foreign affiliates were constrained in the reinvestment of locally generated funds. It was hoped that these limitations would reduce the transfer of capital overseas and force it back to the United States.

The IET aimed at making it more difficult for foreign corporations and foreign affiliates of American corporations to raise capital in this country. This was done by imposing a tax on foreign securities which would reduce the real yield to U.S. investors and make it more expensive for foreigners to borrow money in U.S. markets. The VFCR simply "requested" banks to limit their foreign loans. The limitations were based on historical credit levels.

The net result of these restrictions was to force many companies to go overseas to finance their operations. Many firms switched from the United States to the Eurobond market. The American banks, in turn, had to go abroad to tap foreign sources of funds to finance loans. Foreign assets on the books of the home office were dampened, but overall foreign lending accelerated. In the early 1960s, only New York City banks with some representation from Boston and San Francisco banks operated overseas branches. By 1970, banks from regional money centers such as Chicago, Pittsburgh, and Detroit had physically entered the foreign market. All the credit controls, however, were lifted in 1974.

Another important regulatory factor that induced banks to go overseas was Regulation Q. This regulation puts a ceiling on the rates banks can pay on domestic deposits.[7] There is no such restriction in Europe. When money gets tight and open market rates go above the permissible Regulation Q rate, there is apt to be a run-off of deposits as money chases the more attractive yield. This happened notably in 1966 and 1969–70. Foreign banks and foreign branches of U.S. banks, though, could effectively compete for U.S. dollar deposits. Consequently, many banks, caught in the credit squeeze caused by Regulation Q opened offices abroad, particularly in London, in order to tap the Eurodollar market.

Regulation D, under which the Board of Governors of the Federal Reserve System sets reserve requirements, has also been a factor in inducing banks to seek foreign U.S. dollar deposits. As in any business, banks seek the cheapest source of funds, and while reserve require-

---

[7] Under the Deregulation and Monetary Control Act of 1980, Regulation Q is to be phased out over a six-year period.

ments on foreign deposits have varied over the years, they have always been lower than the requirements on domestic deposits. This obviously has a favorable effect on loan margins and therefore encourages expansion abroad.

There were also some deliberate legislative actions that helped expand international banking. In the 1960s, the attitude of state legislatures began to change, and a number of states allowed foreign banks to open in their states if reciprocal rights were given. Federal regulations were also liberalized. In 1966, national banks were allowed to invest directly in the stock of foreign banks, and in 1970, the Bank Holding Company Act was amended to clarify the regulatory frame of international activities of U.S. bank holding companies. Later, too, in 1979, the Federal Reserve Board issued a new Regulation K, which among other things, authorized domestic branches for Edge Act Corporations.

The creation of the Common Market, too, was in itself an inducement to overseas expansion by U.S. banks. As tariff barriers were lowered within the six countries comprising the Common Market, U.S. corporations moved production to countries within the Common Market to protect their market share. U.S. banks followed their clients to link the client's overseas activities to the domestic relationship. American banks were quite successful in obtaining business from the American industries in Europe by treating the smaller overseas companies as part of a corporate whole and in pricing bank products very competitively with an eye on the total yield on the worldwide business relationship with the company rather than simply the spread on any single transaction in any given country.

Finally, any account of the reasons for the rapid increase in American international banking would be incomplete without mention of the Eurocurrency market, often called the Eurodollar market because most transactions are in U.S. dollars. The Eurocurrency market is a global network of banks, branches, and affiliates that accept deposits and make loans in currencies different than the country in which the loan is booked. Most of the market is located in London, but smaller centers have evolved in Paris, Zurich, Singapore, Hong Kong, and Panama.

It would go far afield to discuss in detail the reasons for the growth of this market, but clearly, a significant boost was given to the market by the U.S. government restrictions discussed previously. The Eurocurrency market grew from $85 billion to over $600 billion in the 1970s, and American banks have played an important part in its development.[8] Today, major money market banks use it as part of

---

[8] *World Financial Markets* (New York: Morgan Guaranty Trust Co., October 1980), p. 3; as of September 1981, the Eurocurrency Market was estimated to be $855 billion, *World Financial Markets* (New York: Morgan Guaranty Trust Co., March 1982), p. 15.

their "liability management" as well as a means to diversify their risk exposure.

FORMS OF INTERNATIONAL BANKING

In the new world of international banking, American banks must compete not only with their domestic counterparts but with financial institutions from other countries as well. Bank customers have choices, and financial services and techniques may vary. European banks, for example, are often regarded as "asset lenders." Japaneses banks may supply permanent working capital by rolling over short-term loans. In contrast, American banks are more likely to emphasize cash flow. To service their clients and meet the competition, U.S. banks have adopted a number of organizational structures. Each of them has inherent advantages and disadvantages.

One of the oldest forms of international banking is the usage of correspondence banks. The arrangment is similar to domestic correspondence bank relationships except that it is international. Typical services involve honoring letters of credit, accepting drafts, supplying credit information, collecting and disbursing funds, and handling foreign investments. Bank customers get the advantages of world-wide financial services, but since correspondents tend to take care of their own accounts before that of the foreign banks, many institutions seek other arrangements.

Some banks, for example, set up representative offices. Although a representative office has severely limited powers—it cannot take deposits, make loans, accept drafts, or transfer funds—some banks established them to take care of the needs of customers of the parent bank. Generally, it is a small, low-cost operation which acts as a conduit for information and contacts. In some cases, as in Mexico, where a foreign general banking business is prohibited, a representative office is the only means of direct bank representation.

Other banks have opted for the agency form. Essentially, it is the same as a branch bank except for one important restriction—it cannot accept deposits from the general public. Some agencies, however, may take time deposits from other banks. Agencies usually may make loans to finance trade with the home country and issue letters of credit. They are often active, too, in the foreign exchange market.

As previously pointed out, foreign branch banking has grown rapidly in recent years, although it should be pointed out that they are heavily concentrated in money market centers such as London and the Caribbean. The advantages of a foreign branch are that a full range of banking services can be provided and the branch benefits from name identification with the parent. The main disadvantages are cost and legal restrictions. They are regulated by the U.S. authorities and the host country. In some cases they are prohibited entirely. In other cases they are welcomed and operate quite freely.

At the close of 1979, the Federal Reserve reported that 131 Edge Act and Agreement Corporations held $17.8 billion of assets.[9] When consolidated with their foreign subsidiaries, however, these companies had assets of almost $44 billion and accounted for 12 percent of the international business of U.S. banks.[10] Edge Act corporations are subsidiaries of parent banks and in a few cases have multiple ownership. They accept deposits that are related to international transactions, make loans, confirm letters of credit, create bankers' acceptances, maintain foreign exchange markets, and act as collection and disbursement agents. Besides overseas subsidiaries, Edge Act corporations may have offices located in cities outside the parent bank's home state.

Foreign subsidiary and affiliate banks have also been formed by U.S. banks. A foreign subsidiary bank is a separate incorporated bank owned entirely or in part by a parent company. It has the advantage of appearing as a local bank in the host country, and usually management is drawn from the local area. It is likely, therefore, to attract local business, whereas a branch may appeal more to a firm with an international business that is headquartered outside the host country. An affiliate bank differs from a subsidiary in that it is not controlled by an outside parent company. Control may be local or by other foreign banks. Its advantage is that besides its local identity, it can draw on the expertise of more than one owner. This, however, may be a source of disagreement, too.

In the mid-1960s, consortia banking was formed in Europe. A consortia bank is a joint venture, separately incorporated and owned by multiple banks, usually from different countries. They were formed to finance large international projects and government development programs. A typical consortia handles underwriting, global syndication, mergers and acquisitions, and equity participations. Examples of consortia banks are Societe Financiere Europeinne, owned by eight banks, with the Bank of America as its American participant, and Orion Bank, Ltd., originally owned by six banks, including Chase Manhattan as its American member. Five of the original banks in Orion, however, eventually sold their shares to the sixth, the Royal Bank of Canada. One of the principal factors that led to the establishment of consortium banks was the raw material shortages forecast by many in the late 1960s ("Limits to Growth," the Club of Rome, etc.) coupled with a shortage of capital. The consortium bank was a logical adjunct to a project in the extractive industries that involved more than one com-

---

[9] *Annual Report* (Washington, D.C.: Board of Governors of the Federal Reserve System, 1979), p. 285.

[10] James V. Houpt, "Performance and Characteristics of Edge Corporations," *Staff Studies, Board of Governors of the Federal Reserve System,* January 1981, p. 1.

pany from more than one country with the financing in more than one currency. The OPEC price increase and the resultant Eurodollar surplus vastly expanded international bank liquidity and the number of banks accepting Eurodollar deposits and making Eurodollar loans.

The recession of 1975 put a number of large projects on the back burner, thus the consortium banks switched their activities from project finance to government and multicorporate lending—the same business their parents were in.

Recently, with the objective of attracting some of the international banking business that occurs overseas, government approval was given for the establishment of international banking facilities (IBFs) at offices in the United States. In many ways, an IBF is similar to a foreign branch except that it is physically located in this country. It is allowed to take time deposits and to grant loans to foreigners, and reserve requirements and interest rate ceilings are waived. Several states, too, exempt earnings of IBFs from state and local income taxes. The full impact of the IBFs on overseas banking arrangements remains to be seen, but as of December 23, 1981, only 20 days after they were authorized, assets of IBFs were over $47 billion.[11]

THE IMPACT OF U.S. INTERNATIONAL BANKING

There can be no doubt that American international banking has scored impressive gains even though, as shown in Table 2, they are not the source of most foreign lending. Clearly, however, they have become a major force in international financial markets, and this movement has been an important contributor to the growth and profitability of the U.S. banking industry. Recently, interest rate margins have narrowed, but overall, international lending has been profitable.

Much has been written about the risk exposure faced by banks who go into the international market.[12] But over the five years 1975–79, a study showed that 10 large U.S. banks reported losses of only $1.144 million on foreign credits. This was equal to 22 percent of total loan losses, although international loans averaged 44.8 percent of the total loan portfolio of the reporting banks.[13] Surely, this is most impressive evidence of good management.

International lending by U.S. banks is highly concentrated. Data supplied by the monetary authorities indicate that the nine largest banks account for 67 percent of the total. The next 15 banks equal 17 percent, and all the other banks generate only 16 percent of foreign

---

[11] International Letter, Federal Reserve Bank of Chicago, January 1, 1982, p. 1.

[12] For a critical review of International Banking, see "Living with a Nightmare," *The Economist,* March 20–26, 1982, pp. 9–100.

[13] *A Profile of Commercial Banking in the U.S.* (New York: Salomon Bros., 1980), table 15.

Table 2
Estimated Lending in International Markets (dollars in billions)

	Changes			Amount Outstanding
Lenders	*1978*	*1979*	*1980*	*1980*
European banks	$145	$165	$127	$ 903
Canadian and Japanese banks	16	15	30	101
U.S. banks (including offshore centers)	54	38	55	319
Total	$215	$218	$212	$1,323
Less double counting due to redepositing among banks	105	88	67	513
Less exchange rate effects	20	5	−20	—
Net new international bank lending	$ 90	$125	$165	$ 810

Source: Calculated from "Estimated Lending in International Markets," *Annual Report, Bank for International Settlements*, 1981, Basle, Switzerland, p. 100.

credits. This breakdown is shown in Table 3. Obviously, then, international lending is particularly important to the big banks. Their significance relative to domestic loans is disclosed in Table 4.

The configuration of international loans booked by American banks shows that most of the money goes to Europe. Furthermore, most of the loans—about 55 percent of the total—are to other banks, and a major part of them are short term. Examination of the data indicate that 72 percent of the foreign loans held by American banks had a maturity of one year or less. The profile of cross border and nonlocal currency claims of U.S. Banks is given in Table 5.

With the growth of international bank activity, problems have also developed. The Eurodollar market, of course, was in existence before OPEC, and while OPEC funds are a very important factor in the market, there are other components. Nevertheless, one difficulty that may get even more troublesome is the recycling of OPEC funds. Mo-

Table 3
Cross-Border Loans by Bank Size, June 1980 (dollars in billions)

Bank Group	*Amount*	*Percent*
First nine banks	$176.7	67
Next 15 banks	45.8	17
All others	43.5	16
	$266.0	100%

Source: *Joint News Release* (Washington, D.C.: Controller of the Currency, Federal Deposit Insurance Corp., Federal Reserve Bank, November 24, 1980), pp. 1–3.

Table 4
International Loans for First Nine Banks, December 1980

	Banks	Percent	
		International	Domestic
1.	Citibank	58.3	41.7
2.	Chase	56.5	43.5
3.	BankAmerica	36.8	63.2
4.	Morgan	55.5	44.5
5.	Manufacturers Hanover	51.0	49.0
6.	Chemical	42.2	57.8
7.	Bankers Trust	48.1	51.9
8.	Continental Illinois	31.1	68.9
9.	First Chicago	38.6	61.4
	All nine banks	48.2	51.8

Source: Annual Reports and 10-K forms—1980.

nies received by OPEC (mostly U.S. dollars) will probably continue to be placed in the banking systems of a few Western countries with sophisticated financial markets, whereas the offsetting deficits will originate from many countries including developing nations. Members of OPEC, in all likelihood, will want to keep much of their receipts in liquid short-term paper. Many of the oil importing countries, however, need long-term funds, so a mismatching of maturities of bank liabilities and assets may be created.

Table 5
Cross Border and Nonlocal Currency Claims of U.S. Banks, December 1980 (U.S. dollars in billions)

Area	Claims On			
	Banks	Public Borrowers	Other Private	Total
Europe	$ 84.4	$ 6.8	$27.3	$118.5
Nondeveloped countries	9.1	6.1	10.9	26.1
Eastern Europe	4.3	3.0	.9	8.2
Oil exporting countries	5.3	7.9	7.5	20.7
Nonoil exporting developing countries: Latin America and Caribbean	17.4	16.1	21.1	54.6
Asia	9.9	5.8	7.9	23.6
Africa	1.0	2.3	.7	4.0
Offshore banking centers	35.3	.9	7.5	43.7
Total	166.7	48.9	83.8	299.4

Source: *Country Exposure Lending Survey* (Washington, D.C.: Federal Financial Institutions Examination Council, May 28, 1981).

Another major issue is whether the growth of international banking has exacerbated global inflation. Have the loans made by the international banks simply postponed the day of reckoning? Have the debtor countries merely bought time by papering over their deficits in their balance of payments and therefore stalled the adoption of anti-inflation policies? Even more, does this cause a "spillover" effect? Do other countries import inflation from those that have been able to forestall the effects of a deficit in their balance of payments by borrowing from the international banking systems?

A related question is the degree of control that national monetary authorities may or may not have over international financial markets.[14] There is some debate on the matter, but many informed observers claim that the Eurocurrency market is beyond the control of any national monetary authority. Even worse, each country has its own techniques for requiring banks to set aside reserves. How does this impact on various money stocks? Is there a multiplier effect, and if so, how much?[15]

SUMMARY AND CONCLUSIONS

Over the years, particularly in the last two decades, U.S. international banking has made tremendous gains. While the big money market banks have been transformed into multinationals, many other banks have shared in this progress. American international banking has not only been an important element in bank profitability, but also instrumental in the development of a truly international market for money and credit. This, in turn, has facilitated the flow of funds across national borders and led to the creation of an efficient market that has aided the economic development of many countries.

U.S. international banking has gone through many changes, and undoubtedly, more will come. The consequences, for example, of a rapidly shifting competitive environment remain to be seen. And, as always, there is the possibility of unanticipated and unplanned strains on the system. So far, American banks have successfully met the challenges posed by international banking. There is good reason to expect that U.S. international banking will continue to flourish in the future.

---

[14] See, for example, Nicholas Carlozzi, "Regulating the Eurocurrency Market: What Are the Prospects?" *Business Review, Federal Reserve Bank of Philadelphia* (March–April 1981), pp. 15–23.

[15] For a comprehensive discussion of this area, see Jack Guttentag and Richard Herring, *Financial Disorder and International Banking* (Philadelphia: University of Pennsylvania, March 18, 1981).

4
The Role of Foreign Banks in International Banking

JOHANN WENDT
Vice President
Comerica Bank, Detroit

Banks vary considerably from country to country in their involvement in the international process. Their patterns depend in general on their history, the level of economic development of the country, the extent of its involvement in transactions with parties in other countries, the volume of its international transactions, governmental limitations or requirements, and factors that may be very special to an individual bank or country. As a general rule the governments of less developed countries exert more control over the international activities of their banks.

Any international banker or businessman approaching a country for the first time is advised to study the banking structure of the country before initiating any contacts. In some countries the branches or subsidiaries of banks foreign to the country may be a wise choice for particular needs; in other cases it might be wiser to develop strong relationships with indigenous banks. The examples given below are not meant to be all inclusive.

BRAZIL

Since the Brazilian financial system developed largely during times of high inflation, one of its important features is inflation indexing, which has been applied to all aspects of finance. High economic growth has successfully coexisted with inflation beyond all expectations. The banking reform law of 1964 created the National Monetary Council and the Banco Central do Brasil. The number of commercial banks was substantially reduced from 328 in 1964 to 108 in 1979, a move supported by the government in order to create large financial conglomerates. Today, however, new emphasis is given to the creation of regional banks mainly to reduce regional imbalances and to halt the concentration process within the financial system as well.

A recent listing shows the following 10 largest banks:

	Assets in U.S. Dollars (millions) as of December 31, 1980
Banco do Brasil S.A.	40,305
Banco do Estado do Rio Grande do Sul	9,164
Banco do Estado de Sao Paulo	6,160
Banco Brasileiro do Descontos	4,079
Banco Itau S.A.	2,839
Banco Real S.A.	2,343
Uniao de Bancos Brasileiros	1,829
Banco de Credito Real de Minas Gerais	1,756
Banco Bamerindus do Brasil	1,704
Banco do Nordeste do Brasil	1,696

Banco do Brasil is by far the largest bank in the country with approximately 1,235 branches in Brazil and abroad. It acts as the main financial agent of Banco Central do Brasil and is a financial agent of the federal government. It plays an important role as an instrument for government credit policies.

In addition, there are 23 state government-owned banks as well as a number of development banks. Investment banks, which are privately held, were established in 1966 to provide medium- and long-term financing.

The Brazilian financial system performs a crucial role in channeling investments to priority sections and neglected regions in accordance with an overall economic strategy of the government. Brazil has, in the past, been an active borrower of foreign funds, particularly in the Eurodollar market. These foreign loans have to be converted into cruzeiros and registered with the government to guarantee repatriation. These foreign loans can either be contracted directly by a Brazilian borrower with a foreign bank or through a Brazilian bank which contracts with a lending bank abroad.

Brazil has a long history of controlling interest rates based on their historical usury law limiting interest rates to 12 percent a year. In recent history, however, the usury ceiling is being circumvented by discounting trade bills.

Authorization to establish a foreign bank is strictly based on reciprocal arrangements for Brazilian banks to operate in the foreign country, provided the foreign bank establishes an investment bank or purchases more than one third of an existing investment bank.

The Banco Central do Brasil performs a rediscounting service in its capacity as the lender of last resort. The rediscounting, however, is determined by the volume of deposits held by the applicant bank.

The Banco Central do Brasil also supports strongly any export financing that is traditionally its responsibility.

Exchange controls are extremely tight, and foreign currencies can only be purchased with the approval of the central bank. The exchange value of the cruzeiro is pegged to the U.S. dollar and depreciated frequently to keep up with the current rate of inflation.

Because of restrictions on capital inflows and outflows, as well as other limitations, it would be advisable for a foreign businessman to use the services of a Brazilian bank.

CANADA

The Canadian banking system is dominated by the 11 chartered banks with a total of 6,969 domestic and about 262 foreign branches. Their charters follow the original charter set up in 1817 for the Bank of Montreal as the first Canadian bank.

Because of diminishing specialization, the chartered banks are increasingly in competition with so-called near banks, such as savings or mortgage loan banks. They do, however, have a large share of the foreign currency business because of economic involvement with the United States as well as close contacts with the New York and London financial markets.

A recent survey shows the following chartered banks:

	Assets in U.S. Dollars (millions) as of October 31, 1980
The Royal Bank of Canada	52,944
Canadian Imperial Bank of Commerce	46,704
Bank of Montreal	41,154
The Bank of Nova Scotia	36,381
Toronto-Dominion Bank	28,515
National Bank of Canada	13,873
The Mercantile Bank of Canada	3,466
Bank of British Columbia	1,970
Continental Bank	1,416
Canadian Commercial and Industrial Bank	761
Northland Bank	213

Although the number of agencies of foreign banks in Canada has been increasing substantially in recent history, it was not until passage of the 1977 revision of the Bank Act that foreign banks were permitted to operate banks in Canada within very well controlled limits.

The Bank of Canada is the country's central bank. It has no powers to selectively control credit but usually implements policies by using moral suasion. There are no foreign exchange restrictions in effect at this time. Accordingly, anyone doing business in Canada and needing financial assistance and/or information has no choice but to use the services of an indigenous bank.

COMECON COUNTRIES

COMECON is an anglicized acronym for "Council for Mutual Economic Assistance"; it was founded in 1949. Members include the USSR, Hungary, the German Democratic Republic, Poland, Romania, Bulgaria, Czechoslovakia, Mongolia, Vietnam, and Cuba. The banking system of COMECON evolved from the nationalization of commercial banks in member countries after the establishment of Communist governments. COMECON supports two regional banks: (1) the International Bank of Economic Cooperation, which is COMECON's trade bank and (2) the International Investment Bank established for long-term credit support by tapping Western money markets. Both banks deal in transferable rubles (TR) and convertible currencies. The TR is a clearing currency between the members for trade purposes only, and credit balances in TRs do not guarantee any true benefit. The banking system of COMECON is used to facilitate the transfer of balances between the various member state's enterprises.

The International Bank of Economic Cooperation (IBEC) was established in 1963 to reorient COMECON members' foreign trade relations. The purpose of IBEC, which handles multilateral payments of Eastern European countries, was to increase volume in intrabloc trade with a more reasonable use of resources and export capabilities. Credit from IBEC is granted automatically to cover imbalances in COMECON countries' commercial payments and receipts in trade with each other. Any credit extended is for less than seven years.

The International Investment Bank (IIB) was established in January 1971 to assist in financing large amounts and for terms of more than seven years.

The individual member state banking systems do not pursue their own courses with their own objectives. Rather, banks are wholly in the service of the economy, and its goals are their goals. There is no competition for customers, and no market competition comes to bear. The banking system is tailored to the needs of the state, because the state is the universal owner.

Besides the two banks that service COMECON, there are usually at least three functioning banks in each member country. These are the state bank, the foreign trade bank, and the foreign exchange bank. The state bank is the absolute center of the banking system and simultaneously serves and protects state interests. The state bank refinances credits granted by other banks or backs up their money deposits.

From the management of foreign exchange holdings to the distribution of exchange balances, the state bank exercises complete control over foreign exchange transactions. This is in close cooperation with the ministry of finance. The foreign exchange bank is a function of this cooperation, while the foreign trade bank is an extension of the state bank's services.

When businesses trade with foreign concerns they must go through the foreign trade corporation established for their industry. Foreign trade corporations divorce domestic prices from the market prices of exports or imports. The foreign trade corporation must then deal with the foreign trade bank.

The foreign trade banks of Eastern European countries, with the exception of Romania, are organized like Western commercial banks. Their capital, however, is held by a number of official governmental institutions, such as the ministries of finance or foreign trade or the state bank. There is no commercial lending or discount credit available as it is known in the West. However, a business concern that produces exclusively for export would not only receive its entitled production costs (normal costs), but also the necessary financing to cover lead time costs between the foreign trade corporation selling its goods, and receiving the proceeds from the sale via trade balance subsidies.

Payments are automatically transferred from purchaser to supplier via the state bank. If the supplier is a foreign concern and a member of COMECON, then the foreign trade bank, state bank, and the IBEC are all involved to effect balance transfers. Otherwise the state bank will handle hard currency transactions, but there will be an effort to barter goods for at least a portion of the original transaction amount in an attempt to preserve hard currency balances. Since domestic prices are set by arbitrary guidelines (i.e., economic plan), they do not correspond directly with a foreign exchange price rate at true market costs.

Some financing is now handled as a loan or specific project subsidy which is in part financed by a loan or commitment from a government agency in conjunction with foreign (mostly Western) financing agreements. There are no foreign banks, however, established in COMECON countries.

GERMANY

The German banking system developed its strength during the 19th century at the time of German industrialization. Banks provided initial finance and subsequently managed the issue of shares to repay the initial loans. This established a close relationship between banks and industrial companies which has continued until today. Banks generally act as universal banks providing a range of financial services which extend beyond that of a typical deposit bank.

The three dominant German commercial banks, Deutsche Bank, Dresdner Bank, and Commerzbank, known as the "Big Three," are considered as the only true national banks in the country. Their importance is evidenced by the classification, with their Berlin subsidiaries, as a separate group in the regularly published official statistics.

As of December 31, 1980 the "Big Three" reported the following:

	Assets in U.S. Dollars (*millions*)
Deutsche Bank (consolidated)	90,001
Dresdner Bank	39,599
Commerzbank	34,136

In addition there are over 100 regional and other commercial banks operating in Germany. The largest banks in this group reported the following at December 31, 1980

	Assets in U.S. Dollars (*millions*)
Wesdeutsche Landesbank	51,641
Bayerische Landesbank Girozentrale	38,224
Bayerische Hypotheken und Wechsel Bank	29,601
Bayerische Vereinsbank	27,028
Hessische Landesbank Girozentrale	24,580
Norddeutsche Landesbank Girozentrale	23,001
Bank Fur Gemeinwirtschaft	22,801
Deutsche Genossenschaftsbank	20,611

In addition to the regular banking services, banks in Germany are also authorized (*a*) to issue and place securities for public authorities and industrial companies, (*b*) to do stockbroking and advise customers on the purchase and sale of securities, and (*c*) to do insurance broking business. Because many of the large German banks have a nationwide branching network and are active in all aspects of domestic and international banking, they are able to respond to virtually any need of a business or a foreign bank.

Some of the relations that German banks have with industry have come under criticism lately because of the significant industrial holdings by the banks. It has been alleged that they exercise excessive control over certain industries. Additionally, there are many bankers present on the supervisory boards of industrial and commercial companies.

Foreign banks are mostly involved in financing imports and exports and servicing the German subsidiaries of foreign companies. They are controlled by the same laws as German banks, and there are no genuine obstacles to their establishment.

The Deutsche Bundesbank is Germany's Central Bank. Although the financial system is subject to controls and regulations, the controls tend to be of a judicial nature and do not interfere with market competition.

As outlined above, a businessman has a variety of German and foreign banks at his disposal to assist him in his business dealings.

HONG KONG

The British Crown Colony of Hong Kong was originally established under the Treaty of Nanking in 1842. It now consists of Hong Kong Island, the Kowloon Peninsula, other land on the mainland up to the China border, and some smaller islands.

Hong Kong has always been a free port, and foreign trade has been very important and crucial to the colony's growth rate. An important activity in the port was the warehousing and the reexporting of goods as well as the necessary interim financing. This activity is called *entrepot.* It was very instrumental in expanding bank credit prior to World War II. Today industry plays a dominant role in the Crown Colony.

The opening of China to the West suggested a lessening of Hong Kong's importance, since financial matters could be handled through Tokyo, London, and New York. Yet, when Hong Kong entrepreneurs opened joint ventures with neighboring China and China began investing in more private companies in Hong Kong, the colony became China's second largest trading partner after Japan. It has also become a most important source of foreign exchange for China.

There are three categories of banks or banking institutions by rules of the Hong Kong Association of Banks to which all licensed banks must belong:

Commercial banks—have a monopoly on deposits up to HK $50,000 and must compete for amounts over this.

Licensed deposit-taking companies—are restricted to accepting deposits of more than HK $50,000.

New deposit-taking companies (merchant banks)—can only accept business deposits of HK $50,000 or more.

The largest local commercial banks are:

	Assets in U.S. Dollars (millions) as of December 31, 1980
Hong Kong and Shanghai Bank Corp.	48,809
Hang Seng Bank Limited	4,693
Grindlays Dao Heng Bank Limited	1,129
Bank of East Asia	1,001

There are a total of 115 fully licensed banks in Hong Kong, 44 local and 71 foreign banks.

Hong Kong has no central banking institution, and until 1965 legal regulations had followed a laissez-faire attitude. Licensed commercial banks could become involved in a wide variety of financial activities, and only on two occasions, when individual banks were unable to meet cash runs, were some of the banking activities regulated.

The central bank functions are handled by the Financial Secretary of the Colony, the office of the Commissioner of Banking and Exchange Fund, and the Hong Kong and Shanghai Banking Corporation, which is also authorized to issue bank notes. There are no foreign exchange controls. The businessman will find a variety of foreign and indigenous banks at his disposal to render outstanding financial assistance.

ITALY

The Italian banking system had its beginnings in the fourth century B.C. Silver dealers accepted deposits, gave loans, bought trade bills, and offered time deposits that paid interest. Deposit slips were transmitted from hand to hand, taking the place of money. Banking regulation was evident when Justinian codified Roman laws in the sixth century and included usury limits.

Until the Bank of Venice was founded as the first State Bank by the Republic of Venice to finance war in 1171, banks serviced personal and commercial needs only. In the 14th century commerce began to flourish, and the Medici, Peruzzi, and Bardi banking families were established.

Early in the 20th century there was heavy bank involvement in industrial financing. This left banks' capital weak and vulnerable to the shifts in fortunes of large industry. It also set the stage for increased governmental regulation and intervention in banking operations.

The extensive involvement of the government in banking is witnessed by the establishment of the Industrial Reconstruction Institute (IRI) in 1933. It is an autonomous agency that holds a majority of shares capital in the country's three largest banks and a large number of industrial, financial, and commercial enterprises.

There are 1069 registered banks, including commercial banks, savings banks, merchant banks, and trade banks. Following is a listing of the largest banks in this group.

	Assets in U.S. Dollars (millions) as of December 31, 1980
Banca Nazionale del Lavoro	42,649
Banca Commerciale Italiana	33,566
Monte dei Paschi di Siena (consolidated)	28,566
Credito Italiano	27,123
Banco di Roma	25,586
Instituto Bancario San Paolo di Torino	25,153
Banco di Napoli	20,911
Banco di Sicilia	14,785
Banca Nazionale dell' Agricoltura	13,918
Banca Popolare di Novara	10,520
Banco Ambrosiano	7,145

Since the Bank Act of 1936, commercial banks have been restricted to short-term credit financing. They number 136 and deal in bonds and stock shares of firms and are the prime source of export financing.

The remainder of banks in this category are those considered to be banks of national interest because they have branches throughout the country. They also include the savings and cooperative banks which are tailored to territorial needs and conditions of crafts and trades associations. These banks are not restricted to short-term financing. They normally handle the medium-term financing needs of their customers in addition to retail transactions.

There are also 90 special credit institutions operating in the country. They provide medium- to long-term credit and loans at subsidized rates to foster governmental development plans. They often take an equity portion in any projects financed. The major banks in this group as of December 31, 1980 are:

	Assets in U.S. Dollars (millions)
Cassa di Risparmio delle Provincie Lombarde	26,241
Cassa di Risparmio di Torino	8,025
Cassa di Risparmio di Roma	7,386
Cassa di Risparmio di Verona, Vicenza e Belluno	4,444
Cassa di Risparmio di Firenze	3,942

The Italian banking system is 66 percent owned by the state. The state-owned organizations receive no special privileges, however. They compete in the same way as private organizations.

There are 18 foreign commercial banks operating in Italy in addition to a number of representative offices. They are mostly involved in wholesale banking due to the nature of their clientele of foreign and domestic companies engaged in worldwide transactions. Most foreign banks depend on the interbank market for funding instead of a retail customer deposit base.

The Bank of Italy, founded in 1893, is the central bank and has the sole right to issue currency. It also authorizes security issues of organizations, sets limits on the credit that a single client may obtain from banks, and sets the ratios and balances that all banks and credit institutions must maintain.

Foreign exchange controls are operated by the Italian Exchange Office. Only authorized banks are permitted to engage in foreign exchange trading.

Any businessman doing business in Italy will find valuable assistance from the Italian banks, in addition to the services foreign banks offer.

JAPAN

The history of some of the Japanese banks dates back several centuries. Although the modern financial system was created after the Meiji restoration of 1868, the most dramatic reconstruction occurred after 1945 during the postwar period when the Japanese financial system underwent drastic reforms. The relative importance of banks in the postwar period arose because of the need for creating credit to repair the destructions of the war. One reform, particularly dramatic for Japan, prohibited banks from the underwriting of securities.

In 1954, the Bank of Tokyo, the former Yokohama Specie Bank, was the only bank able to deal in foreign exchange. However, it did not retain the other privileges the Yokohama Specie bank had held previously. Today, however, a total of 78 banks in the Japanese system, including all the city banks listed below, are authorized to engage in foreign exchange transactions.

In addition to the 13 city banks (page 57) there are 63 local banks, which conduct commercial business principally in local areas.

There are also approximately 55 foreign banks in Japan which (*a*) may not operate a savings or trust bank, (*b*) cannot make foreign currency loans for a term of less than a year, and (*c*) have limitations imposed upon them for converting foreign currencies into yen. We also find the following long-term credit banks: Industrial Bank of Japan, Long-Term Credit Bank of Japan, and Nippon Fudosan Bank.

Although the Zaibatsus (large conglomerations of companies) were outlawed after the war, they live on in industrial groups of which the major city banks are members. One finds, however, only the large corporations involved in such groups.

	Assets in U.S. Dollars (millions) as of March 31, 1981
Dai Ichi Kango Bank, Ltd.	85,867
Mitsubishi Bank, Ltd.	75,450
Sumitomo Bank, Ltd.	74,445
Fuji Bank, Ltd.	73,147
Sanwa Bank Ltd.	67,905
Bank of Tokyo Ltd. (consolidated)	58,009
Tokai Bank, Ltd. (consolidated)	55,393
Daiwa Bank, Ltd.	52,227
Mitsui Bank, Ltd.	51,886
Taiyo Kobe Bank, Ltd.	46,299
Kyowa Bank, Ltd.	30,000
Saitama Bank, Ltd.	24,431
Hokkaido Takushoku Bank, Ltd.	21,152

The Japanese banking system is very closely regulated. The Bank of Japan, specifically, has a large degree of control over the overseas operations of the banks. It also supplements conventional monetary policy with "window guidance" at the central bank rediscount window and by controlling the volume of bank lending by means of moral persuasion.

The foreign exchange control system is operated by the Ministry of Finance, the Ministry of International Trade and Industry, and the Bank of Japan. The authorized banks, however, have been delegated to verify normal international payments. Settlements in yen with foreign countries must be made through a nonresident Free Yen Account.

The increasing importance of the yen as a reserve currency has substantially increased the importance of the Japanese banks, specifically the city banks.

Although it is most valuable for an American businessman to maintain contact with American banks in Japan, especially for informational purposes, any company or bank doing a large amount of business in this country would be well advised to develop strong relationships with local banks.

KOREA

The modern banking system in Korea was patterned largely after the Japanese financial system and dates back to Japan's dominion over this country. Japanese banks opened branches as early as 1878 and engaged in modern banking including issuance of bank notes. Korean banks were traditionally undercapitalized and lacked broad banking experience.

The sudden separation in 1945 of the Korean economy from the

Japanese economy caused serious dislocations in the financial system. This was followed by a period of economic and financial restructuring, the establishment of the Bank of Korea as the central bank, and the strengthening of commercial banks to enable them to do the short-term financing needed for the economic rehabilitation of the country.

The planned development of the financial system by the government has permitted the Korean economy to grow substantially in recent years.

The following five nationwide city banks are the major commercial banks with their head offices in Seoul and branches throughout the country:

	Assets in U.S. Dollars (millions) as of December 31, 1980
Bank of Seoul and Trust Company	6,010
Commercial Bank of Korea	4,475
Hanil Bank	4,363
Korea First Bank	4,013
Cho Heung Bank	3,970

The largest shareholder in the commercial banks is the government.

There are also 10 local commercial banks which are privately owned with a branch system limited to the provinces in which their head offices are located, except for branches in Seoul.

In the 1960s the government established various special banks to facilitate financial support for underdeveloped or strategically important sectors. This was followed in the 1970s by efforts to strengthen nonbank financial intermediaries and the securities market by channeling savings funds into industrial investment.

Presently we find the following special banks:

Korea Exchange Bank	Handles foreign exchange and finances foreign trade.
The Medium Industry Bank	Finances small and medium industry.
The Citizens National Bank	Makes loans to consumers and small enterprises.
Korea Housing Bank	Makes housing loans.
National Agricultural Cooperatives Federation	Makes agricultural and forestry loans.

Additionally, there are a number of nonbank financial institutions such as:

Korean Development Bank	Supplies long-term credit to major industries.
The Export-Import Bank of Korea	Provides medium and long-term credit for export and import transactions.
The National Investment Fund	Channels domestic savings into heavy and chemical industries.
The Land Bank of Korea	Controls efficient use of land resources.
The Korea Development Finance Corporation	Provides medium- and long-term financing to develop private enterprises.

There are also a number of mutual savings and finance companies.

Foreign banks may open branch offices in Korea with the prior approval of the Monetary Board as recommended by the Superintendent of the Bank of Korea. Foreign banks are permitted to engage in commercial banking business without any legal or administrative discrimination.

The Bank of Korea was established in 1950 as Central Bank. It exercises the functions of controlling the money supply and supervising the banking operations. Since businesses rely heavily on local borrowings, banks in turn depend heavily on borrowings from the Bank of Korea, which has been applying varying discount rates to favor certain sectors of the economy. Although the Ministry of Finance sets foreign exchange policy, the Bank of Korea executes most control functions, such as regulating operations in the exchange market. The foreign exchange banks as well as branch offices of foreign banks are authorized to engage in all foreign exchange dealings with the exception of those specifically prohibited.

A foreign businessman can avail himself either of the services of the branches of foreign banks or those of the Korean banks.

KUWAIT

Kuwait has emerged from a desert sheikdom to become one of the world's wealthiest countries. With the income provided by its substantial petroleum reserves, its financial and banking system has paralled this development in growing from its long-standing status as a trading center to its present status as one of the Arab world's most sophisticated financial centers.

The history of Kuwait's modern banking system dates to 1942 when the Imperial Bank of Iran (now the British Bank of the Middle East) formed a branch in Kuwait and conducted domestic and international banking activities until the National Bank of Kuwait was established in 1952.

In 1961 Kuwait ended its status as a British protectorate. In the same year the Currency Board was established. The Board created the Kuwaiti dinar as the country's currency replacing the Gulf Indian rupee. The Central Bank of Kuwait was formed in 1968 to replace the Currency Board and to assume the full duties of a central bank controlling and directing the development of the country's economy and financial system.

At December 31, 1980 the following six indigenous commercial banks had balance sheet totals of:

	Assets in U.S. Dollars (millions)
The National Bank of Kuwait	5,061
The Gulf Bank	4,305
Al-Ahli Bank of Kuwait	3,763
The Commercial Bank of Kuwait	3,704
The Bank of Kuwait and the Middle East	2,029
Burgan Bank	1,508

Kuwaiti law requires that indigenous commercial banks be 100 percent owned by Kuwaiti interests. The government of Kuwait holds a 49 percent interest in the Bank of Kuwait and the Middle East (successor to the British Bank of the Middle East branches in Kuwait), and a 51 percent interest in Burgan Bank.

These commercial banks carry on most traditional banking activities, both domestic and international, with significant portions of their activities devoted to trade, construction, and traditional domestic commercial financing. In recent years the international scope of these institutions has broadened to the point where involvement in international money markets and in syndicated Eurocurrency lending has also become an important activity.

Additionally, in Kuwait there are the following specialized banks created to perform specific functions.

Credit and Savings Bank—Established in 1965 and 100 percent state owned, its purpose is to provide funds to lower income groups for mortgages, establishment or expansion of small businesses, and for agricultural projects.

Kuwait Real Estate Bank—Established in 1973 and 100 percent owned by the Kuwaiti public, its purpose is to provide real estate financing.

The Industrial Bank of Kuwait—Also established in 1973, it is owned 49 percent by the Ministry of Finance and the Central Bank of Kuwait with the balance held by a variety of Kuwaiti interests. Its purpose is to assist the private sector in the development and implementation of industrial projects by providing management and technical advice, medium- and long-term export financing, and in some instances equity participation.

Kuwait Finance House—Established as a bank in 1977 operates under Islamic principles. It is 49 percent owned by the Ministries of Aqwaf and Islamic Affairs, Justice and Finance. Fifty-one percent is held by Kuwaiti nationals.

There are also a number of investment banks in Kuwait. The market is dominated by three of these—the Kuwait Investment Company, the Kuwait International Investment Company, and the Kuwait Foreign Trading Contracting and Investment Company. The government was instrumental in establishing the investment companies with the intent of providing a vehicle for investment abroad of the state's considerable foreign reserves.

Recently, the investment companies have additionally been instrumental in accommodating longer-term private sector demand for Kuwaiti dinar funds as well.

There are no foreign exchange controls in existence, and residents as well as nonresidents may freely purchase and sell foreign currencies. Since foreign banks are not allowed to operate in Kuwait, any business has to be conducted through a Kuwaiti bank.

MEXICO

After the achievement of independence in 1821 and for nearly 50 years thereafter, the financial system in Mexico, because of its inadequacy, limited economic development severely. In 1884 Banco Nacional Mexicano, which was French owned, received powers to act as the central bank. But it was not until 1925 that the most significant step toward the establishment of the modern banking system called for in the 1917 constitution was taken by organizing the Banco de Mexico S.A. Finally the problem of plurality of note issue was solved and the monopoly handed to Banco de Mexico. By the end of the 1930s, Mexico had had a number of unhappy financial experiences, such as bank failures, inflation, and currency devaluations, which had induced widespread distrust of financial institutions and processes.

The trend in the Mexican financial system is towards banks offering multibank services previously performed by specialized institutions. Following is a listing of the seven largest commercial banks:

	Assets in U.S. Dollars (millions) as of December 31, 1980
Bancomer	14,556
Banco Nacional de Mexico S.A.	13,062
Banca Serfin S.A.	5,341
Multibanco Comermex	5,119
Banco Mexicano Somex S.A.	3,801
Banco Internacional S.A.	1,864
Banpais	1,179

In 1934 another important official financial institution, the Nacional Financiera, was established to promote the development of a domestic capital market.

The role of Nacional Financiera became increasingly important over the years, not only because of growth of its own resources and progressive enlargement of the various public trust funds administered by it, but also because of the increase of its capacity as guarantor of the domestic and foreign indebtedness of a variety of public and private enterprises.

Additionally, there are presently approximately 90 financieras in existence which basically raise funds for issuing securities which are authorized by the National Banking and Insurance Commission and are registered with the National Securities Registry. They promote the development of various business enterprises by granting assistance in the organization or reorganization and expansion of businesses and may also purchase equity in that business.

In 1937 Banco Nacional de Commercio Exterior was founded by the government to promote, organize, and develop foreign trade. It is a national credit institution which may grant direct loans to finance exports and imports, production of exports and imports, and issue guarantees and letters of credit to support foreign trade.

In addition to Nacional Financiera and Banco Nacional de Commercio Exterior, there are other government institutions which were formed subsequently for the purposes of developing various sectors of the economy.

Foreign banks are only permitted to establish representative offices in Mexico and since 1979 to incorporate offshore financial operations. They are not permitted to engage in ordinary branch operations nor obtain deposits from local sources. The only exception is Citibank because it was established locally when legislation to exclude foreign banks was passed.

Although a businessman doing business in Mexico may get certain assistance from a representative office of a foreign bank, it is very likely that he must have a good banking relationship with a Mexican bank.

SINGAPORE

Singapore was a small fishing village when first occupied by the East India Company in 1819. From that time on its strategic location on the main Pacific shipping line has only enhanced Singapore's value as a trading port. After independence in 1965, the government embarked upon creating a favorable environment for different types of financial institutions and markets as a means of diversifying their economic development program to become less reliant on entrepot activities for income revenue. Entrepot activities consist of the warehousing and financing of merchandise until shipment to a particular buyer.

To assist in meeting this end, the new government began liberalizing bank licensing, tax laws, and foreign exchange controls. There are currently 100 commercial banks in Singapore, of which 37 are fully licensed and 13 are restricted. There are 50 offshore banks.

> *Full license*—These banks may carry out all types of banking business without any restrictions. They usually make short- to medium-term loans.
>
> *Restricted*—These banks offer all of the above with the exception of being allowed to only accept savings account balances of U.S. $115,000 or more and may not establish more than one branch in Singapore.
>
> *Offshore banks*—They are not allowed to accept savings deposits in any amount, except the fixed-interest deposit for a minimum of S $250,000. These banks are also restricted in their ability to raise Singapore dollar funds for credit offerings.

The three major domestic commercial banks are:

	Assets in U.S. Dollars (millions) as of December 31, 1980
United Overseas Bank (consolidated)	2,889
Oversea-Chinese Banking Corporation (consolidated)	2,631
Overseas Union Bank	1,555

There are also 39 merchant banks in Singapore which are relatively new in the financial sector since being introduced in 1970. They are also allowed to deal in gold and foreign exchange but are prevented from accepting deposits. The major merchant banks are Dresdner Bank, Deutsche Bank, and Commerzbank.

Finance companies rank second to the commercial banks in terms of the amount of money they control. There are currently 34 of them, 16 of which are subsidiaries of local or foreign banks. They are restricted as to the amount they are able to lend on an unsecured basis as well as to gold and foreign exchange dealings. They usually deal in industrial planning, leasing, accounts receivable financing, and inventory and warehouse financing.

In 1968, the Development Bank of Singapore (DBS) was established to provide medium- to long-term financing to promote export-oriented, labor-intensified industries. It is 49 percent government owned and will extend loans up to 10 years on a fixed-rate basis.

There are 87 foreign banks in the country, 24 of which have full licenses. The major foreign banks are Citibank, Bank of America, Moscow Narodny Bank, and Chartered Bank.

The Monetary Authority of Singapore (MAS) was formed in 1972 and performs all the functions of a central bank except issuing currency. It is responsible for regulating and supervising the monetary and financial sectors, but also assists in creating a favorable financial environment. In 1975 all limits on deposit rates and loan rates were abolished. There are no foreign exchange controls in existence at this time.

The foreign businessman will find excellent banking services at his disposal both from domestic and foreign banks.

SPAIN

The banking system of Spain does not have as long a tradition as other banking systems in Central Europe. Interior and exterior wars prevented formation of an extensive credit system until about 100 years ago. Succeeding the Bank of San Carlos, which was founded in 1782, the Bank of Spain became the state bank in 1856. It absorbed many of the smaller banks at that time and acquired the exclusive right to issue notes.

There are 79 commercial banks and 24 industrial banks which, on a combined basis, control 60–70 percent of the total banking service in the country. While involved in extensive retail banking, commercial banks are active in short-term credits and discounting of commercial bills. Unlike their European counterparts, Spanish banks do not allow overdrafts, and interest is charged only on the amount of credit a customer uses, not on the amount available.

Industrial banks lend mostly medium term and, although allowed to accept sight and savings deposits, many function as an arm of a commercial bank in wholesale banking activities. The label of industrial bank is gradually disappearing.

The major banks in this group are:

	Assets in U.S. Dollars (millions) as of December 31, 1980
Banco Espanol de Credito	15,899
Banco Hispano Americano	14,461
Banco de Bilbao	13,438
Banco de Vizcaya	10,143
Banco Exterior de Espana	9,946
Banco de Santander	9,605
Banco Popular Espanol	6,488

The leading Spanish commercial banks maintain 77 foreign branches and 151 representative offices abroad. They primarily service commercial customers abroad and arrange export financing. They are also becoming more involved in the Eurocurrency market, but due to Spanish legislation, they are forbidden to have a net export of capital.

Savings banks are run as nonprofit and public institutions. They are regionally based and lend mostly for social purposes, such as projects that create jobs, agriculture, and small individual enterprises. The two largest savings banks are Caja de Pensiones para la Vejez y de Ahorros de Catalina and Caja de Ahorros y Monte de Pildad de Madrid.

There are six official specialized credit institutions which have their own sphere of activities. They were reorganized in 1972 to fill the void of medium- and long-term financing. Their names and areas of concentration are:

Banco de Credito Industrial	General industrial loans
Banco Hipotecario de Espana	Urban and rural mortgages
Banco Credito a la Construccion	Finances housing, shipping and schools
Banco de Credito Agricola	Agriculture
Banco de Credito Local	Services for provincial and municipal governments
Credito Social Pesquero	Fishing industry

The entry of foreign banks has been held down to those with major international repute and long connections with Spain. They have tended to concentrate on servicing existing clients and operating at the wholesale end of banking. There are 21 foreign banks, and their main innovation has been the introduction of trade acceptances.

Not until the Bank Reform Act of 1962 was the Bank of Spain nationalized and made the central bank for Spain. Its authority includes implementing government credit policy, supervising the whole banking and credit system, as well as establishing deposit and credit ratios for all banking institutions.

Foreign exchange controls are the administrative function of the Ministry of Economy and Commerce with the Bank of Spain executing the operative function. Only authorized banks are allowed to deal in foreign exchange.

Although many of the large foreign banks are represented in Spain, a foreign businessman having business to conduct would be well-advised to also use the services and assistance of a Spanish bank.

SWITZERLAND

The development and existence of Switzerland is closely bound up in its location in the Alps. The strategic importance of Alpine passages was recognized by the important heads of Europe and guided them to be on good terms with the people of Switzerland. Although not free of wars in its history, the various peoples of Switzerland combined voluntarily into one nation, and the permanent neutrality of Switzerland was formally recognized on May 20, 1815, at the Vienna Congress as being in the best interest of Europe. It was against this background that Switzerland developed as a financial center. For centuries it had performed the function of trustee in its capacity of guardian of the Alpine passes and later performed the same function in other capacities.

Geneva may be called the oldest banking center in Switzerland followed later by Basel and Zurich. Switzerland's role as a financial center is built on the old tradition of capital exports, especially during the 18th century at the time of the Spanish War of Succession and another period at the end of that century. In the 19th century Switzerland at first became a capital importing country. Even prior to the establishment of the Swiss franc in 1850, Basel had become an important storehouse of capital, not only for Switzerland, but also the lower part of Germany.

The investing in other countries, especially mortgage investments in Germany and other fixed investments in Austria, caused bitter consequences after World War I, and it was not until 1926 that international transactions were resumed. The famous Swiss banking code of 1934, which protected, for the first time in history, the principle of bank secrecy by penal law was a direct outgrowth of the Nazi infiltration into the Swiss banking system. After World War II the government of Switzerland arranged for so-called swing credits in the trade and payment agreements. Its purpose was to work out an arrangement under which the volume of exports would not depend on the volume of imports. France and Britain used these credits in full. The banks also granted credits to foreign countries, especially France and Belgium, partly to finance Swiss exports.

At December 31, 1980 balance sheet totals of the five large banks are as follows:

	Assets in U.S. Dollars (millions)
Union Bank of Switzerland	44,024
Swiss Bank Corporation	42,083
Swiss Credit Bank	36,045
Swiss Volksbank	10,138
Bank Leu	3,651

The Swiss Banking System has an extraordinarily high density within the country. In addition to the above five large banks, there are 28 cantonal banks, 232 savings and regional banks, and a number of long-term credit institutions and private banks. The Swiss financial system is characterized by the importance of the international business and the lack of official intervention. There is a great degree of international interlocking of interest by bankers with a variety of industrial bank commercial enterprises.

Swiss banks may hold stock in corporations for their own account as well as for their clients. The big banks also act as merchant banks holding stock as underwriters or prior to acquisitions or mergers. There are interlocking directorships by the banks who place personnel on the boards of corporations. One of the specialities handled by Swiss banks is financing by forfeiting, which is basically discount of export receivables evidenced by notes or drafts without recourse to the exporter.

Foreign banks which have been registered as banks in Switzerland are subject to Swiss banking law and can be set up provided that reciprocity is given by the home country of the foreign bank. In December 1979, there were 81 foreign-controlled banks and 15 branches of foreign banks in the country.

The Swiss National Bank is the central bank of Switzerland. Although foreign exchange controls were lifted in August 1980, banks must advise the central bank of bond issues and private placements of SFR 3 million or more. Banks must also ascertain the identity of investment depositors.

Although we find a large number of foreign banks registered in Switzerland which may assist a foreigner in his business transactions, it is very likely that he may have to enlist the assistance of one of the three giants—the Union Bank of Switzerland, the Swiss Credit Bank, or the Swiss Bank Corporation. Their combined assets are more than the assets of all the foreign banks together. This may be especially beneficial if one has to deal with a substantial Swiss corporation or in substantial amounts.

UNITED KINGDOM

The evolution of England's financial institutions stretches over more than 600 years. Until World War I sterling was the currency most commonly used in international payments. Most of the international trade, even that which never touched the shores of the British Isles, was denominated in sterling and was financed with sterling drafts and acceptances. Britain's leading position as an importer-exporter and source of capital, as well as the unrivaled facilities of the London money market, assured that any bills endorsed by any of the British acceptance houses could be discounted at the world's best rates. Britain's predominance in international trade led to the establishment of specialized financial institutions.

The commercial banking system developed a branch banking system with a few giant banks operating many offices throughout the country.

From the number of 600 banks in 1824 we find today eight clearing banks with about 14,000 branches throughout the country. Many of the clearing banks today are trying to establish themselves as one-stop supermarkets for all corporate money requirements and are parts of cross-border financial consortia.

The Clearing Banks Association consists of the Bank of England and the following clearing banks:

	Assets in U.S. Dollars (millions) as of December 31, 1980	
Barclays Bank Limited (consolidated)	88,476	
National Westminster Bank Limited (consolidated)	82,447	
Midland Bank Limited (consolidated)	60,441	
Lloyds Bank Limited (consolidated)	47,380	
Williams & Glyn's Bank Limited	6,133	(9/30/80)
Central Trustee Savings Bank Limited	2,507	(11/20/80)
Coutts and Company	1,523	
Co-op Bank Limited	1,379	

As mentioned before, acceptance houses developed as specialized institutions, financing mercantile activity by accepting and discounting bills of exchange drawn upon them. Originally, the merchants themselves were merely financing their own trading activity. Today we find 17 elite merchant banks as members of the Acceptance House Committee. Traditionally, these merchant banks have been more innovative and responsive in their financing activity than commercial banks. Their endeavors are extremely varied and include banking and acceptance business, dealing in foreign exchange, bullion, bonds, investment management on behalf of private and institutional clients, corporate financial advice on issues, mergers, and money raising as well as export and project financing. The acceptances generated by these merchant banks are automatically acceptable at the Bank of England for rediscount and therefore command the finest rates in the market. The following (page 69) is a listing of the 10 largest merchant banks with assets stated at the end of their fiscal year.

In 1980 there were more than 400 foreign banks in London, of which about 340 were represented directly through a subsidiary branch or representative office. The others have an indirect presence through participation in one of the 30 UK registered joint venture banking groups.

The Bank of England was founded in 1694 and is the country's central bank. It does not formally inspect or supervise the policies or operations of the clearing banks. The governor of the Bank of England influences policies of the clearing banks through frequent meetings with the chief executives of these banks.

Banks	Assets in U.S. Dollars (millions)	Year Ended
Kleinwort Benson	6,470	12/31/80
Schroder Wagg	4,400	12/31/80
Hambros Bank	3,680	3/31/81
Samuel Montagu	3,768	12/31/80
Hill Samuel	3,238	3/31/81
Morgan Grenfell	3,071	12/31/80
Mercury Securities (S. G. Warburg)	2,580	3/31/81
Lazard Brothers	1,753	12/31/80
N. M. Rothschild	1,306	3/31/80
Baring Brothers	1,166	12/31/80

In 1979 all forms of foreign exchange restrictions were abolished. There are no exchange controls on inward or outward investments. There are also no general restrictions on foreign ownership of local business or joint ventures.

The businessman will find some of the finest banking facilities at his disposal when doing business in the UK. In addition to the eight clearing banks, which are certainly well-equipped to assist him, there are a variety of large U.S. banks which, in many instances, can render very valuable advisory service, as well as accommodate most financing needs.

VENEZUELA

Although a private banking system has existed in Venezuela since 1882, it was not until the 1970s that the financial sector experienced rapid growth principally as a result of the rise in oil prices. Latest statistics indicate that there are 34 commercial banks with 1,031 branches and agencies throughout the country. Below is a listing of the 10 largest banks:

	Assets in U.S. Dollars (millions) as of December 31, 1980
Banco de los Trabajadores	3,877
Banco Industrial de Venezuela	2,823
Banco de Desarrollo Agropecuario	2,349
Banco de Venezuela SA	2,282
Banco Union Caracas	2,252
Banco Nacional de Descuento	2,085
Banco Mercantil y Agricola	2,073
Banco Provincial S.A.I.C.A.	1,419
Banco Latino C.A.	1,188
Banco de Maracaibo	1,120

Of these commercial banks, Banco de los Trabajadores' prime function is to provide inexpensive mortgage loans for purchasers of low-cost housing. Banco Industrial de Venezuela which is almost wholly owned by Corporacion Venezulano de Fomento, a government-owned development bank, is involved in industrial and commercial operations of the public sector. It also handles all letters of credit relating to imports by the government and state companies.

There are also four regional development banks affiliated with Banco Industrial De Venezuela. They are Banco de Fomento Regional Guayana, Banco de Fomento Regional Coro, Banco de Fomento Regional Los Andes, and Banco de Fomento Regional Zulia.

A government decree of October 1975, required that commercial banks channel 20 percent of the total lending into agricultural financing. This proportion has not yet been reached but is steadily increasing.

There are 36 financieras engaged in medium-term lending to consumers and industry. These financieras are involved in investment banking, consumer financing, construction financing, issuing of letters of credit, and granting acceptances. They have recently also set up money desks to absorb short-term funds by offering investments in securities for as little as one day.

The foreign ownership of commercial banks has been restricted to 20 percent since 1970. No new banks with foreign capital are permitted, nor are any increases in the foreign capital in existing banks. Banks from other Latin American countries that offer reciprocal treatment, however, have been permitted to exceed the 20 percent foreign ownership limitation. Citibank is the only bank remaining with 100 percent foreign ownership, but it is very severely restricted in its operation.

The central bank, Banco Central de Venezuela, which was formed in 1939, sets rates of exchange for foreign currencies and administers any existing exchange controls. It is also responsible for setting interest rates in relation to a maximum rate published monthly with additional permitted premiums, which effectively raise the interest rates over the maximum 12 percent allowed by the usury law.

Anyone engaging in business in Venezuela would be advised to work with an indigenous bank because of the restrictions placed on foreign banks.

CONCLUDING COMMENT

The intention of this chapter is to give the reader a sampling of a variety of financial systems around the world. None of these systems, however, will permanently remain structured as described above since all of them are subject to evolutionary changes. These changes could be caused by outside political and economic pressures as well as legal and structural changes within a country's environment. A current example is France with its pending nationalization of the remaining private banks by the Mitterand government.

SECTION 2
International Credits

5

The Overall Role of the International Banker and Key Considerations in Lending

HARRY TAYLOR
President
Manufacturers Hanover Corporation
and
DAVID L. PFLUG, JR.
Vice President and Regional Manager
Manufacturers Hanover Trust Company

INTRODUCTION

The essential role of the international banker, and of international lending, has grown notably in both complexity and risk over the past two decades. This is not to suggest that all recent developments are unprecedented in scope and effect. Certain financial transactions undertaken among sovereign entities and private interests in Northern Europe 500 years ago present many parallels to events depicted in today's business press. Indeed, a century and a half ago European bankers were reacting to the repudiation of several millions of dollars in debt by the state of Mississippi, one of the new United States. These obligations remain in default and involve at their essence such now timely phrases as "country risk" and "sovereign immunity."

Even earlier, Alexander Hamilton in 1790 had rendered one of the most eloquent arguments for international financial integrity ever presented in the course of persuading a new Congress to honor America's Revolutionary War debts, largely placed in Europe. However, to point out these and other historical incidents is not to denigrate the great changes which have taken place in the past 20 years. Evolving from a role of primarily providing trade credit, today's banker has assumed a multiplicity of activities involving different types of financing, for a wider range of customers, in a more volatile environment.

Today the diversity and sophistication of borrowers, the uncertainties and fluctuations of the international markets, and the high volume of international lending have added immeasurably to the risk and responsibilities of the international banker.

INTERNATIONAL BANKING TODAY

In the immediate post-World War II period the activities of the international banker centered on financing trade credits to support the flow of goods between nations. Loans were self-liquidating, essentially routine and repetitive, and of generally low concern to the lender. Exchange rates were fixed in accordance with the Bretton Woods Agreement of 1944, and in any event, transactions were carried out almost exclusively in U.S. dollars or pounds sterling, the two surviving reserve currencies. Banks, by and large, conducted their business primarily from home offices and had modest operations overseas. Indeed, a bank would have a foreign department rather than an international division. The financial markets were characterized by excess liquidity with the bulk of banks' liabilities held in demand deposits. In a world of relatively stable interest rates, modest inflation, and ample liquidity, many risks now commonplace to international banking were nonexistent.

Fueled in no small part by the domestic credit provided by the West's banking systems, the spurt in world trade and investment of the early 1960s propelled the world's large banks, especially the Americans, overseas to meet the increasingly sophisticated demands of a newly international and, later, multinational customer base. Politics played an equal and complementary role in facilitating this expansion (as well as the economic boom itself). After 20 years of postwar tension, a general improvement in international politics provided the necessary backdrop against which the banks and their customers could seek new markets and opportunities with general confidence. Ironically the Eurodollar market, which itself had started as a result of East-West tensions and the fear of U.S. expropriation, became, thanks to America's trade and budget deficits, the primary source of liquidity for the world's multinational banks. For the first time, a banker enjoyed a virtually unlimited source of international funds, provided that he was willing to pay a competitive rate. It was this pool which supplied the raw material for international banking's expansion after 1965. It was not until several years later that it became apparent that the pool itself, due to its essentially transnational character and increasing nondollar component, also added new degrees of uncertainty and complexity along with liquidity to the banker's daily business. Indeed, the title of this chapter notwithstanding, many observers of the financial scene now agree that the next collapse of an international bank will occur, not because of mistakes in its lending, but because of problems in the areas of liability management and trading. There is a distinct question in the minds of both bankers and their regulators whether banks today possess sufficient management systems to direct and control adequately these two increasingly important areas of activity.

That said, it is finally necessary to note that any discussion of the role of international banking today while still primarily concerned at essence with the process of taking deposits and making loans subsumes a plethora of new functions and products unknown 25 years ago. Subjects such as cash management, export finance, project lending, co-financing, and foreign exchange trading and advice are treated in depth in later chapters. Suffice it to say that in this decade the most successful banks (with success measured by profits) will be those that are able to successfully integrate these varied activities into a coherent whole servicing their customers in a professional and profitable manner.

KEY CONSIDERATIONS IN LENDING

The bread and butter of any commercial banker remains the lending function. While much useful innovation has come recently from the increased interest in bank marketing, it remains the case that the banker, unlike the soap powder salesman, must be able to secure the return of his "product" from the customer after some agreed upon time. To fail in doing so is to fail at the very nature of his daily business. This is no less true in the international context than it is on the domestic scene. In fact, the differences between lending abroad and at home can be, and have been, overstated. A good lending officer today can be equally at home in both arenas. What does differentiate international from domestic lending is the added complexity of dealing with a larger number of factors which affect the lending decision. These complications, such as cross-national jurisdictions, foreign currencies, and diverse types of borrowers, alter the lending process in degree but not in kind from classic commercial financing. It would be useful for our purposes to examine several of these important considerations in some detail. While any typology of this kind is arbitrary, hardly exhaustive, and in effect ignores the very interrelationships among factors which make international lending so complex, it will hopefully provide us with a systematic base for further examination and thought.

The Borrower

The first rule for any lender, especially in the international sphere, remains "know thy borrower." Since by definition an international borrower is resident in, or has direct ties to, a foreign country this can be a difficult task. It is made no easier by the great diversity in types of international borrowers. These may range from sovereign governments and central banks to joint ventures involving partners from third (and fourth) countries. In between can lie government corporations, supranational entities, local corporations or financial institutions, and foreign subsidiaries. Each type merits a different assessment of credit risk and ultimately, in theory, a different credit decision.

Knowledge of the borrower, however, can be impeded by various circumstances generic to the international status and the particular type of borrower. First, standards of public financial information vary significantly among countries, as do accounting practices. Interpretation of such data requires special knowledge and experience. Second, sovereign governments and their members may have even more starkly set concerns in the matter of full disclosure. It is worthwhile to pause here and consider the very unequal standings enjoyed by foreign sovereign governments and private lenders, the particulars of international law and specific loan agreements notwithstanding. The relationship will always be an unequal one, weighted in favor of the government. Private international banks are reactive not proactive in the political sense. They are most often at a disadvantage when dealing directly in matters of contention with sovereign nations. It is this permanent calculus which encourages most international bankers to urge greater roles for supranational actors like the International Monetary Fund (IMF), World Bank, and Bank for International Settlements (BIS).

Finally, the business and activity of any foreign borrower, public or private, is unalterably linked to the social and cultural milieu within which it operates. At the end of the day certain basic if intangible questions must be answered positively. What is the financial integrity of this customer, demonstrated principally but not solely by its payment history? In rank order of importance for the foreign country involved, how crucial to the central authorities is the specific activity of the customer or its reputation? In a foreign exchange or financial crisis how high a priority would the requirements of this borrower receive? These questions are difficult but answerable. However, they require bankers who are both knowledgeable and skillful. They probably also require in the case of large amounts or complicated terms a resident officer, either as representative or in an operating entity. Today without this direct "experience" true knowledge of any foreign borrower for a bank will be only illusory, as will its accrued profits.

Cross-National Risk

The foreign locus of an international borrower is a central determining factor in the making of any credit decision. This is the case even without considering such various ancillary issues as the residence of the bank's particular lending office, the residence of an interested third party (guarantor or parent), and the actual currency being utilized all of which only further complicate the lending process. The cutting edge of cross-national risk can be usefully subsumed under three subject headings: country risk; regulatory control; and legal jurisdiction. All three impinge importantly on an international banker's day-to-day activity.

First, country risk. It is axiomatic that this much-used phrase concerns the political, economic, and social conditions, present and future, in a particular nation. It is less clear-cut where one goes from there in discussing the subject. Two parallel notions nevertheless seem important. The first is that whatever the type of international borrower, sovereign or private, its credit-worthiness is in some ways inseparable from that of its country of residence. This is hardly an unprecedented idea. For example, a domestic loan decision involving credit for a retail sales corporation based in the American Midwest would always give weight to the fact of a recession in the auto industry. The assessment of country risk at essence involves the same sort of mental process. The second notion is less clear-cut and in some circles less popular. The assessment of country risk must concentrate on those economic, political, and social factors which directly affect the soundness and eventual repayment of the underlying credit involved. Therefore bankers are not economists, political scientists, or sociologists for the sake of those disciplines. Rather the art of assessing country risk involves the use of those and other tools to reach clear credit judgments and business decisions. Stated another way, democracies can default, and authoritarian regimes can be good borrowers. While at the end of the day any decision, credit or otherwise, will have a normative component, professional country-risk evaluations are not popularity contests. They are reasoned business judgments predicated on a deep understanding of particular nations and societies. And, in the long run, their success is most often assured by a long contact with (and residence in) a specific country, rather than by a mechanistic rating system which tends to reduce intangible factors into letter or numerical indexes.

The possible components of a country-risk evaluation are as diverse as any society under study. On the economic side, external and internal characteristics can be of equal importance. Specific judgments about a nation's relative place in the world economy must be reached. National statistics on GNP, GDP, per capita measures, balance of payments and trade data provide an initial base in this regard as do statistics on a country's fiscal and monetary affairs. Several useful standard measures regarding foreign debt service and balance of payments have come under wide use, as have the statistical bases compiled by the major supranational agencies. Numbers, of course, cannot be used mechanically—Japan's foreign debt ratio in the mid-1950s belies the present credit-worthiness of that nation. Put another way, without the foreign financing enjoyed by Japan two decades ago it is very arguable whether Japan would occupy its present preeminent economic position.

Perspective thus must be the key ingredient of any evaluation. A good start in gaining that perspective centers on questioning "the business of a country." What does it do in the world? Are its exports predominantly commodities or manufactured goods? How diverse is the export base? What natural resources does it possess, especially now on the energy side? How well is the economy managed? Who are the managers? Are economic and development plans coherent with reasonable expectations about a nation's resource base and strengths? Are the economic plans supported by the World Bank, IMF, and other multilateral lenders?

A similar exercise needs to be undertaken on the domestic side of the coin, especially in the case of projects involving new or large-scale activities. What is the state of the domestic economic infrastructure; areas such as transportation, power, and labor force? What type of economic ideology and system predominates? Market, planned or mixed? It is probably in the domestic economic component of country risk that a banker feels most at home since his institution routinely, if implicitly, undertakes identical studies of his home country and region.

The aspects of country risk involving politics and social issues are more daunting. Three things need to be said. First, a credit judgment must always be premised on some degree of predictability. Worst case scenarios at a societal level would produce very few international loans. Therefore, constant policy or social changes, motivated by whatever particular political systems or philosophies, tend to produce negative-risk assessments by bankers. Second and related, most bankers applaud governments that actually govern rather than preside. In that sense stability is a misnomer. What many times is at issue on a national scale is political and social inertia. Bankers are not necessarily against change, but they are very much in favor of management and leadership. Third, a country's international politics and associated risks also must play a key, if often unspoken, part in a country-risk evaluation. This is the case not so often with respect to war and peace or East-West tensions, but very often with allocation of scarce resources within a nation and ultimately that nation's relationships with other potential aid donors or financial patrons. Certainly in the past decade no credit has been extended by a Western bank to an East European borrower without a very clear conception of the economic relations obtaining among COMECON and between members of COMECON and the West.

Country risk, then, in a specific case concerns reasoned analysis of those economic, political, and social factors and their combination which intrude directly on a particular credit decision or series of decisions. At a more general level, international bankers manage their institution's portfolio in a prudential manner spreading country risk among various nations. This entails a simultaneous, if inexact, comparison and ranking of risks among different markets, and an individual judgment as to what is a prudent level of risk assets in each country. In the ideal world such exercises would produce not only differentiated lending levels, but also very differentiated pricing. Unfortunately, the last several years have shown a general compaction of interest-rate spreads for international borrowers in the Eurocurrency markets. The reasons for this are numerous and are treated elsewhere in this volume. Suffice to say that until country-risk assessments by international banks are more forcefully translated into their pricing policies, the assessment process itself, no matter how exhaustive, must be termed a sterile exercise on this issue.

The subject of regulatory control has come to be recognized as an important cross-national issue only in the last 10 years. It has generally grown in tandem with the dramatic increase in the number of foreign operating offices of international banks over the same period. Put simply, operating and lending in foreign markets, many times from one into another, enormously complicates the banker's regulatory environment. Different nations have widely varying banking systems, regulatory philosophies, tax laws, and foreign exchange controls. It is not rare that one or more of these factors in a foreign context will be at direct odds with its domestic equivalent in a bank's particular national (or lending) domicile.

While there are formal and informal arrangements among national authorities on these issues, primarily under the auspices of the Bank for International Settlements, the system is far from all-inclusive. It is also strained by any extraordinary event. The 1979 freezing of Iranian deposits in the foreign branches of American banks by the U.S. Treasury is, of course, the best example of this latter point. On a more routine level, the issue of foreign tax treatment, especially for U.S. banks, has been the most widely troublesome cross-national regulatory problem in recent years. Suffice to say that any international lending decision made without due consideration of the regulatory implications in all the concerned authorities will be a flawed one, perhaps fatally so in a profit sense.

Finally, some regulatory factors overseas may not be relevant to the day-to-day operations of the lender, but will impact directly the credit-worthiness of a specific borrower. Rules on foreign exchange controls, tariffs, taxes, and import and export quotas all can exert critical influence on any customer's business. Bankers therefore need to understand the likelihood of potential changes in such regulations and the effect of such changes on a borrower's ability to service its debt. As in the case of a bank's own operations, these issues can involve the interaction of two or three regulating authorities, perhaps even a supra-national institution. While such factors would also apply to any domestic borrower engaged in international business, in the foreign context they present very specialized and multiple concerns.

The problem of legal jurisdiction is closely related to that of regula-tory control. Just as different nations vary as to regulatory environment, so too do they display a wide variety of legal systems. Since the last recourse for every lender resides in the courts, this factor must be taken into account in any credit assessment. In general, international bankers attempt to grapple with this risk by the use of specialized loan agreements and local legal counsel. With respect to dealings with governments it is standard for international lenders to require docu-mentation which establishes the borrower's specific standing in any eventual civil suit and which in many cases mandates the body of law and specific court which would govern that suit. Similar devices are used in documentation for private-sector borrowers. However, as in many other issues, there is no substitute for the lender possessing detailed knowledge prior to making an actual loan. Especially impor-tant are those legal statutes and precedents which impact a lender's ability to perfect its financial and security interests in the assets of a borrower. To cite two very common situations in this area: in many countries it is illegal for a "foreign resident" to own land; and in many countries the foreign exchange reserves of the nation are the property of an independent central bank rather than the national government. It is of course correct to argue that any contemplated resolution of an international loan which includes the foreclosure of foreign land or the seizure of a nation's financial assets says something very negative about the original loan decision, if not the "real world" practicalities involved. However, it is just as true that to totally ignore such issues is to shortchange one's shareholders and depositors.

Purpose

Any lending officer assessing a credit devotes a substantial portion of his analysis to the question of the loan's purpose. Ideally, there should be a demonstrable and positive relationship between the pur-poses to which loan proceeds are put and the eventual repayment of the loan by the borrower. This basic principle is identical in interna-tional and domestic lending. But again, the variety of purposes, and the possible circumstances affecting those purposes, are wider in the overseas context.

On a national level, particular attention needs to be paid to the overall foreign exchange purpose of a borrowing requirement. Al-though it is often times difficult to distinguish the two purposes, nations at times borrow not for specific development objectives but to finance overall deficits in their international balance of payments. This has become more common as a result of the increase in oil prices over the past decade and the resultant "recycling" phenomenon in the world economy. Funds borrowed for this purpose will be repaid on schedule if a nation uses the time provided its national finances to adjust to new economic circumstances by curbing consumption, promoting production and exports, and generally seeking policy solutions to redress the international payments imbalance. Nonetheless, the risks in deficit financing differ from those in specific corporate or project lending since it is often impossible to identify the particular source of repayment of such credits. National economic crises result when a country's economic policies and management fail to make fundamentally good use of balance-of-payments financing. The issue is not so much the oft stated criticism of having to keep borrowing to repay loans. The U.S. government, after all, has not been noteworthy for retiring the principal of its national debt. It does speak, however, to the issue of using the breathing space afforded by balance-of-payments borrowing to effect the necessary market and policy changes that attack and solve a country's underlying economic discontinuities. In cases where those actions are taken, balance-of-payments lending is a prudent activity for private banks, usually in parallel, if not tandem, with multilateral lending agencies.

In recent years a consensus has grown among all lenders, private and public, that the economic solution for national economies with chronic payments imbalances lies in their ability to produce their way out of those difficulties using whatever comparative advantages they possess in the macroeconomic sense. While this conceptual shift has made the analytic process of connecting purpose with repayment no less difficult, it has taken all concerned away from concentration on traditionally narrow technical and structural criteria in judging balance-of-payments borrowing requirements.

At a corporate or project level the analysis of purpose and the ultimate source of repayment can usually be undertaken with more confidence since bankers are on firmer ground in judging these risks. A project whose returns are not projected to commence until 10 years from start-up bears significantly greater risk than a project with a comparable result after three years. In general, specific borrowing purposes are judged best that transform borrowed resources into revenues at least sufficient for debt service with the fewest contingencies over a reasonable period of time.

Foreign Currency Lending

The fact that most international lending entails some aspect of foreign exchange risk presents a marked difference from domestic credit practice. This foreign exchange factor is equally important with respect to the credit-worthiness of the borrower, and the operating viability of the lender. The risks involved have grown markedly since the dismantling of the Bretton Woods system of fixed exchange rates and the subsequent volatility of the currency markets.

On the credit side it is now commonplace for borrowers to incur a built-in foreign exchange gap between their revenue and expense as a direct result of their debt structure. This development is reflected in the activity of almost every type of international borrower. Multinational firms often borrow in second or third currencies for specific accounting purposes, and also in anticipation of profit opportunities afforded by projected exchange-rate movements. Governments operate in multicurrencies not only for balance-of-payments purposes and to match specific trade patterns, but also to diversify the denominations of their international investment holdings. Many Third World enterprises incur exchange risks in their borrowing simply because of the absence of medium- and long-term debt markets in their home economies. In such cases the availability of term financing becomes more important to the borrower than the currency of the debt. Parallel to this wide-spread use of multicurrency borrowing, developments in the foreign exchange markets have provided borrowers with the ability to hedge these and other foreign exchange exposures through a variety of techniques. Two points are relevant, however. First, the availability of hedging devices in general does not guarantee their actual use by specific borrowers. Today lending officers cannot take for granted the effects on creditworthiness attendant to foreign exchange factors. Second, in many currencies, especially in the Third World, the exchange markets necessary to support hedging activities do not exist. In general the weaker the currency the more difficult it is to deal with such a currency exposure. In many senses, the banker's problem is that those borrowers most in need of such protection are least able to secure it. Therefore, consideration of the financial effects of currency-rate movements on specific international borrowers or projects, and ultimately on their ability to repay an obligation, must be a central component of any credit analysis.

Lenders themselves are not immune from similar foreign currency risks in their own operations. The new and generalized threat posed to banks by recent trading volumes was noted above. Less often identified, but almost as important, are the funding risks involved in operating a multicurrency branch system. While theoretically these risks are present when lending in any currency other than that of one's domestic base, in a practical sense the Eurocurrency markets have matured to a point that makes it unlikely that activity in any of the major reserve currencies would pose unacceptable problems to a lender, assuming that its own market reputation was sound. In addition most Euromarket loan agreements contain contingencies for the nonavailability of alternative currencies. In contrast local currency operations in most of the world are of a different character. It is very common for international banks operating with local currency branches in foreign markets to build their core lending businesses faster than their core deposit bases, either retail or wholesale. This arises principally because of usually restrictive branching limits set by local authorities combined with often fragile and heavily regulated money markets. This combination in turn can put at risk in any period of even slight monetary stress the bulk of a branch's liabilities, and ultimately its net lending margins. Perhaps this is an appropriate point at which to note again that the classic definition of banking is to take deposits and make loans. "On the ground" in a foreign country equal attention must be paid to both activities. Solutions involving currency swaps or overnight borrowing are not long-term substitutes for a stable local currency deposit base.

Other Considerations

In a world facing chronic existing and projected shortages of capital, the final consideration in lending for the international banker involves allocating a scarce resource, his capital, to its most profitable use. Today no international loan should be made without that perspective. In essence, a completely sound loan priced at current market terms, may make perfect sense as a credit judgment but no sense as a specific business decision given its inherent level of profitability to the bank. Increasingly international banks have come to gain a more complete knowledge of their profitability by service and by customer. As other financial services expand, and with them discrete costing and pricing, lending will take its place as only one of an array of international activities for banks. It will no doubt remain the most profitable by most definitions, but the era of lending for market share sake, and of general earnings growth based on volume, seems to be at an end. In that respect international banking has matured to a point where the key considerations in lending are approaching a balance between factors external and internal to the various competing institutions. This development is a profound one and augurs a period of much greater selectivity in lending during this decade. Given the heavy responsibilities already borne by the world's private banking system, and the fact that these can only be increased in proportion to individual banks' growth of capital, such a change will be in the long-term interests of lenders and borrowers alike.

CONCLUSION

Of course no article, or even series of articles, of this length can do justice to the mass of relevant detail one could subsume under this title heading. The role of today's international banker and the factors which affect his lending decisions are simply too wide ranging to allow a comprehensive description in the space provided. However, that very diversity may at times mask unnecessarily some basic postulates which are the essence of success in both endeavors. Running through this article are the related themes of perspective and people. In a final sense a successful international bank and a successful loan are direct functions of the abilities of the people who manage and make them. There are no easy formulae which produce good international credit decisions nor is there one ideal background which produces good international bankers. What both have in common is the requirement for a clear perspective that gives order and meaning to an almost endlessly complex environment. The main challenge to all of us who practice international banking today is to avoid the simultaneous pitfalls of self-importance and self-delusion; self-importance in the sense that we must not confuse ourselves and our individual roles with the institutions we represent; self-delusion in the sense that we cannot assume that complete answers in international banking are always available. Very often, knowing the questions is difficult enough.

6
Country Risk Analysis—
Noneconomic Factors

ALLEN S. WHITING
Professor of Political Science
University of Arizona

INTRODUCTION

Judging from the claims of various consulting firms, no task seems
beyond the ability of man and machine when they combine the quantitative analyst with the computer. The forecasting of human behavior,
whether in the aggregate or in the particular, subjects peasant revolt,
military coup, and political assassination to probability estimation.
Armed with impressive print-outs and the latest clips from the *New
York Times,* the intrepid consultant will put your money where his
mouth is anywhere in the world, regardless of a country's ideology,
stage of development, or accessibility. Unfortunately for the consumer,
if not for the consultant, the assessment of political risk is more art
than science. We have advanced beyond the examination of entrails
from a freshly killed goat. But Plato, Aristotle, and Thucydides can
still prove more insightful, and have, than tabulated trend-lines of
Terra Incognita.

Political risk may be associated with a wide variety of developments,
ranging from the minimal modifications in legislation that can affect
profits, through the more far-reaching expropriation of property, to
the extreme terrorist seizure of executives as political hostage. It may
be related to a simple change in policy by key officials or to the overthrow of a regime by internal or external forces. This essay will focus
on the phenomenon of political instability as an important contextual
component of political risk. If one can reduce the uncertainty derived
from basic causes of instability in a society to calculable forecasting,
more rational choices should be possible for economic activity as between one country or another and between differing time perspectives
on the return from investment.

At first glance, the most persuasive mode of probability forecasting is quantitative. Tabular presentations show at a glance the degree of confidence that underlies the analysis. Comparison permits rank-ordering the risk factors for different countries and time periods. The appearance of objectivity and replicability reduces the unease of reliance on experts whose subjective manipulation of sometimes esoteric, if not exotic, information is immune to validation except on faith.

Yet cautions against the use of fine-grained statistics to predict political stability are multiple. The methodology of linking "hard" and "soft" data to numerical probability estimates remains highly experimental. There is no proven way to translate sociological and political phenomena into mathematical data with universally accepted scales. Validation is often just as tenuous for statistics on reported events, such as demonstrations, strikes, riots, and assassinations, as it is for indirect indicators of instability that purportedly measure tension, alienation, and potential dissidence.

Even supposedly hard statistics for many countries vary widely in their reliability, their comparability over time, and their susceptibility to independent verification. Authoritarian regimes deliberately manipulate and manufacture data to serve their needs. Newly emergent regimes lack the human and mechanical resources to collect accurate statistics. Peasant societies traditionally falsify production figures to deceive government and landlord. Industrial output is usually measured in quantitative terms without regard to quality and therefore to cost and utility. Gross national product is notoriously difficult to calculate for socialist systems, particularly where prices are not subject to the marketplace, costs are administrative artifices, and key sectors of the economy are kept secret to maximum possible extent.

Uncertain as is the statistical base for any single country, the uncertainty is compounded when cross-national comparison is attempted. Probability estimation requires a sufficiently large number of cases for generalization. Conceivably, this can be managed for a single country such as China with more than 3,000 years of continuous government. More commonly, however, assumptions which serve as the basis for forecasting must rest on evidence from different countries. Thus, the problem of reliability is exacerbated by aggregation and comparison.

Repeated reference to probability is a useful reminder that predicting a single event that may be determining in its impact on foreign investment is extremely hazardous. No honest estimate of future human behavior can claim total accuracy, or 1.0 probability. Yet the loss for a firm caught in the overthrow of a regime is the same whether the forecast of its stability was offered as .99 confident, .75, or .51. This limitation of statistical probability is a fact of life. Unforeseeable variables, natural or human, cannot be predicted with certainty. The disruptive earthquake or the destructive mobs can hit without early warning indicators, much less be anticipated a year or more in advance.

In short, there is no statistical legerdemain that can by itself provide a wholly reliable guide to political stability. An essential component for such assessment is genuine expertise based on long association with a particular country or region. Such expertise is preferably acquired first-hand through residence. If this is impossible, as with most communist countries, it should be based on total immersion in the country's media, in traveller reports, and in the divergent views of other experts. This last source may be an optional luxury for some countries, but the greater the stakes, the more desirable are several points of expertise. This does not guarantee accuracy, but it can provide alternate avenues of analysis and pinpoint areas of uncertainty.

Recourse to multiple expertise, statistically elevated to the so-called Delphi approach, can also help to reveal respective records of hits and misses, thereby identifying the presence of a better "feel" for the local scene. Such sensitivity is invaluable. The political scientist may be more scientific than political, an attribute for academia but not for the real world. One need not be scientific to be systematic, spelling out one's assumptions, the logic of analysis, and the specifics of a particular forecast. This procedure permits a post mortem of error and comparing it with success so as to identify remediable faults. Expert forecasts inevitably will prove wrong in one instance or another because of the problems adumbrated above, but they should be wrong for the right reasons if they are rationally conceived and explicated.

When time and resources permit, alternative projections should be made on the basis of changed assumptions or different data sets for future developments. There is rarely a single trend line with only one outcome. Instead, competing mixes of variables will offer a range of trend lines with perhaps widely divergent outcomes. If carried to an extreme, this serves little use other than to cover all bets for the forecaster. Within limits, however, it is a useful adjunct to the more conventional single-line statement of things to come.

These caveats will unsettle those looking for a high degree of confidence in political risk assessment. So be it. One need only reflect on the sister discipline of economics and the fate of forecasting in the United States with a large population of experts and an endless flow of data. The 1970s abounded with miscalculations and wrong predictions on major aspects of the American economy. The 1980s began no better. Thus it would be self-deceiving to expect more from a less developed discipline with far greater methodological and analytical problems.

Yet one should not despair of improving over the sheer "gut feeling" of cocktail conversation as a basis for political risk assessment. The relevant internal and external variables are identifiable. Evidence on their evolution over time can be accumulated. A selective checklist can be expanded or contracted according to the need and availability of information for a particular country, region, or time dimension. This checklist can pose relevant questions to be explored. Honest modesty should elicit a frank "don't know" or "impossible to say" response when appropriate. But a political map can at least provide a guide to what remains obscure or uncertain when it does not show how to reach the desired destination of forecasting the future.

INTERNAL FACTORS

The Political System

A primary variable is the political system that prevails in a particular country. Its stability will depend on how successful it is in managing change and adapting to development, whether economic or political. Its responsiveness to demands for participation by various socioeconomic groups, particularly in the sharing of authority and the allocation of resources, may be critical. The system's past longevity is no necessary indicator of its adaptability under contemporary conditions. Hardening of the political arteries may lead to fatal rigidity. Alternately, tradition may constrain the limits of demands and the potential for dissidence.

One of the most dramatic examples of systemic collapse under internal and external pressures occurred in China. In 1911, the fall of the Qing Empire ended more than 3,000 years of dynastic succession. A virtual interregnum lasted until 1949, when the Chinese Communist Party consolidated control over the entire country, an accomplishment unmatched by the Chinese Nationalists. Chiang Kai-shek's writ never extended over more than eight provinces, the remainder being ruled by warlords, communist rebels, or Japanese puppets. His juggling of factions at the center and the ritualistic intonation of loyalty from dissident generals masked the fragmentation and instability that characterized China for nearly half a century.

Alternatively, Thailand has demonstrated considerable adaptability to political and economic change. This permits the continuation of a benevolent monarchy and a quasi-democracy despite a recurring pattern of coups and cabinet resignations. The system's political obituary has been written a number of times since World War II without, however, its demise being realized. Corruption in Bangkok and communism in the countryside have failed to topple it. Strains have occurred from time to time, and they may prove fatal in the future. In retrospect, however, the system has proven remarkably resilient to internal and external challenge.

A key systemic factor is the handling of leadership succession. Paradoxically, coups are not necessarily destabilizing if they are systemically sanctioned, as in much of Latin America. In Africa, however, the absence of a national tradition in newly emergent regimes can cause repetitive coups to paralyze the body politic, as in Uganda. Communist systems, for the most part, have difficulty managing succession. The result is a steadily aging leadership with autocratic power concentrated in one man, as in the Soviet Union and China. When natural causes finally eliminate him, his chosen successor rarely triumphs over competing factions. The resultant power struggle can prove costly in economic as well as political terms. Despite repeated admonitions against the "cult of personality" and calls for collective leadership, this source of instability appears to be inherent in communist systems.

The problem also occurs elsewhere, amply demonstrated by such men as Konrad Adenauer, Charles de Gaulle, and Lee Kuan Yew, all having headed democratic regimes. More commonly found in the Third World, the syndrome of self-perpetuation can create a spurious sense of stability that is singularly dependent on the life of one man. (The closest example of a woman in contemporary times is Indira Ghandi, whose political downfall ushered in a period of immobilism when the leaderless system proved unable to cope with India's massive problems.) Of all the obstacles to forecasting, this is perhaps the most frustrating because it is literally impossible to know how or when that life will end, much less anticipate what individual or group will control the succession.

A less common phenomenon concerns political systems that are dependent on external support, which may be weakened or prove a liability in terms of system stability. Communist rule in Eastern Europe has been a case in point since 1953 when the East Berlin riots first alerted the outside world to the role of Soviet tanks in preserving local power. The subsequent dramas of Hungary (1956) and Czechoslovakia (1968) further proved the point, although Poland (1956, 1980) challenged the generalization. Afghanistan (1979) revealed the hazards of relying exclusively on external support when the political system has no local base whatsoever, resulting in an open invasion and occupation by Soviet armed forces.

Proximity permits the extension of external support through direct means, but this may arouse such internal opposition as not to prove stabilizing beyond the time of foreign presence or military occupation as the case may be. Tanzanian support for the post-Amin regime in Uganda and Vietnamese support for the post-Pol Pot rule in Kampuchea left open the question of what would evolve after the respective armies left the two countries. As against these recent cases, however, stands the unique example of Japan after World War II. There, American occupation forces imposed a new political system at considerable variance from that which had prevailed for more than a decade, including a constitution originally drafted in English. While some occupation rules and values inevitably faded away as too incongruent with Japanese culture, more than 30 years later the basic political system remained intact.

National Cohesion

Marxists and modernizers have forecast the inevitable concentration of power and therefore of control in the hands of the state as technology lessened the power of subnational groups and enhanced the ability of central government to assert its authority. Both have been proven wrong. The proliferation of demands for a share of economic and political power, frequently manifest in acts of violence directed against ruling groups, is worldwide in its impact. While the means of communication and control have extended the potential power of government down to the family and its members, so has the awareness and expectation of subnational groups increased. Anger over perceived mistreatment, frustration over demands not being responded to, and hope that action will bring results prompts these groups to varying degrees of violence with consequent impact on political stability.

The wellsprings of such action may be linguistic, racial, ethnic, religious, or tribal. They have sparked separatist demands in Quebec, violence in South Africa, riots in Yugoslavia, rebellion in northern Ireland, and massacres in Nigeria. Moslems in the Philippines and Basques in Spain share a common bond with the Hutu and the Tutsi's in Ruanda and Burundi, all challenging the legitimacy of authority on grounds of systematic suppression, oppression, or exploitation. The ubiquitous nature of such violence shows it to be independent of political system, ideology, or location. The official dismissal of such violence as sheer terrorism, whether local or allegedly international, rarely reflects reality. More generally, such violence bespeaks a serious schism in the society which must be healed if it is to enjoy long-term stability and growth.

Where available, demographic data can provide important clues to potential trends. An aging, shrinking, ruling group can hope to forcibly suppress demands of a younger, growing subgroup only so long before facing the choice of abdication or compromise. A highly homogeneous nation, such as Japan, has little or no risk in this regard as compared with a heterogeneous state, such as the Union of Soviet Socialist Republics. Endemic racial and religious animosities, as between Malay and Chinese, can actually break up a political system, spawning the city-state of Singapore from the previous Federation of Malaysia. Alternatively, programs may be instituted by a ruling majority against a racial and religious minority where the latter is seen as controlling the economy, as in the Indonesian slaughter of Chinese in 1965.

It may not be enough to demonstrate the existence of an equitable distribution of political or economic rewards. Subjective perception, not objective reality, often determines political action. Moreover, the symbolic manipulation of subgroup representation, as in the Supreme Soviet of Nationalities, or cultural autonomy supposedly manifest in native art forms, may not meet the felt need for genuine autonomy or a greater share of goods and services. Promotion and purge can be differently perceived as between ruled and ruled, regardless of actual statistics or percentages.

National cohesion is difficult to assess when much of the information comes from ruling groups. Dissident demands are often sensationalized by foreign media, whether communist publicity for "national liberation struggles" or noncommunist attention to "terrorism." Croat nationalist airplane hijacking and bombing in the United States proved no more of a threat to Serbian domination of Yugoslavia than did less dramatic Albanian riots in the province of Kossovo. The first captured foreign television and headline attention, but the second elicited doubts in Belgrade over possible survival of the federation.

This illustrates the need for genuine expertise which can differentiate between the sensational and the substantive threat to national cohesion. Someone who is familiar with all the groups in a society and not merely those currently in charge of the economic or political system can better detect the early tremors and divine how deep and long-lasting may be the ultimate shock-waves. The expert should also be better at assessing the long-run effect of regime response, whether repressive or relaxed, as alleviating or exacerbating the sense of grievance and the forcefulness of demand on the part of the dissidents. Power is not readily shared or conceded. Moreover, the confrontation may be unsusceptible to solution with the best of intentions. In many countries, national cohesion presents the greatest political risk and therefore deserves the closest and most careful analysis.

Political Geography

The logistics of control over the periphery are frequently overlooked by foreigners whose contact normally is confined to the capital or the economically developed sector of a country. However, one has only to follow the trials and tribulations of Soviet forces in Afghanistan to appreciate the difference between capturing a few urban areas and being able to suppress guerrilla forces in the remote countryside, much less close the mountain borders to exiting and reentering forces. Similarly, a preoccupation with the politics in Teheran blinded foreign observers to the difficulty of uniting the outlying areas under Ayatollah Khomenei's rule. Subsequently, logistical obstacles frustrated the highly modernized Iranian forces that were unable to concentrate their firepower rapidly and flexibly against the Iraqi invasion.

Afghanistan and Iran also illustrate the importance of political geography in facilitating external penetration that subverts central authority by supporting dissident local groups. Iran and Pakistan provided refuge and supplies for Afghan rebels. Meanwhile, Soviet support was feared in Teheran to embolden Azerbaijani resistance and Pakistani leaders feared potential Soviet aid to Baluchi dissidents.

China presents a classic case of national cohesion being undermined by external activity when central control weakened at the periphery. The Tibetans in the southwest, the Uighurs and Kazakhs in the northwest, and the Mongols in the north have all enjoyed their own imperial past or at least self-rule, independent of Han domination. In the 19th and 20th centuries, as Chinese power from the center has waxed and waned in strength, so too have these non-Han peoples been encouraged to revolt by British, Russian, Japanese, and American support, material as well as political. With most of the country comprised of mountains and desert and lacking modern lines of transportation and communication through these remote peripheral areas, it has been difficult for the center to impose Chinese rule on non-Chinese peoples. When the communists faced a rebellion in Tibet in 1959 and an exodus from Xinjiang in 1962, foreign subversion was perceived as important in both instances.

Ethiopia's problem of national cohesion, already severe with Eritrean separatism, was exacerbated when Sudan and Somalia supported rebellious movements against Addis Abbaba from neighboring territory. The political geography of Africa presents a particularly severe challenge to newly formed governments who inherited purportedly national boundaries from colonial rulers who paid scant heed to tribal groupings and their traditional habitat. The multitudes slaughtered in Biafra's abortive effort at secession foreshadowed a long line of lesser tragedies as the colonial heritage is worked out within and across supposedly sovereign frontiers.

The logistics of political power pose severe natural obstacles to the ruling group. Island regimes, such as the Philippines and Indonesia, face problems of control over widely scattered communities separated by sea. Land regimes must build and maintain costly roads and railroads that tie periphery to center. Mountains in Chile and Peru mock the chimera of national integration forging a single political, economic, and social entity. Desert in north Africa separates nomadic from sedentary peoples, inviting neighboring subversion or outright annexation.

The linkage between problems of national cohesion and political geography tends to blur the distinction between these two factors, and, as our examples illustrate, they are often interrelated. However, it is important to differentiate between them as factors relevant to political stability because they require different responses and may occur in isolation from one another. When they do coincide, the consequences can compound the challenge to central authority.

Traditional Values

Traditional society is antecedent to the contemporary political system in most countries. Its values with respect to authority, rebellion, and violence may exacerbate or mitigate problems of political stability. A checklist of factors does not automatically predict their potential impact. In addition, the tendency toward passivity or action in the society must be assessed in terms of its past ethos and its relevance for present and future behavior.

As an extreme instance, the Buddhism practiced in Tibet proper inculcated an acceptance among the people of whatever conditions prevailed. The endless whirring of prayer wheels, abject prostrations before holy shrines, and absolute belief in fate now and in the hereafter induced the populace of Lhasa and its environs to live with rather than rebel against extant conditions. In like manner, the Dalai Lama refused to arouse resistance against the People's Liberation Army and its imposition of Chinese Communist authority, instead fleeing to India on both occasions that the issue came to a head, in 1950 and 1959. However, less theological Tibetan tribesmen, the Khambas, living to the east fought fiercely when communist practices threatened their way of life, ultimately triggering the revolt and massive exodus in 1959.

The role of religion can provide a critical difference in political cohesion where potential dissidence arises from resentment over inequities of power, status, and wealth. The contrast between Buddhism and Islam in this regard is relevant, depending on local variations in their practice. The relative absence of revolt against authority in Thailand permits the monarchy to survive and even to be an important element in the system when lesser groups contend for power at the elite level. In contrast, the neighboring state of Burma, while also Buddhist, has never known stability since its reemergence as an independent country after World War II because of ethnic revolts against Burman rule by Shans, Karens, and Kachins.

When ideology sanctions rebellion, the consequences can be catastrophic for political stability if confidence in the regime declines as conditions deteriorate. China's traditional Mandate of Heaven concept legitimized overthrowing the emperor if he failed to secure the land against attack or provide an adequate livelihood for the people. In a modern variant, Mao Zedong exhorted millions of young Red Guards to attack the power structure of party and government in 1966 with the slogan, "It is right to rebel!" The result approximated near anarchy in many of China's cities throughout the following 18 months of violence and turmoil.

It is difficult to assess the relative weight of tradition and modernization when the question concerns attitudes, because the test of past versus present values may not come until the decisive moment of mass action. Until that time the observer may be unable to discern the erosion of belief and its replacement with a revolutionary ideology. Sensitivity to the process, however, can illuminate why similar situations evoke different responses in one society as compared with another.

External Threat and Leadership Ability

It is axiomatic that if a ruling group can displace internal tensions and direct them against an external enemy, it can prolong, if not preserve, its power. Scapegoating the foreign devil to explain domestic difficulties is an old and cherished practice, whether the devil is symbolic or real. Calls for sacrifice in the name of national salvation can mobilize a populace to unite its efforts through political exhortation instead of material incentive. Much depends, of course, on the ability of the leadership to manipulate the external threat so as to be credible without inducing panic, on the one hand, or hope on the other. Credibility requires sufficient evidence of an external threat together with a reasonable expectation that the country can cope with it through following its present leadership. Panic can result if the threat seems overwhelming. Hope may seek foreign deliverance from domestic oppression.

The axiom does not always apply. At the turn of the century, Tsarist Russia faced a rising tide of dissident demands for reforms. The threatened autocracy also had growing difficulties with Japan. This prompted the observation by one of the Tsar's advisers that "a nice little war" might be convenient for quelling dissent. Unfortunately, the war was a disaster and further weakened the regime. When Hitler attacked Stalin in World War II, the Kremlin abandoned communist appeals in favor of patriotic propaganda to unite the country. But the hope of escape from the economic chaos of collectivization prompted large-scale Ukrainian defections to the Nazis. Thus, the external enemy appeared preferable to the domestic one until Nazi occupation proved so cruel as to push the populace to resistance.

Xenophobia can be the psychological soulmate of patriotism. Unity for country is readily translated into unity against foreigner. The familiar cry, "united we stand, divided we fall" can serve as an appeal for internal allegiance against external threat whether justified or not. Newly emergent regimes can blame "foreign imperialism" as responsible for their failure to achieve desired goals or to make good on political promises. A traditional foe becomes a convenient whipping-boy for frustration and tension, regardless of his actual intent. Communist countries have a convenient ideology in Marxism-Leninism, which posits conflict as inevitable between socialism and capitalism, thereby making credible warnings of possible war if vigilance and obedience are not maintained.

Such alarms are not permanent placebos; they are no substitute for the successful management of societal problems. Ultimately, a leadership must either provide for its people or prevail through the sheer use of force. This is no easy task in a modern world where communication transmits awareness of values and benefits that are the presumed concommitant of modernization. Whether it is human rights or a rising standard of living, expectations of what regimes should deliver constrain the freedom of ruling groups to define their own terms of success.

But the problems of economic and political development are often not susceptible to successful management sufficient to meet the expectations of all subgroups within a country. We have already seen how such factors as national cohesion and political geography can complicate a regime's task. The economic consequences of drought, floods, and earthquakes are dramatically evident. Less apparent but sometimes more durable are the consequences of location. While collectivization probably hurt rather than helped Soviet agriculture, the USSR would be far better situated if it were at 10 degrees lower latitude. Siberia's vast mineral wealth would be easier to exploit without the climatic conditions and permafrost which raise costs and lower living comfort as compared with European portions of the Soviet Union. Likewise, if China could double its estimated 12 percent arable land, providing for a population of more than 1 billion, this would present fewer problems.

While this chapter's focus is specifically on noneconomic factors, it is impossible to ignore the political consequences of economic problems. Bread and circuses will not suffice in an era when transister radios and television transmit aural and visual images of life in other countries that contrasts vividly with local conditions. As the World War I song warned, "they'll never be happy down on the farm . . ." once rising expectations lure rural youth to urban centers in search of new lifestyles as well as better jobs, housing, and education. In Cairo and Calcutta, Bombay and Beijing, the staggering demands on government that result from mass migration into the modernized sectors of industrializing societies pose a serious challenge to political stability. The aggregation of individual discontents into mass demonstrations can transform unemployed high school and university graduates into rabble-rousing revolutionaries with an explosive impact on the regime.

EXTERNAL FACTORS

Political Geography

Thus far we have examined internal factors and their relevance to political stability. We have necessarily identified linkages with external forces where they intrude upon these factors, but our central focus has been within the bounded limits of national societies. However, our checklist of key variables must also include external factors as such. In an age of growing interdependence, omission of this category would leave a partial picture at best and a wholly distorted one where the threat of war raises the political risk.

This is readily illustrated by the external aspects of political geography. Naturally defined boundaries may provide less of an invitation to attack and more clearly demarcate territorial sovereignty than lines arbitrarily drawn on a map. Where nomadic herdspeople follow their flocks according to pasture and weather across national frontiers, incidents may spark clashes between border guards, accusations of espionage or sabotage can arise, and disputes over the "traditional" boundary can poison relations between neighboring regimes. Troop concentrations increase; tensions rise. This set of conditions contributed to Sino-Soviet confrontation along a 4,500-mile frontier. Fishermen pose similar problems particularly with the expansion of territorial sovereignty from three to 12 miles and the further addition of 200-mile economic zones. Soviet-Japanese relations suffer from these complications.

In the absence of either a natural or an agreed boundary, regimes tend to expand their control as their power permits. Even with such a boundary, there is no guarantee that piecemeal expansion will not occur in remote areas. But where no agreement exists, the balance of power is the only effective constraint on such expansion. Where two states adjoin and experience economic growth, as with India and China, it is almost inevitable that they will push out to probe the limits of their respective domains. Compromise or conflict, or both, may ultimately produce agreement; in the meantime, instability will characterize the frontier and bilateral relationship.

Boundary disputes are commonplace, and while they may capture headlines, they rarely result in major conflict. But territorial disputes are qualitatively different. They usually involve larger areas, and they tend to involve irredentist claims to lands lost by past treaties or defeats. Alternatively, they may rest on allegations of historic precedent and traditional references coupled with contemporary need. China's claims of ownership over islands and reefs in the South China Sea combine several of these characteristics, bringing her into dispute with Vietnam and the Philippines. In fact, Beijing's maps show the entire South China

Sea as within its territorial limits. By linking the territorial sovereignty of 12 miles with the economic zone of 200 miles, Beijing could virtually close the entire waterway to foreign activity except by permission.

Reference to such activity raises an additional impetus to conflict beyond that of nationalistic sensitivity to territorial sovereignty. The importance of ocean resources, particularly fish and oil, promises to supercede questions of political control or strategic utility. The continental shelf can be claimed by the country from which it extends to a depth of 250 meters. When it reaches an adjoining country, separate ownership may be divided along a median line which splits the shelf and waters evenly, provided both sides voluntarily agree. A Law of the Sea has yet to provide universal regulation, despite a decade of negotiation. Unilateral power may therefore determine what international agreement does not achieve.

China, for example, has formally protested Korean-Japanese efforts to explore for oil under the water separating the latter two countries. Beijing's claim is based on the continental shelf extension principle, regardless of the great distance between such exploration and the Peoples Republic of China. This principle also underlies Beijing's insistence of ownership over the unpopulated Senkaku Islands between Taiwan and the Ryukyu Islands. These islands were administered by the United States until Okinawa returned to Tokyo's control at which time Japanese patrolling and administration began. Beijing's relations with the two Koreas, Japan, Taiwan, the Philippines, and Vietnam cover the entire spectrum from ally to enemy, so it is unlikely that a simple and consistent formula will characterize China's ultimate position. However, in the meantime there is considerable potential for conflict involving the exploration and exploitation of off-shore oil in the Yellow Sea, the East China Sea, and the South China Sea.

Political geography thus becomes economic, once again going beyond the "noneconomic factors." But some overlap is unavoidable if we are to identify the factors that pertain to political instability. Similarly, the geography of resources cannot be separated from politics as became dramatically evident during the 1973 OPEC oil embargo. Japan's dependence on Middle East oil, like that of West Europe, determined its reaction to the Arab-Israeli dispute. Closer to home, it affected Tokyo's willingness to extend nearly $4 billion in credits for Siberian development of oil, gas, and coal, together with adequate port facilities. Japan needs to diversify resource dependence and find more proximate sources. The reliability of Middle East production and the vulnerability of lengthy supply lines present Japan with major political as well as economic problems. This helps to explain Tokyo's desire to assist its two communist neighbors in their economic development despite the fact that traditionally hostile relations makes their future power a potential threat to Japan.

Hitler used the term *lebensraum,* or "living space," to justify expansion and the annexation of adjoining countries. The demographics of political geography do not necessarily translate into population pressures from a superior power on less advantaged neighbors. However, perceptions of such a threat can fuel tensions and heighten confrontation, as with Soviet fear that China's vast population surplus will one day overflow into the Siberian wilderness. There is no objective basis for such fear, given the requirements for large capital and advanced technological inputs to make Siberia habitable, both of which are and will remain in short supply for China. Yet we have noted, it is subjective perceptions, not objective reality, which often condition political behavior.

Thus, whether real or perceived, the demographic balance is an important variable in assessing the stability of relations between adjoining states. In addition to size, ethnic factors can contribute to risk where minorities may feel allegiance abroad or be claimed by neighboring regimes. Hitler's proclaimed "protection" of the Sudeten Germans as an excuse for invading Czechoslovakia nearly triggered war in Europe while Hanoi's expulsion of Chinese contributed to Beijing's subsequent invasion of Vietnam.

Traditional Relations

History is taught in nationalistic schools. It is selectively remembered by partial observers who experience it directly or vicariously from the vantage point of their own country. The residual images of other countries provide a filter through which new evidence is screened. If it fits the stereotype, friendly or hostile, it reinforces that image. If not, it is likely to be discounted or explained away so as to fit comfortably with existing preconceptions.

Where there has been traditional enmity, reinforced by war, such images die hard. That they can be overcome is attested to by NATO embracing France and Germany, two antagonists who fought three bitter wars within a century. Egypt and Israel provide an equally dramatic exception, at least under Sadat and Begin. Yet such reversals of relationship coexist with recurring hostility and suspicion based on past experience and present perception. The Franco-German tie is nowhere nearly as firm as the Anglo-American bond while much of what has transpired in Cairo and Tel Aviv is due to the extraordinary efforts and personal chemistry of their two leaders. More common is the hard rock of hatred between Arab and Jew or Pakistani and Indian. In such contexts, nuclear arms carry an extra dimension of threat beyond that inherent in superpower rivalry.

Thus, whether a country enjoys traditional alliances or probable protectors against potential threat on the one hand, as against traditional enemies or hostile coalitions on the other hand, can be a major determinant of its vulnerability and therefore of political risk. Poland's precarious position has led to repeated partition and redefinition of its boundaries as German and Russian pressure, in competition or collusion, has squeezed from both sides. At the opposite extreme, Switzerland has maintained its territorial integrity through centuries of isolation from alliances and surrounding wars, enjoying complete and secure independence.

The past does not necessarily predict the future. Traditional barriers or ties can be transformed through the evolution of new relationships and the exigencies of diplomatic necessity. The latter is the hallmark of a true balance-of-power game where a rising power prompts others to coalesce against its ascendency according to the aphorism, slightly modified, "my potential enemy's enemy is my present friend." Thus, the Sino-American detente was a joint response to perceptions of Soviet expansionism and ended more than 20 years of Sino-American confrontation.

While identifying tradition as a variable, not a constant factor, it nonetheless places constraints on the extent of change and remains a referent in times of trouble. This helps to explain why the Anglo-American alliance could survive the overt crisis of confidence concerning Suez in 1956, while the Sino-Soviet alliance suffered far greater strain from the more subtle differences on India in 1959. National images change so rapidly in the United States as a country remote from others and relatively new in world affairs that it is sometimes difficult to understand the depth and intensity of such images elsewhere. When these traditionally antagonistic relations recur in a contemporary context, as between Cambodians and Vietnamese, they are easily misunderstood as the transient consequences of particular policies or particular leaders. Unfortunately, they more often are the basic cause of tension that can trigger war, in spite of policies and leaders.

INTERNAL-EXTERNAL INTERACTION

While we have touched on a number of instances of interaction between internal and external factors, the phenomenon deserves brief attention in its own right. No country is truly isolated and an island unto itself. Even remote Mongolia cannot escape the vicissitudes of Sino-Soviet conflict and the penetration of foreign values. The permeability of national boundaries to external influences, if not investment, makes such terms as sovereignty and independence increasingly relative.

The economic aspects of the modern world are easily understood. Dependence on external credit, investment, and technology together with the interdependence of monetary conditions and markets makes every regime in some way subject to the decisions of others. Some may be more autonomous, others less, but all are to one degree or another affected by actions taken beyond their own boundaries. But the political implications of modernity are less obvious. The technologies of transportation and communication now permeate entire regions that only decades ago were the exclusive preserve of local rulers. The home was once the traditional transmitter of values. Today it can be penetrated, if not dominated, by messages transmitted by television. These messages may be oriented towards consumption or production for economic or political purposes, but they provide a powerful challenge to parental values wherever they exist. Likewise, stationary satellites instantly relay events to a global village, sending news that was once under the total control of national or local governments.

These multiple stimuli confront those who are responsible for managing change with a continuing and expanding problem. Penetrative technologies will increase their impact as modernization improves local reception through the spread of radio and television. An explosion of consumer expectations may coincide with the expansion of younger groups in the population resulting from lowered death rates due to childhood diseases and infant mortality. Increased education will fuel desire for better jobs where acquired skills can be usefully employed. But for most countries, limited investment capital and a low savings rate will necessitate hard choices at the state level among heavy and light industry, agriculture, and the service sector. Priority for one will impose a slower growth rate on the others with attendant implications for employment as well as for productivity. Moreover, the choice may have to be made with an eye to export markets as well as foreign investment and credit interests, not only according to internal considerations.

As a final fillip, the modernization of defense imposes a soaring burden of advanced weaponry which is necessary for domestic pride as well as for perceived needs of protection against local or distant threats. Arms races feed on mirror-imagery where one country's defense is seen elsewhere as a potential for offense with reactions that spur reciprocal misperception. This proliferation of soaring arms expenditures is stimulated by the competitive marketing of weapons by advanced countries, especially the United States, the Soviet Union, and France.

It is also furthered by the spread of patron-proxy linkages which interlock local rivalries of small powers with larger power competition and confrontation. The multiplier effect of Soviet military aid to Cuba which is then transferred to Angola, Ethiopia, and South Yemen, triggering reactive arms acquistions from NATO members by neighboring regimes is paralleled in Southeast Asia with the Soviet-Vietnamese linkage impacting on the U.S.-Thai military relationship. Clients exploit patron relationships to advance their own interests while patrons find it difficult to disengage locally without risking a perceived loss in their major power competition. In either instance, political stability is threatened. If the Korean peninsula were wholly demilitarized, instead of possessing the most intensive concentrations of arms in the world, how different might be the prospects for internal as well as external stability in South and North alike.

IN CONCLUSION

It is obviously impossible to satisfy the requirements of evidence and knowledge for all of the aforementioned factors, much less to assess accurately their interaction. There are too many unknowns in much of the world and too many uncertainties in much of the future to ensure a consistently high degree of success in forecasting political stability. However, the presence of a theoretical construct with standard categories for comparison across countries and through time permits the systematic collection of data, operationalization of hypotheses, and replication of analysis. Experimentation and *post hoc* evaluation should eventually bring improved results. Provided that the goals are modest and the effort is persistent, genuine expertise should provide a better-than-random assessment of political risk in terms of noneconomic factors.

7
Country Risk Analysis—
Economic Considerations

SHEILA TRIFARI
Senior Vice President and General Manager
International Division
Southeast Bank, N.A.
and
J. ANTONIO VILLAMIL
Vice President and Chief International Economist
Southeast Bank, N.A.

THE BASIC PREMISES OF ECONOMIC RISK ANALYSIS: AN OFFSHORE LENDER'S PERSPECTIVE

Recent developments in Poland, Bolivia, Mexico, and Argentina are suggestive of country risks clearly inherent in offshore credit extension. These risks, whether categorized as economic or political, distinguish international lending activities from purely domestic credit extension. In Poland, poor economic management and systemic political instability have caused the country to seek a restructuring of its external debt obligations. Bolivia and Mexico, for similar reasons, are concluding debt restructuring exercises with offshore bank creditors.

Country risks in international lending activities, therefore, are quite real and primarily stem from the inability of a country to allow its residents to repay external obligations on a timely basis—the so-called economic risk in international credit extension. More explicitly, economic risk occurs when a foreign borrower encounters problems in converting domestic currency into the currency in which the loan was denominated. For example, a U.S. bank, by denominating a loan to a Brazilian borrower in U.S. dollars, can avoid the risk of exchange-rate depreciation of the local currency vis-a-vis the dollar, *but not the risk of repayment in U.S. dollars.*

The essence of country risk analysis at commercial banks, therefore, is an assessment of factors that would allow a country, such as Brazil, to generate sufficient hard currencies to repay external obligations *as they come due.* These factors are both economic and political. Among economic factors are the quality of the public-sector management process, the resource base of a country, and its external financial position. Political factors include the degree of political stability of a country and the regional political environment. Note also the emphasis on timely repayment of external obligations. A bank expects a foreign borrower to adhere to the covenants of the loan agreement and would not extend credit if there is a good probability of a forced refinancing of the loan or of a change in the contractual terms of the loan to keep the borrower solvent (rescheduling). Thus, while actual defaults are few in international lending activities, the primary risk for commercial banks is that the principal on a given loan could be tied up indefinitely in a country.

There are other types of economic risks inherent in offshore credit extension, and perhaps some of these risks will become increasingly important for banks to assess as the decade of the 1980s unfold. An important one is *exchange-rate risk* when extending credit to private-sector borrowers in a country. A depreciation of the local currency to meet public policy objectives could seriously strain the cash flow position of a private-sector borrower with significant external liabilities, even though macroeconomic trends suggest that the country could generate sufficient hard currencies to repay external obligations falling due during the period. There are also *sectoral risks* which could result from changes in the economic development strategy of a country. For example, the lowering of tariff barriers in Argentina during 1976–80 led to a great number of industrial bankruptcies in 1980 and the second half of 1981. Thus, while economic risk was quite acceptable in Argentina through 1980, repayment of many external loans to private-sector entities became a problem. In essence, offshore credit extension requires not only systematic assessment of economic risk for international portfolio decisions, but also *linking* the assessment of country conditions to the analysis of commercial credits.

Much has been written on the appropriate techniques of economic risk analysis since the quadrupling of oil prices in *1973* boosted the growth of international financial intermediation.[1] Experience gained

---

[1] For quantitative approaches to risk assessment see G. Feder, and R. Just, "A Study of Debt Servicing Capacity Applying Logit Analysis" *Journal of Development Economics* 4, no. 1 (1977) pp. 25–38. Also Charles R. Frank, Jr., and William R. Cline, "Measurement of Debt Servicing Capacity: An Application of Discriminant Analysis" *Journal of International Economics* I, no. 3 (1971) pp. 321–344. Finally, see Alice L. Mayo, and Anthony G. Barrett, "An Early Warning Model for Assessing Developing Country Risk" in *Proceedings of a Symposium on Developing Countries' Debt*, ed. Stephen H. Goodman, sponsored by the Export-Import Bank of the United States, August 1977. Excellent criticisms of the rigid quantitative approach can be found in Yves Maroni, "Approaches for Assessing the Risk Involved in Lending to Developing Countries," Board of Governors of the Federal Reserve System, International Finance Discussion Papers No. 112, November 1977, and K. Saini and P. Bates, "Statistical Techniques for Determining Dept-Servicing Capacity of Developing Countries" Federal Reserve Bank of New York, September 1978, unpublished.

during the past eight years in the external debt servicing problems of at least 10 countries has caused the pendulum to swing from a mechanistic ratio-analysis approach, with heavy quantitative orientation, to a structured qualitative approach with emphasis on institutional analysis.[2] From these experiences, the following basic premises of country risk analysis can be derived:

1. The *quality and effectiveness of a country's economic and financial management policies* are almost always the key to economic risk assessment. Political revolutions in Iran and Nicaragua were precipitated by misguided economic policies that did not take into account the factor endowments of the countries or their socio/political institutions. External debt servicing difficulties during the past eight years in Turkey, Zaire, Peru, Bolivia, Poland, Chile, and Mexico were clear cases of endemic economic mismanagement.

2. Economic risk assessment is primarily concerned with *broad* economic changes and with capturing the direction (trend) of events. For example, much time is usually spent on detailed balance-of-payments projections when a statement of direction and its broad magnitudes would suffice. In international economic analysis, where statistical sources are of varying degrees of reliability, the identification of trends and the development of analytical conclusions are of much more intrinsic importance than any simple numerical projections.

3. Economic risk assessment must be forward-looking in its approach and concerned with underlying forces that make events happen. Statistical data are only the end result of such forces. Economic risk assessment, therefore, must be primarily institutional in its analytical approach, with quantitative indicators to cross-check the qualitative analysis.

The above premises offer a framework for the assessment of economic risk in countries where a bank may wish to consider credit extension. The assessment needs to capture a sense of broad direction in key economic risk factors, such as economic and financial policies, the economic resource base, and external financial position. After the underlying factors are assessed, analytical conclusions must be reached as to relative economic risk. A major objective of economic risk assessment, therefore, should be to provide relative risk rankings for each country that the bank extends credit in a currency other than the local one. The chart below illustrates this process.

---

[2] This approach is becoming increasingly preferred by international bank economists. See the excellent analysis by Morgan Guaranty's International Economist Arturo C. Porzecanski "The Assessment of Country Risk: Lessons from the Latin American Experience" in *Financing Development in Latin America,* ed. J. C. Garcia and S. E. Suten (New York: Praeger Publishers, 1980). See also J. Alexander Caldwell of Crocker National Bank and Antonio Villamil of Southeast First National Bank of Miami "Factors Affecting Creditworthiness" in *Assessing Country Risk,* ed. Richard Ensor (Euromoney Publications, March 1981).

TABLE 1
Country Risk Scale, December 31, 1982

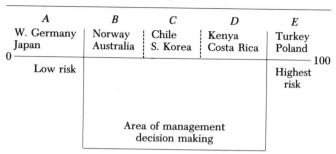

A	B	C	D	E
W. Germany Japan	Norway Australia	Chile S. Korea	Kenya Costa Rica	Turkey Poland

0 ―― 100

Low risk   Highest
                                                                            risk

Area of management
decision making

A number of useful conclusions can be derived from the above illustration. First, systematic analysis of economic risk factors using a structured approach permits relative risk ratings for international portfolio decisions. An A country, for example, would be one where economic risk is lower than in the other categories. These are countries with excellent *structural* attributes, such as outstanding economic management, viable industrial sectors, and strong external financial position. At the other extreme of the relative risk spectrum are countries with poor structural conditions, such as weak economic management, industries that are not competitive on an international basis, and adverse external financial position. These two categories, then, are the extremes in the risk spectrum, as denoted in the graph by the solid lines separating them from the broader B through D categories. From an economic risk perspective they are easy choices.

A second conclusion from an economic risk rating exercise is that the assignment of ratings in the broader middle categories is much more difficult and quite subjective. This is the area for difficult international portfolio decisions. Based on an assessment of structural economic factors, a D country carries greater economic risk than a B or C country. How greater a risk, however, can not be precisely identified. The science of economics is simply not that precise, nor is the subject matter being assessed subject to rigid quantification. This is illustrated in the chart by the broken lines separating the broad B through D categories.

Finally, relative economic risk assessment, and the assignment of country grades, must be based on structural factors that do not change often for effective decision making. A simple illustration may prove this point. A bank observes that country X had a much improved current account position of the balance of payments the previous year and that the outlook for this year is also good. Other things remaining the same, should the relative economic rating of the country be improved? Not necessarily: it would depend on the underlying factors that are causing an improvement on the current account. A country may still be poorly managed, with a narrow export structure, yet due to an unexpected increase in the international price for its main export, a temporary improvement could take place. Moving this country up the risk scale would send the wrong signal to bank management and could result in increased involvement in a country which would still be a relatively weak economic risk. However, if the current account improvement is the result of appropriate fiscal and monetary policies or a more diversified export structure, then an improved rating is warranted. In summary, effective economic risk assessment requires primarily the analysis of structural factors rather than cyclical events. The section below develops further techniques of economic risk assessment with emphasis on structural factors previously discussed.

ANALYZING KEY ECONOMIC RISK FACTORS

Economic risk assessment of foreign economies requires a combination of clear-eyed, no nonsense analysis and the weighing of subjective, intuitive, and judgmental factors. The first procedure is to develop an information system capable of producing a standardized flow of reliable statistical data and country news on a periodic basis. The second step is to insure that the analyst has a good grasp of the institutional characteristics of a country, which can only be acquired through periodic country visits. Finally, the analyst needs a paradigm that is simple, coherent, and robust. If the paradigm is based on sound economics and if the analyst clearly understands it, he will not always make the right judgments, but he will have the odds of making the right judgments on his side.

The start of the authors' suggested paradigm for effective economic risk analysis is an assessment of the resource base of a country—the natural, human, and financial resources available for production. After an assessment of the resource base is presented, economic policies to take advantage of this base must be scrutinized. In fact, the key to effective economic risk analysis is almost always an assessment of the quality of the economic and financial management process. The resource base provides the starting point for a country, but what matters is how the country utilizes that base (management). The Republic of China (Taiwan) is resource poor but extremely well-managed. Zaire is resource rich but not as well managed. At present, Taiwan can tap the international financial markets at much lower spreads than Zaire since it is a superior economic risk.

Finally, the third area of the paradigm looks at the external financial position—or what we may term the *bottom line* of economic risk assessment. As opposed to most economic risk models, however, the external financial position and outlook is deemed to be primarily dependent on endogenous factors such as the direction of economic policies rather than exogenously determined. The key issue, for example, in forecasting the trade balance of Brazil during the early 1980s is not so much the likely behavior of OPEC prices but whether Brazil chooses to adjust structurally to a deterioration in its terms of trade (price exports ÷ price of imports). The likely behavior of external financial variables such as trade balances, therefore, are mostly determined in the medium-term by the domestic structure of economic policies.

Adequacy of the Resource Base

The resource base of a country consists of its natural, human, and financial resources. This base is an important determinant of relative economic risk. Other things equal, a country with a strong resource base is a better economic risk than a country with a poor base. Within a resource-base context, the level of human resource development is of key importance. Zambia is rich in natural resources relative to its small population, but these resources remain mostly untapped due primarily to the low level of human resource development in the country. The Republic of Korea is relatively poor in natural resources but its highly skilled and motivated labor force is better able to utilize natural resources for production. What matters, therefore, is not so much the quantity of natural resources in the ground but the technical and infrastructural capability of a country to take advantage of its natural resources.

Among key natural resources to analyze are the ratio of arable land to population, the availability of energy resources to domestic requirements, and strategic minerals supplies. An assessment of climatic and geographical conditions is also important since many countries have a competitive advantage in the production of tourism and trade services. Furthermore, geographical location *per se* in a world of increased superpower tensions is becoming an important factor to assess. The United States, for example, has a strategic need to see a successful conclusion to the Jamaican experiment in free enterprise as the main engine for development. This need is being translated into increased financial and technological assistance to the country.

The quality of human resources in a country is also quite important from an economic risk perspective as discussed earlier. Focus on an assessment of such factors as the trainability of workers, the quality and depth of technical and managerial personnel, and the availability of entrepreneurship in both the public and private sectors. The rate of population growth is also of critical importance, as too rapid growth (2 percent per annum or above) usually strains the ability of government to provide for social services, including education. Lastly, institutional barriers to labor absorption and mobility need to be analyzed as they discourage the growth of labor productivity and inflate unit labor costs.

A look at financial resources completes the scrutiny of the resource base of a country. The availability of financial resources for investment depends on the ability of a nation to save—that is, to avoid consuming all of a year's domestic production—and to efficiently channel savings into productive investment. The greater the savings rate of a country (gross national savings on a national income account basis relative to gross national product), the higher a portion of a stated investment figure can it meet with its own financial resources. Therefore, the less it needs to borrow from abroad in order to close its savings-investment gap.[3] This relationship between national savings and investment is a key one for economic risk analysis. The present external debt-servicing problems of Poland, Turkey, and Bolivia are directly the result of ambitious investment programs without concomitant national savings efforts. In these countries, the disparity between domestic savings and investment was met through enlarged external borrowings as measured by the current account deficit of the balance of payments. In a few short years, their respective external debt loads became too heavy to service on a timely basis.

The resource base of a country, therefore, is an important determinant of creditworthiness from an economic risk perspective. The critical issue, however, is how the country utilizes its mix of resources

---

[3] Total disposable income of a country is its domestically produced income (Y) *plus* the net transfer payments it receives from abroad (T). According to national income accounting, saving (S) is the portion of total income that is not consumed ($S = Y + T - C$), with C considered both private consumption and net government consumption. We also know that domestically produced Y is equal to consumption (C) plus investment spending (I) plus net exports ($E - M$), with E standing for exports, and M standing for imports. With this background it is now possible to establish the following equations:

$$S = Y + T - C$$
$$Y = C + I + (E - M)$$

and since by algebraic manipulation

$$Y - C = E - M + I$$

We can derive the following equations:

$$S = T + E - M + I$$

or

$$S - I = E - M + T$$

$$\text{Saving investment} = \text{Current account}$$
$$\text{gap} \qquad \text{balance}$$

Therefore: If $S - I > 0$, then $E - M + T > 0$, representing a surplus on current account. If $S - I < 0$, then $E - M + T < 0$, representing a deficit on current account. In summary, a country cannot invest more than it saves without incurring a deficit on current account.

for production. This is the broad area of the quality and effectiveness of economic policies discussed in the next section.

Quality and Effectiveness of the Economic and Financial Management Process

An appropriate structure of economic policies leads to improved country creditworthiness through steadily rising economic efficiency and growing confidence of the international banking community on the long-run viability of a country. Appropriate economic policies require adherence to the following principles of good economic management:

1. A structure of incentives that rewards risk taking for productive endeavors. People on average respond rationally to the structure of incentives they confront and seek to maximize their own welfare, given the resources and information at their disposal. This has been proven true for the peasants of the Guatemala highlands as well as for high-pressure bankers in Miami.

2. A legal structure that allows and stimulates the growth of free markets. Unfettered markets are the most efficient form of economic organization thus far devised. All other forms of organization are to one extent or another either inefficient in resource use or involuntary, and usually both.

3. Where market distortions exist, the appropriate policy response is to correct the distortions at the source. This is called the principle of optimum intervention. For example, a country may be suffering from increased unemployment due to excessive cost of labor. Optimum intervention would remove the distortion at its source, such as reducing social security and other taxes on the use of labor or modifying minimum wage legislation. An incorrect policy response would be to compensate one distortion by adding another, such as subsidizing the consumption of labor-intensive final products. This last response, of course, does not eliminate the source of the distortion, but increases fiscal expenditures and sends the wrong market signals to producers of labor-intensive products. In summary, it fosters economic inefficiency.

4. Simplicity and measurability are basic norms of good management. Complex rules and regulations are confusing, and costly to measure and implement. They are susceptible to centralizing and discretionary authority. Thus they are discouraging to economic enterprise and efficiency.

The above principles are a set of ideal standards from which to judge real-world policies, which are mostly 2nd, 3rd, or 10th best. Poland and Cuba come close to violating most of the above principles of good economic management, while South Korea and Taiwan presently approximate the ideal. It is not by accident that the latter two are considered good economic risks, while the former find it quite difficult to obtain international credits.

The principles of good management provide the economic risk analyst with a broad framework to assess economic policies from a country creditworthiness perspective. But what are the specific policy characteristics that the analyst should center on? It is suggested that at least three specific areas need to be closely assessed before a final determination on the quality of economic management can be arrived at. These three areas are the technical competence of economic management, the long-run development strategy, and shorter-run economic adjustment policies.

The first necessary although not sufficient condition in the design and implementation of effective economic policies is the technical quality of the economic team in the country. To be categorized as an excellent economic team the following characteristics should be met:

1. Key officials at the central bank and the ministry of finance are perceived to be highly competent by both the international and local business community.

2. There is a growing cadre of middle-level officials that gives depth and permanency to economic management.

3. The central bank is de jure independent from the central government and usually pursues independent policies.

4. The levels of bureaucratic red tape and corruption that hinder decision making are minimal.

5. The economic team lines of communication to the politicians in power are deemed to be excellent. These politicians, in turn, have the ability to implement difficult economic policies if necessary. This linkage between excellent policy *recommendations* and actual policy *implementation* is crucial.

A second area for analysis is the development strategy of a country. An appropriate development strategy maximizes output growth, with stable price expectations and manageable external financial position. Such a strategy allows a country to steadily supplement domestic savings with external borrowings at reasonable rates. To be classified as excellent, a development strategy needs to encompass the following characteristics:

1. Appropriate attention to the factor endowments of a country (land, labor, capital, and entrepreneurship). If labor is the most abundant factor, then labor-intensive activities need to be emphasized. In a free market-oriented economy this would tend to occur automatically through relative factor prices. Since most economies in the world operate under government-created market distortions, government policies need to encourage productive activities along factor endowment lines.

2. An "open" economy-oriented development strategy subject to

the discipline and income gains of world trade and investment.[4] Such economies specialize according to the principle of *comparative advantage* (doing what you can do best in exchange—imports—for products and services in which you may not be as efficient). These economies would exhibit a healthy growth of exports on average, high ratio of exports to gross national product, low tariff barriers, and significant levels of foreign direct investment. These economies benefit over time from the technological transfers that result in transnational investments.

3. Reasonable investment expenditures relative to domestic savings as discussed earlier in the chapter. Furthermore, investments must be channeled on the basis of economic efficiency and not in support of prestige projects or to satisfy politically powerful vested interest groups. The efficiency of investment in a country can be roughly measured by the incremental capital-output ratio (ICOR). The ICOR measures new output generated by new investment. In the better-managed economies the ICOR is 2 to 3, while in the worst managed economies ICORs of 6 to 10 are not uncommon—indicating a relatively inefficient use of new investment.

The third area to be assessed is that of economic stabilization policies. These shorter-run policies contribute to smoothing out economic cycles and to adjusting to external shocks, such as the recent sharp increase in oil prices. Thus, they are important determinants of country creditworthiness. In general terms, fiscal, monetary, and exchange-rate policies should provide a stable environment for economic activities and should aid in maintaining the external solvency of a country. An excellent mix of shorter-term policies would include the following:

1. A *fiscal policy* that aims at reducing the share of fiscal expenditures in total economic activity. To the extent necessary by cyclical considerations, expenditure increases should be financed largely by a combination of domestic revenues and domestic borrowing from sources other than the monetary authorities. Excellent fiscal management should show in a declining ratio of fiscal expenditures to GNP, slowing growth of central bank's net credit to the public sector and increasing ability of the private sector to utilize the domestic credit markets.

2. A monetary policy that is not accommodative of inflationary trends. An excellent monetary policy should provide for a relatively stable interest-rate environment, insure credit availability to key productive sectors, and keep the rate of growth of the monetary aggregates

---

[4] For an excellent discussion on the outward model of economic development, and its positive impact on creditworthiness see J. A. Caldwell "The Outward Way to Creditworthiness' *Euromoney*, May 1981.

at a level consistent with reasonable price stability. Interest rate policy should also aim at maintaining real interest rates (adjusted for inflation) to encourage savings and efficient allocation of investment resources. Subsidized credit, even to priority sectors, *is not* a characteristic of excellent financial and monetary policies.

3. An exchange-rate policy that maintains parity between domestic and international prices. A free float of the exchange rate is the preferred policy since it allows for automatic adjustments to parity changes. As a minimum, the exchange-rate regime should be flexible enough to allow periodic adjustments in the rate, reflecting changes in the inflation-rate differential for tradeable goods between the country and its major trading partners. It is not good policy to use the exchange rate to ameliorate domestic economic problems as many countries usually attempt to do. During 1976–80, for example, Argentina allowed a highly overvalued exchange rate as a tool to decrease strong inflationary pressures. This led to a run on the peso in the first half of 1981, and a widening trade deficit. Thus Argentina was forced to sharply devalue in early 1981, with adverse consequences for international confidence in the government, and the very strong inflationary expectations that policymakers had tried to decrease.

In summary, adherence to the principles of good management and policies discussed would significantly minimize economic risk in lending to residents of another country. No country comes close to the ideal set of principles and policies presented, but relative gradations from the ideal set are possible.

The main reason for undertaking an assessment of economic policies is to be able to analyze the likely behavior of the external financial position of a country. Indeed, ultimately, country creditworthiness depends on a viable external financial sector and in noneconomic factors like political developments which are discussed in a different chapter.

Indicators of External Financial Position

The end result of an excellent resource base and appropriate economic policies is usually a favorable external financial position, at least on a medium- to longer-term horizon. In the shorter run, however, adverse world economic conditions, a sharp drop in commodity export prices, or sharp increases in imported energy prices could also strain the external financial position of a well-managed country. Effective economic risk assessment, therefore, requires not only an in-depth view of economic policies, but also of the likely international economic environment confronting the country. The outlook for the external financial position may be arrived at after an analysis of balance-of-payments trends, the external debt burden, the level of international reserves, and potential access to international finance.

The outlook for the balance of payments is of key importance since the future ability of a country to timely service its external obligations will be primarily dependent on key components of the balance of payments. These two key components are the current account and the capital account. The current account measures transactions in goods and services between the residents of a country and the rest of the world. The balance on current account, therefore, is a measure of the *net* change in the external indebtedness of a country. A current account deficit, for example, has to be financed through a net increase in external liabilities or a net decrease in external assets. Forecasting current account trends is complex and requires intimate knowledge of a country's economic policies, the rate of growth of domestic demand, the savings-investment gap, the exchange rate, trends in world prices for its major exports, and the degree of export diversification.

A recurrent-account deficit per se does not imply an adverse trend for the country's creditworthiness. It depends on the cause(s) for such a development, the nominal size of the deficit relative to economic size, and export growth potential. A growing deficit due to a poor development strategy or expansionary monetary and fiscal policies would be a cause for concern. A moderate deficit that can be steadily financed through external inflows and caused by the importation of capital goods for viable projects may actually improve economic risk in the longer term. In fact, developing countries by definition are capital-short countries, and it makes good economic sense to supplement domestic savings with external savings (external borrowings) as measured by the current account deficit. This holds true, of course, as long as the real return on the projects financed by external borrowings is greater than the real cost of these borrowings, which is usually the case in capital-short countries.

Specific components of the capital account need also to be scrutinized. Emphasis should be placed in analyzing the structure of capital inflows to finance projected current account deficits. For example, development projects with a long gestation period and no net foreign exchange generating capacity should be primarily financed by soft loans from multilateral and bilateral agencies. Short-term (less than one year) credits should be undertaken to finance self-liquidating transactions of the same maturity, and so on. In summary, a well-managed capital account will decrease the burden of eventual repayment of most capital inflows by matching the structure (maturity-rate) of external borrowing to specific project characteristics.

The external debt burden is primarily dependent on current account trends and the structure of foreign borrowings. A country with a favorable outlook on current account and a soft external debt profile composed of concessionary loans will probably find it easier to repay external debt obligations than a country with adverse current account trends and a hard external debt profile composed primarily of commercial bank borrowings.

A number of ratios that measure external debt-service burden are used.[5] The table below presents some of these ratios which by themselves mean little unless interpreted in the context of a country. Brazil, for example, is estimated to have an external debt-service ratio (exports of external goods and services ÷ debt-service payments on principal and interest) of over 60 percent in 1981 and is current on its external payments. Turkey had to restructure its external debt with a debt-service ratio of less than 20 percent in the late 70s. The main reason for such a development is that the international banking community perceives Brazil to be a better-managed economy with an excellent resource base and a viable export sector. Turkey is not perceived in the same favorable light. Furthermore, the key to effective economic risk analysis is not the size of a given ratio, but the detection of trends in a number of indicators. Only then can meaningful conclusions as to the external financial position of a country be developed.

Another key indicator of external financial position is the level of international reserves primarily composed of foreign exchange in hard currencies. The level reflects balance-of-payments developments. The international reserve position is really the first line of defense to pay for essential imports and to "finance" a current account deficit if net capital inflows have been insufficient to cover the gap. In most countries it is important to consider not only official international reserves of the central bank, but also the foreign asset position of the commercial banking system. In well-managed countries with favorable balance-of-payments trends, the authorities maintain at least three months of *official* reserve coverage for imports. But again, consideration of institutional factors is important. Panama, for example, can afford to operate with only a few weeks of official reserve coverage since the U.S. dollar, a hard currency, is the medium of exchange in the country.

Finally, access to external financial sources is the second line of defense for countries with adverse balance-of-payments trends. Focus on the ability of a country to utilize its quota at the International Monetary Fund (IMF), borrowing plans for the World Bank, regional development banks, and other multilateral agencies. The IMF provides financial support to member countries with economic stabilization problems, usually in exchange for the development and implementa-

---

[5] Ratio analysis also suffers from the low quality of statistics in many countries, time lags in the production of data, and different country methodologies for data collection and analysis. A certain degree of standardization and timeliness that permits valid inter-country comparisons can be achieved by using the *International Financial Statistics* of the International Monetary Fund, the World Bank *External Debt Reporting System,* and Organization of Economic Cooperation and Development statistical publications for industrialized nations.

Table 2
External Debt-Burden Indicators

Indicator	Characteristic
Total external debt/GNP	Measure of longer-term external debt burden
Total service payments/Total exports	Measure of short-term external debt burden
Total external debt/Amortization payments	Measure of average maturity of the external debt
Interest payments on external debt/International reserves	Short-term measure of ability to meet interest requirements

tion of an economic stabilization program. As of mid-1981, countries could borrow up to six times quota under all available programs, with drawdowns taking place in a three-year period. Furthermore, adherence to an IMF economic stabilization program in many cases is considered a necessity before a country can tap the vast Eurocurrency markets for balance-of-payments support.

The most important source of external finance for most developed and developing countries, however, is the private international credit markets. Therefore, an assessment of the ability of a country to tap these markets for balance-of-payments support is crucial. Among factors to assess are the willingness of a country to implement economic stabilization measures, market perception of the long-run viability of the country, market confidence in the economic team, and the availability of comprehensive financial statistics.

CONCLUDING OBSERVATIONS

Experiences accumulated since 1973 clearly demonstrate that effective international economic risk assessment cannot be subjected to rigid quantification and that an institutional approach with emphasis on analyzing the structure of economic policies enhances predictive ability. An economic risk assessment system can be useful to international portfolio management only to the extent that it can provide relative gradations of economic risk. These relative risk ratings should not change often as their derivation would be based on structural factors rather than cyclical events.

The establishment of country exposure limits requires as a necessary condition an effective country risk rating system. International portfolio decisions, however, should also encompass factors other than country risk, such as return, size of a country using as proxy GNP or import levels, naturalness of a market place to a bank, and the accumulated institutional knowledge of a bank in a particular country.

If bank management decides, for example, that no more than 30 percent of bank capital could be exposed to a given country, then a composite index using the mentioned factors, including relative risk, could be constructed. Such an index could then be used to discount exposure in a particular country from the allowable maximum.

At Southeast Bank of Miami, final determination of country exposure limits is the responsibility of the Country Risk Committee. The subcommittee is made up of the chairman and vice chairman of the bank, together with the senior officers of the international, credit administration, credit policy and economics departments. The Committee meets regularly to consider country exposure limits after receiving the following documents:

1. A country exposure monitoring report prepared by the economics department that keeps management updated on country exposure limits as a percent of bank capital for all the countries in which the bank extends credit. The report also contains comments on important economic and political changes in each country.

2. A country-risk assessment report prepared either directly by the economics department for major markets of the bank or by the international department under the technical supervision of economics. Southeast utilizes a structured qualitative report format, with a methodology similar to the one presented in this chapter but also including political risk considerations.

3. A specific country-risk assessment report and a marketing strategy for a particular country is prepared. The strategy is prepared by the account officer responsible for the country after consultations with senior officers from the international and economics departments. The strategy includes an assessment of marketing opportunities in the country from Southeast's perspective and a table detailing proposed country exposure levels by tenor and type of borrower.

The economics unit is administratively separate from the international marketing function and fully responsible for relative risk ratings. This division of functions assures a strictly independent input to relative risk assessment. However, we encourage strong informal interaction between the international economist and the account officers as both can learn from their respective experiences. In fact, we believe that the quality of our international loan portfolio ultimately rests with the expertise of the account officer and have developed a number of training sessions on country risk assessment for the benefit of international lending personnel.

8
Bank-to-Bank Lending

PHILLIP G. MOON
Senior Vice President
National Bank of Detroit

The international lending activities of most U.S. banks, apart from the major money center institutions, are concentrated heavily in the area of providing a variety of credit facilities to banks in other countries. The purpose of this chapter is to establish the significance of bank-to-bank credit, to describe the facilities offered, and to underscore the risks involved in this type of lending.

The table below uses the approximate outstandings as of December 31, 1980, of the author's bank:

International division assets-total		$2,950,000,000
Loans to and guaranteed by banks	$ 170,000,000	
Export lines of credits and bankers acceptances	325,000,000	
Interbank placements— all currencies	1,275,000,000	
Bank-related credit		$1,770,000,000
Percent of total division assets		60%

As these figures demonstrate, a major portion of the international assets of a typical bank is represented by some form of interbank credit. Consequently, a considerable amount of management time and attention is devoted to this area of the business. The absolute number of dollars involved is large, and the profit potential is significant.

Interest earned on loans, deposit placements, and acceptances are handsomely supplemented by fees derived from other correspondent activities: foreign exchange trading, export letters of credit, collections, payments, and miscellaneous—often one-of-a-kind accommodations.

117

Fee income, however, should be placed in perspective. While significant in total, senior management is keenly aware that related direct expenses, overhead and required safeguards, and expertise mean that measurement of the net return on time assets employed, risk, and so forth, make it difficult to justify a complete international operation unless closely tied to customer demands or to other sources of income, chiefly a sizable portfolio of interest-bearing assets.

Thus, many banks with international activities have developed from an operations-based foreign department to an international division largely focused on credit extension through the natural channel of lending money to their foreign correspondents. The contacts were often in place from years of handling basic export-import documents and payments.

Nondollar-based banks need access to dollar facilities, both short- and medium-term, to finance trade, projects, and liquidity needs. Further, banks have always been considered the finest of risks—if they were considered to be risks at all. Lines of credit permitting direct borrowings by promissory note or telex confirmation was an easy evolution from authorizations in place for overdrafts, confirmation of letters of credit, or acceptance of drafts drawn under those credits.

The point was quickly reached when calling officers of the international division were expanding correspondent banking networks, with lines of credit for untied borrowings being the primary inducement for a foreign bank to open accounts and direct fee-related business to its new correspondents in Chicago, Pittsburgh, Detroit, or wherever.

The number of banks engaged in international finance is very large, and even regional U.S. banks find they must establish correspondent relationships, at least to the extent of exchanging authorized signatures and cable control documents, with upwards of 1,000 banks throughout the world.

The relative amounts of money market type transactions vary with smaller banks and banks in weaker countries doing most of their business by prior, direct arrangements. Larger banks in stronger countries have access to the money market on a daily basis without need for pre-arrangement.

Foreign correspondents, particularly in the developing countries, with limited capital markets and scarce foreign exchange, would on occasion seek U.S. bank assistance in financing a customer import for three to seven years. This was often done by a loan directly to the correspondent or under its guarantee. In this way and others, U.S. banks developed sizable portfolios of bank-related loans often tied to the more traditional documentary services or foreign exchange dealings.

The advent of the Eurodollar market in the early 1960s opened a new era of interbank lending, albeit disguised as the taking and placing of deposits. Banks had rushed to open branches in London and Nassau to escape home-country regulatory restrictions or tax levies. The branches were dedicated to wholesale activities and had no natural base of deposits from which to onlend to corporate or government borrowers. It was also difficult to depend on the head office for funding because of the same regulations that were the cause of the branches in the first place.

Nonetheless, there was a sizable supply of dollars outside of the United States in the hands of foreign governments, central banks, oil companies, and a variety of major corporations heavily engaged in international commerce and investment. A market quickly developed to bid for these deposits on terms of one day to one year. While these .deposits could be onlent to government or corporate users of funds, in many cases they were redeposited in the rapidly expanding inter-bank market, which itself became a major source of profit.

This market developed with relative ease as it bore many similarities to trading in federal funds for American banks and similar instruments for banks in other countries. While it is not the purpose of this chapter to examine the art of making money in deposit dealing, the point is that banks were now lending money in unprecedented volumes to other banks. This meant that loan officers and their credit departments had to establish limits for individual banks and for all banks within a specific country and, in general, to establish suitable criteria and parameters to manage a substantial element of risk that appears on the financial statements as "cash and due from banks."

ASSESSING AND MANAGING RISKS

The reputation of a financial institution is a real asset and critical to its success in maintaining its position in the community and surrounding market area. In its local market, a bank is judged by the community stature of its management, retail efficiency, courtesy, and proper handling of corporate business—such perceptions being enhanced by advertising and involvement in community activities. The national and international arenas are, perhaps, even more demanding of the quality of the "names" that are accepted.

The international—foreign—evaluator of a bank is much less aware, perhaps even ignorant, of the above factors; he is much more conscious of its balance-sheet footings, capital and liquidity ratios, its presence and acceptance in the money markets, loan syndications, and as an aggressive and efficient correspondent in handling payments, foreign exchange transactions, business introductions, and the other essential elements of cross-border dealings.

As a result, the fraternity of international banks, while not an exclusive club, is nonetheless restricted. Membership has expanded rather dramatically in the last 15 years, and most banks have abandoned a credit decision-making process based on asset size or prestige ("They are first class") and have developed their own internal process to avoid those banks considered to offer undue risk.

While systems employed to evaluate creditworthiness vary by institution, certain elements are common to all.

Country Analysis

No bank, or company, can be judged independently of the economic conditions and political environment within which it must operate. Lenders must have a good overview of a country's internal business conditions in order to make judgments on loan opportunities to banks or companies.

The larger U.S. banks have developed rather formal programs to analyze country risks to assist lending officers and senior management, both in their individual credit decisions and in the larger area of asset allocations. The loan officer who travels to an assigned geographic area has considerable responsibility in these programs. In many ways, his trips are similar to visits to factories and plant sites of local companies: first-hand observation of actual conditions.

Asset realization is essential to repay outstanding obligations. Deep recessions, rampant inflation, chaotic political conditions, and threatened revaluations—alone or in combination—create precarious conditions.

Knowledge of a Country's Banking System

A bank can only be judged by first understanding the banking system and regulatory framework within which it operates. Judgments must also be formed on the strength of the government commitment to support individual banks in times of difficulty. This is a very important point as foreign bank lenders do not enjoy the protection of any depositor insurance or other mechanism that might be in place to insure the confidence of the public in the banking system.

Evidence of such support is likely to be derived only from a knowledge of what has happened in recent history, say, the last 10 years. Apart from numerous cases of a central bank quietly helping other banks by permitting loan rediscounts or lending local currency, there are examples in many countries of central bank action such as intervention that resulted in liquidations, mergers, or government ownership. Most of these cases occur in developing countries, and to date, foreign creditors have generally been given favorable treatment in getting outstanding loans paid.

There have been exceptions, however, one of the most notable being

Banco de Guayaquil, Equador, which was closed by the monetary authorities in 1970 reportedly because of fraudulent transactions undertaken by management. The 30-plus foreign bank creditors were able to recover a portion of their loans but, for the most part, were forced to settle for stock in a newly organized bank and a long-term note. Interestingly, the 30-plus banks were still shareholders in the new Banco de Guayaquil in 1981.

The record in the major industrialized countries is considerably different in that central banks and regulators have not felt obligated to give special treatment to bank lenders to a failed financial institution but have rather concentrated on protecting individual depositors. The closing of I. D. Herstatt in 1974 reportedly caused millions of dollars of losses to many banks and precipitated a near financial panic in the London and New York markets.

The Bank of England was also forced to set up a so-called life boat rescue operation to assist ailing secondary banks in England in the late 1970s. While this was generally successful, substantial losses were taken by a number of parties.

Thus, careful lenders will take considerable pains to know the history and present policies of central banks and other monetary authorities before forming judgments on the general soundness of a country's banking system. This consideration is quite apart from assessing the creditworthiness of individual banks.

Analyzing Individual Banks

After the lending officer has satisfied himself on the prevailing conditions in the foreign country and the banking system in general, the next step is to establish the creditworthiness of his prospective bank customer. Bank stock analysts in the United States have developed peer group comparisons for use by investors and depositors. A loan officer evaluating a bank in the United Kingdom or Argentina instinctively develops his own comparisons in order to judge whether the bank in question has a proper balance sheet structure and profit performance.

The analyst must be able to place each bank being scrutinized in its correct relative position in terms of size, market (money center or regional), ownership (public, private, or mixed) and business orientation. This initial screening is necessary to an understanding of balance sheet and operating history.

For example, the largest Italian and French banks are government owned and maintain capital ratios clearly unacceptable in the private sector. Nevertheless, they easily obtain their credit needs in the world's market because lenders or depositors perceive the ownership as tantamount to a guarantee by the government.

Financial Statements

The annual report must be read in whatever language it is published. Banks will typically highlight what they consider to be important to their position, growth, problems, and so forth. Before spreading the statements, one must make sure that the captions are understood. While the terminology may appear similar to that used by American banks, the definitions or standards may not be.

The Robert Morris Associates and some commercial organizations now publish guidelines for the interpretation of bank statements in an increasing number of countries, typically the ones that will concern the analyst the most. A number of large banks have developed substantial in-house expertise on spreading and interpreting bank statements and are generally willing to share their knowledge. The profit and loss statement should receive the same attention as the balance sheet. An analyst must understand the nature of the earnings, the portion derived from loans, fees, foreign exchange, sale of assets, and so on, and whether the mix has changed significantly in recent years. Any notable changes should prompt questions on the possibility that management has undertaken new directions: perhaps efforts were made to prop earnings by engaging in new or more risky fields to offset declining margins and opportunities in a bank's traditional business lines.

Apart from published reports, it is often possible to obtain internally generated financial statements such as those submitted to the central bank or other regulatory bodies which are similar to the call reports of U.S. banks. These statements are often more detailed, thus permitting more in-depth analysis, particularly in the areas of nonaccrual and delinquent loans. The interpretation of financial statements is more meaningful when read in conjunction with calling officer memos which contain comments on recent earnings, balance-sheet change, industry concentration, and loan maturities.

As mentioned earlier, once statements are spread, all banks of a similar category should be compared in as simple but meaningful a way as possible. Deviations from average liquidity and capital ratios, return on assets or equity, and total footings, should be noted. (See Exhibits A and B for abbreviated examples).

Too many ratios or comparison points tend to obscure a quick grasp of the objective: are you dealing with a bank that fits the norm(s) of the banking industry? If it does not, the loan officer must know why or run the risk of unexpected and very public developments.

One caveat—a loan officer is not performing the same function as a bank examiner or a representative of Standard & Poors or Moody's rating agencies. His analysis will be faster and more superficial and thus must be directed at finding trends and highlights that will lead

Exhibit A
Japanese Banks (dollars in thousands, yen in hundred thousands)

	City Banks			Regional Banks		
	Fuji Bank Ltd.	Mitsubishi Bank, Ltd.	Mitsui Bank, Ltd.	Horuriku Bank Ltd.	Joyo Bank, Ltd.	Yamaguchi Bank, Ltd.
Assets						
Cash and due from banks	¥ 2,408,017	¥ 2,390,387	¥ 1,423,052	¥ 149,259	¥ 112,298	¥ 95,891
Loans and discounts—net	8,257,898	8,015,693	5,759,518	1,596,247	1,444,131	996,462
Customer liability for acceptance and guarantee	1,321,050	1,337,095	1,011,791	172,041	36,445	22,036
Total assets	¥15,761,213	¥15,197,455	¥10,497,886	¥2,560,417	¥2,410,286	¥1,542,795
Liabilities						
Borrowed funds	12,249,346	11,755,802	7,813,074	2,117,380	2,152,256	1,340,521
Total liabilities	15,376,392	14,826,716	10,281,286	2,473,496	2,079,964	1,463,008
Net worth	361,157	350,858	200,261	84,558	92,449	79,053
Total	¥15,761,213	¥15,197,455	¥10,497,886	¥2,560,417	¥2,410,286	¥1,542,792
Net profit	21,095	25,929	12,252	5,881	6,935	7,004
Loans/borrowed funds—percent	67.42	68.18	74.11	74.91	67.81	74.33
Capital/total assets—percent	2.3	2.3	1.9	3.30	3.84	5.12
Net profit/total assets—percent	.13	.17	.13	.23	.29	.45
*Stated in U.S. dollars**						
Net profit	$ 84,540	$ 103,800	$ 49,050	$ 24,000	$ 27,760	$ 28,000
Borrowed funds	49,036,610	47,060,860	31,227,780	8,476,000	8,615,920	5,366,000
Total liabilities	61,554,810	59,354,350	41,158,070	9,902,000	9,263,270	5,857,000
Net worth	1,445,780	1,404,560	801,690	339,000	370,090	316,000

* $1 = ¥249.80 as of March 31, 1980.

Exhibit B
Japanese Banks' Results for Six-Months' Term to March 31, 1980

	Yen (billion)			
	Net Income	Percent Change versus Preceding Six Months	Income Excluding Securities Transactions	Percent Change versus Preceding Six Months
City banks:				
Dai-ichi Kangyo Bank	13.5	−2.8	21.8	−37.3
Mitsubishi Bank	13.9	−2.7	23.1	−34.0
Taiyo Kobe Bank	7.1	−0.2	8.7	−53.7
Kyowa Bank	4.6	−0.8	3.4	−52.9
Saitama Bank	4.4	−2.8	4.8	−26.0
Hokkaido Takushoku Bank	4.0	−1.5	2.3	−62.8
Bank of Tokyo	10.5	+8.3	24.1	− 1.5
Long-term credit banks:				
Industrial Bank of Japan	12.81	−6.4	27.52	+12.6
Long-term Credit Bank of Japan	12.09	+1.1	17.92	+74.3
Nippon Credit Bank	8.26	+1.2	6.16	−16.5

to more probing. Generally, the strongest and weakest banks are readily identified; the ranking of those in between is considerably more difficult.

A few simple comparisons have been placed at the end of this chapter for illustration purposes.

Marketplace Reputation

Most leading banks in the United States regularly consult with other known, major lenders to foreign banks on an annual basis to update their files when considering new facilities or renewing existing ones. Such bank checkings are designed to give the loan officer several perspectives including size of facilities generally available to the correspondent under consideration; whether recent renewals are routine; type of facilities used by the bank; and other lenders' impressions of the country in question—whether its banks are readily obtaining the credit they need or if a change in country circumstances is making this more difficult.

In this area of bank checkings, it is much easier to obtain information from other U.S. banks than it is from, say, a major German bank on a smaller regional bank in Germany. The exchange of credit information is not uniquely American, but it is certainly more available here than abroad.

In summary, do not ignore or underrate the value of bank checkings. They are much more important than in the corporate lending field.

It should be noted here that it is important to be open to street rumors that often emanate from trading desks, from foreign representative offices, and from other perhaps unlikely and unofficial sources. The first signs of a bank's difficulties often are picked up long before they are reported in the press or can be deduced from an annual report. The broader your contacts, the more likely you will be forewarned of potential problems.

Officer Visits

Correspondent banking is still a personalized business. The frequent exchange of visits plus social encounters at trade associations and similar conferences tend to cement relationships. It is in these ways that new opportunities for cooperation or additional credit are made known and developed.

A good calling officer will assess the "character" of a bank, know its general customer base and market and the ownership or investor groups with which it is associated. Calls are also the opportunities to discuss balance-sheet changes or unusual developments in the past year. This type of information is invaluable to a proper analysis by the credit department.

CREDIT FACILITIES

Once the judgment is made that a foreign bank meets your requirements, the need remains during the life of the relationship to determine, on an ongoing basis, the type and size of credit facilities. As with corporate customers, initial facilities may be relatively small or at least related to trade or specific transactions. On the other hand, the first credit granted may be strictly money market related or related to foreign exchange limits, deposit placements, or fed funds. Relationships have different starting points, but the objective is generally to achieve a balance among money market, direct lines of credit, and current account activity.

The nomenclature given to facilities by U.S. banks is not necessarily uniform, but they are generally understood to include:

Line of credit or short-term authorization to permit financing of trade transactions. Such lines are used principally for confirmation of letters of credit, which could be payable at sight or against the exporter's draft.

Bankers' acceptance lines of credit or facilities, advised subject to availability and agreement on rate of discount. These are often to refinance other acceptances and frequently are supported by third-country sales and purchases.

Clean loans or advances up to six months to finance specific and identified exports or imports; the guarantee of short-term loans to customers of the bank.

Open facility to borrow in dollars or other currencies for general purposes, which could be a bridge loan pending takedown of a term credit, shortage of local currency, portfolio hedging, etc.

Medium-term loans or guarantees to finance imports from the United States or third countries.

Interbank placements of deposits for periods of up to one year.

Foreign exchange dealing limits.

Overdrafts in deposit accounts.

Daylight overdrafts for payment settlements.

Standby commitments for one to three years.

Term loans to finance acquisitions by borrowing bank.

Clearly, not all of these facilities will be requested or offered when a relationship is being established or is newly developing. The list of possibilities or opportunities is presented to demonstrate the wide range of credit-related activities among banks, a fact that is frequently overlooked. However broad the relationship, the lending bank must have a good internal reporting mechanism and firm control over potential exposure to any correspondent.

The fact that credit may be extended to a correspondent's subsidiaries, affiliates, and foreign branches by the head office, subsidiaries, affiliates, and foreign branches of the lending bank increases the need for such reporting and control. What begins with a small line of credit tends to expand over the years, if circumstances and the relationship are in tune. Since circumstances, such as economic and political conditions, tend to be volatile in many countries, serious judgments have to be made by the loan officer on rather short notice.

The size of any component of the global exposure is not determined by some formula but is based on usage, the size of the lending bank, and the size, capital, government support, and reputation of the borrowing bank. Since many bank-to-bank credits are subject to U.S. banks' legal limit constraints, the management of each bank must develop its own internal guidelines and comfort level.

Paramount in decisions on individual banks is a careful analysis of what one can or hopes to achieve in the relationship—and of a lending bank's view of the risks and prospects for the country in which the borrower is located.

With the advent of the large money markets in New York, London, Nassau, Singapore, and Bahrain, the traditional development of correspondent bank ties has undergone a rather radical change. As new or large regional banks from overseas turn to international dealings and suddenly enter the markets in a significant way, they seek inter-bank funding in such amounts that lending banks must make decisions to start off with limits that they normally would have granted only after getting-acquainted periods of some years. It is again in this area that a lending officer must know the market and the banking system of the country in question.

Often substantial information is available from foreign central banks and bank supervising agencies about the country's banking system and bank accounting statements. Visits with examining officials in some countries can provide much insight on the nature of the examining process and the resultant quality of a bank's operations in general.

RISKS AND REWARDS

The rewards of international bank-to-bank lending come in many forms. Obviously, the direct interest earnings may be a significant part of an international division's gross income and certainly should be large enough to justify the credit risk assumed in such lending.

Beyond basic return there are earnings from the increased corre-spondent network which bank-to-bank lending helps to foster. Among these are the earnings from demand accounts against which must be offset the cost of the reciprocal accounts carried abroad. There are also the numerous fee-producing services previously mentioned which should, in themselves, result in significant net income. These same services provide useful domestic business development tools and en-hance existing corporate relationships.

The growth of foreign investments in the United States has made introductions by correspondent banks of increasing importance. Such introductions by correspondents frequently lead to new accounts and lending opportunities in one's own market area and again build further opportunities for international remittances and related fee-producing business. U.S. corporations value most highly those banks with exten-sive correspondent networks because of their ability to provide impor-tant overseas contacts and facilities.

Profitable foreign exchange trading opportunities and invitations from correspondents to participate in their direct loans and/or syndica-tions are other direct benefits. Reciprocity is both desirable and essen-tial as a bank takes a larger posture in the field of international finance.

While there are these rewards, there are unquestionably risks in bank-to-bank lending. In recent years, there have been a number of bank failures in such diversified countries as Germany, Ecuador, Argen-tina, Spain, and the Philippines, to say nothing of the United States. These insolvencies have led to loan stretchouts, lost interest, charge-offs and foreign exchange settlement failures. The position of foreign creditor banks is uncertain and often untested in the courts of many countries. Thus, the process of recovery may be time-consuming and difficult under the best of circumstances.

Even loans to a strong bank can run into difficulties because of country risk and the possible unavailability of necessary foreign exchange. During 1978 many banks which had advanced funds to Turkish correspondents for onlending to Turkish companies found at the maturity of their loans that the bank involved was able to repay the Turkish lira to the central bank but the latter was unable to provide the necessary hard currency to repay the loan. As a result, what had been short-term, trade-related financing was converted into a long-term, direct credit to the Turkish government with no principal repayment for a number of years.

In the case of I. D. Herstatt (referred to previously), that bank had a number of maturing foreign exchange contracts where payment by the American bank counterparty had been effected in Deutsche Marks that morning in Germany, but the offsetting payment in U.S. dollars had not yet been made in New York because the banks in that city were not open. This clean risk at date of settlement exists in any foreign exchange contract, particularly where different time zones are involved. The multitude (and size) of the resulting claims were the subject of expensive and lengthy litigation. Such costs are never fully recovered.

Other types of risks include the possibility of excessive concentration in assets that produce very small margins. This can be particularly true of interbank time deposits where spreads often are as low as $\frac{1}{16}$th of 1 percent per annum.

As the volume of international payments has increased so dramatically in recent years, U.S. banks have recognized the very real risk in daylight overdrafts and in the failure of a single bank to meet its payment obligations on any particular day. The New York-based CHIPS (Clearing House International Payments Systems) has implemented a mechanism to recall all settlements by computer until a late hour of the day, should one participant fail to receive payments due from a remitting bank. Since payments through CHIPS frequently exceed $100 billion in a single day, the magnitude of the concern is apparent.

Further, the risks inherent in the settlement process are generally not subject to approval by any credit committee, a situation which emphasizes the need for careful selection of a bank's counterparties.

Senior managements of U.S. banks are well aware of the risks in bank-to-bank lending. Internal control and reporting systems have been developed. More emphasis than ever is placed on analysis of financial statements and other information sources, and concentrations in placements or funding reliance are highlighted and avoided. These efforts are made because the importance and necessity of solid relationships with the international banking community are well recognized.

9

Government Borrowing in the International Financial Markets*

JAMES R. GREENE
President
American Express International Banking Corporation

INTRODUCTION

Credit to sovereigns is as old as the existence of sovereigns. It has been sought from wealthy individuals and institutions, and from allies and neutrals, to build armies and navies, wage war, repair devastation, construct public works, and finance exploration and trade.

Contemporary lending to governments and state entities is more sophisticated and institutionalized than in the past; its problems have become more complex as well. Forms of government may have changed, but the risk-reward and lender-protection problems remain. Lending to foreign governments or state entities, therefore, requires a careful assessment of both the country risk involved and the economic, political, and legal standing of the specific borrowing entity. The events of the early 1980s demonstrate that a firm understanding of the nature of lending to governments is essential.

Contemporary commercial bank lending to sovereign borrowers is concentrated in the Euromarkets, and this business has increased extremely rapidly in the past 15 years. This chapter will focus on problems and opportunities presented by present day (i.e., post-1970) Euromarket lending to governments and state entities. After a brief description of recent trends in international financial markets, it will indicate some of the relevant factors in risk assessment. It will describe the different uses for borrowings, outline the components of a rudimentary country rating system, examine some of the legal and political factors

* The author wishes to acknowledge the extensive assistance of Richard O'Brien, Vice President, American Express International Banking Corporation, in the preparation of this chapter through his published and direct contributions.

affecting risk assessment, and cover past, present, and prospective experience with debt-servicing difficulties.

DIMENSIONS OF EUROMARKET BORROWING

Government borrowing in the Euromarkets has grown very rapidly
during the past decade. Gross borrowings by public and private entities
outside of the Bank for International Settlements (BIS) reporting area
(i.e., outside the United States, United Kingdom, Canada, Japan,
France, West Germany, Belgium-Luxembourg, Netherlands, Sweden,
Denmark, Austria, Switzerland, Italy, and Ireland) rose from $75.5
billion in 1973 to $484.6 billion by 1981 (Table 1). The Organization
of Petroleum Exporting Countries (OPEC) and the other industrial
countries are net providers of funds; their deposits exceed borrowings
by $84.8 billion. Nonoil, less-developed countries (LDCs) and Eastern

Table 1
**Financial Flows between Bank for International Settlement Reporting Banks and Groups of
Countries Outside the Bank for International Settlements (billions of dollars)**

Country Group	Stock Position End of 1973	Flows 1980	Stock Position End of 1980	Flows 1981	Stock Position End of 1981
Nonoil LDCs:					
Gross deposits	$27.5	$ 4.1	$ 87.9	$10.4	$ 98.3
Gross borrowings	32.0	39.2	188.5	41.6	230.1
Net deposits	−4.5	−35.1	−100.6	−31.2	−131.8
Memo: Foreign exchange reserves	21.2	−0.9	69.9	0.6	70.5
OPEC countries:					
Gross deposits	16.0	41.6	153.6	3.2	156.8
Gross borrowings	6.5	8.0	67.7	4.3	72.0
Net deposits	9.5	33.6	85.9	−1.1	84.4
Memo: Foreign exchange reserves	12.6	19.4	90.0	−0.2	89.8
Eastern Europe:					
Gross deposits	4.5	0.8	14.7	0.1	14.8
Gross borrowings	9.5	7.0	56.0	4.8	60.8
Net deposits	−5.0	−6.2	−41.3	−4.7	−46.0
Memo: Foreign exchange reserves	n.a.	n.a.	n.a.	n.a.	n.a.
Non-BIS developed countries: and Unallocated					
Gross deposits	34.5	12.6	71.2	14.0	85.2
Gross borrowings	27.5	19.2	98.2	23.5	121.7
Net deposits	7.0	−6.6	−27.0	−9.5	−36.5
Memo: Foreign exchange reserves	23.5	3.4	26.9	−2.2	34.7
Total:					
Gross deposits	82.5	59.1	327.4	27.7	355.1
Gross borrowing	75.5	73.4	410.4	74.2	484.6
Net deposits	7.0	−14.3	− 8.3	−46.5	−129.5

n.a. = not available.
Source: Bank for International Settlements, Annual Report 1981–82.

Europe, in turn, are net borrowers of funds; their borrowings are $177.8 billion greater than deposits.

The most significant group of sovereign borrowers on the Euromarket are the nonoil LDCs. As Table 2, based on International Monetary Fund (IMF) statistics, shows, the total debt of nonoil LDCs rose from $96.8 billion in 1973 to $436.9 billion in 1979. Within this generally rising trend, debt owed to multilateral and bilateral institutions (the World Bank, regional development banks, and governments) has grown from $48.3 billion to $199.5 billion, while debt owed to private financial institutions has grown much more rapidly from $48.5 billion to $305.5 billion. This enormous increase has had large repercussions upon the entire international financial markets, particularly during the world recession of 1982–3.

The bulk of LDC debt is owed or guaranteed by LDC governments—$352.1 billion of the $436.9 billion total in 1981.

United States banks and their foreign branches account for a large proportion of this lending (see Table 6). Of the $195.0 billion in gross claims on nonoil LDCs at end-1980, U.S. banks held $75.4 billion or 38.7 percent. Of the $70 billion in gross claims on OPEC borrowers, U.S. banks accounted for $21.4 billion or 30.6 percent. Of the $118.6 billion in claims on nonreporting industrial countries and other unallocated borrowers, U.S. banks held $29.5 billion or 24.9 percent. Of the gross total of $598 billion borrowed by Eastern European countries only $7.9 billion (13.3 percent) was borrowed from U.S. banks.

SOVEREIGN LENDING

Purposes of Government Borrowing

Governments, government agencies, and government-owned entities account for most Euromarket borrowing. In the 3½ years ending mid-1981 public entities accounted for 59 percent of all borrowing on the Euromarkets, private firms for 32 percent and international organizations for 8 percent. Some 26 percent of all borrowing (nearly half of all public borrowing) was by national or local governments or central banks, another 23 percent (over one third of public borrowing) was by public nonfinancial corporations, and the remaining 10 percent was by public financial institutions (see Tables 3 and 4).

These figures are for *all* Euromarket borrowers: industrialized nations, socialist countries, and less-developed countries (LDCs). There are wide variations between groups of countries. The centrally planned economies, of course, borrow almost exclusively for the public sector,[1]

---

[1] Nevertheless, U.S. government figures indicate that U.S. banks and their foreign branches had nearly $300 million in end-1980 claims on private nonfinancial borrowers

Table 2
Non-Oil Developing Countries: Long-Term External Debt, 1973–82 (billions of dollars)

	1973	1974	1975	1976	1977	1978	1979	1980	1981	1982 (estimate)
Total debt outstanding	96.8	120.1	146.8	181.4	221.8	276.4	324.4	375.4	436.9	505.2
To official creditors	48.3	58.2	67.9	82.2	98.2	117.4	133.3	155.5	175.6	199.5
Governments	35.7	42.6	48.5	57.5	67.4	79.6	88.9	102.1	114.3	128.1
International institutions	12.6	15.7	19.4	24.7	30.8	37.8	44.5	53.4	61.4	71.4
Private creditors	48.5	61.8	78.9	99.2	123.6	159.0	191.1	220.0	261.4	305.7
Unguaranteed debt	20.6	25.3	31.5	38.7	44.0	52.4	58.6	68.8	84.8	101.5
Guaranteed debt	27.9	36.5	47.4	60.5	79.6	106.6	132.5	151.2	176.5	204.2
Financial institutions	14.0	22.8	31.2	41.9	57.5	75.4	101.9	117.4	138.8	162.6
Other private creditors	13.9	13.8	16.2	18.6	22.1	31.2	30.6	33.8	37.7	41.6

Source: International Monetary Fund Occasional Paper 9, "World Economic Outlook" (Washington, D.C., IMF, 1982)

Table 3
Destination of Funds Borrowed on International Capital Markets;
Bonds and Credits to All Countries, 1978–1981 (second quarter)
by type borrower (billions of dollars)

Borrower	Amount	Percent of Total	
Central, state, local governments	$ 89.1	23.0	
Central monetary institutions	11.8	3.0	
Other public financial institutions	40.1	10.3	
Public nonfinancial institutions	88.4	22.8	
Total public	229.4		59.2
Deposit money banks	28.7	7.4	
Other private financial institutions	8.6	2.2	
Private nonfinancial institutions	88.4	22.8	
Total private	125.7		32.4
International organizations	32.4		8.4
Grand total	387.5		100.0

Source: World Bank, *Borrowing in International Capital Markets First Half 1981* (Washington, D.C.: World Bank, 1981), p. 120.

and the LDCs tend to rely relatively more on public sector borrowing than do the industrialized countries. Even within groups there are wide variations. In a recent, rather typical year, Mexico's medium- to long-term Euromarket borrowing was overwhelmingly (86 percent) for government agencies, of which 40 percent was for state development banks, 34 percent for state-owned utilities and industrial corporations, and 12 percent for the central government itself.[2] At the other extreme is South Korea where over half of the medium- and long-term external debt is owed by private corporations.

Government borrowing on the Euromarkets is of three general types: general-purpose or program-related, project-related, and private with government guarantees. The relevance of these distinctions for the lender lies primarily in their identification of how the borrowing government organizes revenue streams. To the lender it matters a great deal whether the central government or some other body has direct control over the borrowed funds and responsibility for their repayments, as well as whether the loan concerns the general credit-worthiness of a nation-state or simply the viability of a particular project

in Poland, the USSR, East Germany, and Hungary. In as much as none of these nations has a conventional private corporate sector, it is difficult to know the meaning of this. It may refer to borrowing by the Eastern European subsidiaries or affiliates of Western corporations or possibly some nonrecourse shipping loans, or it may simply indicate definitional ambiguity. In any event, it points up the complexity of reconciling the various statistical sources.

   [2] Jeff Frieden, "Third World Indebted Industrialization: International Finance and State Capitalism in Mexico, Brazil, Algeria, and South Korea." *International Organization* 35, no. 3 (Summer 1981).

Table 4
Borrowing in Eurocurrency Credits by Governments and Government Entities (billions of dollars)

	1977		1978		1979	
	Amount	Percent	Amount	Percent	Amount	Percent
Central, state, local government, plus central monetary authority	$12.7	45.5	$25.7	45.2	$15.8	33.2
Other government-owned agencies	15.2	54.5	31.3	54.8	31.8	66.8
Total public sector	27.9	100.0	57.0	100.0	47.6	100.0

	1980		1981 (QI + QII)		Total 1977 to QII 1981	
	Amount	Percent	Amount	Percent	Amount	Percent
Central, state, local government, plus central monetary authority	18.7	42.6	$ 9.8	43.0	$ 82.7	41.5
Other government-owned agencies	25.2	57.4	13.0	57.0	116.5	58.5
Total public sector	43.9	100.0	22.8	100.0	119.2	100.0

Source: World Bank, *Borrowing on International Financial Markets First Half 1980* (Washington, D.C.: World Bank, 1980), p. 120.

or corporation. To some extent, the divisions are artificial and overlapping.

General Purpose and Program Loans. Governments will often borrow for unspecified budgetary or balance-of-payments purposes, without reference to an individual development project or state corporation. As indicated in Table 5, between 1977 and 1981 approximately one quarter of all Euromarket borrowing was of this type. Related to this are funds borrowed on the Euromarket and used to finance broad economic or social programs, which may or may not be self-liquidating but which form part of a larger government development plan. It is impossible to indicate with any accuracy which categories of Tables 4 and 5 might be considered program related. Broadly speaking, much of the lending for transportation, utilities, and public services (19 percent of the 1977–81 total) can be considered of the program variety. Lending to public financial institutions (other than central banks) amounted to 10 percent of all 1977–81 lending. Most of these institutions are national development banks, and the lending is largely program related inasmuch as the borrowed funds are usually reloaned domestically to finance government-backed development. General-purpose and program lending might include the following.

Reconstruction and Economic Development Loans. These are usually long-term loans and are general in scope, with interest rates and terms related to the borrower's needs and general creditworthiness. Purposes include reconstruction following natural and human disasters and financing the basic elements of economic growth. Loans often are from public sources but frequently from private as well. They may subsequently be attributed to specific projects, or they may

Table 5
Financing through Bonds and Credits to All Countries, 1977–1981 (through second quarter), by Purpose of Borrower (billions of dollars)

Purpose of Borrower	Amount	Percent of Total	
Banking and finance	$104.9		23.1
Transportation	20.8	4.6	
Utilities	57.9	12.7	
Public services	7.5	1.6	
Total these three	86.2		18.9*
Petroleum and natural gas	36.8	8.1	
Natural resources	6.4	1.4	
Industry	75.8	16.7	
Total these three	119.0		26.2
General purpose	105.1		23.1
International organization	39.8		8.7
Grand Total	455.0*		100.2

* Figures may not add due to rounding.
Source: World Bank, Borrowing in International Capital Markets First Half of 1980 (Washington, D.C.: World Bank, 1981), p. 120.

finance a group of projects which collectively contribute to the achievement of program objectives.

If the foreign exchange cost component of the reconstruction and development activity undertaken is relatively small, the principal financial effect of these loans may be to bolster the borrowing country's foreign exchange reserve position and to permit the exercise of an anti-inflationary influence through additional imports during a period of heavy call on capital construction resources.

A variant of this type is the loan for "general economic development purposes" which may finance construction of new facilities that are specified only in very broad terms.

General Budget Support to Central Government. This financing is ordinarily short term and is extended in anticipation of budgetary receipts. Usually these loans will be repaid out of the country's public sector foreign exchange revenues, such as from petroleum, minerals, or other commodity exports. Depending on the internal legislation and government policy in the borrowing country, this may or may not be attributed to a capital budget.

Loans to Create Foreign Exchange to Finance Seasonal Export/ Import Variations. In the early years of this type of financing, such loans were commonly restricted to short-term financing of anticipated foreign exchange receipts from exports of specific crops. This credit now frequently takes the form of bank credit lines, reviewed annually, to provide for seasonal foreign exchange accommodation on the basis of the borrowing country's overall foreign trade cycle. However, since the first purpose of a country's foreign exchange reserves is to finance just such seasonal swings, the need for this type of financing is prima facie evidence of concern on the part of domestic financial authorities about the level of net exchange reserves or about domestic conditions which could adversely affect reserves.

Economic and Financial Stabilization Financing. Such financing tends to be sourced from multilateral institutions (e.g., the International Monetary Fund) and usually involves a financial package tied to the implementation of a domestic stabilization program. Once the package is agreed to, private lenders often become involved in the provision of some of the external financial resources necessary to support the program.

Project Loans. Lending for specific productive investment purposes is said to be project lending and is generally self-liquidating. Here again, it is difficult to allocate amounts with available data. In Table 5, which allocates borrowing by purpose, it is probably safe to assume that most loans for hydrocarbons, natural resources, and industry (26.2 percent of the 1977–81 total) were for specific projects, but these totals include both public and private borrowers. In Table 3, under types of borrowers, public nonfinancial corporations are most probably involved in project borrowing and accounted for 23 percent of all Euromarket borrowing between 1978 and 1981. Examples are economic infrastructure loans and loans to autonomous state-owned entities.

Economic Infrastructure Loans. These loans finance the construction, expansion, and modernization of airports, subways, railroads, port facilities, and such sophisticated innovations as microwave and other telecommunications projects and atomic energy facilities.

Loans to Autonomous State-Owned Entities. These loans might be to start up or expand the activities of government-owned, raw-material producers in petroleum, natural gas, metals, forestry, or fishing. Also important are loans to state industrial corporations in basic or key sectors—steel, petrochemicals, cement, shipbuilding, aerospace, and transport equipment.

Government-Guaranteed Loans to Private firms. In the interests of general economic development, governments (especially among the LDCs) will often provide guarantees for the Euromarket borrowing of private corporations resident in the country. As indicated in Table 3, borrowing by private firms accounted for 32 percent of all Euromarket borrowing between 1978 and 1981. Inasmuch as these loans are to profit-making firms, it is safe to assume that they are designed to be self-liquidating.

It will readily be appreciated that each loan category implies a different set of factors insuring supervision and repayment. A loan for general budgetary purposes or for a broad development program will be difficult to assess or monitor in its specific implementation, and its evaluation will rest heavily on the creditworthiness of the central government itself. On the other hand, a loan to a private corporation for a specific project with a clearly identifiable stream of income can be evaluated and monitored much more directly. Practice may also vary from country to country; some governments have few autonomous public enterprises and tend to centralize financing, control, and administration, while others prefer a decentralized structure.

Recent Trends with Particular Reference to U.S. Banks

Statistics are available for the claims of U.S. banks and their overseas branches on various categories of borrowers (see Table 6). These claims include both short-term, medium-term, and long-term lending; the data also group public and private banks together into one category. Nevertheless, the differences between and within country groupings are interesting.

In the largest industrialized countries, public borrowers accounted for only 6 percent of all claims of U.S. banks on these countries at the end of 1981; the corresponding figure for nonoil LDCs was 31

Table 6
Claims of U.S. Banks and Their Overseas Branches of Various Categories of Borrowers
(as of December 1981 in billions of dollars)

Borrower	Amount	Percent Claims on Banks	Percent Claims on Other Public Borrowers	Percent Claims on Other Private Borrowers
All countries	$332.1	54	17	29
Group of 10 plus Switzerland	131.4	70	6	24
Nonoil LDCs*	92.8	34	31	35
Argentina	8.4	29	32	40
Brazil	16.8	42	30	28
Mexico	21.5	18	34	48
Peru	2.0	43	42	14
Philippines	5.6	27	39	34
South Korea	8.4	54	16	30
Total for six	63.0	32	31	37
OPEC†	23.0	27	35	38
Algeria	1.4	23	60	17
Indonesia	2.4	14	31	55
Nigeria	1.1	25	66	10
Venezuela	10.5	20	39	41
Total for four	15.6	20	42	38

Note: Totals may not add due to rounding.
* Share of these six in claims in all nonoil LDCs = 67 percent.
† Share of these four in claims in all OPEC = 66 percent.
Source: Federal Financial Institutions Examination Council, *Country Exposure Lending Survey*
(Washington, D.C., various issues).

percent and for OPEC countries 35 percent. Variations among LDCs
are also wide, reflecting differing national development policies and
philosophies. Over half of all claims on South Korea were in the financial sector; claims on other public borrowers amounted to 60 percent
for Algeria, 66 percent for Nigeria, and 42 percent for Peru. In some
LDCs the nonfinancial private sector is not a major short-, medium-,
or long-term borrower (10 percent of the total for Nigeria, 14 percent
for Peru); in others it is predominant (48 percent in Mexico, 55 percent
in Indonesia, 40 percent in Argentina). Again, these differences are
due to wide variations in domestic structure and philosophy.

Changes in the composition of LDC borrowing across time are also
significant, especially when short-term lending is included. Changes
in domestic business conditions or in Euromarket conditions can bring
new borrowers into the market or increase current market actors'
propensities to borrow.

It is useful to look more closely at relevant figures for the largest
U.S. international banks. For the five most active of these—Citibank,
Chase Manhattan, Bank of America, Manufacturers Hanover Trust
Company, and Morgan Guaranty—international operations are of great
importance. For these five banks, loans to foreign governments and

official institutions accounted in mid-1980 for 10.6 percent of all overseas loans, and 5.8 percent of these banks' total foreign and domestic
loan portfolio. The percentage of loans to sovereign borrowers in the
total loan portfolio varied from a high of 8.2 percent to a low of 3.6
percent.

Deposits of foreign governments and other official institutions were
even more significant, accounting for 14.6 percent of the overseas
deposits of the five banks listed above and 8.3 percent of total deposits.
Again, the variation was wide—from a low of 6.9 percent of total deposits to a high of 10.3 percent.[3]

RISKS IN LENDING TO GOVERNMENTS

Almost all governments honor almost all of their foreign debts almost
all of the time. There are strong incentives to service external public
debt or, perhaps more accurately, strong disincentives not to suspend
debt service. The fundamental reward for a good debt service record
is continued, and perhaps less expensive, access to international capital
markets; the fundamental punishment for default is restricted access
to sources of capital. Governments may be able to defer long-term
borrowing, albeit at a cost to economic growth and stability, but short-
term international credit is working capital without which few economies can function.

To obtain new credit, old credit has to be treated reasonably well.
Moreover, if old credit to the public sector is neglected, new credit
may not be made available to the private sector either, or it may
only be made available at a greatly reduced volume. In times of difficulty, governments will usually accord a higher priority to foreign
lenders than to domestic lenders in order to preserve their international credit standing.

However, events beginning with the second oil shock in 1980 have
made a great change in the general ability of developing countries
to service their external debt. The world-wide recession, falling commodity and other export prices, continued high oil prices, and high
Euromarket interest rates have combined to reduce developing country earnings and increase their external payments. At the same time,
many of the Euromarket lenders have restricted their lending to developing countries, which increases their liquidity problems. The result
has been rescheduling of loans to a number of countries.

Therefore, the possibility of debt-servicing problems for a particular
borrowing country must be assessed carefully. The recent international
record demonstrates that individual cases require individual analysis.

---

[3] Salomon Brothers, *U.S. Multinational Banking Semiannual Statistics*, October 24,
1980.

One factor leading countries into difficulties in 1982 was that the ready accessibility of Euromarket funds permitted them to repay one lender by borrowing from another. When credit markets tightened suddenly this option disappeared. This underscores the importance of considering the borrowing histories of the various countries, long-term repayment records, and credit analysis fundamentals; all are key elements of any lending criteria.

Country Risk

Sovereign and Quasi-Sovereign Risks. One factor of importance in evaluating the risk involved in a proposed loan is the borrower's relationship to the central government. Because the central government and its agencies, including the central monetary institutions, are generally synonymous with the nation, loans to these bodies can generally be assumed to have the full backing of the state. In other words, there is no ambiguity about responsibility for the debts of central government institutions: it lies with the central government. The standing of other government-controlled or government-owned entities may be less clear-cut. In some cases, the borrowing may be of such crucial importance to the government as, for example, a state petroleum monopoly in a country dependent on oil exports, that it may be assumed to have full central government support in any eventuality. In other instances, as, for example, in the case of a company in which the state simply owns a minority equity position and exercises little or no control, support may be less complete. The status of "quasi-sovereign" borrowers may be determined by tradition, by domestic law, or by more transient economic and political considerations. In any event, it is crucial that the precise character of central government guarantees be clear to both the borrower and the lender.

Risk Categories. Risks, of course, differ by country. To clarify the type of risks, five categories of borrowing countries are described. These classifications indicate the possible range of debt-servicing difficulties.[4]

Category A is the area of country risk in which we anticipate no financial problems at all. Finance is always available to meet the country's requirements although the price may change. The negotiable securities of these countries are always readily tradeable in the secondary market, and they will always find the new issue market receptive to them. In the event of a major liquidity squeeze these nations would find access to financial and capital markets the least restricted. Most OECD countries would fall within this A group, at least from the stand-

---

[4] What follows draws heavily on Richard O'Brien, "Country Risk and Bank Lending Risk," in *Assessing Country Risk,* ed. Richard Ensor (London: *Euromoney Publications,* 1981), pp. 87–91.

point of a Western bank. Such countries will typically rely on the bond markets for the bulk of their long-term credit requirements, although syndicated credits will also be used. This group would not include all the OECD countries, for some do have large borrowing requirements, and on occasions, the market does get nervous about certain OECD economies. But for the major countries, that nervousness is usually short lived and tends to be related to periods of political speculation over forthcoming elections or particularly bad economic periods.

Category B would include those countries where no great problems are expected. From time to time, however, questions might arise over the country's creditworthiness, and the country's negotiable paper might become less attractive in the short term; such paper might go to unusual discounts. The price of available credit might rise over and above normal market rates, and market conditions might become sticky for these borrowers. There is still no question of default or rescheduling of debt. Into this group would fall some of the less stable or less successful OECD countries for which most lenders have no real qualms about their debt-servicing capabilities over the longer term. Most OECD countries and Group of 10 countries not in the A group should fall into this category.

In the C category would be countries for which there is a reasonable probability of some debt-servicing problems. Such debt-servicing problems are expected to be overcome in a relatively smooth fashion without undue financial stress. Debt problems would be negotiated and resolved by discussions with creditors or with groups of creditors. Meanwhile the country's trade paper would still be negotiated without a punitive premium being imposed. Loans in this category would probably be classified as substandard during any period of debt-servicing problems. Nevertheless, the C category would denote that it is expected that any bad debt provision should not have to be drawn upon. Assets may be nonearning during a crisis, but write-offs are not expected. The countries which would probably fall within this group would be perhaps one or two OECD countries and many of the large developing countries and newly industrialized countries.

The fourth D group presents a much greater probability of debt-servicing problems than countries in the C group. Periodic crises may also set off chain reactions in the financial market. The country's trade paper might become difficult to negotiate at any price during the crisis, for the outcome of debt-rescheduling talks would be highly uncertain. Again, these countries should be sufficiently strong to surmount the debt-servicing problem eventually, but this will require concerted efforts by lenders and borrowers alike. Thus, countries that have experienced rather difficult reschedulings but have eventually solved those problems would be likely candidates for this category.

Finally, high-risk E category includes countries where the possibility of outright default exists, where reschedulings might lead to even lower rates of return on assets remaining in that country, where debt renegotiation becomes prolonged and drawn out, and where the bank is likely to be locked into significant opportunity losses. "Opportunity loss" in this context means that the bank would prefer to be relending those assets to another country for a similar spread, but because of the existing exposure has to continue lending those assets to the troubled country even though the risk reward is no longer as attractive as elsewhere. Within this E group might be the countries whose long-term economic and financial viability is in question. Even though some loans may continue to be organized, they would in most cases be pure rescue loans with very little hope of early repayment. In effect such loans are a patching-up operation. Shorter-term financing may continue and, of course, the countries will need trade finance, but it is most likely that this will require government export credit guarantees or coverage for any reasonable amount to be transacted.

The experienced international lending officer will have developed this type of mental grading of countries according to the attractiveness of the general credit risk they present. An appropriately analytical officer will leave to competitors the risks deemed unduly great. If the officer is too cautious in accepting a reasonable businessman's risk, this will adversely affect the institution's growth, if not its profitability.

Most international bankers in positions of responsibility have grown up with international banking and usually make correct decisions about credit risks to undertake, interest rates to be charged, and investments in affiliates and subsidiaries to be undertaken. However, competition has often played a larger role in these decisions than it should. As modern international banking evolves and lending to governments and official entities worldwide becomes more important, the assessment and comparison of countries will become more sophisticated.

Insurance Programs and Ratings. The concept of ratings, regarded as essential to the operation of domestic money markets, is now being increasingly applied in the private international field to cope with the grades of risk. In addition to bank's own internal ratings, certain export and investment-risk insurance institutions, such as the Export-Import Bank (Eximbank) and the Foreign Credit Insurance Association (FCIA), have utilized country rating systems. These systems are regularly reviewed and revised to accord with current evaluations in order to establish premium charges under insurance programs. Others, such as the Overseas Private Investment Corporation (OPIC), feel that conditions change too much over the life of a guarantee or insurance policy to permit rating, although they may give weight to undue concentration of insurance risks.

Inadequacy of Available Data. A factor which has delayed the use of ratings internationally has been the difficulty of obtaining trustworthy financial information about borrowing institutions expressed in relatively standard accounting terms which can be analyzed on an intercountry basis. Another complicating factor has been the desire for secrecy on the part of institutions and governments in many parts of the world.

It is not likely that governments and other categories of foreign borrowers will soon be rated in public view. Where rating procedures are now utilized, they are for internal use or on a need-to-know basis. The leadership in this area has been taken by the large multinational banks which can justify the effort for their own needs.

For the analyst, the positioning of the potential borrower in an informal or formal rating schedule is a useful scorecard. However, most important to the final credit judgment is detailed knowledge of, and preferably close acquaintance with, the individuals associated with the borrowing—their educational and professional backgrounds, economic and political orientations, and the extent of their individual political authority and influence. In lending to governments and official entities, it is especially important that bankers maintain close and harmonious relationships with ministries of finance; central banks; government development and commercial banks; other ministries of the national, provincial, or state governments; and the official steel, petroleum, airline, and other entities that are actual or potential borrowers. The well-informed analyst can often anticipate accurately the direction of change in the creditworthiness of a country or official entity as a consequence of the appointment of a new finance minister or a new head of a state oil monopoly. As in domestic lending, creditworthiness should be reassessed when there is a change in the management team.

OECD and LDC Borrowers. Although lending to governments and official agencies in the advanced industrial countries is generally less risky than lending to LDCs, risk is not restricted to the LDCs. Uncertainty may exist about the future direction of any government. There may be instability of economic management and policy direction—how will economic programs be recast to meet short-term political pressures or new party platform objectives? Net international trade flows may be unstable; it is always difficult to anticipate commodity and raw material prices and volumes and how domestic economic policies will affect the external sector. The overall balance of payments and exchange reserve position can fluctuate widely in relatively short periods of time. Changes in capital movements may occur, and speculation may affect leads and lags in payments and receipts. There are always uncertainties about inflation, nationalization, labor relations, protectionism, and overvalued exchange rates.

The tendency to lump all developing countries together in the same category must be resisted. The most industrialized LDCs—now often called the middle-income or newly industrializing countries—generally have a far more diversified and sophisticated economic structure than the poorer LDCs. Economic and political management is usually more sophisticated and successful in these nations.

The industrialized and more advanced developing countries generally owe their greater stability to a more highly developed government structure with a trained staff of career technicians and a momentum of its own. If the direction in which the structure is moving is "appropriate," this can favorably influence credit risk; if not, there is likely to be greater difficulty in altering the structure, and the necessary remedial measures are more likely to be drastic.

In less-developed countries where those who participate in the formulation of policy are often also those who implement and monitor it, it is often relatively less difficult to change course. For these institutional reasons, internal political difficulties often tend to have less impact on the foreign sector of the economy of an advanced industrial country than in LDCs, unless of course an economic crisis is the cause of the political difficulties.

Industrialized and more advanced developing countries have two characteristics which provide maneuvering room for managing their external accounts. First, sums entering the balance-of-payments accounts are large, and there is a greater diversity in the trade and invisible accounts, providing more assurance of ability to repay the extension of credit. Second, among countries in which exports and imports represent an above-average percentage of gross national product, there is likely to be a stronger commitment to responsible management of the external sector. However, because of the economic size of some of the newly industrialized countries, their economic problems can be much larger and can cause not only massive loan reschedulings, but can also threaten the foundations of the international economic system.

Differentiating between Government Borrowers

Differences among official borrowers must be recognized when performing analysis, pricing the credit, structuring the loan, seeking protection, and preparing documentation. Broadly speaking, state borrowers which frequently resort to foreign credit markets may be classified as follows:

Central, provincial, state, and municipal governments.

Ministries of the central government and the central bank.

Statutory authorities, boards, and agencies of the central, provincial, state, and municipal governments.

Statutory or chartered joint-stock corporations with full or majority government-equity ownership.

Statutory or chartered joint-stock corporations with minority government-equity participation, whether the government exercises control or not.

Less medium- and long-term Euromarket borrowing is done by government authorities themselves than by decentralized agencies. As Table 4 indicates, central authorities accounted for 41 percent ($82.7 billion) of all such borrowing between 1977 and mid-1981 while other government agencies and corporations accounted for 59 percent ($116.5 billion). These figures include all borrowing countries; generally LDC borrowing tends to involve decentralized government agencies more often than does borrowing by industrialized countries.

As already mentioned, a key question in lending to government entities is the degree to which the central government assumes responsibility under law or policy for repayment of borrowings, and the specific allocation of such responsibility within the central government. This bears directly on protection of the lender and the avoidance of risk. Central government responsibility is neither vague nor intangible; usually it is carefully defined by statute, charter, or regulation. Any ambiguity presents a problem to the prospective lender.

In 1979 the Comptroller of the Currency issued an interpretive ruling of U.S. Law 12 U.S.C. 84 concerning limits on credits made by U.S. national banks to foreign governments, their agencies, and instrumentalities. Three basic conditions must be satisfied in order not to combine, for U.S. legal lending limit purposes, a credit to a foreign borrower in which its national government has any direct or indirect ownership interest. The conditions are:

1. Autonomy—the entity must have some autonomy in order to be considered apart from the central government.
2. Purpose—the loan must be obtained for a purpose consistent with the borrower's general business.
3. Means—the borrower must have sufficient resources or revenues of its own to service its debt obligations. A presumption of dependence arises unless the government's support is less than the borrower's annual revenues from other sources.

Subsequent revisions in Regulation K imply that the maximum liability of any one borrower to the bank and any subsidiary of the bank, including subsidiaries of bank subsidiaries located offshore, is limited to the legal lending limit of the parent bank. Special attention should be given to the Comptroller of the Currency's requirements to secure and retain all required documentation, and to employ the assistance of corporate counsel.

Perhaps the principal reason for needing to know the central government's responsibilities is that there are often gaps in the lender's ability to evaluate the borrower's repayment capability. Some of these may be summarized as follows:

Inadequacy of Financial Statements. Financial statements may be misleading or inadequate for the determination of risk, may be outdated, unduly brief, unaudited, or simply unavailable. Accounting standards and valuation procedures may differ from generally accepted American practice. Political considerations may have colored preparation of the statements. Profit, total assets, net worth, and debt ratios may be unfavorable by standards customary for private borrowers. Cash flow projections may be unavailable or meaningless, and analysis of past flows may be inconclusive.

Government Guarantees. In many cases, the "full faith and credit" of the central government may not be pledged to the borrower. At one end of the spectrum the borrower may enjoy no support from the central government for its external credit operations, except perhaps in the event of liquidation. At the other end, the borrower, may be able to offer the support of the total resources of the government. In between, the lender must determine if a guarantee by another government entity, such as the ministry of finance, central bank, a government commercial or investment bank, or a provincial or state government is available and acceptable.

Borrowing Authority. The authority of the entity to borrow for the purpose intended and under the terms proposed, as well as the authority of the particular officials to commit the entity, must be determined and documented to the satisfaction of the lender. The entity may not normally be eligible to borrow abroad. There may be restrictions on terms or interest rates the borrower can pay for different types of credit. The purpose of the loan may not be adequately founded or authorized in statute, regulation, by-law, or resolution. An inappropriate signature on the loan documentation may render the agreement subject to contest.

Capital Sources. Often the borrowing entity's sources of capital and current operating funds are limited, resulting in a leverage or financial stringency that would normally be unacceptable to lenders. The entity may have a one-time capital allocation from the government, or it may be subject to annual budget allocations of current and capital funds. It may or may not enjoy favored access to the central bank or other government banks to finance special programs or general entity requirements. The entity's prices may be held to unrealistically low levels by the government.

Special Tax or Other Considerations. The would-be borrower may have important tax and import customs that have a favorable impact on its operations. It may be exempt from taxes on interest remitted abroad. There may be preferred access to foreign exchange, or the entity may be under instructions to insist on longer borrowing terms or a rollover of foreign credits outstanding.

Jurisdiction and Choice of Law.   Unless clearly specified in loan documentation, the jurisdiction and the law which is to apply and prevail may be uncertain. Ordinarily the applicable jurisdiction and law is that of the lender's head office, one of its foreign branches or affiliates, or the borrower. This is relevant in determining the priority and rights of various classes of creditors, the worth of liens and collateral, and the degree of difficulty probable in realizing assets if a reorganization or liquidation is undertaken. It may be much easier for a foreign creditor to provoke a bankruptcy proceeding than to benefit from it.

Sovereign Authority.   Finally, responsibility for performance may be avoided or frustrated by the assertion of "sovereign immunity." This may preclude suit against the government for its sovereign acts or their consequences, or it may permit suit against the central government but not attachment of its property. In view of the unique nature of risk in lending to foreign governments and official entities, it is essential that the lender be aware of the borrower's legal status in this regard. This is one of the most complex areas of legal controversy in international trade and finance, touching as it does the core of sovereign power. A government's willingness to waive sovereign immunity is circumscribed by international law, as well as its own constitutional framework, including the extent to which substantive or procedural actions of a government may limit its sovereign immunity if it has not specifically renounced such immunity. Under the law of a given country certain government entities may not have the ability to appeal to the principle of sovereign immunity.

Direct Political Considerations

Lending to sovereign governments quite obviously involves some consideration of political trends in the borrowing country. Apparent or current political stability is no guarantee for the future as recent political upheavals in Nicaragua and Iran have demonstrated.

A special case is presented by lending to socialist countries. Although the Iron Curtain countries, and now China as well, are increasingly integrated into international trade and finance, the level of their economic interaction with the West is largely dependent on the state of East-West political relations. The upheavals in Poland are a good example of the complexity of the political dimension of sovereign lending.

CREDIT AVAILABILITY

The terms and availability of international credit to a sovereign borrower are dependent on two factors: the market's assessment of the reliability of the individual borrower, and the general conditions of the market. Changes in market conditions will to some degree affect terms offered to all borrowers; the degree to which a given borrower is affected depends on its current circumstances. Conversely, if a few major borrowers or groups of borrowers face individual problems, this may affect general market conditions. It is useful to review factors relevant to both specific and general conditions.

Creditworthiness Indicators

Assessment of the creditworthiness of a specific government will depend on a static analysis of the nations' current position and capabilities, and on a dynamic analysis of the nation's position over time. General considerations on the professionalism, experience, and reliability of the economic management team, of the country's political stability, and of the maturity and diversity of the domestic economic system will all enter into an evaluation of credit risk. More specifically, the country's existing stock of external public debt should be examined in relationship to exports and GNP.

Standard indicators include external debt as a percentage of GNP and debt service as a percentage of exports of goods and services. During the 1970s the LDC debt burden approximately doubled. For 87 nonoil LDCs the debt service GNP ratio rose from 1.6 percent in 1974 to 3.0 percent in 1979; debt service/exports went from 7.9 percent to 13.7 percent.[5] These aggregate figures mask country-specific problems. Twelve LDCs were involved in debt renegotiations between 1975 and 1980,[5a] and the figures for these 12 are far less impressive than for other, less troubled, LDCs.[6] For example, between 1974 and 1979 the debt service/exports ratio of these 12 LDCs went from 12.2 percent to 29.1 percent (most analysts consider that a ratio of over 20 percent indicates some danger); the other LDCs' ratio went from 7.5 percent to 12.6 percent.[7]

Apart from specifically debt-oriented indicators, analysis of past, present, and prospective trends in domestic economic activity and the foreign sector are important. Signs of export diversification, a steady increase in total exports, relative stability in the trade balance are all positive indicators.

---

[5] International Monetary Fund Occasional Paper 3, *External Indebtedness of Developing Countries* (Washington, D.C.: International Monetary Fund, 1981), p. 14.

[5a] Since 1980 there have been further debt renegotiations which further demonstrate these principles.

[6] The 12 countries are Chile, Gabon, Jamaica, Liberia, Nicaragua, Pakistan, Peru, Sierra Leone, Sudan, Togo, Turkey, and Zaire.

[7] International Monetary Fund Occasional Paper 3, *External Indebtedness of Developing Countries,* p. 19.

Market Conditions

General market conditions have a major impact on the availability of funds to individual borrowers. Generally tight market conditions will be a disadvantage to all borrowers; a few debt-servicing problems may reduce the market's willingness to take on additional risk until the problems are resolved. From time to time domestic authorities in one of the major capital exporting nations will impose restrictions on the international operations of its lenders; this may lead to a generalized contraction on the lenders' side and a subsequent tightening of terms for less-than-prime borrowers.

The interaction of both general-market and country-specific factors is evident from Table 7, which indicates the maturity distribution of claims of U.S. banks and their foreign branches on borrowing countries. Maturities of all U.S. bank claims on overseas borrowers shortened between 1978 and 1981. This shortening was far more pronounced with the LDCs than with the major industrial countries.[8] Clearly, market conditions in general were tightening. Within this, however, there were significant differences among and between groups of countries. Among non-OPEC LDCs, Mexico, and Peru saw a much more drastic shortening of their debt maturities than did South Korea or the Philippines.

The differential rates of change in maturity distribution are representative either of the market's different assessments of the various countries or of differences in the borrowers' preferences, or both. Indeed, differences in the maturity preferences (or market assessment) of the different borrowing LDCs is evident from Table 7. At one extreme South Korea's liabilities to U.S. banks are 74 percent short term; at the other extreme, Algeria's short-term liabilities are 39 percent of its total.

THE DEFAULT RECORD

In the post-World War II period, multilateral lending institutions have encouraged greater international flows of funds and better borrowing practices and also have taken strong positions that settling defaulted foreign debt is a condition of credit eligibility.

World economic conditions have generally been favorable during most of the 1970s with growing foreign markets providing the exchange earnings necessary to support expanded debt. However, the early 1980s revised this trend. As yet, no general world depression has caused beggar-thy-neighbor trade or exchange policies to threaten the world credit structure. When individual countries have fallen into difficulties, usually due to economic mismanagement, international or

---

[8] *AMEX Bank Review,* vol. 9. no. 4, April 26, 1982, p. 1. American Express, New York, N.Y.

Table 7
Maturity Distribution of Claims of U.S. Banks and Their Foreign Branches, 1979–1980 (percent of total)

	December 1981			December 1980			December 1979		
	Short-Term	Medium-Term	Long-Term	Short-Term	Medium-Term	Long-Term	Short-Term	Medium-Term	Long-Term
All countries	76	18	8	74	19	8	71	22	8
Group of 10 plus Switzerland	84	11	5	84	12	5	83	13	5
Nonoil LDCs*	60	26	14	62	27	11	56	34	11
Argentina	62	31	8	69	25	7	62	30	8
Brazil	46	33	21	47	37	17	39	46	15
Mexico	59	26	15	57	30	13	45	40	15
Peru	73	22	5	70	28	2	58	38	4
Philippines	69	16	15	69	16	15	69	16	15
S. Korea	74	19	8	80	15	5	77	17	6
Total for six	59	26	15	60	28	12	52	35	12
OPEC†	71	23	6	66	27	7	59	34	7
Algeria	39	52	9	31	55	14	22	68	10
Indonesia	59	29	12	57	32	12	56	31	14
Nigeria	44	46	9	39	49	12	22	58	19
Venezuela	74	20	6	71	23	6	67	29	5
Total these four	66	26	7	63	29	8	56	36	8

Note: Totals may not add due to rounding.
* Share of these six in all nonoil LDCs = 67 percent.
† Share of these four in all OPEC = 66 percent.
Source: Federal Financial Institutions Examination Council, *Country Exposure Lending Survey* (Washington, D.C., various issues).

bilateral assistance has been predicated upon corrective measures taken by the beneficiary.

Foreign official borrowers wish to repay external debt and usually make every effort to do so. Not only is the ethical principle of satisfying commitments at issue but national prestige aspects are ever present. At times debtor countries have applied extraordinary discriminatory measures against their own public in order to repay foreign lenders.

Regimes do appear and disappear, however, thereby creating political default and renegotiation problems, even if there is a will to repay by successor political entities. During the 1970s, the default record of sovereign borrowers was, on the whole, good. In the 1980s the problem began to increase with severe world recession bringing depressed commodity prices and slow export growth for most LDCs.

Historical Experience

Few international bankers today have first-hand memories of the widespread defaults of the 1930s, although most are aware of the defaults on czarist Russian bonds, League of Nations-sponsored issues in the Balkans, and the World War I debts to the United States.

After that worldwide rash of bond defaults, negotiations lending to settlement offers and adjustments on many of the less political bond issues were only partly completed before World War II began. According to the 1945 report of the Foreign Bondholders Protective Council, the dollar bonds issued or guaranteed by foreign governments and their political subdivisions outstanding at the end of 1945 amounted to $4,457 million and represented about 65 percent of their original issued amounts. Of the outstanding bonds, $2,041 million or 45.8 percent were in default.

The greatest percentage of defaults outstanding was on national bond issues, accounting for more than 68 percent of the issues in default. On December 31, 1945, 86.8 percent of the European dollar bonds outstanding, 60.1 percent of the Latin American bonds, 56.3 percent of the Far Eastern bonds, and 0.3 percent of the Canadian bonds were in default.

Guatemala was the only country with no dollar issues in default among the 16 borrowing countries in Latin America. Of the 20 borrowing countries in Europe, only Finland, France, and Ireland continued full-dollar service. In the Far East and Africa, which represented 11.7 percent of the dollar bonds outstanding, only Australia and Liberia were paying full service.

Frequently, after years of negotiation, it has been possible to arrive at settlements acceptable to creditors because, in the meantime, debtor governments had taken actions to reduce the magnitude of the bonded debt outstanding. In other instances, the problem has been effectively eliminated by such actions as repurchase by the borrower of its issues in the market at severely distressed prices, repayment of national bondholders in local currency, or unilateral issues of refunding instruments in the local currency at unfavorable exchange-rate equivalents, low interest rates, or at long term.

The reports of bondholder protective councils are required reading for every international lending officer as a constant reminder of the need for careful risk assessment and avoidance of overexuberant sales efforts.

Recent Experience

In the 1970s international experiences with debt-service problems, reschedulings, and refinancings have expanded rapidly. A number of countries—primarily developing nations—have faced debt-related difficulties. In most cases debt renegotiation has taken the form of agreements with international lending institutions, such as economic stabilization packages.[9]

An analysis of the recent experience reveals that five factors are typical causes of debt-servicing problems: commodity price difficulties, inappropriate borrowing strategies, state entities' financial problems, political unrest, and oil price increases. These problems have affected virtually all types of sovereign borrowers. The mention of a specific country below should not be interpreted as a comment on its creditworthiness, because in many cases the debt problem has been resolved, and not all countries encountering such problems have to reschedule their debts as a result.

Commodity-Price Problems.   Problems associated with commodity prices are of two kinds: (*a*) commodity prices moving in the opposite direction from spending plans and (*b*) the sheer vulnerability of single commodity producers. Many LDCs faced a general commodity problem in 1974–75. At a time when oil prices and import costs were rising, other commodity prices were falling sharply. The 1972–73 period had been one of a general commodity price boom; a number of countries' budgets were based on a projection of continually higher prices. Some countries embarked upon overly ambitious spending plans. Examples would include the phosphate producers (for example, Morocco, Togo, and Senegal) after the collapse of phosphate prices (in 1975–76). Copper producers (e.g., Zaire, Chile, Peru) suffered to a varying degree from the sharp decline of the copper price. Zaire in particular ran into debt-servicing problems as the country is 67 percent dependent upon copper for foreign exchange revenues and a number of other measures were also causing economic problems.

---

[9] For a summary, see International Monetary Fund Occasional Paper 3, *External Indebtedness of Developing Countries,* pp. 21–40 and O'Brien, "Country Risk."

The second group of commodity problems is associated with a country's dependence upon one or two commodities, such as Jamaica's current problems associated with the sluggishness of sugar exports.

It should be noted that wide diversification of commodity earnings does not preclude a debt problem. Peru, for example, unlike most developing countries, is not dependent upon a single commodity for its revenues. With silver, copper, fish, and the prospect of oil exports, Peru appeared in 1972–74 to have a diverse export base and thus protection against commodity price falls affecting other LDCs. However the total disappearance of anchovies, the collapse of other commodity prices, and the disappointing results from oil exploration all combined to damage the balance of payments.

Inappropriate Borrowing Strategies.   In this category Turkey stands out as the principal case study. The technique of the short-term convertible Turkish lira deposit has, in retrospect, proved to be both expensive and troublesome for lenders and borrowers alike. There was a high effective rate of return for short-term exposure for the bank, which has since translated into a longer-term position. Such problems are undoubtedly the responsibility of both lenders (who in many cases should foresee the inevitable problems) and borrowers who accept such techniques.

Often a debt problem arises when major state borrowers run into debt-servicing problems with the result that the government itself has to intervene to solve the problem. The prime example of this was Pertamina in Indonesia, where the state oil company's budget became unmanageable, partly due to heavy borrowing and partly due to activities outside its oil sector.

Political Unrest.   It is important to distinguish between political unwillingness to repay debts and a political crisis leading to an inability to meet foreign obligations. Iran was probably the first case since Cuba where the breakdown of political relationships led to financial problems. The political crises in Argentina and Chile in the mid-1970s, Nicaragua in 1980, and Poland in 1981, have impaired debt-servicing capacities due to the economic impact of the respective political crises.

Oil Price Rises.   Oil price rises have affected a wide range of countries. Where countries have little domestic oil and are growing rapidly, the importance of this factor is increased. Ironically, oil price rises have also been responsible for helping to *solve* financial problems (e.g., Gabon, Indonesia, and Peru) as well as directly *causing* them.

The above factors describe some of the specific cases of debt-servicing problems. In practice, debt problems arise from a combination of factors and have varied widely in their severity from smooth refinancing to a drawn-out renegotiation taking considerable management time. Ultimately good country-risk analysis should provide the lender with the ability to anticipate many country-risk problems. Good bank management represents the ability to react effectively to such cross-border problems.

Sovereign Immunity

The law is often dynamic, affected by political, economic, and social factors, the process of negotiation among economic or political power groups, review and reinterpretation by courts, and occurrences of pure chance. Existing law, therefore, does not provide protection in all cases against arbitrary or seemingly arbitrary acts of sovereign states.

The national and international laws pertaining to the characteristics, privileges, responsibilities, and waivers of sovereignty are the domain of the legal and diplomatic professions. Lenders should employ competent counsel in both lending and borrowing jurisdictions.

Marshall's Definition.   While establishing the role of judicial authority in interpreting the Constitution of the United States and setting the course for a strong Supreme Court, Chief Justice John Marshall set forth a description of sovereignty and of the rights and immunities of foreign states that was a landmark in U.S. constitutional law: his 1812 decision in *Schooner Exchange* v. *McFaddon*. It still stands as a good statement of the principle involved.

> The jurisdiction of the nation within its own territory is necessarily exclusive and absolute. It is susceptible of no limitation not imposed by itself. Any restriction upon it, deriving validity from an external source, would imply a diminution of its sovereignty to the extent of the restriction and an investment of that sovereignty to the same extent in that power which could impose such restriction.

> All exceptions, therefore, to the full and complete power of a nation within its own territories, must be traced up to the consent of the nation itself. They can flow from no other legitimate source.

> This consent may be either expressed or implied. In the latter case it is less determinate, exposed more to the uncertainties of construction; but, if understood, not less obligatory.

> The world being composed of distinct sovereignties, possessing equal rights and equal independence, whose mutual benefit is promoted by intercourse with each other, and by an interchange of those good offices which humanity dictates and its want require, all sovereigns have consented to a relaxation, in practice, in cases under certain peculiar circumstances, of that absolute and complete jurisdiction within their respective territories which sovereignty confers.

> This consent may, in some instances, be tested by common usage and by common opinion, growing out of that usage.

> A nation would justly be considered as violating its faith, although that faith might not be expressly plighted, which should suddenly and without previous notice, exercise its territorial powers in a manner not consonant to the usages and received obligations of the civilized world.

This full and absolute territorial jurisdiction being alike the attribute of every sovereign, and being incapable of conferring extraterritorial power would not seem to contemplate foreign sovereigns nor their sovereign rights as its objects. One sovereign being in no respect amenable to another; and being bound by obligations of the highest character not to degrade the dignity of his nation by placing himself or its sovereign rights within the jurisdiction of another, can be supposed to enter a foreign territory only under an express license or in the confidence that the immunities belonging to his independent sovereign station, though not expressly stipulated, are reserved by implication and will be extended to him.[10]

Self-imposed Limitations.   In lending to foreign governments and official entities, the guiding principle for bankers and businessmen is that all exceptions to the full and complete power of a nation within its territory must be the consent of the nation itself. It is the responsibility of the potential lender to clarify the degree to which the nation may have consented to limitations on its sovereign immunity. The consent may lie in the enabling legislation or charter of the borrowing entity, or in the general body of law of the country.

Rulings on State Commercial Activities.   International law allows very great latitude for interpretations of sovereign immunity which involve states of belligerency, revolution, or civil war. It also attaches great importance to the state of political or diplomatic relations between the countries involved, especially whether the foreign country is recognized diplomatically as sovereign.

Much more turbulent and uncertain has been the course of litigation with respect to government activities in international trade and commerce that are similar to those normally or frequently conducted by private interests. It is this area that has attracted increasing international and domestic legal attention in the past 50 years.

Court doctrine with respect to sovereign immunity in the area of state activity similar to international private activity, distinguished solely by the participation of the state, can be characterized as chipping away at the principle of sovereign immunity rather than completely undermining it. Courts have moved slowly and not always in one direction.

The potential lender should understand that it is the judiciary and not the lender that decides immunity. All categories of foreign official entities obviously present sovereign risk. Every banker will appreciate the role played by bilateral diplomatic negotiation and multilateral agreements, conventions, or treaties in establishing common denominators for patterns of permissible conduct in specific areas. The lending officer undoubtedly will conclude also that, in an ultimate legal contest, the relative strengths of the parties are decidedly unequal. As a practi-

---

[10] 7 Cranch 116, U.S. Supreme Court, 1812.

cal matter, therefore, "protection" is the most realistic course to pursue, prior to the closing of a credit agreement.

Waivers of Sovereign Immunity. All nations are jealous of their sovereignty, but those that have experienced what they regard as economic or political colonialism are often especially sensitive. This sensitivity and concern are reflected in the established policies or legal inabilities of some governments, for constitutional or other statutory reasons, to agree to waivers of their sovereign immunity. In most instances, however, waivers of sovereign immunity are now included in international loan documentation. Laws of the United States and Britain now specifically cover waivers of sovereign immunity by sovereign borrowers and clarify some of the previous ambiguities with respect to loan agreements.

Protection

When a credit request seems bankable, the banker must attempt to minimize the overall risk of loss or, more positively, improve prospects for repayment. He should consider the actions he is prepared to take to accommodate the borrower and those he wishes to have available to him. These include features which may encourage the debtor to make the most strenuous efforts to repay, as well as those which become operative in the event of default. The desired features must be incorporated in the loan documentation before it is signed.

Integrity, Ethical and Technical. Insofar as international bankers can protect themselves from the risks of arbitrary action by official borrowers, unnecessary conflicts over the rights and obligations of the contracting parties, and from irresponsibility towards repayment obligations, the best safeguards are basic ethical and technical principles. Loans should only be granted for bona fide, thoroughly defensible purposes; they should be negotiated with integrity and expertise, frankly and openly, and with responsible representatives of the borrower.

Bankers should only accept explicit loan agreements that are clearly understandable in concept and expression when translated into the borrower's language. The agreements must include documentation that is legal in both lending and borrowing countries.

Guarantees and Collateral. Loan documents for international credits usually have standard affirmative and negative covenants, plus guarantees from a suitable government bank or financial institution when appropriate. In today's market it is very difficult to obtain additional assurances such as collateral, although such additional assurances and/ or collateral may be obtained in the case of workout solutions with poor risks. The purpose is not so much reliance on the collateral or guarantee as the resultant increased government commitment to the transaction. Collateral or guarantees provide a more substantial base for negotiation should difficulties arise.

Selection of Borrower.   The borrower should be a continuing incorporated entity such as a central bank, government bank, or state-owned corporation that has the authority to incur foreign debt and possesses independent payment resources. If the lending is to the government or to the ministry of finance, legal authorization for the particular borrowing is desirable; even if by new statute. The authorizing legislation should contain commitments to request budgetary funding and have the necessary amortization appear specifically in annual budgets. In the event that a government's procedures do not permit such an approach, an official opinion of the government attorney should be obtained, and the loan documentation should include a commitment to seek the required funding.

A pledge of the government's full faith and credit is desirable (when it can be obtained) to serve as additional support for the loan. It is not available in all instances, and its absence must be considered an element of further risk. In circumstances in which one entity, such as the central bank, acts as agent for the government, extreme care should be exercised to delineate precisely both the agency responsibility and the government undertakings.

Problems of Successful Protection

Political Undesirability of Enforcement.   The existence of negotiated protection may not itself resolve problems. For example, a lender may find it too risky or difficult to invoke the provisions of a comprehensive and tightly worded loan agreement. In the end, then, the most suitable resolution will involve negotiation to seek the best possible workout for what proved to be a bad loan.

Weaknesses Inherent in Repayment Guarantees.   Repayment guarantees, excluding those covering exchange availability, can also raise questions. They are widely sought and received by lenders, so much so that their inclusion in loan agreements almost appears to be an article of the faith. Yet how much more protection does the lender receive with the guarantee of a government-owned commercial bank, the government development institution, the central bank, the ministry of finance? In practical terms, what will happen as a result of the existence of a guarantee?

If one asks a lending officer in the international division of a large bank why the bank requests a repayment guarantee, the following responses are usually given: "It is desirable because the bank has insufficient experience with the borrower. The guarantor is the largest bank in the country. It's like having two-name paper. The guarantor has a priority access to the country's foreign exchange reserves. If the guaran-

tor cannot honor its commitment, the government would not be able
to pay either, and the bank would be in a salvage operation. The
Eximbank requires the guarantee of this institution, and the bank
should request no less favorable treatment."

If the lending officer is then asked what the experience has been
with guarantees covering official entity borrowing, the usual reply is
that it has not been necessary to invoke a guarantee. If asked how
many times capital and reserves the contingent liabilities for guarantees
outstanding are of the guaranteeing government bank, the banker
may reply half-seriously that it is better not to know. A look behind
the balance sheet might show the lender that contingent liabilities
with respect to outstanding guarantees were 13 times the institution's
capital and reserves, a startling ratio.

Further research might reveal that the foreign government bank
has a legal limitation for outstanding guarantees equal to no more
than three times its capital and reserves, unless the guarantees are
matched by "counterguarantees." If the foreign bank's guarantee portfolio could be examined, it might be found that the majority of guarantees apply to special development, industrialization, or medium-size
industry promotional programs sponsored by the government and that,
consequently, the ministry of finance, in turn, has guaranteed repayment to the bank. When such counterguarantees are taken into account, the analyst may find that the outstanding guarantees of the
bank total just under three times its capital and reserves.

Evaluating a Guarantee.   How useful are guarantees? Are government entities preferred borrowers for which the repayment risk is
minimal? Has provision been made within the country to permit the
borrowing entity to repay, regardless of its balance-sheet position (without recourse to the guarantee) because national honor and prestige
are involved and any sacrifice is justified to preserve international reputation? Are the country's overall international financial and domestic
monetary positions adequate to permit repayment, despite any illiquidity of the borrower? Does the combination of available credit lines,
borrowing possibilities from aggressive new foreign credit sources, and
liquidity in the Eurocurrency capital market permit flexibility for a
government's management of its public sector?

It has been mentioned that, in some countries, a government institution is designated as an official guaranteeing body. This raises another
question regarding the value of the guarantee. Does the guarantee
of a highly leveraged government development institution with total
capital and reserve of perhaps only $25 million give additional protec-
tion to a lender who is providing substantial credit of tens of millions
of dollars to a state enterprise which possesses a tangible net worth
of, say, $200 million?

Merits of Guarantees.   The record in recent years suggests that, despite some misuse or even abuse by both lenders and borrowers, the guarantee concept does have merit. In some instances, the designated institution's guarantee is accorded on behalf of the government and therefore commits the full faith and credit of the government.

Even though guaranteeing government institutions may be overextended to a degree that would not be tolerated in a private bank by its foreign correspondents, and even though their financial statements may not demonstrate the strength to warrant significant reliance for large borrowings, it does not deny the desirability of a lender seeking the guarantee. Nor does it necessarily follow that, if there has been little or no resort to the guarantor, the guarantee is of minor value. The influence of the guarantor with the borrower is often greater than that of the creditor. No guarantor, if he can help it, is going to repay the borrower's obligation. As a domestic banker, when dealing with the borrower, the guarantor is often in a position to be more hard-hearted than the foreign banker and usually will have obtained his own protection for the contingent liability assumed. The general record, indicating that loans to state entities are repaid without recourse to the guarantor, does not imply that the guarantee is of minor value, but rather that it probably has a real value.

A guarantee does not ensure repayment, however. In a foreign debt-scheduling or refunding exercise, when the borrowing country has exhausted its repayment capability, the most the guaranteed lender can expect is a preferred position in a general misery, and it may not get even that. Short of debt reorganization at a time of major external payments problems, a guarantee by one government entity to support the borrowing by another serves to double the commitment to the national prestige of the borrower's country. By the extension of the guarantee, one government entity or ministry assumes a degree of interest in the affairs of another that it may not have for any other reason. At a minimum, it implies that in the event of differences between the two, an "official" position is determined by more than one ministry or senior financial officer of the government.

Along with the increasing sensitivity of many governments to matters concerning their sovereignty and the integrity of their judicial system, there is increasing sensitivity to the responsibilities involved in assuming foreign obligations. Aggressive ministers of finance, strongly supported by the international lending institutions, are asserting greater control over the international borrowing activities of their public sector. An obvious implication of organizing and institutionalizing such control is that a government authorization for a public entity to borrow abroad tends to become a broad governmental commitment to repay, not necessarily in terms of a specific undertaking to the lender, but in terms of overall public-sector financial management to keep commitments in line with resources so that the loan can be repaid by the borrower. To promote this process, it is desirable that lenders seek a guarantee where possible.

Multilateral Institutions.   In recent years there has been much discussion of the role of international lending institutions, specifically the World Bank and the IMF, in supervising or safeguarding current and future sovereign borrowing. As the financing requirements of the nonoil LDCs increase the World Bank should aid in both the provision of funds and the supervision of borrowing and repayment.

Suggested roles for international institutions include:

1. Co-financing, in which the institution would participate with private lenders in providing funds to borrowers.
2. IMF borrowing from private sources for lending to major sovereign borrowers.
3. Guarantees granted by international institutions for private bank loans.

There is some controversy over each of these proposals, although some movement to implement them has taken place. Nevertheless, the role of multilateral institutions in relations between sovereign borrowers and private lenders remains restricted. The private lender remains more or less on its own in the provision of funds and supervision of repayment—and this is a powerful argument for careful and complete analysis.

10
Project Financing

LOUIS G. SCHIRANO
Vice President
Bankers Trust Company

DEFINING PROJECT FINANCING

Courts, writers, and an entire generation of lawyers attempted to define pornography. None did so satisfactorily. None except one Supreme Court Justice who proclaimed, "I know it when I see it."

Project finance has much the problem of definition, but most observers do "know it when they see it." However, for the purposes of this chapter it is appropriate for the subject area to be more clearly delineated.

Perhaps the most useful situation for example purposes is an extractive mineral development project in a host (less-developed) country. The focus is on the capital formation for such a project with the understanding being that the suppliers of the debt capital are repaid only if the cash flow from sale of the output of the mine is sufficient. Project finance will therefore mean "cash flow lending" *not* lending supported by the underlying credit of the host country whose purpose happens to be for a specific project or the development of infrastructure to support various "projects."

THE NATURE OF A PROJECT

Regardless of size, location, or mineral resource, certain elements are common to every project. There will always be a host country (according to the definition). The project will have "sponsors" or investors whose interest may be varied both as to amount and as to their reasons for investment. There will be purchasers of the product, and there will almost certainly be suppliers of equipment and services to the project. It is not unusual for the roles to be combined. For example, the host country will often, through a government-owned corporation, act as a sponsor as well as a host. A sponsor may also be a supplier, and it is not uncommon to find a sponsor fulfilling the important role of a purchaser of the output.

When there exists a comingling of roles such as has been described, confusion, uncertainty, and often conflict—potential or real—can be the result. From a banker's standpoint the evaluation of the project's viability becomes extremely difficult, and financing can assume substantial risks. The project as a viable entity can be subordinated to the individual requirements and desires of the various parties, particularly if the profit potential for the participants is outside of the project itself. Should, for example, the off-take from the extractive project be sold to a purchaser who is also a project sponsor, it may well be in the interest of this purchaser/sponsor to structure a capital and pricing mechanism which limits profitability within the project and maximizes it at the level of the ultimate product. Similarly, a host country sponsor rarely has little interest in anything but maximized project profitability and market stability for a variety of reasons which we shall explore later. Understanding and reconciling these competing interests can often be most difficult, and, in several cases, impossible by the participants themselves. We shall explore one approach to solving this dilemma; however, at this time let us take a banker's view as to the evaluation and the financing of a project risk.

EVALUATION OF THE PROJECT

Prior to the structuring of the financing plan, an evaluation of the project must be made not so much from the standpoint of how the project should be financed, but from the standpoint of whether the project should be financed at all. It is almost axiomatic that, if the project makes sense to the various participants, many of the problems associated with the accompanying financing can be overcome. Conversely, with ill-conceived concepts, the result is often confusion, dissention, and, in some cases, abandonment on the part of one participant in the process.

Assuming that basic agreement between a host and the project sponsor can be achieved, the economic factors in the analysis of any project for the sponsor are entirely similar to any capital expenditure analysis. This is expressed in the context of a discounted cash flow analysis whose main components are:

1. The estimation of future cash flows.
2. Determination of the translation rate.
3. Comparison of material rate as related to the required rate of return.
4. Risk analysis (which shall be dealt with later).

The estimation of future cash flows and the effect of risks thereon calls for combining of practically every skill factor associated with a project, as well as the willingness (and nerve) to make substantial assumptions. Interpretation of geological data, estimating future markets, estimating future transportation availability, as well as assumptions as to the speed of infrastructure development and the ability of an indigenous labor force to operate sophisticated equipment, must be factored into the equation. Needless to say, assumptions and considerations as to the price that can be obtained for the product is critical. Essentially, the result is a sensitivity analysis coupled with risk analysis and the examination of different scenarios relating to various combination of factors.

This exercise can be undertaken either by the project participants or by an advisor—preferably by both—so that the greatest objectivity and expertise can be brought to bear. The findings will often be critical in the decision to proceed or not to proceed, but in some cases may be overruled by other considerations. For example, if the product (such as iron ore to a new steel mill) is of critical importance to the project sponsors, sensitivity-analysis results may be accepted which produce a risk profile that might otherwise be unacceptable given less-pressing needs.

The determination of the translation rate or the appropriate return on investment is largely an exercise that project sponsors and host governments must work out for themselves in light of their critical needs. Should the product be in short supply, a sponsor may accept a return far below a corporate norm merely to achieve a source of supply. By the same token, a host may accept a less than totally satisfactory arrangement to obtain critically needed foreign exchange or the development of infrastructure, personnel training, and so on, which otherwise would not occur. Suffice it to say the external factors influencing this decision are too many to collate. From the standpoint of a creditor these factors may be relatively unimportant as they may not impact upon a lender's risk, except in those cases where the returns are so imbalanced as to lead to a scenario of a simple "walk away" at some future date at the first sign of a negative change. Also unimportant is the question of appropriate returns which is largely an internal view and not germane to the financing of any particular project.

RISK ANALYSIS AND FINANCING

The actual financing of a project is in some ways anticlimactic to the project's evaluation. While the evaluation stage is very much an intellectual exercise, the financing is mechanical, and as for most mechanical things, the parts must be installed properly and in correct sequence in order for them to run. The intellectual freedom creating scenarios involved in evaluation is not present; instead the hard reality of risk analysis and financial structuring prevail. It is important to keep in mind that, if the financing requires a syndicate of banks, the financial structuring must be satisfactory to the entire syndicate. What an individual bank may accept is often far different from colleagues in the industry. Should one be in the position of an agent bank, the lending criteria must change to reflect the most conservative view.

Any lender in the official sector, such as an export agency or a private institution, will generally adopt an overview analysis which is concerned with six major risk areas. These are:

1. The *Supply* Risk.
2. The *Completion* Risk.
3. The *Technology* Risk.
4. The *Market* Risk.
5. The *Political* Risk.
6. The *Currency* Risk.

If the project members and a project advisor have done their jobs, a well-conceived financing plan has been drawn up that identifies each of these risks and presents them in a manner that will be accepted by potential lenders. It is at this stage that the role of an advisor can be critical. If he is unaware of market conditions or practices, or, if on behalf of his client, he attempts to cut "too fine a deal," the entire project may be jeopardized. (This advisory role will be discussed later.) The assumption or the sharing of the above risks and their documentation is a key ingredient in the plan. The cost to the project and the return to the lenders will be the indicators as to where the burden of those risks lie.

From the standpoint of the project itself, assuming that the requisite guarantees are available, it is almost a sine qua non of project finance to maximize the amount of export credit to take maximum advantage of favorable financing terms. It is indeed not unusual, given quality of equipment and services, to secure equipment from suppliers on the basis of competitive export-financing schemes available from the supplier's country. This situation has resulted in fierce competition from export credit agencies around the world. In times of high volatility in interest rates and the absolute level of such rates, the value of fixed-rate, long-term debt cannot be overemphasized. The myriad of approaches that can be used in developing sound export-financing schemes, using official agencies, is a major subject in itself. Sufficient for our purposes is the understanding that export finance is a vital element in any successful plan, and one which requires a highly sophisticated team of professionals to be put in place properly. Without such help, confusion, delay, and even disaster are the results.

Concurrent with the development of the export-financing plan will be the development and placement of institutional debt. The sources can be varied. While recognizing the availability of such debt financing in various local markets, the international capital market, and domestic private placements (invariably with a corporate or bank guarantee), for the purposes of this chapter nonofficial (institutional) debt will be considered as bank debt. This component accounts for the majority of project debt. Not surprising, therefore, is the awareness that the six major risk areas mentioned above are drawn up with the banker in mind and will be discussed from the standpoint of a commercial bank lender. Although there are other sources as mentioned above, access to markets other than commercial banks requires a credit that in the parlance of the trade is undoubted.

It is important to understand that, for any major project today, the commercial bank exposure, be it direct or indirect, will be high in terms of absolute amounts. With the numbers with which we must deal, it makes no sense for bankers to approach project sponsors as partners in a great venture.

The sponsors wish to have the bank's money at the lowest cost and no risk; the banks wish high return and low risk. The proceeding is an adversary one and should be approached as such. This is not to say that it need be contentious; on the contrary, the ability of the banker and the sponsor to bring to the negotiations a spirit of forthright competitiveness, rather than hostility, can spell the difference in the success or failure of the financing, as many of us have experienced.

It is difficult to remain objective at this point. Having watched and having been party to a number of such proceedings, one develops views which are difficult to sublimate. To begin, the equation is unbalanced. A strong, financially sound sponsor holds most of the cards if he wishes to play them in the assigning of risk elements. It is more and more common to see the risk placed almost entirely on the shoulders of commercial lenders *in every category*, rather than it being shared or apportioned among those parties who are best able to evaluate and control such risks. Bankers, of course, are not adverse to taking risks. It is the nature of our business; but the risks should be intelligent ones, and banks should be properly compensated for assuming them. Too often the compensation received today is not adequate for, or reflective of, the risks undertaken. In addition to assuming both supply and production risks as is common in production-payment financings, we have recently seen a project in which the continuing economic attractiveness of the project to the sponsors was a basis upon which the project could be abandoned with impunity as to the in-place debt. By any objective standard that is an equity holders' risk, but the lenders were not to be compensated through a profit-sharing plan but strictly through an interest-rate calculation that yielded a margin of slightly above 1 percent over cost of funds. That return is grossly inadequate for the risk assumed, and while it must be admitted that the project in question appears undoubted, one must ask why the sponsor demanded such protection. Was the situation more uncertain than it appears, or is a principle being established for future negotiations? And why would lenders accept such a situation? Perhaps because the situation is so secure that option is meaningless. But even if that is so, having once agreed to such a principle, will one be able to resist a like situation on a later, less favorable project? This remains to be seen.

Beset with the difficulties of modern-day competitiveness, the banker's traditional role of balancing the acceptability of risks with benefit to his shareholders and depositors becomes more difficult. More often than not, the risk is weighed against the value of the overall relationship with a particular sponsor or host, with the final decision being influenced by factors unrelated to the project itself. But, irrespective of the banker's decision, the evaluation of the risk factors must be undertaken and are reviewed here.

The banker must be satisfied with the supply and completion risks, which are interrelated. The supply risk is simply the actual availability of product at acceptable quality levels, while the completion risk is the ability to produce and/or refine the product. The first is essentially a geological determination, while the second can be a mixture of geology, chemistry, and legal draftsmanship. In many cases, however, our hypothetical ore body will probably not be owned by the project sponsors. More likely, the case will be that the ore will be considered the "patrimony of the nation" (host), and therefore, the contractual rights and obligations of the various parties will play an important role in judging the supply risk. The evaluation of these supply contracts is just as vital to the understanding of the supply risk as in the underlying geology.

At this point we should bring into focus an important consideration which can be discussed in the context of the evaluation of the supply risk. In the capacity of an individual lender, each bank would have to make an individual decision as to the supply risk, but for a lead or agent bank the problem becomes considerably more complex. A bank in the lead position generally is larger and more experienced than other participants in the credit. Often, the available talents will include the presence of staff geologists in a mining or project-financing group who can properly evaluate raw geological data and work in conjunction with staff mining engineers as to the creation of a full-risk analysis. While very useful internally, there can be dangers to other banks. Participant banks tend to rely on the opinions of agents as to the technical viability of a project, especially if the agent is known to have a particular expertise in house or advertises the same. If something is wrong with the analysis and the financial viability of the project is put in jeopardy, there is certain to be substantial dissension within a lending syndicate at precisely the time dissension is not needed. The approach followed at Bankers Trust is to have the syndicate rely on the opinions of independent mining engineers as to the technical evaluation of the supply risk, reviewing those opinions with our internal experts for our internal use only. We feel our qualifications are in the field of finance, not mining, and as a result the integrity of both the project and lenders is better served through independent evaluation.

The second critical risk is the assurance that the project will be completed to enable it to supply the product. In most every case a completion guarantee will be required by lending syndicate of the project sponsors.

Such a guarantee can take many forms, but in general, it is usually a quantitative and qualitative test extending over a period of time from the outset of production. In short, in our example, a minimum amount of ore of a specified grade must be mined and, if necessary, refined which, under cash flow scenarios developed, will produce sufficient income to generate debt-amortizing cash flow. Or, to generalize, completion can be defined as the ability to design, engineer, and construct a facility within a time frame consistent with project cash flows and to produce the right product as called for by specifications. Careful coordination between banker, engineer, and lawyer is required here to insure a viable and enforceable test which can be considered meaningful in light of the nature of the product and the technology involved.

A properly drawn completion guarantee can serve another purpose. During the construction period it can, in a somewhat perverse way, minimize a political risk. The ultimate political risk is of course expropriation by a suddenly hostile host, but it is almost an axiom of the business that incompleted projects are not expropriated. The existence of a tight completion guarantee will almost invariably delay the actions of a host government until its terms have been fulfilled or until the project is abandoned, at which point the issue becomes academic.

In some cases where the sponsoring group is particularly strong, where the technical supply issue is undoubted, and where all other risk elements are minimal, a requirement for an outright guarantee (save war, insurrection, or natural disaster which can be covered by insurance) may be reduced, but for many institutions, a full-completion guarantee is as a matter of policy and a prerequisite to the extension of credit.

The technology risk can, to an extent, be referred to as the true nature of project finance. Of all the risks, this is the one which is the most difficult for a banker to evaluate and one which is nearly impossi-

ble to "draft away," short of requiring either a full process guarantee
or incorporating within a completion guarantee the full technology
risk.

It is also the most difficult risk to isolate in risk assessment. Intermin-
gled as it is with supply and technology, it must be viewed in the
light of the proceeding two and dealt with concurrently. It is a risk
which can, for the most part, be covered by an inclusive completion
guarantee, provided the lenders are aware at the outset of the presence
of new technology or technology which, because of a unique set or
combination of factors, poses a threat to the operation of the project.
The unveiling of an entirely new process is, of course, simple to spot
and protect against. However, the difficulty arises where a well-developed process suddenly becomes extremely risky due to a certain set
of circumstances present at a single point in time. In a silver-extractive
process we have seen a perfectly tried and true leaching process rendered unusable for the separation of silver oxide due to the creation
of poisonous gases formed from arsenic in the ore. While no financing
was involved in the project, there is some doubt as to whether a standard completion guarantee would have covered that situation. Silver
would have been produced in sufficient quantities with only the death
of employees to interfere with the smooth running of the mine!

In the above example the company involved was one of the finest
in the world and operating in North America. While the project was
financed internally, it is illustrative of a technology risk which probably
would not have been foreseen and therefore not guarded against. In
addition it was in no way related to the physical location of the project.
There is an element of "they know (or don't know) what they're doing,"
in every analysis. Where there exists a market leader as a sponsor,
the element of sponsor reliance often assumes a larger than appropriate
position in the decision-making process. Comfort can, and should, be
gained from working with a top-class sponsor, but the risk perspective
must not be lost.

The degree by which a market risk can vary is large. The marketing
or sale of the product can be set in such a manner as to place lenders
fully at the mercy of the free market, or so as to practically eliminate
every other risk associated with the financing. Most commercial banks,
as a minimum, will require long-term sales contracts whose minimum
terms will provide sufficient cash flow to amortize debt in a "worst
case scenario." Obviously, where market conditions dictate, there may
be some relaxation of this concept, but the availability of "commercial
sales contracts" whose proceeds are assignable to the lenders is generally standard. Often, however, the initial term of these contracts is
insufficient to amortize the entire debt, and at this point, the lenders
had best be familiar with the market for the product or prepared to
force the project to enter into debt-amortizing contracts. Often sound

economic sense will dictate against such contracts as the general expectation may be a rise in market price.

On the other end of the spectrum, particularly where the purchasers are the project's sponsors and where all the leverage is with the lenders, there exists the concept of the "hell-or-high-water" take or pay contract. The difference between this and a full guarantee is virtually nil, for with such an agreement the purchasers (sponsors) commit to purchase an amount of product at a price and within an agreed-upon time frame so that all debt will be amortized *whether the product is available or not for whatever reason.* Clearly, an arrangement of this nature shifts the credit risk entirely to the purchasers, and the project for all intents and purposes becomes a corporate loan. Not surprisingly, such agreements are rare, but between this hell-or-high-water agreement and the commercial sales contract there exist as many different arrangements as the imagination of the parties and their lawyers will allow.

Most common, perhaps, for the situation where the purchasers are the sponsors, is what can be defined as the "commercial take or pay." If available, the purchaser agrees to take a specific amount of product or pay the project the contract price. In such an agreement it is often common to find that the project is under no obligation whatsoever to attempt to find an alternative purchaser and often need not reduce the original purchaser's obligations from the proceeds of subsequent sales. However, the definition of availability is, as one might guess, critical and can vary in its test from force majeure to ore quality levels.

Not surprisingly, some of the best advice either a project or its lenders can have is "get a lawyer." The *very* best advice is "get a *good* lawyer." Until one has been involved in the actual negotiations and drafting of completion guarantees, sales contracts, take or pay agreements, and the like, there can simply not be the appreciation of how vital the presence of capable counsel on both sides is to the successful completion of the process. More importantly, however, is the certainty that an inexperienced counsel will wreck the process entirely and, in some cases, poison the atmosphere to an extent that the project becomes irretrievable. While the role of attorneys in project finance is a major subject in itself, suffice it for us to recognize that they are vital—and if good, worth the price.

For the international banker the evaluation of the political risk of a host country in relation to its effect upon the ability to finance a project, while important, is hardly as critical an exercise as it is from a sponsor's standpoint. A host's stability will obviously impact upon the ability of a project to operate properly, but clearly, the major political risk is that of expropriation which can be a far greater event to sponsors than to lenders. The substitution of ownership need not interfere with the ability to service debt, provided sufficient infrastructure, technical expertise, and marketing ability are present and, as such, is not the end of the world from a lenders' standpoint. But it is an event which deserves closer scrutiny as there are subtle issues which should be explored.

Barring a radical change in government (such as in Cuba in the 1950s or in Chile in the 1970s) few projects are expropriated. Expropriation is an extreme act which will generally result in international repercussions such as witnessed against Chile. Projects are nationalized, however, with the difference of course being that compensation (fair or otherwise) is paid to the project sponsors.

Often however, nationalization is in itself a step most governments are loath to take. Far better to receive an offer to sell than to present a demand to buy—particularly when one can arrange such an offer. A host simply has to create conditions in which the continued investment becomes unattractive by, for example, increasing taxes or royalty payments. If faced with these circumstances, the sponsors can be assured that the remaining benefits of the project, such as, for example, the supply of product, can be maintained after transfer, and if the sale price is reasonable the result is generally a rapid change in ownership. A lender's attitude should therefore be one of "what when," rather than "what if," with an understanding that the political risk of the host country should be viewed in light of the potential assumption of sponsor roles within the project. Stated another way, the existence of a project will not improve the political risk of a host country. If the political risk is unacceptable at the outset, a negative conclusion in regard to the financing of the project should result.

It should be mentioned at this point that the political risk can, to varying degrees, be covered by political risk insurance, but care must be used in placing too much reliance on such coverage. Expensive and extremely limited in scope and more attuned to an equity investor than a provider of debt, it is nonetheless available and should not be dismissed out of hand. Both private sources as well as public agencies such as the Overseas Private Investment Corporation (OPIC) formed under the Foreign Assistance Act of 1969 provide this coverage. From the standpoint of major international banks, however, such coverage is rarely used.

From the viewpoint of an international lender, the currency or foreign exchange risk is not a risk in most cases simply because most refuse to take it! It is rare to see the financing (other than export financing from official agencies) denominated in anything but dollars and rarer still to find an exchange risk lodged anywhere but with the project. As a practical matter most sale contracts are denominated in dollars; hence there will be an automatic cover for dollar debt. Debt, other than export-related debt, in currencies other than dollars should properly be considered currency speculation. This is not to imply that such an approach is incorrect; on the contrary we have often provided multicurrency facilities. It is the view of Bankers Trust that exposures in currencies other than the currency of the cash flow is to be assumed by the borrower and not the lenders.

THE ROLE OF THE PROJECT ADVISOR

In a project situation where there exist elements of extreme diversification, such as different nationalities, financial interests, and social systems, the role of an independent advisor can prove critical to the project's ultimate success. The term *project advisor* has been used, rather than *financial advisor,* for the latter is too limiting. The ability of the project to be financed will very often be dependent upon the structure of the project as agreed to in the prefinancing stage, and experience has shown that mistakes made by project sponsors and host governments during this phase have doomed what could have been a viable venture.

Very often the advisor's role transcends the financial plan. The advisor often negotiates between the various parties in structuring agreements, assists in creating the legal structure under which the project will act, and, from the standpoint of an international bank (this is critical), advises the host country as to consequences of the project in regard to the credit standing of the host and its ability to engage in other borrowing exercises should these be required. Timing is important. If a project advisor is deemed necessary and, in most cases, one is advisable, this appointment should be made at the earliest possible date so that the full benefits accruing from such an appointment can be obtained. The advisor is the buffer between the parties and can prevent false starts and early disagreements which, because of the parties' lack of familiarity with one another, can often occur.

Clearly, to do all these things and do them well, the advisor must be independent. Unfortunately, the reality of many situations is that, while an advisor may attempt to be independent, there exist pressures which become so great as to decrease (if not destroy) the independence and limit the ability of the advisor to orchestrate. This reduces him to the role of an arranger of meetings. It is very difficult, for example, for a commercial bank, acting as a project advisor, to take a neutral position between a host country and various project sponsors where the host country and the sponsor are the bank's clients and where there exists major disagreements over such items as royalty payments, ownership percentages, infrastructure development, or a myriad of other important items. The advisor often wins the battle but loses the war, leaving behind a well-structured project but a half dozen ex-clients as well. Faced with this fact situation, advisors often have been unable to stand the heat.

The situation described above often is faced by large international commercial banks and is, therefore, tailor-made for the entry of investment or merchant banking institutions who can, in some cases, remain more independent than their commercial counterparts. Balanced against this, however, one will generally find that, except for all but a few such houses, the depth of knowledge and expertise is far greater in commercial institutions, plus they probably have a longer track record in dealing within the host country. It is my opinion that the benefits offered by a commercial banking advisor far outweigh the drawbacks—especially if the issue of divided loyalties can be set aside or minimized.

CONCLUSION

This chapter has presented, in the briefest possible format, an overview of project financing from the standpoint of an international banker. Clearly the approach is not all-inclusive, and important elements, such as lease financing, currency swaps, international arbitration, and governmental export-financing agencies, have been only briefly mentioned or not mentioned at all. The subject is so broad that it was not feasible to cover it exhaustively. We have attempted to convey, however, the complexity which can surround even the simplist of fact situations, such as the extractive-project example. This type of finance is not to be approached lightly, but only by individuals and organizations who have the experience and resources to face difficult and interrelated problems and the fortitude to see them through to their conclusion. It is not an easy business and is often filled with frustrations and disappointments. But when done and done well, few things in the banking business can be as rewarding.

11
International Leasing

KARL M. PARRISH
Chairman and Chief Executive Officer
Manufacturers Hanover Leasing Corporation

In its various forms, leasing has provided borrowers worldwide with a steady supply of term financing during periods of credit scarcity and interest-rate volatility. This service has proven to be invaluable to many borrowers in recent years, at a time when government deficits and tight monetary policies have crowded out many firms from the more traditional term credit markets. Certainly a vast majority of the needs of such firms was supplied through short-term commercial bank or commercial paper borrowings. However, a growing number of firms have made use of some form of secured-asset financing as a means of extending the average term of their liabilities.

Moreover, in recent years there has been a growing trend among large multinational firms to diminish the working capital demands which have been created by financing their product sales internally. Volatile interest rates, a thin fixed-rate term credit market, and pressure on earnings caused by an economic slowdown have all contributed to such companies seeking to refinance their existing portfolio of term sales agreements and developing reliable external sources of term financing for their customers.

INTERNATIONAL LEASING

Within the context of this article, leasing is defined to include a multitude of financing forms tied directly or indirectly to asset financing. These are finance leases, tax leases (single investor and leveraged), operating leases, conditional sales contracts, loan and security agreements and bareboat charters. A use of lease financing may be categorized into one of three uses:

Financing the acquisition of new equipment or other assets.

Obtaining additional working capital by selling existing assets and leasing them back (sale and leaseback).

Vendor discounting of installment sales portfolio.

While this list represents the most common uses of leasing, the reasons why leasing is chosen vary considerably from lessee to lessee, country to country, asset to asset. Many times it is assumed that a "lease versus buy" analysis is performed, with the leasing being selected for its superior economics. Certainly some types of leasing, such as short-term operating leases and leases for potentially obsolete equipment, require the user to compare ownership and renting. When the trade-off of tax benefits to a lessor would result in cost savings, leasing may be more attractive than ownership. Internationally, however, lease agreements frequently provide ultimate transfer of ownership at known, and often nominal, cost. This kind of lease receives the same accounting and tax treatment as bank financing and allows the lessee to take the tax benefits associated with economic ownership. Therefore, leasing more often represents an alternative form of borrowing than an alternative to ownership.

The leasing industry has its roots in ancient civilizations that used lease arrangements for shipping and real estate. Leasing land has been more common, but equipment leases can be traced to the 1800s. Nonetheless, the dynamic nature of the industry really began in the 1950s in the United States when tax incentives for investment were created.

Internationally, the growth of leasing accelerated in decades of the 60s and 70s, depending on the individual country. Growth was marked primarily by the emergence of leasing companies to provide financing to companies within their own countries and to conduct cross-border transactions. At present, the leasing industry is undergoing "internationalization": the expansion of leasing companies into countries outside their headquarters. Today, the largest markets are in the United States, the United Kingdom, Japan, West Germany, Italy, France, Canada, Brazil, and Mexico.

This pattern of industry evolution has produced several types of companies. Leasing participants may be segregated into three broad categories:

Large, multinational independent or bank-affiliated leasing companies.

Leasing companies and intermediaries whose activities abroad are limited to a few countries within one continent.

Smaller, single-country leasing companies and intermediaries.

BANK-AFFILIATED LEASING COMPANIES

Bank-affiliated leasing companies were formed in the United States after the Comptroller of the Currency gave federally chartered banks the authority to act as direct lessors in 1963. Subsequent regulations including those incorporated in the Bank Holding Company Act permitted the establishment of separate subsidiaries to engage in lease financing. Banks in other countries followed suit by forming their own lease financing operations. Although not covered by the same regulations as banks, leasing companies became subject to their own set of rules.

Commercial banks entered the leasing market as a natural extension of their credit activities. There was a distinct need for the banks to expand their financial services in order to meet the needs of their customers and compete more effectively. Quite often, the leasing subsidiary enters markets where the parent company has already established branches or representative offices. Bank-related leasing companies have the advantage of an inexpensive and reliable source of funds as well as a built-in customer base.

Sometimes the subsidiary will enter markets not previously penetrated by the bank. This may occur when the leasing operation can fill a particular void in the marketplace, usually in countries where the leasing industry has not reached maturity. Also, due to the fact that leasing companies are not viewed as banks by many foreign governments, it is easier for them to enter markets where banks are faced with a much more restrictive regulatory environment.

Originally, most U.S. commercial banks entered the leasing market by participating as equity and debt participants in leveraged lease transactions, first for domestic and subsequently for foreign lessees. In time such activities became housed in special departments of the banks. Ultimately, banks either established separate leasing subsidiaries or separate divisions within the banks. Most U.S. banks have chosen to form separate subsidiaries for their leasing operations. Such operations usually consist of a domestic subsidiary and one or more international subsidiaries to hold investments in foreign leasing operations. Often, a separate department or division is retained for the leveraged leasing activities.

With an international banking presence already established, leasing companies of money center banks quickly sought to establish their presence in the international marketplace. This movement began in the early 1970s. Leasing companies of U.S. money center banks quickly established a predominant position in international leasing. Their success can be attributed to a number of factors including the predominance of the U.S. dollar as the world currency, the use of U.S. tax-based leveraged leases for foreign lease transactions, and the size and depth of the U.S. leasing market. These resources and professional expertise have become additional products that banks can rely upon to serve their international customers.

It is the intention of most bank-affiliated leasing companies to own 100 percent of their foreign subsidiaries wherever possible. However, the laws of many countries are written such that the majority ownership must be held by a local entity. Foreign investment, whether by one or multiple investors, must be less than majority. Bank-affiliated leasing companies will generally enter into a joint venture only when required to do so. However, there are advantages for certain companies to enter into a joint venture agreement. Should a company not have the complete expertise necessary to enter a particular market, it might seek a partner or partners whose areas of expertise compliment its own. For example, one partner may be able to provide local currency funding, and another may have an existing prospect base or expertise in the credit function. The obvious disadvantage of the joint venture is that control is not complete. Control is shared at the board-of-directors level and down through the executive level of the company.

CONSIDERATIONS IN ESTABLISHING A FOREIGN OPERATIONS NETWORK

For some commercial banks, establishing local leasing companies in foreign countries has provided a means of gaining access to foreign markets which were, and often continue to be, closed to the establishment of full bank branches. This has been true largely because countries consider leasing a commercial activity rather than a financial enterprise. For example, most countries allow lessees to fully deduct lease payments against other taxable income. Such financings are almost always treated as off-balance-sheet financing. Additionally, where local tax laws allow the lessor to fully depreciate the asset on a straight-line basis equal to the lease term, regardless of the normal depreciable life of such assets, the leasing industry may offer lease financing as a tax product. That is, a lease can be structured for a shorter term and as a full-payout lease to accelerate the write-down of the asset by the user (lessee) via full deduction of rental payments.

Because of its quasi-commercial status, the leasing industry has been free from restrictions often levied on local bank operations. Leasing, however, is still subject to regulations governing the treatment of the companies and transactions. The major regulation issues include:

Definitions of leasing products.
Foreign ownership of local leasing companies.

Lessor's rights in case of default.

Rights of creditors.

Assets eligible for lease financing.

Lessor and lessee tax and accounting treatment of transactions.

Reporting requirements and maximum leverage ratio guidelines for the leasing company.

The tax and accounting regulations can be many. In this area would fall the treatment of deductions for lease payments and depreciation, withholding taxes on dividend and interest remittances, duties on imported equipment, and distribution of retained earnings.

Once the regulatory issues have been identified and evaluated, there remain the risks of financial, economic, and company operations. In the financial area, a leasing company faces potential problems in funding and foreign exchange.

Traditionally, companies have looked to lease financing as a means of accessing medium-term financing. Medium-term financing is often not available or, if it is, is available only to the private sector. Additionally, firms have historically sought fixed-rate financing in the form of a fixed-rental contract as a means of locking in their future funding costs. As the lender under such agreements, the lessor is cast in the role of serving as an intermediary between the short- and medium-term credit markets and the borrower. This potential funding risk must be carefully balanced with business and credit objectives.

Operating in inflationary economics is a reality for multinational leasing companies. Countries such as Brazil, where the leasing industry's net investment totals more than $2.0 billion, have experienced excessive levels of inflation. For example, in Brazil inflation has ranged from 75 percent to 100 percent over the past few years. Such inflation rates have served as a destabilizing force in the local credit markets. As stated, local currency funding is virtually unobtainable in many markets on a medium-term basis. When such funding is available, it is unlikely to be on a fixed-rate basis. As a result, early on in their operations, multinational leasing companies developed methods of indexation which allow a lessor to pass on foreign exchange risks to the lessee. A variable (floating) rate lease agreement requires the lessee to pay rentals which are comprised of principal repayment together with accrued interest charges most often priced at some margin over the London Interbank Offered Rate (LIBOR). Under such a contract, principal may be amortized through equal installments or through a step-up amortization similar to the principal retirement standard in most homeowner's mortgage agreements in the United States. In its more complex form, indexation may involve linking lease obligations, fixed or variable rate, to variations in currency exchange rates. The result is that a lessor may use foreign currency borrowings to support lease contracts which may be denominated in the local currency with payments indexed to the foreign currency.

The complexity of managing contract billings and payment receipts is directly correlated with the frequency of exchange-rate variations. For instance, where the local currency has a history of multiple devaluations relative to the foreign currency within a 30-day period, it is usually necessary to bill the client a second time for any foreign exchange losses incurred between date of billing and date the payment is received in available funds.

With a foreign investment, a company's capital is subject to the swings of currency. Indexation will address the ongoing foreign exchange risk, but the risk on equity itself cannot always be hedged. This is a risk that must be factored into the analysis of international leasing from the beginning and assumed to be a cost of doing business.

Since multinational leasing companies have found it necessary to pioneer the establishment of leasing industries in most foreign markets, implicit with that pioneering has been the need to train personnel locally. By its nature a large part of international lease financing involves marketing to local middle-market-size corporate clients. The most effective sales force to accomplish this are local nationals whose training usually is provided through a series of training programs established at the local level. Training focuses on developing greater technical skills such as selling, negotiating, credit, market planning which will enhance the inherent knowledge of the local business community. Training may also be provided for management and staff areas, such as the controller's function, to assure the multinational parent of compliance with parent country requirements and company policies and procedures.

Training in sales and other staff areas becomes more important as the reliance on expatriates declines. Minimizing the use of the expatriates is a sound practice given two factors. One is the local expertise offered by local professionals. The other is that the ratio of personnel to other operating components is considerably higher for a leasing company than for a comparable bank operation.

In the initial stages of development, most leasing companies begin operation with a hand full of professionals, each with an expertise in one or more disciplines, such as general management, marketing, finance and treasury operations, accounting and tax, credit, contract administration, or legal. As the organizations fill out, complete departments for each one of these areas is established, and specialists are hired. Some of the most important areas are accounting, billing, and collections.

Commonly the size of individual lease transactions booked by local leasing subsidiaries have ranged from $100,000 to $2.5 million with the average for most countries at about $250,000. That small size per transaction implies a medium-size leasing subsidiary, usually defined as having a net investment of $30 to $50 million, which must process 120 to 200 contracts, usually with monthly billings. This requires a sophisticated back office operation prepared to handle the record keeping that is unique to leasing. The requirements of the business are significant and, if met properly, command large resources and high-level management attention. When the back office issue is addressed, the following three solutions have been used alone or in combination:

Increased staff, to handle increased work.

Decentralization of authority, to streamline processing.

Automation, to facilitate large-volume processing.

INTERNATIONAL LEASING-PRODUCT PROFILE

Multinational leasing companies have an array of financing products to choose from including finance leases, true leases, and conditional sales contracts. The choice of which legal form to choose must be made with an eye towards enforceability of such contracts under local laws. Issues such as lessor rights to: (*a*) repossess assets in case of the lessee's (borrower's) default; (*b*) enforce claims of variable rate interest charges; and (*c*) accelerate payments in the event of lessee default. All are important for determination of which form of contract is appropriate for each country or state of jurisdiction. Additionally, other issues, such as the varying practices of assessing value added taxes (VAT), sales taxes, or withholding taxes depending on type of contract, quite often lead to a choice of one legal form over others. Finally, in several countries the leasing industry is restricted to offering only one form of lease agreement.

Certainly the simplest and most common form of lease financing is a full-payout finance lease (as defined by the U.S. Financial Accounting Standard Board) with a nominal purchase option at the end of the term of the lease. Under U.S. accounting standards such financing must be capitalized by the lessee as debt. A portion of the rental charges is recorded as interest expense while the remainder is recognized as principal repayments. However, quite often under foreign tax and accounting rules, such agreements are treated as off-balance-sheet financing for the local borrower. Such agreements are commonly referred to as true leases, and almost universally the lease payments are 100 percent tax deductible under local laws. Where such financing is undertaken by the foreign subsidiary of a U.S. company, the lease obligation may be viewed by the multinational borrower as both a true lease (by the foreign subsidiary) and a finance lease (by the U.S. parent).

Single investor tax leases are well known in the United States. Under such an arrangement the lessor (owner) provides 100 percent of the equity. As owner, he receives 100 percent of the cash flow from depreciation and investment tax credit. The lessee acquires the use of the equipment by the payment of rent to the lessor.

Tax leasing of a similar nature exists in other countries, such as Australia, Canada, France, Japan, and the United Kingdom. Common to all of these markets is that tax-based leasing is limited by the availability of investors seeking tax shelter via leasing. In order to compete in these foreign markets, U.S. bank-affiliated leasing companies have had to scramble to construct three-party financings accessing a third-party's tax shelter to construct a tax lease bearing a low interest rate charge. This concept has been most successfully applied in the United Kingdom where the tax-based leasing market represents a vast segment of the overall market.

The leveraged lease is another type of tax lease. This form of financing involves three parties: a lessee, a lessor (equity participant contributing at least 20 percent of the purchase price), and a long-term lender (typically a bank or insurance company who contributes the remainder of the purchase price). Internationally, leveraged leasing has played a predominant role as a vehicle for financing the aircraft of airlines. The high cost of such equipment precludes most carriers from purchasing their planes. The lessor can offer a financing rate significantly lower than that available through other forms of financing because the equity is highly leveraged. The lessor receives all the tax benefits of ownership even though it contributes only a portion of the investment, resulting in a quick return of the investment plus additional revenues from rental payments from a long-term agreement.

Lease financing is particularly suited as a complementary financing vehicle for the export subsidy programs offered by most industrialized countries around the world. The linking of a lease financing vehicle with export financing has been of growing importance. This provides support for exports which can be financed from one country into another in which the leasing company operates. The export program which has been used most successfully with lease financing is the United Kingdom's (Export Credits Guarantee Department (ECGD) program. In such instances a foreign lessor becomes the borrower under an ECGD facility, receiving funds generally equal to 60 percent to 65 percent of the equipment cost in the form of low fixed-rate financing. The lessor may then "top up" such funding with additional monies to provide the borrower (lessee) with 100 percent financing. Additionally, where the export subsidy program is of a shorter term than the financing desired by the lessee, rental payments may be flattened and "stretched" to produce a lease payment stream acceptable to the lessee.

In some cases such *top-up and stretch programs* may be constructed in multiple currencies and rate bases to meet the requirements of the borrower. Multicurrency financings, however, are not limited just to export programs. Indeed, in some countries, such as the Republic of Korea, the government requires that all local costs, such as inland transportation, insurance, and installation costs (ancillary costs), must be financed via local currency transactions without indexation to a foreign currency. The result is that in such countries imported equipment will always require two separate lease payment agreements.

One rapidly growing area of importance within international leasing is the use of residual value insurance to cover residual risks otherwise borne by the lessor. Simply stated, the use of such insurance allows U.S. bank-affiliated leasing companies to write considerably shorter-term leases whose rental payments, by themselves, do not fully repay the lessor's original investment in the equipment plus interest. As a result the lessee is required to pay fewer lease payments. Additionally, if the lessee is a subsidiary of a U.S. company, this form of lease financing would have the added advantage of being off-balance-sheet financing.

If properly structured such residual value insurance permits U.S. bank-affiliated leasing companies to write lease transactions which, from the lessee's perspective, are nonfull-payout leases; while from the lessor's viewpoint, they are full-payout leases. Under U.S. Federal Reserve Board regulations U.S. bank-affiliated leasing companies must write full-payout leases which are defined by the Federal Reserve as leases in which the cash flows will return to the lessor the full cost of the asset, the cost of financing and administering the asset, plus a satisfactory return.

Leasing companies worldwide have long sought to establish formal financing programs (vendor programs) with manufacturers of heavy industrial equipment, construction equipment and other types of equipment suitable for lease financing. Often these agreements have been difficult to structure, particularly in the U.S. market, with many manufacturers choosing instead to establish their own in-house customer finance divisions or captive finance companies. However, such manufacturers have recently begun to reassess their customer financing policies with a view toward lessening the financial burden assumed by the parent multinational company which funds the receivables portfolio of its foreign operations.

The advantages to a manufacturer of establishing a vendor relationship with a multinational lessor depend on the country in which the sales are made, the type of equipment sold, and the creditworthiness of the customer base. Nevertheless, a fair generalization may be that such programs often provide one or more of the following advantages:

Medium-term local currency funding, either fixed or variable rate.

Lessor's credit expertise in assessing creditworthiness of customers.

Off-balance-sheet financing for the lessee, in some cases with a built-in tax advantage.

Smaller investment exposure in countries by the parent company.

Credit facilities of the local operation or the parent available for other purposes.

Bareboat charters have provided long-term financing for charterers of vessels. Although structured similar to a finance lease, this financing vehicle was created to give charterers an alternative to short-term time-charter financing. The charter hire (rent) is normally such that, at a minimum, it covers the debt amortization of the vessel. The bareboat charter is considered a project finance type transaction in that the lessor looks to the revenue that will be generated by the vessel rather than the balance sheet of the charterer in order to determine the viability of the transaction.

FUTURE PROSPECTS

The trend among the larger bank-affiliated leasing companies is clearly toward incorporating more foreign subsidiaries and affiliates and relying less on large cross-border deals to sustain their international operations. As in the past, that expansion will be predicated on the prospects for long-term profitability of the leasing market in countries targeted for new operations. With such expansion, however, additional opportunities are likely to unfold. A well-developed network of international subsidiaries and affiliates should allow a multinational leasing company to compete ever more effectively for the companywide relationship with multinational corporations. Additionally, other areas of business development will surface, such as using a well-developed customer base to capture a larger share of the term import-export financing market.

The attractiveness of international leasing heralds a future of increased competition. Unfortunately, the industry will be joined by some institutions who will not understand or heed the points made in this article. These are the competitors who are likely to be short-lived for lack of appreciation of the true risk and cost of the funding, credit, and operations of a foreign leasing company. Their situation, and that of other better-positioned leasing companies, will be affected by slower economic growth. The rapid industrialization and growth that is occurring in spite of tight monetary markets will not persist. So there will be more leasing companies competing for smaller shares of a market.

Finally, as leasing becomes a regularly utilized financing alternative in most countries, it is expected that the host countries will develop regulations that govern all aspects of leasing. Some of these regulations may in fact turn leasing into a banking or near-banking activity. If it can be said that the term *banking* confers a primary position to a type of financing, then perhaps such a distinction for leasing recognizes the vital role that leasing plays worldwide.

12
Tanker and Shipping Loans

LESTER D. ANDERSON, JR.
Vice President
Chemical Bank

INTRODUCTION

Ship financing has long been considered by many banks and other lenders to be a particularly attractive form of lending. The industry is heavily capital intensive, and ship loans are typically larger and longer in term, and carry somewhat higher spreads, than other common types of loans. Collateral in the form of a vessel mortgage and assignment of various cash flows is perceived as adding safety to profitability, offsetting in part the inherent cyclicality of the industry and complexity of documentation. Further, the heavy concentration of shipowning activity in a few geographic locations, and the predominance of a relatively small number of companies and groups, puts the building and maintenance of a sizable shipping portfolio within the grasp of any institution willing to invest the required money and manpower and accept the attendant risks.

In this chapter we will attempt to describe the industry briefly and to discuss several approaches to analyzing and structuring ship loans. We will concentrate primarily on the tanker segment as a microcosm of the industry which is more simple (though not necessarily more stable) than many segments of the industry. However, many of the lessons learned in the tanker market apply across all segments of the industry.

A short glossary of terms appears at the end of this chapter. While every attempt has been made to minimize the use of industry lingo, to some extent it is a necessary part of understanding ship financing, and it is entirely necessary to the marketing effort in any part of the world or segment of the industry.

183

Definition of Breadth

The shipping industry may be defined in several ways, to be as broad or as narrow as anyone might wish. The narrow definition might be limited to just those vessels which provide deep-sea transport of goods in international commerce. Using this definition one would include most oil tankers, coal carriers, and container ships plying ocean trade routes, but would not include fishing boats, offshore supply and tug boats, or holiday cruise ships. The narrowest view might even exclude Great Lakes ore boats which never reach the ocean and the transatlantic passenger liners whose cargo is mostly human.

On the other hand a broad definition might include virtually anything that floats and which has any revenue-producing business purpose. Thus we might include not just all those things mentioned above but also inland river barges, seismic research boats, and perhaps self-propelled semisubmersible drilling rigs.

Whatever the definition used, it is clear that the shipping industry is not a simple, monolithic entity but rather is composed of a group of widely differing types of assets and businesses related to each other by similar economics, similar technology, and of course the water. While the degree of interaction and interrelation among various industry segments can be high, it does not at all follow that strength in one market segment is accompanied by strength in any other segment.

Specialization

Until the early part of this century there was little specialization of ship designs for the particular cargoes they were intended to carry. The need for protection resulted in the galleons of the 1500s and 1600s; the East Indiamen were developed in the 1600 to 1700s to handle larger cargoes and the long distances of the East Asia trades; the Clipper ships of the late 1800s were designed to speed the movement of Chinese tea and other more valuable products; and by 1900 steam propulsion was replacing sail, providing dependability unknown in prior centuries.

But none of these developments rivals the specialization which has taken hold during the 20th century. There are now tankers which carry liquids by the shipload in bulk; there are dry bulk carriers which carry bulk coal, ore, and grain by the shipload; there are ships designed to carry nothing but 20- and 40-foot containers, or only automobiles, or refrigerated goods, or solely huge, bulky items like drilling rigs or power generating plants.

Within each segment of vessel type there are further subcategories of size or specifications relating to specific cargoes or expected trade routes. For example, a dry bulk carrier intended for carrying iron ore might have a specially strengthened and somewhat smaller hull than one designed to carry the same tonnage of grain, as grain represents more volume for the same weight as compared to ore, and applies less strain on the hull in loading and unloading operations.

Size of ship is another important factor as economies of scale of a larger vessel are balanced against the limitations of port or canal size, or against normal trading quantities of particular cargoes. For example, a 60,000 to 70,000 dwt. (deadweight ton—see Glossary) dry bulk carrier is a popular size because it is the largest such vessel able to traverse the Panama Canal. Orders for larger bulkers which will not use Panama are generally for vessels of 120,000 dwt. or more where other port restrictions begin to be encountered. The size of an ocean-going ship may be anywhere between 3,000 to 5,000 dwt. for a short distance feeder-ship or coaster to the 560,000 dwt. Seaside Giant, the world's largest supertanker.

The ship lender is of course very interested in the size and type of ship being financed inasmuch as its value as collateral is a source of strength in the loan package. The market must be studied and followed on a continuing basis, and any part of the industry which shows probable weakness over the term of the proposed financing should typically be avoided unless there are carefully considered reasons to the contrary.

THE TANKER MARKET

For lack of space we will concentrate here on tankers and the economics and financing modes which apply to this segment of the shipping industry. Much of the discussion here applies or can be extrapolated to the remainder of the industry as well.

Tanker is a term which describes in general any ship which is designed to carry liquid cargo in bulk. By far the highest-volume liquid bulk cargo is crude oil, which is carried in whole shipload quantities in tankers of virtually every size in existence. But other liquid cargoes are also carried in tankers, often with more sophisticated specifications than crude carriers.

Refined petroleum products, such as gasoline, require tanks coated with compounds which protect against corrosion. Such product carriers also often have several separate tanks making it possible to carry several grades of product on the same voyage. More sophisticated liquid chemical tankers may have as many as 48 or more separate tanks, with several choices of coatings or stainless steel construction, and several separate piping systems to avoid contamination problems.

Other liquid cargoes include molasses, edible oils, various ammonia compounds, molten sulphur, and even fresh water, each of which has special technical handling and tank-cleaning requirements. For the moment let's look at a crude oil carrier.

Operations

A tanker owner has two basic alternatives for employing his ship: he can arrange for long-term employment at rates fixed from the start by signing a long-term time charter, or he can opt to seek only short-term employment and depend on a continuing ability to arrange satisfactory consecutive short-term charters for the life of his investment. Every owner has a predilection for one or the other method, a philosophical predisposition which dictates his response to opportunities in a normal market. The "spot" (short-term) market operator hopes to make more than enough profit in boom times to cover losses in slow markets, though it could obviously go the other way in the wide swings that make up the shipping cycle.

On the other hand a long-term charter is intended to create a buffer from the extreme highs and lows of the cycle, providing sufficient cash flow to cover operating expenses and debt service and perhaps provide a bit extra over time, with the real profit coming from residual value after the ship has been paid for. While long-term employment is generally considered a more conservative mode of operation, it is not difficult to imagine cost inflation wiping out small projected cash surpluses over 6 to 10 years and causing losses on long-term charters.

There are times when no long-term employment is available in the market, and there are medium-term options which are somewhere between the two outlined above. The truly conservative owner is probably one who has a mix of long-, medium- and short-term employment in his fleet, thereby ensuring his market timing will never be entirely wrong.

Economics

The tanker market is an excellent example of an ideal market (in the economists' sense of perfect competition). It has a wide diversity of supply (many ships, many owners), a wide diversity of demand (many oil companies, refiners, power companies, speculators, etc.), and a nearly perfect flow of information (a worldwide net of brokers who are involved in virtually every charter and sale/purchase, and who publish details of nearly every transaction). There are no real barriers to entry other than minimum capital levels—technical expertise can be hired, second-hand ships can be purchased to avoid the lead time required for new deliveries, and vessels can be taken in on longer-term charters to avoid the significant capital cost of a purchase.

Freight rates (the price a company shipping oil pays to carry each ton of crude between two points) are strictly a function of supply and demand. For example, if 30 large tankers are waiting in the Persian Gulf to find a cargo and only 20 loads are available, freight rates will drop as shipowners compete for limited business. The opposite will occur if the supply of tanker tonnage exceeds demand: rates will increase. In fact, supply and demand are constantly changing, and so are freight rates. And swings in these rates can be massive.

The demand for tankers to move crude oil is not very responsive to the cost of using those tankers because demand for crude oil itself is not affected much by the cost of transportation. Freight represents a relatively small portion of total cost and is far smaller than the cost of starving a refinery or a national economy. World demand for crude oil rises or falls most often for reasons unrelated to shipping, such as politics and international economics, and any adjustment required to correct an inbalance between supply and demand for ships must be made on the supply side.

In the very short run little can be done to adjust the supply of tanker tonnage. To the individual shipowner whose fixed costs are extremely high in a bad market, it is advantageous to operate a vessel for a time at very low freight rates, as long as variable costs can be covered with a small contribution toward fixed. Over a somewhat longer period continuing losses will force less efficient ships into layup and eventually illiquid owners will sell tonnage, and the least efficient vessels will be scrapped. Inasmuch as the final solution to oversupply can take a significant amount of time, freight rates can remain depressed for a significant period.

Undersupply, on the otherhand, which can result in quite high freight rates and booming profits to the owner, can only be solved by converting vessels from other trades—a partial solution at best— or by ordering new buildings to meet excess demand. Inasmuch as construction of a new ship may take 6 to 12 months, and shipyards may have an order backlog of two to three years or longer, the solution to undersupply comes only over time. However, it generally takes less time for owner optimism to lead to new orders than for owner pessimism to lead to scrapping. Thus, the boom times are generally more intense but shorter in duration than the bust periods.

The causes and effects of changing supply and demand for ship tonnage represent the specific economics of the shipping industry and result in the extreme cyclicality endemic to the industry. While this description has been greatly simplified, its elements represent the core of shipping economics which must be understood by anyone playing a financial role in the industry.

Employment

Highly cyclical and quickly changing freight rates can be a problem, or an opportunity, to the tanker owner operating in the spot market, fixing his ships for one voyage at a time. But other employment arrangements can be made to transfer away from the owner some of the risk of a bad freight market. Most common alternatives to the single-voyage charter are longer-term time or bareboat charters and various types of contracts of affreightment (COA).

In its simplest terms a voyage charter provides for a specific vessel to carry cargo for the charterer from one point to another. The charter rate is meant to include the owner's capital cost as well as the cost of crew, fuel, and port charges, and the charter may call for one or several consecutive voyages.

A time charter is similar in that the owner provides a particular ship with crew and agrees to carry cargo on instructions of the charterer, but it is effective for a specified time period rather than for a specified voyage(s), and fuel costs and port charges are for the account of the charterer. A time charter may be as short as 30 days or as long as 25 years.

Under a bareboat charter the charterer must provide his own crew and is responsible for all fuel and other operating and maintenance costs with the charter rate covering only the owner's capital cost. It is very similar to the "dry lease" of aircraft.

Often a shipper has substantial cargo movement requirements in one direction but nothing for a return trip, and often he would prefer not to become involved in the details of shipping but would still like to arrange a longer-term agreement for transportation of his cargoes. He might sign a contract of affreightment (COA) under which he would agree to provide a specified amount of cargo on some regular schedule while the shipowner would agree to provide transportation for that cargo on schedule. Freight rates might be established in advance or tied to some published market rate from time to time. The shipper is happy because he has covered his transport requirements on a term basis without getting into the shipping business himself. As no specific vessel is named, the shipowner is able to increase his profitability through creative scheduling of his fleet to carry various contract cargoes as well as spot cargoes to fill otherwise empty return trips. He need not dedicate a specific vessel to a specific contract.

THE ANALYSIS

In the normal ship loan the lender is able to look to three distinct sources of repayment. Without regard for relative importance, which can vary from deal to deal, the three sources are the general corporate strength of the borrower (and any guarantors), the vessel's income stream (net cash generated), and the collateral value of the vessel itself. In a particular transaction any one or two of these sources may be so strong as to make a thorough analysis of the other(s) unnecessary. On the other hand the combined strength of all three may be insufficient, and additional outside support may be needed to construct an acceptable transaction.

The ship loan analysis should look at all three aspects, each in as much detail as is required by the degree of support provided by it. The following structure might be helpful in doing such an analysis.

Introduction—The "3 × 5 Card"

The analysis should open with a brief description of the transaction to set the stage for the remainder. It is almost axiomatic that if the essence of the deal cannot be written in the space of a 3 × 5 card, then the writer does not fully understand the transaction. This brief description should include borrower, amount, interest rate, term and purpose of the loan, and brief description of the asset, its intended use or employment, and the parties involved in the underlying transaction.

The following is an example of a 3 × 5 card introduction:

> Approval is requested for a $20 million 8–year term loan at 1.5% over LIBOR to a subsidiary of Bulbous Shipping Co. to finance 80% of the purchase price of the 1980-built 80,000 dwt. tanker M/T "Coburn," which will be on full-payout time charter to National Shipping for onward 5-year charter to National Oil. Final loan maturity is February, 1990.

Before beginning the detailed analysis, it can be helpful to put the proposal into perspective by discussing the lender's historical relationship to the borrower, or marketing or other reasons for considering the proposal favorably. Expectations relative to asset growth and profitability targets should also be discussed here.

Company Analysis

Next it is usually helpful to look at the borrowing company or group. The standard requirement of *knowing your borrower* is as important in ship lending as it is in any banking situation. No matter how much policing is done and insurance arranged, the lender cannot avoid exposure to bad faith or bad management except by choosing his clients carefully. There is no substitute for good character and little substitute for proven industry knowledge and experience. The lender should do complete checkings with industry sources—charterers, vendors, other owners, trade publications, brokers, insurance underwriters— as well as banks and other lenders, and should develop enough personal understanding and rapport with the borrower to assure his good character and capacity.

Understanding the borrower's legal *corporate structure* is also critical. Frequent use is made of offshore incorporation and ownership in countries which provide an attractive tax environment, convenient vessel registry, and relatively unregulated operations. The lender must know and understand the legal system within which his borrower may have to operate.

Further, owners often establish separate corporations for each vessel in a fleet in order to isolate each ship from potential liabilities of the others. These separate companies may be organized in a complex series of interlocking superior and subordinate holding companies or they may be completely independent entities with similar or identical ownership. Moreover, such purely operating responsibilities as crewing, provisioning, bunkering (fueling), engineering, maintenance and repair, freight collection, and cash management are often centralized in one or two nonshipowning companies which act as agent for the owning companies.

The lender must be completely aware of the corporate structure in order to understand which entities are responsible for maintaining seaworthy condition of collateral, for acceptable performance under a charter, and for availability of excess liquidity when needed. If general corporate financial strength is an important credit consideration, appropriate specific guarantors should be chosen.

Several examples of common corporate structures are shown below. The chart form is usually the simplest and clearest way to collect and present such information. Like the 3 × 5 card, if the analyst cannot draw the chart, he doesn't understand the corporate structure.

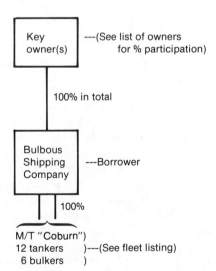

Simple structure: one company owns all ships; shareholders (may include public listing) and vessels listed separately if too numerous to show without cluttering chart. Here if Bulbous is the borrower, any excess liquidity or equity in assets is equally available to service debt on all vessels.

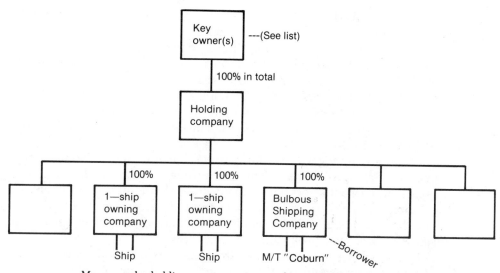

More complex holding company structure: here if Bulbous is the borrower, the lender is shielded from the liabilities of other shipowning subsidiaries in the group but is also isolated from any excess liquidity or equity in other assets. The guarantee of the holding company, and others if available, is advised to draw added support from the group.

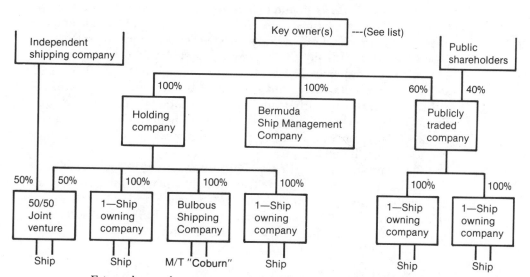

Extremely complex structure: includes a 50/50 private joint venture, controlled public company, and an offshore management company which may handle some or all technical and financial affairs for the shipowning companies. How the management company is used, and which shipowning company is the actual borrower, has a significant influence on appropriate loan structure.

Parallel with the determination of corporate structure, a *financial analysis* should be done based on audited statements if these are available. However, in the shipping industry book values of fixed assets are largely unrelated to market values. Further, decisions motivated by cash flow economics more often than not are misrepresented by generally accepted accounting principles, and local accounting practices and tax systems are not only different but often allow or enforce special treatment of shipping assets. Thus, financial statements must be handled carefully.

For example, negative working capital is common in shipping company financials, as current liabilities include 12-months' debt installments but current assets normally include only the next month's charter hire (a charter may be cancelled for nonperformance). Also there may be substantial "hidden equity" in fixed assets as vessel market values may exceed book values significantly.

Equally important as understanding the financial statements, a cash flow projection should be prepared showing all known and expected revenues and expenditures. Where employment or interest rates are not fixed, estimates must be used, and the sensitivity of the bottom line to changes in those estimates should be tested. Remembering the cyclicality of the industry, the ability of a borrower to withstand the pressure of a bad market is critical. Projections covering both the borrowing company and the group in total are needed as the two can seldom be separated except to the disadvantage of the lender.

Next a *fleet analysis* should be done, to include both a brief description of each vessel with its associated debt and employment and an analysis of charter runoff and debt-service requirements over the proposed loan term. Ideally the borrower's fleet should contain a mix of several types and sizes of vessels, a mix of long-, intermediate-, and shorter-term employment, and a spread of business over several different strong charterers with no undue concentrations. Charters and debt should run off fairly regularly over the period in question. The potential impact of any concentrations of charter renewals or debt refinancings required must be analyzed.

Finally any other particular corporate strengths or weaknesses should be noted and assessed. These might include, for example, an especially strong owner or customer relationship, unusual market position, or limited management depth. Occasionally the credit decision is based entirely on the contents of this section.

Project Analysis

In this section all aspects of the proposed transaction itself are analyzed. It is a detailed expansion of the introductory 3 × 5 card and should include a discussion and analysis of:

The vessel: type, size, age, flag, important technical specifications and operating characteristics, current physical condition and survey status (if not new), world fleet size and order book, expected market movements (demand/supply) over the loan term, flexibility of usage and potential alternative uses and users, expected future value as loan collateral, and so forth.

The employment: type, duration, rates, description of parties involved (who takes what risk/responsibility/reward), operations and cost escalation, cargo and marketing considerations, options and renewals, residual values, pertinent market factors and expectations and other risks involved over the loan term, and so on.

The cash flows: complete analysis with specific market- and interest-rate assumptions as needed, with sensitivity analysis on assumptions, showing capacity to service loan with comfortable margin.

The loan: pricing, fit within credit and portfolio policy guidelines, special amortization provisions, financial or market value covenants, any unusual terms or conditions, and so forth.

Summary and Recommendation

This is a summary of the strengths and the risks in the proposed transaction, with a brief reminder of how each risk is covered or why it is left uncovered. A restatement of the marketing, profitability, policy, or other overriding reason for approving the loan should be followed by an unequivocal recommendation. A detailed outline of terms can then be attached.

STRUCTURING THE LOAN

A ship financing facility may take on many different forms, from a standard term loan to a lease or a guaranty of financing from elsewhere (as for export credit on a newbuilding), or less commonly a revolving credit or working capital line or advance. It might also be a short-term advance to be repaid from proceeds of a sale, or scrapping, or a refinancing.

In general, shipowners are very highly leveraged, and virtually all of their financing is obtained on a secured basis covered by mortgages on vessels. Each credit facility is tied to an underlying asset or contract, and such facilities are normally designed to be paid out as a result of operation of the asset or completion of the contract.

In the case of short-term advances, each deal should be structured to ensure that the projected source of payout is indeed used to pay out the lender. Credit lines and revolving credits are less common and are generally available only to the largest and strongest of borrowers for well-defined purposes. Term loans and guaranties (and leases as an alternative variation) represent the most common form of ship financing and in many ways the most complex.

Appendix I contains a sample outline of terms for a typical secured term ship loan. The following section contains a commentary on the various segments of the outline describing the structure and rationale of each. Please refer to Appendix I while reading the following.

The Outline of Terms

Each section of a term sheet like the one in Appendix I, has a specific purpose. Many provisions are obvious while some are very special and should be carefully written.

The *Borrower* designated here should be the legal borrower for whom the proposed loan will be a general obligation. To reinforce an earlier comment, the Borrower's place within a corporate organization should be clearly identified by the lender.

The *amount* is obvious, but it may be written to allow a switch into other Eurocurrencies to take advantage of interest rate differentials.

A clear statement of the *purpose* is important to the analyst's understanding of the entire package. The "80% of purchase price" might be expanded to include a further limitation of "80% of market value" on the drawdown date in order to provide additional protection to the lender.

Drawdown and *Commitment Fee* are standard—suffice to say any firm Commitment should be paid for and should be available for a finite period of time.

The *amortization* of loan principal is an area where considerable creativity can be utilized. Level installments are common but are often not well suited to the particular cash flow situation of a vessel. Monthly charter hire, or in fact regular income from any source, can be matched conveniently with a rear-weighted principal payment schedule calling for larger installments in the later years when the interest burden is relatively lower. The level of any balloon payment should be carefully considered inasmuch as residual values, and even scrap values, are difficult to project 8 to 10 years in the future.

It should not be difficult to justify a 15-year or longer economic life for most vessels, and thus in most cases the *final maturity* should occur within the first 15 years of a ship's life. On an older ship of 12 to 15 years, financing of 3 to 4 years is not uncommon if the physical condition of the vessel is good and employment is secure. Often this is a case of an owner prolonging the useful life of a ship to take advantage of a particularly attractive charter. In such a situation a large balloon would make little sense. At the same time newbuilding costs have risen so much in the past 7 to 10 years that a typical vessel now requires 10 to 12 years to pay out its 75 percent financing as compared with the 7 to 10 years which was applicable in the early 1970s. For the lender whose comfort level terminates at 8 years, the answer may be a newbuilding financing of 8 years with a 33 percent balloon payment at final maturity—the equivalent of a 12-year payment schedule with an exit option to the lender after eight years.

The *interest-rate* provision is no different from the standard Eurodollar loan except that shipping credits normally command a premium for their complexity and perceived risk. In a world of large differentials between interest rates in various currencies, the multicurrency option is becoming more common and even standard in some markets. Under a multicurrency provision the borrower has the option to switch into or stay in one of a series of specified currencies at each interest rollover date. While substantial interest savings can be obtained by choosing a currency with low rates, the exchange rate could move enough to eliminate any interest differential and even cause a loss. As most shipping revenue is denominated in dollars, great care must be exercised in borrowing in other currencies.

The *security* of a first preferred ship mortgage is as important to the ship lender as is the home mortage to a savings bank. Because the financing represents a relatively high percentage of market value of the asset, and because a ship is a registered asset easy for other creditors to locate and attach, it is important to have a prior claim on the ship via a first mortgage. Since each country which registers ships has its own law relating to vessel mortgages, the maritime law of the country in question should be checked for its clarity and support to the mortgagee prior to agreeing to take a particular mortgage. A mortgage may be of little use to a lender in a country which allows only its own citizens to own ships in its registry. Two of the most commonly used and most supportive and convenient registries are Liberia and Panama.

Similarly, an *assignment of the proceeds* of any employment gives the lender a prior claim to cash flows received. However, should the owner fail to perform on a time charter, for example, the charterer can terminate the contract. Where possible the lender should take an assignment of the charter party (the actual agreement) as well as the charter hire (the cash payment), so that should the owner/operator fail to operate the vessel as required, the lender as assignee can step into the shoes of the borrower and operate the vessel (through a competent consultant) to keep the charter alive. Acknowledgment and consent of the charterer is necessary to ensure payments are made directly to the lender.

Where there is an onward charter, particularly from a shipping company charterer to an end user, an *assignment of both charter parties* and all charter hire can add strength to a credit.

Guarantees of payment from parent companies are common where the borrower is an isolated single-shipowning company. The need for guarantees is dependent on strength in other areas.

Assignment of all related *insurances* is obviously necessary. If a ship is lost the insurance pays off the financing (presumably), and an assignment perfects the claim. War and pollution risk coverages are relatively inexpensive in most locations at most times but should be mandatory. It should be noted that war risk insurance can be cancelled by the underwriters upon the outbreak of a war. Minimum coverage of 115 percent of loan values ensures that interest will be covered.

The *Representations and Warranties* are fairly typical for a Eurodollar loan agreement except for mention of a class certificate, which refers to a periodic certification of acceptable seaworthy condition of a ship by an internationally recognized classification society.

The *Covenants* contain one provision somewhat peculiar to some shipping transactions. They require that additional collateral be posted should the value of the pledged asset fall below 133 percent of the outstanding loan (in which case the loan would exceed 75 percent of the current collateral value).

Events of Default, Expenses, Taxes, and *Availability* are all rather standard for Eurodollar loan agreements. For reasons of control over security and perhaps profitability, all related charterhire should pass through the borrower's deposit account with the lender.

The law governing the ship mortgage must be that of the country in which the vessel is registered. The law governing the loan agreement may be any one acceptable to both parties, though English and U.S. are used most often in international loan agreements.

DOCUMENTATION

Once the outline of terms has been accepted by both borrower and lender, documentation should be drafted by someone familiar with maritime law. The complexities of ship loan documentation are not evident from a brief summary term sheet; by way of example, Appendix II contains a list of the various items which were signed or changed hands at a typical ship loan closing, which coincided with a vessel purchase. Actual requirements are voluminous and exacting. Further, the closing is not the end of the process but really is just the beginning.

In order to ensure that the provisions of the loan agreement are being followed, tracking systems should be developed and implemented so that, for example, annual insurance renewals are not missed, financial statements are received, and charterhire flows through the proper account on schedule. Market values should be compared to collateral margin requirements on a regular basis, and a program of continuing calls on each borrower will help to spot potential problems as well as new financing opportunities early.

As a final remark, one of the keys to effective ship financing is the ability to identify the various risks inherent in any lending situation and to create covers for each area of risk to construct a strong credit. In many respects "credit is credit is credit"—no matter what industry or country or asset one looks at, the basic principles remain the same. Still in order to identify and protect against the risks of the shipping cycle, the lender must develop an expertise and familiarity with the industry. It can be a highly rewarding challenge.

APPENDIX I

OUTLINE OF TERMS
For A Sample
8-YEAR SHIP LOAN
To The
BOW & STERN GROUP

BORROWER:	Bulbous Shipping Co., Ltd. (Monrovia, Liberia).
AMOUNT:	US$20,000,000.
PURPOSE:	To finance 80% of the purchase price of the 1977-built 80,000 dwt. tanker m/t "Coburn" from Anglo Shipping.
DRAWDOWN:	In total on closing of purchase, not later than June 30, 1980.
COMMITMENT FEE:	½ of 1% p.a. on the commitment amount from the date hereof until the date drawn.
AMORTIZATION:	In 16 semiannual installments commencing 6 months from drawdown as per the following schedule:

Pd. 1–$	500,000	Pd. 9–$	1,250,000
2–	500,000	10–	1,250,000
3–	750,000	11–	1,250,000
4–	750,000	12–	1,250,000
5–	750,000	13–	1,500,000
6–	750,000	14–	1,500,000
7–	1,000,000	15–	1,500,000
8–	1,000,000	16–	4,500,000
		Total	$20,000,000

FINAL MATURITY:	June 30, 1988.
INTEREST RATE:	1.375% p.a. over London Interbank Offered Rate (LIBOR) for Borrower's choice of 1, 3, or 6 months interest periods, payable at the end of each interest period.

SECURITY:	A.	First preferred Liberian ship mortgage on the vessel;
	B.	Assignment of time charter and charter hire between Borrower and National Shipping Corp., with acknowledgement and consent of National;
	C.	Assignment of charter hire between National Shipping and International Oils Ltd., with acknowledgment and consent of International;
	D.	Unconditional guarantee of payment of Bulbous Holdings Ltd. (Liberia), of Bow & Stern Group, Inc. (U.S.) and of Capt. D. Rollins;
	E.	Assignment of all insurances on the vessel, including Hull & Machinery (including War Risk) and Protection & Indemnity (including Pollution Risk), placed with underwriters acceptable to the Bank, maintained in amounts never less than the market value of the vessel and in no event less than 115% of the loan outstanding at any time.
REPRESENTATIONS AND WARRANTIES:	1.	That Borrower and the corporate guarantors are duly organized corporations in good standing and fully qualified to perform under contracts to which they are parties.
	2.	That the loan agreement, guarantees, mortgages, and other documents are legal and binding obligations of the Borrower, the corporate guarantors, and the personal guarantor.
	3.	That there are no pending or threatened actions before a court which would affect the financial condition or operations of the Borrower, any of the corporate guarantors, or the personal guarantor.
	4.	That all copy documents produced to the bank are complete and have not been cancelled or terminated; that there are no other documents or verbal arrangements or agreements which would adversely affect the transaction evidenced

by such copy documents or the security of the lender.

5. That the vessel upon delivery is unencumbered (except for the Mortgage), seaworthy, properly registered, classified, and insured.

CONDITIONS PRECEDENT:

Prior to drawdown the Bank shall have received:

1. The mortgage on the vessel, executed and registered in accordance with the laws of Liberia.
2. A signed certificate by the Borrower and the guarantors stating that no event has occurred nor is continuing which would constitute an event of default.
3. Appropriate legal opinions from counsel to the Borrower as well as its own counsel.
4. Such documents, resolutions, and evidences in connection with the execution and delivery of this agreement as Bank requests.
5. Class certificate from Lloyd's, ABS, or Bureau Veritas on the vessel.

COVENANTS:

1. Usual protective covenants including provision of audited annual and certified semi-annual financial statements of the Borrower and Guarantors and any other information reasonably requested by the Bank.
2. No charter changes, extensions, or replacement without the prior written consent of the Bank.
3. The total loan outstanding shall at no time exceed 75% of the charter-free market value of the vessel, as valued by independent brokers. In case the 75% ratio is exceeded, Borrower shall pledge to the Bank additional satisfactory collateral, or prepay a portion of the loan.

EVENTS OF DEFAULT:

Shall include:

A. Any breach of any of the assignments, the mortgage or any other security documents by the Borrower or the guarantors,

B. Breach of any representations and warranties,
C. Breach of any of the covenants, and
D. Cross acceleration of the Borrower and the Guarantors.

ACCOUNT: The Borrower shall establish a U.S.-dollar account with the Bank into which all charterhire in respect of the vessel shall be deposited.

EXPENSES: All expenses for the preparation, execution of the appropriate documentation of the loan will be for the account of the Borrower.

TAXES: All payments of principal and interest by the Borrower shall be free and clear of any present and future taxes, duties including stamp duties, and reserve requirements (excluding taxes on corporate net income).

AVAILABILITY: The facility is subject to the execution of formal documentation which includes but is not limited to a loan agreement, guaranties, general assignment, assignment of charter party and charterhire as well as mortgage to reflect the contents of this proposal and which shall be prepared by our legal counsel and be acceptable to the Bank in its sole discretion.

GOVERNING LAW: Loan Agreement: The laws of England. Mortgage: The law of Liberia.

APPENDIX II

List of Required Documentation for Typical Ship Financing

Security Documents:
1. Loan Agreement.
2. Note (under U.S. or U.K. law).
3. First preferred ship mortgage (with English translation if required).
4. Assignment of charter party with Consents of guarantors/charterers.
5. Assignment of charterhire with Consents.
6. Certified copy of time/bareboat charter(s).

7. Letter from borrower and charterer(s) directing charterhire to Bank.
8. Insurances, noting Bank as co-assured and sole loss-payee.
9. Guarantees.

Vessel Documents:
10. Memorandum of Agreement.
11. Bill of sale.
12. Confirmation of Class Certificate.
13. Statement of delivery and acceptance (buyer-seller).
14. Certificate of delivery and acceptance (borrower-charterer).
15. Valuation Certificate.
16. Certificate of Ownership & Encumbrance.
17. Provisional Certificate of Registry.
18. Affidavit of Freedom from Liens.
19. Notice of Preferred ship mortgage.
20. Master's receipt (of Certificate of Registry, Mortgage & Notice of Mortgage).
21. Export license.

Corporate Documents:
22. Secretary's Certificate of Incorporation of borrower.
23. By-Laws of borrower.
24. Certificate of Board Resolution of borrower (& guarantor).
25. Certificate of Good Standing of borrower and guarantor (from country of registry).
26. Incumbency Certificate of borrower (& guarantor).
27. Certificate of Signatures of Officers of borrower (& guarantor). If guaranteed:
28. Certified copy of Articles of Association of guarantor.
29. Certified copy of Memorandum of Association of guarantor.

Legal Opinions:
30. Country of Registry.
31. Country of Prior Registry.
32. Country of Guarantor.
33. Bank's Counsel.
34. Borrower's Counsel.

GLOSSARY OF SHIPPING TERMS

A. **Ship Types**
   1. **Liners:** Vessels which ply their trade on a regular scheduled service between groups of established ports of call. Liner services are common carriers which offer cargo space or passen-

ger accommodations to all shippers or passengers requesting them.

Cargo Liners (freighters): Are generally designed to carry general cargo, operating on fixed routes and regular schedules. These vessels can be tailored to fit a particular geographical trade pattern by including, for instance, refrigerated capability, container handling facilities, or tanks for liquid cargoes.

2. **Trampers:** Differ from liner vessels in that they do not operate on a fixed sailing schedule. They generally carry *bulk cargoes* including coal, timber, ores, fertilizers, etc. These vessels tend to operate under *charter* arrangement (time or voyage).

3. **Specialized Vessels**
   a. **Tankers:** This tonnage comprises over 45 percent of the shipping tonnage in the world today. The vessels tend to be specialized, designed to carry heavy bulk liquids and capable of speedy loading and discharging.
   b. **OBO's (ore/bulk/oil carriers):** Are multipurpose bulk carriers designed for switching between the above bulk shipments. Higher operating costs hopefully are covered by economies of scale.
   c. **Bulk Carriers (dry bulk):** Designed for carriage of ore and grain; designed with wide hatches over large holds, where the holds have longitudinal bulk-heads for strength and for carrying ballast.
   d. **Gas and Chemical Carriers:** Designed for specific cargoes conveyed under exacting temperature and pressurized conditions. Very sophisticated technology and high operating costs.
   e. **Refrigerated Vessels (reefers):** A liner vessel configurated to carriage of meats, fruits, and other perishables.
   f. **Container Ships:** An increasing trend in cargo liner trades where this type of tonnage permits improved integration with other forms of transport thereby offering "door-to-door" service.

B. **Tonnage Measurements**
   1. **Deadweight—DWT:** The number of tons (1 ton = 2,240 lbs.) which a vessel can transport of cargo, stores, and bunker fuel. Deadweight tonnage is the difference between the volume of water a vessel displaces "light" and the volume it displaces when loaded to her loadline.
   2. **Cargo Tonnage:** A weight or measurement:
      a. U.S. ton (weight)   = 2,000 lbs. (short ton)
      b. English ton (weight)   = 2,240 lbs. (long ton)

  c. Measurement ton = 40 cubic feet
  d. Metric measurement ton= 1,000 kg.

3. **Displacement:** The weight of water a ship displaces.

4. **Gross Tons:** Refers to vessels, not to cargo. Determined by dividing the *contents in cubic feet* of a vessel's closed-in space by 100. Called GRT (gross registered tons). A vessel ton is 100 cubic feet. Used for dry docking and pilotage purposes.

5. **Net Tonnage:** The space available for passenger accommodations and cargo stowage. Defined as a vessel's gross tonnage less the total space occupied by crew, fuel, stores, machinery, and other non-earning spaces aboard the ship.

13
Security Underwriting and Syndicated Loans

DENIS NEWMAN
Managing Director
The First Boston Corporation

The international financial markets are comprised of various instruments of which bonds and syndicated loans are the most prominent. International bonds are those issued by a borrower who is of a nationality different than the country of the capital market in which the bonds are issued. Foreign bonds are those issued in a single national market on behalf of nonresident borrowers and are usually underwritten and sold by a group of financial institutions of the market country and are denominated in that country's currency. The other international bonds are those underwritten and sold in various national markets simultaneously, usually through international syndicates of banks. Both types of bonds are credit instruments which contain a promise to pay a specified amount of money at a fixed date and to pay interest periodically at stated intervals. They are usually issued in standard denominations, are negotiable, and either publicly issued (offered for sale to investors at large and usually quoted on a stock exchange) or privately placed (taken entirely by institutional investors and not listed).

Eurocurrency loans are granted by banks out of Eurocurrency funds on deposit with them or borrowed by them in the Eurocurrency market. Eurocurrency loans are typically granted by syndicates of banks formed ad hoc for each loan and are always granted in a currency which is not native to the country in which the bank office making the loan is located.

THE INTERNATIONAL BOND MARKET

Eurobonds, that is, international issues whose distribution is managed by banks and institutions located in European financial centers,

International Capital Markets by Type of Instrument (U.S. dollars in billions)

	1977	1978	1979	1980	1981†
Foreign bonds					
Industrial countries	$10,157	$13,057	$12,301	$ 9,127	$12,155
Developing countries	1,609	2,584	1,668	1,036	1,241
International organizations	4,748	5,706	6,959	5,995	5,878
Other*	96	196	77	51	133
Total foreign bonds	16,610	21,543	21,105	16,209	19,407
Eurobonds					
Industrial countries	13,167	9,832	14,214	17,631	22,844
Developing countries	2,617	3,183	1,885	1,425	2,297
International organizations	2,412	2,719	3,064	2,924	2,805
Other*	1,289	206	374	194	260
Total other international bonds**	19,485	15,940	19,537	22,174	28,206
Total international bonds					
Industrial countries	23,324	22,889	26,515	26,758	34,999
Developing countries	4,225	5,767	3,554	2,461	3,538
International organizations	7,160	8,425	10,023	8,924	8,683
Other*	1,386	401	550	245	393
Total international bonds	36,095	37,483	40,642	38,388	47,613

* Centrally planned economies and others.
** Primarily Eurobonds.
† Preliminary.
Source: World Bank, *Borrowing in International Capital Markets,* various issues.

constitute the largest single category of international bonds. The forerunners of today's Eurobond issues were bond issues by governments in a foreign capital market and sold entirely (at least theoretically) within such a market. In particular, the most immediate predecessors were foreign issues in the United States domestic capital market to which European governments turned after World War II. The access to the market was relatively simple as the Securities and Exchange Commission (SEC) was dispensing with most of its onerous disclosure requirements for such issuers and capital was available in sizable amounts. In addition, the U.S. dollar was a currency acceptable not only to the borrowers and the domestic investors but also to foreign investors, which was a significant factor for the future direction of international financing.

It was soon recognized that a great proportion of the foreign bonds which were issued in New York were flowing back through the European financial centers to individual and institutional investors scattered around the world. They were attracted by the quality of the paper, the currency in which the bond was denominated, and the fact that it was listed on a stock exchange in bearer form and that payments were made free of withholding taxes, which are normally imposed in the issuer's country of origin. New York was, in effect, providing a means through which high-quality borrowers of diverse nationality could issue debt securities with particular characteristics to widely dispersed "retail" investors.

In 1963, foreign issues in the New York market were singled out by the Kennedy administration as having as unfavorable impact on the capital account deficit in the United States, which the administration was seeking to redress. The result was the imposition of the Interest Equalization Tax (IET), which made it impractical for foreign borrowers to issue bonds in New York by making these bonds unattractive to domestic investors through yield-reducing fiscal penalties. Domestic investors would not buy the paper (unless induced to do so by the compensation of a higher coupon which was unacceptable to the issuer), and consequently, the New York Stock Exchange would not list the issues since one of its requirements for the listing was that at least 20 percent of an issue should be held by U.S. residents.

The natural response to such a move was to relocate the base of the financing operations to the European financial centers and tap the investment demand of international investors directly, offering the bonds to a wide group of financial institutions through which this demand was channelled—especially the Swiss banks, as a result of their extensive management of international investment portfolios. This development was made inevitable as no other single domestic capital market was capable of providing funds in the size, regularity, and with the ease of the procedure desired.

The first international issue, launched in Europe in 1963 after the introduction of the IET in the United States, which therefore can be considered to mark the opening of the public Eurobond market, was for a government institution—Autostrade, guaranteed by IRI, the Italian State holding company. Public-sector financing continued to constitute almost all public Eurobond issuing activity until 1965. In that year, the concern of the U.S. authorities to check capital outflows from the country, the same concern which had given birth to the IET, led to a voluntary program of restraint on the export of capital by U.S. industry to fund its international expansion which became mandatory in 1968. The resultant entry of the U.S. corporations into the public Eurobond market broadened access to this type of financing, and the U.S. corporations were soon joined by public European corporate borrowers.

Today, the public international bond market caters to a diverse range of borrowers from all parts of the world issuing debt securities in amounts of between $15 million and $400 million at one time and with maturities ranging up to 15 years. The volume of new issues of securities in the international bond market is a measure of the already considerable and growing importance of international investors. Approximately $25.1 billion equivalent of new internationally syndicated international bond issues was completed in 1981 alone, which represented an increase of approximately 44 percent over the volume of approximately $17.4 billion equivalent in 1980.

Size. The aggregate annual volume of international bond issues, starting with an $800 million equivalent in 1963, had risen to $7.0 billion by 1975 and was approximately $49.7 billion equivalent in 1982. U.S. issuers accounted for a record $3.6 billion equivalent principal amount of international bond issues in 1980, nearly 21 percent of the total bonds issued by U.S. borrowers in 1980. As the Eurobond gained credence as a secure investment medium (defaulted issues of roughly $400 million through November 1982 representing a tiny fraction of the total volume issued) and with a sufficient degree of liquidity by an increasingly sophisticated over-the-counter secondary market, a number of investors have entrusted a significant proportion of their surplus liquidity to this market. A cross-section of long-term buyers of bonds from a new issue today might include a private individual whose money is handled on a discretionary basis by a bank, the pension fund of an international company, an insurance company with long-term foreign currency liabilities, and a central bank. An important aspect of this market is the relatively high proportion of bonds placed with individual investors and, conversely, the relatively low institutional participation compared with the U.S. domestic capital market.

There has been not only remarkable growth in the aggregate annual volume of new issues since the inception of the Eurobond market, but also an equally dramatic increase in the size of individual financings.

International Bond Issues by Type of Borrower (U.S. dollars in millions)

Type of Borrower	1977	1978	1979	1980	1981	1982
Central and provincial governments	$2,781.42	$ 2,966.71	$ 1,950.26	$ 2,060.30	$ 2,113.45	$ 4,983.24
Government agencies	1,827.02	1,127.64	810.97	2,161.54	925.04	40.78
Municipalities	156.94	109.54	157.76	207.51	162.11	347.26
International and European agencies	1,514.09	1,417.20	1,575.19	2,254.90	2,511.65	1,492.23
Industrial and financial companies:						
Straight debt	8,578.12	5,171.64	8,156.02	7,874.67	15,462.79	39,364.09
Straight debt with warrants*	125.00	—	380.00	—	1,000.00	2,265.65
Convertibles	792.17	1,146.38	1,092.45	2,793.42	2,569.79	1,153.09
European depositary receipt	—	—	—	—	336.19	46.95
Totals	15,774.76	11,939.11	14.122.65	17,352.34	25,081.02	49,693.29

* Equity linked.
Source: Credit Suisse First Boston Limited.

As witness to the increased capacity of the Eurobond market, in the first eight days of 1981 alone over $1 billion aggregate principal amount of new issues were floated in the market. Whereas even at the beginning of the present decade the average size for a Eurobond issue was in the $20–30 million range, during the past couple of years, financings of $100 million and over have been common occurrences in the market, which has absorbed, for example, a $350 million financing for the Commonwealth of Australia, $500 million for Royal Dutch Shell, $300 million for Citicorp, and $300 million and $500 million tranches, sold two weeks apart, for the European Economic Community and $500 million for the World Bank. In early 1982, the market further demonstrated its ability to absorb not only large issues, but large issues in quick succession.

Currency. The range of currencies in which international issues are denominated is wide, thereby providing at any given time a vehicle reconciling the requirements of borrowers and investors. The U.S. dollar has been joined by the deutsche mark and other leading European currencies (excluding the Swiss franc because Swiss authorities forbid the use of their franc for Eurobond issues, although they allow foreign borrowers to float Swiss franc issues in their domestic capital market), the Canadian dollar, Middle Eastern currencies (notably the Kuwaiti dinar), and various currency-linked composite units (the most widely recognized being the European Unit of Account and the International Monetary Fund's Special Drawing Rights and increasingly in European Currency Units).

Nevertheless, the U.S. dollar remains the single most important currency in this market due to the importance of the U.S. economy in world trade and the recent balance-of-payments deficit which has created a considerable U.S.-dollar liquidity outside the United States. It is also due to the inherent stability of the U.S. economy coupled with the relatively low degree of manipulation of the currency by domestic monetary authorities that the U.S. dollar is a favored investment medium for international investors.

As a result, the U.S.-dollar markets are broadest in terms of the range of investors participating in them and thus in terms of the amount of funds available to potential borrowers.

Dollar deposits represent the most important sector of the Eurocurrency market, and an active secondary market in Eurodollar bonds can be maintained since market-makers can easily obtain short-term funds to refinance their positions in bonds. This consideration is of importance to investors concerned about the liquidity of their portfolios and to borrowers whose credit standing is in part a function of the secondary market performance of their paper.

The size and timing of bond issues in the Eurodollar sector are subject only to market forces, while issues in other sectors which make a meaningful contribution to overall activity in the Eurobond market, such as the Euro-deutsche mark sector, are additionally subject to close control by the monetary authorities of the denominating currency's country of origin. For example, in the case of the deutsche mark, issues must be submitted for the approval of the Capital Markets Sub-Committee set up by the Bundesbank. This considerably reduces the prospective borrower's flexibility on the timing and size of issues denominated in Eurocurrencies other than the dollar.

Total International Bond Issues and Placements by Currency of Denomination by All Countries (U.S. dollars in millions)

Currency	1976	1977	1978	1979	1980	1981	1982
Deutsche mark	2,821	5,215	6,531	5,881	4,254	1,055	4,272
French franc	62	—	103	374	1,002	513	—
Japanese yen	—	111	79	184	301	535	549
Netherlands guilder	467	363	384	308	788	453	552
U.S. dollar	9,999	12,336	7,693	11,095	13,664	23,024	40,249
Composite currency units	103	34	235	413	99	818	1,862
Canadian dollar	1,450	654	—	468	270	649	1,083
Kuwaiti dinar	304	130	481	384	26	26	81
British sterling	—	221	287	291	1,089	826	981
Saudi Arabian riyal	—	103	95	—	—	—	—
Austrian schilling	—	—	—	—	235	—	—
Norwegian krone	—	—	—	—	100	78	32
Other currencies	162	317	52	139	346	229	31
Totals	15,368	19,484	15,940	19,537	22,174	28,206	49,692

Source: World Bank, *Borrowing in International Capital Markets*, various issues.

Maturity. The Eurobond market was, in its early years, a relatively long-term market, with issuing activity concentrated in the 10- to 15-year maturity range; medium-term financings, with maturities of 10 years and under, accounted in 1969, for instance, for only 14 percent of all new issues. In 1973–74, however, with the impact of inflation and high short-term interest rates, the focus was suddenly shifted to

Straight Debt International Bond Issues by Maturity Excluding Straight Debt Issues with Warrants and Convertible Issues (U.S. dollars in millions)

Maturity (years)	1976	1977	1978	1979	1980	1981	1982
0– 5	3,043.22	3,015.01	2,624.79	2,871.21	3,585.01	6,105.38	8,332.81
6–10	7,249.04	8,259.21	5,170.92	7,017.10	9,484.30	13,278.61	30,066.50
11–15	1,012.68	3,299.51	2,872.02	2,686.89	1,489.61	1,669.04	7,310.59
16–20	20.71	283.86	125.00	75.00	—	40.00	200.00
21–30						82.01	—
Totals	11,325.65	14,857.59	10,792.73	12,650.20	14,558.92	21,175.04	45,909.90

Source: Credit Suisse First Boston Limited.

the shorter end of the conventional maturity range, and in 1974 medium-term bonds represented 69 percent of new issue activity. Current concern in the international investment community over the renewed high levels of inflation has accounted for a definite concentration of demand in medium-term paper, although long-term issues by the best-rated borrowers are also salable to investors from time to time. The U.S. domestic market is also experiencing a trend toward somewhat shorter maturities.

Type of Instrument. While fixed-rate, medium- to long-term straight debt offerings constitute the most considerable proportion of issuing activity, more complex instruments have either been borrowed from domestic capital markets and adapted for use in the international market, or invented in this latter market—and have been readily absorbed by investors. Paper can be offered today in the Euromarket covering the whole maturity spectrum, from short-term securities (London Dollar Certificates of Deposit for banks with branches in London: one month to five years; and Euro-commercial paper for corporations: 90 to 270 days—although neither is publicly distributed) to medium- and long-term securities, with retractable or extendable maturities with equity features (convertible bonds, bonds with warrants attached—usually with maturities of between 5 and 20 years) and so on. In addition to the many fixed rate issues, beginning in 1970 there have been a large number of issues of Floating Rate Notes (FRN's). FRN's are securities on which the quarterly or semi-annual interest rate is linked to a short term rate such as the London Interbank Rate for three or six month dollar deposits. In all other respects, FRN's are structured and distributed like fixed rate issues. Issuers of FRN's range from corporations and banks to governments and agencies, and maturities range from medium to long term.

Marketplace. There is no single marketplace. Various centers, of which London, Amsterdam, Brussels, Dusseldorf, Frankfurt, Luxembourg, New York, Paris, Zurich/Geneva, Singapore, Hong Kong, Kuwait, and Abu Dhabi are the most important, provide the technical facilities and channel the funds. The degree to which any given center provides technical services or funds varies with each issue and depends on such factors as the country of origin and quality of the borrower, the currency of denomination of the issue, the stock exchange (if any) on which the issue is to be listed, and the location of the managers, in particular the lead manager, of the syndicate of financial institutions through which the bonds are sold. The market is really a massive telephone, and perhaps more important, the telex network connects banks and other financial institutions throughout Europe, the Middle East, the Far East, the United States, and Canada.

Listing. With the exception of Euro-Dutch guilder issues, virtually all Eurobond and FRN issues are listed on one or more stock exchanges, usually London or Luxembourg (except Euro-deutsche mark issues, which are listed on one or more German stock exchanges). Despite the fact that little trading of an issue takes place on the stock exchange on which it is listed, listing is undertaken for a number of reasons. First, some institutional investors (most often pension funds and insurance companies) are not permitted to buy, or are restricted on the amounts they may buy, of unlisted issues. Also, a stock exchange listing guarantees investors that certain minimum reporting and financial standards will be met by the borrower throughout the life of the issue (e.g., satisfactory auditing of its accounts, making available its annual reports and other information).

Form. Eurobonds are usually in denominations of $1,000 or equivalent and are almost without exception in bearer form (unlike the U.S. domestic market, in which corporate bonds are issued predominantly in registered or nominative form). Retail Eurobond investors have shown their strong preference for bearer paper by ignoring issues of registered bonds, which have consequently been very few in number and have been taken up mainly by banks.

In the case of a U.S. borrower, the bonds are represented initially by a single temporary global bond without interest coupons. The borrower exchanges the temporary global bond for definitive bonds in the form described above, with interest coupons attached, not earlier than 90 days after the completion of the distribution of the bonds. Such exchange is made only upon certification that the beneficial owners of such bonds are not nationals nor residents of the United States.

Payments. Payments on bonds are made through banks (Paying Agents) located in the financial centers of Europe and the country of the currency in which the bonds are denominated. Payments are invariably made free of withholding taxes imposed at source in the issuer's country of origin (though this exemption is not valid for bondholders who are nationals of, or resident in, the issuer's country), issuers being liable either to bear the burden of any such withholding taxes that may be imposed or to redeem the issue.

Distribution. The placing of issues is spread over a wide number of countries, though the extent of the distribution will naturally vary from issue to issue, depending on factors such as the currency of denomination, the credit of the borrower, and whether the issue is public or private.

Secondary Market. As in the U.S. market, secondary trading activity in issues generally does not take place on the stock exchange on which the issues are listed but in an international over-the-counter market, consisting of financial institutions around the world linked by telephone and telex. The foundations of the secondary bond market are the so-called market makers—dealers who actively buy and sell bonds as principals rather than as agents or brokers.

International Bond Issues by Nationality of Borrower or Guarantor
(U.S. dollars in millions)

Nationality	1976	1977	1978	1979	1980	1981	1982
United States	265.00	1,039.99	1,081.68	2,637.02	3,698.09	5,751.48	17,838.38
International and European Agencies	1,695.22	1,537.87	1,722.16	1,413.53	2,466.66	2,788.76	4,070.15
United Kingdom	657.24	2,430.83*	748.15	835.22	1,482.66	1,100.55	568.23
France	1,253.20	975.84	622.23	1,346.16	1,357.16	1,806.66	4,959.16
Canada	2,772.34	1,798.23	774.87	1,351.99	1,325.67	4,970.86	6,365.95
Japan	940.31	1,106.28	1,511.88	1,238.45	1,268.20	2,604.03	2,207.10
Sweden	512.49	842.01	239.36	459.43	987.90	903.60	1,327.22
Austria	271.62	520.75	252.35	213.78	703.38	407.44	783.17
Netherlands	239.30	254.14*	99.98	322.57	698.60	405.12	2,180.26
Norway	825.97	1,042.85	1,043.43	827.10	440.92	159.51	403.23
Australia	602.16	576.34	476.94	130.00	390.14	431.88	628.25
Denmark	326.08	175.98	294.64	201.31	330.03	191.18	521.20
Italy	85.00	190.00	50.00	249.76	328.98	595.82	1,527.87
Mexico	150.02	627.00	207.08	225.00	300.70	999.48	1,021.91
Switzerland	300.01	170.00	108.00	314.90	241.16	—	491.45
Belgium	—	—	—	—	200.00	227.56	—
South Africa	25.00	—	—	—	170.98	—	89.39
Brazil	183.23	483.71	501.94	330.05	169.66	50.00	—
Finland	135.02	213.52	293.54	358.50	145.35	350.16	1,063.05
New Zealand	279.52	139.14	423.47	164.52	139.55	307.81	780.97
Spain	166.46	172.78	149.61	101.53	107.61	142.82	225.79
Venezuela	—	100.00	228.32	20.00	78.52	45.30	—
Chile	—	—	—	—	57.53	30.00	—
Costa Rica	—	—	20.00	—	50.00	—	—
Israel	—	30.00	110.00	125.00	50.00	50.00	170.00
Luxembourg	57.45	207.20	—	143.20	47.89	224.65	—
Colombia	—	—	—	—	30.00	—	—
India	—	—	—	—	30.00	30.00	30.00
Portugal	—	50.00	—	—	30.00	—	—
Taiwan	—	—	—	—	25.00	—	—
Germany	80.00	245.28	120.00	405.64	—	46.99	1,138.39
Argentina	—	43.04	182.89	262.99	—	95.00	—
Ireland	—	30.00	—	110.00	—	169.36	304.14
Philippines	—	43.43	48.69	100.00	—	—	30.00
Algeria	—	98.59	226.82	55.00	—	—	—
Thailand	—	—	—	55.00	—	—	—
Yugoslavia	—	80.00	80.00	50.00	—	—	—
Singapore	129.13	42.22	25.00	45.00	—	75.00	75.00
Malaysia	—	43.17	—	30.00	—	—	580.00
Panama	—	25.00	102.36	—	—	30.00	—
Indonesia	—	—	51.61	—	—	—	200.00
Trinidad & Tobago	—	—	37.11	—	—	—	—
Poland	30.00	35.00	30.00	—	—	—	—
El Salvador	—	—	25.00	—	—	—	—
Egypt	—	—	25.00	—	—	—	30.00
Kuwait	—	—	25.00	—	—	—	—
Hong Kong	—	128.05	—	—	—	30.00	—
Iran	30.00	80.92	—	—	—	—	—
South Korea	25.00	70.10	—	—	—	60.00	—
Hungary	—	44.57	—	—	—	—	—
Iceland	33.73	40.93	—	—	—	—	83.03
New Guinea	—	25.00	—	—	—	—	—
Bolivia	—	15.00	—	—	—	—	—
Totals	12,070.50	15,774.76	11,939.11	14,122.65	17,352.34	25,081.02	49,693.29

* U.S. $882.71 million equivalent was jointly guaranteed by United Kingdom and Netherlands entities, but has been included in this table under United Kingdom only.

Source: Credit Suisse First Boston Limited.

Lead-Managers and Co-Managers of Internationally Syndicated Eurobond Issues in 1982 (U.S. dollars in millions)

	U.S. $	Can $	DM	Dfl	Other	Total	Number of Issues Lead/Co-Managed	Number of Issues Lead/Co-Lead Managed
Overall Totals								
U.S. dollars in millions	40,249.05	1,083.21	4,272.35	552.35	3,455.30	49,612.26		
Number of issues	325	33	94	12	52	516	516	516
1. Credit Suisse First Boston Limited	27,702.30	323.44	748.69	464.13	1,028.06	30,266.62	246	91
2. Deutsche Bank AG	25,151.80	94.95	2,979.77	414.75	1,114.24	29,755.51	252	70
3. Swiss Bank Corporation Intl.	22,954.55	413.39	1,046.42	459.99	741.84	25,616.19	244	19
4. Union Bank of Switzerland Ltd.	21,805.00	373.68	651.61	407.99	115.30	23,353.58	198	16
5. Morgan Stanley Intl.	21,109.00	74.57	296.08	204.22	329.87	22,013.74	158	59
6. S. G. Warburg & Co. Ltd.	17,378.00	308.34	747.79	93.42	1,914.09	20,441.64	179	30
7. Merrill Lynch Int. & Co.	18,266.75	609.45	169.29	—	1,282.27	20,327.76	172	30
8. Salomon Brothers International	18,848.55	217.34	121.78	—	451.40	19,639.07	148	35
9. Banque Nationale de Paris	15,505.00	115.75	183.49	—	1,311.51	17,115.75	146	13
10. Algemene Bank Nederland N.V.	12,910.00	765.49	275.41	513.61	1,501.58	15,966.09	149	10
11. Societe Generale de Banque S.A.	13,405.00	969.45	207.68	108.64	1,239.78	15,930.55	155	8
12. Morgan Guaranty Ltd.	13,664.55	—	154.04	111.62	586.18	14,516.39	128	35
13. Banque de Paris et des Pays-Bas	11,524.00	91.96	126.34	—	1,609.12	13,351.42	101	8
14. Banque Bruxelles-Lambert S.A.	10,415.00	945.52	258.92	60.40	1,253.91	12,933.75	129	6
15. Goldman, Sachs International Corp.	11,980.00	40.77	192.22	—	168.46	12,381.45	95	24
16. Orion Royal Bank	10,923.55	400.84	299.61	242.96	101.83	11,968.79	113	11
17. Credit Lyonnais	9,114.55	431.97	570.64	—	1,470.89	11,588.05	129	7
18. Amsterdam-Rotterdam Bank N.V.	9,225.00	755.62	223.55	513.61	688.61	11,406.39	109	9
19. Manufacturers Hanover Limited	9,595.00	—	241.43	38.74	131.72	10,006.89	79	7
20. Nomura International Ltd.	7,775.00	204.44	161.00	200.88	444.41	8,785.73	80	12

Source: Credit Suisse First Boston Limited.

All Notes and Bonds (including floating rate notes, but excluding New York Issues, January–December 1982)*

Rank	Managing Bank	Number of Loans	Total ($ millions)	Percent
1.	Credit Suisse First Boston Ltd.	92	12,559.70	18.79
2.	Deutsche Bank AG	70	8,249.71	12.34
3.	Morgan Stanley International	59	5,997.98	8.97
4.	Salomon Brothers International Ltd.	40	4,388.45	6.57
5.	Morgan Guaranty Ltd.	40	4,316.77	6.46
6.	Merrill Lynch International & Co.	36	3,427.32	5.13
7.	Swiss Bank Corp. International Ltd.	22	2,533.89	3.79
8.	Goldman Sachs International Corp.	27	2,324.42	3.48
9.	Warburg S.G. & Co. Ltd.	34	2,258.87	3.38
10.	UBS (Securities) Ltd.	15	1,594.94	2.39
11.	Credit Lyonnais	13	1,546.60	2.31
12.	Societe Generale	25	1,534.79	2.30
13.	Banque Nationale de Paris	14	1,369.77	2.05
14.	Commerzbank AG	20	1,303.61	1.95
15.	Citicorp International Bank Ltd.	11	1,200.00	1.80
16.	Orion Royal Bank	16	1,142.87	1.71
17.	Dresdner Bank AG	19	933.80	1.40
18.	Bank of Tokyo International Ltd.	8	925.00	1.38
19.	Banque Paribas	11	905.72	1.36
20.	Hambros Bank Ltd.	10	856.85	1.28
21.	Manufacturers Hanover Ltd.	8	815.00	1.22
22.	Wood Gundy	14	811.39	1.21
23.	Nomura International Ltd.	17	791.13	1.18
24.	Amsterdam Rotterdam Bank NV	19	785.33	1.17
25.	Algemene Bank Nederland NV	19	775.31	1.16
26.	Samuel Montagu & Co. Ltd.	6	725.00	1.08
27.	Daiwa Europe Ltd.	14	719.45	1.08
28.	Credit Commercial de France	8	717.85	1.07
29.	European Banking Co. Ltd.	8	680.65	1.02
30.	Societe Generale de Banque SA	12	646.16	0.97
	Total all issues	707	66,838.33	100.00

* Preliminary.
   Note: Sole lead managers receive *full* amount of the issue, joint lead managers receive *equal* amounts.
   Source: *Euromoney,* London, England, February 1982.

Legal Covenants.   Eurobonds are rarely secured by specific assets of the issuer, since the fact that the bonds are in bearer form and widely dispersed would make such security difficult to administer. Instead, Eurobonds typically carry a pari passu provision (according to which the securities rank equally among themselves as well as at least equally with all other unsecured obligations of the borrower) and a "negative pledge" covenant, the borrower thereby undertaking that it will not secure present or future indebtedness without granting the same security, equally and in the matter of rate, to that debt to which the negative pledge applies. These provisions together ensure that the bonds enjoy and will continue to enjoy, at least equal status with the issuer's other unsecured indebtedness and that the bonds are not, in effect, subsequently downgraded in terms of security. Additional standard terms and conditions relating to an issue of Eurobonds include withholding tax indemnification provisions for events of default (including a cross-default provision), a force majeure clause, and other covenants generally contained in the issuer's domestic debt, as appropriate.

FOREIGN BOND MARKETS

Foreign bonds are international bonds issued in a single national market. Such issues are usually underwritten and sold by a group of banks of the market country and are denominated in that country's currency. The most important foreign bond markets are in the United States (Yankee bonds) and Switzerland and the foreign bond markets in Japan (Samurai bonds), Great Britain (Bulldog bonds) and other overseas countries are of a lesser importance.

The Foreign Dollar (Yankee) Bond Market

The public debt market in the United States is the largest and most liquid capital market in the world and offers a wide variety of financing alternatives to the international borrower. This is largely possible because of the important role played by the institutional investor, such as commercial bank trust departments, life and health insurance companies, fire and casualty insurance companies, public and private pension funds, investment advisors, and mutual funds, all of which control billions of dollars of investable assets and together comprise by far

Foreign Bond Issues (U.S. dollars in millions)

	1977	1978	1979	1980	1981
Austria	—	29	100	81	—
Belgium	43	148	161	—	52
France	62	231	365	94	89
Germany, Federal Republic of*	1,511	1,677	2,296	3,496	1,604
Japan*	1,394	4,687	2,985	1,731	2,562
Luxembourg	80	206	218	159	123
Netherlands	182	352	466	325	539
Saudi Arabia	645	246	86	21	—
United Kingdom	—	56	—	178	803
Switzerland*	4,959	7,553	9,637	7,488	8,120
United States*	7,688	6,359	4,602	2,637	4,959
Other countries	66	—	189	—	557
Total	16,630	21,544	21,105	16,209	19,408

* Comprised of both public offerings and private placements, various issues.
Source: World Bank.

the largest segment of investable funds in the United States. As a result of the active participation of these institutions, the U.S. public debt market provides larger amounts of fixed-rate capital for longer maturity at more competitive rates and with less volatility of supply than any other capital market.

The foreign sector of the U.S. domestic capital market has been a traditional source of capital for foreign borrowers seeking intermediate- and long-term dollar-denominated debt.

The Yankee bond market has recently declined in importance relative to the U.S. public debt market and the international bond market. Issuing activity was relatively high through 1979 but declined substantially in 1980 and 1981. This decline is attributable partly to rates that in many circumstances were not competitive to those available in other capital markets and partly to regulatory requirements (which have since been somewhat modified to alleviate the situation) that impeded foreign issuers from responding to attractive rates as quickly as domestic borrowers.

The traditional issuers in the Yankee bond market are foreign governments, international institutions, government-owned or guaranteed entities, municipalities, and, to a much lesser degree, corporations. Most of the market's expansion over the past years has come from return borrowers whose names are already well established in the market. The private-sector borrower considers the market less inviting due to the necessary application for a rating and compliance with the disclosure requirements of the Securities and Exchange Commission.

The main reason for obtaining ratings by Moody's and Standard & Poor's is to broaden the distribution and the appeal of the issued securities. Public ratings are a large factor in the investment-decision process of the U.S. institutions. Many of them lack the staff to undertake independent credit analysis and are legally restricted in the purchase of nonrated securities. Except for Mexico and Brazil, which elected to come to the market without a rating, and for Finland, which has a split rating, all of the issues of the sovereign governments, government agencies, or international institutions have carried triple-A ratings. Corporate issuers, of which only a very limited number have come to the market, have been ranked lower, as well as several Canadian entities which, however, are considered much more American than foreign.

In contrast to the Eurobond market, Yankee issuers are subject to the filing requirements under the Securities Act of 1933 and the Securities Exchange Act of 1934. In general, the Securities Act provides that a registration statement which contains a prospectus is filed with the SEC in connection with every public offering in the United States. Under the Act, an initial filing, containing a preliminary prospectus, is made with the SEC, and offers of the securities can thereafter be made by the prospective underwriters orally or by the preliminary prospectus. No actual sales of the securities can be made, however, until the registration statement becomes effective. A final prospectus will be part of the registration statement when it becomes effective, and a copy of this final prospectus must be delivered to each purchaser.

The registration statement is essentially a disclosure document, and the SEC has no power to approve or disapprove of the securities themselves. However, the SEC undertakes a review of the registration statement after its initial filing and then issues comments upon the disclosures made. In general, the comments of the SEC must be complied with because of the power the SEC has over the timing of effectiveness. The period between initial filing and the declaration of effectiveness should be expected to be 30 days for a first-time foreign issuer. The applicable registration statement form for a first-time issuer would be Form S-1. Periodic reporting requirements under the Securities Exchange Act will be triggered both by the filing of a registered statement under the Securities Act and by a listing on the New York Stock Exchange. These requirements will be fulfilled by the filing of an annual report on Form 20-F and the filing from time to time of reports on Form 6-K. The SEC is currently holding public hearings with respect to the revision of the various forms for foreign issuers, and it appears that some of the changes may be substantial.

Besides the rating, filing, and reporting requirements and the substantial costs associated with them for a first-time issuer, there are considerable advantages associated through a financing in this market.

The market has developed the depth and the capacity to absorb large and frequent issues. Offerings of $100 million are common, although substantially larger offerings have been made by the World Bank ($500 million) and the United Kingdom ($350 million). The U.S. market represents for many governments and international institutions an alternative pool of funds for their tremendous financing needs which cannot be satisfied by other foreign bond markets and the Eurobond market.

The maturities in the Yankee bond market are particularly suited to long-term fixed funding requirements and can reach 30 years, unknown in any other capital market in the world.

Interest rates are quite competitive although foreign borrowers will have to pay a premium over a similarly rated domestic borrower. The spread between Yankee bonds yields and U.S. Treasury bonds has become progressively narrower.

Underwriting commissions are substantially lower and range from 0.5 percent to 1.5 percent as compared to 1⅞ percent to 2.5 percent for most Eurobonds and up to 3.5 percent for foreign Swiss franc bonds. Interest, however, is paid semiannually, while it is standard practice in Europe to pay interest on an annual basis.

The Yankee bond market is the most difficult of all markets in which to gain acceptance, and the resulting prestige of an issue will be conferred in all markets which will reinforce the borrower's credit standing and will reduce his borrowing costs in these markets.

SYNDICATED EUROCURRENCY CREDITS

Over the past decade, the syndicated Eurocurrency bank loan has developed into one of the most important instruments for international lending. The market, which started in the late 1960s, involves the granting of credits by syndicates of banks out of Eurocurrency funds. These funds are either on deposit with the lending banks or are borrowed by them in the Eurocurrency market, which has developed as an offshore market outside the United States. The lending will be arranged in the form of loans, lines of credit, or other forms of medium- and long-term credits. The bank syndicates making the credits are not permanent groupings but are formed in each case by banks willing to take participations of varying size in a particular credit.

There are several features that distinguish the Eurocredit market from the international bond market. Eurocredit lending is the wholesale sector of the international capital market, as banks alone provide the finance, in contrast to the bond markets where most capital is supplied by individual investors and certain institutions. The loans are generally priced at a spread over the interbank interest rate in the Euromarkets and are adjusted every three or six months as market rates vary, unlike the international bonds which consist mostly of fixed-rate capital. Amounts of individual loans can vary enormously. The most recent months have shown that even sizes of up to $6 billion can be arranged within several days without indigestion in the market. While at its inception the market was highly quality conscious and only prime sovereign credits, agencies, and corporations were able to raise funds, the syndicated credit market has now become an important pillar in the recycling process where surpluses from oil-exporting countries are channeled to oil-importing countries to finance their deficits.

Market Development. Since its inception, the market has grown rapidly to $70.3 billion in 1980. This increase does not merely represent new incremental borrowings, since the market has now a substantial impetus from maturing loans which have to be refinanced. Syndicated loans now provide approximately 50 percent of the medium- and long-term borrowings in international capital markets. More important, however, is their role in financing lesser-developed countries and centrally planned economies for which they have provided more than

Eurocurrency Bank Credits (dollars in millions)

	1979	1980	1st Half 1981
Industrialized Countries	19.0	29.9	12.8
Nonoil exporting LDCs	50.0	39.3	20.2
Oil-exporting countries	0.7	0.4	0.2
Others	0.5	0.7	0.1
Total	70.2	70.3	33.3

Source: World Bank, *Borrowing in International Capital Markets*, various issues.

85 and 95 percent of medium- and long-term funds during the 70s, respectively.

As the market has matured, it has become much less concentrated. While in 1970 the top 10 borrowers accounted for 84 percent of total Eurocredits, their share had dropped to approximately 55 percent in 1980.

Instruments. There are two principal types of syndicated Euro-credits—the term loan and the revolving-credit facility. Under the term loan, which is the more common form of loan, funds can be drawn down by the borrower within a specified period of time after signature of the loan agreement and repaid according to an amortization table, which can start at any time after drawdown.

Another form, which is frequently used by borrowers for funding balance-of-payments deficits, is the revolving-credit facility. The banks will commit themselves to make funds available to the borrower up to a certain date until which the borrower is free to draw down, repay, and redraw the funds by giving appropriate notice. The commitment by the banks is subject to amortization, just as in a term loan. The borrower must pay a fee on undrawn commitments to the banks on such facilities.

A combination of term loan and revolving credit is also possible, under which the banks' commitments expire after a given period, and any part of the commitment drawn down on the date of expiration is converted into a term loan at that time; any undrawn commitment is cancelled.

Syndication. There is generally a multi-tier system of banks involved in the syndication of a Eurocredit which can extend to over five levels depending on the size of the transaction. The principal syndicate members are the lead managing banks, the managing banks, and the participating banks. Most loans are led by one or two banks that negotiate to obtain a mandate from the borrower to raise funds. Often a borrower announces a competitive bidding procedure through which the lead banker will be determined. After the preliminary stage of negotiation with the borrower, the lead bank will assemble a management group to underwrite the loan. Once this is in place, a placement memorandum is prepared by the lead bank outlining the terms of the loan, a description of the borrower, the latest financial statements of the borrower or the economy if the borrower is a government, and any other material which may be useful to the banks for their evaluation. In addition, the lead manager assists in the preparation of the loan documents and in the signature of the loan agreement by the borrower and all participating banks. All banks in the syndicate sign a common loan agreement with the borrower, but the contractual relationship is between the borrower and each bank individually. Each lending bank is therefore responsible for its own credit assessment of the borrower, its own decision to participate in the loan, its own surveillance of the borrower, and its own risk.

Most Eurocredits are unsecured, and special attention is therefore attached to the covenants and default terms. The covenants usually stipulate the maintenance of certain financial ratios as well as that no liens on property or revenues will be given to new creditors without being offered to existing creditors. The cross-default clause stipulates that a default on any loan will be a default under the loan agreement of the syndicated Euroloan.

After the loan is arranged, one of the banks serves as agent assuming many of the responsibilities of a fiscal agent in a Eurobond issue. The agent controls payments of interest and principal and handles other relations between the borrower and the participating banks over the life of the loan.

The timetable to syndicate a loan takes anywhere from several days for repeat high-quality borrowers to several months for a first-time issuer with a complex credit situation.

Pricing. Interest on syndicated loans is computed by adding a spread to the London Interbank Offered Rate (LIBOR), which is the rate at which banks lend funds to other banks in the Euromarket. The spread is negotiated by the borrower before the loan is granted and can either remain constant over the life of the loan or may change after a certain number of years to a predetermined level. The margin is usually between ¼ to 1 percent, depending on the market's assessment of the creditworthiness of the borrower, the maturity of the loan, and the prevailing market conditions. While LIBOR is changing continuously, the rate on any loan is readjusted only every three months or six months. The borrower is usually given the choice between the two readjustment periods. The new base rate is calculated two days prior to the rollover date as the average of the offer rates of several reference banks which are specified in the loan agreement.

In addition to the interest costs on a syndicated Euroloan, there are also commitment fees, front-end fees, and occasionally an annual agent's fee. Commitment fees are charged as a percentage of the un-drawn portion of the credit and are typically ½ percent annually; front-end management fees are one-time charges imposed when the loan is signed and range between ½ to 1 percent of the loan.

Payments have to be made net of withholding taxes, and usually a reserve requirement clause is included which allows for an adjustment if the cost of funds increases because of an imposition of reserve re-quirements. There is generally no prepayment penalty on syndicated Euroloans.

Implications.   There are several reasons why syndicated loans have emerged as one of the prime lending vehicles in the international capital markets. From a borrower's viewpoint, the syndication of the loan allows for the arrangement of a large amount which no single lender could supply or which could be arranged through a bond offer-ing. This is of utmost importance, as the financing needs imposed by balance-of-payments deficits or large development projects combined with a lack of other financing alternatives create the demand of billion-dollar loans. While certain industrial-country borrowers' only financing alternative is very often the syndicated Euroloan market, very often they are used by borrowers new to the international market as an introduction to major institutions and as a stepping stone to other forms of borrowing if the quality of the borrower thus allows. In addi-tion, the instrument gives borrowers the flexibility to select the length of the rollover periods, to choose different currencies at such periods, and to prepay or cancel the agreements after a short notice period without penalty.

From the lenders' viewpoint, the syndication procedure allows them to share large credits with other banks, leaving them room to partici-pate in many financings and to diversify their risks. Moreover it allows different-sized banks to participate in the market. A syndicated Euro-loan is underwritten by a small group of banks that often resell portions of their loan commitments to other banks. The main attraction, how-ever, is the profitability as costs are relatively low in comparison to the onlending rates and a heavy volume often guaranteed. The spread over LIBOR paid by the borrower understates the banks' actual return on the loan as the offered rate is generally ⅛ to ¼ percent above the rate at which banks purchase funds from large depositors (LIBID).[1]

The various markets described above have emerged during the last several decades. While the numbers are impressive and large in size, they cannot be compared to the U.S. bond market, and they tend to be at times occasional and fragmented. However, with careful planning and organization, these issues can be brought to market from time to time, usually within the timing needs of borrowers.

---

[1] London Interbank Bid Rate.

SUMMARY

As can be noted from the material in this chapter, considerable progress has been made in the development internationally of instruments and mechanisms which work well for longer-term funds. Although these markets are not as broad and constant as localized or shorter-term markets, they can be reached with careful planning and placement for each issue.

14
Foreign Currency Loans and Eurocurrency Markets

HORST DUSEBERG
Executive Vice President
European American Bank

INTRODUCTION

The origins of the Euromarket occurred during the 1950s when the Cold War with the United States prompted the Russians to place dollar deposits with banks outside the United States fearing their assets could be expropriated by the U.S. government. The growth of the offshore market for dollars as well as other currencies stemmed from several factors. The surge of foreign trade and the internationalization of businesses during the 1960s largely contributed to this expansion. In the United States, the Federal Reserve Bank's imposition of Regulation Q (interest-rate ceiling on domestic deposits but not on Eurodollar deposits) and Regulation D (reserve requirement on domestic deposits) made domestic deposits more costly for banks, while the Euromarket remained free from such regulations. And later, the large divergences of interest rates among major countries and the volatility of foreign exchange and interest rates led to further expansion of the market.

Today's Eurocurrency markets are actively used by U.S. multinational corporations. The scope of the market has broadened, and although the U.S. dollar remains the dominant currency, activity has increased in the major European currencies. To a lesser extent, deposits and loans are also available in many other currencies, and the list continues to grow.

The major market centers are in Europe, with smaller markets existing in the Far East and the Middle East. To expand their participation in the Eurocurrency markets, U.S. banks and foreign banks also have offshore branches in such places as Nassau and the Cayman Islands, selected because of the same time zone, freedom from regulations, and favorable tax structures. However, the need for these offshore branches has now lessened because the Federal Reserve Board, as of December 3, 1981, permitted the establishment of International Banking Facilities (IBFs) by banks in the United States. The creation of the IBFs allows offshore transactions to be conducted in this country.

Deposits taken by the IBFs will be considered offshore transactions and exempt from the reserve requirement under Regulation D and from the interest-rate limitations of Regulation Q. An IBF will, however, only be permitted to accept deposits from nonresidents and lend only to nonresidents, including foreign subsidiaries of American companies.

This chapter discusses the structure of the Eurocurrency markets and the funding alternatives of banks; the various participants and uses of the market; the practicality of loans over one year; and the operational procedures.

INTEREST-RATE STRUCTURE OF THE EUROCURRENCY MARKET

To understand a bank's role in the Eurocurrency market, one must have a clear knowledge of the interest-rate structure of this market. While each country's domestic or internal market is controlled and monitored by the central bank, there is no such governing body for the Eurocurrency or external market. While central banks can curb or increase domestic liquidity and restrict resident as well as nonresident usage of the local market, their ability to influence the external market in the same manner is limited. Even where central banks or governments have acted in the past to regulate the use of the Euromarket, their restrictions apply only to resident banks and branches for which they have jurisdiction. For instance, the United States may mandate a reserve requirement on Eurodeposits owned by the foreign branches of U.S. banks but cannot impose the same on a dollar deposit on the books of a London bank. Likewise, in the early 1970s the German Bundesbank's imposition of the Bardepot scheme was designed to curb capital inflows into the DM.[1]

Thus, restrictions on local markets and the influence of central bank monetary policy on domestic markets can create a spread between the domestic rate and the Euro rate. This spread is also affected by other factors. Reserve requirements on domestic deposits increase the cost of such funds, while the Euromarket is virtually free from such costs. Additionally, other factors such as FDIC insurance premiums and taxes add to the cost of domestic U.S.-dollar deposits.

[1] The Bardepot was introduced in 1972 and represented a compulsory interest rate free deposit at the central banks system to be maintained by a German company which borrowed funds abroad.

As is true in any free market, the Eurocurrency market is influenced by supply and demand. While the Euro rates may normally tend to parallel and be influenced by domestic market rates, external pressures may create wide divergences between the two.

As any currency available in the Euromarket has a floating exchange rate, the interest rate may be influenced by pressure on that currency. For instance, if the German mark is appreciating in the exchange market vis-a-vis the U.S. dollar, we would also expect that Euro-DM rates might decline as market participants would prefer to hold DMs on deposit to benefit from further appreciation, thereby increasing the supply of funds in the market.

This brings us to the interrelationship between the foreign exchange market and the Eurocurrency market. The difference between the spot exchange rate for a currency and the forward rate is called the swap. The swap rate is the cost of exchanging one currency into another for a specified period of time. The swap will represent an increase in the value of the forward exchange rate (a premium) or a decrease in the forward exchange rate (a discount). What determines whether a currency is at a premium or discount in the forward market is the interest rate for that currency in the Euromarket versus the Eurodollar rate. That is, the difference between the Eurodollar rate and any Euro-currency rate for a given period will be equal to the forward discount or premium in the forward market.

Interest rate differential = Swap rate
(in the Euromarket)   (in the foreign exchange market)

The currency with the higher interest rate in the Euromarket will be at a discount (less expensive) in the forward market and the currency with the lower interest rate will be at a premium (more expensive). In other words, both markets offset and serve as an alternative for the other. Exhibit 1 illustrates this point.

This concept is reviewed further in the discussion on bank funding.

Exhibit 1

Euromarket:
1-year Eurodollar rate:	18%
1-year Eurosterling rate:	13%
Interest Rate Differential =	5%

Foreign Exchange Market:
Spot sterling	= $2.0000/U.K.
1-year swap rate	= + .1000 (premium)*
1-year forward sterling	= $2.1000/U.K.

* Exchange rate × Interest rate differential × $\dfrac{\text{Number of days}}{360 \text{ or } 365}$ = Swap rate

2.0000 × .05 × 1 = .1000

This relationship forces one market to move in tandem with the other. If, for example, there is substantial demand for Eurosterling loans outweighing the supply of deposits, interest rates would rise, adjusting to the demand pressure. As Eurosterling rates rise and assuming Eurodollar rates remain the same, the interest-rate differential between the two currencies will narrow. Likewise, the sterling premium in the forward market will also narrow. Exhibit 2 illustrates this point.

Exhibit 2

Euromarket:	Before	After Adjusting
1-year Euro$ rate	18%	18%
1-year Euro£ rate	13%	14%
Interest rate differential	5%	4%
Foreign Exchange Market:		
Spot sterling	$2.0000/U.K.	$2.0000/U.K.
1-year swap rate	+.1000	.0800*
1-year forward sterling	$2.1000	$2.0800

$$* \ 2.0000 \times .04 \times 1 = .0800$$

As a general rule, if the Eurorate is substantially higher or lower than the domestic rates, we can assume that the currency in the spot exchange market is under downward or upward pressure, respectively. A prerequisite for this scenerio is exchange controls limiting capital movement. However, if the Eurorate is closely in line with domestic rates, the reverse may be true. Very high rates in both markets may reflect a tight monetary policy of the central bank which may be attracting substantial flows into that currency, thus maintaining a strong exchange rate.

Interest rates in the Eurocurrency market are actively quoted for fixed periods of 1-, 2-, 3-, 6-, 9-, and 12-month periods. Therefore, a corporation can lock in the cost of a foreign currency loan over a specific period of time. Major foreign exchange banks will be able to quote its customer a rate for any specific period, that is, for 3 months and 5 days.

FUNDING A FOREIGN CURRENCY LOAN

U.S. banks can fund a foreign currency loan by: (1) taking a deposit in that currency (borrowing in the interbank market) or (2) taking a deposit in Eurodollars and swapping the dollars for the foreign currency in the foreign exchange market. A third alternative is to fund the foreign currency loan with domestic dollars plus the swap; however, because of the additional costs and restrictions involved, this is not likely to be a profitable alternative.

Financing a loan with a deposit is the simplest form of matched funding. A bank will pay less for the deposit than it will offer or lend the funds, and therefore lock in a profit from the spread. Using the Euro-DM rates, Exhibit 3 shows the bank obtaining the deposit and relending the funds to a corporation.

Exhibit 3

Euro DM	Bid:	12¹⁄₁₆% (Deposit)
	Offer:	12³⁄₁₆% (LIBOR)*
Bank accepts DM deposit @	12¹⁄₁₆% (if obtainable at bid)
Bank lends DM @	12⁹⁄₁₆% (+⅜ spread)
Spread or profit	½%

* London interbank offered rate.

The other alternative would be for the bank to accept a dollar deposit, sell the dollars spot, purchasing DMs and simultaneously selling the DM forward against U.S. dollars to the maturity of the loan. Access to dollar deposits may be easier or the cost of this operation may be less than funding with a deposit in the same currency. From the following market rates we will determine the Euro-DM rate for one year.

Exhibit 4

Euro$ rate:	18.00%
Spot DM:	2.0000 DM/$
Swap:	1000
1-year forward outright rate:	1.9000

Formula:

$$\frac{\text{Euro\$ rate} \times \text{forward outright rate}}{\text{Spot rate}} - \frac{360 \times \text{swap}}{100 \times \text{days} \times \text{spot}}$$

Calculation:

$$\frac{18 \times 1.9000}{2.0000} - \frac{360 \times 1000}{100 \times 365 \times 2.0000} = \text{Euro rate}$$

$$17.1 \quad - \quad 4.9315 \quad = \underline{12.1685\% \text{ or } 12³⁄₁₆\%}$$

This formula includes the coverage of the interest in the swap.

To substantiate this calculation, Exhibit 5 shows that a Euro-DM rate of 12.1685 percent will result in the required dollar earnings to the bank. That is, the dollar cost of obtaining a Eurodollar deposit at 18 percent is the same as the dollar earnings that result from lending Euro DM at 12.1685% provided the swap was locked in through the foreign exchange market.

Exhibit 5

Cost of dollar deposit:	18.0000%
Cost of $/DM swap:	(5.8315)
Euro DM rate:	12.1685%

Principal + interest

$1,000,000 + ($1,000,000 @ 18.00 ÷ 360 × 365) = $1,182,500

DM 2,000,000 + (DM 2,000,000 @ 12.1685 ÷ 360 × 365)
= DM 2,246,750.13 ÷ 1.90
= $1,182,500

If the Euro-DM deposit would have cost more than 12.1685 percent in the Euromarket, the bank would use this alternative. If there were no Euro-DM deposits available in the market at that particular time, the bank would base its pricing on the swap alternative which resulted in a Euro-DM rate of 12.1685 percent. For additional formulae see the appendix.

In addition to the bank's decision on which method to use for funding a foreign currency loan, there is also the option of funding on a matched or unmatched basis. Matched funding is locking in all cash flows at the origination of the loan as illustrated in Exhibit 6.

Exhibit 6

A. *Funding DM Loan Through DM Deposit*

		Today	At Maturity
1.	Take 6-month DM deposit	+DM	−DM
2.	Make 6-month DM loan	−DM	+DM
		0	0

B. *Funding DM Loan Through $ Deposit and FX Swap*

		Today	At Maturity
1.	Take 6-month $ deposit	+$	−$
2.	Sell $/buy DM spot	−$/ +DM	—
3.	Buy $/sell DM 6-month forward	—	+$/ −DM
4.	Make 6-month DM loan	−DM	+DM
		0	0

Matching of loans is most common; however, some bank's internal guidelines permit some unmatched funding. For example, if a bank made a six-month DM loan but expected Euro-DM rates to decline next month, they may take a DM deposit for one month in anticipation of refunding the remaining five months at a lower rate. The same can be achieved if the funding is through a dollar deposit and foreign exchange swap by creating the swap for only one month. (See Exhibit 7.)

Exhibit 7
Unmatched Funding

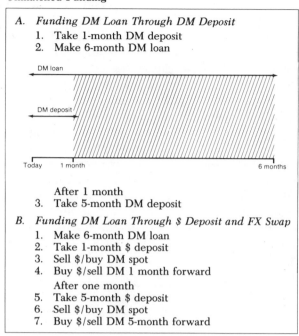

A. *Funding DM Loan Through DM Deposit*
1. Take 1-month DM deposit
2. Make 6-month DM loan

After 1 month
3. Take 5-month DM deposit

B. *Funding DM Loan Through $ Deposit and FX Swap*
1. Make 6-month DM loan
2. Take 1-month $ deposit
3. Sell $/buy DM spot
4. Buy $/sell DM 1 month forward
After one month
5. Take 5-month $ deposit
6. Sell $/buy DM spot
7. Buy $/sell DM 5-month forward

In this example, the bank has created an interest-rate risk. The loan has been made with a fixed-interest rate for the six-month period while the bank has fixed its interest-rate cost for only one month. However, there is no foreign exchange risk. Exchange risk would occur only if the bank were to make a foreign currency loan by funding in dollars and converting the dollars to the foreign currency without selling the currency forward. Open positions involving currency risk are handled by the foreign exchange trading department. This department will also monitor the changes in interest rate differentials and position itself accordingly.

USES OF THE EUROCURRENCY MARKET

Banks engage in foreign currency deposits and loans basically for two reasons:

1. Money market operations—spreads and arbitrage.
2. To serve its corporate customers needs.

In the interbank market participating banks buy and sell money among themselves; that is, they take or accept deposits and place deposits or lend funds to other institutions. As is true in the domestic markets, banks will attempt to pay a lower interest rate on deposits and lend the funds at a higher rate. The spread from such an operation is the profit to the bank. In the Eurocurrency market the spread between the bid (interest rate paid on a deposit) and the offered rate (interest rate on a placement) is generally very narrow. For Eurodollars and other active and liquid Eurocurrencies the spread is generally ⅛ percent. The bank must generate a high volume of turnover to be worth the costs and risks of rates moving against them.

Some banks also engage in covered-interest arbitrage by taking advantage of disequilibrium between the Eurocurrency market and the foreign exchange forward market. This operation is technically similar in nature to funding a foreign currency loan through a dollar deposit and a swap. This arbitrage opportunity exists when the swap rate is not equal to the interest rate differential. Referring to the details of the Euro-DM loan in Exhibit 4, and adding for this example that the Euro DM rate is 12.50 percent the bank can take advantage of the differential as illustrated in Exhibit 8.

Exhibit 8

Euro $ 18%	*Euro-DM 12.50%*
Spot DM:	2.0000 DM/$
Swap:	1000
1-year forward outright rate:	1.9000

Cost of Euro DM calculated from Exhibit 4 = 12.1685

Covered Interest Arbitrage

1. Borrow Euro$ @   18.00%
2. Sell $ spot/buy DM
   Buy $ 1-year forward/sell DM   5.8315%*
3. Lend Euro DM in Euromarket   12.50%
   Profit from arbitrage   =   .3315%

* Calculated DM rate 12.1685 is subtracted from 18.00.

Real arbitrage opportunities are rare, and when they do occur, the market tends to move into equilibrium rather quickly. If this opportunity did exist, market participants would, in this example, be borrowing dollars (pushing up the Eurodollar rate); swapping dollars for DMs (widening the swap rate); and lending DMs (push down the Euro-DM rate). These rates would adjust until the arbitrage opportunity disappeared.

If markets are not in equilibrium, the spread is usually very small, possibly 1/16 percent, and market participants who engage in arbitrage must watch for these opportunities closely and be able to act instantaneously. Another disadvantage is that by engaging in covered-interest arbitrage opportunities, banks are inflating their balance sheets and affecting their ratios.

Corporations generally borrow Eurocurrencies (1) to eliminate a foreign exchange exposure (as an alternative to the FX forward market); (2) to tap another source of funds to support their foreign operations based on their need for working capital, liquidity, and inventory financing; and (3) to take advantage of interest rate differentials while accepting the foreign exchange risk.

1. Many multinationals prefer to borrow foreign currencies to hedge a net asset position instead of selling the foreign currency in the forward market. Because of the assumption that markets are in equilibrium, each market serves as an alternative for the other. In assessing which alternative to use a corporation should consider the following:

a. If the company is a net borrower of dollars, the cost is approximately the same as the forward market. If the company does not need the dollars and engages in this transaction for hedging purposes only, the cost is higher than the forward market because of two factors: (1) the credit margin over LIBOR; and (2) the dollars would then have to be invested, thereby incurring another cost—that of the spread between the bid and offered rate.

b. Further, if a corporation is a net borrower that has access to the commercial-paper market, its cost of funding is generally lower than the Eurodollar borrowing rate, making the forward market a more attractive hedging alternative.

c. From an administration standpoint, it could be argued that borrowings require additional work, such as loan agreements, booking transactions, notes, and so on. Also for a company that is not a net borrower of funds, using this method inflates the balance sheet.

2. Where country exchange and credit controls allow, a company may choose to finance part of its operation through the Euromarket rather than the domestic market. This could be due to a more attractive rate in the Euromarket or the lack of availability of local funds.

3. During the early 1970s many corporations borrowed long-term Swiss francs and deutsche marks to finance their dollar needs and to take advantage of the lower interest rates. This created an exchange risk as the borrowings ultimately were to be paid in SFRs and DMs and had to be purchased with U.S. dollars. During the same period the U.S. dollar fell sharply, more than offsetting the benefit of the interest-rate differentials and resulting in foreign exchange losses for these companies.

It is important then to recognize the exchange risk involved in such a borrowing. Borrowing foreign currency for purposes of using dollars for the life of the loan is comparable to speculating in the foreign exchange market by selling the currency forward. The risk is exactly the same. However, some corporations engage in such an operation successfully by carefully evaluating the outlook for a currency and monitoring the market.

The effective cost of borrowing a foreign currency instead of dollars includes the interest paid and the change in rates of the currency. For example, if the Eurodollar rate is 18 percent and the Euro Swiss franc rate is 8 percent, an actual savings would only occur if the Swiss franc appreciated against the dollar by less than 10 percent.

EUROCURRENCY LOAN AGREEMENT

In order to enable its corporate customers to borrow foreign currency, a bank is likely to structure a credit facility to include multicurrency borrowings. These agreements are similar in content to a domestic or dollar-borrowing agreement; however, some terms are unique to this facility.

Typically, the pricing of a domestic loan would be based on the prime lending rate of the bank and would normally include a compensating balance requirement. The pricing of a Eurocurrency loan would be based on the LIBOR (London interbank offered rate) or IBR (interbank rate), plus a credit margin. It is common for banks not to require compensating balances for such a facility.

In a domestic dollar borrowing the rate may be fixed for up to three months or change as the prime rate changes, depending on the agreement. In a Eurocurrency borrowing the rate may generally be fixed up to 12 months, and the agreement may state that the borrowing will be fixed for specified periods such as 1, 3, 6 or 12 months. This would generally be the case for a revolving credit. Foreign currency loans with maturities over one year may be rolled over every three months, in which case the interest rate is fixed for only a three-month period at a time.

Eurocurrency agreements may also state that the borrowing may take place in certain currencies only or in any currency, if available. Also, because the markets trade in percentages as small as $\frac{1}{16}$ percent, the agreement may state that the rate will be rounded up to the nearest $\frac{1}{8}$ percent.

PREPAYMENT OF FOREIGN CURRENCY LOANS

When a bank makes a foreign currency loan to a customer it is for a fixed period of time at a fixed rate. Theoretically, and for the most part, in practice, the bank has funded this loan with a matched deposit or through a swap, thereby fixing the costs associated with the funding.

If a corporation wishes to pay the loan prior to the maturity, it may incur a penalty fee as per the loan agreement and additionally have to pay the cost to the bank for relending the funds at current market rates. Assume that a corporation has borrowed DMs at 12 percent plus a credit margin for one year and that the bank has funded that loan with a one-year DM deposit at 11.875 percent. It is now six months later, and the corporation decides to prepay the DM loan. The current rate for six months DM (the remainder of the period for which the bank must relend the funds) is 10 percent. The bank must incorporate in the penalty charges the 2 percent penalty add-on (12% − 10%) for the remaining six-month period.

LONG-TERM LOANS

With the growth of the Euromarket, fixed maturities in recent years have extended beyond 12 months. While the markets are far less liquid beyond a year, it is possible to fund a foreign currency loan on a matched basis under certain circumstances. The dollar, DM, SFR and U.K.£ are available in the Euromarket for up to five years. Banks are not active in trading among themselves in the longer periods but do so primarily on behalf of corporate customers seeking to fix interest costs for long-term financing requirements. Also the Eurobond market may be better suited to meet these corporate needs.

An alternative to a long-term, fixed-rate loan for a bank would be to commit to lending funds for an extended period but to set the rate for a fixed period of only three months with continuous rollovers. An option for fixing the interest rate by rollovers of up to one year could also be incorporated into the agreement. While the corporation is then subject to rate fluctuations, the funding is easier for the bank, encouraging the commitment to longer-term credit facilities.

OPERATIONS

When a Eurocurrency transaction is originated the trader will complete a form to submit to the operations department for processing. This must include the following details:

1. Name and address of counterparty.
2. Currency and amount/U.S.-dollar equivalent.
3. Trade date.
4. Value date.
5. Maturity date.
6. Interest rate.
7. Settlement instructions.

The operations department then is responsible for all aspects of processing, including all accounting entries, the delivery or receipt of funds, confirmations, and administration of the bank's records. This unit will also generate reports to the traders and management. These include position sheets, various maturity and counterparty listings, limit records, and the profit and loss statements for the department.

APPENDIX

Calculating the appropriate interest rate for a currency based on the foreign exchange swap.

Formula:

$$\left[\frac{\text{Euro\$ rate} \times \text{Outright rate}}{\text{Spot rate}}\right] - {}^{(A)}\left[\frac{360^{(B)} \times \text{swap}}{100 \times \text{days} \times \text{spot}}\right]$$

Example:

6-month Euro $ rate:	17.75%
Spot DM:	2.4500
6-month DM Swap ($ discount):	597
Outright rate:	2.3903
6 months equal 182 days	

$$\frac{17.75 \times 2.3903}{2.4500} - \frac{360 \times 597}{100 \times 182 \times 2.4500}$$

$$17.317 - 4.8190 = \quad 12.498\%$$
$$\text{Euro-DM rate}$$

Note:

A. If the swap reflected a dollar premium, then this should be added rather than subtracted.
B. Eurocurrency rates are calculated on a 360-day basis except for the U.K. sterling and the Belgian franc where 365 days are used.

Calculating the appropriate Eurodollar rate based on the Eurocurrency rate and the foreign currency swap.

Formula:

$$\left[\frac{\text{Eurocurrency rate} \times \text{Spot rate}}{\text{Outright rate}}\right] + {}^{(A)}\left[\frac{360 \times \text{swap}}{100 \times \text{days} \times \text{outright rate}}\right]$$

Example:

6-month Euro DM rate:	12.498%
Spot DM:	2.4500
6-month DM swap ($ discount):	597
Outright rate:	2.3903

6 months equals 182 days

$$\frac{12.498 \times 2.4500}{2.3903} + \frac{360 \times 597}{100 \times 182 \times 2.3903}$$
$$12.810 + 4.940 = \underline{\underline{17.75\%}}$$
$$\text{Euro \$ rate}$$

Note:

A. If the swap reflected a dollar premium, then this should be sub-tracted rather than added.

Calculating the foreign exchange Swap based on the Eurodollar rate and the Eurocurrency rate.

Formula:

$$\frac{\text{Spot} \times \text{Days} \times \left(\dfrac{\text{Interest rate differential}}{100} \right)}{360 + \left(\text{Days} \times \dfrac{\text{Euro \$ rate}}{100} \right)}$$

Example:

6-month Euro $ rate:	17.750%
6-month Euro-DM rate:	12.498%
Spot DM:	2.4500

6 months equals 182 days

$$\frac{2.4500 \times 182 \times 0.05252}{392.305} = 0.059695$$

or

$$\underline{\underline{597}}$$
$$\text{Swap points}$$

GLOSSARY

Arbitrage: Locking in transactions to take advantage of temporary imperfections in the market to yield a profit without incurring a risk.

Exchange rate: The price of one currency expressed in terms of another currency.

Hedging: The process of eliminating an exchange risk by entering into a transaction to match cash flows in foreign currencies or to offset an exposure.

Outright rate: The spot exchange rate plus or minus the swap. The exchange rate for a specific date in the future.

Spot rate: The rate at which a currency is converted based on a delivery date of two business days from the date of the transaction. (One business day for Canada and Mexico).

Swap rate: The differential between the spot rate and the outright rate.

Swap transaction: The simultaneous sale and purchase of a currency for different maturity dates.

Value date: The date at which funds are actually delivered and exchanged.

SECTION 3
International Banking Services

15
Commercial Letters of Credit

JOSEPH A. COLLERAN
Vice President
Irving Trust Company

FUNCTIONS OF LETTERS OF CREDIT

The basic function of letters of credit is to act as a means of ensuring payment to a seller upon shipment of merchandise to a buyer. Under a letter of credit, the buyer requests his bank to establish a letter of credit in favor of the seller. In the letter of credit the bank (in place of the buyer) promises to pay the seller a specified amount if the seller presents documents which evidence that the shipment has taken place. Letters of credit can be, and are, used to effect payment for domestic shipments of merchandise, but the majority of letters of credit are used to settle payments in international trade.

The classic problem for merchants in international trade has always been, "Who is to act first?" Is the seller expected to ship merchandise to a foreign country in the hope that the buyer, upon receipt of the merchandise, will remit funds in payment? Is the buyer expected to remit funds to a foreign country in the hope that upon receipt of the funds the seller will ship the merchandise? Obviously, neither would be fully comfortable in initiating the transaction.

One solution to the problem would be to have the seller send his documents for collection (see Chapter 17); but the protection afforded the seller under a collection is somewhat limited. The letter of credit offers a solution which affords protection to both buyer and seller.

The bank, the buyer, and the seller constitute the three basic parties to a letter of credit. In letter of credit terminology, the bank is known as the "Issuing Bank" or the "Opening Bank," the buyer is known as the "Account Party," and the seller is known as the "Beneficiary." Usually the letter of credit specifies the latest date on which shipment can take place; it always specifies the latest date on which documents can be presented.

Under the letter of credit, the beneficiary (the seller) has the assurance of the issuing bank that he will be paid if he ships merchandise described in the letter of credit to the account party (the buyer) within the time frame specified in the letter of credit and if he presents documents evidencing such shipment to the issuing bank prior to the expiration of the letter of credit. The buyer is assured that payment will be made only if the documents specified in the letter of credit are presented to the issuing bank within the time frames permitted by the letter of credit.

Thus the letter of credit overcomes the reluctance of both parties to initiate action. It affords protection to both parties because the seller is assured by a bank that he will be paid if he ships in accordance with the terms of the letter of credit and the buyer is assured that payment will be made only when documents evidencing the shipment are presented to the issuing bank.

Since letters of credit are essentially bank instruments, the discussions that follow will be made from a bank's point of view. However, the interests of other parties can be discerned from the examples. Moreover, while letters of credit can give rise to bankers acceptances, these instruments are covered elsewhere in this book (see Chapter 16). Therefore, the discussions will be limited to sight (demand) transactions.

IMPORT LETTERS OF CREDIT

Presumably, for each merchandise transaction a contract of sale exists between the buyer and the seller. However, since this instrument does not involve the bank directly, the bank does not see the contract of sale, and technically, the bank has no interest in it. The letter of credit transaction, as such, is initiated by the buyer.

The buyer prepares a formal application for a letter of credit. The application is addressed to a bank where the buyer maintains a demand deposit account. The application is signed by the buyer and specifies in detail the terms and conditions of the letter of credit that the buyer wishes the bank to issue for his account (hence the term *Account Party*).

Based on the credit standing of the buyer, the bank will issue the letter of credit against a line of credit previously established for the buyer. Since the letter of credit the bank will issue will be irrevocable on the part of the issuing bank (the credit cannot be cancelled), the bank will create a contingent liability on its books in the name of the buyer.

Let us presume that the buyer wishes to import radio equipment from Japan at a cost of $100,000. The application will give the full name and address of the beneficiary (the seller), give a brief description of the merchandise, specify the documents which are to be presented,

indicate the latest date for shipment, and the expiration date of the
letter of credit. The application will also authorize the bank to debit
the buyer's demand deposit account for all payments made by the
bank under the letter of credit.

Based upon the details in the application, the issuing bank will issue
a letter of credit and forward it to the beneficiary probably through
a bank in the beneficiary's locale. The issuing bank may forward the
letter of credit by mail or by telecommunication, based on the instruc-

Exhibit A

Irving Trust

Irving Trust Company
One Wall Street
New York, NY 10015

SPECIMEN

EXHIBIT "A"

Credit Number 000553   March 15, 198 7
of Issuing Bank   Date
of Advising Bank

Irrevocable Documentary Credit

Advising Bank	Applicant
Commercial Bank of Japan Tokyo, Japan	Dynamic Radio Co. 51 West 36th Street New York, New York 10020

Beneficiary	
Tokyo Electric Co. 30 Imabashi 3 Chome Tokyo, Japan	Amount **U.S.$100,000.00** Expiry June 30, 198_ At Our Counters

Gentlemen:

We hereby issue in your favor this documentary credit which is available by your drafts drawn on us at sight

All drafts must be marked: "Drawn Under Irving Trust Company New York Credit...(indicating the number and date of this credit)...." Your drafts must be accompanied by the following documents (complete sets unless otherwise stated; alternatively, if any document is issued as a single original only, such original shall be deemed a complete set).

Commercial Invoice.

Customs Invoice.

Packing List.

Insurance policy/certificate issued by an insurance company, in negotiable form, covering marine and war risks.

Onboard ocean bills of lading made out to the order of Irving Trust Company, New York, indicating the number of this credit and marked notify applicant as indicated above, marked "Freight Prepaid".

Covering Radio Equipment - C.I.F. New York.

Shipment From Japan	Latest Date	Partial Shipments
Shipment To New York	June 1, 198_	(X) Are Permitted ◯ Are Not Permitted

Presenting bank must send all documents to us in one airmail.

Except so far as otherwise expressly stated, this documentary credit is subject to the "Uniform Customs and Practice for Documentary Credits" (1974 revision) International Chamber of Commerce Publication No. 290.

Advising Bank's Notification

We hereby engage with drawers and/or bona fide holders that drafts drawn under and in compliance with the terms of this credit will be duly honored on presentation.

Yours very truly,

Place, date, name and signature of the advising bank.

3780/00 (Rev. 3-81)   Authorized signature

tion of the buyer. A specimen of such a letter of credit advised by mail is attached as Exhibit A.

Upon receipt of the letter of credit from the issuing bank, the bank in the beneficiary's locale (the Advising Bank) will inform the beneficiary of the establishment of the letter of credit either by remitting to the beneficiary the original instrument received from the issuing bank or by preparing their own advice addressed to the beneficiary.

With the letter of credit in hand, the beneficiary may now ship the merchandise with assurance that if he fulfills the terms of the letter of credit he will be paid. Accordingly, he ships the merchandise on a vessel bound for the United States and receives from the steamship company a bill of lading attesting to this shipment and indicating the date the merchandise was loaded on board. An insurance company provides him with an insurance policy covering the merchandise against certain losses while en route. The invoice and the packing list are prepared by the shipper on his own letterhead.

The beneficiary then draws a sight draft on the issuing bank for the amount of the shipment and presents the draft and documents to his local bank who forwards them to the issuing bank with a request for payment.

When the draft and documents are received by the issuing bank, they must be examined to determine that the documents conform to the terms of the letter of credit. If the documents do conform, the issuing bank debits the account of the buyer for the amount of the draft plus the issuing bank's charges and credits the account of (or remits proceeds to) the foreign bank who forwarded the documents. The foreign bank will, in turn, remit proceeds to the beneficiary. The issuing bank stamps the draft "paid" and retains it in files. The documents, together with an advice of debit, are sent to the buyer, and the contingent liability in the name of the buyer is removed from the books of the issuing bank.

Now that the buyer has possession of the shipping documents, he is able to take possession of the merchandise when it arrives, and the transaction is complete.

EXPORT LETTERS OF CREDIT

Just as the import letter of credit covered a shipment of merchandise into the United States, so the export letter of credit covers a shipment of merchandise out of the United States. However, the role of the U.S. bank is somewhat different. Again the transaction is initiated by the buyer who requests a bank in his country to establish a letter of credit in favor of the seller in the United States. The issuing bank will issue an irrevocable letter of credit and advise it through one of its correspondent banks in the United States.

Upon receipt of the letter of credit the U.S. bank will forward it to the beneficiary. If the issuing bank instructs it to do so, the U.S. bank will confirm the letter of credit. That is, the U.S. bank will engage itself to honor the beneficiary's drawings under the letter of credit. By so engaging, the U.S. bank is committed to honor drawings regardless of the financial condition of the issuing bank at the time documents are presented. This commitment is undertaken against the line of credit that the U.S. bank has established for the issuing bank. A specimen

Exhibit B

 Irving Trust

EXHIBIT "B"
Irving Trust Company
One Wall Street
New York, NY 10015

7

SPECIMEN

Confirmed Irrevocable Credit	Our Credit No. 047328	Correspondent's No. 164-3891	Date September 15, 198_

Beneficiary	Correspondent
Eagle Export Co. Lexington Avenue New York, New York	Banco de Caracas Caracas, Venezuela

Gentlemen:
We are informed by our correspondent that they have issued an irrevocable credit in your favor, available by your drafts on us

at _____ sight, to the extent of   **$100,000.00**

for account of Casa de Aire, Caracas, Venezuela

accompanied by the following documents (**complete sets unless otherwise stated**) evidencing shipment(s) of:
ROOM AIR CONDITIONERS AS PER PROFORMA INVOICE NO. 107-61 FROM ANY U.S.A. PORT TO LA GUAIRA, VENEZUELA

Partial shipments are not permitted.   Transshipment is not permitted.

Signed commercial invoice in original and two copies.

Invoices must state that merchandise and invoices are in accordance with Proforma invoice No. 107-61.

Packing list in duplicate.

Insurance policy/certificate issued by an insurance company in negotiable form covering marine and war risks.

Fullset clean onboard ocean bills of lading issued to the order of Banco de Caracas marked "Notify Casa de Aire" and "Freight Prepaid" dated onboard not later than December 15, 198_.

Drafts must clearly specify the number of this credit and be presented at this Company not later than December 30, 198_.

                    ****

This credit is subject to the uniform customs and practice for documentary credits (1974 Revision), International Chamber of Commerce Publication No. 290.

At the request of our correspondent we confirm their irrevocable credit and engage with you that all drafts drawn under and in compliance with the terms of this credit will be duly honored.

Note   RM
Documents must conform strictly with the terms of this credit. If you are unable to comply with its terms, please communicate with us and/or your customer promptly with a view to having the conditions changed.

Yours very truly,

3809/00 Rev. 3-80

_____
Authorized Signature

of an irrevocable credit which has been confirmed is attached as Exhibit B.

Once the bank has confirmed the letter of credit, it has incurred a contingent liability. This contingent liability will be recorded on its books in the name of the issuing bank.

The domestic seller now has the commitment of the U.S. bank that, if drafts and documents in conformity with the terms of the credit are presented to the domestic bank, the seller will be paid. Accordingly, the seller effects shipment and obtains the necessary documentation as specified in the credit. He draws a sight draft on the U.S. bank and presents this draft, together with the documentation, to the bank for payment.

If the documents meet the requirements of the letter of credit, the U.S. bank will effect payment to the beneficiary by debiting the account of the issuing bank and will remove from its books the contingent liability in the name of the issuing bank. The debit advice and the documents will be mailed to the issuing bank who will examine the documents to verify that they conform to the terms of the letter of credit. After verifying that the documents are correct, the issuing bank will debit the account of the buyer and turn the documents over to him. The shipping documents enable the buyer to take possession of the merchandise when it arrives.

In the forgoing example the U.S. bank acted in the capacity of an advising bank since it advised the letter of credit to the beneficiary. Since the domestic bank added its commitment to that of the issuing bank, it also acted in the capacity of a confirming bank.

However, all letters of credit advised through U.S. banks are not confirmed by them. In many instances, the domestic bank advises the letter of credit to the beneficiary without any engagement or responsibility on its part. This type of letter of credit is an "unconfirmed letter of credit."

The mechanics of the unconfirmed letter of credit are exactly the same as the mechanics of the confirmed letter of credit except the U.S. bank does not incur any contingent liability. Therefore, when advising such a credit, the bank does not record a contingent liability on its books. Nevertheless, many U.S. banks have automated their letter-of-credit bookkeeping systems, and these banks usually show the letter of credit on their books in the name of the issuing bank, but the entry will be coded in a fashion that will indicate that no liability has been incurred under the credit. In this way the bank will have a record of all letters of credit which it has advised for its foreign correspondents, broken down into the categories of "confirmed" and "unconfirmed." In determining its outstanding contingent liabilities, the U.S. bank is concerned only with the confirmed credits.

The beneficiary of an unconfirmed letter of credit does not have any commitment from the advising bank, but he does have the irrevocable undertaking of the foreign issuing bank. Thus, when he ships and presents documents to the U.S. advising bank, the bank is under no obligation to effect payment to him. Nevertheless, if his documents conform to the terms of the credit, in all probability he will receive payment.

The foreign issuing bank is a correspondent of the U.S. advising bank and probably maintains a demand deposit account with the bank. The U.S. bank does not wish to disparage the reputation of its foreign correspondent and therefore will effect payments under the correspondent's irrevocable unconfirmed credits even when such payments occasionally overdraw the demand deposit account. After all, if the advising bank had no intention of effecting payment under the unconfirmed credit, it should not have advised the credit in the first place.

Nevertheless, there are situations when the U.S. bank will refuse to effect payments under credits which it has advised but not confirmed. If the issuing bank were to collapse between the time the credit was advised and the time documents were presented, the U.S. advising bank would not honor drawings under credits it had not confirmed. Other situations indicating an unstable or uncertain condition in the issuing bank or in the issuing bank's country might also cause the U.S. bank to refuse to honor drawings under unconfirmed credits. Such situations include a deteriorating political situation, the outbreak of war, and so on. While in practice advising banks usually refuse to honor drawings under unconfirmed credits only in extreme situations, it must be remembered that the U.S. bank may legally refuse to honor drawings under *any* credit which it has not confirmed.

AMENDMENTS

Since the letter of credit is irrevocable on the part of the issuing bank, it cannot be amended without the consent of all parties concerned. An amendment usually is initiated by the buyer, and therefore his agreement is evidenced by his request for amendment addressed to the issuing bank. If the issuing bank acts on the amendment request and issues the amendment to the beneficiary, the issuing bank's agreement is evidenced by the amendment itself. If the credit were confirmed and the confirming bank passes the amendment to the beneficiary, then the confirming bank's agreement is evidenced by the advice of amendment to the beneficiary.

But what of the beneficiary? How do we know he has agreed to the amendment? In many cases the question is moot. The most common amendments to letters of credit are increases to the credit amount and extensions of the expiration date and/or shipping date. Since these amendments are beneficial to the beneficiary, most banks do not require the beneficiary to signify his agreement to them in writing; rather, the banks assume these amendments will be accepted by the beneficiary. However, when an amendment obviously is detrimental to the beneficiary, for example, a decrease in the credit amount or a shortening of the expiration and/or shipping date, banks will require the beneficiary to signify his agreement in writing.

A problem arises for banks when they are unable to determine if a specific amendment is beneficial or detrimental to the beneficiary. An amendment may delete a "certificate of weight" from the documentary requirements and require instead a "certificate of inspection." The bank is in no position to determine if this amendment is beneficial or detrimental to the beneficiary. In such cases, the bank's best approach is to require the beneficiary to signify his agreement to these amendments in writing.

Certain amendments will affect the liability of the issuing and confirming bank. As mentioned above, the most common amendments are increases to the credit amount and extensions of the expiration date. Both of these amendments alter the contingent liability of the banks involved: in the first instance by increasing the amount of the contingent liability and in the second instance by extending the time the contingent liability is outstanding. Thus, when a bank processes such amendments, it must make the proper adjustments on its liability records.

DISCREPANCIES IN DOCUMENTS

All parties to a letter-of-credit deal in documents only. Therefore, payment will only be made if the documents conform to the requirements in the credit. Conversely, an issuing or confirming bank *must* pay if the documents conform to the credit terms. Therefore, prior to the effecting payment, the bank must examine the documents against the letter of credit to determine if the documents conform. All too frequently, discrepancies are found in the documents on first examination.

The method of handling discrepancies is different in an export letter of credit and an import letter of credit. Let us look first at the export letter of credit. A U.S. bank has confirmed an irrevocable letter of credit issued by one of its foreign correspondents in favor of a U.S. exporter. The exporter ships the merchandise, prepares his documents, and presents the documents to the domestic bank with a request for payment. Fortunately most discrepancies can be corrected easily. These include such discrepancies as: failure to endorse the bills of lading; failure to sign the commercial invoice; failure to present one or more of the required documents, and so forth. When the bank finds such discrepancies it will inform the presenter immediately, preferably by phone. Upon notification of such discrepancies, the presenter, in all probability, will wish to make the necessary corrections.

In many cases the beneficiary will come to the bank and correct the documents as necessary. In other cases he may have the documents picked up by messenger, or he may request the bank to return the documents to him by mail. In the latter two cases the bank must take care that the corrected documents are re-presented before the credit expires; otherwise a new discrepancy has been created which, of course, cannot be corrected. If the corrections are made properly the U.S. bank will effect payment by debiting the account of its foreign correspondent bank and mailing the debit advice and documents to the issuing bank.

Many discrepancies cannot be corrected by the beneficiary. These include late shipment, credit expired, excess drawing, and so on. When the bank finds these discrepancies, it again must notify the presenter immediately. Since the bank cannot pay because the terms of the letter of credit have not been complied with, the presenter has the option of reclaiming the documents without payment or seeking other means of getting payment under the letter of credit. The vast majority of presenters will seek to obtain payment through the letter of credit.

The bank can assist the presenter in any of the following ways, based on the presenter's instructions. The bank can send a telecommunication to the issuing bank describing the discrepancies and requesting authorization to effect payment despite the discrepancies. If the issuing bank waives the discrepancies, the U.S. bank will effect payment under the letter of credit and mail the documents to the issuing bank. If the presenter prefers, the bank can send the documents to the issuing bank by mail accompanied by a covering letter describing the discrepancies and requesting authority to pay. If the issuing bank gives the authority to pay, the U.S. bank will make the payment under the letter of credit.

In some cases the presenter may not wish to wait for a telecommunication exchange between the U.S. bank and the issuing bank nor for the mail time involved in sending the documents on approval; rather he may wish to receive payment immediately. In this case he may offer the U.S. bank a guarantee in which he agrees to refund the payment, plus interest, in the event the issuing bank refuses to honor the documents because of the discrepancies. The domestic bank will accept the guarantee if the presenter is known to them and is creditworthy; otherwise the bank will insist that the guarantee be issued by a bank known to them. When the bank accepts the guarantee, it will effect payment by debiting the account of the issuing bank. The documents and debit advice will be mailed to the issuing bank, and the debit advice will indicate that the U.S. bank has paid against a guarantee because of the discrepancies. If the issuing bank does not wish to honor the documents because of the discrepancies, it must inform the U.S. bank of such refusal within a reasonable time. Upon receipt of such notice of refusal, the U.S. bank will use the guarantee to obtain a refund from the presenter. If no notice of refusal is received, the payment under the letter of credit would stand.

Under an import letter of credit, the presenter of the documents is in a foreign country. If the domestic bank finds discrepancies in the documents, the procedure will be somewhat different. The U.S. bank, as issuing bank, has an irrevocable commitment to pay if the documents conform to the credit terms. If, however, the U.S. bank finds discrepancies in the documents, it is that bank which must reject them. Since the presenter is in a foreign country it would not be practical to notify the presenter of this rejection without checking with the buyer. Therefore, the U.S. bank will inform the buyer (usually by phone) that discrepancies have been found in the documents. The bank will ask the buyer if payment may be made notwithstanding the discrepancies. If the buyer approves, the bank will debit the buyer's account and forward the documents to him. The debit advice will mention the discrepancies and state that these discrepancies were waived by the buyer. Payment will be made to the presenter in accordance with his instructions. The payment advice will also mention the discrepancies and indicate that payment was made despite these discrepancies. It must be noted from the forgoing that the rejection was made by the U.S. bank. The approach to the buyer was made only to seek his waiver of the discrepancies, not to invest the buyer with the decision to reject or accept.

In both the export letter of credit and the import letter of credit, if the documents are rejected, the U.S. bank must hold the documents at the disposal of the presenter or return the documents to the presenter.

FOREIGN CURRENCY LETTERS OF CREDIT

Up to this point we have been discussing letters of credit denominated in U.S. dollars, and the preponderance of credits involving our banks would be handled in that currency. However, occasionally letters of credit denominated in foreign currencies are handled by U.S. banks, and such credits may cover either imports or exports.

A domestic buyer may have entered into a contract to purchase goods from London payable by means of a letter of credit in pounds sterling. At the request of the buyer a U.S. bank could issue an irrevocable letter of credit denominated in pounds sterling. To accomplish this, the bank would utilize the services of one of its correspondent banks in London where the bank maintains a pound sterling account. The letter of credit would be issued for account of the U.S. buyer in favor of the London seller and require a sight draft drawn on the London bank. The U.S. bank would instruct the London bank to pay the draft by debiting the pound sterling account maintained by the bank in London. Thus, when the seller presents his draft and documents to the London bank, the London bank must examine the documents; if the documents are in accordance with the credit terms, the London bank will pay the seller immediately by debiting the U.S. bank's pound sterling account at the London bank. The London bank will mail the documents and debit advice to the U.S. bank.

Upon receipt of the documents and the debit advice, the U.S. bank will examine the documents to verify that they conform to the credit terms. If the documents are in order, the bank will debit the account of the buyer and send a debit advice and the documents to him. However, the debit to the domestic bank's account in London was in pounds sterling, whereas the debit to the buyer's account was in dollars. The U.S. bank will determine the amount of dollars to be debited by converting the pounds sterling to dollars at the spot rate prevailing on the date of the dollar debit. For purposes of discussion only, let us assume that pounds sterling are trading at $1:2$ versus the dollar, that is, one pound sterling equals two U.S. dollars. Thus, if the letter of credit were issued for £100,000, the U.S. bank would debit the buyer's account $200,000. This debit alone would not be sufficient to reimburse the U.S. bank for its part in the transaction, because it was the bank's funds (pounds sterling) that were used to pay the letter of credit in London several days prior to debiting the buyer's account in this country. In effect, the U.S. bank made a pound sterling loan to the buyer in order to effect payment under the letter of credit. Therefore, in addition to the debit for the spot rate on pounds sterling, the U.S. bank would debit the buyer's account interest for the number of days that the bank's sterling account was out of funds.

In the transaction described above, the buyer is taking an exchange risk, since his account will be debited on the day the U.S. bank completes its examination of the documents at the rate of exchange prevailing on that day. For example, if the rate prevailing moves from $1:2$ to $1:2.1$, then the buyer will be debited $210,000 for the cost of the pounds sterling. The buyer can protect himself against this risk to some extent by entering into a forward exchange contract with his bank at the time the letter of credit is issued. Under the terms of this contract the bank agrees to *sell* pounds sterling to the buyer, at a rate fixed in the contract, for delivery whenever the letter of credit is paid. Thus the buyer knows exactly how much he will be debited regardless of the actual spot rate prevailing on the date of payment. This contract only fixes the rate of exchange; the buyer must still pay interest for the time the U.S. bank is out of funds.

In recording such a letter of credit on its liability records the U.S.

bank will convert the foreign currency to dollars at a nominal rate at the time the credit is issued. This rate may remain in effect throughout the life of the credit if the particular foreign currency does not fluctuate to any great degree from the nominal rate. However, all letters of credit which are issued in foreign currency must be reviewed periodically to determine that the dollar value recorded in liability reasonably reflects the current exchange rates. In the event any rate has fluctuated to a large extent, the necessary adjustments must be made on the liability records. In a reverse situation where a U.S. seller has contracted to ship goods to a buyer in London payable in pounds sterling, the transaction can also be handled through a letter of credit. In this instance the London buyer would instruct a London bank to issue an irrevocable letter of credit in favor of the shipper for account of the London buyer. The letter of credit would require sight drafts on the London bank in pounds sterling, and the credit would be advised to the beneficiary through a U.S. correspondent of the London bank.

After shipment, the seller would bring his documents and the sight draft on London to the U.S. bank. Since the draft is not drawn on that bank, it cannot be paid by them; it is payable only in London by the London bank. This being the case there are several ways in which the transaction may be handled. The seller's bank can send the draft and documents to the London bank under the letter of credit and instruct the London bank that payment is to be effected by crediting the pound sterling account maintained by the U.S. bank in the London bank under telecommunication advice to the U.S. bank. Upon receipt of the documents the London bank would examine them to verify that they conform to the letter-of-credit terms. If the documents are in order, the London bank would debit the buyer's account £100,000 and send him the debit advice and the documents. The London bank would credit the account of the U.S. bank £100,000 and send a wire to that bank informing it of its action. Upon receipt of the wire, the U.S. bank would purchase the sterling from the seller at the bank's spot rate for sterling on that date. Assuming a rate of 1:2, the seller's bank would purchase the pounds sterling by crediting the seller's account $200,000.

In the above example, the seller was forced to wait an unspecified number of days before receiving payment because of the mail time from the U.S. to London, plus the time the London bank takes to examine the documents and send a wire to the U.S. bank. This time period could be anywhere from several days to a week or more. Many sellers do not wish to wait this long to receive their funds. In those instances the seller may request the U.S. bank to negotiate the draft. If the bank is agreeable, it will first examine the documents to ascertain that they are correct. If the documents are correct, it will negotiate by converting the sterling to dollars at its buying rate for sterling drafts on London.

In negotiating the pound sterling draft under the letter of credit, the bank negotiates with full recourse to the beneficiary. In the event the draft is not paid by the London bank, the U.S. bank has legal recourse to the beneficiary for the amount of the negotiation, plus interest. To overcome this, the beneficiary may request that the U.S. bank add its confirmation to the credit. If all parties agree and the U.S. bank confirms the credit, it has committed itself to negotiate "without recourse." Under these circumstances, the bank *must* negotiate the draft when it is presented, and such negotiation is without recourse to the beneficiary. Thus, if after negotiation by the U.S. bank, the London bank fails to pay the draft, the U.S. bank has no legal right to proceed against the beneficiary. It must be noted that, by confirming the credit, the U.S. bank has taken on only the obligation to negotiate without recourse. The confirmation does not fix the rate at which negotiation will be accomplished. This rate is determined by the rate prevailing at the time of negotiation.

As with the import letter of credit, there is an exchange risk involved under the export letter of credit. This risk must be borne by the seller. If the rate of exchange moves from 1:2 to 1:1.9 then the beneficiary will receive $190,000 for his documents. The beneficiary can protect himself against this risk by entering into a forward exchange contract with the U.S. bank. The contract will be the reverse of the one the importer entered into because in this case the bank agrees to *purchase* pounds sterling from the beneficiary, at a rate fixed in the contract, for delivery whenever the letter of credit is paid.

Liability entries will be maintained by the U.S. bank similar to the method used under the foreign currency import letter of credit. The bookkeeping entries will be made in dollars at a nominal rate, which must be checked periodically to insure reasonableness. The type of liability recorded would depend upon whether the U.S. bank advised the credit unconfirmed or whether it added its confirmation.

SUMMARY

There are many other types of letters of credit which cannot be discussed here because of space limitations. These include back-to-back letters of credit, revolving letters of credit, red clause letters of credit, and stand-by letters of credit, among others. The durability of the letter of credit as a mechanism for financing international trade has been well established. As new techniques are developed for increasing the efficiency of the international movement of goods, the letter-of-credit instrument will continue to evolve to meet these needs. The use of the letter-of-credit instrument can expand as far as the imagination of bankers will allow.

16
Bankers' Acceptances

JOHN M. CHALK
Vice President
Wachovia Bank and Trust Company, N.A.
and
WILLIAM F. HAMLET
Vice President
Wachovia Bank and Trust Company, N.A.

The use of eligible bankers' acceptances by American banks as a means of financing has increased dramatically in recent years, from $2 billion in 1960 to slightly less than $19.0 billion in 1975, and to over $60 billion in 1980. This rapid growth has resulted largely from the recognition by banks and their customers that bankers' acceptances need not be the cumbersome letter-of-credit-related transactions they once were but rather can be used flexibly to the benefit of both bank and customer for a variety of financing purposes.

The rules governing the creation and use of bankers' acceptances, with one exception, have not changed. But the understanding of the ease with which the rules can be observed has.

Basically, a banker's acceptance is a time draft, or a time bill of exchange, drawn on and accepted by a bank. It is distinguished from a trade acceptance simply by the fact that the accepting party is a bank rather than a buyer of goods.

Bankers' acceptances are either eligible or ineligible for rediscount by Federal Reserve banks, depending on their compliance with the eligibility requirements set forth in Section 13, Regulation A, of the Federal Reserve Act. As indicated later in this chapter, the issue of eligibility is central with respect to the use of bankers' acceptances as a financing tool. Put simply, eligible acceptances are attractive to bank and customer alike, and ineligible ones are significantly less so. For the most part, any casual discussion of acceptance financing by bankers and their customers is in reference to eligible acceptances.

This chapter is intended to demonstrate how banks can employ eligible bankers' acceptances to assist their customers with a range of financing needs at good profit to themselves. It specifies the legal and practical limits of bankers' acceptances and establishes eligibility criteria; it indicates advantages and disadvantages to borrowers; and it demonstrates how banks can benefit from a successful knowledge and use of this unique financing vehicle.

ELIGIBILITY

Section 13 of the Federal Reserve Act of 1913 (12 U.S.C. Section 372), as amended, provides:

> Any member bank may accept drafts or bills of exchange drawn upon it having not more than six months sight to run, exclusive of days of grace, which grow out of transactions involving the importation or exportation of goods; or which grow out of transactions involving the domestic shipment of goods; or which are secured at the time of acceptance by a warehouse receipt or other such document conveying or securing title covering readily marketable staples.

A bankers' acceptance is "eligible" for discount at a Federal Reserve bank if it arises from a transaction meeting the guidelines of the Federal Reserve Act. The purpose of the guidelines is to insure that the financing is self-liquidating; that is, that the underlying transaction will result in a sale, the proceeds of which will be used to repay the maturing acceptance and thus retire the obligation. These guidelines, described in paragraphs 7 (12 U.S.C. Section 372) and 12 (12 U.S.C. Section 373), divide eligible transactions into four broad categories.

Determining eligibility requires a thorough knowledge and understanding of Regulation A and the subsequent rulings and amplifications the Federal Reserve has issued on the subject. If neither party to the transaction intends to rediscount the draft, eligibility is irrelevant. It is important to remember that, as explained later, ineligible acceptances are not unlawful but rather forfeit some of the advantages attendant to their eligible cousins.

The chart below shows bankers' acceptances outstanding by category in the United States:

	March 31, 1981 (000s)
Imports	$13,292,056
Exports	13,451,030
Goods stored in or shipped between foreign countries	31,452,672
Domestic shipments	210,421
Domestic storage	1,557,200
Dollar exchange	36,000
Total	$60,089,379

Source: Federal Reserve Bank of New York.

Further explanations and examples from some of these categories follow.

IMPORT AND EXPORT TRANSACTIONS

As the chart shows, the financing of imports and exports represents the predominant use of bankers' acceptances in the United States. The third category, "goods stored in or shipped between foreign countries," is comprised almost exclusively of foreign trade; that is, imports and exports not involving the United States. Grouping this category with the first two, we find that imports and exports constitute about 95 percent of the national market.

A traditional use of acceptance financing is by importers in conjunction with a letter of credit. For example, a U.S. retailer opens a sight letter of credit in favor of a Taiwanese manufacturer of Christmas toys. The Taiwanese manufacturer ships the toys and presents his documents in August. Payment is due from the U.S. retailer, but he is not able to finance his inventory buildup without borrowing. Rather than borrow under his seasonal line of credit, the retailer draws a draft for 120 days on his bank. The bank accepts the draft, charging the retailer a commission for acceptance. The draft, now significantly strengthened (from an investor's point of view) by the addition of the bank's name, is sold by the bank (rediscounted) to a broker. The bank uses the proceeds to pay the sight obligation due the Taiwanese manufacturer. The broker sells the draft to an investor. In December, the retailer uses the proceeds from sale of the toys to pay the bank when the acceptance matures. The bank passes these funds through to the investor who presents the draft.

Acceptance financing is not limited to letter-of-credit sales. For instance, a U.S. tobacco company can use acceptance financing to buy leaf inventory for export. The regulations require that the exporter have a firm contract of sale from the foreign buyer in order to qualify the transaction as eligible. When such a contract is in place, the exporter draws a usance draft on his bank to cover the period from purchase of the tobacco domestically until shipment and receipt of proceeds from abroad. The exporter is able to finance his inventory buildup period and his receivable period, although the total may not exceed 180 days.

Acceptances can be used to finance shipments between two foreign countries. A Japanese importer needs dollars to pay for a shipment of oil from Kuwait. Rather than borrow Eurodollars, the importer draws a draft on his bank. The Japanese bank simultaneously draws a draft on a U.S. bank. The U.S. bank accepts the draft, rediscounts it with a broker, and pays the proceeds (less the acceptance commission) to the Japanese bank. The Japanese bank pays the Kuwaiti supplier, is repaid at maturity by the Japanese importer when the oil is sold, and then repays the U.S. bank which honors the investor's draft. This type of bank-to-bank lending to finance trade is a very important part of the acceptance market.

In summary, trade transactions involving imports and exports easily meet eligibility requirements, either in conjunction with letters of credit or not.

TRANSACTIONS INVOLVING GOODS IN TRANSIT

The Export Trading Act of 1982 amended Section 13 of the Federal Reserve Act. One of the major changes incorporated was the determination of eligibility for this class of transactions. Previously, banks were required to have at the time of acceptance "shipping documents conveying or securing title." However, most domestic carriers do not issue receipts that meet this requirement. Consequently, domestic shipments were rarely financed with acceptances. As amended, the eligibility and documentary requirements will be similar to those applied to import and export transactions. This change will undoubtedly increase the use of acceptances to finance domestic shipments.

TRANSACTIONS INVOLVING GOODS IN STORAGE

Banks providing acceptance financing for stored goods must have documents conveying or securing title to the goods. The security must be a "readily marketable staple," which is defined by the Federal Reserve as "an article of commerce, agriculture, or industry, of such uses as to make it the subject of constant dealings in ready markets with such frequent quotations of price as to make (a) the price easily and definitely ascertainable, and (b) the staple itself easy to realize upon by sale at any time." Cotton, potatoes, coal, and flour are prime examples. In practice, the document used to convey title is usually a warehouse receipt. Additionally, the financing must be in anticipation of a reasonably immediate sale, and not to carry the goods for speculative purposes or for an indefinite period of time.

TRANSACTIONS FOR DOLLAR EXCHANGE

Some countries, mainly in Latin America, are very dependent on one or two commodities for export earnings. With preapproval from the Federal Reserve, these countries are allowed to use acceptance financing as a source of working capital. The dollars are used to bring the commodities to market, and the resulting export earnings are used to retire the acceptances. Maturities are limited to three months. Transactions of this nature are a very small part of the total market.

ELEMENTS OF COST FOR THE BORROWER

A borrower incurs two distinct costs in obtaining acceptance financing. The first is the acceptance commission. This is the bank's charge for lending its name to that of the borrower; that is, guaranteeing that the borrower's obligation will be repaid. The bank is lending its name not its funds.

The second cost, the cost of funds, is the interest cost of discounting the draft. The source of funds is usually an investor, represented by a broker, who purchases bankers' acceptances for the same reason he buys bank certificates of deposit. In the case of bankers' acceptances, not only is the bank an obligor, but the maker of the draft is also secondarily liable. The result is that the investor normally has an extremely safe and liquid investment.

The total cost to the borrower is the commission plus the discounted rate of interest. Usually, the bank does not inform the customer of the commission, but rather adds the discount rate and the commission together to arrive at an all-in discount quote.

In marketing acceptance financing it is important to explain the discounting process to the customer and perhaps to provide him with the discount to interest adjustment. A chart for making this conversion is provided in Exhibit D.

ADVANTAGES/DISADVANTAGES FOR THE BORROWER

One factor which reduces the cost of funds for eligible acceptance financing is the absence of reserves if the draft is rediscounted with investors. When the accepting bank sells the draft to the broker to fund the transaction, the proceeds are not deemed a "deposit" by the Federal Reserve and are not, therefore, subject to reserve requirements. As the level of interest rates has risen over the past few years, the nominal cost of reserves has increased. When interest rates are at 5 percent, a 3 percent reserve requirement increases the cost of funds by 15 basis points. $(.05 \div .97 = .0515)$. When rates are 15 percent, the reserve requirement adds 46 basis points to the cost of funds $(.15 \div .97 = .1546)$. On the other hand, an *ineligible* bankers' acceptance, when rediscounted, *is* deemed a deposit and *is* subject to reserve requirements.

Another advantage for the borrower is that banks providing bankers' acceptance financing normally do not require compensating balances in addition to the acceptance commission. For borrowers required to increase compensating balances when borrowing, this feature of bankers' acceptance financing can be very attractive.

Still another factor which serves to reduce the cost of funds for bankers' acceptance financing is the participation of the Federal Reserve in the rediscount market. Henry Harfield, commenting on the Federal Reserve Act of 1913, stated:[1]

> the Act was not intended as a statutory grant of power to create acceptances, but rather as a stimulus to their use. . . . To facilitate as well as to encourage the participation of American banks in acceptance financing and thereby to promote the expansion of American trade, Congress created within the Federal Reserve System a support mechanism for United States bank credit. The Federal Reserve banks were authorized to purchase bankers' acceptances, thus providing a considerable measure of liquidity to the selling banks.

Historic "cost advantages" of acceptance financing are depicted in the following chart:

Date	Average Prime	Adjusted Prime*	Average 90-day Banker's Acceptance Rate	Account Commission	Total Banker's Acceptance Cost (4 + 5)	Adjusted Banker's Acceptance Cost†	Columns 3–7 Cost Difference
1958	3.83%	4.40%	2.04%	1.50%	3.54%	3.62%	.78%
1959	4.48	5.15	3.49	1.50	4.99	5.12	.03
1960	4.82	5.54	3.51	1.50	5.01	5.14	.40
1961	4.50	5.18	2.81	1.50	4.31	4.42	.76
1962	4.50	5.18	3.01	1.50	4.51	4.62	.56
1963	4.50	5.18	3.36	1.50	4.86	4.99	.19
1964	4.50	5.18	3.77	1.50	5.27	5.41	(.23)
1965	4.54	5.22	4.22	1.50	5.72	5.88	(.66)
1966	5.62	6.46	5.36	1.50	6.86	7.08	(.62)
1967	5.63	6.47	4.75	1.50	6.25	6.44	.03
1968	6.28	7.22	5.75	1.50	7.25	7.49	(.27)
1969	7.95	9.14	7.61	1.50	9.11	9.45	(.31)
1970	7.91	9.10	7.31	1.50	8.81	9.13	(.03)
1971	5.70	6.56	4.85	1.50	6.35	6.54	.02
1972	5.25	6.04	4.47	1.50	5.97	6.14	(.10)
1973	8.02	9.22	8.08	1.50	9.58	9.95	(.73)
1974	10.80	12.42	9.89	1.50	11.39	11.89	.53
1975	7.86	9.04	6.29	1.50	7.79	8.06	.98
1976	6.84	7.87	5.19	1.50	6.69	6.90	.97
1977	6.78	7.80	5.59	1.50	7.09	7.32	.48
1978	9.06	10.42	8.11	1.50	9.61	9.98	.44
1979	12.67	14.57	11.04	1.50	12.54	13.12	1.45

Note: Average cost difference in favor of bankers' acceptance—.21 percent.
* Column 2 × 115%
† Bond Equivalent Rate
Source: *Business Statistics, Survey of Current Business,* and First City National Bank of Houston Economics Department. Used with permission from Jasper H. Arnold, III, Vice President, First City National Bank of Houston. The chart appeared in "Banker's Acceptance: A Low-Cost Financing Choice," an article by Mr. Arnold in *Financial Executive,* July 1980, p. 18.

A final advantage of acceptance financing is that it can be used to go beyond the normal legal lending limit of banks to a single entity.

---

[1] Henry Harfield, *Bank Credits and Acceptances* (New York: Roland Press, 1974) pp. 125–26.

The regulations state that if "the bank is secured either by attached documents or by some other actual security growing out of the same transaction as the acceptance," then the bank can, in effect, double its legal lending limit to a customer.

There are, to be sure, some potential disadvantages for the borrower

Exhibit A
Acceptance Credit Agreement

Wachovia Bank and Trust Company, N.A.
Winston-Salem, North Carolina   _____
                                                                    Date

  We hereby request you from time to time to accept, for our account, drafts in United States Dollars drawn on you by us or by persons designated in writing by us to you upon or after the date hereof.

  In consideration of your accepting any such draft, we hereby agree as follows:

  1. As to such drafts or acceptances, to pay to you, at your accepting office, in United States legal tender, an amount sufficient to cover any such drafts or acceptances, your commission, interest at the prevailing rate where chargeable and all pertinent expenses, on demand, but in any event not later than on day of maturity, or, in case the acceptance is not payable at your said office, then on demand, but in any event in time to reach the place of payment in the usual course of the mails not later than on day of maturity.

  2. We certify that each draft, which may be designated by us for acceptance by you hereunder, will have not more than six (6) months sight to run, and will grow out of a transaction involving the importation or exportation of goods.

  3. We agree that in the event of any extension of the maturity or time for presentation of drafts, acceptances or documents, or any other modification of the terms of any transactions hereunder, at the request of any of us, with or without notification to the others, this agreement shall be binding upon each of us with regard to any transactions hereunder so modified, to drafts, documents, and property covered thereby and to any action taken by you or any of your correspondents in accordance with such extension or other modification.

  4. We shall request acceptance of drafts by telephone. We shall instruct you to complete one or more drafts drawn on Wachovia Bank and Trust Company, N.A., Winston-Salem, N.C. signed in blank by us and held in your custody for our account. All requests for acceptances will be confirmed in writing and include the certification that 1) no other financing is concurrent, 2) that the transaction has not been refinanced, and 3) the import or export of a product is involved.

  5. This agreement shall be binding upon us, our heirs, executors, administrators, successors and assigns, and shall inure to the benefit of, and be enforceable by, you, your successors, transferees and assigns. If this agreement should be terminated or revoked by operation of law as to us or any of us, we will indemnify and save you harmless from any loss which may be suffered or incurred by you in acting hereunder prior to the receipt by you, or your transferees or assigns, of notice in writing of such termination or revocation. If this agreement is signed by two or more parties, it shall be the joint and several agreement of such parties and whenever used herein, the singular number shall include the plural, and the plural the singular. This agreement shall be governed by and construed in accordance with the law of the State of North Carolina.

                                           By _____

                                           By _____

in using acceptance financing. Before examining these we should note two perceived disadvantages that are more apparent than real. The first is that acceptance financing involves complicated documentation and handling. In fact, an acceptance arising from a letter-of-credit transaction would require, at most, an additional draft. Acceptance financing, independent of shipping documents ("clean" acceptances), generally can be accomplished with: (1) an acceptance credit agreement: the borrower's promise to repay the bank when acceptances mature; (2) a draft; (3) a purpose statement: a letter from the borrower describing the underlying trade transaction being financed and certifying that no other financing is outstanding on the transaction and that the transaction has not been refinanced.

These documents can be constructed and handled by bank and borrower in a way that makes clean acceptance borrowing hardly more troublesome than borrowing in the commercial paper market. The acceptance credit agreement can be a continuing agreement lodged with the bank to support all acceptance borrowing. It can have much the same content as a standard bank letter-of-credit agreement, or it can be simplified to delete language pertaining to security and to focus on debt acknowledgment. Exhibit A is an example of a very simple acceptance agreement.

The draft is also simple, as per Exhibit B. To facilitate borrowing, blank drafts can be held in custody by the bank, to be filled in when transactions are consummated.

Finally, the purpose statement is also a simple document, although it contains key information governing the transaction. Exhibit C is illustrative. Most banks will accept by phone the information contained in the purpose statement, under subsequent written confirmation. When this is the case, and when presigned drafts are in bank custody, along with a continuing acceptance agreement, a financing can be arranged in minutes by phone. An explanation of how this occurs is

Exhibit B
Illustration of a Bankers' Acceptance

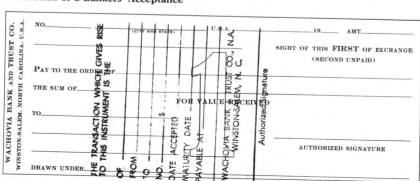

Exhibit C
Purpose Statement

Wachovia Bank & Trust Company, N.A.
P.O. Box 3099
Winston-Salem, North Carolina 27102

ATTENTION: International Department

Gentlemen:

Please create Bankers' Acceptance (s) by means of a draft (s) drawn by you on our behalf and pay the discounted proceeds to our account. The amount should be $5,000,000.00 and the value dates are from August 10, 1981 to October 30, 1981 .

We hereby certify that no other financing is outstanding nor has this transaction been refinanced and that the proceeds will be used to finance the following:

Export of _____tobacco_____
from _U.S.A._ to _France_ .

Very truly yours,

XYZ Company

By _____
       Authorized Signature

---

contained later in the discussion regarding bank involvement in acceptance financing. Suffice it to say here that acceptances can easily be arranged by borrowers if they work closely with their banks to establish an appropriate understanding of documentation and processing.

The second perceived (but misunderstood) disadvantage of using acceptance financing is that the borrower might somehow run afoul of the Federal Reserve's eligibility requirements and consequently incur a costly penalty. In fact, absent fraud on the borrower's part, this will not occur. Precedent indicates that the penalty for erroneously creating ineligible acceptances, and treating them as if they were eligible, is the retroactive imposition of a reserve requirement on the accepting bank (not on the bank customer). If the bank creates the acceptance on the basis of accurate information provided in the purpose statement, only to learn subsequently that it has erred in considering the transaction eligible, no compensation from the customer for the reserves is warranted. In short, the relationship between borrower and bank in acceptance financing protects the borrower from adverse consequences arising from ineligibility.

Having pointed out the cost and other advantages of acceptances, and having dealt with two perceived disadvantages, it is finally appropriate to acknowledge the existence of a few actual disadvantages to the borrower in using acceptance financing.

One limitation of bankers' acceptance financing is that the maximum term for eligible bankers' acceptances is 180 days. This is imposed by the Fed because most trade transactions, even when the transactions cover an inventory and a receivable period, are completed in six months. Transactions requiring more than six months of financing may not, therefore, be suitable for bankers' acceptance financing.

Another limitation is that prepayment is normally not permitted. Because the discounting of the draft results in a fixed-rate loan to the borrower, it is not surprising that prepayment (at least without penalty) is not allowed.

A final disadvantage has been largely eliminated by the Export Trading Act of 1982. Previously, banks had been limited in their capacity to accept and rediscount acceptances to 100 percent of their capital and surplus. This limitation was significant, with most large banks at their limits and consequently rationing acceptance financing, largely on the basis of price. The new regulations allow banks to go to 150 percent of capital and surplus and up to 200 percent with special permission of the Federal Reserve. The removal of this constraint, coupled with the liberalization of eligibility requirements regarding domestic shipments, will probably lead to explosive growth in acceptance financing in the next few years.

ACCEPTANCES PROVIDE OPPORTUNITY FOR BANKS

The preceding paragraphs have indicated both the ease with which eligible acceptances can be created for bank customers and the substantial benefits—including reduced costs—available to the customers therefrom. As with most banking transactions, however, the viability of bankers' acceptances depends upon the presence of benefits to customer and bank alike. While some banks have barely used their acceptance capacity, others have learned that a properly organized marketing and funding effort can produce significant profits and customer relationship benefits. The rest of this chapter identifies various benefits available to banks from the effective use of bankers' acceptances and addresses organizational issues that should be considered by banks contemplating the wholesale marketing of acceptance financing.

BENEFITS TO BANKS

The primary benefit to banks in the provision of bankers' acceptance financing is profit. Prior discussion identified two costs to the borrower from acceptance financing: the acceptance commission and the discounted interest charge. There is opportunity for profit in each.

As explained earlier, the acceptance commission is the fee the bank charges for taking the credit risk of its customer. It takes this risk by accepting a draft, thus creating a marketable instrument upon which it becomes the primary obligor. Historically, the minimum commission banks would charge was 1½ percent per annum. The 1974 explosion in oil prices changed that. Because oil is usually priced and paid for in dollars, the price explosion brought about an associated boom in the use of bankers' acceptances to finance oil trade, and competition among banks put substantial pressure on the traditional fee. Currently, commissions of as little as ½ percent per annum on interbank transactions are not unusual. Indeed, the spreads might be even lower except that as previously indicated the Federal Reserve limits aggregate eligible acceptances that each bank can create. This de facto rationing of acceptance financing appears to have placed a shaky floor under commissions. At present most still exceed ½ percent per annum, and frequently they are greater than 1 percent per annum. Successful negotiation of the commission is important to banks because commissions represent the total profit on acceptance transactions. As previously indicated, compensating balances are generally not exacted, and incremental income results only from incurrence of rate risk in the funding of the transaction—a dangerous proposition at best.

Before addressing the profit available to banks willing to incur this rate risk, it is useful to reiterate that in the process of accepting a draft, thereby earning its commission, the bank provides no funds and the customer receives none. Financing occurs only when the holder of the accepted draft has it discounted. Generally, this will occur simultaneously with the act of acceptance and at the accepting bank. It could occur subsequently, however, and at a different bank (or with someone else) willing to invest in the accepting bank's paper.

This explanation specifies the role of the accepting bank in creating an eligible acceptance and differentiates that role from the discounting process. Now assume that the customer does indeed want financing. It can ask the bank to discount the draft at the "prevailing market rate." To accomplish this, the bank must ascertain what, in fact, the prevailing market rate really is. For drafts of $1 million or greater, there is an active broker market to which the bank can refer. The brokers will provide a discount rate for the acceptance. After adding its commission, the bank passes this rate on to its customer. As explained later, the discount rate differs from bank to bank, giving some a competitive advantage over others. In any event, in discounting the draft, the bank provides the borrower with financing. It is at this point that the bank must decide either to rediscount the draft immediately at the quoted market rate, or hold it in portfolio. If it rediscounts the draft immediately, the only profit in the transaction is the acceptance commission.

If, however, the bank holds the draft in its own portfolio, the transaction assumes the characteristics of a fixed-rate advance, with the attendant rate risk. That is, holding the draft creates opportunity for future profit or loss arising from the interest-sensitive funding of the asset being held. While it can be argued that any resulting profit emanates from the original acceptance transaction, in our view it is more logically accounted for as a trading profit. It should accordingly be divorced from the acceptance financing profit.

In summary, banks can derive profit from two sources in acceptance financing—the acceptance commission and by incurring the rate risk on discounted drafts held in portfolio either temporarily or until maturity. The commission is true profit and should alone provide incentive to banks to do acceptance financing.

Another incentive to banks is the potential goodwill to be obtained from providing customers with acceptance financing. In enumerating advantages to the borrower who uses acceptance financing, we pointed out that relatively low cost is perhaps the most important. Moreover, we indicated that the perception that acceptance financing is somehow mechanically difficult to accomplish is, in fact, a misperception. The combination of being able to show a customer how relatively low-cost financing can be arranged through acceptances, and without cumbersome documentation, represents an excellent marketing opportunity that can produce significant goodwill for banks. It can also work as a door opener with a competitor's customer.

Another incentive to banks is that acceptances can be effectively used to satisfy customer financing needs in periods of tight money (if such periods ever again occur). This results from the fact that financing is available through the rediscount market, providing the bank with a nondeposit source of funds.

There are, then, clear benefits to banks which actively provide acceptance financing to their customers, not the least of which is profit opportunity. These benefits are most likely to accrue to those banks which effectively organize their marketing and funding efforts with an eye to operating at the lowest possible cost. Doing so will enhance competitive position and profitability.

BANK ORGANIZATION AND MARKETING

Banks which are successful at acceptance financing differ substantially in the organization of their money management and marketing efforts. But they have at least one thing in common: their money managers obtain funds at the lowest possible cost, and their marketers generally place these funds at the disposal of customers who are willing to pay the most for them (credit considerations being equal). Before commenting upon various organizational alternatives available to banks interested in developing wholesale acceptance financing programs, key funding and marketing considerations should be addressed.

Regarding funding of bankers' acceptances, we previously outlined the basic funding process to include: acceptance, discount, and rediscount. In attempting to obtain funds at the lowest possible costs, the banks' funds managers usually focus on discounting and rediscounting, leaving the process and pricing of acceptance to the marketers. As we described, when the marketers seek a discount rate from the funds manager, the latter can obtain this rate from brokers in New York and other money centers.

It is important to note, however, that these brokers rarely buy bankers' acceptances for their own account; rather, they purchase them for resale to investors at a profit. In quoting discount rates to banks (rediscount rates from the bank's viewpoint) they are, accordingly, oriented to the investor appeal of the underlying draft. This appeal differs based upon numerous variables including: perceived credit strength of the bank; volume of acceptances the bank offers the market; draft amount; draft tenor; and draft delivery date.

With regard to bank creditworthiness, there can be a significant difference in the discount rate accorded by investors. Most institutional portfolio managers (and indeed most individual investors) who invest in acceptances are name conscious. They usually undertake a formal review process to develop a list of acceptable banks in whose paper they will invest. Because the strong credits are favored, the resulting demand for their paper gives them a relative cost advantage versus weaker banks.

Volume considerations are of similar significance. Frequently investors will go to the trouble of qualifying a bank's name only if the bank provides substantial paper to the market. Banks with lower volumes may experience a thinner market and thus incur a cost premium.

The dollar amount of drafts offered to the market is also important, with investors generally favoring large transactions of $1 million and above. Smaller acceptances and odd amounts can incur a price disadvantage as can acceptances with shorter maturities. Generally speaking, acceptances with maturities shorter than 30 days incur a price disadvantage. Both size and maturity must be weighed against the fixed costs of completing a transaction.

Finally, the operational ability of the bank to make timely delivery to the broker of the drafts is important, since the broker is intent upon selling and delivering them to an investor as soon as possible. Convention calls for delivery of drafts and settlement two days after the dealing date. There can be advantages to being able to deal for earlier delivery, and there are significant disadvantages to dealing for later delivery. (In all cases, the bank must be able to deliver on settlement date, or a substantial penalty will result.)

It is not necessary for bank money managers to sell all acceptances through money center brokers. Frequently, better rates can be obtained locally, where investors are already accustomed to purchasing the bank's CDs and other investments. Local investors can be reached easily, through bank bond, trust, and retail departments and without a broker intermediary, thereby reducing cost. And smaller transactions are frequently of greater appeal to local investors. Local rediscounting probably best serves to complement rather than to replace the broker market, however, since local markets tend to be thin and will not absorb a high volume of paper at the most competitive rates.

Regardless of which approach a bank's funds management team favors—dealings through money center brokers or directly at the local level—they must always strive to get the best possible rediscount rates if their marketing counterparts are to be effective.

Turning, then, to the marketing group, it is equally important for banks interested in developing successful acceptance financing programs to effectively *identify, solicit,* and *service* their target markets.

We previously stated that banks that are successful at acceptance financing generally direct their efforts at those customers willing to pay the most, credit considerations being equal. This arises from the aggregate limits imposed by the Federal Reserve, causing no bank to have an inexhaustible ability to create acceptances. In practice, of course, pure price allocation of any scarce resource rarely prevails. So it is with acceptance financing.

Candidates for acceptance financing include corporations and foreign banks. As is true with most other financing instruments, acceptances generally do not command as great a spread in the interbank market as is available from corporate clients. But, the interbank market provides a more consistent borrowing base and is accordingly worthy of attention. Most banks that market acceptances aggressively allocate a high percentage of their capacity to foreign banks.

Turning to corporations, opportunity exists with large and small domestic companies and with foreign companies as well. Again, strict price allocation is probably too stringent an approach for most banks, particularly if they are concerned with servicing a variety of corporate customers. Thus, a small customer with relatively nominal acceptance financing eligibility might be as good a prospect as a larger client with significantly greater needs if good will and other considerations are factored in.

Each bank must devise its own strategy with respect to acceptance financing allocation. While price is a useful tool for allocation, it need not be the sole determinant. Fortunately, for banks just starting to exploit the market opportunities that acceptance financing can provide, the problem of allocation is far from acute. Only as the marketing program begins to take effect does the allocation issue arise. Each bank should have ample time to fine tune allocation criteria as the acceptance portfolio builds. Initially, the challenge is simply to book profitable business from each market.

Not only must each bank choose its own approach to identifying prospective acceptance financing clients, it must also develop its approach to the solicitation and servicing of this business.

With respect to solicitation, the role of the lending officer is crucial. He must be able to demonstrate a thorough knowledge of acceptance financing; assist customers in determining eligibility of their transactions; and demonstrate an ability to provide competitive quotes on a timely basis. Concerning servicing, the lending officer's role is also key. Emphasis must be placed on the continuing provision of acceptance financing with a minimum of effort from or disruption to the borrower. Documentation must move on an orderly basis, and must be kept appropriately simple. And funds must be made available when and as agreed.

Returning to the issue of organization then, successful banks must structure themselves to be able to discount their paper at the most attractive rates available without losing competitive position in the marketplace. Various structures will accommodate these goals.

In preparing for this article, the authors contacted a number of medium-sized regional banks, several larger regional banks, and a few money center banks to ascertain how different banks organize their acceptance trading activities. Most of the larger regional and money center banks have the bankers' acceptance trading function as part of their domestic money markets operations (funds trading area), whether it is part of the bond department or an investment department. These traders are responsible for contacts with brokers and other potential investors in bankers' acceptances and the supplying of rates to the lending staff throughout the bank. With this organizational structure, the bank is assured of access to various sources of funds, control of the bankers' acceptance funds position, and the compatibility of that position with the rest of the bank's policies, objectives, and overall liability structure.

Another structure which is utilized is to have the bankers' acceptance trading function located in closer proximity to key lending areas, perhaps as part of the international department. The attractiveness of this arrangement is that it facilitates the timely and accurate communication of rates to lending officers. It also puts the trader in an environment in which he can be attentive to the needs of the lending officer.

Various organizational arrangements seem to work for banks. Regardless of the structure utilized, success depends on two key factors. First, the funds management group must actively seek and provide the best rates available. This is accomplished by building rapport with brokers and investors, by broadening the market through the brokerage community and the education of local investors, and by aggressively trading when opportunities arise.

Second, rates must be available on a timely basis. This aspect of acceptance financing has become more important, even crucial, as financial markets have become increasingly volatile. Acceptance rates are money market rates and may move rapidly in a very short time. A quote made at 9:30 A.M. may be well off the market at 10:30 A.M. If rates have moved up significantly in that hour, the bank may lose its entire acceptance commission as the funding cost rises. If rates fall during that hour, almost certainly another bank will get the business by lowering its quotation.

A bank which is able to bring to bear on its marketplace knowledgeable account officers, timely information, and an aggressive funds management team can find acceptance financing an extremely profitable product.

CONCLUSION

Eligible bankers' acceptance represent a vigorous growing class of financing that offers benefits to borrower and bank alike. While the benefits to each are numerous, focus can be placed on reduced cost to borrowers, profit to lenders.

We have indicated that eligibility criteria are easy to understand and meet; that import and export transactions support most acceptances; that customers can operate with their banks in a relatively unencumbered manner and that banks can effectively organize their marketing and funding operations to exploit acceptance financing opportunities. In addition, considerable attention has been paid to the documentation, discounting and rediscounting aspects of acceptance financing.

In conclusion, it is perhaps useful to trace a typical transaction from start to finish, indicating customer and bank involvement.

Transaction

XYZ Company exports cars to Europe. The cars are invoiced monthly, with the current month's invoices totalling $9,389,000. The exporter wishes to obtain 180-day financing to cover the receivable liquidation period.

1. XYZ Company provides bank with acceptance credit agreement and presigned drafts to be held in custody.
2. XYZ Company telephones bank lending officer requesting 180-day financing in amount of $9,389,000 and asks for a rate indication.
3. Lending officer obtains indication of discount rate from funds management area, and adds predetermined acceptance commission.

Prior to providing lending officer with discount rate, funds management may have obtained indications from brokers. Broker could indicate preference for nine $1 million drafts and a $389,000 odd-lot draft, or funds management may have its own preference.

4. Lending officer communicates all-in rate to XYZ Company, which computes simple interest equivalent. XYZ Company may reject the rate as too costly. If the rate is accepted, XYZ Company provides information for the purpose statement which lending officer also makes available to whomever is responsible for draft preparation.

5. Lending officer indicates draft amount preference to customer (i.e. 9 × $1MM, 1 × $389,000) and advises draft preparer of same.

6. XYZ Company forwards purpose statement to bank, bank credits discounted proceeds to XYZ Company account, or otherwise pays per XYZ Company instructions.

7. Funds management either maintains discounted paper in portfolio or confirms rediscount sale and delivery with broker or other purchaser.

8. At maturity, ultimate holder/investor presents draft through its commercial bank for payment. Bank pays face amount of draft to presenter; charges XYZ Company account in same amount.

Exhibit D
Discount/Effective Annual Interest Rate (days)

Annual Discount (percent)	30	60	90	120	150	180
4.00	4.01	4.03	4.04	4.05	4.07	4.08
4.25	4.27	4.28	4.30	4.31	4.33	4.34
4.50	4.52	4.53	4.55	4.57	4.59	4.60
4.75	4.77	4.79	4.81	4.83	4.85	4.87
5.00	5.02	5.04	5.06	5.08	5.11	5.13
5.25	5.27	5.30	5.32	5.34	5.37	5.39
5.50	5.53	5.55	5.58	5.60	5.63	5.66
5.75	5.78	5.81	5.83	5.86	5.89	5.92
6.00	6.03	6.06	6.09	6.12	6.15	6.19
6.25	6.28	6.32	6.35	6.38	6.42	6.45
6.50	6.54	6.57	6.61	6.64	6.68	6.72
6.75	6.79	6.83	6.87	6.91	6.95	6.99
7.00	7.04	7.08	7.12	7.17	7.21	7.25
7.25	7.29	7.34	7.38	7.43	7.48	7.52
7.50	7.55	7.59	7.64	7.69	7.74	7.79
7.75	7.80	7.85	7.90	7.96	8.01	8.06
8.00	8.05	8.11	8.16	8.22	8.28	8.33
8.25	8.31	8.36	8.42	8.48	8.54	8.60
8.50	8.56	8.62	8.68	8.75	8.81	8.88
8.75	8.81	8.88	8.95	9.01	9.08	9.15
9.00	9.07	9.14	9.21	9.28	9.35	9.42
9.25	9.32	9.39	9.47	9.54	9.62	9.70
9.50	9.58	9.65	9.73	9.81	9.89	9.97
9.75	9.83	9.91	9.99	10.08	10.16	10.25

Exhibit D (*concluded*)

Annual Discount (percent)	30	60	90	120	150	180
10.00	10.08	10.17	10.26	10.34	10.43	10.53
10.25	10.34	10.43	10.52	10.61	10.71	10.80
10.50	10.59	10.69	10.78	10.88	10.98	11.08
10.75	10.85	10.95	11.05	11.15	11.25	11.36
11.00	11.10	11.21	11.31	11.42	11.53	11.64
11.25	11.36	11.46	11.58	11.69	11.80	11.92
11.50	11.61	11.72	11.84	11.96	12.08	12.20
11.75	11.87	11.98	12.11	12.23	12.35	12.48
12.00	12.12	12.24	12.37	12.50	12.63	12.77
12.25	12.38	12.51	12.64	12.77	12.91	13.05
12.50	12.63	12.77	12.90	13.04	13.19	13.33
12.75	12.89	13.03	13.17	13.32	13.47	13.62
13.00	13.14	13.29	13.44	13.59	13.74	13.90
13.25	13.40	13.55	13.70	13.86	14.02	14.19
13.50	13.65	13.81	13.97	14.14	14.30	14.48
13.75	13.90	14.07	14.24	14.41	14.59	14.77
14.00	14.17	14.33	14.51	14.69	14.87	15.05
14.25	14.42	14.60	14.78	14.96	15.15	15.34
14.50	14.68	14.86	15.05	15.24	15.43	15.63
14.75	14.93	15.12	15.31	15.51	15.72	15.92
15.00	15.19	15.38	15.58	15.79	16.00	16.22
15.25	15.45	15.65	15.85	16.07	16.28	16.51
15.50	15.70	15.91	16.12	16.34	16.57	16.80
15.75	15.96	16.17	16.40	16.62	16.86	17.10
16.00	16.21	16.44	16.67	16.90	17.14	17.39
16.25	16.47	16.70	16.94	17.18	17.43	17.69
16.50	16.73	16.97	17.21	17.46	17.72	17.98
16.75	16.99	17.23	17.48	17.74	18.01	18.28
17.00	17.24	17.50	17.75	18.02	18.30	18.58

The effective cost of acceptance financing can be calculated as follows:

$$\frac{\text{All-in-rate}}{1 - \left(\text{All-in-rate} \times \dfrac{\text{Days financed}}{360}\right)} \times 100 = \text{Effective interest rate}$$

For example, effective cost of a 180-day transaction with a 1 percent commission and 9 percent discount rate could be calculated as follows:

$$\frac{.10}{1 - .10 \times \left(\dfrac{180}{360}\right)} \times 100 = 10.53$$

17
International Collections

LEONARD A. BACK
Vice President
Citibank, N.A.

Collection terms are a common sales device but are not exclusively related to international export sales. Such terms, for example, can cover a sale of goods between an exporter in New York and an importer in California or, for that matter, can be a term of sale between two businessmen selling and buying goods within a single city in the United States. Our treatment of the subject in this book will be from the viewpoint of a seller in one country to the buyer in another under collection terms of sale. However, except for the difficulties which are sometimes imposed by differences in language, in currencies, and in cultures, the collection term, as a basis for payment, operates similarly whether or not the transaction is international or domestic.

EXPORTERS' OPTIONS FOR PAYMENT

Cash Advance Terms

Before an exporter would agree to collection terms of sale, he might strive to sell on terms more favorable to him. Given a choice, the first choice of anyone selling anything is to be paid in advance. For an exporter this virtually means receiving payment with the purchase order. But if the payment is in the form of the buyer's check, that is, a check drawn on the buyer's account with his bank, the exporter will need to have that check sent for collection. An exporter receiving such a check turns it over to his own bank with instructions to handle it for collection. His bank will then route it for payment to the bank on which it was drawn by the buyer, and when paid and the funds remitted from the buyer's bank to the exporter's bank, the check will be considered collected. The exporter will then ship the cash-in-advance order.

Rather than make payment in the form of the buyer's check, the buyer may effect payment by acquiring and remitting a bank cashier's check payable in the exporter's country and payable to the exporter, or alternatively, the buyer might arrange for an international-funds transfer for payment to the exporter. Payment either in the form of bank cashier's check issued by a bank in the exporter's country or of a funds transfer would avoid the need to have the buyer's check "collected" prior to shipping the order.

Letter-of-Credit Terms

Many buyers of goods do not want to give up funds in advance but are willing to arrange irrevocable letter-of-credit terms which provide for payment to the exporter at the time shipment of the order is effected. This payment to the exporter under an irrevocable letter of credit would be effected immediately against documents covering the shipment of the order. When discussing letter-of-credit terms with the buyer, the exporter may be willing to grant terms to the buyer wherein under the letter of credit the exporter presents the shipping documents and receives an accepted draft (banker's acceptance) instead of actual payment. The banker's acceptance may have terms such as 90 days or possibly as much as 180 days (depending on the originally agreed terms between buyer and seller), but the exporter knows that he can sell the banker's acceptance immediately to obtain funds rather than wait until the banker's acceptance matures for payment.

Open Account Terms

Instead of either receiving funds prior to shipment (cash in advance) or at the time of shipment (irrevocable letter of credit), the exporter may be requested to ship on open-account terms. This simply means that the exporter will ship without having received payment or a bank assurance of payment but will get paid under the usual payment terms of the buyer, perhaps 60 days from the bill-of-lading date or some other established term. Open-account terms require the exporter to have complete faith in the buyer's honesty for payment.

Collection Terms

In negotiating the terms of an export sale, the buyer may insist that the sale can only be made on collection terms. What are collection terms?

Collection terms mean that the exporter will draw a draft (also called a bill of exchange) on the buyer who will honor that draft when it is presented to him (pay it, or accept it if a term draft) after the export order has been shipped. An illustration of a draft drawn by the exporter-seller on the importer buyer is depicted on page 273. If the buyer and seller agree on collection terms of sale, the term or tenor of the draft instrument, as well as the documents to accompany the draft, are elements which should be clarified in the early collection-terms discussion between the parties.

COLLECTION DRAFTS

Sight or Usance Drafts

A brief definition of the parties and elements that comprise the banking instrument called a "draft" or "bill of exchange" is the basis of our further discussion and illustration:

Maker or drawer	The party in whose name the draft order is drawn (usually appears in the lower right of the form, like a check).
Drawee	The party on whom the order is drawn.
Payee	The party to whom the order is payable (usually the drawer or a bank).
Tenor	The term for which it is payable (sight or a time period).
Date and place	Date issued and locale at which drawn.
Number	Optional reference number of drawer.

The first essential point to be settled between the buyer and seller is the term of the collection draft (sometimes called a trade draft or a commercial draft). Will the buyer pay the draft when it is presented by a bank in his country? If the answer is yes, the term or tenor of the draft should be "payable at sight," which means payable on demand or upon presentation. If the buyer requires longer terms of payment, he may request that the draft drawn against his account bear terms anywhere from 30 days to 180 days or longer. The exporter will need to decide if he can agree to await payment for such longer term.

Drafts draw on a term basis are called time drafts or usance drafts. They are presented to the drawee-buyer to be "accepted." The acceptance notation across the face of the instrument, when made by the drawee-buyer, represents a legal acknowledgment of his obligation to pay the draft at its maturity at his place of business. The drawee, when adding the acceptance notation, may also inscribe "payable at (his bank)." Noting a collection draft as payable at a bank enables the holder of the accepted instrument to present the draft at maturity to the bank on a collection basis. The named bank will effect payment provided the drawee-acceptor has made arrangements with that bank for such draft(s) to be paid.

Illustration of a Collection Draft (bill of exchange)

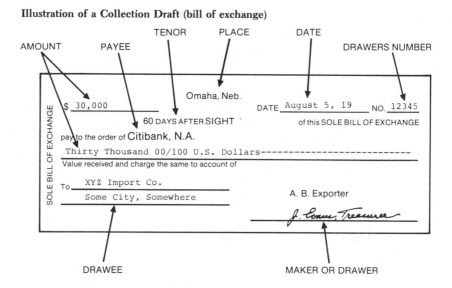

Understanding Draft Terms

Whether you are the importer or the exporter, it is important to be able to distinguish between a draft term *days after sight* and one drawn *days after date.* Draft terms, for example, 30 days sight (actually days *after* sight) will cause a draft to mature 30 days from the date accepted. Thus a draft 30-days sight, dated March 15 and accepted April 1, matures for payment April 30. The same draft, if drawn for terms 30 days date and dated March 15 and if accepted April 1, will mature 30 days from the draft date of March 15. That maturity date will be April 14.

From the foregoing explanation it is important to remember that drafts with terms "x days sight" mature based on the dates *accepted.* Drafts "x days-date" mature x days from the date of the draft regardless when it is accepted but provided that it is accepted on some day during its life. To illustrate further:

	Draft Date	*Amount*	*Term*	*Date Accepted*	*Maturity*
Days sight*	September 1	$100,000	90-days sight	September 15	December 14
Days date†	September 1	$100,000	90-days date	September 21	November 29

* (September, 15 days + October, 31 days + November, 30 days + December, 14 days = 90 days)
† (September, 30 days + October, 31 days + November, 29 days = 90 days)

Checks for Collection

It was previously mentioned that a seller might receive a check in payment of an order, a check which the seller would arrange to have "collected" before filling the order. A U.S. supplier of goods who received a check drawn on a U.S. bank might instead choose to deposit the check and, realizing the time required to prepare to ship the order covered by the check, assume that if the check is not returned unpaid before the shipment is made, that it is a paid check. Yet, if the supplier wants to be absolutely certain that the check is paid, he will send it on a collection basis via his own bank, which bank will notify the supplier when the check has been finally paid.

In the instance of considering the check as a deposit, the supplier (as depositor) takes the risk that the check will be returned unpaid. In the instance of having the check collected, that risk is eliminated once notice of final payment from the bank is received, but the supplier pays a collection fee to his bank for the service. The fee may also include an amount charged by the bank on which the check was drawn.

Whatever benefit may be realized from a check received from a domestic buyer being handled as a deposited check, that benefit is unavailable if the check received is from an overseas buyer and is payable at a bank overseas because such checks are not handled for deposit in U.S. banks (U.S.-dollar checks on Canada may be deposited at some banks). The only method available to an exporter to assure that the funds represented by the check are good funds is to send the check "for collection."

The process of collection of a check is shown in the diagram on page 275.

Bank fees for the collection of checks are rather modest, but when check amounts are less than a few hundred dollars, the fees might represent a significant percentage of the amount being collected. The supplier who receives checks for relatively small amounts would do well to request such payments in the form of an airmail transfer of funds directly to his bank account or by a check drawn in U.S. dollars on a U.S. bank, thereby avoiding bank collection of a check payable overseas.

Clean and Documentary Drafts

A buyer and seller may agree on the use of a collection draft payable at sight or on a term basis but may further agree that delivery of the shipment will not be contingent upon payment or acceptance of the draft. In effect, that type of agreement is a combination open account shipment payable on collection terms. Whatever label may be applied to this type of arrangement, from a bank's viewpoint it will be classified as a clean draft collection; that is, one without documents except possibly for an invoice attachment. The documents covering title to the goods will flow directly from the seller to the buyer. Then the draft drawn for the value of the order will be presented to

Collection of a Check-Flow Diagram

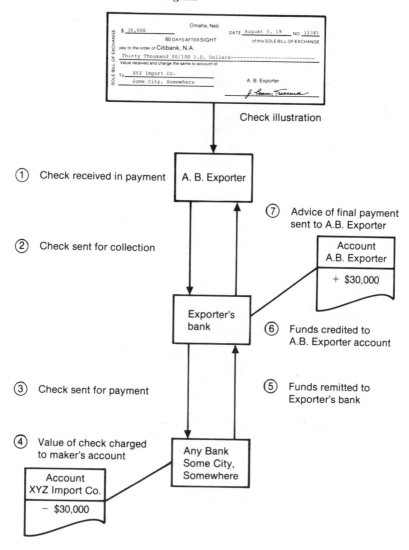

Check illustration

① Check received in payment — A. B. Exporter

⑦ Advice of final payment sent to A.B. Exporter

② Check sent for collection

⑥ Funds credited to A.B. Exporter account

③ Check sent for payment

⑤ Funds remitted to Exporter's bank

④ Value of check charged to maker's account

the exporter's bank to be sent for collection from the buyer. Additional types of collection transactions typified as clean include the collection of promissory notes and other instruments.

The clean collection draft is less prevalently used than one wherein the seller agrees to send the *draft and shipping documents* covering the order on a collection basis. The so-called documentary collection will have attached to the draft not only invoices but the bills of lading, insurance documents, and any other documents necessary for the buyer to obtain the goods, but usually only after he honors the draft by having paid it (if payable at sight) or having accepted it (if payable on terms).

COLLECTION INSTRUCTIONS FOR THE BANK

We will discuss shortly the relative importance of the various documents which accompany a documentary collection draft, but for now the point to be emphasized is that with a documentary collection, the drawee of the draft, who is usually the buyer, does not acquire the documents attached to the draft until he honors the draft. When the draft and documents are sent by the exporter or the exporter's agent to the bank to be remitted for collection, specific instructions should be given to the bank. These are usually:

Deliver documents against payment (if sight draft).

Deliver documents against acceptance (if a term or usance draft).

In Case of Dishonor

Once having instructed the bank (who will remit the collection overseas) whether to release the documents against payment or acceptance, what if the draft is not paid (or not accepted)? How should the overseas collecting bank report such notice of dishonor, by airmail or by cable? Instructions to the bank should so indicate.

Remittance of Proceeds

When payment is made, should the proceeds be remitted by airmail or by cable? Unless the amount is small, the cost of money and the possible reinvestment return usually recommend that proceeds be returned by telex or cable. However, specific instructions must be given to the bank, otherwise airmail remittance will be the method used.

Who Pays Bank Fee

Who is to pay the banking fees of the exporter's bank? Who is to pay the fees of the overseas bank? What if the drawee is to pay them but refuses to do so? Can payment of the fees be waived?

Answers to the above questions must be decided upon before the draft and documents are sent for collection. These instructions and some additional ones appear in the illustration on page 278 of a typical, remitting bank collection-instruction form which is prepared by the exporter or his agent.

Protest Instructions

A protest is a certificate of dishonor issued by a party legally authorized within a country to issue such a certificate at the place where the dishonor occurs. Such notice of dishonor has little practical value in a collection transaction unless the drawer plans to institute legal action against a drawee who dishonors a draft. If a draft were payable at sight, the drawer would need more evidence in court than the certificate of dishonor to prove any claim. Proof of breach of contract undoubtedly would need to be established. However if the drawee had accepted the draft and failed to pay it at maturity, the payee or other endorser of the draft as legally entitled to the funds would have a claim merely in the dishonored draft.

Protest action can be expensive in some countries and in others can also be damaging to the business reputation of those against whom such action is taken. It is therefore wise for exporters to investigate the implications of protest action before giving a bank such instructions.

Hold for Arrival of Merchandise

It is a practice in some countries to honor collection drafts only after the related merchandise has arrived in that country's port. In recognition of this practice and to avoid needless presentations of the collection draft to the drawee, the exporter will normally instruct the bank to hold off effecting collection until the arrival of the merchandise.

Provisional Deposit

When the seller's draft is denominated in a strong currency (often called a hard currency), such as the U.S. dollar has been for many decades, it can happen that the buyer's country is in short supply of that currency. If that is the case, the central bank in that country will ration U.S. dollars, and drafts payable in dollars temporarily will be paid in local currency. Such temporary payment is known as a provisional deposit which is held by the collecting bank in the buyer's country until the dollars are made available by the central bank in that country. Provisional deposits should be required to be accompanied by the drawee-buyer's written agreement to supply additional local currency, if necessary, to buy the required dollars to cover the value of the draft when finally paid in dollars.

Discount or Interest

Depending upon the agreement between the buyer and seller, the collection transaction may contain instructions to the collecting bank

Remitting Bank Collection-Instruction Form

Item 313700 (FOB 608(L) Rev. 7-79

Telex from Overseas No. 420392/235530   **1**
Attn: NYCLC

TO: **Citibank, N.A.**
           NBG COLLECTION OPERATIONS
           111 WALL STREET, NEW YORK, N.Y. 10043

COLLECTING BANK		DATE
(IF BLANK, YOUR CORRES- PONDENT)		

WE ENCLOSE THE FOLLOWING ITEM FOR [ ] COLLECTION AND [ ] CREDIT TO OUR ACCOUNT NUMBER
[ ] AN ADVANCE   REMITTANCE TO US BY CHECK

Subject to Uniform Rules for the Collection of Commercial Paper, International Chamber of Commerce, Publication No. 322   IO. 254

DRAWERS REFERENCE NUMBER	DATE OF DRAFT	TENOR	AMOUNT
DRAWER		DRAWEE	
ADDRESS			

BILLS OF LADING ORIG. / DUP.	PARCEL POST RECEIPTS	INSUR. CERT'S.	INVOICES	CONSULAR INVOICES	PACKING LISTS	WEIGHT CERT'S.	CERT'S. OF ORIGIN	OTHER DOCUMENTS	
DELIVER DOCUMENTS AGAINST			ACCEPTANCE	PAYMENT	YOUR CHARGES			DRAWEE'S EXPENSE	DRAWER'S EXPENSE
ADVISE BY CABLE			NON-ACCEPTANCE	NON-PAYMENT	MAIL DOCUMENTS			DRAWEE'S EXPENSE	DRAWER'S EXPENSE
REMIT PROCEEDS BY CABLE			DRAWEE'S EXPENSE	DRAWER'S EXPENSE	FOREIGN BANK CHARGES			DRAWEE'S EXPENSE	DRAWER'S EXPENSE
REMIT PROCEEDS BY AIRMAIL					WAIVE CHARGES IF REFUSED				
PROTEST			NON-ACCEPTANCE	NON-PAYMENT	DO NOT WAIVE CHARGES				
DO NOT PROTEST					HOLD FOR ARRIVAL OF MERCHANDISE				

IF DOLLAR EXCHANGE IS NOT IMMEDIATELY AVAILABLE AT MATURITY (OR ON PRESENTATION IF DRAWN AT SIGHT) AND IT IS NECESSARY TO PROVISIONALLY ACCEPT LOCAL CURRENCY PENDING AVAILABILITY OF DOLLAR EXCHANGE, IT MUST BE DISTINCTLY UNDERSTOOD THAT THE DRAWEE SHALL REMAIN LIABLE FOR ALL EXCHANGE DIFFERENCES. AT TIME OF DEPOSIT OF LOCAL CURRENCY OBTAIN FROM DRAWEES THEIR WRITTEN UNDERTAKING TO BE RESPONSIBLE FOR ANY EXCHANGE DIFFERENCES. THE DRAFT MUST NOT BE SURRENDERED TO DRAWEES UNTIL FINAL PAYMENT FOR FACE AMOUNT IN U.S. DOLLAR EXCHANGE.

ALLOW A DISCOUNT OF		IF PAID	
COLLECT INTEREST AT THE RATE OF		% FROM	

IN CASE OF NEED REFER TO		WHO IS EMPOWERED BY US: TO ACT FULLY ON OUR BEHALF I.E. AUTHORIZE REDUCTIONS, EXTENSIONS, FREE DELIVERY, WAIVING OF PROTESTS ETC.	WHO MAY ASSIST IN OBTAINING ACCEPTANCE OR PAYMENT OF DRAFT, AS DRAWN, BUT IS NOT TO ALTER ITS TERMS IN ANY WAY.

OTHER INSTRUCTIONS

_____
AUTHORIZED SIGNATURE

to allow the drawee-buyer a discount of some percentage, say 2 percent, (or a fixed sum), if paid immediately or within a specified time period.

On the other hand, additional to the draft amount the buyer/seller agreement may be that the drawee-buyer is to pay interest at a specified rate computed from the date of the collection, the date of the bill of lading, or some other date, until paid. Thus the longer payment is delayed, the more costly the interest to the drawee-buyer.

If a discount is to be allowed or if interest is to be collected, instructions to the bank must so state.

In Case of Need

If for any reason the drawee-buyer refuses to honor the collection draft, it is often useful if the seller has an agent in the buyer's country to whom the collecting bank can refer the matter for assistance. The agent can either be empowered to assist the collecting bank or to have full authority over the collection transaction. With full authority the agent can give full instructions to the collecting bank just as if the instructions originated from the seller.

Legal Action

In the event that the seller decides to take legal action against the drawee for refusing to honor a collection draft and the seller has been advised that the draft has been protested as instructed by the seller, the next step would be for the seller to issue instructions to his bank to have the transaction turned over to an attorney in the drawee's country. When that has been done, both the collecting bank overseas and the seller's bank will close their records on the transaction, and the attorney and the seller will deal directly between each other.

Principal/Agent Relationship

It is important for anyone who gives a bank a check or draft for collection to understand that the bank who sends the collection to the collecting bank as well as the collecting bank itself both act only as an agent for the customer. It should be emphasized that the banks are not collection agencies in the sense that they will apply pressure tactics to achieve payment. Except for routinely tracing or presenting an unpaid collection for payment, the banks will usually initiate no action on an unpaid transaction unless instructed by the principal, the bank's customer who originated the collection.

SHIPPING DOCUMENTS

There are no prescribed documents which accompany a documentary draft for collection. Whatever documents are agreed between buyer and seller for a particular shipment appropriately can be attached to a collection draft. We shall, however, briefly discuss some of the more commonly used documents covering a shipment.

Commercial Invoice

A document listing the merchandise by description, quantity, and price, totaled for the amount of the sale, is called a commercial invoice. Depending upon the quantities of the merchandise ordered, the listing may consist of one or several pages.

Bill of Lading

The document issued by the transportation company covering carriage of the goods from one point to another is called a bill of lading.

For transportation over land it may be a truck bill of lading or railroad bill of lading. If over water it may be an ocean bill of lading or barge bill of lading. If by air, it will be an air waybill.

Bills of lading may be issued in negotiable form or nonnegotiable form. The latter are known as "straight consignments," and the party to whom such goods are consigned can often acquire the underlying merchandise without having to submit the related bill of lading.

If issued in negotiable form, bills of lading are issued consigned "to order" of a named party. In that form title to the goods is passed only by endorsement of the bills of lading by the "to order" party. Goods transported under negotiable bills of lading are not to be released by the transport company until the bills of lading have been surrendered bearing the endorsement of the party claiming the goods. Unless such "to order" bills of lading are presented, the transport company will require presentation to it of a bank guarantee or indemnity bond covering a release of the merchandise in the absence of the bills of lading.

Thus when a shipment is effected under collection terms, it is usually negotiable bills of lading which are attached to the draft. With negotiable bills of lading the drawee-buyer generally cannot pick up the goods unless he honors the collection draft and thereby acquires possession of the bills of lading properly endorsed along with the related documents.

The manner in which merchandise is consigned should be carefully considered by the exporter. Shipments by air cannot be made on negotiable bills of lading, and when shipped by that mode, the exporter will need to consign the goods to someone other than the buyer if control over the goods is to be retained until the buyer honors the draft. If the exporter has no agent in the buyer's country to whom he can consign the goods, he may inquire whether the overseas collecting bank will serve as consignee.

Insurance Certificate or Policy

In a sale of goods where the exporter and the importer agree that the exporter should insure the goods and add the insurance premium to the selling price, among the documents sent with the collection draft will usually be an insurance certificate. Certificates are more prevalent than use of the policies themselves since an exporter generally insures all of his exports under an open policy. The insurance certificate is issued for the coverage of one shipment under that open policy. Certificates are issued in negotiable form so that by endorsement on the reverse of the form the insured party can transfer his rights. With a negotiable insurance certificate properly endorsed, if the buyer having paid the collection draft has an insurance claim, the certificate can be used to file the insurance claim.

If the buyer is arranging for insurance coverage, the exporter would not supply any insurance documents with the collection draft.

Consular Invoice or Customs Invoice

Customs officials in most importing countries require one or more of the export documents to be submitted to clear entry of the goods into the buyer's country. A special document called a consular invoice is required by a few countries of the world. This special document, after preparation, must be visaed (officially stamped) by the consulate of the importing country domiciled in a city in the exporting country. Most countries have done away with special consular documentation although many continue to require that a commercial invoice be visaed by the consulate nonetheless. For imports within the United States, the exporters of some types of merchandise must prepare a form known as the U.S. Customs Invoice, but there is no visa required of that form.

Inspection Certificate

An importer, who requires evidence that the quantity or quality of a shipment meets the exact standards specified in the contract, may require the exporter to have the goods inspected either for quantity or quality or both and require that an inspection certificate accompany the export documents. It is also usually agreed between buyer and seller that the inspection firm be independent of the seller. Obviously there is a cost for such inspection which the seller will add to the price of the goods. The banks handling inspection certificates with collection drafts do not accept any responsibility for the contents of those certificates.

COLLECTION PROCESS FOR EXPORTERS

Having discussed many aspects of collection terms, let us now look at the process from the beginning to the end on an export transaction.

Agree on Terms

With any type of export sale, the seller and buyer must first agree on the terms, not only whether they will use collection terms but what specific collection terms. Is the draft to be paid at sight? If not, what terms? What will the agreed-upon price cover? Only the cost of the goods or including the freight cost? Or including cost of goods, insurance premium, and freight (CIF)? How are the goods to be shipped by air, by sea? How will they be consigned? These and perhaps other questions need to be answered *before shipment arrangements are begun.*

Effect Shipment

Once the time or approximate date for shipment is known, the exporter can arrange for the actual export. If the exporter does not have an export department, the details of handling the export order will likely be turned over to a freight forwarder. Freight forwarders make all the arrangements for shipment and for sending the collection draft and documents to the exporter's bank.

From a business viewpoint it is important that the shipment be effected in a timely manner. The buyer-importer, who is expecting the shipment, may have a need to reach his market within a certain time frame and any delay in shipment of the goods could produce a reason for nonpayment of the collection draft.

Dispatch Collection to the Bank

Either the exporter or the exporter's forwarding agent will prepare the bank-transmittal collection letter and together with the draft and documents deliver or mail it to the bank where the exporter does his banking and maintains an account. The exporter's bank will complete the transmittal letter which will accompany the draft and documents being sent to the collecting bank. If the exporter does not give instructions to his forwarder as to which bank the forwarder should send the collection transaction, the forwarder will likely send it to a bank of his choice.

Many banks offer a service which enables the exporter or his forwarding agent to send the collection draft and documents directly overseas on a prenumbered form. The banks make these direct collection forms available. For each collection transaction sent overseas on this form, a copy of the form is sent to the exporter's bank (supplier of the forms) who records the transaction on its books and handles all other bank collection procedures from that point forward. The benefit of the direct collection service to the exporter or his forwarding agent is that it expedites transmittal of the draft and documents to the overseas bank by anywhere from one to three or four days, the amount of time saved often depending on the proximity of the sender to the exporter's bank.

Receive Advices/Give Instructions

The role of the overseas collecting bank is to present the draft and documents to the drawee (buyer) for payment or acceptance as called for by the transaction. If for some reason the draft is not honored on first presentation, the overseas bank will notify the originating bank (exporter's bank) by airmail or by cable as instructed. When received by the exporter's bank, such information will be passed along to the exporter. When the exporter decides to take some action involving a need to instruct the overseas bank, he will do so through his own bank who has a record of the collection transaction and should be the communications intermediary between the exporter and the overseas collecting bank. As stated earlier, the exporter's bank will precipitate no action of its own except to routinely trace for payment or acceptance, other than eventually to recall the collection as unpaid if all efforts to collect are considered fruitless.

Receive Payment

Every collection has the objective of realizing payment. The exporter or forwarding agent should give clear instructions to the exporter's bank specifying how payment to the exporter is to be rendered. Is the exporter's account to be credited with the proceeds? Or is the exporter to be paid by cashier's check? If so, what is the mailing address?

If the draft sent for collection is payable on a term basis, the draft will first be presented for acceptance to the drawee. Once the drawee has accepted the draft, the overseas collecting bank will advise the exporter's bank of the acceptance and also provide the date of maturity, the date the draft is due for payment. The exporter's bank will relay this information to the exporter.

DRAFTS FOR NEGOTIATION OR PURCHASE

It is sometimes possible for an exporter to arrange with his bank to finance his export-collection drafts. Such financing usually has the bank advancing to the exporter the amount of each draft (or some percentage of the draft) given to the bank on a collection basis. When a draft is collected and ultimately paid, the exporter will be charged the agreed interest rate between the period of the advance and date of final payment. Advancing the amount of the exporter's draft to the exporter but reserving the right to recover such advance if the draft should ultimately be unpaid is called negotiation of the exporter's draft with recourse.

If instead of advancing funds against the draft at an agreed interest rate, the bank were to discount from the face amount interest at a fixed rate for a fixed period of time, the bank could be said to have purchased the bill. Whether such purchase is with recourse or without recourse will depend upon whether the risk of nonpayment falls on the exporter (with recourse) or the bank (without recourse). In the latter case the bank would assume any losses due to nonpayment. The purchase by a bank of collection drafts without recourse is much less common.

Uniform Rules for Collections

A series of rules have been published by the International Chamber of Commerce entitled, "Uniform Rules of Collections, ICC Publication No. 322." These rules became effective January 1, 1979, as a revision of rules which had been in effect since 1967.

The rules govern practices and procedures between banks engaged in handling collection transactions, but exporters and importers are well advised to become aware of the rules to gain a better understanding of the manner in which banks will service their collections. (See Appendix.)[1]

COLLECTIONS FOR IMPORTERS

We have reviewed the process whereby an exporter sends for collection a draft drawn on an importer on terms and for an amount previously agreed upon in a purchase order or other contractual arrangement between the buyer and seller. When the draft and documents arrive at the collecting bank in the importer's country, the manner by which presentation will be made to the importer may vary by country. In many countries a messenger from the bank will make a presentation to the drawee-importer. In other countries the importer may be advised by telephone or mail that documents together with a draft drawn on the importer have arrived. The importer would then be expected to give the bank instructions for payment or would arrange to stop at the bank to effect payment or acceptance of the draft as the case may be. In the United States the draft and documents are sometimes given to the importer on a messenger's "left out," a form of receipt. The messenger would return later that day for either the payment or the accepted draft (or return of the documents if the draft is dishonored).

The collecting bank is responsible for the documents and their release to the importer only against payment or acceptance of the draft as instructed. However, responsibility for the related merchandise is beyond the purview of the bank and only in exceptional circumstances will a collecting bank follow any instructions concerning care of the merchandise itself.

---

[1] A complete catalog of publications of practical use to the world business community is available from the ICC Publishing Corporation, Inc., 801 Second Avenue, Suite 1204, New York, New York 10017. Uniform Rules for Collections (ICC Publication No. 322) may be purchased from the ICC Publishing Corporation at a cost of $3.50 and $1.00 postage and handling, plus sales tax if applicable.

Except for open-account terms, collection terms are those most favorable for the importer. Once an importer pays a sight draft or accepts a time draft, any claims with regards to the merchandise must be settled directly between buyer and seller. The fact that business firms continue to handle collection-term sales between each other year after year attests to the fact that such claims are settled and that the collection term plays a necessary role in international trade as well as in domestic trade.

SUMMARY

The contents of this chapter give a brief overview of the most typical aspects of collection terms. However, both importers and exporters should be aware of the legal fabric and options governing each step in this type of activity as the differences can vary widely.

APPENDIX

United States Council
of the
International Chamber of Commerce
1212 Avenue of the Americas
New York, New York 10036
Telex 14-8361 NYK   Tel. (212) 354-4480

Uniform Rules
for Collections
I.C.C. Publication No. 322
EFFECTIVE JANUARY 1, 1979

The International Chamber of Commerce published its "Uniform Rules for the Collection of Commercial Paper" for the first time in 1956. They were revised in 1967, the revision being effective from 1st January 1968, as Publication No. 254.

The present revision was approved by the Council of the ICC in June 1978 to be in force from 1st January 1979. It is being issued with the title "Uniform Rules for Collections" as Publication No. 322.

These rules are also available in a French as well as a German-English edition.

Foreword

These new ICC "Uniform Rules for Collections" enter into force as from 1st January 1979.

This development will interest bankers throughout the world since the new Rules replace the existing "Uniform Rules for the Collection of Commercial Paper" (Publication No. 254), which have been widely used since their introduction in 1967.

The new title was chosen since, in practice, documents collected are as likely to have as much a financial as a commercial character.

In making this revision, the ICC's Banking Commission has taken into account both the evolution in practice since 1967 and specific problems that have arisen that could not be solved by the existing rules. An example is the course of action presenting banks should follow when the collection order requires the payment of interest that the drawee refuses to pay. The revised Rules give a clear ruling on this problem.

This revision reflects the policy of the ICC to stay abreast of changes in international commerce.

Carl-Henrik Winqwist
Secretary General
of the ICC

General Provisions and Definitions

A These provisions and definitions and the following articles apply to all collections as defined in (B) below and are binding upon all parties thereto unless otherwise expressly agreed or unless contrary to the provisions of a national, state or local law and/or regulation which cannot be departed from.

B For the purpose of such provisions, definitions and articles:

1. **i** "Collection" means the handling by banks, on instructions received, of documents as defined in (ii) below, in order to

a) obtain acceptance and/or, as the case may be, payment, or

b) deliver commercial documents against acceptance and/or, as the case may be, against payment, or

c) deliver documents on other terms and conditions.

ii "Documents" means financial documents and/or commercial documents:

a) "financial documents" means bills of exchange, promissory notes, cheques, payment receipts or other similar instruments used for obtaining the payment of money;

b) "commercial documents" means invoices, shipping documents, documents of title or other similar documents, or any other documents whatsoever, not being financial documents.

iii "Clean collection" means collection of financial documents not accompanied by commercial documents.

iv "Documentary collection" means collection of

a) financial documents accompanied by commercial documents;

b) commercial documents not accompanied by financial documents.

2. The "parties thereto" are:

i The "principal" who is the customer entrusting the operation of collection to his bank;

ii The "remitting bank" which is the bank to which the principal has entrusted the operation of collection;

iii The "collecting bank" which is any bank, other than the remitting bank, involved in processing the collection order;

iv The "presenting bank" which is the collecting bank making presentation to the drawee.

3. The "drawee" is the one to whom presentation is to be made according to the collection order.

C All documents sent for collection must be accompanied by a collection order giving complete and precise instructions. Banks are only permitted to act upon the instructons given in such collection order, and in accordance with these Rules.

If any bank cannot, for any reason, comply with the instructions given in the collection order received by it, it must immediately advise the party from whom it received the collection order.

Liabilities and Responsibilities

Article 1

Banks will act in good faith and exercise reasonable care.

Article 2

Banks must verify that the documents received appear to be as listed in the collection order and must immediately advise the party from whom the collection order was received of any documents missing.

Banks have no further obligation to examine the documents.

Article 3

For the purpose of giving effect to the instructions of the principal, the remitting bank will utilize as the collecting bank:

i the collecting bank nominated by the principal or, in the absence of such nomination,

ii any bank, of its own or another bank's choice, in the country of payment or acceptance, as the case may be.

The documents and the collection order may be sent to the collecting bank directly or through another bank as intermediary.

Banks utilizing the services of other banks for the purpose of giving effect to the instructions of the principal do so for the account of and at the risk of the latter.

The principal shall be bound by and liable to indemnify the banks against all obligations and responsibilities imposed by foreign laws or usages.

Article 4

Banks concerned with a collection assume no liability or responsibility for the consequences arising out of delay and/or loss in transit of any messages, letters or documents, or for delay, mutilation or other errors arising in the transmission of cables, telegrams, telex, or communication by electronic systems, or for errors in translation or interpretation of technical terms.

Article 5

Banks concerned with a collection assume no liability or responsibility for consequences arising out of the interruption of their business by Acts of God, riots, civil commotions, insurrection, wars, or any other causes beyond their control or by strikes or lockouts.

Article 6

Goods should not be dispatched directly to the address of a bank or consigned to a bank without prior agreement on the part of that bank.

In the event of goods being dispatched directly to the address of a bank or consigned to a bank for delivery to a drawee against payment or acceptance or upon other terms without prior agreement on the part of that bank, the bank has no obligation to take delivery of the goods, which remain at the risk and responsibility of the party dispatching the goods.

Presentation

Article 7

Documents are to be presented to the drawee in the form in which they are received, except that remitting and collecting banks are authorized to affix any necessary stamps, at the expense of the principal unless otherwise instructed, and to make any necessary endorsements or place any rubber stamps or other identifying marks or symbols customary to or required for the collection operation.

Article 8

Collection orders should bear the complete address of the drawee or of the domicile at which presentation is to be made. If the address is incomplete or incorrect, the collecting bank may, without obligation and responsibility on its part, endeavour to ascertain the proper address.

Article 9

In the case of documents payable at sight the presenting bank must make presentation for payment without delay.

In the case of documents payable at a tenor other than sight the presenting bank must, where acceptance is called for, make presentation for acceptance without delay, and where payment is called for, make presentation for payment not later than the appropriate maturity date.

Article 10

In respect of a documentary collection including a bill of exchange payable at a future date, the collection order should state whether the commercial documents are to be released to the drawee against acceptance (D/A) or against payment (D/P).

In the absence of such statement, the commercial documents will be released only against payment.

Payment

Article 11

In the case of documents payable in the currency of the country of payment (local currency), the presenting bank must, unless otherwise instructed in the collection order, only release the documents to the drawee against payment in local currency which is immediately available for disposal in the manner specified in the collection order.

Article 12

In the case of documents payable in a currency other than that of the country of payment (foreign currency), the presenting bank must, unless otherwise instructed in the collection order, only release the documents to the drawee against payment in the relative foreign currency which can immediately be remitted in accordance with the instructions given in the collection order.

Article 13

In respect of clean collections partial payments will be accepted if and to the extent to which and on the conditions on which partial payments are authorized by the law in force in the place of payment. The documents will only be released to the drawee when full payment thereof has been received.

In respect of documentary collections partial payments will only be accepted if specifically authorized in the collection order. However, unless otherwise instructed, the presenting bank will only release the documents to the drawee after full payment has been received.

In all cases, partial payments will only be accepted subject to compliance with the provisions of either Article 11 or Article 12 as appropriate.

Partial payment, if accepted, will be dealt with in accordance with the provisions of Article 14.

Article 14

Amounts collected (less charges and/or disbursements and/or expenses where applicable) must be made available without delay to the bank from which the collection order was received in accordance with the instructions contained in the collection order.

Acceptance

Article 15

The presenting bank is responsible for seeing that the form of the acceptance of a bill of exchange appears to be complete and correct, but is not responsible for the genuineness of any signature or for the authority of any signatory to sign the acceptance.

Promissory Notes, Receipts and Other Similar Instruments

Article 16

The presenting bank is not responsible for the genuineness of any signature or for the authority of any signatory to sign a promissory note, receipt, or other similar instrument.

Protest

Article 17

The collection order should give specific instructions regarding protest (or other legal process in lieu thereof), in the event of non-acceptance or non-payment.

In the absence of such specific instructions the banks concerned with the collection have no obligation to have the documents protested (or subjected to other legal process in lieu thereof) for non-payment or non-acceptance.

Any charges and/or expenses incurred by banks in connection with such protest or other legal process will be for the account of the principal.

Case-of-Need (Principal's Representative) and Protection of Goods

Article 18

If the principal nominates a representative to act as case-of-need in the event of non-acceptance and/or non-payment the collection order should clearly and fully indicate the powers of such case-of-need.

In the absence of such indication banks will not accept any instructions from the case-of-need.

Article 19

Banks have no obligation to take any action in respect of the goods to which a documentary collection relates.

Nevertheless, in the case that banks take action for the protection of the goods, whether instructed or not, they assume no liability or responsibility with regard to the fate and/or condition of the goods and/or for any acts and/or omissions on the part of any third parties entrusted with the custody and/or protection of the goods. However, the collecting bank must immediately advise the bank from which the collection order was received of any such action taken.

Any charges and/or expenses incurred by banks in connection with any action for the protection of the goods will be for the account of the principal.

Advice of Fate, etc.

Article 20

Collecting banks are to advise fate in accordance with the following rules:

i *Form of advice.* All advices or information from the collecting bank to the bank from which the collection order was received, must bear appropriate detail including, in all cases, the latter bank's reference number of the collection order.

ii *Method of advice.* In the absence of specific instructions, the collecting bank must send all advices to the bank from which the collection order was received by quickest mail but, if the collecting bank considers the matter to be urgent, quicker methods such as cable, telegram, telex, or communication by electronic systems, etc. may be used at the expense of the principal.

iii a) *Advice of payment.* The collecting bank must send without delay advice of payment to the bank from which the collection order was received, detailing the amount or amounts collected, charges and/or disbursements and/or expenses deducted, where appropriate, and method of disposal of the funds.

b) *Advice of acceptance.* The collecting bank must send without delay advice of acceptance to the bank from which the collection order was received.

c) *Advice of non-payment or non-acceptance.* The collecting bank must send without delay advice of non-payment or advice of non–acceptance to the bank from which the collection order was received.

The presenting bank should endeavour to ascertain the reasons for such non-payment or non-acceptance and advise accordingly the bank from which the collection order was received.

On receipt of such advice the remitting bank must, within a reasonable time, give appropriate instructions as to the further handling of the documents. If such instructions are not received by the presenting bank within 90 days from its advice of non-payment or non-acceptance, the documents may be returned to the bank from which the collection order was received.

Interest, Charges, and Expenses

Article 21

If the collection order includes an instruction to collect interest which is not embodied in the accompanying financial document(s), if any, and the drawee refuses to pay such interest, the presenting bank may deliver the document(s) against payment or acceptance as the case may be without collecting such interest, unless the collection order expressly states that such interest may not be waived. Where such interest is to be collected the collection order must bear an indication of the rate of interest and the period covered. When payment of interest has been refused the presenting bank must inform the bank from which the collection order was received accordingly.

If the documents include a financial document containing an unconditional and definitive interest clause, the interest amount is deemed to form part of the amount of the documents to be collected. Accordingly, the interest amount is payable in addition to the principal amount shown in the financial document and may not be waived unless the collection order so authorizes.

Article 22

If the collection order includes an instruction that collection charges and/or expenses are to be for the account of the drawee and the drawee refuses to pay them, the presenting bank may deliver the document(s) against payment or acceptance as the case may be without collecting charges and/or expenses unless the collection order expressly states that such charges and/or expenses may not be waived. When payment of collection charges and/or expenses has been refused the presenting bank must inform the bank from which the collection order was received accordingly. Whenever collection charges and/or expenses are so waived they will be for the account of the principal, and may be deducted from the proceeds.

Should a collection order specifically prohibit the waiving of collection charges and/or expenses then neither the remitting nor collecting nor presenting bank shall be responsible for any costs or delays resulting from this prohibition.

Article 23

In all cases where in the express terms of a collection order, or under these Rules, disbursements and/or expenses and/or collection charges are to be borne by the principal, the collecting bank(s) shall be entitled promptly to recover outlays in respect of disbursements and expenses and charges from the bank from which the collection order was received and the remitting bank shall have the right promptly to recover from the principal any amounts so paid out by it, together with its own disbursements, expenses and charges, regardless of the fate of the collection.

ICC Services to Business

The International Chamber of Commerce is the world business organization. It acts to promote the greater freedom of world trade, to harmonize business and trade practices, and to represent the business community at international levels. Paris based, the ICC is represented by National Committees and Councils in over 50 countries and also has members in over 40 others.

The ICC Banking Commission

The Uniform Rules for Collection found in this brochure were developed by the ICC Commission on Banking Technique and Practice. This Commission brings together bankers from throughout the world with the aim of:
- defining, simplifying and harmonizing the practices and terminology used in international banking;
- expressing the views of bankers before relevant international organizations, in particular the United Nations Commission on International Trade Law (UNCITRAL);
- serving as a meeting ground for the bankers of the world to discuss common problems.

Some Publications

Uniform Customs and Practice for Documentary Credits
These Rules designed to simplify and facilitate commercial documentary credit operations are now universally adopted by banks and professional associations. The 1974 revision came into force on 1st October 1975. English, French, German, bilingual English-German, Spanish and Arabic editions.   **No. 290**

Guide to Documentary Credit Operations
This new guide explains the role of documentary credits and, in a practical, step-by-step manner, how they work. International businessmen and bankers will find it invaluable in their daily professional life. It includes the Uniform Customs and Practice contained in publication No. 290.
English and French editions   **No. 305**

Standard Forms for Issuing Documentary Credits
With help of banking authorities throughout the world, the ICC has recently completed work on new standard forms for issuing documentary credits. In addition, practical advice for their use is given in an explanatory booklet. The increasing use of ICC standard credit forms is a further contribution to uniform documentary credit practice.
English and French editions   **No. 323**

Uniform Rules for Contract Guarantees
The result of 12 years of work by the ICC Commissions on Banking and Commercial Practice, this new brochure presents Rules designed to regulate contract guarantees as well as an introduction explaining their use. The Rules cover tender bonds, performance guarantees and repayment guarantees given by banks, insurance companies and other guarantors to ensure the fulfillment of a tender or a contract. They invest these guarantees with a moral content and strive to achieve a fair balance between the legitimate interests of the parties involved.
English and French editions   **No. 325**

18
Funds Transfer and Corporate Cash Management

DON A. RESLER
Vice President
First National Bank of Chicago

INTRODUCTION

The ability to transfer funds efficiently is a key element in a company's overall cash management plan. Funds transfer is a standard banking service which when used properly can facilitate effective cash management.

The basic transfer procedures for both intracountry and cross-border funds movement have existed in the present form for quite some time. Use of these services, particularly for international transactions, has on many occasions been a frustrating experience for companies which lack a clear understanding of how the mechanisms work. Recent developments in telecommunication and computer processing in conjunction with an inclination to a more "paper-free" business environment portend a greater emphasis on funds transfer payment mechanisms for both intracountry and cross-border funds movements.

This chapter treats the topic of funds transfer in two ways. First, it provides general background including a description of procedures and mechanics involved. Secondly, it addresses various aspects concerning funds transfer as a corporate cash management tool.

By way of general definition the term *funds transfer* as discussed here includes those mechanisms used to move funds excluding currency, check, draft, or similar instruments. The procedures are characterized by a heavy dependence on electronic processing and/or telecommunication networks.

The author is indebted to Andries, H. J. Jansma, Vice President, Antoine G. Soussa, Vice President, and others in the Cash Management Consulting Division of Continental Illinois Bank for valuable comments during the preparation of this chapter.

It is necessary to distinguish between two broad categories of such transfers: intracountry and cross-border. The distinction is straightforward but very important from a cash management perspective. As a general rule, funds movements within a single country tend to be more easily accomplished than those which cross country boundaries. While in many countries the internal-funds transfer techniques may be far from well developed, they are not encumbered by currency control or foreign-exchange conversion considerations that may complicate cross-border movements.

When considering use of funds transfer as a cash management tool, a company must recognize that what may currently be possible within a country may not be available when cross-border movements are involved. Additionally, different management and control techniques may be required.

The focus of this chapter is on cross-border movements of funds. The primary objective will be to insure that the reader obtains a clear understanding of these mechanisms and the applicable cash management principles and techniques. We shall also discuss future developments and the opportunities that they may provide.

Another general consideration as a company reviews its use of funds transfer procedures is whether the transactions involve outside third parties or are exclusively intracompany. Evaluation of the technique to be used may be based on slightly different considerations in each situation. If the items are for intracompany funds movement, the company has some control over both ends of the transaction. This means the company should be able to obtain full cooperation and support as well as enjoy all benefits accruing as a result of the procedure. In situations involving outside parties the company has control over only one side of the transaction. As a consequence there may be trade-offs which must be evaluated.

CROSS-BORDER TRANSFERS

Before addressing the cash management implications of cross-border funds transfers, we think it would be useful to describe how such transfers occur. Having a familiarity with the basic mechanism, the reader will be able to understand the comments concerning cash management more readily. In its simplest form an international-funds transfer would have the following steps:

1. Payer requests transfer from payer's bank.
2. Payer's bank then:
   a. Debits payer's account.
   b. Credits correspondent bank's account on its books.
   c. Informs correspondent bank that its account was credited and requests it to effect the payment.

3. Correspondent bank responds to the entry passed by the payer's bank and:

   a. Debits that bank's account on its books.

   b. Credits the payee's accounts.

   c. Advises payee of payment details.

Exhibit 1 shows these steps schematically.

If the payer's bank is not a direct correspondent of the payee's bank (that is, it does not have an account with the other bank), then the payer's bank will route the transfer through a common correspondent bank. Hence, Steps *2b, 2c* and *3a* may be repeated as banks pass the payment through a correspondent chain to the ultimate destination. Likewise, the chain may be extended if either the payer's or payee's account is at a bank's branch office rather than its head office. The basic transfer procedure can vary depending on (1) the method the payer uses to request or initiate the transfer and (2) the method the payer's bank uses to execute the payment.

International Funds Transfer

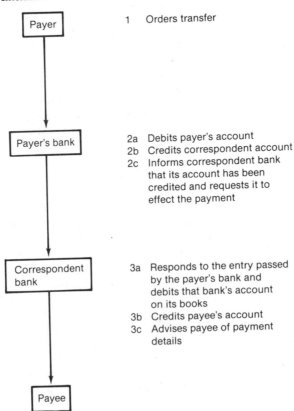

1   Orders transfer

2a Debits payer's account
2b Credits correspondent account
2c Informs correspondent bank
     that its account has been
     credited and requests it to
     effect the payment

3a Responds to the entry passed
     by the payer's bank and
     debits that bank's account
     on its books
3b Credits payee's account
3c Advises payee of payment
     details

Methods of Request. The method a payer uses to initiate an international transfer may depend on one or more of several different variables, such as, availability of a particular method at its bank, agreements with its bank, common business practices in the locale, cost and convenience for the company, and so on. Several relatively common methods exist including telephone, letter, tested telex, timesharing computer terminal, and standing order. The methods are procedurally straightforward and will be discussed when appropriate later in the chapter.

Methods of Execution. Customarily a bank executes an international transfer via either airmail or cable. As far as bookkeeping entries to the bank accounts the mechanisms are the same. They differ with respect to the method used to notify the receiving bank of the transaction. For the airmail transfer the payer's bank sends an advice of the transaction by airmail. For a cable transfer the payer's bank advises via electronic medium (such as, Telex/TWX or SWIFT message).

Usually a company specifies whether airmail or cable advice is desired when initiating a transfer. The method used depends upon a company's situation and cash management considerations as discussed in the next section of this chapter.

A cross-border funds transfer usually will entail at some point a conversion of funds from the currency of the payer to the currency of the payee. Exactly when the conversion takes place is definitely a cash management consideration, and the question is addressed in the following section of this chapter.

CORPORATE CASH MANAGEMENT CONSIDERATIONS

Simply stated the underlying objective of the use of funds transfers as a cash management tool should be to move funds as cost-effectively and efficiently as possible. When funds transfers have been deemed the most effective method to make or obtain payment, a company wants the transaction to resemble that shown in Exhibit 1 as nearly as possible. The company should attempt to keep the number of banks through which a payment passes to a minimum.

As we consider funds transfers as a cash management tool, we shall discuss several topics with regard to policy and technique. In some situations a company will be constrained by conditions beyond its control; however, to the extent possible a company should develop a policy of what it would like to do and modify it as required by current conditions while working toward the desired situation. This means that a company may raise issues in an effort to improve payment services provided by its banks.

Cash Inflow/Outflow Perspective. A company's attitude toward funds transfer as a payment mechanism often depends on whether the transaction results in a cash inflow (the company is the payee) or outflow (the company is the payer) or is an intracompany transaction (the company—usually subunits within it—is both payee and payer). Since cable transfers should accelerate the flow of funds, as a general rule payees would encourage their use while payers might tend to prefer other methods (i.e., checks or drafts). Although this general rule based on funds-flow implications may seem to be paramount, other factors, such as increased control, contract requirement, and so on, may override this consideration in certain circumstances. If the transaction is intracompany, at the subunit level the decision to use the method extensively may usually be based on other factors such as enhanced control; however, a company should realize that the potential for accelerating funds flow and eliminating cash trapped in the banking system also has relevance for intracompany transactions.

Instructions for Transfers.   One of the more apparent reasons which give rise to problems with international-funds transfer is incomplete or vague instructions. Whether the company is a payee providing information to the payer or the payer issuing instructions to its bank, a company can reduce errors and consequent delays in funds' flow by insuring that instructions are clear, concise, and contain all necessary data so the bank can correctly route the payment, and the payee can properly identify and process it upon receipt.

A simple format for transfer instructions which includes the required data elements is shown below:

Remit (type of currency   to   (exact name and address
      and amount)   of payee's bank)

For account of (exact title of account to be credited)

Account number: (exact number of bank account)

by: ☐ bank cable transfer
        or
    ☐ bank airmail transfer

Reference: (enter payee's invoice or other reference numbers)

If a payee is to be notified by its bank upon receipt of the payment, such instructions can be put in the reference area so they become part of the transmission from the payer's bank.

In addition to giving its customers proper instructions for remitting payments, a company should review procedures for handling inbound payments with the bank which will receive them. A company can take the opportunity to determine that the bank's standard processing will meet its needs and, if not, can establish standing instructions which will do so. This is especially critical regarding procedures for notifying a company of credit to its account.

When a company is responsible for initiating a transfer, it should attempt to obtain complete data from the payee so it can issue proper instructions to its bank. Although a company may assume the attitude that the responsibility lies with its counterparty, this is short-sighted. Payment delays which might have been prevented or reduced by proper initial instructions may cause unnecessary discord with suppliers. At the very least, tracing problem payments wastes staff time that could be used more effectively on other tasks.

As discussed previously, several methods exist for initiating transfers. A company should endeavor to make requesting transfers as routine and simple as possible while maintaining security and audit controls. For instance, if a high percentage of a company's transfers are between the accounts of the company or to the same party, the use of preauthorized transfers is an extremely effective way of controlling transfers. With this technique, the company sends to the bank a list of transfers with complete instructions that identify the debit and credit side of the transaction. With this list the company provides a statement authorizing the transfers to be made from time to time.

The bank will generally assign a code number to each transfer. To initiate a transfer, the proper code number and the amount of the transfer are given to the bank. In addition to better control, this procedure facilitates transferring funds and reduces errors as the bank may standardize its processing. By preauthorizing as many transfers as possible, it is easier to establish special procedures for handling exceptions.

A number of banks have developed systems whereby a time-sharing terminal can be used to initiate transfers. The transfers made on these systems are usually preauthorized. The computer systems are designed with a number of controls and checks which make them very attractive from the security point of view. These systems also reduce or eliminate the potential for garbling of messages as occurs on Telex/TWX transmissions and have the ability to accept and store requests for future payments.

Timing. Timing of requests for cross-border transfers may be more troublesome for two reasons. First, because a company may be issuing requests to a bank in a different part of the world, it will have to allow for time differences and insure that it issues instructions in sufficient time to meet deadlines in the bank's time zone. Secondly, if funds conversions are involved, additional time may be required. In either case a company may have to prenotify its bank or issue instructions a day or two earlier.

Security. The question of the security-of-payment mechanisms has become more topical in recent years as banks and their customers, including companies and other banks, have begun to use more automated and impersonal payment mechanisms. Both parties have a vested interest in making the payment mechanisms as secure as possible while keeping the restrictions to a minimum so as not to impede payment flow. The two groups will need to cooperate and do their share to work toward this goal.

Historically banks relied on knowing their customers who requested transfers either by personal recognition or by verifying the signature on a document against a specimen signature on file at the bank. As Telex/TWX communication developed, testing arrangements were established whereby codes were exchanged between communicants so that they could verify the authenticity of a message as well as validate the amount involved.

From a company's perspective it should insure that its internal controls are sufficient to prevent misuse of company funds. Where possible it should separate the functions of payment request, authorization or verification and reconcilement. It must also safeguard all codes or testing arrangements to insure that only personnel with a need to use them know them. One useful technique is to preauthorize as many transfers as possible. Since complete instructions except the amount and date of execution are lodged with the bank, this method both makes the payment more secure and facilitates its execution.

Cost-benefit evaluation.   Usually the payee is the party who encourages the use of funds transfers rather than another mechanism for payment. The four elements to be considered are: payment size (P), days gained on use of funds over current payment method (D), current short-term cost of funds or interest rate (R), and the incremental cost of the alternative payment method (C). The basic mathematical relationship is shown below:

$$P = \frac{C}{\dfrac{D}{360} \times R}$$

If a company knows or estimates three of the variables, it can make a cost-benefit evaluation to develop strategic parameters concerning the fourth variable. For example, suppose a company wants to determine when to encourage the use of cable transfer instead of airmail transfer. The cost of the cable is customarily deducted from the remitted amount by the paying bank. The payee should be willing to bear this expense if the cable cost is less than or equal to the potential gain resulting from more timely information and use of funds. Assuming a cable cost (C) of $10, days gained ($D$) of five, and a cost of funds (R) of 15 percent, the company can calculate the minimum size of payment (P) for which cable advice is cost effective as follows:

$$P = \frac{\$10.00}{\dfrac{5}{360} \times \dfrac{15}{100}}$$

$$P = \$4,800$$

Based on these assumptions, a payee should request that a payment of $4,800 (or equivalent) or larger be made via cable transfer even if the payer is authorized to deduct the cable cost from the invoice amount. Smaller payments can continue to be remitted by airmail transfer and the cost assumed by the payer.

A payee can encourage the payer to use cable transfers by offering to accept the cable costs. In most cases such costs will represent the payer's incremental cost over other methods of payment because normally the payer's account will be charged immediately for a mail transfer or to purchase a draft.

Value-Dating.   Value-dating practices differ from country to country. In several countries it is common to back-value debits and future-value credits to an account. In some situations the value-dating terms are negotiable. A company should be aware of the prevailing value-dating procedures and, where possible, negotiate the terms with its banks to obtain the best terms available. This is especially important if the transfers are intracompany because the company should minimize the loss of use of funds on internal-funds movements.

Value-dating rules do change from time to time. For example, the change in settlement procedure for the New York Clearing House Interbank Payments System (CHIPS) scheduled for October 1981 may have an effect on the value-dating conventions used by participant banks. A company *must* keep itself aware of such situations so it can adjust its strategies accordingly.

Foreign Exchange Implications.   The topic of foreign exchange exposure-management policy and procedure is covered in another section of this handbook; however, two aspects of foreign exchange deserve comment here: foreign exchange control regulations and the conversion of funds.

Where foreign exchange control regulations exist, a company should review the requirements and insure that funds flow will not be impeded by failure to understand and/or comply with them. In some countries banks have the responsibility for making sure the control requirements are fulfilled. In such cases it may be possible to prepare documentation in advance and lodge it with the bank so that the bank can process a payment immediately upon receipt without waiting for the arrival of documentation.

The strategy concerning conversion of funds should be an integral part of a company's foreign exchange exposure-management policy and procedures. From a cash management operational perspective a company must decide when and how the funds conversion should occur and insure that correct instructions are lodged with the appropriate banks and that adequate follow-up procedures exist to monitor the transaction flow. This is especially crucial if a company wants to shop for the optimal foreign exchange deal. In such cases care must be taken to insure that a bank does not automatically convert an inbound payment to local currency for credit to the company's account. It is also important if the company is using forward foreign exchange contracts to hedge exposure although use of contracts with an optional delivery date can help alleviate some of the timing pressure.

CONCLUSION

The effective use of funds transfers as a cash management tool depends on several factors. A company must evaluate its situation to determine how funds transfers fit into its overall cash management operation procedures. It should develop and maintain a good working relationship with its banks which are the primary resource for information and developments in funds-transfer services. Because transfers usually involve relatively large transaction amounts a company which invests the time to develop proper strategy and procedures will find the benefits worthwhile.

19
Merchant Banking

H. G. ASHTON
Director
J. Henry Schroder Wagg & Co. Limited

INTRODUCTION

A primary difficulty in describing the activities of a merchant bank is to identify the subject matter. For the purpose of this chapter the definition has been restricted to describe those banks which are members of the Accepting Houses Committee and of the Issuing Houses Association. The members of these two institutions, both of which limit membership to U.K.-controlled bodies, are engaged in all those activities that are seen as quintessential merchant banking: namely, commercial banking (the accepting-house aspect), corporate finance activities (the issuing-house aspect), and investment management.

It should be stressed at the outset that the services merchant banks offer are continually changing. A few decades ago the role of the merchant banks was materially different from that today. At that time the involvement of merchant banks in the financial advisory business was small, the investment management side was even smaller, and the issuing business was exclusively in sterling. Lending was predominantly through acceptance credits which had been the basis of merchanting finance provided by merchant banks at the beginning of this century; at the stage bill financing was mainly for raw materials purchased abroad or finished goods sold abroad.

The changing nature of the activities of merchant banks emphasizes the central reason for their success. Their strength lies not in the size of their balance sheets, which are relatively small, but in their ability to exercise skill and inventiveness for the benefit of their clients and to adapt and change the emphasis of their business to suit the markets in which they operate.

The merchant banks in the United Kingdom have origins that are based on the development of world trade from the 16th and 17th centuries; they were international from the outset and depended on their overseas contacts. Now, the merchant banks are represented throughout the world. Indeed it is their international outlook and expertise that allows them to provide the comprehensive service to their clients, which is the basis for their existence. The operations that are described below are primarily aimed at the activities provided in the United Kingdom. However, there is not only an international thread running throughout, but it should also be emphasized that these U.K. activities are mirrored or complemented by world-wide representation. For example, Schroders has substantial commercial banking, corporate finance, and investment management operations in New York and has similar operations either through subsidiaries or affiliates in Switzerland, Australia, Hong Kong, Singapore, and 11 other countries worldwide.

As a last word on the problem of identifying the subject matter of this chapter, it should be kept in mind that there is no uniform merchant bank; indeed many of them have operations which, while perhaps logical extensions of the central services, cannot be described as merchant banking—for instance, life assurance, insurance-broking operations, and bullion dealing. The ensuing paragraphs therefore represent the core services which are common to most merchant banks and which are divided into the headings:

Commercial banking.
Corporate finance services.
Investment management.
Project finance.
Other.

COMMERCIAL BANKING

While the international banking market has grown enormously since the early 1960s, the major international banks have fought aggressively to maintain and expand their market share. The merchant banks have participated in this growth both by exploiting perceived opportunities and by reacting defensively to the encroachment by the international banks on what had been their exclusive preserves. As a result of this highly competitive market, the range and type of credit facilities offered by both types of banks are now very similar. These have been described fully elsewhere in the Handbook and it is only proposed to list them here:

Case-to-case loans in sterling and foreign currencies.
Committed short-term sterling and foreign currency facilities.

Committed medium-term sterling and foreign currency facilities.

Syndication of short-term and medium-term sterling and foreign currency facilities.

Back-to-back loans and currency swaps.

The opening and confirming of letters of credit.

The provision of guarantees.

Major leasing transactions.

Interest rate swaps.

It is interesting to examine briefly how the merchant banks are able to compete with major international banks in lending money when their financial resources are so much smaller. Since banking is largely a service industry, the quality of service is clearly of paramount importance, and it is here that the merchant banks can claim to have a significant advantage. Their compact size facilitates the provision of a service which emphasizes innovation, flexibility, and speed of response. In today's highly competitive market these qualities are essential in meeting the challenge of the other international banks.

There are two areas where merchant banks have a competitive advantage which is more tangible than quality of service. The first of these is the all-round financial service that is provided and which is described in detail in the rest of this chapter. The contacts and relationships of the other divisions of the bank provide a useful source of introductions for banking officers and of particular significance in this context is the close relationship that is formed by the company finance division with a customer. This relationship is particularly beneficial in three ways, namely:

It ensures that the merchant bank is one of the company's recognized banks, and, as such, will usually be asked to quote when the company has a financing requirement.

It ensures that there exists within the bank an independent and in-depth source of expertise and information about a customer, on which (confidentiality permitting) it is possible to draw when making a credit decision.

This great in-depth knowledge of the company leads to the provision of a better and more imaginative banking service.

A further advantage enjoyed by merchant banks in the U.K., although less so now than hitherto, is their prominent role in the London bankers' acceptance market. For over 150 years the major merchant banks have played a central part in financing domestic and overseas trade by accepting and arranging the discount of sterling bills of exchange. Until recently these merchant banks were members of a relatively select group of U.K. and other banks whose acceptances were eligible for rediscount at the Bank of England. While this "eligible" status has now been extended to the U.K. branches of a number of foreign banks, the merchant banks continue to exert a considerable influence on the acceptance market and, in so doing, substantiate their traditional relationships with their customers.

The provision of credit facilities is by no means the only source of income for the banking division of a merchant bank. Foreign exchange dealing and deposit taking are of themselves an important source of profit as well as being essential parts of the mechanics of lending money. Section 4 of the Handbook gives a description of foreign exchange transactions and functions, and it will be seen from this that the volatility of exchange rates means that there is considerable potential for incurring losses as well as making profits. Having relatively little capital, the merchant banks must be careful not to take unduly large risks and profits can be made by effecting a large number of deals in which an open position of any magnitude is only taken for a matter of minutes or hours. The provision of foreign exchange dealing facilities for customers is also an important part of the all-round service provided.

The retail business of the large international banks has played an important role in their development in that it has provided them with a large source of interest-free deposits from current (demand) accounts. Historically the merchant banks have not had many retail customers, and consequently they have had to rely more on the money markets as a source of funds. The management of liabilities has therefore played an important role in their operations for longer than for most of the other international banks and, with the increasing volatility of interest rates, has become as important a source of profits as foreign exchange dealing.

CORPORATE FINANCE SERVICES

The corporate finance division of a merchant bank carries out work in several fields on behalf of its clients. In many respects the nature of these activities is similar to that of a U.S. investment bank. In the United Kingdom there is no restriction, as there is in the United States, preventing merchant banks from underwriting securities in addition to carrying out commercial banking operations. The most publicized areas of this activity are new issues and mergers and acquisitions. However, the merchant bank would generally, on a continuing basis, advise its clients on a wide range of financial matters. The merchant bank can offer its clients not only its technical expertise, but also provide experience over a broad spectrum of problems.

New Issues

New-issue business principally involves the sponsoring of capital issues and the sale of securities to the public, either in the United Kingdom or in international capital markets. In this context, it is primarily the job of a merchant bank to bring investors and issuing organizations together.

There are a number of different types of capital-raising issues made to the public, which are described below:

Equity Issues in the United Kingdom.   Companies coming to the stock market for the first time will normally be involved in the sale of ordinary shares to the public. This can either take the form of a sale of existing shares, if the present shareholders wish to realize all or part of their investment, or the issue of new shares to raise funds for the company.

A merchant bank will normally have been associated with its client for a considerable time before an issue is contemplated. It would advise on the timing and, most importantly, the pricing of an issue and the most appropriate form it should take. During the issue itself, the merchant bank will be closely involved in the preparation of a detailed prospectus about the company and will ensure compliance with the necessary regulations.

The success and future marketability of an issue can depend to a very large extent on the reputation of the merchant bank associated with it; investors will pay considerable attention to the reputation of the sponsoring merchant bank when making the decision whether or not to invest. For this reason, the investigations carried out prior to an issue are very thorough, and indeed, the reputation of a merchant bank associated with issues that have failed would very soon suffer.

There are three main methods of obtaining a listing on the London Stock Exchange for the first time: the commonest is an offer for sale. In this case, the merchant bank normally contracts to purchase on its own account all the shares to be issued and then sells them on to the investing public. It is also normal for the bank to arrange for such an issue to be subunderwritten by other financial institutions. Subunderwriting is simply a method by which the primary risk is laid off on other parties.

The second method, which is in practice little different from the first, is where the company offers its own securities to the public for subscription. In this case, the merchant bank would normally underwrite the issue and, in the event that part or all of the issue were not subscribed, would buy the securities.

The third method, an introduction, does not involve the sale of shares. It requires the preparation of a full prospectus about the company, and provided the shares are widely held, The Stock Exchange will then admit the company to a listing. This method is particularly appropriate for corporations with an existing listing on an overseas stock exchange. In the case of companies listed on the major U.S. exchanges, the listing requirements are not onerous. In the case of an introduction, the merchant bank involved does not take any financial risk in the issue, and its primary responsibilities are to ensure that the necessary documentation has been completed and regulations complied with. However, in the same way as for an offer for sale, by associating its name with the introduction, the merchant bank will be risking its reputation on the ultimate success of the company.

There is a further, albeit rare, method, a placing. In this case the merchant bank will contract with the issuing company to place the securities directly with a number of major investing institutions. However, in the case of equity issues this method is not common because The Stock Exchange imposes restrictions on the amounts that may be raised and in any event will only allow such a method to be used where there is unlikely to be significant public demand for the securities.

Companies which are already listed on The Stock Exchange can also raise funds by a rights issue of new equity capital. Except with shareholders' approval, the rules of The Stock Exchange and of new U.K.-company law provide that these must be offered pro rata to existing shareholders. A merchant bank will normally advise on the timing and pricing of such an issue. Again, so that the issuing company can, from the outset, be assured of the funds that will be raised, the merchant bank will normally underwrite the issue; the merchant bank, with the assistance of a stockbroker, will then arrange to subunderwrite the issue. In the United Kingdom, an offer is generally open for three weeks; this is therefore the period for which the merchant bank is at risk.

Debt Issues in the United Kingdom.   There are two main types of marketable debt issued by companies in the United Kingdom: straight-loan stock and convertible-loan stock. Either form of debt can, but does not have to, be secured by a charge on the company's assets. Convertible-loan stock gives the added attraction to an investor of the right to convert the debt into equity at some future date, thereby allowing him to participate in the capital growth of the company; it therefore normally carries a lower coupon than straight debt. Another example of the innovative aspect of merchant banks has been the different types of instruments that have been designed to balance the particular needs of the borrower with the requirements of the investor. Apart from convertible debt, other new instruments include sterling-dollar convertible stocks, loan stocks with warrants to subscribe for ordinary shares and oil-production stocks which give a direct interest in North Sea oil production.

Loan stocks are issued in the United Kingdom either by an offer for sale to the public or by the placing method referred to above. It is priced in consultation with the merchant bank, with reference to the term, security, debt-equity ratio and, critically, yield. In the case of convertible-loan stock, particular attention needs to be paid to the existing shareholders' rights vis-a-vis those of the potential shareholders after conversion. Again, the reputation of the merchant bank is important to the success of an issue of loan stock: both investors and issuing organizations would very soon become wary of dealing with a bank that had been associated with issues that had either been wrongly priced or faltered for some other reason.

As a matter of history, until very recently, the level of long-term interest rates in the United Kingdom since the early 1970s has been such as to discourage most borrowers from tapping the domestic sterling market. It is only since autumn 1982 with a fall in the long-term interest rates that there has been a significant number of issues by U.K. corporations and there have been very issues by industrial companies in that number. The principal exception has been the U.K. government which has followed its long-standing practice of funding the majority of its borrowing requirements on a long-term, fixed-interest basis. In this period, issues by the U.K. private sector have fallen in absolute terms and, in any case, have been dwarfed by the growth in government borrowing. Since the abolition of U.K. exchange controls in 1979, there has been a number of domestic sterling issues by foreign borrowers. It is interesting to note that the procedures and structure of these bulldog issues have imported elements from those used in the Eurobond market, which is discussed below.

Issues in the International Capital Markets.   The international bond market, specifically the Eurobond market, provides a further major source of capital and is an area in which the merchant banks have played a significant role. Eurobonds are bonds held by persons or institutions who reside in countries other than those in which the issuing entity is resident; they are normally issued through a syndicate of international banks and sold to investors in two or more countries.

The Eurobond market opened in 1963 and since that time has developed into a major source of finance. The initial growth of the market was encouraged by the United States' imposition of a taxation penalty on foreign borrowers raising money in the U.S. capital market. Although this tax has now been abolished, the Eurobond market has continued to thrive because it offers considerable flexibility, competitive rates, and often requires less disclosure and documentation than issues in domestic markets.

When the Eurobond market opened, among its chief proponents were the U.K. merchant banks who, although relatively small in financial power, had a major competitive advantage over the other European competition because of their technical expertise. The merchant banks were joined in these early days by some of the American investment banks who had transferred their operations outside the United States. Although the U.K. merchant banks had a considerable advantage at the outset of the Eurobond market, the premium that had existed for technical excellence has been matched by the far greater financial power of the European banks, which allows them greater capital for trading in these bonds. The greatest advantage of the European banks over the U.K. merchant banks is their immense placing power through their own and clients' portfolios. Such has been the rise to power of the German and Swiss banks, that at the present time only one U.K. merchant bank remains in the top 10 of lead managers of Eurobond issues. In the face of this competition the merchant banks have tended to specialize in particular types of issues and particular markets. For example, Schroders have developed a particular expertise in the management of convertible bond issues.

In common with the U.K. debt market, the Eurobond market provides two main types of debt; straight Eurobonds and convertible Eurobonds. In addition to these types of debt, the relative freedom from restrictive regulations has encouraged the introduction of a great many new instruments such as floating-rate notes, currency convertibles, commodity-linked bonds, and many hybrid instruments. The Eurobond market is principally a dollar market; however, a significant proportion of the market has been denominated in other currencies including deutsche marks, Japanese yen, French francs, Dutch guilders, sterling, and composite currency units.

There is a broad range of practices in this market; however, a classically-structured issue would typically proceed in the following manner. The lead bank managing the issue works closely with the issuer, advising him on the structure, magnitude, timing, and pricing of the issue, and assuming responsibility for the preparation of the necessary documentation and the coordination of the sale and distribution of the securities. In consultation with the issuer, the lead manager forms a group of, say, 4 to 10 international banks to act as co-managers; these banks underwrite the issue and provide further advice on timing and pricing. On the announcement of the issue, it is subunderwritten by a large group of, say, 30 to 50 banks and sold through a group of 100 to 200 banks. The final terms of the issue are set in the light of market conditions at the end of the selling period.

Eurobonds are normally listed in London or Luxembourg, and the international banks participating in the original placing of the issue maintain a secondary market in the securities.

Mergers and Acquisitions

Probably the most publicized activity of a merchant bank is its involvement as adviser in the field of mergers and acquisitions. While merchant banks do not have a monopoly for this type of advice, they have the technical expertise and experience which has made their presence almost invariable, particularly where quoted companies are involved. Furthermore, in the majority of cases the merchant bank's involvement with either party to a takeover will have sprung from its role as financial adviser to that client over a period of years.

The traditional work in this field involves the negotiation of the terms for an acquisition, either on behalf of an offeror or an offeree company, the preparation of the formal documentation necessary for the offer to be made, and advice on the legal and regulatory aspects of a takeover.

It is common for a merchant bank to be involved with its clients from the earliest stages leading up to an acquisition. This often involves giving advice on the development of a suitable corporate strategy, including consideration of economic and political factors as well as particular business opportunities. It may also include a search for suitable acquisition candidates before the detailed negotiation stage begins; indeed many of the merchant banks have personnel assigned specifically to this type of operation.

Even where a merger is being conducted on a willing basis, the negotiations leading up to the merger can very often be an anxious time for the directors of both companies involved. The advantages in carrying out negotiations through independent advisers are that they provide a forum for unemotional argument and also enable the directors to continue running their respective companies efficiently. Also, even with an approved bid, a heavy responsibility rests with the merchant bank to ensure that the terms are fair for the shareholders of the offeree company as a whole and are not simply designed to suit the interests of one or more large shareholders.

Almost invariably, the merchant bank will make the formal offer on behalf of the offeror company and will play a leading role in presenting the rationale for the merger and in setting out all the relevant facts so that shareholders in the offeree company can properly assess the offer. The merchant bank will also play an important part in advising its client on the most appropriate form of consideration for the acquisition balancing on one side the effect on the offeror's balance sheet and earnings with the likely requirements of shareholders in the offeree company.

The majority of takeovers nowadays are agreed by both parties involved. However, on some occasions, an offeree company may oppose a takeover. There are a variety of reasons for this: the directors of the offeree company may, for example, consider the price too low or they may have a differing view on the prospects of the merged business. In these cases, the merchant bank advising the offeree company will assist in the development of a coherent and practical defense strategy.

To a large extent the regulations governing the conduct of a takeover in the United Kingdom are laid down not by statute but by rules promulgated and supervised by the Panel on Take-overs and Mergers and The Stock Exchange. In a very real sense the system is self-regulating in that the main burden for ensuring that the system works is borne by the major merchant banks. It is generally considered that a nonstatutory framework of rules, which depends as much on an observance of the spirit as on the letter, is more effective in controlling and regulating the conduct of mergers and takeovers.

In summary, takeovers and mergers are an area which requires considerable expertise to overcome financial, technical, and administrative complications. The nature of this type of activity means that it is unlikely to be an expertise possessed by the parties to the takeover. It is this expertise which the merchant bank provides.

General Financial Advice

In addition to their role as advisers in capital-raising exercises and mergers and acquisitions, merchant banks provide advice on a wide spectrum of financial matters. This can involve matters such as developing long-term financial and business strategies or advice on a capital reorganization; the variety of different financial problems is limitless. Aside from the major exercises that a merchant bank would perform for a client, the cornerstone for the relationship is the close contact that is built up between the bank and the client as a result of continuous advice on financially-related matters.

INVESTMENT MANAGEMENT

The history of U.K. institutional investment management over the last 50 years provides an excellent example of the trend-setting tradition of the merchant banks. The early 1930s saw the beginnings of the pension fund movement in the United Kingdom; even at that stage, when pension funds were invested entirely in government securities, merchant banks had already begun both to advise upon, and manage, their assets. Shortly after World War II, it was a merchant bank that led the first pension fund into equities.

But it has been the last 20 years that have seen the major transformation in investment management and the emergence of merchant banks

Table 1

	U.K. Equity Ownership	
	1957	*1979*
Pension funds	3.4%	22.0%
Insurance companies	8.8	19.5
Investment trusts	5.2	5.0
Unit trusts	0.5	3.5
Total Institutions	17.9%	50.0%
Persons	65.8	30.5
Others	16.3	19.5
Total	100.0%	100.0%

as a dominant force. Table 1 shows the change in ownership of U.K. equities between 1957 and 1979.

As can be seen from Table 1, institutional ownership of U.K. equities has almost tripled over the last 20 years from 17.9 percent to 50.0 percent, while personal ownership has more than halved from 65.8 percent to 30.5 percent. Among institutions, the greatest growth has been in pension funds, which have increased their share more than sixfold.

An indication of the degree to which merchant banks have participated in—indeed led—this transformation can be gained from Table 2, showing the estimated distribution of U.K. pension funds by manager in 1980.

Table 2 demonstrates that merchant banks dominate in the management of noninsured, nonself-managed pension funds, taking a market share of more than 65 percent. Of that share, more than 90 percent is accounted for by 10 merchant banks.

Although the prominence of the merchant banks is in large measure due to their trend-setting role in the pension fund movement, the endurance of their market leadership owes much to other factors. In particular, their close and long-standing connections, with companies on the one hand and with financial markets on the other, have provided them with the experience and expertise to offer a service which is tailored to the individual requirements of each client. At the same

Table 2

	Pension Fund Management (1980)
Self-managed	34%
Insured	35
Independently managed	31
Merchant banks	21
Others	10
Total	100%

time, because of their own limited financial resources but strong international bias, the merchant banks have long been accustomed to the need to balance financial risk and return; this has meant that they have generally resisted the urge to sacrifice investment prudence for the sake of short-lived performance, and so have provided pension fund clients with a consistent and reliable product.

Indeed, for the majority of U.K. pension fund clients, merchant banks still play the dual role of investment adviser and investment manager. This contrasts sharply with the relationship between many North American investment institutions and their corporate clients—where increasingly the client company retains its own in-house team of investment advisers who select their managers according to whether the manager's product fits the advisers' investment approach.

If, however, merchant banks are a dominant force in pension fund management, they are not, by any means, an insignificant force in other areas. In 1979 some 60 percent of the funds under management with the top 10 merchant banks was accounted for by pension funds, the remaining 40 percent representing investment trusts, unit trusts, charities, insurance funds, and private client accounts. Moreover, as the pension fund movement in the United Kingdom begins to mature in the early 1980s, signs have emerged of increasing activity by the merchant banks in other areas—new unit trusts, heavy marketing of unit-linked life assurance schemes, promotion of personal financial services, reorganization of investment trusts.

However, perhaps the greatest new area of investment management activity for the merchant banks in the 1980s lies in offshore funds. The internationalization of economic trends in the 1970s—stimulated particularly by oil crises and financial crises—has brought with it the internationalization of fund managers' and trustees' investment horizons—in North America, Europe, the Middle East, the Far East. At the same time, the combination of international expertise, experience and connections, and a prestigious professional reputation as a fund-management institution have been hard to find—except, that is, among the British merchant banks and a few others. Consequently the merchant banks are once again in the forefront of a development which may yet prove to be as important and far-reaching in its consequences as the emergence of pension fund management in the United Kingdom 50 years ago.

PROJECT FINANCE

Commercial Project Finance

Project finance has come to be understood to be commercial lending to a project without the need for overall guarantees or substantial balance sheets in which a lender can put its faith. Instead reliance is put on the innate ability of the project to generate a cash flow sufficient to service its own debt.

Project lending is described in detail in Section 2, Chapter 11 of this book. However, it is necessary to reintroduce some of the basic principles in order to reveal the role of the merchant bank in project finance. Most merchant banks have small balance sheets and would not be in a position to engage in project lending on a large scale. They are, however, particularly well suited to act as agents since the role demands flexibility, imagination, attention to detail, and professional expertise.

In proposing a project financing the project sponsors will have certain aims in mind. It may be that no one party is prepared to guarantee the whole project, that the sponsors wish to avoid encumbering their own balance sheets or that the project is large relative to any individual sponsor although well within their joint capabilities.

At the same time the syndicate of banks that the sponsors hope will fund the project will not be prepared to take any extraordinary risks.

If a mining, industrial, or infrastructural project is planned to be undertaken by a newly incorporated company without shareholder or external guarantees we might consider that the following broad categories of risk exist:

That the equity might not be subscribed.

That the construction phase might not be completed.

That any new technology employed might be faulty.

That the management might be inadequate.

That raw materials might not be available.

That the product might not be saleable at an appropriate price.

Before lending to such an enterprise, banks will expect to see these risks minimized. The role of the merchant bank acting as agent is to devise a structure which minimizes the risks sufficiently to persuade other banks to lend to the project but which avoids impinging on the basic requirements of the project sponsors.

In order to produce an effective compromise, the merchant bank will have to produce a different financial structure for every project. The principle employed is to introduce as many constraints as possible in order to limit the risk and then to subdivide the risk that remains until each element can be taken on by one party. Thus, in the case of a new mine an independent geological survey might be commissioned. If the standing of the consultant is high, a favorable report might reduce the risk that the deposit has been poorly assessed. Project revenue may well depend largely on the availability and cost of raw materials and the sales revenue. It may be possible to arrange long-term supply and sales contracts with several different parties which give security of supply, ensure demand, and place limits on the prices.

Having designed a package, the merchant bank will syndicate the funding to the large international banks and in so doing will have to demonstrate the sensitivity of the debt-service capability to changes in the project parameters and may well have to convince them that the project can service its debt under the worst possible circumstances. In order to do so it will certainly be necessary to produce a computer model to project the accounts of the company under a variety of circumstances.

Having "sold" the project risk to the banks, the merchant bank would then act as agent leading the syndicate in the normal way. Its main income would be in the form of negotiation and management fees.

Project financing is most common in countries such as Canada and Australia where the political risk is small and where greenfield projects, mainly natural resource-based, are still common.

Export Credit

Export credit is credit guaranteed by a state agency or private insurance company which is extended to buyers as an incentive to purchase capital goods. The loans may be funded by the government of the exporting country or by commercial banks, often with government support in order to allow a low fixed-rate of interest. The international consensus on export credit terms between the export credit agencies of most major exporting countries restricts competition on credit terms by the imposition of minimum interest rates and maximum credit periods.

The export credit schemes of various countries operate in slightly different ways but most involve commercial bank funding either in whole or in part. Merchant and other banks have therefore set up teams to offer financial packages, including export credit, in support of bids for major export contracts, to advise the exporter on the financial aspects of his bid, and to arrange and manage the loans if the bid and financial offer are accepted. The loans arranged are usually syndicated in the usual manner but with the added complexities of dealing with the export credit agency. Again the main aim of the merchant banks is to derive fee income from their services although they may take small participations. They tend to specialize in arranging credits through their own domestic-credit agency although most would have a fair knowledge of other export-credit systems and would occasionally arrange a foreign export credit. They also tend to concentrate on the larger, more complex deals which have more need of their skills and can bear their fees rather than on the smaller, stereotyped export credit which remains the prerogative of the larger banks.

Export credit is a favoured source of finance for projects since it is often provided on concessional terms. Export credit and commercial-project finance teams are therefore often merged into one division.

Advisory Work

With their expertise in commercial project and export finance and their ability to draw on the banking, corporate finance, and leasing knowledge of their colleagues, the project divisions of merchant banks are particularly well placed to advise project sponsors on matters such as the best source of funds, the most advantageous way in which to structure the project company, currency strategies, the merits of the various export-credit agencies, and of competing loan offers. The fact that they are not particularly concerned to act as lenders to the project gives them an independence and impartiality which is of particular value to the project sponsor.

The merchant bank may be retained to advise one party in the project on its interests or by all the sponsors to advise on the project as a whole. The brief may be very specific or may cover all financial matters including assisting the borrower in negotiations with potential lenders.

OTHER SERVICES

The services offered by the merchant banks, other than those already described in the preceding sections, are legion. They range from bullion dealing and commodity trading, activities exemplifying the historical merchanting activities of the older banks, to life assurance, insurance broking, and leasing, fields that a number of merchant banks have entered in the last two decades.

It is not within the scope of this chapter, nor would it be appropriate, to describe all these different activities. The point to be made is that these different, but related, financial services are a demonstration of the flexibility shown by the merchant banks. The following paragraphs on currency management are an illustration of just one new financial service provided by the merchant banks.

Currency Management

The persistent instability of the foreign exchanges and of short-term money markets since the early 1970s has caused great problems to those who must make decisions, the outcomes of which are partially dependent on these volatile markets. There is therefore a growing demand for advisory services that specialize in addressing the problems faced by international asset and liability managers. A number of leading London merchant banks have established divisions that work in this field.

The clients advised by these divisions are drawn from both the government and private sectors, and include central banks, monetary agencies, public investment and development funds, and multinational corporations. The problems may range from the investment of the surplus reserves of an oil-producing state to advice on the hedging alternatives that are open to reduce the currency risk faced by an international company. Common to all these institutions, however, is their exposure to the uncertainties imposed by volatile international markets. The London merchant banks, with their historically international orientation and their experience of financial markets derived from their other activities, are well placed to provide advisory services of this type.

Some of these money market advisory groups manage reserve funds, on either a discretionary or a nondiscretionary basis, while other groups provide market advice and comment to assist their clients, but do not directly manage money. In either case, the markets that must be monitored by these groups include the foreign exchange markets, all major domestic money and bond markets, and the offshore or Euro-money and bond markets. At a tactical level, advice to clients about how they should invest new moneys or maturing funds clearly depends on expectations about future rate movements, and economic and market developments must therefore be monitored closely in order to assess the signals they provide for future policy. Some of these advisory groups have developed econometric models with which they attempt to forecast future rate movements.

Tactical advice on hedging or money management decisions thus forms a large part of the work done by these groups. However, central banks and other international institutions have additional requirements in their asset and liability management activities. They may require a computerized-portfolio information system to process and display all the complex information that can be derived about the structure and performance of the portfolio. Similarly, a problem faced by many central banks in developing countries is a shortage of people with adequate experience of the foreign exchanges and the short-term markets. These problems are all aspects of the demands imposed by asset and liability management, and the reserve asset-management advisory groups frequently develop ancillary services that can address these problems—advising on computerizing a central banks's operations and information systems, or arranging to train the bank's personnel either by seminars at the central bank itself, or while the staff are seconded to a major financial center.

In general, therefore, the range of money market advice and related services now available from these groups provides a good manifestation of the capacity of the merchant banks to use their experience and background knowledge to advise on new problems as they are encountered by their customers.

THE FUTURE

Merchant banks would not have survived on financial muscle alone. In the United Kingdom, the clearing banks have very much larger resources and the added advantage of having many billions of pounds of interest-free deposits from customers on current accounts. Many overseas banks also have very much larger financial resources than the London merchant banks. In the past, the latter have survived by expertise in the most complicated forms of financial transaction, through their reputation for integrity and, above all, by innovation and an ability to react to changing markets. To prosper in the future, merchant banks will have to continue to demonstrate their fleetness of foot and their ability to serve the changing needs of their clients on an international basis. It is this flexibility, the range of financial services offered, the speed of service, and the personal quality of these services which will offer the merchant banks a bright future in spite of intense competition.

SECTION 4
Foreign Exchange

20
A General Description of Foreign
Exchange Transactions
and Functions

ARTHUR H. MEEHAN
Executive Vice President
Bank of New England, N.A.

Foreign exchange has often been described as a difficult and mysterious area of international finance. It has been characterized by some commentators as being in the world of the occult. Fortunately, much of this mystery has been removed in recent years since foreign exchange is often the lead story on the financial pages of daily newspapers. More information is now available; thus, it is no longer necessary for the interested reader to labor through material written in the 1920s and 30s.

This chapter has been written to introduce the subject of foreign exchange primarily by describing its function and by outlining seven typical foreign exchange transactions. It is the writer's experience that these seven transactions could categorize in general all foreign exchange operations.

WHY FOREIGN EXCHANGE?

The foreign exchange markets are among the oldest in existence. Their foundations are firmly rooted in trade transactions and cross-border finance. The nature of each of these activities requires the expenditure and the acceptance of funds by either a buyer or seller of goods, by parties to some other financial transaction, or for services (such as accommodations) which any traveler might require. There is no common medium of exchange for payment of such transactions today nor has there been in the history of commerce. Gold, silver, and other precious metals came very close to universal acceptance, but even these metals required foreign exchange transactions to effect final settlement. This came about because metals commonly used in cross-border transactions were minted in various places and had different degrees of fineness, purity, and desirability. In short, there is no issuance of coin, currency, or any other vehicle for payment of services or merchandise with universal acceptance on a global basis; hence, all such transactions require an exchange involving the conversion of one unit of value for another. This necessity gave rise to markets for foreign exchange and to a profession which is very much a part of commercial banking, foreign exchange dealing.

Commercial banks and their early ancestors were natural creators of foreign exchange markets given the intermediary role they play in commerce and their interest in earning profits for such services. They have become the middlemen and have assumed the risk of holding inventory of various methods of payment commonly referred to as money or foreign exchange. Foreign exchange exists, therefore, simply because commerce moved away from the early barter arrangements and there was no common denomination for payment across borders either in precious metals (coins) or later in paper issued by acceptable local issuers, such as banks or various governing bodies. The desire for travel and the appetite, as well as the necessity for buying and selling items, produced beyond the horizon of one's own locality, is and remains the foundation stone of why foreign exchange markets exist.

WHAT IS FOREIGN EXCHANGE?

Foreign exchange is someone else's money. Money is a subject which we will discuss later in this chapter but for now shall be left undefined. Most will know or recognize what is meant by the term *money* for purposes of defining foreign exchange. We could define foreign exchange as being shells, feathers, or other items used as exchange in antiquity; but this is beyond the scope of this writing. Paul Einzig's *History of Foreign Exchange* is a good reference for those interested in that subject.[1]

Foreign exchange is by definition foreign to the holder; otherwise, it would be domestic exchange or, in modern practice, local currency and legal tender. Foreign exchange typically is not legal tender and is therefore not acceptable in exchange for goods and services to whom it is being offered; hence, the desire to exchange it into something closer to home in terms of acceptability. Foreign exchange markets are nearly always markets that convert issues of foreign money for local units. The New York foreign exchange market, for example, is essentially a market for exchanging foreign currencies against the U.S.

---

[1] Paul Einzig, *The History of Foreign Exchange*, 2d ed. (London: Macmillan, 1970).

dollar. It is possible in New York to exchange French francs for Swedish kroner, but the normal practice would be sell French francs for U.S. dollars as a first step and then sell U.S. dollars and buy Swedish kroner as a second step in order to complete the transaction. Markets in other countries would be similar in structure and mechanical operation.

FOREIGN EXCHANGE AS MONEY

We have interjected the notion of money into this discussion of foreign exchange, and it would seem appropriate to define it. I have read many definitions of money over the years, but the best for me is found in H. E. Evitt's *A Manual of Foreign Exchange:*

> . . . money as something which is accepted generally by a community as a measure of value and a medium of exchange of goods and services. It is a measure of present value; but should also be a measure of future value, a store of value, that is. It gives the owner a command over the goods or services of other members of his community, which command he should be able to exercise at his option. Anyone who has exchanged his goods or his labour for money should have obtained something which he can again exchange for the goods or services of others to an extent which satisfies him that he has received a fair return.[2]

This book is also an excellent, if dated, work on foreign exchange.

It is essential when discussing foreign exchange to understand that it is money. This can be important in several ways. It is important because it demonstrates that foreign exchange is involved with the sovereignty of a nation. This distinguishes it from other markets, such as commodities. Foreign exchange is subject to control, regulation, interest-rate movements, and money supply concepts due to its essence as a currency issued by a sovereign entity. It is viewed by most governments in a very proprietary sense. Governments do not take kindly to anyone interfering with their prerogative as it relates to the governance of the coin of the realm. Speculators and others, for example black-market operators, have learned this lesson with extreme penalties when forgotten in some foreign exchange markets. Governments view foreign exchange as intimate to their ability to controlling their economic destiny and to fulfilling the economic expectations of their people. Therefore, even in free markets, the government is always present. This fact is central to exchange operations and should never be forgotten by anyone dealing with foreign exchange transactions. Foreign exchange is unique in this sense and exchange markets differ radically from stock markets and other markets from which one can draw parallels due to this unique feature. The foreign exchange operator can confront this fact in the market in a direct way such as in the form

---

[2] H. E. Evitt, *A Manual of Foreign Exchange* (London: Sir Isaac Pitman & Sons, 1938), p. 2.

of exchange controls or indirectly via interest-rate policy or other actions by governments or their agencies, such as central bank intervention in the marketplace.

FOREIGN EXCHANGE AS A COMMODITY

We have just said that foreign exchange is money and that it is important to remember that when dealing in it. It may then appear contradictory to some that we will now discuss foreign exchange in a commodity sense. This is done for two reasons: First, I have found in learning about foreign exchange, in trading foreign exchange, and in training young foreign exchange dealers that it is easier for many people to work with exchange as though it were a commodity and to put away the notion that it is money in the corner of one's mind. It is easier to think of the exchange markets as similar to markets for corn or soybeans and to equate French francs as just another commodity than to concern oneself about the French franc as money. As one other dealer in a major dealing room once said to me in a moment of confusion, "Just think of it as so many oranges and apples." In fact, exchange markets do operate much like markets for commodities with a cash market, a forward market, currency swaps (which resemble commodity straddles), and other similarities readily apparent. The second reason, however, is a more practical issue: that of legality. Foreign exchange contracts are treated legally in many jurisdictions as contracts under the commodities section of the law, not as negotiable instruments as is the case with most money market instruments. This is a very important distinction to be aware of if one is dealing actively in foreign exchange transactions and markets.

A good way to introduce the subject of foreign exchange is to describe typical transactions common in the day-to-day foreign exchange markets. All foreign exchange transactions can be divided into seven typical operations. It could be argued that some of these operations are redundant or that additional types of transactions exist distinct from those outlined by me in this chapter. The seven transactions identified as typical of all exchange transactions are derived from my particular experience in several active commercial bank dealing rooms. The experience of others might raise issues as to my arbitrary categories; but, nonetheless, these seven will achieve our purpose which is to describe foreign exchange and its functions as an introduction to the more detailed and technical chapters which follow.

The Cash Transaction

Most markets in which a commodity is actively traded usually consist of a cash or spot market and a related market for future or forward delivery of the commodity. The foreign exchange market is not an exception to this rule. This is a large market in a physical sense for cash foreign exchange. In fact, it is this aspect of the market that most people become somewhat familiar with since all of us have received Canadian coin in our change or have had some other cash exchange experiences. This cash market for notes and coin is, of course, a common experience for any business person or tourist. Indeed, business people dealing in very complex exchange transactions routinely are active in the operations. The cash market in exchange parallels other commodity markets in that it tends to be separate from the larger forward market and can be characterized as having rates of exchange which differ quite significantly from the larger market. The cash market will have rates which vary even from the more closely related spot market. The spot market can be thought of as short-date forward market in that settlement normally occurs two days after agreement, or it can be considered as an electronic cash market via telegraphic debits and credits passed over a commercial bank's books. It is not a physical cash market but straddles the cash market and the forward market. The cash market in physical exchange has different rates due to insurance, counterfeit risks, lost interest on the inventory and the cost of shipment of the physical cash to the market of issue by the holder. Operators in the cash market tend to be specialized firms, although commercial banks worldwide are involved as a customer service. Some commercial banks operate actively in this market in direct competition with these specialized nonbank firms. The commercial banks in Switzerland are a good example in that many Swiss commercial banks are active in the cash market for physical exchange.

Some readers might say to themselves, "Why so much written about a small, unimportant aspect of exchange which consists purely of small transactions for tips at the airport and other routine tourist concerns?" My response is that this cash exchange market is more important than that and can influence the larger market. Attacks on the Italian lira, for example, commenced in spring or summer are largely frustrated by the cash market for lira and the traditional strong demand for cash lira by vacationing non-Italians during the spring and summer months. Other markets, the black market or any other market in cash, whether illegal or sanctioned by government, can directly influence all exchange transactions and are frequently more indicative of market trends than officially posted rates by the central bank or by the commercial bankers. Along certain borders, the cash market is traditionally extremely active. The French and Italian borders with Switzerland have always been very active due to economics, political uncertainty, or exchange controls. We again saw this traditional reaction in early-1981 due to the financial markets' internal reaction to recent French electoral results.

It would be a mistake for anyone operating in foreign exchange to ignore the physical market in any currency and not to gain knowledge of it since this market can be central to understanding the currency. Large corporations have had to conduct large multimillion dollar transactions in those markets from time to time in my experience. This market is, of course, always active wherever you have illegal trade, smuggling, closed borders, exchange controls, or tight limitations on the amount of foreign currency nationals may hold, not to mention political, economic, or social instability. For instance, Miami has currently received widespread press coverage concerning the large cash market conducted in that city derived from both the drug trade and flight capital from South American countries now encountering political instability.

The Commodity Transaction

Large commodity-trading organizations and some major corporations actively engaged in commodity trading are major players in foreign exchange markets. The activity described here is in some respects similar to the import-export transaction to be described in the following section of this chapter. The major distinction to be made is volume. The transaction known as the commodity transaction takes place in unusually large volume and on a daily basis. The operators involved are typically doing business in a widely traded global commodity which moves in bulk or in very large quantities such as grain, cocoa, copper, and so on. Foreign exchange is required essentially for two purposes in this context. The commodity-producing nations and the large dealers rarely share the same currency; hence, these trading firms or entities need to acquire foreign exchange to pay for their raw material. The currency can be sterling in the case of Nigerian cocoa or the U.S. dollar in the case of American wheat. Foreign exchange is needed in the second case because in their global trading activities, these commodity dealers frequently sell their raw material for currencies other than those which they used for acquiring the commodity initially.

It is not unusual for a silver operator to buy silver in New York City against payment in dollars and to sell silver in London against payment in sterling. The margins on the commodity are typically quite small so that any movement in the exchange rates could erase any profit; hence, exchange operations are normally concluded simultaneously with the commodity operation in order to ensure a profit. These transactions are usually for delivery some time in the future; thus most of the activity takes place in the forward exchange market, although not always. Option contracts are very common in this end of the foreign exchange business to more closely tie the transaction to commodity-market practice. Commodity markets typically trade for months while the interbank exchange markets trade for particular dates within a month. A banker's willingness to give a commodity house an exchange contract covering all dates in a given month at the commodity's firm option effectively places the terms of the two separate and distinct markets at parity.

The commodity transaction should be watched for by all other exchange operators since it is typically large and high in volume. It can also be sudden and seasonal such as when the United States concludes a large grain transaction with the Russians. Commodity operators will also move to the exchange markets for pure speculation if their markets are quiet or if the margins in exchange begin to exceed their profit margins on the basic commodity. These companies and organizations already have a fixed overhead in place with staff and communications established to conduct their basic commodity business, but it is very easy for them to redirect that staff and communication network to the foreign exchange markets should the potential profits in foreign exchange exceed those available in their basic business.

The Import-Export Transaction

The import-export transaction is general in scope since by nature this market is very broad and diverse. The classic import-export house is a small, privately owned company with specialized expertise in a particular business field, for instance, toys, novelties, baby furniture. The company capitalizes on its expertise to capture price advantage or quality disparities in markets. This market tends to be difficult to classify as it can be cyclical with a large dependency on exchange-rate relationships, economic activity, and the business cycle, or it can be purely seasonal as, for example, the Christmas market in this country. The importer or exporter operates in the exchange market frequently but without the high volume or tendency to speculation prevalent in the commodity markets. In fact, the typical operator in this end of the market is usually a reluctant player often willing to take exchange risks only if absolutely necessary. Importers prefer to pay in their own currency, and exporters prefer to get paid in their own currency; hence, a stalemate is the negotiating starting point. The party that accepts the exchange risk ultimately becomes the party least able to bargain or the party with less leverage. The issue generally is decided by who needs to buy or sell more aggressively. In either case, the exchange transaction is married to a particular invoice evidencing a specified shipment of merchandise. Depending on the result of the negotiation as to the terms of trade, the importer will become a buyer in his local exchange market for the exporter's currency or the exporter will become a seller of the importer's currency in his

local market. The terms of trade plus individual preference will tend
to determine whether the transaction is done in the spot or forward
market.

The exporter may agree to be paid on an open-account basis which
means that he will ship merchandise against payment of an invoice
enclosed with the merchandise or billed directly to the importer. In
consideration of his willingness to ship on open account, however,
he may insist on payment in his own currency. The importer can in
this case wait to receive the invoice and buy a draft in the exporter's
currency to airmail to him or arrange a telegraphic transfer of spot
exchange in the exporter's currency. The importer could also determine at the time the terms are set that the exchange risk is uncomforta-
ble and subsequently arrange with a bank to cover the invoice amount
in the future market for the exporter's currency for delivery about
the time receipt of the invoice is expected. In this event, upon the
receipt of the invoice, the importer would arrange with his bank to
have the forward contract liquidated and the proceeds remitted to
the exporter. This latter example is a case of pure hedging which is
a very large and continuing aspect of all exchange markets.

It is an interesting aside to note here that hedging risk, which is
often described as riskless, can backfire. In this case, if, after the importer arranges a hedge, the exporter's currency were to drop in value
against the importer's currency, competitor importers who did not
hedge but waited for the invoice to pay would automatically have a
price advantage which could place a tremendous strain on the hedged
importer in turning over his inventory. The import-export transaction
has many variations depending on the terms of sale and other factors.
It can involve drafts, letters of credit, forward contracts, or none of
these things. What is important to remember is that this basic merchandise transaction is a big and continuing factor underlying foreign exchange transactions and is the link between exchange markets and
world trade. Trade flows will react to exchange rates and vice versa.

The Corporate Transaction

The three transactions described in the prior sections represent traditional and repeated kinds of foreign exchange transactions, the very
root of foreign exchange markets for centuries. The corporate transaction is a relatively modern phenomenon and is directly connected to
the rise of the multinational corporation. These corporations clearly
conduct transactions similar to those described in the prior sections.
Corporations do export and import. Indeed, some of our largest corporations account for a very heavy percentage of U.S. export trade.

The corporate transaction in foreign exchange markets differs markedly from those previously described in that they rarely are tied to a

specific piece of business, such as an invoice of a commodity movement. The corporation tends to act as a clearinghouse for internal exchange transactions; and when the corporation enters the marketplace, the transaction frequently represents a netting of foreign exchange risk by currency within the organization. The corporation has assets, liabilities, income, expenses, and other relationships in foreign currencies; and their foreign exchange involvement tends to be the net result derived from internal accounting systems designed to reflect for the corporate treasurer's staff the net foreign exchange risk in a particular currency. Corporations also use nonmarket techniques for solving exchange problems such as increasing assets to offset liabilities or other similar balance-sheet techniques. The goal of most modern corporations is to have a zero sum by result currency. In terms of foreign exchange risk management, hedge transactions are utilized to accomplish that end. The foreign exchange dealer in a commercial bank rarely knows why a particular corporation is calling to sell one-year lira forward. On occasion, it is tied to an identifiable transaction such as an anticipated dividend remittance from an Italian subsidiary company. More often, however, no explanation is given, and the transaction is an attempt to offset a net internal long position in lira which will be offset by the lira sale contract.

The Financial Transaction

The financial transaction is a relatively modern phenomenon in that it is dependent upon modern, rapid communication of information and risk evaluation. The financial transaction has the unique characteristic of almost always involving a swap which is simply the simultaneous purchase and sale of the same foreign currency for two different dates in time. Commodity traders would refer to this type of operation as a straddle. Financial transactions represent opportunities to employ funds at marginally higher rates. The below-listed example will demonstrate a typical swap transaction utilizing a hypothetical investment decision involving a Canadian versus a U.S. investment. I should point out that the example is deliberately simple in terms of the rates and the interest differentials utilized in order to establish the principle.

Step 1

An investor has U.S. $1 million to invest. Rates in United States are 10 percent. An investment in U.S. dollars for one year (365 days) produced interest of U.S. $101,388.89.

Step 2

An alternative would be taking an investment in a Canadian-dollar instrument with an interest rate of 14 percent.

A. Convert U.S. $1 million into Canadian dollars at a rate of .8350 producing Canadian $1,197,604.79.

B. Invest Canadian $1,197,604.79 at 14 percent for one year (365 days) producing interest of Canadian $169,993.35.

C.   In order to eliminate exchange risk, the investor sells Canadian principle and interest
     in the forward market at .8200:

Canadian-dollar principle	1,197,604.79
Canadian-dollar interest	169,993.35
Canadian dollars	1,367,598.14

Canadian dollars 1,367,588.14 times .8200 equals U.S. $1,121,430.47. Thus, the U.S.
dollars earned on this investment are $121,430.47.

Summary
Thus, the Canadian fully hedged investment produces interest income of U.S. $121,-
430.47 versus the U.S. $101,388.89 on a comparable U.S. investment. The above example
assumes the credit risks are identical and does not consider the issue of taxation.

This example demonstrates that by the simultaneous purchase of
Canadian dollars along with the sale for future delivery of the resultant
principle and interest, an investor can significantly increase his yield
via this fully hedged financial transaction. Opportunities such as this
exist for sophisticated and informed investors where forward exchange
markets are available in the currency involved. The foreign exchange
operator executing such financial swaps typically does so for very marginal increased yields. The large differential used in the example was
done so for convenience and simplicity and would not exist under
real market conditions except rarely since the professionals operating
in markets today would never allow the disparity to remain so large.

This example demonstrates why forward exchange markets are so
clearly tied to interest movements in modern exchange practice. The
action of the swap technique in the marketplace tends to bring the
forward exchange markets into line with interest differentials existent
between two currencies. This is not always the case, and the operator
in foreign exchange should be cautious in concluding that interest
rates are the sole determinant of forward exchange-rate movements.

The Professional Arbitrage Transaction

Professional operators in foreign exchange during the course of their
daily work will note market discrepancies which allow for immediate
arbitrage potentials. The rapid dissemination of information has narrowed these opportunities considerably in recent years. No time will
be spent on the classic arbitrage example found in many older foreign
exchange textbooks involving a series of spot transactions through several currencies which can yield a minimal profit upon conclusion.

The most obvious modern-day arbitrage opportunity exists between
two foreign exchange markets. This arbitrage has been quite profitable
in recent years. It involves the arbitrage into the interbank, informal
foreign exchange market by operators on the formalized commodity
markets, such as in Chicago. These markets, with a standard commodity-market approach to future trading, tend to be dominated by individ-

ual trading activity. The arbitrage opportunity develops due to market practices and structural differences which create significant variations in exchange rates between the two markets.

Arbitrage opportunities develop quickly, and the dealer in commodity-exchange pits who has access to the interbank foreign exchange market via an active commercial bank can often simultaneously buy or sell currency in his market and offset the transaction with an immediate profit. This type of activity has tended to significantly increase volume, particularly in the afternoons, in the New York market during some periods. As more people have become aware of the arbitrage situation, the opportunities have become limited and the profitability has narrowed considerably. The professional arbitrage transaction by definition is constantly changing as professional operators in the marketplace perceive and create arbitrage opportunities. This situation is mentioned as a class of transactions because it clearly adds to foreign exchange volume and market liquidity but differs from most other transactions in that it has no particular connection with trade or other more normal motivations for accomplishing foreign exchange transactions. The motivation tends to be internal to the marketplace itself and restricted to professional operators with instant profit the singular goal.

The Speculative Transaction

Pure speculative transactions account for some undeterminable percentage of foreign exchange activity. Speculation involves the taking of a view on a particular currency by establishing either a long or short position in that currency for pure speculative profit. These transactions can be initiated by commercial banks, although most commercial banks avoid a purely speculative posture in the marketplace and function most frequently as intermediaries satisfied with marginal profits from that role. Corporations, rarely, as a matter of philosophy, speculate.

In my experience, some corporations, particularly those accustomed to market kinds of risks, will attempt to earn profits from purely speculative foreign exchange positions. Individuals normally have difficulty establishing a speculative position with a commercial bank since most banks, as a matter of policy, will not accept a counterparty to a foreign exchange contract whose sole purpose is purely speculative and where the credit decision involved with extending a foreign exchange limit to the counterparty cannot be clearly established via normal financial analysis as is possible through the analysis of a corporation's balance sheet and income statement. Individuals, however, do have access to speculative positions in foreign exchange via investment banking firms and other special trading firms who are members of commodity ex-

changes. This market provides a vehicle for individual speculation provided the person can establish credibility as to financial strength with
the brokerage house, is willing to pay the appropriate commissions,
and will put up the required margin. It is my experience that individual
speculative activity has markedly increased in recent years through
the mechanism of the foreign exchange future contracts offered by
commodity exchanges and that this has spilled over into the interbank
market indirectly via the professional arbitrage transaction described
in the section immediately preceding this one.

These seven typical exchange transactions will, hopefully, aid the
reader in coming to understand the more detailed chapters which
follow this one on the subject of foreign exchange.

21
The Major Foreign Exchange Markets

DAVID E. BODNER
President
Baer American Banking Corporation

Foreign exchange transactions are an integral, even essential, part of international trade and finance. As those functions have grown during the past 30 years, foreign exchange trading has assumed a progressively more important role. In the immediate aftermath of World War II, foreign exchange trading was relatively limited, as most major currencies were subject to extensive exchange controls, and the opportunities for the movement of funds across national boundaries were severely limited. The subsequent recovery and growth of the world economy brought a gradual relaxation of these controls, and, as a result, foreign exchange trading became more and more active. The really explosive growth of the exchange markets began, however, with the advent of floating exchange rates following the collapse of the Bretton Woods system in the early 1970s. Since then, not only has world trade continued to expand very rapidly, but international financial transactions have grown exponentially and with them, the foreign exchange markets. Moreover, not only has volume grown, but the markets have become increasingly volatile, and that, in itself, has drawn in additional players to the market, both for defensive and aggressive trading.

The objective of this chapter is to outline the basic structure of the major foreign exchange markets. The first section will be devoted to a review of the participants in the market and their various roles. This will be followed by sections on the mechanics of foreign exchange trading, which currencies are traded, where they are traded, and when. Thereafter will be a tour of the major markets, following the sun around the world.

MARKET PARTICIPANTS

Participants in the foreign exchange market fall into five broad categories: commercial customers, banks, brokers, central banks, and the International Monetary Market in Chicago. From the point of view of a trading bank, a customer is a commercial firm, a correspondent bank which does not participate in the interbank trading market but simply covers its own commercial customers' needs, a nonbank financial institution, or a foreign central bank. Commercial firms are participants in the market through their banks primarily to provide cover for trade and financial transactions. Their needs may be in the spot market to meet current invoices for trade transactions or to acquire currency needed for current financial transactions, or in the forward market to hedge against an exposure arising from either a trade or a financial transaction. For example, importers whose goods are invoiced in foreign currencies will have to acquire those currencies either on a spot basis to pay for goods upon delivery or on a forward basis in order to guarantee to themselves the foreign exchange rate at which they will ultimately have to pay for those goods. Exporters may find themselves in a parallel situation if they are dealing in markets which require them to invoice their transactions in the importer's currency rather than in their own, thereby forcing them to absorb the exchange risks.

These requirements for foreign exchange transactions arising out of international trade provide the underlying basis for the foreign exchange market and, indeed, its original rationale. Trading companies naturally looked to their banks to provide foreign exchange service, just as they did for other financial services. It was these needs that brought the banks into the foreign exchange trading business in the first instance. Even today, when the volume of foreign exchange trading far exceeds that required to provide for customer transactions, such business continues to represent the fundamental rationale for banks' participation in the markets.

Another set of foreign exchange transactions which emerges from the commercial side is hedging transactions in the forward market to protect capital exposures or other investment exposures. Particularly in the United States, since the introduction of specific accounting standards covering foreign transactions, firms have found it desirable to take hedge positions against their overseas capital or inventory exposures, selling forward amounts equal to the value of their foreign currency assets. Transactions of this type were particularly substantial in the period immediately following the advent of these accounting rules, and, although less important on an ongoing basis today, they remain a significant element in the market.

In addition to these trade- and translation-oriented transactions, commercial customers may also have international financial transactions which require foreign exchange. For example, the manager of a diversified international investment portfolio may need Japanese yen, German marks, pounds sterling, Hong Kong dollars, Singapore dollars, or other currencies in order to acquire securities traded in those markets. Depending upon the nature of the portfolio, he may also want to sell those currencies in the forward market in order to hedge his exchange risk. If not, he will again come into the spot market as a seller of those currencies when he liquidates his portfolio. The remittance of earnings from overseas subsidiaries provides another important base of commercial transactions that flow into the market, as companies convert their foreign currency earnings into the home currency.

Finally, there is outright position taking by commercial customers. This type of trading is perhaps less common in the United States than it is elsewhere in the world, but is certainly not unknown in this market. Position taking is simply the acquisition or sale of a currency on an outright basis by a company that has no underlying commercial or financial transaction requiring such a purchase or sale. The transaction is entered into purely in an attempt to profit from an anticipated change in the exchange rate for a particular currency. There is, of course, a variety of ways in which corporations can take "speculative" positions without entering into outright foreign exchange transactions, including not covering an exposure which exists as a result of a commercial transaction, but the primary concern in this chapter is those elements which actually come into play in the market, and it is for that reason that we concentrate on the positive transaction rather than the negative one.

The major players in the market are the banks who make up the interbank market. International banks participate in the foreign exchange markets for three basic reasons. First, banks need to service the customer requirements outlined above. Second, banks have their own financial transactions involving foreign currencies and, therefore, may need to operate in the market in order to meet their own internal requirements for current transactions or for hedging future transactions. In particular, banks may raise funds in a variety of currency markets around the world where they can find liquidity at an acceptable price and use those funds in other markets, converting them into the necessary currencies through swap transactions in the foreign exchange market. Finally, and now most important, the banks make the foreign exchange market by trading among themselves.

It is the banks' role as market makers that puts them in a position to provide effective service to their commercial customers and maintain a broad and deep market in which large volumes of foreign exchange requirements can be covered. In effect, by standing ready to meet their customers' requirements for foreign exchange, the banks act to absorb the foreign exchange risks of the customers and take them onto their own books, trading those risks for the possibility of earning profits within the risk parameters set forward by individual bank management. Indeed, in recent years more and more banks have come to look upon their foreign exchange trading operations as independent profit centers which can contribute significantly to bottom-line earnings.

Banks' appetites for foreign exchange risk vary very widely around the world and from institution to institution. Some participants in the market act primarily to service customer requirements and very quickly pass the positions into the market so as to minimize the risk taken on their own books. Others are more aggressive participants in the market and frequently will take large open positions for their own account. Bank trading styles also vary significantly, not only among institutions, but even from trading room to trading room within the same institution. Thus some operate in an extremely aggressive, high-volume manner—with or without large overnight positions—while others trade on a more modest scale.

In the United States there are now some 175 commercial banks which are reasonably regular participants in the foreign exchange market. Of these, however, probably not more than 40 could be classified as active market makers, including several branches of some major foreign institutions. Around the world there are hundreds of banks that have some role in the market and probably something on the order of 200 institutions that could be considered to be active market makers.

Another perspective on the size of the worldwide market is gained by looking at the people involved: there are some 7,500 foreign exchange traders and brokers who are members of the International Association of Foreign Exchange Traders and probably a similar number who are either local "national" members or dealer participants who are not yet full-fledged members of the Association. Considering the number of institutions and individuals involved in these markets, it is not surprising that turnover is as large as it appears to be. There are no good international data on total turnover in the foreign exchange markets, but a survey of 100 active banks in the U.S. market in April 1980 showed a daily turnover of approximately $20 billion, and it seems reasonable to assume that the turnover in the rest of the world must amount to at least four times that amount, thus a total of some $100 billion per day.

The next major set of participants in the market is composed of foreign exchange brokers who provide an essential link among banks, both in the individual domestic markets and internationally. The role of the brokers will be covered in detail in Chapter 23. Suffice it to say here that brokers are an important part of all of the major foreign exchange markets, providing an efficient link for dealing among banks. Their role has expanded considerably in the last 10 years. This is especially true on the international scene in that most of the major brokerage firms now operate on a worldwide basis and provide direct links between the markets in different parts of the world. For example, a German bank can make an offer in the market in Frankfurt and find a broker returning with a counterparty from London or New York as easily as from within Germany. As a result, prices in the various markets around the world have tended to get closer and closer together, and there is now very little difference in the quotations that one will find at any moment anywhere in the world.

The next major set of actors in the foreign exchange market is the central banks. They have a dual role, both to provide for the foreign exchange requirements of their governments and investment authorities on a regular basis and a special role in intervention. Under the Bretton Woods arrangements, central banks were obligated to intervene in the foreign exchange markets at fixed levels in order to preserve the established parities of their currencies against other major currencies. In general, this obligation no longer exists, and most currencies are now allowed to float freely against other currencies. Nevertheless, many central banks have retained the option to intervene in the markets to influence the level of the exchange rate for their currencies. Some central banks do so frequently. Moreover, within the European monetary system there remain fixed obligations of the participating central banks. Overall, while the current monetary system is one of very considerable flexibility and latitude for the central banks in choosing when and whether to intervene, there remains a significant volume of official intervention.

The level of the exchange rate is an important policy issue in many countries, and the central banks are frequently in the market to try to influence that level. In general, the role that the central banks have adopted is a defensive one; that is, they confine their intervention to periods when they believe that the exchange markets have become too volatile or disorderly and require intervention in order to smooth the flow of international transactions, or, for those countries which have assumed fixed obligations, when they are required to intervene in order to maintain the agreed exchange rates. Some central banks, however, will intervene under other circumstances, in particular, when they or their governments believe that the exchange rate is reaching a level where the potential economic consequences are unacceptable. Then an attempt is made to influence the market to move the rate to a more comfortable zone.

The final major participant in the markets is the International Monetary Market (IMM) in Chicago. The IMM is a subdivision of the Chicago Mercantile Exchange. It was established some years ago in order to provide individual traders and speculators access to foreign exchange transactions. In the United States, in contrast to other countries, commercial banks generally have been reluctant to deal with individuals in foreign exchange, especially if they did not believe that those individuals had an underlying commercial or financial transaction involving foreign exchange but rather were simply taking speculative positions. The IMM filled that vacuum, creating a market in which the individual speculator could be active. Floating exchange rates, and their accompanying volatility, attracted a large volume of business to the IMM, as individuals saw the opportunity to profit from exchange trading in the same way that they could from commodity trading. At the same time, commercial banks began gradually to deal with various arbitrage companies which came into being on the IMM, thus providing a link between the IMM and the interbank market, thereby helping to insure the liquidity of the IMM. As a result, the volume of business on that market has grown very significantly over recent years. Transactions initiated on the IMM have come to play an important role in influencing the interbank market.

MECHANICS OF FOREIGN EXCHANGE TRADING

The mechanical arrangements for the conduct of foreign exchange business have become increasingly sophisticated in recent years, but the basics remain simple. The bulk of foreign exchange trading is conducted by telephone or by telex. In general, commercial customers deal with their correspondent banks by telephone with transactions subsequently confirmed in writing. Banks traditionally have dealt with each other by telephone in local markets, usually through brokers, and by telex in international markets. In recent years, with the improvement of telephone service and the advent of direct international dialing, bank-to-bank dealing has been conducted increasingly by telephone even internationally, although the traditional telex links continue to be used.

Dealing through brokers is usually done by telephone. Banks and brokers maintain direct private lines between themselves, and in recent years many of these have been augmented by loudspeaker systems which enable the brokers to communicate instantaneously with a number of banks on the prices they receive. Indeed, as the markets have become more and more volatile, the pressure to develop high-speed communication links has grown, and a variety of techniques have been employed to increase the speed of dealing response. The latest addition in this respect is the Reuters Money Dealing Service, which provides a high-speed computerized telex system enabling banks who are members of the arrangement to access each other over computer terminals at high speed and with ease of communication. But with all of the increased sophistication, the traditional image of the foreign exchange trader as a man with a telephone in each ear remains reasonably accurate.

CURRENCIES TRADED

The who and the how of foreign exchange trading have now been reviewed. What foreign exchange trading consists of was covered in detail in the previous chapter. To complete the picture only a brief review is needed of the currencies that are the major ones traded in the markets and those which play a secondary or tertiary role. Ever since World War II and the development of the Bretton Woods System, the dollar has been the world's primary trading and financial currency. As a result, it also fulfills the role of the world's major reserve currency. Consequently, the vast majority of foreign exchange trading is of individual currencies against the dollar, and central banks traditionally have kept the bulk of their foreign exchange reserves in dollars. Because of the historic role of Great Britain as a trading country and the continuing role of London as a financial center, sterling has remained a major international currency even after its decline as the dominant currency of the world's international trading markets. Thus, sterling also continues to be actively dealt in all of the major financial centers.

However, the role of sterling as the lead currency whose exchange rate against the dollar would be key to the establishment of other rates has been taken over now by the deutsche mark. With the growth of West German trade and finance in the postwar period and the country's now-sustained history of monetary stability, the deutsche mark has become increasingly important. Moreover, within the European Monetary System, the mark is the key to the whole block of associated European currencies. This central role of the mark is exemplified by the fact that, when the Federal Reserve System in the United States chooses to intervene in foreign exchange markets to protect the value of the dollar or to curb exchange-rate volatility, the focus of that intervention is the deutsche mark. As a result of this increasing role in recent years, the mark is now one of the most actively traded currencies in the world's exchange markets.

Two other currencies that are actively traded in most centers around the world are the Swiss franc and the Japanese yen. Switzerland, of course, is an active commercial trading country, but on a world scale it is relatively small. The importance of the Swiss franc comes from its historical role as a haven currency and as a financial dealing currency rather than directly out of its trade role. Switzerland's long history of political neutrality and of banking confidentiality have given the Swiss franc a special role around the world as a safe-haven currency.

Although there are signs that this unique role of the Swiss franc is beginning to fade, the Swiss franc remains a significant trading currency. In most markets, however, the volumes traded in Swiss francs are significantly less than those traded in deutsche marks, and in general, the Swiss franc tends to be traded in relation to the dollar-mark rate because of the very close trade ties between Switzerland and Germany.

The Japanese yen is a relatively new arrival on the scene as an internationally traded currency. In the immediate aftermath of the war, the yen was a highly restricted currency, subject to extensive exchange controls and with limitations of the ability of nonresidents to hold yen balances. In recent years, however, as the Japanese economy has grown and the trade role of the yen consequently has expanded, the Japanese authorities have progressively unwound their exchange control restrictions. Today the yen is traded not simply to finance current trade transactions, but also for financial needs because of the extensive growth and internationalization of the Japanese securities markets. Most trading in yen takes place in Tokyo and the other Far European markets and in London and in New York. It remains true today that, despite the yen's growing importance, the volume of interbank trading in yen among continental European banks is relatively low.

This small group of currencies—sterling, the deutsche mark, the swiss franc, and the yen—constitute the core of the interbank exchange market trading against the U.S. dollar and account for the bulk of interbank trading. Of course, there also are significant amounts of trading done in other European currencies and in the Canadian dollar, but these can legitimately be considered second-tier currencies in that they are not of worldwide interest, either because of exchange control restriction or because of a lack of sufficient volume of trade and financial transactions denominated in those currencies. Included in this list would be the Belgian franc, French franc, Italian lira, and the Canadian dollar, which is essentially traded in the North American market. In that market the Canadian dollar remains a very major part of the total business, but the currency is not actively traded in the rest of the world.

In the third tier would be the currencies of smaller countries whose banks are active in the markets and in which there are significant local markets and some international scale trading. In this group one would include the Austrian schilling, the Hong Kong dollar, the Singapore dollar, the Scandinavian currencies, and some of the Middle East currencies, especially the Saudi rial and Kuwait dinar.

Finally, the fourth tier would consist of what are called the exotic currencies, those for which there are no active international markets and in which transactions are generally arranged on a correspondent-bank basis between banks abroad and local banks in those centers to meet the specific trade requirements of individual clients. This group would include the majority of the Latin American currencies, the African currencies, and the remaining Asian currencies.

THE WHERE AND WHEN OF FOREIGN EXCHANGE MARKETS

The where of foreign exchange markets, as is implied from the above sections, is individual bank trading rooms and commercial firms treasurers' offices. With the exception of the IMM, there is no central marketplace. The interbank market is a telephone-telex market and business is conducted around the world from individual dealing rooms. Indeed, business can be conducted from any place there is a telephone and that includes the homes of individual dealers or anywhere they can have access to a phone. Normally, trading takes place from the established locations of the individual banks, but it is common practice for many banks to have senior foreign exchange traders maintain contact with the worldwide market even when they are at home. The possibility exists for dealers to enter into trades from any location. Such off-premises dealing has become increasingly common in recent years because the market is now active almost 24 hours a day.

In the 1950s and 60s, foreign exchange trading took place primarily in Europe and to a lesser extent in New York, and once the New York market closed, there was virtually no trading until Europe opened the following morning. Over the last 10 years, however, markets in the Far East have grown significantly. Tokyo, Hong Kong, and Singapore now represent important foreign exchange trading centers. As a result, there is almost no time during the day when foreign exchange trading is not taking place. The only meaningful gap that remains is between the close of the New York market and the opening of the Far East markets. Even during that period there is some trading taking place on the West Coast of the United States, but that market has never become a significant factor on the worldwide scene. Thus, from the point of view of active dealing, there is a brief gap between New York and the Far East. Otherwise, there is continuous trading as the markets overlap each other, and the center of the trading shifts from location to location following the sun.

THE OPERATION OF THE MAJOR MARKETS

A broad perspective on the major markets and the flow of trading can, perhaps, best be obtained through an imaginary tour of the world, beginning in Tokyo. Since the only significant gap in trading activity takes place following the close in New York, one may say that the day begins with the opening in the Far East. Of course, traders in

Tokyo are aware of what happened in the New York market the previous afternoon and where rates closed. From that information they can key their starting quotations. In addition, many banks in Tokyo will have had overnight orders from their U.S. offices or correspondents, and will be receiving telephone calls from their associates in American and foreign banks with additional orders, as well as information. The opening of the Tokyo market is frequently quite hectic as much will have changed in the marketplace since its close the previous day, and traders may well have to adjust their positions to account for significant overnight changes.

The principal activity in the Tokyo market is in dollar-yen, although there is gradually beginning to be some dealing in the dollar against the major European currencies. The yen remains dominant, however, not only because this is the Tokyo market, but also because the market is peculiarly customer oriented. As indicated earlier, in most of the world's exchange markets interbank trading constitutes the bulk of the volume, with the commercial customers providing a base but a small part of the total turnover. Tokyo, on the contrary, has a very high percentage of business stemming from customer activity; thus it is not uncommon for 30 or 40 percent of the turnover of a Japanese bank to be accounted for by customer orders, in comparison with 3 to 6 percent in the rest of the world's major markets. This is in part a function of the fact that a major proportion of Japanese trade, both imports and exports, continues to be dominated in U.S. dollars. These proportions are quite different from those prevailing in most of the rest of the world's markets. This means that both importers and exporters have significant requirements for foreign exchange transactions.

As the Japanese economy has grown, and in particular as in recent years the Japanese securities markets have become of great interest to nonresidents while the Japanese authorities have liberalized their exchange control rules, financial transactions have become increasingly important. Thus "natural" business is very large in Tokyo. Finally, Japanese banks traditionally have not been active interbank traders, in part because of the history of exchange control and in part because the yen was not actively traded abroad until recent years. On balance, as the yen has grown in importance, the Tokyo market has expanded. Nevertheless, even today, turnover in the Tokyo market remains small relative to some of the other major exchange markets. Typical volume in the interbank market as reported through the brokers in Tokyo runs about $1 billion per day. This, of course, does not account for the total activity of banks operating in that market, since a significant volume of business is done with banks in foreign centers and is not included in the above total.

The Tokyo market over recent years essentially has been a brokered market, with transactions between banks in Tokyo being intermediated by a group of local foreign exchange brokers. The typical transaction is $1 million, although $3–$5 million transactions are not uncommon. The Tokyo market was the last major market to receive the participation of international brokers. The first foreign broker set up shop in Tokyo in 1980, and the second opened in 1981. Their role remains limited to dealing within Tokyo, however, as the Japanese authorities have been reluctant to permit a true internationalization of the market in which the brokers could service banks abroad.

Consequently, international transactions that do occur are done directly on a bank-to-bank basis. At the same time, the increasing number of foreign banks operating in Tokyo has begun to introduce additional changes in local market practice, so that there is now beginning to be some direct interbank trading outside of the brokers' market. This trading has tended to be concentrated in currencies other than the yen, however, and the bulk of the dollar-yen trading within Tokyo continues to be done through the brokers. One of the major constraints on the further growth of the Tokyo market is the fact that it officially closes for lunch time from 12:00 to 1:30 P.M. and for the day at 3:30 in the afternoon, when the brokers cease dealing and the banks have to report their closing foreign exchange positions to the Bank of Japan. Thus, Tokyo remains the only significant market in the world in which there is an official closing time. On balance, while the Tokyo market is beginning to conform more and more to international practice and to get away from rather specialized local customs, the market is not yet fully international.

About one hour after the opening in Tokyo, the Hong Kong and Singapore markets start their trading days. Both of these markets are more free wheeling and less regulated than the Tokyo market, and of course, it is entirely possible for banks in those centers to begin dealing earlier in the day so as to be available for the actual opening in Tokyo. Nevertheless, banks in Hong Kong and Singapore normally do start about one hour after the Tokyo opening. It is with the opening of these two markets that active trading in the Far East begins in deutsche marks, Swiss francs, and sterling. Both Hong Kong and Singapore are relatively new exchange markets on an international scale, but both have been growing rapidly in recent years. In the case of Singapore, this is a result of a decision by the Singapore government to make the "Lion City" a financial center for South Asia by inviting foreign banks to come into the country to set up offshore banking units and become active in foreign exchange and deposit trading.

In the case of Hong Kong, development was less a question of conscious policy than a function of the fact that Hong Kong had an open and largely unregulated banking environment and provided a natural base of commercial business growing out of the colony's active manufacturing and trading role. The development of Hong Kong has been greatly facilitated, however, by the decision of the authorities to permit foreign banks to open branches, rather than only finance company subsidiaries. This has made it possible for those branches to trade much more actively, since the credit facilities available to them as branches are much greater than those that had prevailed when they were subsidiaries.

The combination of a friendly regulatory environment and the very rapid growth of the economies of Southeast Asia has meant that both of these markets have grown rapidly in recent years and are now significant factors in the world's exchange markets. The Singapore market is almost entirely a brokered market. Banks in Singapore tend not to deal on a direct basis with each other but to confine their direct dealings to banks outside of Singapore. Hong Kong, on the contrary, is more open and deals both through brokers and on a direct basis. Both markets include local and international brokers, although the local brokers are more important in Hong Kong than in Singapore, in part because there is a significant trade in Hong Kong dollars which tends to be dominated by the local brokers. Another difference between the two markets is that the Singapore market is largely an English-speaking one, while the Hong Kong market conducts the bulk of its business in Chinese.

The early morning in both Singapore and Hong Kong tends to be extremely active as traders catch up with developments in the Tokyo market, execute orders passed on from Europe and New York, and deal with the early volume of commercial business.

Although activity has grown significantly in these markets, it remains true that they are much smaller than the European and North American markets and, as a consequence, tend to be somewhat more volatile. After the initial rush of activity, the typical pattern is for the markets to turn quiet in mid-day and for very little to happen until other markets begin to have an impact. About that time the Bahrain market opens, but because that market itself is not well developed, it only feeds a limited amount of business into Hong Kong and Singapore. Moreover, at the same time the Tokyo market officially closes for lunch, both the dollar-yen business and the other activity emanating from Tokyo disappear.

The volume in the Far East markets tends to pick up again in mid-afternoon, particularly as Europe begins to open. As the volume in the Far East has grown and those markets have developed the capacity to handle larger transactions, more and more banks in Europe have begun to arrange for early-morning teams of traders to deal in to the Far Eastern markets. Thus, it is not uncommon for Hong Kong to get quite hectic from about 3 P.M. onward as European banks begin to funnel large-scale business into that market. As the normal European business day begins, however, the focus of activity shifts to the west, and business in Asia dies down.

Trading activity in Europe develops gradually in the early morning, in part because the various banks begin trading at different hours of the day, depending upon their short-term requirements as well as their long-term trading strategies. There are no official opening and closing times, and therefore, banks are free to begin and end dealing as they see fit. Because European banks can begin early by trading with the Far East or stay late to trade with New York, they have a wide range of options as to how they manage their trading activities and the length of the dealing day.

For the trader in Europe, as for his Far Eastern counterpart, much may have changed since the previous day's close, depending upon activity both in New York the previous night and that morning in Asia. However, unlike the Asian dealer, who can be said to start the day's trading, the European trader comes into a market already functioning, with prices appearing firm the various brokers and with calls coming in from banks in the Far East and Middle East.

Because of the tremendous importance of international trade and finance in the economies of Western Europe, as well as the long history of such trade and foreign exchange trading, there are active markets in virtually all European countries, and a very large number of banks participate in the markets. Thus the broadest and deepest exchange market in the world can be said to be the European market. That market, of course, is a collection of a large number of individual national markets, some of which are more active and freer than others. Although exchange control has played a diminishing role in recent years, it remains a significant constraint on activity in a number of centers, particularly with respect to dealing in the local currency against the dollar. Belgium, France, Italy, and Spain all maintain a degree of exchange control that has an impact on the freedom of banks in those centers to participate in the market. Scandinavian banks are also subject to significant restrictions. The rules applied by the central banks in Scandinavia have tended to significantly reduce the ability of banks in those centers to participate actively in the markets and has reduced the ability of foreign banks to trade in the Scandinavian currencies. Nevertheless, major banks in Sweden, Norway, and Denmark continue to be meaningful participants in the world's exchange markets.

The most important trading centers are in the United Kingdom, Germany, and Switzerland, three countries which do not maintain exchange control and where there are both major and lesser banks with long histories of participation in the foreign exchange markets. In the case of Germany and Switzerland, there is no single foreign exchange center as London is in the case of United Kingdom. While Frankfurt is, perhaps, the principal banking center in Germany, all of the major banks maintain large trading activities in the other important German cities, and there are, as well, significant smaller institutions located in those centers. Thus, Hamburg, Dusseldorf, and Munich also are significant centers for foreign exchange trading. Similarly in Switzerland, while Zurich is the main foreign exchange trading center, Basle and Geneva also play important roles in the market.

Trading throughout Europe is a mixture of brokered and direct dealing. All of the markets are well served by active international brokers, while at the same time banks are free to trade on a direct basis with counterparties in their own markets and abroad. The only exception to this practice remains London which is an almost wholly brokered market. In the last year it has been possible for banks in London to deal with each other on a direct basis, but this remains a relatively limited practice and the bulk of trading in London continues to be done through brokers.

One anachronism that remains unique to the Continental markets is the daily "fixing." Around mid-day representatives of the major banks, plus the central bank, meet at the stock exchange and under the guidance of an official broker establish, or "fix," exchange rates for the dollar against the local currency and for the local currency against all other major currencies traded. This fixing represents a balance of bids and offers for currencies put into the fixing by the participants. Naturally, the rate set will be close to the rates prevailing in the international market immediately prior to the fixing, since any significant variation would lead to arbitrage possibilities. Indeed, in many centers participating banks maintain continuous contact with the international markets during the fixing process.

Should there be an imbalance in the market that might require the rate to be fixed significantly away from established levels, the central bank may use the opportunity to intervene to set the rate, although in the normal course of events the central banks do not participate actively. The purpose of fixing is not to set rates for transactions among banks, but rather to establish an official rate for transactions with commercial customers. Thus, it is possible for a customer to send an order in to a bank asking that it be executed at the fixing or at the fixing rate. This can be done at any time prior to the actual fixing. Most large transactions are no longer done through the fixing because the more sophisticated customers are aware of the possibility of trading directly with their banks at other times during the day and, perhaps, obtaining a better price than that available at fixing time. Fixings remain significant, however, because they have a legal status within the country as an official rate. Thus, many contracts call for settlement at the fixing rate, which has the advantage of providing both sides of the transaction with a transparent and published rate that leaves no question on either side as to how the exchange rate was established.

As is the case in the Far Eastern markets, the European markets tend to open with a surge of activity which carries through a good part of the morning, followed by a lull during lunch time. Activity then picks up again as the New York market comes into play. The New York market is also an unregulated one in which banks are free to trade at any time of the day. Some occasionally begin as early as 3 A.M. to participate in the opening of the European markets. More typically, however, trading rooms begin to be staffed from 7 A.M. onward, and by 8 o'clock, most are fully staffed.

Nevertheless, the real activity in New York tends to begin after 8 o'clock, with traders employing the early period as they filter into their offices to catch up with their colleagues abroad on the prior activity in the Far East and in Europe and to decide upon opening tactics. The International Money Market in Chicago opens at 8 A.M. New York time, so that it can participate fully in the New York market activity and in the late afternoon business from Europe. Because the European banks have not only themselves to trade with in the afternoon but also the large and growing U.S. market, activity tends to remain high in the European markets through the close. Typically, banks in Europe will cease dealing activity around 5 P.M., although that varies considerably, for there is no official closing time. On days when there is little going on and nothing exciting happening in the markets, traders may cease dealing earlier in the day. On the other hand, on those days when there is much news and a high level of activity, it is not uncommon for banks in Europe to continue dealing into New York well into their evening. New York banks may receive telex and telephone calls from European banks at 7 and 8 P.M. European time. Generally, trading ceases at more normal business hours, and at that time activity in the U.S. markets also tends to slow down as the lunch hour approaches.

The afternoon volume in the U.S. market normally tends to be rather small. Once Europe has closed, there is a sharp drop in the number of active dealing banks, and the market then has to rely entirely on its own resources. Since there is a limited number of active dealing banks in the United States, afternoons can be very quiet. If there are no large orders or important news to move the market in one direction or another, there is not much incentive to trade. On the other hand, at times of intense and very hectic market activity, banks may also decide to cease active dealing early in the day because they are concerned that, with a limited number of participants, they may have difficulty reversing positions that might develop. Generally, however, there is a reasonable volume of business that carries on through the afternoon, and in recent years that volume has increased significantly.

There are essentially three reasons for the continued growth of the New York market. First, international trade and finance have become increasingly important in the United States, and therefore, the natural volume of commercial business has grown. Further, an increasing portion of U.S. trade is denominated in currencies other than the dollar (as a result of the decline in the value of the dollar since the early 1970s), and this, in itself, means that more U.S. companies have foreign exchange requirements. A second major factor has been the influx of foreign banks to the United States. A large number of banks from Europe and the Far East have opened branches in the United States in recent years, and almost all have established foreign exchange trading rooms as a natural extension of their worldwide business. This has meant a significant increase in the number of participants in the market, especially of banks that have a long history of foreign exchange trading. Therefore they expect to play an active role in the market. The foreign banks also have brought with them a number of expatriate dealers, augmenting the supply of dealers in the United States and the level of experience with European and Far East markets. Finally, the growth of the markets in Hong Kong, Tokyo, and Singapore has meant greater flexibility for U.S. banks in managing their own positions.

Historically, the New York market would tend to thin out in the afternoon, and a bank, unless it was very cautious, might find itself with a significant overnight position because it was unable to find a counterparty in the afternoon. An overnight position occurred because the next real market activity would not take place until the opening in Europe, which was the middle of the night New York time. Typically, a bank with a position could come in the following morning to a market that might be quoting rates significantly different from those of the night before; therefore, the risk in carrying a position was substantial.

The development of the Far East markets, however, has given the U.S. bank with an overnight position the opportunity in the early evening to be in touch with the Far East at its opening. The bank then could reduce its exposure by dealing in those markets without taking the risk of carrying the position during an extended period when it could not readily be monitored. The result is greater willingness on the part of banks dealing in the U.S. market to continue to trade later into the afternoon with the assurance that they will not have to wait 12 hours before they can cover their positions. As a consequence of all these elements, the New York market has grown significantly, and the afternoon market is more meaningful than it once was.

Like the European and most Asian markets, the North American market is one in which there are active foreign exchange brokers and in which dealing banks also may trade directly with each other. Until 1979, banks in New York did all of their business with each other through the established foreign exchange brokers, and direct dealing was confined to international and out-of-town transactions. At the same time, the brokers in the New York market did not work on an international basis but confined their activity to banks in the United States and Canada. Beginning in 1979 direct links were established by the brokers with their counterparts or partners in Europe so that the two markets were linked even more closely than in the past. At the same time, the banks in New York began to deal on a direct basis with each other outside of the brokers' market. Overall, this improvement in communication has led to a further increase in volume, as the brokers now intermediate directly between European and New York banks while the New York banks are no longer confined to dealing only on prices appearing in the brokers' market.

In the late afternoon activity dies down in New York and the market effectively comes to a close. Major American banks located in the Midwest and on the West Coast that are active participants in the foreign exchange market operate essentially on New York time, work through the New York-based brokers, and deal directly with the New York banks, so that their business does not tend to continue after the New York close. Trading activity on the West Coast is predominantly customer oriented, with a significant focus on dealing in Japanese yen, Mexican pesos, and Canadian dollars. In general, however, the West Coast banks tend to try to cover exposures with Chicago and New York rather than staying on to wait for the opening in the Far East. As a result of this focus on the tie to the New York money and exchange markets, the West Coast markets have never developed a significant independent presence.

Overall, as one looks at the pattern of trading around the world, it becomes clear why the foreign exchange markets react instantaneously to political and economic developments anywhere in the world. The market is almost always open, and there are banks in a position to trade or take positions in response to any news as it develops. Thus, almost any dealer coming in to start his trading day does not himself start up the market fresh where he left it last night, as in the case with the domestic money markets. On the contrary, he comes in to a dynamic and moving market which may be trading at quite different levels from those prevailing when he went home the night before. And he may have to respond to a whole new set of forces that have emerged during the previous 12 hours.

22
Exchange of Minor Currencies and Special Exchange Systems

EARL I. JOHNSON
Assistant Vice President
Harris Trust and Savings Bank

INTRODUCTION

There are over 140 currencies in the world, although global foreign exchange activity is dominated by transactions in about 10 major currencies. A 1977 Federal Reserve study of turnover in the U.S. foreign exchange market revealed that four currencies—the German mark, Swiss franc, British sterling, and Canadian dollar—accounted for nearly 80 percent of the total volume.[1] Nine currencies accounted for more than 97 percent of U.S. volume; the prior four plus the French franc, Dutch guilder, Japanese yen, Belgian franc, and the Italian lira. In addition to these major currencies, there are about 20 to 25 currencies which are actively traded in the world foreign exchange market which encompasses a global network of national and regional foreign exchange markets.

This second tier of so-called minor currencies includes Scandinavian and European currencies, as well as the currencies of Asia, the Mideast, and Latin America. Most of these currencies are not actively traded in the U.S. interbank market since U.S. banks normally conduct limited exchange operations in these currencies, primarily as a service to their corporate customers. Nevertheless, many of these minor currencies have become increasingly important in world trade and finance during the 1970s and 80s, and consequently, the scope of interbank trading in these currencies has expanded significantly during the past decade. Large international banks have created limited markets in these lesser-

---

[1] Roger M. Kubaryah, *Foreign Exchange Markets in the U.S.* (New York: Federal Reserve Bank of New York, 1978), p. 48.

traded currencies in order to satisfy the requirements of multinational corporate customers who operate subsidiaries throughout the world.

CHARACTERISTICS OF MINOR CURRENCY MARKETS

The key distinction between major and minor currencies (or primary and secondary currencies) involves the degree of free tradability or convertibility that an individual currency possesses. Major currencies normally can be freely converted into other currencies, while minor or secondary currencies often possess only limited or partial convertibility due to deliberate policy actions or institutional inadequacies. Transactions in the so-called minor or lesser-traded currencies are normally conducted in foreign exchange markets which lack the depth of primary currency markets since there are a limited number of participants, and relatively immature domestic financial markets prevail. Many of these secondary currency markets are located in less developed countries in which foreign exchange transactions are closely regulated and strictly administered by government officials. The central bank will often specify who is eligible to participate in the local markets, set trading rules for local banks, and designate specific transactions which can legally be executed.

Hyperinflation and balance-of-payments problems often force monetary authorities in developing nations to erect exchange controls in an effort to restrict arbitrage flows between domestic credit markets and international financial markets. Exchange-rate arrangements in developing countries may take various forms, but they normally exhibit certain common characteristics. Central banks normally set fixed buying and selling rates on a daily basis for the guidance of banks authorized to deal in foreign exchange. Local commercial banks typically conduct business at fixed margins around these official buy-and-sell rates. Monetary authorities often pursue a flexible exchange-rate policy involving periodic adjustments in the value of the exchange rate. Monetary officials may regulate financial flows of dividends and royalties, the repatriation of investment capital, and the repayment of foreign loans.

Exchange markets in developing countries are often characterized by embryonic or nonexistent forward markets due to constraints upon arbitrage flows between domestic and external financial markets. Central banks often restrict forward market access to corporate merchandise trade transactions and may require corporations to provide documentary evidence to support forward contracts. Some countries allow residents to conduct forward transactions but prohibit nonresidents from participating in the forward market. In such circumstances an offshore or parallel forward market often evolves in which foreign banks conduct limited trading operations in forward contracts.

EXCHANGE RATE ARRANGEMENTS AND POLICIES

The International Monetary Fund (IMF) is the global institution which is charged with responsibility for regulating the exchange-rate arrangements and policies of its member countries. Under Article IV of the IMF Articles of Agreement, fund officials are required to conduct surveillance procedures over exchange-rate systems to avoid excessive rate volatility or undue rate rigidity. The Articles grant member countries considerable freedom to select the format of their exchange-rate arrangements, but the IMF retains the authority to police exchange-rate regimes and ensure that they are consistent with IMF exchange-rate guidelines. Monetary authorities in developing countries are often unwilling to allow free market forces to dictate movements of their currencies and may attempt to minimize the impact of exchange-rate fluctuations upon the domestic economy by adopting multiple-currency practices. This all-encompassing term embraces a variety of exchange-rate systems which utilize different exchange rates to discriminate against certain types of transactions. Prior approval must be obtained from IMF officials before multiple-currency practices can be adopted. An IMF study of the 1970–80 period revealed that the yearly percentage of its members engaged in multiple-currency practices varied from 25 to 48 percent, although the fund detected a reduced reliance upon these practices by 1980.

Detailed descriptions of the exchange-rate practices of member nations are contained in the Annual Report on Exchange Arrangements and Exchange Restrictions issued each summer by the IMF. The major world currencies have been floating relatively freely since 1973, but the exchange market systems for secondary currencies are normally characterized by a significant degree of government intervention. This governmental regulation may take the form of a controlled central bank float; unofficial or official rate pegging; dual exchange-rate systems; or various adjustable peg systems involving disclosed or undisclosed adjustment formulas. Countries which utilize a dual exchange-rate system attempt to channel commercial and financial transactions into separate currency markets involving different exchange rates. A growing number of countries who wish to achieve a controlled depreciation of their currencies have adopted a crawling peg system involving small, frequent exchange-rate adjustments—perhaps weekly, biweekly, or monthly minidevaluations. Global exchange markets have been characterized by considerable exchange-rate volatility in recent years and many monetary authorities have attempted to stabilize the value of their currencies by linking them to a single key currency like the dollar, to the IMF special drawing right (SDR), or to a currency basket composed of the currencies of their major trade partners.

SPECIAL DRAWING RIGHT (SDR)

The special drawing right is an artificial reserve asset created by the IMF in 1970. The SDR serves as the unit of account for fund transactions, and a number of developing countries have chosen to fix the value of their currencies in terms of the SDR. The value of the SDR was originally set at parity with the dollar, but in 1974 it was redefined as equivalent to the daily weighted average of 16 major currencies. On January 1, 1981, IMF authorities decided to simplify the computation of the SDR by reducing the SDR currency basket to five currencies. The five currencies are the U.S. dollar, deutsche mark, French franc, Japanese yen, and the British pound sterling. The specific weightings of the five currencies are based upon the relative importance of these currencies in world export trade; dollar 42 percent, mark 19 percent, franc 13 percent, yen 13 percent, and sterling 13 percent.

The 1981 Report on Exchange Arrangements reported the increased tendency for member countries to substitute individual currency baskets of single-currency pegs in an effort to cope with increased exchange-rate flexibility. The 1981 report indicated that as of March 1981, 58 countries had chosen to peg their currencies to a single currency. Forty member currencies were pegged to the dollar, and 14 were pegged to the French franc. Fifteen currencies utilized an SDR peg for their currencies, while twenty-two countries linked their currencies to other currency composites. (See Table 1.)

EUROPEAN SECONDARY CURRENCIES

Virtually all of the Continental currencies are traded on a global basis with worldwide corporate interest fostered by extensive trade relationships among the European economies. Several of the minor or secondary European currencies are freely convertible, but generally they are traded in markets that lack the depth of the major currency markets since these secondary currencies play a more limited role in international trade and finance. The movements of these secondary European currencies are primarily dictated by the fluctuations of the European Monetary System (EMS) currencies. The second tier of European currencies includes the Spanish peseta, Greek drachma, Portuguese escudo, Austrian schilling, Irish pound, and the Scandinavian currencies.

Scandinavian Currencies

The Scandinavian currencies include the Swedish krona, Norwegian krone, Danish krone, and the Finnish markka. Trading in the markka

Table 1
Exchange Arrangements of Member Countries on March 31, 1981[1]

Currency Pegged to					Exchange Rate Adjusted According to a Set of Indicators	Cooperative Exchange Arrangements	Other Arrangements
U.S. Dollar	French Franc	Other Currency	SDR	Other Currency Composite			
Bahamas	Benin	Equatorial Guinea[2]	Burma	Algeria	Brazil	Belgium	Afghanistan
Barbados	Cameroon	The Gambia[4]	Guinea	Austria	Colombia	Denmark	Argentina[3]
Burundi	Central African Rep.	Lesotho[6]	Guinea-Bissau	Bangladesh[5]	Peru	France	Australia
Chile		Swaziland[6]	Iran	Botswana	Portugal	Germany, Fed. Rep. of	Bahrain[7]
Costa Rica				Cape Verde			Bolivia
Djibouti	Chad		Jordan	China, People's Rep. of		Ireland	Canada[8]
Dominica[9]	Comoros		Kenya	Cyprus		Italy[10]	Ghana[8]
Dominican Rep.	Congo		Malawi	Fiji		Luxembourg	Greece
Ecuador	Gabon		Mauritius	Finland[11]		Netherlands	Iceland
Egypt	Ivory Coast		São Tomé and Principe	Kuwait			India[12]
				Malaysia			
El Salvador	Madagascar		Seychelles	Malta			Indonesia
Ethiopia	Mali		Sierra Leone	Mauritania			Israel[8]
Grenada[9]	Niger		Uganda	Norway			Japan[8]
Guatemala	Senegal		Viet Nam	Papua New Guinea			Korea
Guyana	Togo		Zaïre				Lebanon[8]
Haiti	Upper Volta		Zambia[13]	Singapore			Maldives
Honduras				Solomon Islands			Mexico
Iraq				Sweden			Morocco
Jamaica				Tanzania			New Zealand
Lao People's Dem. Rep.				Thailand			Nigeria
Liberia				Tunisia			Philippines
Libyan Arab Jamahiriya				Zimbabwe			Qatar[7]
Nepal[14]							Saudi Arabia[7]
Nicaragua							South Africa[8]
							Spain

Oman	Sri Lanka
Pakistan	Turkey
Panama	United Arab
Paraguay	Emirates[7]
Romania	
	United Kingdom[8]
Rwanda	United States[8]
Somalia	Uruguay[3]
St. Lucia[9]	Western Samoa
St. Vincent and	Yugoslavia
the Grenadines[9]	
Sudan	
Suriname	
Syrian Arab Rep.	
Trinidad and	
Tobago	
Venezuela	
Yemen Arab Rep.	
Yemen, People's	
Dem. Rep. of	

[1] No current information is available on Democratic Kampuchea.

[2] Pegged to the Spanish peseta.

[3] Member maintains a system of advance announcement of exchange rates.

[4] Pegged to the pound sterling.

[5] Changes in the exchange rate generally occur when the effective exchange rate, as calculated on the basis of the weighted currency basket, deviates by more than plus or minus 1 percent from the pegged level.

[6] Pegged to the South African rand.

[7] Exchange rates are determined on the basis of a fixed relationship to the SDR, within margins of up to plus or minus 7.25 percent.

[8] Official exchange rates are not fixed or quoted.

[9] The currency is the East Caribbean dollar.

[10] Margins of plus or minus 6 percent are maintained with respect to the currencies of other countries participating in the exchange-rate mechanism of the European Monetary System.

[11] The fluctuation band of the Bank of Finland's currency index is currently about 6 percent (equivalent to margins of plus or minus 3 percent).

[12] The exchange rate is maintained within margins of 5 percent on either side of a weighted composite of the currencies of the main trading partners.

[13] The exchange rate is maintained within margins of plus or minus 2.5 percent in terms of the fixed relationship between the kwacha and the SDR.

[14] A fixed rate for the Nepalese rupee is also maintained vis-à-vis the Indian rupee.

Source: Annual Report on Exchange Arrangements and Exchange Restrictions, International Monetary Fund, 1981.

is quite limited, but the other Scandinavian currencies are the most widely traded of the European minor currencies. Relatively active spot trading prevails in the Scandinavian currencies during European trading hours, but the North American market for the Scandinavian currencies becomes extremely thin after Europe closes. Extensive trade relations link the Scandinavian economics to the major industrial nations of Europe, hence the Scandinavian currencies tend to fluctuate along with the EMS currencies against the U.S. dollar. Denmark is the only one of the Scandinavian currencies that remains within the EMS. Sweden left the EMS in August 1977, while Norway departed in December 1978.

Norwegian and Swedish authorities have chosen to peg their currencies to trade-weighted currency baskets in an effort to stabilize currency fluctuations. The Norwegian trade-weighted basket includes 12 currencies, of which the most important are the U.S. dollar, Swedish krona, deutsche mark, and British pound sterling. The U.S. dollar, British pound sterling, Norwegian krone, and Danish krone are the dominant currencies in Sweden's basket, which includes the currencies of 15 major trade partners. The Danish krone has participated in the EMS virtually since its inception in 1972. Danish authorities are thus obligated to intervene regularly to ensure that the krone spot rate remains within 2.25 percent margins around the EMS central rates, which are expressed in terms of the European currency unit (ECU).

Relatively liquid 1- to 12-month forward markets exist for the Norwegian krone and Swedish krona, but the forward market for Danish krone is tightly regulated by the Danish Central Bank. Forward Danish contracts with 1- to 12-month maturities are available for commercial trade transactions, although strict documentation is required by the Central Bank. Forward Danish contracts beyond one year are unavailable. Two-year forward contracts for the Norwegian krone and Swedish krona can be negotiated, although interest in these maturities is limited.

Spanish Peseta

Since 1974, the Spanish peseta has been allowed to float relatively freely in the foreign exchange markets, although Spanish authorities periodically intervene in the markets to ensure orderly trading conditions and to control peseta fluctuations. Prior to 1981, Spain operated a dual exchange-rate regime involving A and B pesetas—for resident and nonresident transactions—however early in 1981 these currencies were merged into a single currency. The Bank of Spain announces official buying and selling rates for the peseta against various currencies including the dollar, which is Spain's major intervention currency. A forward peseta market exists for commercial deals with maturities up to 360 days, although the market for 6- to 12-month maturities is quite thin.

Greek Drachma

Greece has traditionally maintained a restricted foreign exchange market, but late in 1980 monetary officials began to liberalize external financial transactions to coincide with Greece's entry into the European Economic Community (EEC) on January 1, 1981. Existing exchange-control measures will be phased out over several years, but in November 1980, Greek officials permitted an embryonic interbank foreign exchange market to commence in Athens. Commercial banks are free to quote spot exchange rates among themselves, although the Bank of Greece continues to provide guidance by quoting daily drachma rates. The bank is guided by a currency basket composed of the currencies of Greece's major trade partners—the deutsche mark, British pound sterling, U.S. dollar, French franc, Belgian franc, Japanese yen, and Saudi riyal.

Portuguese Escudo

Since 1978, Portuguese authorities have implemented small monthly downward adjustments in the value of the escudo. These monthly devaluations averaged 1.25 percent in 1978, but they were progressively reduced to .5 percent by December 1980. The escudo is informally linked to a trade-weighted currency basket which includes the British pound sterling, deutsche mark, Dutch guilder, and the French and Belgian francs.

Austrian Schilling

The Austrian schilling is a fully convertible currency. A well-developed spot and forward market exists, although the volume of trading in the schilling is relatively modest, especially after the European market closes. Movements of the Austrian schilling are largely dictated by deutsche mark fluctuations due to close trade and financial ties between Austria and Germany. Austrian authorities adhere to a so-called hard schilling policy, which involves maintaining a relatively fixed parity rate for the schilling against the deutsche mark.

Irish Pound

The 150-year old linkage of the Irish pound (punt) with the British pound was broken on March 31, 1979, when adherence to the 2.25

percent EMS trading bands forced Irish authorities to float the punt. Since 1979, the Irish pound has floated at a substantial discount—35 cent average 1980–81—against the pound sterling, reflecting oil-in-duced strength of sterling and fluctuations of the EMS currencies against the dollar. Irish authorities continue to exercise exchange con-trol over certain trade and financial transactions. The forward markets for Irish pounds are extremely thin since the Central Bank exercises tight control over forward transactions. Trading banks require full doc-umentation for merchandise trade transactions. Forward contracts for maturities up to 12 months can be negotiated, but contracts beyond 12 months are virtually impossible to obtain.

MIDEAST AND AFRICAN CURRENCIES

The Saudi Arabian riyal is the major currency in the Middle East, but considerable Mideast business is conducted in other currencies including the Kuwaiti and Jordanian dinars and the UAE dirham. Multi-national banks in the U.S. and London, as well as Zurich and Frankfurt, regularly transact business in the major Mideast currencies, although the largest volume of trading in these currencies is conducted in re-gional finance centers. The accumulation of massive OPEC oil revenues and extensive Mideast economic development programs have fostered the evolution and expansion of several money and foreign exchange centers in the Gulf region. Sophisticated financial institutions and active money market facilities have developed in Kuwait and Abu Dhabi, but a rapid influx of foreign banks into Bahrain has enabled it to become the largest financial center in the Middle East.

Bahrainian authorities legalized offshore banking units in 1975, and by 1981 more than 60 foreign banks had established offshore units to transact money market and foreign exchange business. These foreign offshore banking units are responsible for establishing relatively active forward markets for the major Mideast currencies. The establishment of these markets was facilitated by local regulations that require foreign contractors to receive payment in local currencies. Forward contracts for Saudi riyals can be negotiated for maturities up to five years, and 3-year forward Kuwaiti dinar contracts have been transacted. Twelve-month forward contracts are available for most of the other Gulf cur-rencies.

Saudi Arabian Riyal

Since 1975, the Saudi riyal has been linked to the SDR, although Saudi officials have allowed the currency to fluctuate within a 7.25 percent trading band around a central rate determined by the SDR basket. The riyal is carefully managed by SAMA, the Saudi Arabian

Monetary Agency, which conducts small periodic adjustments in the value of the riyal based on fluctuations in the value of the dollar. These small periodic adjustments typically average about .01 riyals per dollar. An active, unregulated spot and forward foreign exchange market exists in Jeddah, and spot and forward quotations are readily available in London, Zurich, and in the North American marketplace.

Kuwaiti Dinar

The Kuwaiti dinar is pegged to a currency basket containing the currencies of Kuwait's major trade partners, and the Central Bank quotes daily buy and sell rates for the dollar—which is the major intervention currency—based on the value of the basket. Foreign currencies may be freely bought and sold in Kuwait by residents and nonresidents.

South African Rand

The South African rand is widely traded in global markets reflecting foreign investor interest in gold stocks, as well as corporate plant and equipment investments. The fortunes of the rand are inextricably linked to the price of gold bullion and, to a lesser extent, capital flows associated with foreign investments and disinvestments. In January 1979, South African authorities introduced extensive monetary reforms which modified the existing dual exchange-rate system into a new two-tier rate system involving a managed commercial rate and a floating financial rate. South African officials intervene to support the commercial rand, while the financial rand has traded at a substantial discount relative to the commercial rand. The commercial rand is utilized for merchandise trade transactions, debt servicing, and dividend repatriation, while direct and portfolio investments by nonresidents are effected through the financial rand. South African officials strictly regulate resident operations in forward market transactions, but an external forward market in commercial rands has evolved which includes 1- to 12-month maturities.

ASIAN CURRENCIES

Corporate interest in the Asian currencies has escalated during the 1960s and 70s, reflecting the rapid growth of many economies in the Pacific region. Important Asian currencies include the Hong Kong, Singapore, Australian, and New Zealand dollars, as well as the Malaysian ringgit and the Indian rupee. Singapore and Hong Kong are the major international finance centers in Asia. Both of these centers are primarily renowned as the headquarters for the Asian dollar market, but foreign exchange trading facilities have grown rapidly in both centers. Hong Kong abolished all foreign exchange controls on January 1, 1973, while Singapore lifted exchange controls in June 1978.

Hong Kong Dollar

The external value of the Hong Kong dollar is basically determined by supply and demand forces, although Hong Kong monetary authorities occasionally intervene to ensure orderly market conditions. The Hong Kong dollar is significantly influenced by international arbitrage flows; with movements primarily dictated by fluctuations in U.S. short-term interest rates and Hong Kong money market rates. Forward exchange contracts with 1- to 6-month maturities are readily available, but the market for 6- to 12-month contracts is extremely thin.

Singapore Dollar

U.S. money market rate fluctuations are the dominant factor influencing movements of the Singapore dollar, which has been allowed to float relatively freely in the foreign exchange markets since 1973. Singapore officials are guided by a trade-weighted currency basket which includes the U.S. dollar, Japanese yen, Australian dollar, deutsche mark, and British pound sterling. Singapore authorities lifted all exchange control regulations in 1978 and created a free interbank exchange market in which banks are free to quote spot and forward exchange rates with maturities up to one year. A well-developed external forward market exists for 1- to 6-month maturities, but it is difficult to negotiate longer-term maturities.

Australian Dollar

The Australian dollar is one of the most widely traded of the Asian currencies, and global interest in the Australian dollar is likely to intensify in the 1980s due to an anticipated influx of foreign investment capital to develop Australia's mineral and energy resources. The Australian dollar is carefully managed by the Reserve Bank and is unofficially linked to a trade-weighted currency basket, which is dominated by movements in the Japanese yen, U.S. dollar, and British pound. Prevailing trade patterns indicate the yen and the U.S. dollar would each receive a 23 percent weighting in the basket compared to 8 percent for sterling. In actual practice, the dollar is undoubtedly given a larger weight since the majority of Australia's foreign trade transactions are invoiced in dollars. A well-developed external forward market exists for maturities up to six months, but the market becomes extremely illiquid in the 6- to 12-month maturities. Forward contracts with maturities beyond one year can be negotiated with major trading banks, and there is strong corporate interest in these far-date forwards.

New Zealand Dollar

New Zealand monetary authorities utilize a trade-weighted currency basket to establish a daily exchange rate for the New Zealand dollar against the U.S. dollar, which is the intervention currency. The most important currencies in the basket include the Australian dollar, British pound sterling, U.S. dollar, and the Japanese yen. Since 1978, New Zealand authorities have employed a mini-crawling peg system involving small, monthly devaluations. These monthly devaluations initially totalled about 1.25 percent in 1978, but by mid-1981 they had shrunk to .5 percent. The forward market for the New Zealand dollar is relatively liquid up to six months, but it becomes quite thin in the 6- to 12-month period. Longer-term forward contracts can be negotiated only with great difficulty.

Malaysian Ringgit

The Malaysian dollar severed its historic parity with the Singapore dollar in 1973 and was allowed to participate in a managed float until 1975. In 1975, Malaysian authorities officially changed the name of the Malaysian dollar to the ringgit and pegged it to a trade-weighted currency basket. The currencies in the basket have not been disclosed, but recent trade relationships indicate it would include the Australian dollar, Singapore dollar, U.S. dollar, and the Dutch guilder. In practice, the U.S. dollar probably plays a proportionately larger role than its percentage weighting since a significant portion of Malaysia's foreign trade is invoiced in U.S. dollars. Prior to 1981, Malaysian ringgit movements tended to parallel Singapore dollar trends, but this year the ringgit has slumped sharply against the Singapore dollar. A limited forward market exists for 1- to 6-month maturities.

Indian Rupee

India maintains the value of the rupee within 5 percent of the midpoint of a weighted basket of currencies of its major trading partners—the United States, Japan, Germany, United Kingdom, and France. Indian officials frequently change the exchange rate of the rupee against its intervention currency, the pound sterling. Spot rupee quotations are readily available from major trading banks, but an active external forward market for rupees does not exist.

LATIN AMERICAN CURRENCIES

The major Latin American currencies include the Mexican peso, Brazilian cruzeiro, Argentine peso, and the Venezuelan bolivar. The Mexican peso and Venezuelan bolivar are freely traded in the North

American market, but most of the other Latin American currencies are closely regulated by monetary authorities and usually are only traded in local markets. Since the Latin American economies are typically characterized by chronic inflation and balance-of-payments problems, most Latin American governments are forced to regularly depreciate their currencies to offset the eroding influence of inflation upon the external values of their currencies. Historically, many of the South American currencies have experienced large, one-shot devaluations which have adversely affected foreign investor confidence. In recent years, many Latin American governments have implemented crawling-peg exchange-rate systems to foster more predictable, less disruptive adjustments in the external values of their currencies.

Mexican Peso

For nearly a quarter of a century, Mexico maintained a fixed parity of 12.5 pesos per dollar, but mounting inflationary pressures forced Mexican authorities to adopt a more flexible exchange rate policy in 1976. In August 1976, the Echeverria administration devalued the peso by 43 percent to 8 pesos per dollar prior to the inauguration of the new Lopez Portillo administration. Mexican officials held the peso steady near 23 pesos per dollar from 1977 until mid-1980 when they allowed the peso to depreciate about 1.6 percent against the dollar as inflation reached 30 percent. In 1981, Mexican authorities enacted a "mini" crawling peg exchange rate regime which yielded an 11.6% depreciation of the peso to 26.24. Prior to 1982, an active, well-developed forward exchange market existed within North America including a bank market with 1–12 month maturities and a currency futures market in the Chicago Mercantile Exchange. North American peso trading slackened dramatically in 1982 as Mexico's debt servicing problems fostered modified financial regulations, payment delays and the imposition of exchange controls. On December 20, 1982, a new two-tier exchange rate system was implemented which included a sliding preferential rate of 96 pesos per dollar and a free market rate which closed the year at 155 pesos per dollar—a yearly depreciation of 83%.

Brazilian Cruzeiro

Sizable U.S. direct investments in Brazil have fostered rising corporate interest in the Brazilian cruzeiro, although cruzeiro transactions continue to be closely regulated by Brazilian officials. Spot foreign exchange transactions can only be conducted with the government or with authorized banks and exchange houses. Official buying and selling rates are quoted by Brazilian monetary authorities. There is no local or external forward exchange market for the cruzeiro.

Since 1968, the Brazilian Central Bank has pursued a flexible exchange-rate policy involving small, periodic reductions in the value of the cruzeiro relative to the U.S. dollar. Until recently, this crawling-peg, exchange-rate system normally involved a yearly series of minicruzeiro depreciations based upon a preannounced devaluation schedule. In 1979, surging inflation forced Brazilian officials to announce a late-year, one-shot 30 percent maxidevaluation. Minidevaluations continued in 1980, and in 1981 Brazilian officials altered the devaluation mechanism slightly by stating that the cruzeiro depreciation would be an unspecified magnitude based upon the differential between Brazilian and global inflation. Brazilian inflation averaged 100% during 1981–82 and consequently the pace of minidevaluations accelerated and the size of devaluations increased.

Argentine Peso

High inflation has traditionally eroded the external value of the Argentine peso and forced officials to periodically implement large peso devaluations to maintain the competitive posture of Argentine exports. During 1980, the pace of depreciation lagged far behind the yearly inflation rate—28 percent compared to 100 percent—which heightened market concern about the overvalued condition of the peso. Yearly peso devaluations averaged 80% during 1981–82 and the Viola Government was forced to implement a two-tier exchange rate system to stem speculative capital outflows. The dual-rate system involves a managed commercial rate and a floating financial rate. An external forward market for pesos does not exist. Forward contracts with one-year maturities can be negotiated in an extremely thin local market, but this market is not extensively utilized by resident companies.

Venezuela Bolivar

During the past decade, the Venezuelan bolivar has been one of the most stable of the Latin American currencies due to the supportive influence of oil revenues. The bolivar has remained steady near 4.2925 per dollar since 1976 although devaluation rumors intensified in 1982 as slackening oil revenues fostered debt servicing problems. Venezuelan authorities impose no foreign exchange controls, although the Central Bank does set official buying and selling rates for the dollar and other major currencies. Spot and forward quotations up to 12 months are available in the North American market, although the depth of the market is limited.

23
Foreign Exchange and International Money Broking

DAVID H. RILEY
Joint Managing Director
Tullett and Riley International Limited

What is a money broker? What does he do? Who needs him and why?

A broker is an intermediary between two principals, for example, two banks, a business house and a bank, or even two business houses. He brings the parties together and takes a commission in payment for his intermediary services in putting counterparties together in deposits and foreign exchange transactions in the main trading currencies of the world. In the international foreign exchange and currency markets the broker does not take a position as a principal at any time. His role is strictly that of an "in-between party." His task is to present to his customers the information, facts, opinions, rumors, and sometimes he proffers his advice. But it must be remembered that, in the final analysis, it is the principal and not the broker who has to take full responsibility for dealing decisions.

A BACKWARD GLANCE

In order to understand the broker's role, it is necessary to review briefly the history of broking. Before World War II, there were some 36 brokerage companies in London—mostly partnerships—operating with a small staff and usually specializing in one or two specific areas. For obvious reasons the market closed down for the duration of the War to reopen in 1952 with some nine broking firms. Since then the numbers have increased, and currently there are 13 members of the Foreign Exchange and Currency Deposit Brokers Association in London. Some overseas broking companies also intermediate on behalf of London banks and do a substantial amount of business. Over the last 20 years the Eurocurrency deposit and foreign exchange markets have grown dramatically. This growth was stimulated by the volatile, gyrating exchange and interest rates which encouraged many banks, large and small, attracted by the profit opportunities, to join the fray. The explosion in volume and personnel in the banks, new and old, had to be matched by an expansion in the activity of brokers to provide effective services. In the mid-1960s an average-sized London foreign exchange and money brokerage house would have employed about 8 to 10 people. Today that figure can run to several hundreds. If you include the domestic markets and the overseas offices, the figure can be more than doubled. The small broking houses of the past have developed into large-sized international companies.

HOW DO BROKERS OPERATE IN THE FOREIGN EXCHANGE AND INTERNATIONAL CURRENCY DEPOSIT MARKETS?

By far the largest part of a broker's business is done bank to bank; this is the main area which this chapter will examine.

There is, of course, a considerable amount of direct dealing between banks, located in different countries, and sometimes between banks in their home market. The two systems—that is, through brokers and direct bank to bank—complement each other and business done directly is frequently covered in the market through the broking system.

A banker may deal direct because he feels he is able to transact a larger amount in one deal without disclosing his interest to the market as a whole. Or the bank may have long-established contacts with other banks that it wishes to maintain and protect. However, the banker will use the broking system because it is physically impossible for any bank to call the large number of dealing banks in his own and the other major financial centers of the world.

The broking network provides broad cover so that the dealer has instant access to hundreds of banks in many centers simply by calling his broker. Further, the bank will use the broker because it may wish to be anonymous until a firm interest has been identified by the broker. In the foreign exchange market anonymity is preserved, for a bank's name is identified only when a deal is about to be closed with a counterparty. In the deposit market the bank's name is withheld when the bank is a lender. When the bank is a borrower, the name is passed to a potential lender only when the price and the amount have been agreed.

There are limits which banks impose upon themselves on the amount of foreign exchange or deposit trading they are prepared to do with other banks. It is quite a normal occurrence for a borrower to have its name checked and turned down by lenders in the market because they have used the limits for the borrower. A lender has the privilege of checking a borrower's name, having disclosed its interest as a lender at a specific price which the borrower has agreed to pay. The bank can be secure in the knowledge that its name will not be passed to any of the borrowers that it has turned down unless it gives prior permission. The bank can, therefore, operate in the market in a major way, and the only people who will know that it is active are its broker and the banks with whom it has concluded deals.

The volume of money traded during the dealing day by a major international broker can run to several billion dollars. These vast sums of money are traded at a very brisk pace and, to the casual observer, perhaps in a rather haphazard manner. The system places an enormous responsibility on the broker. The market is a word of mouth market since the majority of deals are transacted over the telephone. The transactions are subsequently comfirmed in writing, within the square mile of the city of London, or by telex. Written confirmations are dispatched by messenger to insure that details can be checked for accuracy as soon as possible. Although much care is taken, mistakes can and do occur, and these can be very costly, particularly if funds are not applied by having been routed into the wrong clearing bank. Because of the large sums involved, the lost interest income can amount to many thousands of dollars even on one-day money.

The broker, therefore, must not only be quick thinking in order to take advantage of the rapidly moving markets but, at the same time, has to be thorough in the execution of orders received for the mutual protection of the customer and his own company. The inefficient broker will soon find business dropping away, because it is essential that the banker has absolute confidence in the broker's ability and integrity. A brilliant individual broker who does not pay sufficient attention to detail after the deal has been concluded can lose money as well as the confidence of his customer.

Major international broking companies today, have offices or associates in all the major financial centers of the world. They are linked with direct telex and telephone lines so that they have instant communication round the world. The broker obtains quotations by a combination of his own interpretation of the facts and figures that are available to him and by discussion with responsible and knowledgeable dealers. In the morning when he opens for business, he will normally talk with his principal banks to discuss the closing rates, let us say in New York, and the impact of any regulatory changes, perhaps from the Federal Reserve, the money supply figures, trade figures, or any other relevant financial or political data. Prior to talking with New York, he will already have spoken with his Far Eastern and Middle Eastern offices. These markets, which are much smaller than the European market, nonetheless, will have a real effect on the early morning rates.

HOW DOES THE BANK DEALER OPERATE?

The dealer in a London bank collates the outside information, adds this to his own sources of information from his network of branches and correspondents, discusses the market conditions with his colleagues and management, and evaluates the bank's dealing posture for the day.

Many senior dealers in the banks are in constant touch with their overseas offices even during the hours when their local market is closed. The dealer often receives telephone calls at home from New York, Toronto, San Francisco, and so on, and he is usually well primed before he leaves his home in the morning. It is only if something dramatic occurs very late that he is likely to be caught in a bad market position. In normal times, subject to checking overnight cables from the bank's American offices when he reaches the office, he already knows the fundamental position from which he must deal during the day. As soon as the banker-dealer compares the brokers' early morning rates with rates received direct from other banks, and with his own ideas, he will start dealing.

DEALER-BROKER INTERACTION

The broker will quote his rates to the bank dealer; for instance the one-month dollar deposit 10 to 10⅛ percent. These are indication rates not firm dealing prices, because, as already mentioned, the broker is not a principal. He can only suggest what the rate should be and then try to obtain firm orders from the bank dealers which will enable him to firm his prices. If he quotes 10 to 10⅛, the banker may agree with the price structure and, should he be a lender, may tell the broker that he wishes to lend at 10⅛ the top of the market, a specific amount of, say, $10 or $20 million. The broker has then established one side, that is, 10⅛, and hopefully will find at least one borrower to come into the market. The early borrowers will probably place themselves into the market at 10 percent, thereby substantiating the prices at 10 to 10⅛. These are then firm, and the broker can quote them as such. If the market moves, or the original lender takes the view that the market is going to move downward fairly soon, he will come back to the broker and ask him what his price is now. The broker will again quote 10 to 10⅛. The conversation would probably go: Question: "Is that a firm price?" Answer: "Yes sir, it is." Question: "How much for?" Answer: "say $20 million." The banker dealer may then ask the name of the borrower. If it is acceptable, he may give the borrower whatever amount his limit allows up to the specified borrowing amount.

If the lender satisfies all the borrowers in the market at, say, 10 percent, and still has funds to place, obviously he has initiated a major move in the market. If he continues to lend, the market is now offered at 10 percent, and the broker has to scour the world rapidly to find borrowers to take his lender's funds. In all probability, the broker will be countered with bids at $9\frac{7}{8}$ or $9^{15}\!/_{16}$. The market will then become quoted at 10 to $9\frac{7}{8}$, possibly 10 to $9^{15}\!/_{16}$. The dealer will expect the broker to keep him updated so that he knows that the order that he has placed with the broker is being looked after and that the broker is working for him. The fact that the bank puts "something into the market" by placing a firm order with the broker encourages the broker to repay this trust by increasing the frequency of the information service, giving all the changes in the market, and keeping the dealer informed of the strength of the bids and the way he feels about possible movements or the weight of other lenders coming in. This information will enable the banker to assess whether he should continue lending, if necessary at a lower price, or whether he should hold off and perhaps move his price back up to $10\!/_{16}$ to encourage the borrowers that have reduced their prices to $9\frac{7}{8}$ or $9^{15}\!/_{16}$ to increase bids to 10 percent.

The element of co-operation between the banker and a good broker is very strong. For the broker this is essential. Without the co-operation of, and firm orders from, the banker, the broker will not be able to quote prices. Being able to quote prices is essential in order to maintain a strong presence in the market. For the banker, by putting something into the market with a trusted broker, he is insuring that the bank's interests are being looked after by someone other than his own staff. Effectively, the banker-dealer is using his broker as an extension of his dealing staff.

By using broking services a bank can maintain lower staff levels in its dealing rooms than would be required if it concentrated on direct bank-to-bank dealing. For instance, if a bank employs five or six dealers who use the broking services extensively, to change to direct dealing exclusively, in all probability, would necessitate a personnel increase to 20 or 30 people without a commensurate wider-market coverage. Bank management has to decide on the basis of economics whether it prefers to have a large, highly paid staff, with pension and other fringe benefits, plus the extra space that is required to house the extra staff, plus extra communication equipment (telephone lines, telexes), back-up staff, and so forth. This has to be balanced against the brokerage bills which are incurred by utilizing that service. In practice, banks tend to take a middle-of-the-road route, doing some direct dealing as well as utilizing the broking service, depending upon which is more appropriate at the time.

SETTLEMENT PROCEDURES FOR ERRORS

Because of the speed with which markets move and the complexities of operating a worldwide system, it is obvious that mistakes may occur.

A dealer may "give" a London broker on his price at the very moment when the borrower, who may be located in Singapore, removes his bid with the Singapore intermediary. By the time the message at each end is relayed, the broker, that is, the middle man, is literally stuck in the middle. He has been given by the London bank, and now he has no where to place the funds, and he feels obliged to justify his price. Because the relationships between the individual broker and dealer are carefully built up over a period of time, a bond of understanding is reached and a set of informal rules established on ethics, terminology, and so on.

At moments such as we have described, where a problem arises, the informal system is put to the test. The broker would immediately go to his bank, tell the dealer exactly what has happened, and ask him if he, the banker, is committed to a customer. If he is so committed, the broker will unquestionably stand by the deal. If the banker is committed, the broker will ask him to forget that particular name that was quoted and allow him to try and find a replacement. Sometimes the broker is unable to find another name acceptable to the bank at the price quoted. He will then tell his banker that he is only able to find a suitable name at a lower price and offer to make good the difference between the original price quoted and the one at which they will be forced to deal. It is the banker's decision whether or not he claims the difference from the broker. Frequently the banker, in understanding the problem, will refuse if he is not committed, but there are also occasions when the individual banker is committed and has to substantiate the price to his customer.

Different money centers have varying procedures for settling differences. On occasions like these, the London procedure is as follows: Since London brokers are members of the Foreign Exchange and Currency Deposit Brokers Association, the member firms put all difference payments due to their customers through the association. In effect, the association acts as a clearing house. The broker will notify the association of the problem, how it occurred, and how it is being remedied. The bank will write to the brokerage house claiming the net difference and set out the reasons why. The broker will send a check for the amount of the difference to the Broker's Association, and the association will send its check directly to the bank.

This rather complicated procedure insures that a high standard of professionalism is maintained. No broker or dealer likes to go through these formalities! The fact that all member firms of the association are entitled to see what went wrong and how the problem arose acts as a real incentive towards greater professionalism in the market. It is a broker's pride that he stands by his prices, although there are occasions when it is extremely difficult to do this. No major firm of brokers can allow comment to circulate within the market that it does not substantiate quotations. Accordingly, brokers are very quick to offer differences, as appropriate, to their banks through the established machinery.

CONTROL AND SUPERVISION IN LONDON

Control and supervision in the London market are maintained through four groups. These are the Brokers Association, the Central Bank, the Banker's Association, and the Joint Standing Committee.

The Brokers Association (FECDBA) exerts its own control over member firms and can exact severe penalties for major breaches of its rules.

The Bank of England, the licensing authority, prefers not to play too direct a disciplinary role, opting instead for the less direct, but equally effective, influence it exerts through the Joint Standing Committee (JSC) of which it holds the chair.

The JSC is made up of representatives of the members of FECDBA and the Bankers' Committee. It is concerned with running an orderly professional market through joint consultation between banks and brokers. Standards, ethics, market practice, terminology, brokerage scales, and so on, are covered and any other area which would be of benefit to the market in particular and the city of London in general.

THE BROKER AS AN INDIVIDUAL

Generally speaking, high academic qualifications of an aspirant broker (and many bank dealers) have been regarded as less important than the capability to think and act quickly and responsibly. A sense of humor and an appreciation of the need for discretion are essential. Hectic, volatile markets can be very trying on the nerves. Confidentiality is one of the corner stones of the market. Hence a pleasant personality and the capacity for sustained hard work are essential.

With the continuing growth of the market, there is a corresponding need for greater management skills. In time, this will necessitate additional specialized academic qualifications. Most broking houses run in-house training courses, but in the foreseeable future these will have to be supplemented by industrywide courses resulting in professional examinations on the lines of the Institute of Bankers or the Stock Exchange Examinations.

COMPOSITION OF A BROKER'S OFFICE

London

Because of the wide range of services offered, staffing has become highly specialized and sectionalized. The typical London brokerage house employs several hundred people, some engaged in functions which are "loss leaders." These unremunerative activities are necessary to supply a comprehensive range of services to the banks, as banks often have to deal in these areas on behalf of customers. A bank that provides a retail service hopes to obtain more remunerative business from his customer because of the retail service. The broker, in turn, expects to earn a profit from the banks in other more profitable areas. It is an unspoken, but mutually understood business, of "swings and roundabouts."

The early initiative of the London brokers resulted in their offices in London becoming the main clearing station for European and overseas brokers. This is still the case, but there has been rapid and increasing growth in centers such as New York. If we look at the London broker's office rather like the head and body of an octopus with many tentacles leading to overseas brokers and banks, we can see how the orders are drawn from those services and passed out again to each and every one.

Overseas

There are indigenous brokers operating in local markets in areas such as the Far East, Middle East, and so forth, but they have tended to remain domestically orientated. Several years ago the London broking firms began cautiously opening offices in places like Hong Kong, Singapore, Kuala Lumpur, and other developing financial centers. This meant bringing the European and North American practices to these developing areas. There has been a steady expansion both as branches of the U.K. Company and as joint ventures with local brokers in the Far East, Middle East, and in South America.

Continental Brokers

In general, the continental broking house will offer a narrower range of services and tends to specialize in one or two specific areas, frequently attaining a high level of proficiency in these markets and, consequently, contributing a valuable service to the international market. Specialization enables them to maintain smaller staffs, and, because the banks have become accustomed to this system over the years, these brokers may generate higher profits. Suprisingly, few continental brokers have used their greater profitability to expand into other countries. They have generally been content to leave this to the British firms.

In helping to introduce world markets to the emerging and developing financial centers, and vice-versa, the international broker must work in close cooperation with the financial authorities (central banks or monetary authorities of the nations involved), as well as with local

and international banks. The broker will help to acquaint local banks
and the central bank with international market practices, customs,
ethics, terminology, procedures, credit and exposure risks, and profit
potentials. He may also assist by discreetly locating senior staff for
the local institutions, instigating training schemes for inexperienced
local staff, and offering technical advice and guidance.

INTRODUCING NEW BANKS TO THE INTERNATIONAL MARKET

Experienced international banks entering new markets usually have
their own senior staff already, but a broker may help these banks in
finding accommodation, arranging introductions to organizations able
to assist the newcomer with professional advice (e.g., lawyers, accountants, telecommunication companies), staff, and property arrangements.

Local banks, joint local/international banking ventures and sometimes even full branches of established international banks may benefit
from being introduced to the market. Circulating information such
as balance sheets, profit and loss accounts, parentage, management,
and so on, to the market at large can rapidly improve the acceptance
of the banks and speed up the establishment of trading limits with
the international banking community. This helps the bank to trade
and, hopefully, to make profits. The broker benefits from the goodwill
generated and brokerage subsequently earned.

We have, so far, only mentioned foreign exchange and international
currency deposits as the main areas in which the brokerage houses
are involved. While these form the mainstay of the industry, there is
strong growth in both traditional instruments and the newer forms
of negotiable securities.

The certificate of deposit is just one of the instruments in which
an emerging bank, and, for that matter, any bank with a small capital
base, can find particularly useful to help develop a trading book. The
reason for this is that a small bank may have great difficulty in trading
off its low capital base, but in the CD market the bank dealer would,
in effect, be trading off the limit and the name of the major bank
that issued the paper. The smaller bank must, however, be careful
only to trade in first class name paper which is readily acceptable in
the secondary market, thereby insuring that the position can be liquidated when desired.

LONG-TERM PROSPECTS FOR BROKERS

Assuming continued, steady growth in the world markets and a
keen awareness by the management of broker firms in developing

new products and trading areas, the future looks bright. In the United States, because of the structure of the banking system, there is enormous opportunity for change. Branch banking across the United States and the merging of banking with investment and insurance interests will create stronger groupings and the need for increasingly diversified brokerage services.

The Middle East is gaining in market professionalism and, like the Far East, has enormous potential.

Central and South America are virtually virgin ground and Africa is still undeveloped. Let us stop here. The long term holds great promise and the future poses an exciting challenge to the banking and brokerage industries. The future should see more brokerage houses in different countries merging and forming a few large worldwide groupings.

The range of services are, and will be, extended by forging links with companies in allied fields (stockbroking, commodities, financial futures, etc.). With consolidation in these and other ways, further confidence will be built into the brokerage system, and employees will have greater career opportunities with increased security.

To sum up, the brokerage industry has grown rapidly and substantially over the last few years. Naturally, there have been and still are growing pains. With the opportunities for expanding overseas lending in a real and meaningful way, despite the present problems with LDCs, the professional international brokerage companies can view the future with confidence.

MARKET CUSTOM, PRACTICE, AND ETHICS

Everyone in the international money markets—bankers and brokers, management, and dealers—should be constantly aware of the need for constant vigilance. No one wishes to have repressive rigid and hyperrestrictive dealing constraints imposed. All of us have a vested interest to insure that the market which provides our livelihood is run in accordance with sound dealing practices, sensibly controlled by alert management, and in strict accordance with prudent banking principles and ethics.

POSSIBILITIES FOR THE FUTURE

In conclusion, let us consider the alternatives to the broking system and as prospects for the future.

Direct Dealing

We have already mentioned dealing done directly from bank to bank. Direct dealing either in large amounts or small amounts, or in exotic currencies, in a way assists brokers to be more effective in the wholesale volume markets. Thus, direct dealing itself does not present a danger for the brokers; in fact it strengthens the overall market.

Central Clearing Houses

The Canadian Bankers' Association has a central clearing house that handles the banks' foreign exchange business. The staff are employed collectively by the banks and conduct the business in a central pool. While some of the banks have reservations and only put modest business through the system, it appears to work reasonably well. It should be clearly understood, however, that this is purely an internal system and handles only Canada to Canada business. There are real doubts about the effectiveness of this system when applied in an international context.

Another experiment along the same lines was organized during the 1960s by the London Foreign Exchange Brokers Association. They joined forces to set up a company called FEBA London Limited. This company was discontinued when competitive forces and the necessity for greater freedom and flexibility brought it to an early end.

Reuters Proposed System

This is a proposed extension of the 'monitor' visual-display information service to banks. Again the idea is a good one, but many banks doubt that it will meet all their requirements and do more than supplement the international broking service. Although automated systems will be installed, and will, undoubtedly, be very useful, it is difficult to see this system being more than an additional, and welcome, tool for the money dealer, taking its place alongside traditional direct dealing on telephone and telex and the international money brokerage houses.

24
Managing the Exchange Risk

DONALD R. MANDICH
Chairman
COMERICA, Incorporated

The trading of foreign exchange is invariably performed by banks as principal dealing with principal, whether it is bank to bank or a bank dealing with a nonbanking entity. There is no automatic or customary commission for traders in foreign exchange;[1] currencies are bought and sold at market prices, and, what with fast-moving markets, there can be sizable losses. Losses are a part of the business and must be taken in stride and evaluated within the context of the overall trading results during a period of weeks or months. However, losses beyond the expectations of management or losses due to inadequate controls are most unwelcome and can be avoided or minimized with the proper techniques. Such techniques are not meant to restrain traders in any way but rather should provide an environment in which they can concentrate entirely on the marketplace and not be concerned with recurring loose ends or errors.

POLICIES

Due to the significant financial risks that can be present in any trading operation, the cornerstone of any operation should be the development of clearly written policies that are approved by senior management (preferably chairman and/or president); it is highly desirable for the mutual protection of the foreign exchange trading operation and the earnings of the entire bank that top management understand the risks involved and the significance of each part of the trading policy.

---

[1] Note that in some markets (e.g., the United States and England) brokers do act as intermediaries between banks to facilitate trades. However, they do *not* act as principals, and they *do* exact a nominal commission for their services.

Financial risks divide into two categories: the risk of fluctuation in the value of a currency bought, held, or sold for one's own account and the credit risk of dealing with a party that may not be able to settle his side of a transaction; this in turn may create a risk of currency fluctuation.

The greatest financial risk in trading is the size of the positions taken. Any fluctuation in market prices for individual currencies could create profits or losses. In approving policy limits for such exposures, managements should understand the possible magnitude of rate fluctuations under varying conditions and the financial implications. Ordinarily, within the tastes of a given institution, the policy for the limits of any open positions would be determined by the maximum loss the institution is willing to tolerate, particularly vis-á-vis the normal size of that bank's profits.

The exercise of calculating maximum possible losses obviously involves estimates and assumptions of possible events. A matrix might be developed for each currency showing the possible losses per $1 million for each type of position under various scenarios. In a calm trading day, a currency might fluctuate a few points which might gain or lose a few hundred dollars per million U.S. dollars—certainly an amount that could be tolerated by virtually any trading bank. However, on June 3, 1980, British sterling opened at 2.3450 and dropped within a few hours to 2.2900 due to a dramatic statement on the outlook for interest rates by the prime minister. If a U.S. bank owned spot sterling outright during those hours, it would have lost $55,000 for each million pounds! Forward rates can also shift dramatically. If a dealer purchased 10 million deutsche marks in June 1980 for delivery in six months, the rate would have been approximately 1.7500 ($5,714,285.71 equivalent). Subsequently, the dollar strengthened measurably, and if the dealer had chosen to carry the open position to maturity expecting the mark to return to its former levels, he would have received marks worth about 1.9600 ($5,102,040.82 equivalent) in December of 1980, causing a loss of over $600,000 on the position.

Bank policy should consider approval of limits for:

A. Overnight net open positions for each currency.
B. Overnight net open positions for all currencies.
C. Overnight spot positions for each currency.
D. Overnight net forward positions for each currency. Note that limits might be given for both short or long forward positions for specific periods and they may not necessarily be for the same amounts.
E. Total overnight net forward positions for all currencies.
F. Time gaps in forward positions, i.e., a long forward position being covered by a short position of a significantly different date.
G. Total time gaps for all forward positions.

H.   Intraday trading positions which might be significantly larger than overnight positions.

A well-written trading policy should provide limits on the amount of uncleared spot or forward transactions that the bank will have with each counterparty, whether it be a bank or nonbank entity. Obviously, there are credit risks in dealing with anyone, and the size of risk taken should depend upon a credit appraisal of the trading partner. The amount of risk would be the loss taken from a fluctuation in currency rates if the trading partner should become bankrupt and never settle the contract.

The entire question of the status of claims against a bankrupt for unsettled foreign exchange contracts has never been very clear. Despite the efforts of the writer and several others to include rules regarding claims for foreign exchange transactions in the recent major revision of the U.S. federal bankruptcy law, such rules were omitted due to the apparent complexities of the issues. Precisely, the position of a trading partner with a subsequent bankrupt counterparty is uncertain for the following reasons:

A.   The amount of the claim is uncertain. It cannot be anticipated whether the court will decide whether the claimant should have covered his position as soon as the bankrupt status was known or whether he should cover on the maturity date of the contract. Hindsight might be used to the detriment of the claimant.

B.   The question of the right of offset is uncertain where a bank has numerous contracts, buy and sell and spot and forward, with the bankrupt. Can all exposures be covered and the entire net loss (if there is one) be a single claim; can similar currencies only or similar dates only be netted; can the trustee in bankruptcy choose as time passes to settle only those contracts where the bankrupt has a profit and ignore those that have losses?

Since no answers exist to the above questions, every trading institution should review the creditworthiness of all trading partners and recognize the risks of large involvements with trading partners with marginal credit standing.

Finally, the written trading policy should require a separate procedures and controls manual which is prepared to the satisfaction of all parties concerned: the foreign exchange trading department, the officer to whom the chief foreign exchange trader reports, the bank comptroller, the bank auditor, and outside auditors.

PROCEDURES AND CONTROLS

Discipline and thoroughness in all trading procedures and controls provide a sound backdrop for a business that at times can be erratic, widely fluctuating, and hectic. Beginning with the decision-making process, there should be a regular routine to review and revise all currency trading limits periodically within the prescribed written policies. There should be regular reporting of all trading positions to appropriate levels of management on at least a weekly basis if the bank is more than a very minor and occasional trader. The aggregate gains or losses should be measured (i.e., the trading book should be revalued) no less than twice monthly and in very active operations the management may prefer to do it weekly or even daily. Such gains or losses should be entered into the general accounts of the bank at least monthly.

Aside from the very general measurements and reports described above, an excellent control is the preparation of a daily trading summary which lists each trade by name, amount, currency, price, and settlement date. (Most active trading operations are computerized and such a daily summary should not be burdensome.) The daily report should be scanned by the chief trader and one other senior person, perhaps the chief trader's immediate superior, to see that prices seem reasonable and with whom trades were made: Are there any surprises? Is there any sudden flurry of activity with a marginal counterparty? Are there any apparently large amounts for a given name suggesting that they're overtrading? Is there any undesirable flurry of trading in a weakening currency suggesting caution? Are the prices within the day's market?

Exceptions to written limits may be required from time to time to accommodate good customers or to avoid unnecessary expense in a difficult market. In such cases, a mechanism should exist where the traders can obtain approval promptly.

Routine operational procedures and controls should follow the usual principles of good internal control,[2] but recognition should be given to the fact that traders might at times be under more than a little pressure, both due to abrupt and wide market swings and the need to produce earnings. In recognition of the potential pressures, it is suggested that any approach to managing the operations be one of tighter routines and controls rather than the opposite. Such requirements as prenumbered trade tickets and other forms and prompt recording of transactions will help to avoid loss of control of positions as well as failures to settle contracts due to errors. Daily reconcilement of all positions would seem mandatory, and special recordings should be made of all trades after hours, after a cutoff time, or from places outside the bank, such as at home. Some banks have the servicing

---

[2] *The Comptroller's Handbook for National Bank Examiners—Commercial International* (Englewood Cliffs, N.J.: Prentice-Hall, 1981) is an excellent reference for elements of sound control of a trading operation as well as the examination of it.

section (back office) report directly to the chief trader. It is the writer's preference that the traders be relieved of such administrative burdens and concentrate on the marketplace; separation also provides better internal control.

It is recommended that every bank making loans in a currency not funded by the same currency adopt a policy of requiring that the currency exposure be hedged by executing an "internal contract" at arms-length rates between the bank loan department and the exchange trading department. The trading department can assume such exposures within its authorized limits or cover on the outside. However, this practice places the exposures on the records of the traders who can follow them closely and take action if necessary. It also sorts out the profit on the lending part of the transaction from the premium or discount for the difference in currencies.

SPECIAL PROBLEMS

Special problems can arise due to errors, and invariably they will be costly. Internal errors in processing can be minimized if confirmations are promptly sent and incoming confirmations are checked immediately. Similarly, "due-from" bank accounts should be reconciled promptly to detect possible errors.

External errors, such as misunderstandings with counterparties on verbal aggreements, can not only be costly, but can create bad feelings and loss of future business. The number of such misunderstandings has surged in recent years and is attributed to the increased number of less experienced traders who allegedly feel pressures to create earnings. This trend is unfortunate as it is contrary to all banking traditions, and such traders usually do not survive in the relatively close fraternity of traders. More and more dealing rooms are electronically recording their activities to provide documentation in case of disputes. Experienced traders will settle the occasional misunderstanding by splitting any cost. Experienced traders will also point out any market quotation that is obviously an error even if it is to their disadvantage.

The constant intake of economic information or news is crucial to every trader. Hence, every dealing room has at least one or more news reporting machines so that the house is not disadvantaged in the marketplace. In addition to news received from the various news services, the marketplace constantly abounds with speculations and rumors. Business ethics prohibit the repeating or initiating of irresponsible rumors or speculations.

A major problem and risk is the possibility of a counterparty becoming a bankrupt on the day when a trading partner has transmitted funds to settle its side of the transaction, and the bankrupt has failed entirely to perform its side of the deal. In this case, the possible loss is the entire principal, rather than a small percentage due to fluctuation in the value of the currency. In such cases, the dealers must be alert to news reports of failures and react promptly to arrange the retrieval of funds that may have been paid in settlement of their side of any transactions with the bankrupt.

25
Multicurrency Reserve Assets

A. D. ORSICH
General Manager, Treasury Division
Standard Chartered Bank Limited

INTRODUCTION

Since the fixed exchange-rate system finally collapsed in 1973, fluctuating currencies have posed new challenges to all involved in international trade and finance. Even at the basic level of exporting or importing, the two parties' currencies may move sharply against one another between the time an agreement is signed and final delivery. Most transactions are far more complicated, perhaps involving suppliers in half a dozen countries, phased payments, and so on. At each stage some currency risk is incurred. Unless companies cover themselves against those risks, they may find a potentially profitable, well-executed deal turned into a loss-maker by factors outside their control.

For banks and other financial institutions the position is similar. Their business is accepting deposits and making loans. The volatility they face is not confined to currencies. In each national market, interest rates have also become more volatile (a function chiefly of higher and more variable inflation). Financial institutions therefore must balance both interest rate and currency considerations to obtain the best combined yield on their assets.

There are basically three types of cover against currency risk.

1. *Forward cover.* Forward exchange markets exist to provide guaranteed prices for currencies at some future date. For many purposes, they satisfy the needs of companies and banks. However, there are no forward markets for several of the minor currencies; and even in the major currencies, it can sometimes be difficult to buy or sell more than 6 or 12 months in advance.

2. *Using a single, universal currency.* For 25 years after World War II, the dollar was the cornerstone of international finance. It was extensively used to denominate trade between third parties, international

bank loans, and official debts between countries. Even when floating rates replaced fixed rates, the dollar could theoretically have maintained this dominance. It did not wholly eliminate exchange risk, of course: traders or borrowers wanting to convert dollar receipts into their domestic currencies still faced uncertainty about the dollar value of those currencies. But the widespread use of dollars for settling intermediate accounts greatly reduced the range of uncertainty.

However, the dollar's preeminence has gradually been eroded. Since it devalued against gold in 1971, it has come to be treated more and more like other currencies. It has fluctuated sharply, both against individual currencies (falling by 5 percent against the Deutsche mark in one day in April 1980; by 40 percent against the Swiss franc in five months in 1973); and in trade-weighted terms. It has been the subject of (often successful) speculative pressure. No bank or international company could afford to hold dollars in the belief that they would maintain their value in the long term.

Neither forward markets nor (still less) a single, dominant currency are therefore proof against exchange risk.

3. *Multicurrency baskets.* This third approach aims to reduce rather than eliminate exchange risk and is the subject of the rest of this chapter.

THE EVOLUTION OF CURRENCY BASKETS

At the beginning of 1973, the world's central bank held some 85 percent of their foreign exchange reserves in dollars. This proportion actually increased for a time, to nearly 87 percent at the end of 1976. Since then it has fallen steadily. By the end of 1980 it had reached an estimated 76 percent; if the European currency unit (discussed below) is included, the dollar's share had fallen below 65%. These figures probably understate the degree of international diversification out of dollars. Between 1976 and 1979, the leading central banks intervened heavily to support the dollar. In a sense, they were forced buyers of dollars, while other central bankers were shifting their portfolios to include other currencies (and often gold as well).

No comprehensive data are available on the currency mix of private holdings of foreign exchange, but it seems certain that they too were reducing the weight of dollars. As Table 1 indicates, the dollar element in deposits with banks operating in the Euromarket has fallen from its peak in 1976.

As other currencies have come to play a growing role in both official and private foreign exchange holdings, banks in particular have faced new challenges. The range of financial instruments varies from country to country, as does the degree of access permitted to outsiders. Yet there was a growing demand from depositors and borrowers to spread

Table 1
External Liabilities of Reporting European Banks in U.S. Dollars and Other Currencies
(percentage in each currency)

Year	U.S. Dollars	Deutsche Marks	Swiss Francs	Pound Sterling	Dutch Guilders	French Francs	Yen and Others
1973	68.2	16.8	8.9	2.5	1.2	1.2	1.2
1974	70.7	15.5	8.3	1.6	1.2	1.0	1.7
1975	73.2	15.4	5.9	1.2	1.4	1.3	1.6
1976	74.1	15.2	5.1	1.3	1.1	1.0	2.2
1977	71.2	16.9	5.4	1.5	1.3	1.1	2.6
1978	68.2	18.2	5.5	2.0	1.4	1.4	3.3
1979	65.5	19.2	6.1	2.3	1.3	1.7	3.9
1980	68.5	15.7	6.4	3.0	1.0	1.8	3.6

Source: Bank for International Settlements

currency risk. The de facto spreading of currency risk was sooner or later bound to encourage the use of special instruments.

SPECIAL DRAWING RIGHTS

Created by the IMF in 1968, special drawing rights (SDRs) were intended in time to take over some of the reserve asset role of the dollar. Their use was, and is still, confined to transactions between official holders of SDRs, mainly central banks of countries belonging to the Fund. Many members thought they had a right to extra liquidity to finance expanding world trade. The French objected that this was inflationary, and the right should be granted only in special circumstances; the title of the SDR reflected the eventual compromise.

The SDR was initially valued against gold at 1 SDR = 0.888671 grams of fine gold, which, in 1969 was the same as the par value of the U.S. dollar. Thus one SDR equalled one U.S. dollar. Once the United States had abandoned the $35-an-ounce official gold price and let the dollar float, it became necessary to adopt a new method of valuation to ensure the stability of the value of the SDR against currencies in general. In 1974 it was therefore recommended that the value of the SDR should be based upon the value of a group of major currencies in specified proportions. Under this method one SDR equalled the sum of specified quantities of the 16 currencies whose issuers accounted for more than 1 percent of world trade in the period 1968–72. The weightings used to determine the quantities of each currency were determined by their countries' share of world exports of goods and services. For some countries—particularly the United States—the weightings were adjusted to take account of that currency's importance in financial dealings.

After 1974, therefore, the SDR was indeed a multicurrency asset.

But it still had several significant shortcomings for any private institution wishing to denominate its assets or liabilities in SDRs. With 16 currencies it was very difficult for banks to match assets and liabilities, or even to quote a precise market rate; the IMF announced a rate only once a day, based on exchange rates prevailing in London five or six hours earlier although for the yen the average price in the Tokyo market, which had closed some 13 hours earlier, was utilized.

To correct these weaknesses, the SDR has been radically reformed. From the beginning of 1981, it has been composed of only five currencies (U.S. dollar, deutsche mark, yen, French franc, and sterling). The IMF has also gone most of the way toward market interest rates for the SDR. From May 1, 1981, members whose holdings rise above a certain level will receive a return of 100 percent of the weighted interest rates on the five currencies. Instead of calculating SDR interest rates on the basis of averages in the preceding quarter, they will now be based on the preceding three weeks.

The weights of the five currencies which were to compose the SDR from January 1, 1981, were announced by the IMF in September 1980; these were U.S. dollar 42.0 percent, deutsche mark 19.0 percent, yen 13.0 percent, French franc 13.0 percent and sterling 13.0 percent. The weights loosely reflect the relative importance of the currencies in international trade and payments, based on the value of goods and services of the countries issuing these currencies and the balances of the currencies held as reserves by members of the Fund over the five-year period 1975–79.

On December 31, 1980, the Fund made the necessary calculations to convert the agreed percentages into units of each of the five currencies in the new basket on the basis of exchange rates over the preceding three months. The amounts are 0.54 U.S. dollars, 0.46 deutsche marks, 34 yen, 0.74 French francs, and 0.071 pounds sterling. To determine the dollar value of the SDR the individual amounts of currency are converted at current market rates. By adding these dollar equivalents the exchange rate between the U.S. dollar and the SDR is arrived at. Because currencies vary, the dollar value of these components changes from day to day, thereby changing their weights in the SDR. Table 2 shows the value of weights of the currencies comprising the SDR on January 2 and June 2, 1981.

The simplicity of the calculation is obvious. It is reinforced by the fact that the SDR interest rate is computed from the same five currencies, each of which has an active Eurodeposit market. Banks are therefore able to offer immediate, precise quotes to customers; as a result, the spread between bid and offer price has narrowed significantly, and is now comparable to the spread on heavily traded instruments in national markets.

The SDR's role in the international monetary system has thus far

Table 2
SDR Composition, Weights, and Value

		Weight Percent	
	Composition	January 2, 1981	June 2, 1981
U.S. dollar	0.54	42.5	46.1
Deutsche mark	0.46	18.3	16.9
French franc	0.74	12.8	11.4
Yen	34	13.2	13.0
Pound sterling	0.071	13.3	12.6
		100.0	100.0
1 SDR =		U.S. $1.27174	U.S. $1.17020

disappointed its architects. In 1978–80, the IMF considered the introduction of an SDR substitution account as a way of relieving some of
the downward pressure on the dollar. Central banks would be able
to exchange part of their dollar holdings for SDRs. The proposed account was to contain some $15 to 20 billion—relatively small, compared
with official dollar holdings about 15 times as large and private holdings
that were larger still. In the event, the substitution account was shelved,
but that has not stopped the SDR from making considerable advances
both as a public and private medium.

A EUROPEAN COUNTERPART: THE ECU

The European Monetary System (EMS) was started in March 1979.
Its main initial purpose was to provide a quasi fixed-rate system for
EEC member currencies. But unlike its predecessor, the European
"currency snake," the EMS has ambitions to develop more formal monetary links within the EEC.

A European currency unit (ECU) is at the center of the EMS. Its
value and composition are identical to that of the European unit of
account (EUA) which is equal to the sum of 3.66 Belgian francs, 0.14
Luxembourg francs, 0.286 Dutch florins, 0.217 Danish crowns, 0.828
German marks, 109 Italian lire, 1.15 French francs, 0.0885 pounds
sterling, and 0.00759 Irish pounds. The amounts broadly reflect the
relative importance of the currencies concerned but because currencies vary, the weight of each component in the ECU changes from
day to day, in the same way as the weights of the currencies making
up the SDR vary. Table 3 shows the value and weights of the currencies
comprising the ECU on January 2 and June 2, 1981.

The ECU's dollar value is calculated on a similar basis to that used
for the SDR. That value in turn can then be used to calculate the
ECU value of any other currency. In this case the reason for arriving
at a dollar value, rather than say a deutsche mark value, is that the

Table 3
ECU Composition, Weight, and Value

		Weight Percent	
	Composition	January 2, 1981	June 2, 1981
Deutsche mark	0.828	32.39	32.5
Pound sterling	0.0885	16.14	16.8
French franc	1.15	19.46	19.0
Italian lire	109	9.00	8.7
Dutch florin	0.286	10.31	10.1
Belgian franc	3.66	8.90	8.8
Danish crown	0.217	2.74	2.7
Irish pound	0.00759	.72	1.1
Luxembourg franc	0.14	.34	0.3
		100.0	100.0
1 ECU =		U.S. $1.31040	U.S. $1.07505

U.S. unit is recognized in the foreign exchange market as the vehicle currency for trading.

The composition of the ECU is the same as that used for the European unit of account—which was an accounting device for denominating budgetary transactions within the EEC. The shares of individual currencies have been fixed according to various criteria, such as GNP, participation in intra-EEC trade, and so on. However, they are subject to review every five years, and a member state may request reexamination of the ECU's composition if the weight of a currency in the basket changes by more than 25 percent. Any change in the composition of the basket is subject to the agreement of all member states.

The ECU occupies a central place in the European Monetary System. Members acquired ECUs through transferring 20 percent of their *dollar and gold* reserves to the European Monetary Cooperation Fund (EMCF) in exchange for ECUs. (Even though Britain has chosen to stay out of the EMS, it is a full participant in the EMCF.) These transfers take the form of three-month revolving swaps, so as to avoid legal complications about the permanent transfer of national assets. The ECUs that members acquire are then used to settle accounts between one another on the basis of what they borrowed or lent for intervention purposes.

Members regularly have to adjust their contribution to the EMCF to ensure that it represents at least 20 percent of their gold and dollar reserves. Gold is valued at its average price for the preceding six months (or its price on the penultimate day of the six-month period, whichever is lower). The dollar is valued by its market rate two days previously.

Individual contributions to the EMCF earn interest according to what was the prevailing dollar interest rate (three-month U.S. Treasury bills) in the preceding quarter. But if a member becomes a net borrower of ECUs from the EMCF, it has to pay an interest rate which is the weighted average of all members' official discount rates.

The ECU is used as one of the numbers for determining whether countries have to react to currency fluctuations within the EMS. However, in terms of the development of multicurrency assets, the ECU's two most significant features are:

a. It withdraws some dollar reserves from European central banks; in that sense it performs the same "laundering" function as was intended for the IMF's substitution account.

b. By allowing members to exchange gold for ECUs, the EMS has partially remonetized gold. ECUs are usable liquidity—they can settle accounts between member countries—whereas gold holdings had generally been regarded as inert. The Europeans have therefore done in a roundabout way what many small countries have been doing directly—diversifying their range of usable assets to include gold.

THE PERFORMANCE OF THE SDR AND THE ECU

In international terms, the value of a financial instrument depends on two joint variables—its value against other currencies and its yield. On both counts, the two major currency baskets have fulfilled their function. They have been less volatile than individual currencies but over time have offered competitive joint returns (currency plus yield).

As far as the SDR is concerned, the weight of the dollar is the dominant factor in determining both its value and yield. The SDR's behavior as a 16-currency basket was actually very similar to what it would have been had it all along been composed of its present five currencies. It has outperformed each of the major currencies for at least one year in the five-year period 1976–80. This is not at all surprising. The nature of the foreign exchange market is such that at least 90 percent of trade involves only the five largest currencies. By definition, therefore, their trade-weighted values cannot all be rising or falling simultaneously (and it is of course logically impossible for all five to rise against each other). When some of the big five are strong some or all of the others will be weak.

The SDR's interest rate has also moved to offset some of the volatility of currency movements. Since October, 1979 short-term dollar rates in particular have fluctuated sharply. While three-month Eurodollar rates ranged from over 20 percent to under 10 percent between April and June 1980, the SDR rate moved within a narrower band of 15.5 percent down to 11 percent. That was still superior to the yields obtainable in the major currencies' bar sterling and (for some of the time) the dollar.

Nonetheless, yields on the official SDR have still been somewhat below what would have been obtained in the private market. The official SDR rate is computed from treasury bills or interbank deposits in the five countries concerned; these carry a lower rate than could be obtained in their respective Eurocurrency markets, and because the official rate is derived from historical averages (explained above), in a period of rising interest rates it will also be below the market equivalent.

The ECU's performance should be judged on different criteria to those applied to the SDR. Since the EMS is intended to ensure long periods of near-stability between member currencies, the ECU itself will remain even more stable. (Within the European context, that is, it will of course fluctuate vis-a-vis currencies like the dollar or the yen). As a European currency hedge, the ECU comes into its own when an EMS realignment occurs (in September 1979, for example). Its value against member currencies then changed less than the cross-rates of those currencies that were realigned. The quasi fixed-rate nature of the EMS makes it easier for markets to anticipate which currencies may be realigned. They are therefore less in need of a currency hedge against the vagaries of fully floating currencies. For that reason, the ECU is (and will probably remain) less in demand than the SDR for short-term transactions. For long-term business, however, the ECU is valuable cover against EMS realignments—and, the sceptic would say, against the possibility that the EMS will break up altogether.

MARKETABILITY

Currency performance and yields are both important considerations for depositors and borrowers, but the size and strength of the market will also condition their attitudes. Both the SDR and the ECU were created by official institutions, and for a while their use was restricted to official purposes, but more important, private markets have recognized the virtues of multicurrency assets, and adapted the SDR and the ECU to their specific needs.

Even as recently as mid-1980, the SDR was still a relatively untried instrument. About SDR16 billion were held by central banks in their official reserves; an estimated $1 to $2 billion of SDRs were held on deposit with commercial banks. In private markets the first SDR-denominated bond issue had been made in 1975, but very few issues had followed, raising a total not much over SDR250 million. The secondary market was thin largely because of the complexities involved in valuing a 16-currency instrument.

Since the SDR was streamlined, however, its use has spread considerably. There is an active market in SDR certificates of deposit (CDs) in London, and one seems to be developing in the Far East as well.

SDR floating-rate notes were issued for the first time in January 1981. The SDR deposit market has expanded rapidly; by May 1981 its size had reached an estimated $4 to $5 billion. A forward market in SDRs is also operative.

The SDR market will in due course be boosted by the appearance of the International Monetary Fund as a significant borrower. The IMF has been instructed by its member governments to raise a large (but unspecified) amount of extra money to meet demands on it in the early and mid-1980s. In April 1981 the IMF announced a bilateral loan from Saudi Arabia, denominated in SDRs and extending for two or possibly three years. It will total at least SDR4 billion a year. However, the IMF has also indicated that it intends to supplement this loan with market borrowing, probably before the end of 1981. It may take the form of a syndicated credit or a bond issue. The World Bank may also borrow in SDRs from the bond market. The addition of these two international institutions to the list of borrowers will increase the marketability of SDRs and will almost certainly be followed by further borrowing by them.

THE MECHANICS OF MULTICURRENCY BUSINESS

The official origins of both the SDR and the ECU explain why their interest rates were calculated by cumbersome procedures and were long held well below market rates. The private markets need have no such inhibitions. In just the same way as in individual currencies, they quote a variety of interest rates for different types of instruments, so they can do the same for currency baskets. All that is needed is an agreed composition for the basket; thereafter the components can be valued according to the relevant interest rates to produce a market rate for a multicurrency instrument. It is thus possible to devise SDR interest rates on money-market deposits ranging from overnight to 12 months or more; on CDs; on short bills; on medium-term credits; and on long-term bonds.

In developing a market for multicurrency instruments, intermediaries initially had to match liabilities by making separate individual loans in the currencies concerned. Thus, for example, a bank accepting an SDR deposit of SDR1 million may have had to match this with five separate loans in dollars, yen, deutsche marks, French francs, and sterling, according to their respective weights in the SDR. However, as the different markets grow, it becomes increasingly easy for intermediaries to borrow and lend in SDR-denominated terms. At that state, the currency basket ceases to be treated as a synthetic creation. It takes on a market identity of its own, with just the same convenience and marketability as any national currencies.

OTHER CURRENCY BASKETS

The SDR and the ECU are the two most prominent currency baskets at the moment, but that does not prevent others from emerging. There are no conceptual reasons why a variety of baskets should not be developed, tailored according to individual needs. Like any other market, all that is required are willing buyers and willing sellers. Examples of possible baskets include the following:

a. Regional currency baskets. A company trading in a specific region might find a use for a basket consisting of the main currencies of the area, plus one or more internationally traded currencies (e.g., the U.S. dollar).

b. Gold component. A gold component could be included in the basket. In recent years, many outright buyers of gold might have been satisfied with holding only some fraction of their purchases in gold, the rest being held in interest-bearing currency form. This would, of course, provide a less effective hedge against currency fluctuations.

c. Other commodities. In just the same way as gold has often been advocated as the best reserve base for the monetary system, so other commodities could perform some of the same role. Unlike paper currencies, they cannot be created at the whim of national governments, but the large fluctuations that occur in their price would inevitably mean that any basket with a commodity component could not be used as a hedge against exchange risk.

These different mixtures essentially reflect what happens already in less formal ways. Investors prefer to spread their portfolios to contain equities, bonds, liquid assets, different currencies, gold, and other commodities. Multicurrency units offer a portfolio mix; while it is unlikely that efficient markets can develop for every combination, they could do so for a few.

SUMMARY AND CONCLUSIONS

There is no real prospect of a return to fixed exchange rates so long as inflation remains high and variable. The currency risks involved in floating rates will therefore continue, highlighting the need for exchange-rate cover. The multicurrency basket offers one form of cover. Its attractions depend on how easy it is to use, and how tradeable it is in secondary markets.

The streamlined SDR is now a usable basket, and its use is spreading quickly into private markets. The ECU provides a European alternative to the SDR, though the total exclusion of the dollar means that it is unrepresentative of international trading and financial realities. Other currency baskets could easily be devised.

The key to developing wide use of multicurrency assets lies with nonbank borrowers and lenders. It is easy to see rapid growth in the interbank market, but it needs to be complemented by nonbank business. Multicurrency units are increasingly appreciated by corporations, government borrowers, and others; their participation will ensure the strength of secondary markets, and the gradual emergence of currency baskets as independent entities.

SECTION 5
Special Institutions and Programs

26

The Export-Import Bank of the United States

TURHAN TIRANA
General Manager
Pittsburgh International Bank

INTRODUCTION

Since its founding during the Depression, the Export-Import Bank has become a significant factor in the financing of the United States' export trade. However, controversy has accompanied the bank's growth from time to time, and today some changes in its role and possible effectiveness are likely.

Over the years Eximbank has been responsible for more than $100 billion of U.S. sales overseas, much of it equipment requiring long deferred payments. No knowledgeable export manager or commercial bank lending officer would provide a customer with a financing bid on a U.S. export sale without at least considering whether the bid could be improved by one or another of Eximbank's programs.

The controversy Eximbank faces concerns the magnitude of its programs, which are included in the U.S. government budget. An Office of Management and Budget document on Eximbank concludes, "While export promotion is a desirable activity, the Export-Import Bank is a very weak instrument for achieving any significant gains. . . . Capital raised in the U.S. markets at high rates of interest is the major export promoted by the Export-Import Bank."[1]

On the other hand, major U.S. manufacturers, labor unions, and both Republican and Democratic senators and congressmen are calling for an increase, not a decrease, in Eximbank funding. If the Reagan administration goals are realized, they argue, orders either will be lost to foreign competitors whose governments provide subsidized export credit, or they will be subcontracted to overseas subsidiaries or

---

[1] Eximbank Report, February 9, 1981, p. 2.

foreign-owned manufacturers. The result will be the loss of U.S. sales and jobs and an increased trade deficit.

Eximbank's legal existence is based on the Export-Import Bank Act of 1945, as amended on numerous occasions since. However, the act is simple and remarkably broad. The act decrees that the purpose of the bank is to "aid in the financing and to facilitate exports and imports and the exchange of commodities between the United States . . . and any foreign country or national thereof."[2] To accomplish this purpose, it is authorized to do a "general banking business" which comprises virtually every banking function except the issuance of currency.

The operating charter is renewed periodically, most recently in 1978 with a five-year extension to 1983. However, program limitations are recommended annually by the Office of Management and Budget and acted on by the Congress. In addition, the Senate and House banking committees are charged with overseeing Eximbank's performance.

The bank is designated as an independent agency of the United States government, the powers of which are not to be transferred to any other government entity. There is a president and first vice president, both of whom are directors, and three other directors. All five persons are appointed by the president of the United States and confirmed by the Senate. They serve without term as long as the president decides. No more than three directors may be from the same political party. None of the directors has any loan authority; a majority vote is required to approve a loan.

The bank's capital stock is $1 billion, subscribed by the United States. The bank has the authority to borrow from the Treasury another $6 billion at any time. This facility is used primarily for short-term borrowings. Longer-term borrowings are arranged through the Treasury's Federal Financing Bank.

There are several key constraints and directives, dictated by the charter and by policy set in large measure by Congress.

1. *Self-sustaining:* The bank is expected to operate on its $1 billion capital without coming to the taxpayers for appropriations. In fact, until recently it has done a remarkably good job in this respect. During the life of the bank profits have amounted to more than $3 billion of which more than $1 billion has been paid to the Treasury in dividends and the balance added to retained earnings.

2. *Reasonable assurance of repayment:* The bank's loans and guarantees must meet this criteria, as defined with varying degrees of stringency by different boards of directors. The pressure to extend loans varies, partly with the attitude of the political party in power toward government involvement in the economic affairs of the nation, and partly with concerns about the status of the nation's balance of interna-

---

[2] Export-Import Bank Act of 1945, Sec. 2(a)(1).

tional payments. In any event, the record here has also been good. Most U.S. financing assistance to countries with obvious and substantial difficulties has been allocated to the Agency for International Development, the purpose of which is more the financing of economic development.

3. *Private competition:* The bank is to complement but not compete with private sources of finance. The result is that it is denied the best credits, as well as the worst. If a private lender is prepared to extend a credit and foreign competition does not require Eximbank's usually lower interest rate to obtain a contract for the U.S. seller, Eximbank is not supposed to become involved. Because of the availability of private capital, Eximbank does not finance imports into the United States, although reportedly the bank extended one credit during World War II for the import of fish from Iceland.

4. *Meeting foreign competition:* The bank's statute now requires it to attempt selectively to meet subsidized, concessionary financing terms of its official counterparts in other industrial exporting nations. This directive, as other nations have stepped up their own export financing activities, has produced an increasing drain on Eximbank's resources.

There are a number of other, less important constraints which nevertheless either complicate the loan approval process or the obtaining of an overseas order. For example, products directly financed by Eximbank must be shipped on U.S. flag vessels, which often are more expensive, unless a waiver is obtained from the Maritime Administration. Environmental impact statements are required for nuclear power and certain other projects which may pose a health hazard in the borrower's country. Consideration must be given to the possibility of a loan having an adverse impact on the U.S. economy, especially with regard to loss of jobs. Loans to the Republic of South Africa and loans to Communist nations carry additional review procedures.

Credits of $30 million and more are reviewed by the National Advisory Council on International Monetary and Financial Policies (known as the NAC), the chairman of which is the secretary of the Treasury. The purpose is mainly one of providing information and coordination among interested U.S. government agencies, but objections occasionally are raised on policy grounds. Pressure to authorize certain loans for diplomatic or business reasons is imposed occasionally on the Eximbank board but before the loan arrives at the NAC for review. Credits of more than $100 million must be additionally reviewed by the Congress which has up to 35 days in which to comment; no comment within that time signifies no objection.

Eximbank's sources of funding, besides its capital and retained earnings, are mostly the U.S. Treasury through the Federal Financing Bank, as shown on the balance sheet below. A relatively small amount is

Export-Import Bank, December 31, 1980 (millions of dollars)

Cash	5	Accrued interest	96
Loans	14,286	Due private and other lenders	596
Accrued interest	324	Notes payable to Federal	
Other	102	Financing Bank	10,654
		Notes payable to U.S. Treasury	142
		Other	26
		Total liabilities	11,514
		Capital	1,000
		Retained earnings	2,203
		Total capital	3,203
		Total liabilities	
		and capital	14,717

Source: Export-Import Bank of the United States, *Financial Highlights for the Period Ending January 31, 1981*, p. 9.

due directly to the Treasury; as mentioned earlier, this could be substantially increased, and other, lesser sums are owed to private purchasers of participations in Eximbank's loans.

Rising interest rates have complicated Eximbank's funding activities. As of January 31, 1981, the weighted average cost of the bank's liabilities was 9.5 percent; including equity, the effective cost was lowered to 7.5 percent. At the same time, the bank's lending rate was 8.75 percent, but rates on loans authorized earlier and still on the books were even less. The General Accounting Office in a report to Congress estimated that Exim's reserves would be depleted by 1985. Subsequently, interest rates for nonaircraft credits were raised to 12.0 percent, and a one-time 2 percent fee was imposed on the amount of each credit, to be paid at authorization. For the moment, these charges exceed the bank's average borrowing costs but not its marginal costs. Moreover, the bank's ability to carry out its mandate is reduced.

The bank obviously is caught between its directives to be competitive and to be self-sustaining. If lending rates are set too high, the overall costs of the exports the bank is expected to finance will become excessive; if rates are too low, earnings are jeopardized.

Operating earnings for the fiscal year ending September 30, 1980 were $110 million, down from the $158 million earning the previous year. That year the bank's dividend was passed for the first time in 30 years. Operating earnings of $12 million were reported for fiscal 1981, and the first loss ever of $160 million was estimated for fiscal 1982. The new, higher lending rates will help, but not on the outstanding portfolio which remains under water. In addition, there are potential loan defaults in several countries.

The General Accounting Office, in its report, stated,

"We believe Eximbank's current financial dilemma has intensified to the point where Congress needs to clarify its intent. If the mandate to meet competition is emphasized over self-sufficiency, some form of subsidy for the Bank's lending activity with public funds could be necessary. If Congress does not intend that meeting the competition should be given predominance in the current situation, then it should affirm that fact by indicating what it believes is acceptable lending policy.[3]

EXPOSURE

The bank's exposure of $34.5 billion in loans, guarantees, and insurance, including undisbursed portions, as of December 31, 1980, was as follows, in percentages:

	Total	FCIA Short Term	FCIA Medium Term	Exim Medium Term	Financial Guarantee	Direct Loans
Africa/Middle East	17	0.8	0.7	0.6	3.4	12.2
Asia	27	1.2	0.2	0.3	4.4	20.7
Europe and Canada	25	2.4	0.3	0.3	5.0	16.8
Latin America	22	3.6	2.0	2.0	2.1	12.0
Discount loans	3	—	—	—	—	2.6
Other	6	5.9	—	0.3	0.1	0.1
Total	100	13.9	3.2	3.5	15.0	64.4

Source: Export-Import Bank of the United States, *Financial Highlights for the Period Ending January 31, 1981*, p. 9.

Direct loans and loan commitments comprised about 64 percent of the total, and financial guarantees another 15 percent. Short-term FCIA insurance was the next largest category, with 14 percent. Geographically, the exposure was spread fairly evenly, with Asia the highest and Africa and the Middle East the lowest. Discount loans are a separate risk category, as they are extended to U.S. commerical banks.

The economic sectoral breakdown was as follows:[4]

Agriculture	2%	
Communications	3	
Construction	6	
Electric power	27	
Nuclear		17
Other		10
Manufacturing	7	
Mining and refining	14	
Transportation	27	
Commercial jet aircraft		21
Other		6
Other	100%	

[3] *To Be Self-Sufficient or Competitive*, General Accounting Office, June 24, 1981, p. 35.

[4] Export-Import Bank of the United States, *Financial Highlights for the Period Ending January 31, 1981*, p. 11–1.

Two thirds of Eximbank's direct loans in fiscal-1980 financed exports of seven major corporations, comprising Boeing, McDonnell Douglas, Lockheed, Westinghouse, General Electric, Combustion Engineering, and Western Electric.

The two single largest components are nuclear power plants and commercial jet aircraft, comprising 17 percent and 21 percent of total exposure, respectively. Large exporters argue, however, that their employment rolls count, too, and in any event much of their business in subcontracted to smaller companies.

The 10 countries in which Exim had the greatest exposure as of year-end 1980 are shown below, in millions of dollars.[5]

Korea	$3,352
Mexico	2,452
Taiwan	2,262
Spain	1,755
Brazil	1,681
Algeria	1,637
United Kingdom	1,041
Canada	1,013
Yugoslavia	996
Israel	955

The loan loss record has been good. Out of $35 billion in total loan disbursements, only $8 million has been written off. However, most major credits in difficulty, such as those to the governments of Poland, Zaire, and Turkey, are rescheduled with longer maturities. Supplier credits involving smaller private-sector borrowers find themselves in difficulty more often. As of the end of 1980, $5 million in claims had been paid, net of recoveries. Arrearages on January 30, 1981, totaled $343 million, but of this, $310 million was in the form of accelerated Iranian debt.

HISTORY

Eximbank was founded in 1934, within the context of the New Deal recovery program. At the time, competition for diminishing trade resulted in import barriers and currency depreciation, and exchange controls were adopted to stem capital flights. U.S. exporters, who previously had conducted much of their business on a cash-against-documents or a letter-of-credit basis, found sales difficult without the extension of credit. At the same time, few U.S. commercial banks, even if they were in a position to extend new credit, had the experience to do so overseas. It was hoped that the bank would encourage exports and at the same time stimulate employment in idle U.S. factories.

[5] Ibid. p. 11–2 through 11–7.

Ironically, Eximbank was created essentially to undertake business with the Soviet Union, the government of which had been recognized by the United States the year before. By executive order, President Roosevelt directed the secretaries of state and commerce to organize a District of Columbia banking corporation, funded by the Reconstruction Finance Corporation, the main financial arm of the New Deal. The new bank was to finance what was expected to be a large volume of trade with the USSR. Advice was obtained from the American Bankers' Association on the operation of the bank. However, there was a falling-out with the Soviet Union on the question of settlement of Imperial and other debts, and it was not until 1972 that the first Exim credit was extended to the Soviet Union.

Subsequent to the falling out with the Soviet Union, emphasis was switched to the Good Neighbor policy in Latin America. Cuba was Eximbank's initial beneficiary with a loan of $4 million to finance the purchase and minting into Cuban pesos of silver from the Philadelphia mint. The loan, followed by four others in the next four years, was used to stabilize a new but friendly government in Havana which was facing a critical budget deficit as well as domestic unrest.

Since then the bank has undergone several reorganizations and changes in emphasis, adapting to the requirements of the time and the attitudes of its boards of directors. Throughout, however, two purposes have existed. One is the need of a government agency to stimulate U.S. exports, and the other that the bank would complement U.S. foreign policy objectives. In the bank's early years the latter objective was more prominent than now.

Following the German invasion of Poland, credits were extended to Scandinavian nations which were suffering from trade dislocations. Lending in Europe subsequently was closed down, and Eximbank shifted its emphasis to financing resource development in Latin America. In the postwar period the financing of reconstruction in Europe became the principal focus, followed by the Cold War when Congress authorized the bank to lend to Greece and Turkey, then struggling with Communist subversion and the prospect of economic collapse. The bank assured the financial underpinning of Israel in 1948 when that nation was created with $100 million of long-term development loans. Yugoslavia's break with the Soviet Union the next year led to the first of a long and substantial lending relationship there. A little later the governments of Iran and Spain and then Indonesia became a major focus of U.S. foreign policy, and at the same time Eximbank creditors.

Throughout this period purely commercial credits were extended as well, but generally for large industrial, power, mining, and oil and gas projects, often publicly owned or controlled. The bank was little known except to major overseas borrowers and their governments and large U.S. manufacturing and engineering concerns. The bank's borrowers were first class, and the bank was managed easily by a staff of about 50 persons.

However, in the 1950s, with Europe and Japan back in business, the seller's market our exporters had enjoyed began to change, and Eximbank was directed to do more. The result was the introduction of supplier credit programs designed to encourage private financing of exports. The medium-term guarantee program was established, and in 1961 the Foreign Credit Insurance Association (FCIA) was formed by about 50 private insurance companies to write short- and medium-term credit insurance policies, coinsured and reinsured by Eximbank.

As the balance of payments deteriorated in the 1960s and 1970s, additional pressure was placed on the bank. Its role and lending authority continued to expand with an often perplexing and sometimes overlapping array of programs.

At the same time and partly in response to Eximbank's activities, U.S. commercial banks were expanding or starting international departments. No longer content to act solely as recipients of Eximbank guarantees and FCIA insurance, they demanded and obtained a role in Exim's direct lending program. Heretofore, Eximbank had extended 90 to 100 percent of every direct loan. Hereafter, commercial banks were invited to participate in most of these loans, at first on a 50/50 basis and then in a more flexible range.

Programs were developed to increase private involvement, including the discount loan program to provide commercial bank's fixed-rate funding commitments ostensibly to be used when funds are scarce, and the Cooperative Financing Facility, a rather cumbersome program by which Eximbank and commercial banks jointly lent to foreign banks.

The liability side of the balance sheet was not ignored either in the search for private help. Participations in specific Eximbank loans, guaranteed by Eximbank, were sold to private investors, as were debentures. Then, in 1971, the Private Export Funding Corporation (PEFCO) was established to mobilize for export financing capital held by insurance companies, pension funds, and other institutions. PEFCO is discussed in Chapter 28.

CONGRESSIONAL AND PUBLIC RELATIONS

Until the 1960s, annual hearings on Eximbank on Capitol Hill rarely called for debate and consisted mainly of an exchange of accolades. The bank was earning money, it was doing generally what was expected of it, and there were no problems that went so far as to attract the attention of the constituents of the congressional committeemen responsible for Eximbank. Annual reports were kept brief and arcane, and the press was not encouraged to take an interest in the institution.

In addition, the bank's beneficiaries, both borrowers overseas and domestic suppliers, were satisfied with its performance, which was not rivaled anywhere in the world.

A startling interruption of this congenial state of affairs occurred when President Eisenhower took office; the bank was virtually liquidated for a while. There were two reasons. First was an effort to restrain government expenditures much like what is taking place now. And second, there was a dispute with the World Bank.

The World Bank's practice was and still is to require competitive worldwide bidding for the projects it finances, which produced some conflicts with Eximbank and its more parochial objectives of fostering U.S. sales abroad. Moreover, the World Bank believed it had the right to control borrowing by member nations. It had succeeded in blocking several Eximbank loans.

What happened was that Exim's supporters turned to the Republican chairman of the Senate Banking and Currency Committee, who in turn ordered a study which included a committee mission to Latin America. There Exim's role was praised beyond all expectations. The result was legislation killing the president's "reorganization plan" for the bank. The same legislation also declared Exim an independent agency of the U.S. government, which has allowed it to this day an unusual degree of flexibility.

In the years of the Johnson and Nixon Administrations pressure to accelerate Exim's support of exports increased. Exim resisted initially. One result was another reorganization plan, this time for the bank to be controlled by the Commerce Department. This failed, but the bank further expanded its activities, resulting in still other difficulties.

Among the difficulties was aircraft financing. Criticism came from several sources. The domestic airline industry complained that government loans at rates of 6 percent and 7 percent to their foreign competitors did not seem an appropriate use of public funds. The Treasury added that it did not see the need for concessionary financing for aircraft in the first place; sales of U.S. medium- and long-range commercial jet aircraft then faced little competition from abroad.

Other criticism was directed at military lending which Eximbank had undertaken in Western Europe in cooperation with the Defense Department. Also criticized were loans to Communist nations begun in 1972 after the Nixon-Brezhnev summit meeting. Later the General Accounting Office, an arm of the Congress, was asked to investigate Eximbank. The result was a report that the risk inherent in the bank's loan portfolio was such that its capital was impaired. A professional Congressional relations staff was formed whereas relations with the Congress previously had been handled in most cases directly by the bank's chairmen with the advice of the general counsel.

Partly as a result of these issues, the bank underwent another change

of direction during the Ford Administration. The then chairman of
the bank declared, "Most United States exports do not require Eximbank support," and loan authorizations were in fact reduced.[6] During
the Carter administration lending resumed on a large scale, increasing
about 600 percent in four years. The Reagan administration is now
reevaluating the bank's role, seeking to ascertain how it might be reduced. Congress has approved for fiscal 1982 and 1983 a lending authority of $4.4 billion, compared with the $5.461 billion authorized
for the previous fiscal year. In any event, the bank has been examining
more closely the need for direct credits, especially to buyers in wealthy
nations and of equipment for which our exporters have a competitive
edge. Financial guarantees also may be used more than before.

The administration initially took what some would call a laissez-
faire view toward Eximbank. "A dollar's worth of exports adds no
more to GNP than a dollar's worth of production of domestic consumption," a Treasury official testified. "At the same time, subsidizing exports
transfers resources from domestic sellers to export sellers."[7] However,
active lobbying by exporters, especially Westinghouse and Boeing, has
pursuaded the administration to amend at least partially its posture
on Eximbank. This lobbying was based essentially on the fact of concessionary financing offered by Eximbank's foreign counterparts.

COMPETITION

Competition with Eximbank's counterparts has become an increasing difficulty, especially those in countries with commitments to full
employment and also to expanding their economies at a time of weak
domestic and international demand. Some of these agencies were created before Eximbank, in the depression of the late-1920s in the case
of Germany, Italy, and France. However, they did not acquire financial
muscle until recently.

Some describe what is occurring now as a credit war between the
official export-finance agencies, with the French as the major aggressors
and the Americans as their principal competitors. In the effort to sell
overseas, repayment terms have been extended and interest rates reduced to the point that exports are being subsidized by the taxpayers
of many exporting nations. The cost of these subsidies in 1980 alone,
according to the Organization for Economic Cooperation and Development, was $5.5 billion.

The extent of the interest rate subsidies is shown in the table below.

---

[6] Export-Import Bank of the United States, *1976 Annual Report*, p. 3.

[7] Statement of John D. Lange, Jr., Acting Deputy Assistant Secretary of the U.S.
Treasury before the Subcommittee on International Trade, Investment, and Monetary
Policy of the Committee on Banking, Finance, and Urban Affairs of the U.S. House of
Representatives, April 28, 1981.

For the past three years Eximbank has sought to bring lending rates and repayment terms closer to market conditions through what is called the "International Arrangement on Guidelines for Officially Supported Export Credits." Some minor progress has been achieved, but significant changes have been vetoed or subverted by the French and others blending aid grants or credits with standard export credits. The French call this mechanism a *crédit mixte*.

Currency	Export Credit Rate Most Frequently Charged (as of early 1981)	Long-Term Government Bond Yield (February 1981)	Subsidy Difference
French franc	8.35%	15.05%	6.70%
British pound	8.10	13.84	5.74
Deutsche mark	8.90	9.80	0.90
Japanese yen	7.85	8.79	0.94
U.S. dollar	8.60	12.23	3.63

Source: U.S. Treasury Department.

As a result, Eximbank decided in certain cases to match the competition. In one such case Eximbank offered against French competition a $100 million credit to the Tunisian government, half at a rate of about 7½ percent with a term customary for the equipment being financed, and half at 3.75 percent with repayment over 25 years. The blended rate was about 5½ percent.

Eximbank also lengthened terms further rather than reduce rates in other cases. Long maturities appeared to be more difficult for most of the other agencies. The administration decided not to cut back on the bank's budget as much as it would have otherwise to be able to continue its fight against foreign subsidization.

"If there is to be a credit war, we are certainly prepared to defend United States economic interests," a Treasury official said. "Our competitors will find that our pockets are far deeper than theirs."[8]

The response of the other countries' export finance agencies has varied, partly with their budget limitations and partly with need. Canada, for example, has not been a major disruptive force, but the decline in its dollar has helped their exports in the same way financing subsidies would. In general, however, most of the agencies have stayed in the game by maintaining low rates.

The procedures for providing the subsidies vary somewhat, attracting differing attention to the problem. In Eximbank's case, because of accumulated earnings and a large capital base, calls on Congress

---

[8] Excerpt of remarks by R. T. McNamara, Deputy Secretary of the U.S. Treasury, before the Institutional Investors' Conference, Cannes, France, June 12, 1981.

for appropriations have not been required. In France, financing is passed by the commercial banks through the Banque Francaise du Commerce Extérieure directly to the Banque de France and is accordingly hidden. On the other hand, the Export Credit Guarantee Department pays the British banks the difference between the rates to the borrowers and a notional cost of funds. The difference comes from the British Treasury and is highly visible. In fiscal 1981, this charge was close to £500 million.

Another drain in the credit war has been the costs of increased risks taken to support export drives. Last year Britain's ECGD paid £264 million in claims, £80 million of which was for losses on credits to Iran, substantially more than the income from insurance premiums, and in France, COFACE paid $770 million, twice the amount lost in 1979. Substantial additional French losses were expected this year for Iran, by one account as much as $1.2 billion, which could endanger COFACE's economic self-sufficiency.

Obviously, these costs cannot continue increasing forever without becoming politically embarrassing, as has happened already in the United States, and eventually, logic dictates, the war will wind down. One evidence of this is a unilateral agreement by France, Britain, and the United States to increase interest rates to 12 percent on loans financing sales of the Airbus, as well as Boeing, McDonnell Douglas, and Lockheed aircraft competing with the Airbus.

EXIMBANK PROGRAMS

Although there are numerous Eximbank programs, most can be divided into two categories, direct credits and supplier credits.

Direct Credits

These credits are extended by Eximbank directly to overseas buyers. They are generally in amounts covering export sales of more than $5 million and include repayment terms in excess of five years. They finance the sale of capital goods, usually made to order and comprising part of a specific project, such as a manufacturing facility, mine, power plant, or other such entity. Large commercial jet aircraft and locomotives also may be financed through direct credits. Because of the size and complexity of the credit, Eximbank prefers what it calls "privity," or a direct relationship, with the borrower.

Repayment usually is based on the debt-servicing capability of the project, with most terms between 5 and 10 years in semiannual installments beginning six months from the time the equipment is delivered or the project completed. Occasionally, as in the case of nuclear power plants, terms are extended to 15 years following completion of the plant. Interest rates are fixed for the life of the loan but vary depending upon the country to which the export is sold. At the time of this writing, the standard rates are 12.4%, 12%, and 11%, depending on the per capita GNP of the country.

The portion of a sale Exim will cover also varies from 42½ percent to 85 percent, depending upon how competitive the bank wants to be, the type of project, and Exim's budget position. In almost all cases, a so-called cash payment of 15 percent is required which may be financed independently by a commercial bank or other lender.

When foreign competition has warranted, the maximum Exim contribution recently has been 65 percent, with that portion increased to 75 percent if the exporter finances another 10 percent at Eximbank's interest rate. In that case, the foreign buyer can obtain 85 percent financing. The exporter would obtain a repayment guarantee from Eximbank so he could sell his loan to a commercial bank, PEFCO, or an insurance company, arranging to pay the buyer of the loan the difference between the negotiated rate and the rate on the promissory note. The exporter probably would increase his price to reflect his financing costs.

Where there is private financing, Eximbank will accept payment over the latter maturities, thereby reducing the overall costs of the credit as Exim's less expensive money is outstanding longer. Progress payment by the buyer to the seller before shipment may be financed; this provides the seller with working capital.

Loan disbursements by Exim and other lenders usually occur simultaneously. Disbursement is usually through a letter of credit issued by a commercial bank. Alternatively, the foreign buyer may pay for the equipment first and come to Eximbank and the other lenders for reimbursement, with receipted invoices as documentation.

In some cases, Eximbank provides what it calls a financial guarantee in lieu of a loan, especially for aircraft sold to European airlines. Here PEFCO often assumes the financing at a fixed rate, albeit a higher one than Eximbank's. Eximbank's guarantee fee is generally ½ of 1 percent per annum on outstanding amounts.

In all cases there is a commitment fee on undisbursed balances. For direct loans it is ½ percent per annum, and for financial guarantees, ⅛ percent.

There is no standard application form for a direct loan. The information required depends to some extent on the project to be financed but is generally obvious and can be reviewed in advance with the loan officer for the appropriate country at Exim. However, in most cases Exim requires engineering and market data demonstrating the feasibility of the project to be financed and financial projections, as well as information on any foreign competition for the sale.

If the sale is in the marketing or bid stage, Exim may provide what is known as a "preliminary commitment." This letter states the financial terms that would be offered if the borrower meets certain conditions. A preliminary commitment usually has a life of no longer than six months but may be extended.

The preliminary commitment is not legally binding and may be requested by a commercial bank, the exporter, or the foreign buyer. The final loan must be requested directly by the borrower. The loan agreement, once the loan is approved, is prepared by Eximbank for all the lenders.

A theoretical example of a direct loan is shown below. The main possible variation is in the percentage of the Eximbank participation which, as stated above, could be increased, when justified, to 75 percent.

Direct Loan

Project:	$10,000,000 sale of equipment for a steel rolling mill.	
Financing:	15% cash payment	$ 1,500,000
	42½% Eximbank	4,250,000
	42½% for commercial bank	4,250,000
		$10,000,000

Interest Rates:	12% for Eximbank.
	1½% over six-month London interbank offered rate (LIBOR) for commercial banks.
Term:	Eleven years, with repayment in sixteen semiannual installments after a 2½-year grace period to permit time for construction with the commercial bank portion being repaid over seven years.
Fees:	½% commitment fee for Exim and commercial bank.
	¾% one-time financing fee for commercial bank.
	⅛% letter of credit negotiation fee for the commercial bank on the total credit.
	2% front-end fee for Exim on its portion.

Note: All commercial bank charges are negotiable with the borrower. The commercial bank also may negotiate a separate credit for the $1,500,000 cash payment and perhaps some of the local construction costs of the project as well.

Supplier Credits

Supplier credits are credits arranged by a supplier for the borrower with a commercial bank agreement to purchase a promissory note in favor of a supplier, endorsed by the supplier with partial or no recourse. Exim provides several types of assistance in these cases.

Excluded from this consideration will be short- and medium-term credit insurance provided by the Foreign Credit Insurance Association and partially underwritten by Eximbank. FCIA is described in Chapter 27. Eximbank has no short-term coverage but does provide commercial banks with guarantees of medium-term supplier credits, overlapping the FCIA medium-term program.

Medium-Term Guarantees

Eximbank's Commercial Bank Guarantee Program provides commercial banks with coverage from 181 days to five years and, at times, to seven years if the product warrants. Coverage is provided for most but not all countries. The actual term depends mostly on the cost of the goods being financed.

After a 15 percent cash payment, the exporter takes 10 percent of the commercial risk, unless the commercial bank and Eximbank agree that the commercial bank may assume it. The commercial bank must assume from 5 to 15 percent of the balance of the commercial risk, as shown in the example below.

Any losses due to war, revolution, civil strife, revocation of import license, and inability to convert local exchange into U.S. dollars would be covered by the political risk portion of the contract. Commercial risks include insolvency or simply protracted failure to pay. Not covered, unless a waiver is obtained, are losses due to a dispute between the buyer and seller. Interest up to 1 percent above the U.S. Treasury borrowing rate is guaranteed.

Some special requirements prevail. In many cases of sales to government agencies, a ministry of finance or central bank guarantee is required. Sometimes specified foreign commercial bank guarantees are needed. Generally, no military products are eligible for coverage. Also products must be of 100 percent U.S. origin, with a few exceptions in which a small portion may be of foreign origin. Repetitive sales to dealers or distributors can be financed under one guarantee covering all such sales for a year. Special dealer floor-plan coverage is available.

The procedure is for the commercial bank and Eximbank to enter into a master agreement which specifies the general conditions of the program but is not issued until the first guarantee has been approved. An application is submitted by the commercial bank for each sale. When the guarantee has been approved, the commercial bank may purchase the note from the U.S. supplier at or after shipment, and then notify Eximbank and pay the guarantee fee.

Many banks have received delegated authority to commit Eximbank to guarantee certain loans without first receiving Eximbank approval. Eximbank's principal liability in these cases may be as high as $750,000 per credit to a government buyer or a sale guaranteed by a foreign commercial bank, and $500,000 otherwise.

The guarantee fee is costly, although the risks it covers may be significant. Accordingly, the program is used usually as a last resort. A partial schedule of fees follows.

	Private Buyer	Private Buyer with Financial Institution Guarantee	Sovereign Public Buyer
1 year	1.88%	1.5%	1.31%
3 years	2.88%	2.3%	2.01%
5 years	4.38%	3.5%	3.06%

The fees are based on the financed amount of the export. The commercial bank may retain 15 percent to 25 percent of the fee, depending upon whether it assumes 5 percent or 15 percent of the commercial risk.

If there is a default, the commercial bank is repaid usually within a month of filing a claim. If in certain specified countries the nonpayment is due to lack of foreign exchange, the commercial bank must wait 60 to 360 days before its claim is honored. Interest at 1 percent above the U.S. Treasury borrowing rate will be paid by Eximbank when the claim is honored.

Guarantee

Export:	$1,000,000 of tractors	
Financing:	Cash payment (15%)	$150,000
	Financed portion (85%)	850,000
	Exporter retention of commercial risks (10%)	85,000
	Balance	765,000
	Commercial bank retention of commercial risks (5% of $765,000)*	38,250
	Eximbank coverage of commercial risks	726,750
	Eximbank coverage of political risks	850,000
Term:	Five years with repayment in 10 semiannual installments.	
Guarantee fee:	Assuming private buyer without local bank guarantee, the fee is 3.5% of $850,000, or $29,750, of which 15%, or $4,462.50, is rebated to the commercial bank.	

* If the commercial bank assumed 15 percent instead of 5 percent of the commercial risks, Eximbank's liability for commercial risks would decrease from $726,750 to $650,250.

As part of the Commercial Bank Guarantee Program, Eximbank will issue a guarantee of repayment to a U.S. commercial bank on a medium-term line of credit which the U.S. bank issues to a bank in a lesser developed country. All sales under this mechanism, which is called a Bank-to-Bank Guarantee, are automatically guaranteed by Eximbank without prior approval. No fee is charged by Eximbank for this facility unless the line is actually used.

Discount Loans

The Discount Loan Program provides commercial banks with a standby fixed-rate source of funds to enable the banks to lend at fixed interest rates. The commercial bank borrows directly from Eximbank for a term parallel with the supplier credit, submitting to Eximbank its own promissory note or the buyer's note with recourse to the commercial bank. The U.S. bank may draw on its loan from Eximbank at any time after shipment and may prepay the loan. Presently, the maximum loan amount is $2.125 million (85 percent of $2.5 million), although these limits fluctuate with budget availability.

The word *discount* is a misnomer; there is no discount. The commercial bank pays Eximbank a rate of interest in effect at the time Eximbank's discount loan is approved. The commercial bank may charge its borrower one percentage point more. Thus, if Exim's rate is 12 percent the foreign borrower could be charged 13 percent. The discount loan may be combined with an Eximbank Commercial Bank Guarantee or FCIA policy.

At the beginning of 1983 the program was limited to providing support for sale by small manufacturers (companies with gross sales of $25 million per year or less). A similar program, the medium-term credit program, is available to provide fixed interest rate support for exporters forcing subsidized, officially supported export credit competition from abroad.

The Future

What is Eximbank's future? For the time being, it is clearly to have a continuing role in financing the nation's exports, albeit likely a reduced one.

In testimony before Congress, a Treasury department official said, "We are committed to a strong export policy—one based on removal of both disincentives and artificial stimulants to exports and greater reliance on market forces."[9] This portends, as during the Ford administration, an attempt to shift more export financing and also risk taking to the private sector.

Specific changes in the bank's policies and programs remain to be determined, although the general course has been set. Whatever happens, these changes will not be the last. The bank has shifted in direction from being virtually liquidated under the Eisenhower administration to a policy of providing the maximum credit possible in the Nixon administration.

One constant has been a competent staff that is hard working and responsive to the bank's mandate. Turnover is low and a tradition of high performance is passed from one generation to another.

---

[9] Statement by John D. Lange, Jr.

27
Foreign Credit Insurance Association

ROBERT KEENAN
President
Foreign Credit Insurance Association

Despite an ever increasing demand abroad for American-made goods and services, a number of U.S. companies and financial institutions have been reluctant to compete in world markets. In addition to concerns over the creditworthiness of foreign buyers, changing economic and political conditions can block numerous sales and profit opportunities.

Executives reviewing their firms' export portfolios should ask themselves several questions: Has competition offered better repayment terms abroad? Is financing difficult to obtain? Have financial institutions reached their "country lending limits?" Can exports add a significant contribution to profitability or productivity? The following chapter will help to answer these and many more questions.

FCIA—HISTORY AND ORGANIZATION

During the early 1960s, an emerging U.S. balance-of-trade problem prompted the Kennedy administration to look into competitive credit at the international level. The private insurance industry was asked to establish, in cooperation with the federal government, a credit insurance program that would protect U.S. companies in the event foreign buyers defaulted on their obligations for unforeseen reasons. The result was the Foreign Credit Insurance Association (FCIA)—an association today consisting of a number of the nation's leading marine, property and casualty insurance, and reinsurance companies. In cooperation with the Export-Import Bank of the United States (Eximbank), a statutory U.S. government agency, FCIA reinsures U.S. exporters and financial institutions against the risk of nonpayment by foreign buyers for commercial and political reasons. FCIA members underwrite the overseas commercial credit risks, and Eximbank insures all political risks.

FCIA and Eximbank operate under a reinsurance and agency agreement, under which Eximbank insures the member insurance companies for certain excess commercial credit risks. The agreement is amended periodically to reflect expanding needs of the association and states the participation amounts of the insurance companies, the annual stop losses by policy, buyer, and country, and the parameters of operation.

FCIA is a member of the Berne Union, an international organization of official export credit insurers around the world. The purpose of the union is to work for the international acceptance of sound principles of export credit insurance, and the establishment and maintenance of discipline in the terms of credit for international trade. This organization has been in existence since 1934.

FCIA is also a member of the International Credit Insurance Association, an international organization of private credit insurers. This association studies questions relating to credit insurance, and initiates means whereby the members can develop their mutual relations in the interest of their insureds, and in the safeguarding of their own positions. Membership in both the Berne Union and the ICIA provides FCIA with up-to-date country and buyer information, which in turn brings improved service to its insureds.

BENEFITS OF FCIA COVERAGE

FCIA insureds have benefited from export credit insurance in a variety of forms. A manufacturer of semiconductor processing equipment was generating $1.2 million in annual sales. Due to economic conditions, the company was experiencing a difficult period. In order to sustain operations, the firm needed a working capital facility. An FCIA policy was issued to insure shipment of semiconductor processing equipment to foreign markets. The export receivables were insured against commercial and political risks and could be used as collateral for low-cost working capital. The company established a relationship with a local bank to finance 100 percent of their foreign receivables. When the domestic market declined, the firm was prepared to solicit additional business outside of the United States. Within several years, the company's sales reached $20 million, 35 percent of them overseas.

Extending adequate credit terms is also important. A computer manufacturer with a large distributor network was interested in penetrating the international market more effectively. To help their distributors along, the company provided every trade-financing benefit available. The FCIA export credit insurance program proved to be a crucial ingredient in supplying this type of support. During the firm's first year of using FCIA insurance, distributor sales grew over 200 percent. One important criterion in selling equipment overseas is financial support in the form of adequate credit terms. Assessing the financial needs of the distributor as well as the market place are essential in determining appropriate credit terms. Further, the company was able to monitor its risk from the standpoint of asset exposure—a benefit during a time of rapidly developing and unpredictable international events.

Insurance Protection

The most fundamental attribute of export credit insurance is the protection it gives a company for what is typically a risky part of its asset portfolio, foreign receivables. Such insurance, of course, is not a substitute for an exporter's good in-house credit management. However, overseas political and commercial developments can unfold, despite the exercise of normal credit judgment, and generate unacceptable losses for otherwise prudent manufacturers or financial institutions. Iran, Lebanon, Nicaragua, and Turkey are examples of political risk areas where FCIA has paid claims. War, riots, insurrection, transfer risk, and nationalization are common forms of political risk. Protracted default and outright insolvency are the two most common forms of commercial risks covered by FCIA. In all of these instances, export credit insurance fulfills a vital function. It protects the U.S. seller against overseas events beyond his control.

Financing Assets

The proceeds of an FCIA policy are frequently assigned to a commercial bank or other financial institution as security against a discounted receivable. The receivables generated from an export transaction are sold on a nonrecourse basis. The savings in corporate cost of capital are usually significant and result in an improved corporate cash flow, attractive off-balance-sheet financing, and better application of the resulting inflow of corporate funds. Each of these improvements can increase profitability. In addition to the insured's financing advantages are those extended to the foreign buyer through the insured's policy. Local credit facilities may be difficult to secure for an insured's buyer and even if obtained, they may be prohibitively expensive. Since the U.S. exporter does not have to carry the receivables while extending terms, both the insured and the overseas buyer benefit.

Marketing Tool

The advantages of knowing that financing packages can be arranged while in the field are obvious. Increased inventory and/or buyer financing can result in improved sales by both the insured and buyer. The buyer is able to extend terms to its own customers. The U.S. exporter then is able to meet foreign competition, which has offered such credit terms for years and which is quickly reaching parity with the quality of U.S. manufactured goods. The ability to extend terms becomes crucial in the effort to make an overseas sale against tough competitors from other industrialized countries. New and existing markets can be added or expanded through use of an FCIA policy.

Benefits To Commercial Banks

There are actually several ways that the commercial bank can adapt the exporter's FCIA protection to benefit its operation. FCIA-insured exporters have additional security to offer lending institutions because their export transactions are protected against both commercial and political risks. With the benefit of FCIA protection, many banks are able to develop new business while expanding present business with exporting customers and prospects. Other bank services, such as letters of credit, acceptances, collections, and wire transfers can be included in a full-service program to FCIA insured customers.

COVERAGE

FCIA insures U.S. exporters against the risk of nonpayment by foreign buyers which may result from a wide range of commercial and political causes. Commercial risks include losses resulting from a buyer's insolvency or failure to pay within six months after the due date of an insured obligation. Political risks involve losses not due to the fault of the buyer or any of its agents, from any of the following events:

Transfer risk (inconvertibility of currency).

The cancellation or nonrenewal of an export license or the imposition of restrictions on the export of products subject to license or restriction prior to shipment.

The cancellation of a previously issued and valid authority to import.

War, hostilities, civil war, rebellion, revolution, insurrection, civil commotion, or other like disturbances.

Requisition, expropriation or confiscation of, or intervention in, the business of the buyer or guarantor by a government authority.

Products Covered and Terms Extended

Credit terms acceptable to FCIA for coverage of products generally cannot exceed the terms commercially customary in international trade for the products in question. An exporter selling a product on credit terms up to 180 days qualifies for short-term coverage. At least 50 percent of the product value, exclusive of price mark-up of such product, must be added by labor or material exclusively of U.S. origin. A medium-term product, (credit terms from 181 days to five years), must normally be 100 percent of U.S. origin, but special consideration can be given, upon application, to contracts with a minor foreign content percentage.

Virtually any product is eligible for coverage, although there are some exceptions:

> Military or defense-related equipment is generally not eligible for coverage. (Exceptions require advance approval.)
>
> Used equipment and cattle/livestock require the completion of special questionnaires to be submitted with each application for coverage.

FCIA Short-Term multibuyer policies, discussed later in this chapter, typically cover transactions with terms of payment not exceeding 180 days from the date of arrival of products at the port of importation. Products such as agricultural commodities, fertilizers, insecticides, and some consumer durables may qualify for terms up to 360 days by special endorsement. The Short-Term–Medium-Term Master, also to be explained later in the chapter, differs slightly and covers transactions with repayment terms of up to five years.

FCIA's Single Buyer Policies typically cover transactions with terms of repayment running between 181 days and five years. Goods eligible for cover are generally capital or quasi-capital goods having relatively high unit value. The size of the contract is important in determining the appropriate repayment terms as follows:

Contract Price	Repayment Term
Up to —$ 50,000	Two years maximum
$ 50,001—$100,000	Three years maximum
$100,001—$200,000	Four years maximum
$200,001—and over	Five years maximum

A minimum down payment of 15 percent is required from the buyer on or before shipment. The balance of the transaction is payable in approximately equal installments, usually made monthly, quarterly, or semiannually, and must be evidenced by a promissory note.

OVERVIEW OF POLICIES

FCIA's policies are categorized in two groups: multibuyer and single buyer. The multibuyer program insures all, or a reasonable spread, of an exporter's sales under a single policy. Normally, FCIA indemnifies an exporter for 90 percent of a commercial loss and for 100 percent of a political loss. Available credit terms range from sight drafts to five years. The five policies available to exporters in the multibuyer program are: the Short-Term Deductible (SD), Short-Term-Medium-Term Master (CMR), Medium-Term Deductible (MD), Comprehensive Services (CV), and Small Business (SB). Issued as part of the policy, the declarations detail variable provisions in order to meet the specific requirements of the exporter.

The Single-Buyer Program (Medium-Term Program) insures a transaction between buyer and supplier, and differs from FCIA's Multibuyer Programs by not requiring whole turnover. In most cases, transactions are covered for 90 percent of a commercial loss and for 100 percent of a political loss. Capital or quasi-capital goods are insurable on terms of 181 days to five years and require a 15 percent cash down payment on or before shipment. A transaction endorsement, which accompanies the policy, details specific terms of cover authorized. The three separate policies available for single-buyer insurance are the Medium-Term Single Sale (MTS); Medium-Term Repetitive (MTR), and Combined Short-Term–Medium Term (MSC).

Exhibits 1 and 2 detail the eligibility requirements and parameters for FCIA's policies.

MULTIBUYER POLICIES

The Master Policy

Companies exporting U.S. goods on credit terms can both insure their foreign receivables against loss and expand their global marketing

Exhibit 1

Industry	*Policy Type*
Manufacturer	Master Policy
Consumer goods* (multibuyer)	Short-term deductible
Capital goods† (multibuyer)	Medium-term deductible
Consumer and capital goods (multibuyer)	Short-term–medium-term master
Bank	Short-Term Comprehensive Policy
Service (management consultants,	Services policy
architectural design, engineering)	
Small business/new exporters	Small business policy
Manufacturer/banks	
Capital goods sold to	
End-users (single buyer)	Medium-Term Single Sales
Dealer/distributor (single buyer)	Medium-Term Repetitive
Consumer and capital goods sold to	
Dealer/distributor (single buyer)	Short-Term–Medium-Term Combination

   * Consumer goods—products such as raw materials, parts, software, chemicals, light steel, small tools.

   † Capital goods—heavy machinery such as cranes, bulldozers, tractors aircraft.

Exhibit 2

Type of Policy	Multibuyer or Single Buyer	Policy Aggregate	Discretionary Credit Limit	Special Buyer Credit Limit	Deductible	Premium
Short-term deductible	Multibuyer	—	—	—	—	Composite
Medium-term deductible	Multibuyer	—	—	—	—	Composite
Master short-term medium-term	Multibuyer	—	—	—	—	Composite
Small business	Multibuyer	—	Case-by-case	—	n.a.	Schedule
Services	Multibuyer	—	Case-by-case	—	—	Case-by-case
Medium-term single sale	Single buyer	n.a.	n.a.	Per buyer Commitment Notice issued.	n.a.	Schedule
Medium-term repetitive	Single buyer	n.a.	n.a.	Per buyer Transaction Endorsement issued. Per buyer Transaction Endorsement issued.	n.a.	Schedule
Short-term–medium-term combination	Single buyer Multibuyer/ Single buyer	n.a.	n.a.	—	n.a.	Schedule
Political only	Single buyer	—	n.a.	—	n.a.	Case-by-case

Note: n.a. = not available.

Deductible—The policy deductible, similar to major medical or automobile insurance. It does not apply to political coverage. Political risks are normally of the unforeseen type, and losses in this area should not penalize the exporter's full scope of coverage. The deductible does apply to commercial coverage on a first dollar aggregate policy year basis.

For example, an exporter with a policy deductible of $20,000 incurs $30,000 in eligible commercial losses attributable to a certain policy year. First, the normal 10 percent retention reduces the $30,000 in eligible losses to $27,000. The $20,000 deductible is then applied, leaving a net amount of $7,000 to be paid by FCIA. Should further commercial losses be incurred during the same policy year, FCIA would be liable for 90 percent of those losses, as the deductible would have been satisfied.

Aggregate Limit—Represents FCIA's maximum liability under the policy.

DCL (Discretionary Credit Limit)—The DCL quoted is the highest amount of credit that an insured may extend to any buyer at any one time without prior FCIA approval. FCIA determines the amount of an exporter's DCL authority based on the credit level needs and expertise of the exporter. Usually, the DCL authority eliminates the majority of an exporter's buyers from direct FCIA review.

SBCL (Special Buyer Credit Limit)—Insureds needing credit limits for buyers in excess of the insured's DCL may be covered under the policy through an SBCL. The SBCL is a revolving dollar limit approved by FCIA upon the insured's submission of an application with the corresponding credit and financial information.

Premium—Composite premium rates are determined by the terms of sale being offered by the exporter, although total volume to be insured and the exporter's past history are taken into consideration.

Interest—"FCIA insures interest on short term shipments made on or after April 1, 1982, at a rate not to exceed The Chase Manhattan Bank Prime Rate in effect on the date of shipment or, if lower, the rate specified in the contract of sale. Interest on medium term transactions is insured for up to 1 percent above the U.S. Treasury Borrowing Rate for borrowings having the same maturity as the remaining repayment term of the written obligation. The remaining term is the period commencing on the due date of the installment in default and ending on the due date of the final installment.

base with the security of a Comprehensive Master Policy. In the early 1970s this deductible policy was developed to allow lower premiums, independent credit decision making by the exporter, and faster service to overseas buyers.

The Master Policy is a blanket-type policy. It is written for shipments during a one-year period and may cover all, or a reasonable spread, of an exporter's eligible sales of both short- and medium-term credits up to five years. A broad spread of risk enables FCIA to quote a low premium rate and to offer a fully comprehensive insurance package for an exporter's sales. FCIA's Master Policy can be tailored to the needs of an exporter selling U.S. products on the following conditions:

> Short-term sales only—This policy is called Short-Term Deductible (SD)—for consumer goods with repayment terms ranging from sight to 180 days after the arrival of goods. (Quasi-capital goods, initial inventory, and fertilizers are eligible for 360 days)

> Medium-term sales only—This policy is called Medium-Term Deductible (MD)—for capital goods with repayment terms ranging from 181 days to five years after the arrival of goods.

> Combination of short- and medium-term sales—This policy is called Short-Term–Medium-Term Master (CMR)—Mainly for companies with diversified product lines, or those selling through dealers and distributors.

Short-Term Comprehensive

The Short-Term Deductible Policy issued to commercial banks is very similar in concept to the SD Policy issued to non-bank insureds. The policy covers export sales transactions made to more than one buyer during a given year on terms of credit usually not exceeding 180 days. The declarations of the policy issued to an insured bank at the inception of a policy expand the general provisions outlined in the policy to meet the specific requirements of the bank, that is, the period of coverage, products, exclusions, and additions to cover. The policy will be endorsed to cover the specific business that the bank does, such as buyer credits, supplier credits and agricultural commodities.

Buyer Credits

The endorsement allowing coverage of a buyer credit transaction provides insurance for banks which have agreed to lend directly to the foreign buyer to finance the import of U.S. goods. The bank pays the supplier in cash upon presentation of documents evidencing the supplier's compliance with the terms of the contract of supply. The supplier's financial interest in the transaction then ceases, (unless a sharing of the uninsured retention has been agreed to), and the principal participants in the transaction become the bank insured and the foreign buyer. Their relationship would be specified in a loan agreement.

Supplier Credits

The endorsement allowing coverage for supplier credit transactions covers export shipments of U.S. suppliers under the policy of a commercial bank. The bank must agree to either finance, or guarantee, without recourse, the U.S. exporter's overseas portfolio. FCIA must be assured that the exporter is offering a reasonable spread of overseas export business to the insured bank for financing. In principle what is offered for coverage on that exporter should not be less than if that exporter had its own FCIA policy. All exporters must be preapproved by FCIA.

Although no bank actually exports, the bank, as named insured of the policy, is responsible for paying the premium, reporting procedures, and adhering to any other provisions established in the policy.

Agricultural Commodities Program

Upon request, an endorsement can be issued to a bank's policy for all export sales of bulk agricultural commodities sold on irrevocable letter-of-credit (ILC) terms. Such sales of most commodities qualify for 98 percent coverage of the insured loss for commercial risks, and for 100 percent for political risks.

Coverage becomes effective at the date of shipment, or on the date the U.S. bank gives a commitment, whichever is first. This commitment would include confirming the letter of credit of the issuing bank, granting the U.S. exporter an unconditional commitment to honor drawings made under the letter of credit, or assuming a direct interest by financing 100 percent of the drawings to be made under the letter of credit all without recourse to the U.S. supplier.

The uninsured commercial retention of 2 percent under the policy is retained by the bank and cannot be shared or passed back to the seller. Also, the issuing bank must be located in a country listed on the Country Limitation Schedule.

Agricultural commodities are those commodities so defined by the U.S. Department of Agriculture (e.g., grains, raw sugar, rice, cotton, leaf tobacco, soybean oil, tallow, and peanuts). All commodities must be of U.S. origin.

The maximum term of credit under the irrevocable letter can be up to 360 days from the date of importation.

Procedure For Approval Of Limits

Coverage under the Agricultural Commodities Program can be obtained as follows:

A telex containing the following information should be sent to the attention of the Underwriting Group of FCIA:

Issuing bank/country.

Amount.

Product.

Terms.

L/C number; Expiration date.

Bid order number.

Approximate utilization date.

Supplier.

If the bank cannot provide any of this information immediately, FCIA still might issue a commitment with the understanding that the missing information, when later provided, does not have any adverse bearing on the commitment.

Prequalified Foreign Banks

FCIA has prequalified over 100 foreign banks. When the amount requested for approval is within the prequalified limit set for the issuing bank, and all other specifics of the request are acceptable, FCIA will immediately send a telex outlining its commitment. Notification of the amount of premium payable for the transaction will be given at that time. This commitment is binding for a period of 30 days from the date of the telex.

Premium

Premium for agricultural commodities coverage is payable at the appropriate rate per $100 of the gross amount of all indebtedness arising from eligible shipments made under the ILC, excluding interest.

Small Business Policy

The Small Business Policy allows companies new to exporting, or which have only occasionally exported in the past, to insure their sales of U.S. products against loss and to develop an effective export sales program. FCIA requires a company to insure all, or a reasonable spread, of eligible sales under a policy. FCIA indemnifies the insured for 95 percent of an insured obligation in the event of a commercial loss (an increase over the standard 90 percent) and for 100 percent on a political loss. A further improvement in the coverage of commercial risks is the deletion of the deductible requirement for first dollar losses.

Because the Small Business Policy is a special program for small or new exporters, all companies applying for the policy must meet the following requirements:

Net worth not exceeding $2 million.

Average annual export sales during the preceding two fiscal years not exceeding $750,000.

No prior coverage under any FCIA insurance program, either through the company's own policy or through a commercial bank or merchant exporter policy.

FCIA will continue coverage on the Small Business Policy for a period of five years. The policy must then be converted to a standard multibuyer policy with commercial losses protected for 90 percent of their value, and with the inclusion of a first-loss policy deductible.

The Services Policy

A Services Policy is available to companies providing U.S. expertise and technology on credit terms. Industries benefiting from this coverage include management consultants, engineering service firms, and design consultants. The policy insures the service company against failure of its clients to make agreed-upon progress payments caused by defined commercial and political risks. Services must be performed by U.S. personnel or with equipment of U.S. origin. It can be tailored to the needs of any company performing services overseas and receiving progress payments at regular intervals ranging from payment on receipt of invoice to payment at 180 days after the invoice date. In general, FCIA requests that a company submit all of its overseas projects for consideration of coverage.

SINGLE BUYER POLICIES

The single buyer policy is a medium-term program designed to cover the export of capital goods with repayment terms ranging from 181 days to five years. Maximum terms are dictated by the contract price as described previously. The Medium-Term Single Sale (MTS), Medium-Term Repetitive (MTR), and Short-Term–Medium Term (MSC), insure an exporter's transactions with a particular buyer for 90 percent of a commercial loss and 100 percent of a political loss. A cash down payment of at least 15 percent of the contract price is required on or before shipment. The balance, or financed portion, must be evidenced by the promissory note or notes of the foreign buyer.

Promissory notes must be dated within 30 days of shipment and should specify the amount of principal and interest. The note should be drawn and executed in the English language, be made payable in U.S. dollars at a specified bank in the United States, and require equal monthly, quarterly, or semiannual installments. Sales denominated in a foreign currency may be eligible if approved by FCIA.

Both manufacturers and commercial banks can obtain policies in their own name. If a commercial bank is a policyholder, it must finance, without recourse to the exporter, 100 percent of the financed portion of the goods shipped.

Medium-Term Single Sales (MTS)

The MTS policy is designed to extend coverage for capital goods on a single transaction basis to a particular buyer or end user. Separate shipments can be made during the policy period (usually six months) but FCIA can extend this period if a delay in shipment is expected. The policy requires promissory notes to be executed within 30 days of shipment. Upon application, FCIA can consider cover on multiple shipments evidenced by a single note.

The following is an example of a MTS transaction to an end-user:

> A manufacturer has a potential sale of four trucks to an end-user. The contract price for the trucks is $50,000, to be paid over two years (semi-annual installments). FCIA reviews the proposed transaction upon receipt of an application, two current credit reports, and financial statements for at least the most current year. The criteria for determining a good risk are based on the buyer's reputation, past payment history, liquidity and debt positions in addition to the overall equity of the company. Credit and financial information differ per country and are evaluated accordingly. If acceptable, FCIA issues a commitment notice, which acts as FCIA's agreement to insure according to the parameters designated (e.g., contract price $50,000, down payment (15 percent) $12,500, financed portion $37,500, terms—four semiannual installments, coverage, products—four trucks, premium rate, and special conditions, if necessary). The commitment notice is generally good for six months to allow the insured sufficient time to obtain a firm commitment from the buyer and arrange financing. Once this is completed, the insured submits notice to FICA, with the premium due, to issue a transaction endorsement. Generally, the commitment notice and transaction endorsement contain the same information, although they may differ slightly.

Medium-Term Repetitive (MTR)

The MTR policy is designed to extend coverage for capital goods shipped to a particular buyer on an ongoing basis. The buyer is generally a dealer or distributor who will resell the goods locally. The policy contains a final shipment date or one year from the date of issue, and is renewable each year. Because the MTR involves repetitive shipments to a buyer, FCIA issues a transaction endorsement initially reflecting the maximum credit limit, product, terms, coverage, final shipment date, and special conditions for coverage. An example of an MTR policy is the sale of cranes to a dealer/distributor. The cranes are shipped throughout the course of a year. The exporter continues shipments until the credit limit is reached. At any time during the policy year, if the credit limit is paid down, additional goods can be shipped.

Short-Term–Medium-Term Combination Policy (MSC)

The MSC policy covers sales to overseas dealers and distributors on a continuing basis. The policy covers spare parts and accessories usually sold on short terms and capital goods equipment sold on either short or medium terms of credit. There is an added provision to allow capital goods sales to be converted from short-term to medium-term coverage following an initial "floor plan" period. The combination policy permits liberal financing to overseas dealers and distributors. U.S. manufacturers which previously sold on very secure terms can now improve the sales capacity of their overseas dealer network markedly. Like the MTR policy, once a credit limit has been approved by FCIA, a transaction endorsement is issued setting forth the individual terms of policy coverage.

Coverage under this policy provides a benefit to the exporter in the following ways:

Financing for normal short-term shelf items, spare parts, and capital equipment.

Inventory financing, where the exporter may ship goods under a floor plan arrangement. Initial coverage is for up to 270 days with no down payment.

Medium-term receivable financing is available following a minimum cash down payment upon resale by the dealer or at the end of the inventory period.

An example of the Combination Policy is the following: An exporter ships a tractor to a dealer/distributor to be in a showroom during a 180-day floor plan period; within 10 days after the due date of the short-term obligation the dealer has the following options:

1. Obtain payment (sold to an end-user).
2. Convert the obligation to a medium-term commitment—a 15 percent cash down payment is required. Drafts must be cancelled and promissory notes issued.

3. Extend drafts an additional 90 days to 270 days. At the 270th day, the following options apply:
    a. Obtain payment.
    b. Convert the obligation to a medium-term commitment—a minimum 15 percent cash down payment is required. Drafts must be cancelled and promissory notes issued.

Sometimes the agreed floor-plan period is 270 days. In that event the bank can, at the end of that period, either extend the drafts to 360 days, or convert the obligation to medium term. Once the drafts are extended to 360 days there is no option to convert to medium term at the end of that period. The dealer must pay the outstanding obligation in full.

POLITICAL ONLY POLICIES

All policies mentioned offer comprehensive coverage—commercial and political. Insurance is also available for multibuyer policies to cover all or a reasonable spread, of an exporter's product, against political risks only. Political only coverage is also available to insure an exporter's transactions to one buyer. FCIA will indemnify the exporter for 100 percent of a political loss as defined in the policy. In actual practice, many losses which might be considered "political" may in fact only be eligible for payment under commercial coverage. For example, transfer risk or currency inconvertibility is eligible for political coverage only if the dollar equivalent of the currency of the buyer's country was deposited on or before the due date, or within 90 days thereafter. In the event the currency is deposited on the 91st day, political coverage is no longer in effect. Under the political only policy the exporter would not be reimbursed. If the exporter had a comprehensive policy, the loss would qualify under the commercial credit risk coverage.

SPECIAL COVERAGES

In addition to the basic policy provisions, FCIA offers special coverages to insure against other risks. The following is a brief summary of these coverages which are added by endorsement to the policy.

Nonacceptance

FCIA may issue nonacceptance cover under both short-term and medium-term comprehensive insurance policies. Coverage is in effect for a loss to the insured from failure or refusal of the buyer to accept the products, after shipment has been made, when such is not due to the fault of the insured or the insured's failure to comply with the terms of the contract of sale.

For example: An insured ships $80,000 worth of spare parts to a distributor under his Short-Term Deductible Policy. The goods are not accepted by the foreign buyer for some unknown reason, not due to the fault of the insured, and they cannot be resold. The exporter then files a claim under his policy including a written order or other document evidencing a contract to purchase the products. Assuming the insured's deductible is fulfilled, FCIA indemnifies the insured for a maximum of 60 percent of the financed portion for the products which have not been accepted less any amount received from resale of the products. In this example, the insured is reimbursed $48,000.

Nonacceptance coverage is not offered under political only policies, and usually is not provided when used products are to be shipped.

Preshipment Coverage

Preshipment, or contracts, coverage insures against specified risks from the date of execution of the sales contract until the date of shipment (maximum time period of 18 months). The additional insurance protects an exporter against both the political risks incurred in accepting an order for an export shipment and against the commercial risk of the buyer going insolvent prior to shipment. Preshipment coverage is designed for exports which involve specially or custom fabricated goods which are not readily resalable on the open market should the order be cancelled.

Preshipment coverage protects the exporter against political risks such as cancellation of an import or export license, war, revolution, expropriation, or similar instances which would result in the exporter's inability to ship to his buyer. Additionally, coverage extends throughout the preshipment period against loss due to the insolvency of the buyer. Preshipment does not apply to transfer risks (inconvertibility of currency), a buyer's arbitrary cancellation of a sales contract, or the buyer's nonacceptance of the goods.

Preshipment coverage is available on a selected basis or on all transactions under a multibuyer policy.

Consignment Coverage

FCIA may approve applications for consignment coverage and for sales out of consignment. The insured is indemnified for 100 percent of the loss incurred due to specified political risks while the products are in consignment stock. Shipment of an eligible consignment begins when the products in question are shipped to the country in which the products are to be held in consignment stock on the order of the insured or its agent. Coverage begins on the date of shipment and terminates no later than 180 days thereafter. The insurance can be renewed for an additional 180-day period, subject to payment of additional premium.

Trade experience plays an important role in determining a customer's moral and financial position. FCIA realizes the significance of this experience, as evidenced by the "uplift provision."

The uplift provision can be added to multibuyer deductible policies upon approval from FCIA. The special endorsement allows the insured to increase the Discretionary Credit Limit available under the policy for a buyer who has proved to be a good credit risk based on his own trading experience. If the insured has had satisfactory trading experience with a buyer who has paid promptly, within 60 days on unsecured transactions, or within 20 days after arrival on secured transactions, he may increase the outstanding credit limit for that buyer in increments of 25 percent up to a maximum of $100,000 on unsecured terms, and $200,000 on secured terms.

To illustrate, assume the insured's policy has a $50,000 discretionary credit limit and the buyer has repaid a $48,000 transaction promptly. He can then increase the authorized limit by 25 percent to $64,000 for that buyer. As long as the buyer continues to pay promptly, the limit may be increased in 25 percent increments over the highest amount outstanding at any time during the previous two years.

Assignments

A bank may also use an exporter's FCIA policy by taking an assignment of the policy proceeds. The bank can finance its clients who export by using the assigned right to the policy proceeds as collateral. The exporter must, of course, retain a financial interest in the transaction in order to qualify for FCIA insurance. Whether a bank offers financing on a total recourse or nonrecourse basis, the insured exporter remains at risk for the uninsured percentage of the sale; or if the buyer purchases without recourse the uninsured portion, the insured exporter must retain the risk of the deductible.

An assignment of the proceeds of an FCIA policy will not give the bank any greater rights than those held by the policyholder. Also, the insured's failure to comply with the terms of the policy could prejudice the right to recovery under a policy whether the insured or an assignee is to be the beneficiary. Therefore, an assignee bank should typically have a close working relationship with its exporting customer, including an assurance that all parties are familiar with FCIA programs and procedures. An assignment may encompass a single transaction, transactions with selected buyers, transactions with buyers in specified countries, or all transactions under the policy.

CLAIMS

When an overdue account is eligible for claim filing, a Proof of Loss form should be completed and submitted to the claims department for investigation. The Proof of Loss form calls for the details of the transaction, the apparent reason for nonpayment by the buyer, and requires copies of all documentation evidencing the transaction.

Some of the documentation required for claims investigation includes bills of lading, invoices, purchase orders, contracts of sale, debt instruments in force, proof of acceptance by the buyer, evidence of collection efforts, and prior ledger experience.

Default claims are eligible for payment six months after the due date of the obligation. All other claims are eligible on the maturity date of the obligation, unless a waiting period is imposed by the applicable policy or the Country Limitation schedule. The deadline for submitting a claim is generally eight months from the due date, but it can be longer if a waiting period for filing is imposed.

SUMMARY

FCIA, in conjunction with the Export-Import Bank of the United States, offers a wide variety of policies and services to assist its customers in promoting exports. The coverage provides comprehensive insurance for both short- and medium-term transactions against nonpayment by foreign buyers for commercial and political risks. FCIA insurance is a highly useful tool enabling U.S. exporters to extend terms, protect themselves against unforeseen global conditions while meeting intense competition, and arrange advantageous financing.

Exporters in all industries have taken advantage of FCIA's policies, whether it be to increase sales, protect assets, or improve cash flow. Based on a company's needs, a multibuyer or single buyer policy can be designed. Many companies have adopted an active program toward increased export sales in order to compete effectively in the overseas marketplace, with FCIA insurance providing the ways and means to take advantage of the export market while generating greater productivity and profit.

28

Private Export Funding Corporation

FRANK W. NEE
Senior Executive Vice President
Private Export Funding Corporation

INTRODUCTION AND SUMMARY

Private Export Funding Corporation (PEFCO) was established for the purpose of mobilizing nonbank funds in the bond and money markets for the financing of U.S. exports. All of its loans carry the unconditional guarantee of the Export-Import Bank of the United States (Eximbank) as to principal and interest. The corporation was designed to be a supplemental lender in the sense that it makes loans only when funds are not available from traditional private-sector sources on normal commercial terms and at competitive rates of interest. It provides a reliable source of funds during periods when other facilities are overburdened and when the traditional export lenders seek participants for loans in which the amounts and terms exceed their capabilities.

To date PEFCO's principal value to banks and the export community has been its readiness to make loans at fixed rates of interest during periods of tight money and to make loans with long commitment periods and with final maturities beyond the normal range acceptable to commercial banks. These terms are generally not available to exporters from other lenders in the private sector. PEFCO's activities have also been useful to the U.S. government. Where borrowers have been willing to accept U.S. government-supported financing which included both Eximbank direct loans and guarantees, PEFCO's guaranteed loans can be said to have "stretched" the impact of Eximbank's limited direct-lending capacity. Guarantee and commitment fees paid by PEFCO and its borrowers have created a source of revenue for Eximbank and, therefore, the U.S. Treasury. By raising funds in the private sector, PEFCO's loans are not a charge against the cash budget of the federal government as direct government loans are. Another beneficial effect of PEFCO's loans is that they have encouraged some unguaranteed export lending on the part of commercial banks which would not have materialized without the financing by Eximbank and PEFCO of part of the project.

ORIGIN AND RELATIONSHIP WITH EXIMBANK

PEFCO was established in 1970 at the initiative of the Bankers' Association for Foreign Trade. Its shareowners today consist of 54 commercial banks, seven industrial companies, and one investment banking firm. It was created with the active support of the Eximbank and the U.S. Treasury Department. This support was essential at the corporation's inception because of the high risk inherent in making fixed-rate loans with long repayment and disbursement periods. A portion of this support has been waived, and PEFCO's ultimate goal is to receive no special assistance from the public sector. In return for its support, Eximbank has earned fees aggregating $43 million since 1971. Eximbank exercises a broad measure of supervision over PEFCO's major financial management decisions. Eximbank's approval is required for individual loan commitments and for the terms and timing of PEFCO's long-term debt issues. The investment of PEFCO's surplus funds is limited to instruments approved by Eximbank, and the bank sends representatives to meetings of PEFCO's Board of Directors and Advisory Board.

LENDING OPERATIONS

General Characteristics

PEFCO's loans, the bulk of which have been to industrialized and developing countries such as Brazil, Republic of China (Taiwan), France, Italy, Korea, Mexico, Spain, and the United Kingdom, have financed a wide variety of capital goods especially power plants, aircraft, mining and petroleum projects, industrial plants, communications facilities, and railroad equipment. During the 10 years of operations since 1971, PEFCO's loan commitments have aggregated about $3.6 billion, mostly to developing countries.

PEFCO is generally part of a lending group which includes one or more commercial banks as well as Eximbank as a guarantor and usually co-lender. The corporation's share of individual loans has ranged from a modest to a substantial percentage of the total financed portion of the project. PEFCO usually takes the middle maturities between those assumed by the commercial banks and Eximbank. Final maturities have ranged from approximately 5–22 years from date of acceptance and have averaged 7.5 years. PEFCO will not make loans of less than $1 million, but there is no upper limit with respect to the size of its participations. In the past, individual loan commitments have ranged from approximately $1 million to $224 million with the average loan amounting to about $23 million.

PEFCO's Fixed Interest Rate

The fixed interest rate provided at the time PEFCO makes a firm loan offer is based on the current estimated cost of funds at the time the rate is established plus a spread for profit and risk. All fixed rates are established at a differential over yields of U.S. Treasury securities with maturities similar to the average maturity of the loan being financed.

Deferred Pricing

Under an alternate type of offer, provision is made for the fixed interest rate to be established at a future time. Whenever a borrower accepts a PEFCO offer on this basis, PEFCO will commit to establish a fixed interest rate (using the same formula applicable to new loans) on a "fixing date" selected by the borrower. Fixing dates are generally the 15th day of January, April, July, or October of each year subsequent to acceptance of PEFCO's offer and prior to the first disbursement of PEFCO's funds. Generally the borrower must establish the fixed rate for the entire PEFCO loan at one time. The first disbursement by PEFCO can be delayed until the end of the disbursement period (as specified in the loan agreement) if the borrower arranges for the temporary financing of shipments with his own funds or those borrowed from others. This arrangement helps to lengthen the time during which a fixing date can be selected, and it thereby gives the borrower maximum flexibility to obtain an attractive interest rate on his loan.

Commitment Fee

PEFCO charges a commitment fee which accrues from the date the PEFCO offer is accepted by the borrower. This fee continues to accrue on the committed but undisbursed amount of the PEFCO loan commitment until disbursement of the funds or the cancellation or expiry of the commitment. The commitment fee is ½ percent per annum for PEFCO commitments which carry an established fixed interest rate. It is ¼ percent per annum during the period prior to establishing the fixed interest rate under the deferred pricing alternative.

When and How to Approach PEFCO for an Offer

A foreign borrower will usually find it practicable to approach PEFCO through a commercial bank or the U.S. exporter. The initial contact generally occurs when the borrower, his bank, the exporter, and Eximbank have agreed on the various components of a proposed financing and when there is at least an informal indication of the amount which Eximbank is willing to guarantee. With a minimum of information in hand (amount of the loan, disbursement, and repayment schedule) PEFCO can give an informal indication of its fixed lending rate. Thereafter, if a firm commitment is requested, additional information about the loan must be provided, including the status of Eximbank's commitment. If requested PEFCO can then make a firm offer to the borrower through and in cooperation with the U.S. exporter or his commercial bank. This offer is subject only to Eximbank's approval of PEFCO's loan participation and is generally valid for acceptance by the borrower within a period of up to 45 days. If the borrower does not accept the initial offer, one or more subsequent offers may be obtained, if requested. These subsequent offers are similar to PEFCO's initial offer except that they are valid for a maximum of only up to 30 days and that the fixed interest rate is recomputed each time a new offer is made.

Loan Agreements and Other Documents

After an offer has been accepted by the borrower, PEFCO becomes a party to the final negotiations on the form of the loan agreement and other required documentation. PEFCO is a party to the same loan agreement as Eximbank. If Eximbank is not a lender, PEFCO may be a party to the commercial bank's agreement. No special loan covenants are required by PEFCO since it relies on Eximbank's guarantee.

Disbursement Procedures

When all conditions precedent to the first utilization of a loan have been fulfilled, PEFCO will respond to requests for disbursement. Under the terms of most loan agreements, the borrower sends the documents relating to a specific disbursement to either the co-lending commercial bank or to Eximbank, as appropriate, for review and approval. Upon approval, the examining party notifies PEFCO of the amount and the date on which a disbursement is to be made. On that date, PEFCO makes payment in immediately available funds.

Disbursements may take the form of funds paid to the account of the borrower to reimburse him for payments previously made to U.S.

suppliers for the equipment, or, at the request of the borrower, PEFCO will disburse funds directly to the supplier. An alternate procedure is for U.S. suppliers to draw against letters of credit issued or confirmed by preauthorized agent banks in their favor. Under this procedure PEFCO normally issues an undertaking to reimburse the agent bank for PEFCO's pro rata share of the payments made under the letters of credit.

PEFCO'S LOAN PURCHASE PROGRAM (LPP)

In addition to its regular loan program PEFCO will purchase without recourse from banks or other acceptable institutions, outstanding debt obligations of foreign importers, or participations therein, which have been guaranteed by Eximbank. The purpose of this program is to establish a secondary market in which lenders can sell existing export loans in order to obtain liquidity for making new ones. The essential details and procedures of the LPP are as follows:

Debt obligations eligible for purchase by PEFCO are those evidencing the indebtedness of foreign obligors. They must be guaranteed by Eximbank. At present this means that PEFCO will purchase obligations partially guaranteed by Eximbank under its Commercial Bank Guarantee Program (supplier credits), or fully guaranteed under its Financial Guarantee Program. With respect to the former, PEFCO will purchase a participation for the amount of the fully guaranteed portion only. With respect to the latter, PEFCO will purchase the obligations themselves or a participation therein. Only the principal amount of the obligations is included in the purchase. There are no maximum limits for the size of the purchases or the maturities of the obligations. However, purchases are limited to obligations or packages thereof totalling not less than $1 million of principal amount, and to maturities not earlier than one year from date of purchase by PEFCO.

PEFCO will purchase obligations which bear interest at either fixed or floating rates. It will, however, offer to purchase these obligations only at a fixed rate of interest based on market rates at the time of purchase and calculated by using the same rate determination procedure as PEFCO applies to its normal lending operations. The price at which PEFCO will purchase the obligations is the present value of PEFCO's participation on the day of purchase computed by discounting the participation to yield PEFCO the desired rate of interest.

PEFCO will make no prior commitments to buy obligations under the LPP. Its decision about whether to conclude a purchase will be entirely at its discretion, and each purchase is subject to prior approval by Eximbank. PEFCO will not resell any loans purchased but will hold them to maturity. It will generally purchase loans from those institutions which provided the original export financing. The sellers of the obligations will generally continue to service them for PEFCO.

HOW PEFCO FUNDS ITSELF

PEFCO has funded itself principally by selling secured debt obligations with maturities from 5 to 12 years in the public financial markets through underwriters and securities dealers. A total of $1.25 billion of these securities which carry the highest bond ratings from Standard & Poor's and Moody's have been placed to date principally with institutional investors and DISCs (Domestic International Sales Corporations). The principal of these notes is collateralized by assignment to a trustee of the corporation's guaranteed export loans. The payment of interest carries a direct guarantee of Eximbank. The collateral trust includes at all times scheduled maturities sufficient to ensure that before the maturity of each note issue the trustee will have cash from maturing collateral sufficient to pay the principal amount of the debt. Many of the purchasers of these secured obligations are not directly involved in nor conversant with export financing. By creating a debt instrument with which these investors are comfortable, PEFCO has made additional resources available for the financing of U.S. exports.

PEFCO also sells unsecured notes through private placements with maturities of up to five years. It issues commercial paper with maturities of from 60 to 270 days. On average, $200 million to $300 million of this commercial paper is outstanding. It carries the highest ratings from Standard & Poor's and Moody's and can be obtained direct from the corporation or through commercial banks or other dealers in money market instruments.

DISCs AND PEFCO'S DEBT OBLIGATIONS

Since PEFCO's debt obligations may constitute "qualified export assets" under existing tax legislation for Domestic International Sales Corporations (DISCs), they may be an appropriate investment for some of the funds of these corporations. In particular, DISCs have been buyers of PEFCO's commercial paper, and they also hold the private placement notes and a portion of PEFCO's secured notes. PEFCO's ability to borrow from DISCs has broadened the market for its debt and has favorably affected the corporation's cost of money. PEFCO's lower cost of money, in turn, has helped to keep the interest rates on PEFCO's export loans as low as possible.

Exhibit 1

PRIVATE EXPORT FUNDING CORPORATION
Statement of Financial Condition
as of December 31, 1981 ($000)

Assets

Cash	$ 4,464
Short-term investments	961,564
Interest and fees receivable	54,871
Export loans guaranteed by Eximbank	1,549,410
Other assets (including $5,430,000 of unamortized debt issue costs; $5,185,000 in 1980)	6,180
Total assets	$2,576,489

Liabilities and Shareowners' Equity

Liabilities

Short-term notes	$ 881,753
Interest payable	41,956
Accounts payable and accrued expenses	358
Dividend payable	1,280
Income taxes payable	9,242
Payable to Eximbank	54,138
Medium-term notes	262,550
Long-term secured notes (principal amount less unamortized discount of $640,000; $815,000 in 1980)	1,249,360
	2,500,637

Undisbursed export loan commitments ($1,492,599,000; $1,824,990,000 in 1980)

Shareowners' equity

Common stock—no par value; authorized 40,000 shares, issued and outstanding 14,221 shares	14,189
Retained earnings	61,663
Total shareowners' equity	75,852
Total liabilities and shareowners' equity	$2,576,489

Exhibit 2

PRIVATE EXPORT FUNDING CORPORATION
Statement of Income and Retained Earnings
Calendar Year 1981 ($000)

Financing revenue

Interest	$202,875
Commitment fees	5,898
	208,773

Financing expense

Interest	174,278
Commitment and other fees	1,103
	175,381

Net financing income	33,392
General and administrative expenses	1,985
Income before income taxes	31,407
Provision for income taxes	14,464
Net Income	16,943
Dividend declared on common stock ($90 per share)	1,280
Retained earnings beginning of year	46,000
Retained earnings end of year	$ 61,663

Net income per share	$1,191.41

Statement of Changes in Financial Position

Funds were provided by

Net income	$ 16,943

Charges to income not requiring cash outlay

Amortization and depreciation	1,607
Total funds from operations	18,550

Net changes in

Short-term debt	384,159
Medium-term debt	17,800
Long-term debt	60,175
Payable to Eximbank	54,138
Other liabilities	12,609
Total funds provided	547,431

Funds were used for

Net changes in

Export loans guaranteed by Eximbank	242,338
Interest and fees receivable	15,377
Dividend paid	1,280
Other items	1,791
Total funds used	260,786
Increase in cash and short-term investments	286,645
Cash and short-term investments beginning of year	679,383
Cash and short-term investments end of year	$966,028

29
Overseas Private Investment Corporation

JAMES L. KAMMERT
Executive Vice President
Equibank

PURPOSE AND BACKGROUND

Overseas Private Investment Corporation (OPIC), a self-supporting agency of the U.S. government, was created in 1969 by amendment of the Foreign Assistance Act of 1961 and began operations in 1971.[1] However, the main activities in which OPIC engages generally have been carried out in some form by various U.S. government entities or programs since the Marshall Plan in 1948. OPIC's basic purpose is to encourage private U.S. investment in friendly foreign nations.

More specifically, the Foreign Assistance Act of 1969 states that OPIC's purpose is "to mobilize and facilitate the participation of United States private capital and skills in the economic and social development of less developed friendly countries and areas, thereby complementing the development assistance objectives of the United States."[2] To carry

The author wishes to thank OPIC staff members, Robert L. Jordan, Director, Public Relations, Charles F. Lipman, Assistant General Counsel for Finance, and David M. Fields, Assistant Treasurer, for their suggestions and support in writing this chapter. However, all contents, including any errors, are solely the responsibility of the author.

[1] Subsequent to preparation of this chapter for publication, the President of the United States on October 16, 1981, signed into law the Overseas Private Investment Corporation Amendments Act of 1981 (herewith cited as 1981 OPIC Act) further amending certain sections of the Foreign Assistance Act of 1961, which along with various intervening amendments forms the basis for OPIC's authority. Accordingly, several significant provisions of this latest amendment are mentioned in footnotes to this chapter, based upon a Memorandum from Craig A. Nalen, President of OPIC, Passage of Overseas Private Investment Corporation Amendments Act of 1981 (October 20, 1981) (hereinafter cited as Nalen). In addition to various changes in OPIC's authority, the 1981 OPIC Act extends the existence of OPIC for another four years.

[2] Foreign Assistance Act of 1969, Pub. L. No. 91–175, sec. 105, sec. 231, 83 Stat. 809 (codified at 22 U.S.C. sec. 2191 (1976)). For a detailed treatment of the legislative

out its purpose OPIC engages in two main activities. First, it insures eligible U.S. investors in overseas projects against certain defined risks, basically of a political nature, and second, it provides direct financing or loan guaranties to selected foreign companies or ventures.

The insurance program, which is now OPIC's largest and most important function, dates back to the Marshall Plan. Immediately after the Second World War, U.S. foreign development assistance policy was directed mainly toward rehabilitation of Western European countries. During the 1950s after the recovery of Europe and Japan, however, emphasis on U.S. policy for encouraging foreign investment through government development assistance programs shifted to developing nations. By the late 1950s the U.S. government's foreign investment insurance program had been redirected to focus on friendly, developing countries consistent with the changed direction in overall U.S. foreign assistance policy. By 1961 the insurance program had been extended in scope to cover losses due to expropriation and war, revolution and insurrection in addition to losses from currency inconvertibility, which was the original insurance coverage offered by U.S. government programs preceding OPIC.[3]

Loss from currency inconvertibility under an OPIC insurance policy arises when the foreign investor in a host country has received in local currency sums representing dividends, equity shares, interest or loan repayments, but is unable to exchange the local currency for a currency which can be used outside the host country. Inconvertibility might result, for example, from foreign exchange shortages by a host country's central bank caused when foreign currency payments for imports and government debt service exceed foreign currency proceeds from exports and new borrowings or other receipts. Due to the complexities of analyzing and coping with the causes and solutions for such events, which are closely related to political and economic policies in each country, most private insurers generally have tended to avoid underwriting in this area and leave the field to government programs. However, during the last few years some private insurers and insurance brokers have become more active in providing increasing types of political insurance coverages.

During the last 20 years in addition to insurance, various loan, guaranty, and other incentive programs, which are now administered by OPIC, have been authorized by the U.S. Congress. After dealing with the insurance and finance programs, other activities will be discussed

---

authority and history of OPIC and its predecessor organizations and programs see Charles F. Lipman, "Overseas Private Investment Corporation: Current Authority and Programs," *North Carolina Journal of International Law & Commercial Regulation* 5, no. 3 (Summer 1980), hereinafter cited as Lipman.

[3] Lipman, pp. 337–39.

near the end of this chapter, since they are newer and more related to OPIC's future role in development finance.

While all of OPIC's activities revolve around the theme of encouraging U.S. private investment, the benefits of OPIC programs do not flow exclusively to U.S. private investors. Host country equity investors, project sponsors, suppliers, customers, and citizens obviously benefit from OPIC supported projects, and third-country investors and lenders from around the world, among others, receive important advantages, as do exporters, labor, and suppliers of numerous specialized services in the U.S. For this reason not only U.S. direct investors but many others, including international bankers, have occasion to work with OPIC to assist their customers and thus need to understand the programs and requirements for using OPIC services.

Various units of this chapter describe OPIC's operations, financial resources, organization, and management policies followed by sections which examine OPIC's insurance, loan, guaranty, and other programs. Finally, the chapter discusses the future role of OPIC and explains how to contact OPIC personnel for further information.

OPERATIONS AND RESOURCES

OPIC now operates in approximately 90 developing nations around the world.[4] Together these countries constitute the fastest growing market for U.S. exports. This market already purchases more U.S. exports than the European and communist nations combined. Increasingly, developing countries also are becoming vital sources for energy supplies, mineral ores, and other raw materials upon which the U.S. economy depends.

In order to extend its programs to a particular country OPIC must be permitted to operate in the country by the Foreign Assistance Act, which created OPIC, or amendments to this Act, and for OPIC insurance and guaranty operations the host country and the United States must have entered into a treaty dealing with such OPIC operations. The Foreign Assistance Act permits OPIC operations in various developing countries. However, in the case of the People's Republic of China, it was necessary to amend the Act in 1980 to include China, as well as enter into a treaty.[5]

Countries where OPIC operates, obviously, must permit private foreign investment in some form. In most nations with domestic legal, and economic systems which allow for establishment of privately owned, limited liability entities, no technical problems are presented

---

[4] Overseas Private Investment Corporation, *Overseas Private Investment Corporation Country and Area List* (FCIA, Washington, D.C.: August 1980).

[5] Overseas Private Investment Corporation, "U.S. and China Sign OPIC Pact," *OPIC TOPICS* 9, no. 3 (September-October 1980), p. 1.

in accommodating international investment. However, in the People's Republic of China, Romania, and Yugoslavia it has been necessary to await enactment in these nations of laws authorizing joint ventures or similar contractual relationships with foreign investors.

Since its start-up in 1971 OPIC has written more than $10 billion in political risk insurance, provided more than $265 million in financing commitments, and OPIC and its predecessors have paid, guaranteed, or provided indemnities for more than $373 million to settle 111 insurance claims. During the period up to September 30, 1980, only 18 insurance claims were denied, and only five were contested.[6]

Total assets of OPIC were $668 million at the end of the 1980 fiscal year (September 30, 1980), and net income has exceeded $50 million in each of the past three years reaching a record $65.8 million for fiscal year 1980. OPIC's capital and reserves amounted to $649 million out of a total of liabilities, capital, and reserves of $668 million. Of this $649 million, $452 million represented an insurance reserve and $123 million a loan guaranty reserve. At fiscal year-end 1979 these reserve amounts were $405 million (insurance) and $113 million (loan guaranty), respectively. At the close of fiscal year 1980, OPIC had $23 million in retained earnings to be allocated by its Board of Directors.[7]

OPIC's issuance of investment insurance is limited by the Foreign Assistance Act which created OPIC, amendments to the Act, and by various prior authorizations (related to predecessor programs) to a total of $9.7 billion. Of this amount $4.3 billion is uncommitted, and $5.4 billion is outstanding. It is important to note, however, that OPIC as did its predecessors, usually insures the same investment against three different risks (inconvertibility of currency, expropriation, and war, revolution, or insurrection, often abbreviated as inconvertibility, expropriation, and war).[8]

Under some predecessor contracts investors theoretically could make successive claims under more than one coverage for the same investment, although it is improbable that multiple payments would be made. Also, the outstanding insurance amount reflects amounts for which OPIC is not at risk currently but is obligated to cover upon future request by investors to include increases in retained earnings and accrued interest. For these reasons OPIC believes that $3.1 billion represents a more accurate representation of its maximum potential

---

[6] Overseas Private Investment Corporation, *1980 Annual Report* (hereafter cited as *1980 Annual Report*), (Washington, D.C., 1980), p. 45.

[7] *1980 Annual Report*, pp. 60–61. The 1981 OPIC Act, however, requires that 25 percent of net income from each preceding year be paid to the U.S. Treasury (after making suitable provisions for transfers to reserves and capital) until the approximately $106 million appropriated to OPIC prior to January 1, 1975 is repaid (Nalen, point 6).

[8] *1980 Report*, Note 5, p. 65.

liability as of September 30, 1980. Thus, the $452 million reserve at year-end 1980 should be compared to this number of $3.1 billion.[9]

The Foreign Assistance Act further requires that at the time OPIC commits to issue any loan guaranty the guaranty reserve must be equal to at least 25 percent of guaranties then issued, outstanding, or committed. At September 30, 1980 the $123 million guaranty reserve exceeded the required minimum by $49 million. Total legislative authorization at September 30, 1980 amounted to $765 million with $465 million uncommitted. Thus, $299 million was outstanding of which $103 million was then currently at risk.[10]

In considering the size of OPIC's reserves in relation to outstandings it is important to note that OPIC insurance coverage and guaranties constitute obligations of the United States because the full faith and credit of the United States of America is pledged for the full payment and performance of these obligations. The Foreign Assistance Act provides that both the insurance reserve and the guaranty reserve may be replenished or increased either by transfers from retained earnings or from new appropriations by the U.S. Congress. At September 30, 1980 retained earnings available for transfer were $23 million.

ORGANIZATION AND POLICIES

U.S. foreign aid policies and programs have undergone numerous changes, and the size and scope of U.S. aid programs have changed tremendously since the late 1940s. Beginning with an unprecedented effort to help restore the war-torn but once highly developed economies, U.S. policy rapidly changed to assisting less developed nations anywhere on the globe. This assistance now involves creating and encouraging the entire national economic development process in nations which previously have had various degrees of effort underway in this regard. Helping these developing nations, many of which have little or no experience with the development process, is vastly different from restoring once modern, developed nations.

Accordingly, over these last three decades various U.S. government institutions and organizational units emerged and evolved to carry out extensive programs in the developing nations. OPIC's role for the last 10 years has been largely the result of a trend to concentrate programs to encourage private investment in one specialized agency. However, many other activities of U.S. bilateral aid programs remain under the aegis of the Agency for International Development (AID) and other government units, including the Agriculture, Commerce, Defense, and Treasury Departments.

Furthermore, certain aspects of various U.S. aid programs are inex-

---

[9] Ibid.

[10] Ibid., Note 6, p. 65.

tricably linked with important domestic political considerations. Inevitably, some overlap, and even conflict is bound to result from such far-reaching activities which are subject to extensive public examination in the context of the U.S. political process. Understandably, various criticisms have been voiced along with suggestions for improving the effectiveness of the entire U.S. foreign aid effort.

During the 1980s the U.S. will be spending less for bilateral aid programs due to other spending priorities, such as defense, and efforts to cut back total government spending in general as a result of current U.S. domestic economic difficulties. To take up the slack created by the decline in government-to-government assistance programs, greater emphasis will be placed on the management of more private investment.

In addition to the Administrator of the International Development Cooperation Agency (now the administrator of AID) who serves as the chairman of OPIC's board of directors, other members of OPIC's 13-member board include the U.S. trade representative (as vice chairman of the OPIC Board), OPIC's president (a full time OPIC employee), under assistant secretaries representing the Departments of Commerce, State, and Treasury and seven private directors. Government directors are appointed by the president of the United States and thus change with their respective positions within the government. The private directors are nominated by the U.S. president and confirmed by the U.S. Senate to represent business, labor, and cooperative groups, and variously have included business executives, labor leaders, heads of cooperative organizations, accountants, and attorneys among others. Until 1980 the board consisted of only 11 members, but in accordance with the President's Reorganization Plan Number Three of 1979 two additional members, including the U.S. Trade Representative as vice chairman and one new director from the private sector, were added.[11]

As of September 1981 the major operating units of OPIC continue to be the Insurance and Finance Departments. The Finance Department headed by a vice president has about 15 professionals. The Insurance Department also headed by a vice president has a division for minerals and energy activities and two regional divisions. The first regional division is responsible for insurance activities in Latin America and Asia and the second unit covers Africa and the Middle East and European countries such as Portugal, Yugoslavia, and Romania, where OPIC conducts insurance programs. OPIC also has a Marketing Department and an Office of Operations, an Office of Development and an

---

[11] Overseas Private Investment Corporation, *1979 Annual Report* (hereinafter cited as *1979 Annual Report*), p. 2. In addition by the 1981 OPIC Act the OPIC Board of Directors was expanded by two more members (to a total of 15), one representing the Department of Labor and the other experienced in small business (Nalen, point 8.).

Office of Personnel and Administration, all headed by vice presidents. Additional staff support is provided by the Office of the General Counsel, headed by the vice president and general counsel, and the Office of the Treasurer, headed by the treasurer. Total OPIC staff numbers about 125, and no offices are maintained outside its headquarters in Washington, D.C. However, OPIC does have access to other U.S. government departments and agencies including U.S. embassies, and OPIC staff travels outside the United States as necessary to accomplish its tasks.[12]

In evaluating OPIC's overall effectiveness in helping foreign nations and its usefulness, particularly to international bankers and their U.S. investor customers, OPIC's general policies must be kept in mind. First, OPIC requires mutual advantages to both the host nation and U.S. participants. Projects involving OPIC services must contribute to the economic development of the less developed host nations with nonexclusive preference for projects in countries with lower per capita incomes.

Second, beyond its humanitarian aspects, or benefits to the host country, economic development projects involving OPIC assistance must not only help individual U.S. private investors but also further U.S. policies and not conflict with or harm various U.S. interests. For example, OPIC is interested in projects which find and develop new sources of raw materials to supply imports vital to the U.S. and projects which improve host nations food systems in order to increase U.S. agricultural exports. In recent years increased emphasis has been placed on mineral and energy projects. At the same time OPIC rejects projects which will hurt the U.S. economy by shifting U.S. industrial plants overseas or causing job loss domestically. Thus, applications have been declined for manufacturing textiles and electronics products where OPIC determined that U.S. markets and domestic companies would suffer, U.S. exports would be displaced, or U.S. jobs would be lost.

Third, OPIC policies have been recast to provide increased support for smaller U.S. investors, namely these smaller than the Fortune 1000 in size.[13]

---

[12] Overseas Private Investment Corporation, *Organizational Directory*, September 1981.

[13] Overseas Private Investment Corporation, *Private Investment: Helping People to Help Themselves* (Washington, D.C., December 1979) (hereinafter cited as *Private Investment*), pp. 5–6. The 1981 OPIC Act contains provisions which enjoin OPIC from supporting investments subject to performance requirements which would reduce substantially the positive trade benefits likely to accrue to the United States from the investment. Local procurement requirements might be an example of such a restriction. Also the 1981 OPIC Act contains a mandate for OPIC to support projects having positive trade benefits for the United States (Nalen, points 4 and 7).

BASIC INSURANCE DEFINITIONS

This and the next section deal with the definitions and coverages for the basic insurance program, which applies mainly to manufacturing and service projects. A subsequent section deals with fees for the basic and special programs followed by a section on special insurance coverages for contractors and mineral and energy projects, especially for oil and gas. These special programs are based upon modifications of the basic program, which preceded them.

Before examining insurable events for the three coverages (inconvertibility, expropriation and war, and revolution and insurrection) and the costs of coverage, it is necessary to understand OPIC's requirements for eligible investors, less developed countries, new investments, the form of insured investment, co-insurance, and the nature of OPIC insurance coverage. OPIC's tests must be met with regard to these factors in order for insurance to be issued.

Eligible Investors. The law under which OPIC operates specifies that insurance be issued only to "eligible investors." Since there is no requirement that the project in which the insured investment is made be a project owned or even controlled by U.S. investors, OPIC may insure an investment by an eligible investor in a project controlled by foreign interests. However, only the eligible investor's investment is insured, not the entire project.

To be an eligible investor it is necessary to pass one of three tests. Thus, eligible investors may be either (1) U.S. citizens, or (2) corporations, partnerships, or other associations created under the laws of the United States or of any state or territory of the United States, which are substantially beneficially owned by U.S. citizens, or finally, (3) foreign businesses at least 95 percent owned by investors eligible under the first two tests.

OPIC deems a corporation organized under U.S. law or the laws of any U.S. state or territory to be substantially beneficially owned by U.S. citizens if more than 50 percent of each class of issued and outstanding stock is owned by U.S. citizens either directly or beneficially. For making this determination in cases where shares of corporations with widely dispersed public ownership are held in names of trustees or nominees, including stock brokerage firms with U.S. addresses, such shares will be deemed to be owned by U.S. citizens unless the investor has knowledge to the contrary. OPIC also allows the beneficial ownership of U.S. corporations to be determined by tracing back through any foreign corporate ownership of the shares to the ultimate beneficial owners.[14]

---

[14] Lipman, p. 343.

Less Developed Countries. OPIC may insure investments only in "less developed friendly countries and areas" where agreements exist between the host country and the United States for operation of OPIC programs. These intergovernment agreements usually provide that the host government must approve the issuance of OPIC insurance and guaranties for each specific project. Availability of insurance coverage in countries with per capita gross national product over $1,000 (in 1975 dollars) is limited to projects sponsored by U.S. small businesses or cooperatives, minerals, or energy exploration and development projects in non-OPEC and other projects deemed by OPIC's Board of Directors to merit insurance, such as those offering exceptionally significant development benefits. Small businesses are generally defined as industrial companies with less than $124 million of consolidated revenues or other businesses with less than $39 million in equity.

Other statutory or policy constraints also may limit OPIC programs at various times in some eligible countries. For instance, its statute requires OPIC to "conduct financing, insurance, and reinsurance operations with due regard to principles of risk management." Thus, from time to time if OPIC has reached self-imposed insurance limits in otherwise eligible countries, it may not issue further coverage until better balance, spread of risk, or reduced exposure is reached. Accordingly, investors or their bankers should contact OPIC early in the consideration of any project to determine whether a particular country is eligible.[15]

New Investments. OPIC only insures new investments, which may include a significant expansion, modernization, or development of an existing enterprise as well as a "greenfield project." Accordingly, investment will be eligible for insurance if used for enlarging an existing plant, modernizing existing equipment, or adding working capital in an expanded business. In some cases investment to acquire ownership of an existing enterprise will qualify for insurance coverage if new capital contributions by the applicant for insurance will expand the business.

However, in order to be eligible for insurance, an investor must apply for and receive an OPIC Registration Letter before the investment is made or irrevocably committed. In addition sufficient insurance coverage must be obtained before starting a project to cover possible cost overruns. Otherwise, a subsequent application for further insurance coverage may fail to pass the new investment criteria.[16]

---

[15] Overseas Private Investment Corporation, *Investment Insurance Handbook* (Washington, D.C., August 1980) (hereinafter cited as *Insurance Handbook*), pp. 2–7. The 1981 OPIC Act modified the per capita restriction for OPIC's insurance and other programs. Although the $1,000 per capita limit was not removed entirely, the present per capita restriction was raised to $2,950 in 1979 dollars. As a result OPIC programs will operate free of restriction in an additional 17 countries (Nalen, point 1.).

[16] Ibid., pp. 5–6.

Investment Form. OPIC does not require investment in any fixed form to be eligible for insurance coverage. Thus, coverage is available for conventional equity and loan investments, as well as other exposures of funds, goods, or services under various types of contractual agreements. OPIC has insured investments resulting from licensing and technical assistance agreements, construction and service contracts, production-sharing agreements and special forms of agreement such as the joint venture agreements provided for under the foreign investment laws of Yugoslavia.[17]

Co-Insurance. OPIC's statute requires that the insured bear the risk of loss of at least 10 percent of the total investment of the insured and its affiliates in a project. Therefore, the most OPIC will cover of any proposed investment is 90 percent with the sole exception of loans to unrelated third parties which may be insured for the full amount of their interest and principal. This single exception for loans, however, is obviously extremely important for international bankers and their customers, since total insurance coverage by OPIC may make acceptable an otherwise unreasonable risk for the banker.

OPIC may not issue cover to its 90 percent maximum for various reasons. For large investments, especially in countries where OPIC already has heavy portfolio concentration, and for projects considered to be highly sensitive, OPIC coverage might be limited to less than 90 percent.[18]

Co-insurance must not be confused with reinsurance. In an effort to be of greater service and stretch its resources to cover more projects, OPIC in recent years has reinsured with other insurers, including private insurance companies, analogous to a lender participating out a loan. Reinsurance generally is not of importance to applicants with regard to extent of their coverage. Rather the significant point in reinsurance involves the knowledge which other parties might obtain about the project as a consequence of their reinsurance function. This aspect merits some consideration by investors with regard to the type of reinsurance entities which may become involved. Foreign private firms, as well as firms owned by foreign governments have been involved in this activity. To the extent that risk is spread to different entities with various nationalities the safety of the project may be strengthened; but the factor of confidentiality also must be weighed carefully.

Nature of Coverage. OPIC insurance covers direct investments and rights under related securities or contracts. In most cases, for example, OPIC will issue insurance for retained earnings on equity and accrued interest on loan investments. OPIC may issue insurance commitments for up to 270 percent of the initial investment with 90 per-

---

[17] Ibid., p. 6.
[18] Ibid., p. 6.

cent representing the original investment and 180 percent representing standby commitments to cover future earnings or accrued interest. OPIC insurance may run for the length of contractual obligations but, by statute, may run for only 20 years for equity investments. Larger and more sensitive projects often involve less than the maximum duration.[19]

BASIC INSURANCE COVERAGE

The exact terms of an insurable event always must be examined thoroughly in any insurance contract, and OPIC insurance contracts are not exceptions to this general rule. However, in order to better understand OPIC's functions in the context of international banking activities, this unit reviews in a general way the main aspects of the relatively unique events which OPIC insures. Mention is made of some areas where OPIC may modify its standard terms, but special situations should be explored with OPIC staff on a case-by-case basis.

Inconvertibility. OPIC inconvertibility coverage is designed to assure that earnings, capital, principal and interest, and other eligible remittances such as payments under service agreements, can continue to be transferred into U.S. dollars to the extent transferable under exchange regulations and practices in effect at the time the OPIC insurance policy was issued. The blockage which entitles the insured to exchange local currency for dollars through OPIC may be either "active" (e.g., action by exchange control authorities denying access to foreign exchange on the basis of new, more restrictive regulations) or "passive" (e.g., failure of authorities to act within a specified period— usually 60 days—on an application for foreign exchange).

OPIC inconvertibility insurance also protects against adverse discriminatory exchange rates but is not designed to protect against devaluation of the foreign currency. For example, subsequent imposition of a two-tier exchange system distinguishing between commercial or trading and investment or financial transactions might be discriminatory. Local currency held by the investor for more than 18 months is not eligible for transfer by OPIC. OPIC makes dollar payments upon receipt of the local currency. The exchange rate used for determining the amount of dollars payable is fixed with reference to the rate in effect on a date which is generally 30 or 60 days prior to the date the claim is made against OPIC.[20]

Expropriation. OPIC insurance contracts define the insurable event of "expropriatory action" to include not only the classic nationalization of the enterprise or the taking of property, but also a variety

---

[19] Ibid., p. 7.
[20] Lipman, pp. 347–48.

of situations which might be described as "creeping expropriation." An action, "taken, authorized, ratified, or condoned" by the project country government is considered to be expropriatory if it has a specified impact on either the properties or operations of the foreign enterprise, or on the rights or financial interests of the insured investor. Insurance contracts typically provide that for an action to be considered expropriatory it must continue for at least one year. This period is reduced to three months or less in contracts covering institutional loans (loans by third parties, such as commercial banks or other institutional lenders, otherwise unrelated to the project as sponsors, owners, or partnerships).

Important limitations in the definition of expropriatory action include exceptions for proper regulatory or revenue actions taken by host governments and actions provoked or instigated by the investor or foreign enterprise. In certain situations specific actions may be insured against at the request of the investor and rated separately.

In the event of expropriatory action, compensation by OPIC is based on the original amount of the insured investment, adjusted for retained earnings (or losses) or accrued interest (and, of course, for any prior recoveries of investment) as of the date of expropriation. Except for coverage against the seizure or freezing of certain funds, OPIC pays expropriation compensation on investments only against assignment to it of the securities evidencing the entire insured investment and any related claims or rights. The coverage therefore does not permit an equity investor both to retain his ownership interest and to be compensated by OPIC for governmental actions resulting in lost profits or reduced investment values.[21]

War, Revolution, and Insurrection. Compensation is provided under war, revolution, and insurrection coverage (or war coverage for short) for loss due to bellicose actions occurring within the project country. There is no requirement that there be a formal declaration of war. Coverage extends to losses from actions taken to hinder, combat, or defend against hostile action during war, revolution, or insurrection.[22]

Insurance of equity investment, certain kinds of debt investment, and construction contracts, pertains to specific "covered property." The basic measure of compensation is the original cost of the covered property. Compensation is limited to the insured's proportionate interest in the assets of the foreign enterprise.

---

[21] Ibid., pp. 348–350.

[22] The 1981 OPIC Act broadens OPIC authority to insure against losses from "civil strife" for the first time in addition to losses from war, revolution, and insurrection. "Civil strife" includes violent action by political organizations trying to influence a government policy or, in short, "terrorism," according to an interpretation of the Act by *Middle East Business Intelligence* 1, no. 1 (October 15, 1981).

Coverage of debt under some forms of contracts is neither limited to nor measured by the loss sustained to the physical assets of the foreign enterprise. Rather, an act of expropriation, war, revolution, or insurrection occurring in the project country is compensable if it directly causes a default on a scheduled payment of principal or interest for a period of three months (or for one month in the case of subsequent, consecutive default) for institutional lenders, or six months for parent company lenders. Compensation is paid in the amount of the insured portion of the defaulted installment. Debt investors can purchase either the "covered property" coverage or the "installment default" coverage.[23]

BASIC AND SPECIAL PROGRAM COSTS

With an understanding of the requirements for obtaining basic insurance and the insurable events for OPIC policies it is now appropriate to consider the current costs of OPIC insurance. As customary in the industry OPIC insurance contracts generally require that insurance premiums be paid annually in advance. Premiums are computed for each type of coverage on the basis of a contractually stipulated maximum insured amount and a current insured amount which may, within the limits of the contract, be elected by the investor on a yearly basis. The current insured amount represents the insurance actually in force during any contract year.

The difference between the current insured amount and the maximum insured amount for each coverage is called the standby amount. The major portion of the premium is based on the current insured amount, with a reduced premium rate being applicable to the standby amount. For expropriation and war coverage the insured must maintain current coverage at a level equal to the amount of investment at risk.

Base rates for manufacturing and services projects and institutional loans are shown in Tables 1 and 2. These base rates shown in Tables 1 and 2 and the rates in Tables 3, 4, and 5 for the special coverages discussed in the next unit of this Chapter may be increased or decreased by up to one third depending on the risk profile of the specific project. The rates for natural resource and hydrocarbon projects (Tables 4 and 5) may vary by more than one third of the base rates. OPIC insurance contracts, except for those covering institutional loans and certain service contracts, contain provisions allowing for an increase in the initial current coverage rate by up to 50 percent during the first 10 years of the contract period and another 50 percent during the second 10 years of the contract period.

---

[23] Lipman, pp. 350–351.

Table 1
OPIC Insurance Base Rates for Manufacturing/
Services Projects

Type of Coverage	Current (Percent)	Standby (Percent)
Inconvertibility	.30	.25
Expropriation	.60	.25
War, Revolution & Insurrection	.60	.25

Table 2
OPIC Insurance Base Rates for Institutional Loans Coverage

Single Coverages	Current (Percent)	Standby (Percent)
Inconvertibility	.25	.20
Expropriation	.30	.20
War, Revolution & Insurrection	.60	.20
Combined Coverages		
Inconvertibility and Expropriation	.50	.30
Inconvertibility, Expropriation and War, Revolution & Insurrection	.90	.50

Table 3
OPIC Insurance Base Rates for Contractors' & Exporters'
Guaranty Coverage

	Current (Percent)	Standby (Percent)
Bid, Performance, and Advance Payment Guarantees	.60	.25

Table 4
OPIC Insurance Base Rates for Non-gas/Oil Natural
Resources Projects

Type of Coverage	Current (Percent)	Standby (Percent)
Inconvertibility	.30	.25
Expropriation	.90	.25
War, Revolution & Insurrection	.60	.25

Table 5
OPIC Insurance Base Rates for Oil and Gas Projects

Type of Coverage	Exploration (Percent)	Development/ Production (Percent)
Inconvertibility	0.1000	0.3000
Expropriation	0.4000	1.5000
War, Revolution & Insurrection (WRI)	0.6000	0.6000
Interference with Operations (IWO)	0.4000	0.4000
Primary Standby (per coverage)*	0.0750	0.2500
Secondary Standby (per coverage)	0.0075	0.0075

* For Primary Standby premiums, WRI and IWO are treated as one coverage.

All rates in the following tables are, of course, subject to change, but were taken from the latest OPIC publications, as of fiscal year end 1980.[24]

SPECIAL INSURANCE COVERAGES

After extensive experience with insuring investments in projects along the lines described in the preceding sections on the basic insurance program, OPIC initiated its first special program for contractors in 1972. Subsequently special coverages were tailored for mineral projects and oil and gas projects. The special coverages for these three areas are described in this section.

Contractors' Coverage. The purpose of this special program is to cover bid, performance, and advance payment obligations or guaranties which are required to be arranged by U.S. construction and service contractors and exporters in favor of host government owners. OPIC insures these obligations, which often take the form of letters of credit, against drawings which are not justified by the contractor's or exporter's actions.

Typically, in large international projects, especially in Middle Eastern or North African nations, host governments require that at the time of submitting bids to supply services for a project, the bidder must arrange for its bank to issue a letter of credit in favor of the project owner, which is often the host government or a government-owned entity. At the time a contract is awarded an additional letter of credit may be required from the successful bidder's bank covering

---

[24] *Insurance Handbook*, pp. 9–12.

satisfactory performance of the contract. Also, in order to obtain advance payment monies from the owner for use in starting work contracts, another letter of credit may be required in favor of the owner, which is making partial payment before work is actually performed.

Host government or other project owners who are the beneficiaries of these letters of credit usually may draw under these credits by presenting to the issuing bank, drafts accompanied by signed statements stating that the contractor failed to perform some service or performed in an unsatisfactory manner some service specified under the separate contract between the contractor and the host government. If the documents presented to the bank comply with the listing and description of documents described in the letter of credit, the bank must pay under the letter of credit. The bank then charges the account of the contractor which arranged for the letter of credit in accordance with an agreement established between the bank and the contractor at the time when the letter of credit was issued. Should the contractor believe that a drawing was unjustified, it may make a claim for reimbursement for the drawing in accordance with its insurance contract with OPIC since the bank which issued the letter of credit has already paid the beneficiary of the letter of credit and collected a like amount from the contractor.

In these circumstances, if the contractor's claim is proper and all other matters are in order, OPIC will compensate the insured for up to 90 percent of the amount drawn provided the applicable disputes procedure contained in the contract between the contractor and the owner: (1) results in an award to the insured which is not duly paid; (2) is frustrated by the host government; or (3) results in an award in favor of the host government which is demonstrably the result of fraud, coercion, or corruption or is unsupported by substantial evidence in the record.[25] Table 3 shows the cost for this coverage. In addition OPIC offers insurance coverage for political risks associated with an underlying construction or service contract.

Mineral Projects.   OPIC now also offers special terms and conditions on coverage for natural resource projects. Previously these projects were handled with certain modifications to the basic program. Unless otherwise mentioned from this point on the criteria and rules described under the preceding section on the Basic Insurance program apply to these nonoil and gas mineral resource projects.

Due to the higher risk, and generally larger size and increased sensitivity of mining projects, OPIC will cover only 50 to 90 percent of the initial investment plus an equal amount for retained earnings. The exact percentage of investment and retained earnings which OPIC

---

[25] Overseas Private Investment Corporation, *OPIC Programs for Insurance of Contractor's Bid, Performance and Advance Payment Guaranties* (Washington, D.C.: November 1979) (hereinafter cited as *Contractor's Program*), pages not numbered.

will insure depends upon OPIC's assessment of all risk factors in the project, including the nationalities of equity and loan investors. For instance, as a general rule the greater the number of different nationals represented as owners and lenders and the greater the differences in geographical location, economic and political systems between them, the lesser the risk is perceived to be. The theory is that host countries will be reluctant to risk cutoff of aid and investment inflows from around the world by behaving unreasonably with respect to the project which has numerous diversified investors.

OPIC will issue insurance coverage against all three risks (inconvertibility, expropriation, and war) during the exploration phase for intangible costs as well as tangible assets. Special additional coverage may be provided against losses resulting from the breach of certain host government undertakings identified by the project sponsor at the outset as vital to the successful operation of the project. There are no set fees and coverages for this type of coverage which must be negotiated case by case with OPIC.

Beyond the standard war, revolution, and insurrection coverage (WRI), OPIC may provide insurance coverage for consequential loss due to closing of operations caused by WRI events in the project country or by certain specified WRI events in another country. Each of these situations must be tailored to the circumstances involved by creating special contractual wording and using experienced legal counsel to represent the investor and work with OPIC's lawyers.[26] The base premium rates for mineral resource projects are shown in Table 4.

Oil and Gas Projects. OPIC's new program for this industry insures all forms of investments in exploration, development, and production of oil and gas, including production-sharing agreements, service contracts, risk contracts, and traditional concessions. OPIC covers up to 90 percent of the insured's net unrecovered costs taking the sum of (1) the value of Covered Property (i.e., tangible property as to which the insured bears the risk of loss) plus (2) Operating Costs (direct costs other than for Covered Property, plus a six percent allowance for U.S. overhead), and subtracting from that sum the total of (3) the value of recoveries (i.e., Cost Oil received under a production-sharing contract or a portion of receipts attributable for such purposes under the terms of the OPIC insurance contract), and (4) any Return of Capital. (These capitalized words represent defined terms in OPIC contracts.)

Intangible exploration costs are treated in two different ways based upon the time when a claim arises. If a claim arises before the initial discovery of commercial quantities of gas or oil, intangible costs are covered only if they are not related to drilling a dry hole. If a claim arises after discovery, all intangible drilling costs, including those related to dry holes, are included in Operating Costs, except that Operat-

---

[26] *Insurance Handbook*, p. 13.

ing Costs may not exceed the value of the insured's interest in the proven reserves of oil and/or gas.

Insureds may select one or more coverages, including inconvertibility, expropriation, WRI (war, revolution, and insurrection), and IWO (interference with operations). The insured may independently elect maximum levels of insurance. Coverage is issued for a term of 12 years, at the end of which OPIC, in its sole discretion, may offer insurance for an additional eight years.

The base premium rates for oil and gas projects are shown in Table 5. The insurance coverage for these projects is structured to provide current coverage, adjusted on a quarterly basis, equal to 90 percent of what is actually at risk. The low secondary standby premium shown in Table 5 is intended to cover amounts that will be needed only after commercial quantities of oil or gas have been discovered. When amounts are transferred from secondary standby to primary standby or current coverage the insured must pay the difference between the secondary and primary standby fees for such amounts from the date when the insurance was issued.

WRI (war, revolution, and insurrection) coverage for oil and gas projects insures tangible assets against physical damage. Compensation normally is at least equal to the cost of repair or replacement, or if equipment remains commercially operable, the reduction in the fair market value of the damaged asset.

IWO (interference with operations) coverage insures WRI-caused cessation of operation for six or more months with compensation equal to 90 percent of net unrecovered cost. If within five years of payment the WRI situation abates and the insured can resume operations, the insured must return the compensation to OPIC without interest.

Expropriation for oil and gas projects includes abrogration, impairment, repudiation, or material breach of a production-sharing agreement which for a six-month period directly results in certain effects, including preventing the insured from effectively exercising fundamental rights with respect to the production-sharing agreement (including the rights to take and export oil or to be paid for it). The insurance contract for a concession agreement provides that unilateral changes by host government in terms of the agreement do not give rise to a claim unless they prevent the insured from realizing a share of the economic benefits from the project that is equitable and reasonable, taking into account all then-available information with respect to project and industry factors. Expropriatory action for all types of agreements includes confiscation of tangible property and bank accounts. Compensation for confiscated property is based on the value of the assets in question. Compensation for other types of expropriatory action generally is based on net unrecovered costs.[27]

---

[27] Ibid., pp. 13–17.

INSURANCE APPLICATION PROCEDURE

As mentioned above when discussing the new investment requirement in the section on the basic insurance program, investors considering possible use of OPIC insurance in any project must obtain an OPIC
Registration Letter before any investment has been made or irrevocably committed. An agreement to invest subject to obtaining OPIC
insurance coverage is not considered a disqualifying commitment, and
a commitment to enter into the exploration phase of a natural resources
development project is not disqualifying with respect to coverage of
investment in the production phase. As the main purpose of the Registration Letter is to establish the timeliness of an application for OPIC
insurance coverage, it is issued promptly, usually within a few days,
on the basis of a brief submission of data.

A request for a Registration Letter must contain: the identity of
the investor, citizenship eligibility of the investor, the location of the
investment project, a brief description of the project, a statement that
the investment has not been made nor irrevocably committed, the
type of investment contemplated (equity, loan, or other), the kind of
coverage sought, and the estimated amounts under each kind of coverage. OPIC prefers that investors complete in triplicate a one-page
application entitled "Request for Registration for Political Risk Investment Insurance" (OPIC Form 50). A registration fee of $100 must
accompany the application if the investor has annual revenues over
$100 million and the proposed investment is $100,000 or more. Otherwise a fee of $50 must be submitted with the application.

If all is in order OPIC sends in reply its Registration Letter, which
is valid for six months, but is not a "binder" and in no way constitutes
a commitment to issue insurance. Neither is the Registration Letter
evidence of an affirmative determination with respect to satisfaction
of any eligibility criteria for an investment. Accordingly, the investor
may at a later time change both the coverages and the amounts of
coverages required. Unless cancelled by reason of a denial of the investor's application for insurance, Registration Letters normally may be
extended, if necessary, for such periods as may be appropriate. After
sending the Registration Letter the OPIC Application officer usually
sends insurance application forms which should be completed and returned to OPIC as soon as the final form of the investment is reasonably
clear.

Finally, it is the applicant's duty to obtain the foreign government
approval (FGA) for OPIC's insuring the project. FGA's typically are
required under the intergovernmental agreement between the host
country and the United States. OPIC provides pertinent data on obtaining the FGA when it issues its Registration Letter. The original signed

copy of the FGA is delivered through U.S. government channels, usually the U.S. Embassy in the host country, to OPIC.[28]

FINANCE PROGRAMS

In past years OPIC has provided financing in the form of loans from its Direct Investment Fund (DIF) and loan guaranties issued to private U.S. financial institutions, including commercial banks, making eligible loans.[29] In certain situations OPIC also has provided financing for feasibility studies and is becoming much more active in this area. This section describes the criteria for OPIC financing, including project ownership, economic soundness, development contribution to the host country, types of businesses OPIC finances, financing plans, and the extent of OPIC's participation. Then OPIC loan terms, guaranty terms, and finally the application process for obtaining OPIC financing assistance are explained. Unless otherwise mentioned these criteria apply to both the loan and loan guaranty programs.

Project Ownership.   OPIC finances wholly U.S.-owned projects, but encourages joint ventures between U.S. investors and host country nationals, where U.S. investors assume a meaningful share of the risk. Usually purchase of at least 25 percent of the equity by U.S. investors is required. Under certain circumstances OPIC may guarantee loans of U.S. financial institutions to businesses owned by host-country investors. As a rule at least 51 percent of the voting shares must be held by privately owned firms or individual persons. However, a guaranteed loan may be made to an entity in which local government ownership of voting shares represents a majority, if it is agreed by contract that management will remain in private hands and there is a strong showing of direct U.S. interest in other respects. On the other hand, wholly government-owned projects are not eligible for OPIC financing, since OPIC's role is to encourage private investment.[30]

Economic Soundness.   In addition to U.S. ownership OPIC financed projects must be financially and commercially sound and within the demonstrated competence of the proposed management, which must

---

[28] Ibid., pp. 18–20. Also see Lipman, pp. 342 and 344. In connection with the concept of requiring an OPIC Registration Letter before an investment is made or irrevocably committed it should be noted that the 1981 OPIC Act requires that OPIC prepare and submit to Congress by June 30, 1982, a report on methods for estimating the probability that particular investments or types of investments will or will not be made if OPIC insurance or other support is not provided (Nalen, point 5).

[29] By provisions of the 1981 OPIC Act, OPIC is required to transfer to the DIF at least 10 percent of annual net income plus amounts repaid to the DIF from outstanding DIF loans to the extent or in such amounts as provided in advance in appropriation acts. (Nalen, point 3).

[30] Lipman, pp. 354–56.

have a proven record of success in the same business, as well as a significant continuing financial risk in the project, usually evidenced by equity ownership as already discussed.

Local Development Contribution. Beyond examination of U.S. ownership and the economic soundness of the project, OPIC requires that the host country approve both the project and OPIC's commitment. But in addition to review of host-government agreements or concessions, OPIC makes its own examination of the benefit to be provided by the project to the host-country economy. In this examination OPIC considers whether the project will increase the host country's supply of goods and services at better quality levels or at lower costs, create employment opportunities and develop skills through training, transfer technological and managerial skills, increase foreign exchange earnings, savings, or local taxes, and stimulate other private enterprises. Projects in the developing countries with per capita income of less than $680 (in 1979 dollars) and those involving smaller U.S. firms as sponsors are of particular interest.[31]

Eligible Enterprises. OPIC provides financing to manufacturing, agricultural production, fishing, forestry, mining, energy, processing, storage, and certain service industries involving significant capital investment such as hotels, tourist facilities, and equipment maintenance and distributorship facilities. However, from time to time internal policies or statutory provisions exclude certain types of businesses from consideration for OPIC financial participation. Current examples include projects involving gambling facilities, projects producing munitions, alcoholic beverages, or producing or processing palm oil, sugar, or citrus crops for export to the U.S. Runaway plants or projects which are substitutes for existing U.S. facilities and produce for the same U.S. or export market also are prohibited. Nor does OPIC generally finance housing and infrastructure projects; programs for financing these activities exist within AID, the World Bank Group, and other organizations, and OPIC does not wish to duplicate these efforts.[32]

Adequate Financing Plan. OPIC requires sound debt/equity ratios for projects it helps finance. OPIC may not purchase equity in a project, but may hold convertible notes or other debt instruments with profit participation features. In some cases such instruments may be considered as quasi-equity and help increase the equity base for a project. In addition convertible notes may help achieve or increase local ownership by eventual sale to local investors. Use of combinations of such instruments may be necessary to provide suitable grace periods and repayment schedules consistent with sound credit practice and princi-

---

[31] Overseas Private Investment Corporation, *Finance Handbook* (OPIC, Washington, D.C.: May, 1980) pp. 6–8 (hereinafter cited as *Finance Handbook*). Also see footnote 15 above regarding changes in the per capita income restriction.

[32] Ibid., pp. 5–6.

ples for some projects. Moreover, the financial structure of each project naturally varies with the type of the business and other factors, including the existence of long-term sales contracts. Generally, OPIC requires a ratio of no more than 60 percent debt to 40 percent equity.

Beyond funds to cover feasibility studies, organizational expenses, and costs for loans, construction, machinery, equipment, training, market development, interest during construction, and start-up expenses, including any initial losses and adequate working capital, OPIC requires adequate provision for cost overruns and contingencies. As a rule OPIC requires that project sponsors enter into an agreement under which they are obligated to provide sufficient financing to complete a project and have adequate working capital after certain operating levels have been achieved.

OPIC requires data from project sponsors to substantiate raw material sources, technical feasibility, market demand, cost estimates, and projected cash flow. OPIC may retain independent consultants in various disciplines to help analyze this information since OPIC does not employ specialized technical personnel. However, to a large extent, OPIC has designed its financing programs to compliment and supplement the lending and investing capabilities of commercial banks, local, regional and international development banks, and bilateral agencies such as the Export-Import Bank of the United States.

By law for the projects it finances, OPIC must consider the balance-of-payment and employment effects on the U.S. and host nation economies, the extent of U.S. procurement, net financial flows, and net project exports to the U.S. Also OPIC expects quality standards and specifications in design, engineering, and construction plans for project facilities, and that work be within the capabilities of the contractors and supervised carefully by the projects' sponsors.[33]

OPIC Participation. The size of OPIC's commitment to a particular project varies based on numerous factors, including the contribution to the host country's development, financial requirements, risks and benefits of the project, and the role of other participants and lenders. Because OPIC programs are designed to support facilities of other institutions, OPIC encourages joint participation with others and for appropriate projects will actively assist U.S. sponsors in obtaining debt and equity financing from other institutions. In fact OPIC financings typically involve at least one or more other lenders, and OPIC often accepts longer or more flexible maturities or provides fixed-rate loans in order to facilitate participation by other financial institutions.

Because its programs support private-sector investment in financing economically viable projects, OPIC does not provide concessional terms often associated with bilateral government-aid programs. Nor

[33] Ibid., pp. 7–8.

does OPIC offer financing specifically for export sales unrelated to long-term investment in overseas business. However, export of U.S. equipment, goods, and services for a project is certainly a positive factor which is considered by OPIC, and OPIC works with both multilateral and bilateral international lending institutions.

While OPIC's financing commitment to a new venture often amounts to as much as 35–45 percent of total project costs, OPIC seldom has provided more than 50 percent of total costs. Larger participations may be considered for expansions of existing projects, but smaller participations are the rule for new ventures, and project sponsors are encouraged to arrange for additional financial participations from other international and local sources.

OPIC loans usually range in amount from $100,000 to $4 million but may be used only for financing projects sponsored by or significantly involving U.S. small businesses or cooperatives. Terms generally range from 5 to 12 years based upon the cash flow projections for the project for both direct and guaranteed loans. OPIC as a rule requires approximately equal semi-annual principal payments after a suitable grace period. In some cases longer maturities may be permitted. Interest rates for direct loans vary based upon OPIC's assessment of financial and political risks. The interest rate on convertible loans is lower than on straight loans, and rates also vary based on market trends and whether the credit of a U.S. sponsor or only the project itself is involved.

Except in the case of convertible subordinated notes, OPIC expects that its financial participation in a project will be on a senior basis, *pari passu* with other senior creditors and will share in a first lien on fixed assets and when appropriate other collateral. Although a host-government guaranty normally is not required, OPIC is not prohibited from taking such guaranties. OPIC charges normal commitment and out-of-pocket fees, such as outside legal expenses. Because OPIC funds are not strictly tied to U.S. procurement, as in the case of the Export-Import Bank, proceeds of OPIC financing may be spent for capital goods and services in the United States, host country, or other less developed countries. However, if a project involves substantial procurement from an industrialized nation other than the United States, OPIC expects financing for that procurement to come from other sources.[34]

While direct loan funds generally are limited to the $4 million level for any one project, OPIC assists financing in amounts ranging up to $50 million by use of OPIC guaranties to U.S. financial institutions. Projects must meet OPIC's criteria as detailed above and additionally OPIC must approve the U.S. institution's loan terms. While several of the largest U.S. banks use OPIC programs to insure their direct investments in branches, affiliates, and other equity ventures abroad,

---

[34] Ibid., pp. 7–13.

many U.S. banks and other financial institutions of all sizes may utilize the OPIC loan-guaranty program to benefit their customers. Loans to economically viable entities in nations perceived as high political risks may become feasible for a commercial bank's portfolio with OPIC's guaranty. OPIC's guaranty covers nonpayment for any reason, commercial or political.

OPIC's guaranty is an irrevocable commitment to the lender that principal and interest will be paid by OPIC, if the borrower fails to pay in accordance with the loan agreement. The guaranteed lender will be paid promptly by OPIC and need not pursue remedies against the borrower before making demand on OPIC. OPIC's guaranties are backed by the full faith and credit of the United States of America in addition to the guaranty reserve mentioned earlier in this chapter.

In order to obtain a loan guaranty a U.S. lender must be more than 50 percent beneficially owned by U.S. citizens, corporations, or partnerships. Foreign lending institutions that are at least 95 percent U.S. owned also are eligible to obtain loan guarantees. In addition to U.S. commercial banks, guaranteed lenders have included savings banks, insurance companies, and pension funds. For U.S. commercial and savings banks OPIC guaranteed loans qualify as legal investments and as exempt securities under applicable Federal securities regulations.[35]

For sponsors or lenders with customers interested in considering use of OPIC finance programs, the usual information required by any banker for a loan request should be submitted to OPIC with particular emphasis on the criteria mentioned. Preliminary information would typically include:

The name, location and business of the proposed project.

The identity, background, and financial statements of the principal sponsors.

The planned sources of supply, anticipated output and markets, sales channels, and basis for projected market share.

The costs and sources of capital goods, services, and other key components of the project.

A proposed financing plan indicating OPIC's share and financial projections; and

Statements indicating the expected contribution the project will make to local economic and social development.[36]

CONTACTING OPIC

Inquiries about OPIC programs should be directed either to the Information Officer (telephone (202–632–1854) or addressed to the Fi-

---

[35] Ibid., pp. 10–11. Also see Lipman, pp. 357–59.

[36] Ibid., pp. 14–15.

nance Application Officer or Insurance Application Officer, Overseas Private Investment Corporation, 1129 20th Street N.W., Washington, D.C. 20527. Small businesses are encouraged to use OPIC's toll free "Hot Line" for their inquiries (telephone 800–424–OPIC). This chapter is based on the most recent information available. However, OPIC programs change from time to time, and therefore review of OPIC's published materials could be useful before meeting in person with OPIC personnel.

In addition to comprehensive *Annual Reports,* OPIC publications include an introductory brochure entitled "Overseas Private Investment Corporation," an "Investment Insurance Handbook," detailing OPIC's political risk insurance programs, a "Finance Handbook," describing OPIC's loan, guaranty, and feasibility study financing programs, a booklet summarizing the "OPIC Program for Insurance of Contractors' Bid, Performance and Advance Payment Guaranties," an OPIC "Country and Area List" listing the nations where OPIC programs are in effect, and a "Guide for Executives of Small Companies." OPIC also publishes a bi-monthly newsletter named "TOPICS," usually about eight pages in length for each issue, which describes new projects and program developments and announces personnel changes. All of these materials are free of charge.

FUTURE TRENDS

OPIC is in good financial condition, exhibits sound trends in earnings and operations and continues to carefully develop new programs to serve the needs of U.S. private investors and private enterprises in developing nations. However, OPIC's greatest problem probably is the need for periodic extension of its authority at the hands of the U.S. Congress. In spite of the fact that OPIC is self supporting, has demonstrated the success and usefulness of its programs, has increasing net income, and maintains an extremely small staff (about 125) for a 10-year-old agency in comparison with other government agencies, it has a relatively small constituency due to the specialized nature of its work. However, some analysts predict that during the 1980s OPIC will grow in importance.[37] Because it is a successful and self-supporting agency, OPIC should fare better than agencies and programs which depend upon increased government appropriations to expand activities.

In the last several years, in addition to new programs for contractors,

---

[37] Richard F. Janssen, "Business Role Abroad," *The Wall Street Journal,* April 14, 1981, p. 56. Also see "New Business for OPIC," *The New York Times,* October 24, 1982, p. 20F in which OPIC President, Craig A. Nalen reported that more than $3 billion in insurance was written during fiscal 1982, surpassing the previous record of $1.48 billion for the preceding year. New emphasis on the private sector and a change of attitude toward American investors by many developing countries were cited by Nalen as the main reasons for the dramatic increase in OPIC's business.

natural resources, and oil and gas projects, OPIC has increased its emphasis on encouraging small businesses in the United States to invest in the developing world. A new incentive program provides commission payments to insurance brokers who help small businesses purchase political risk insurance policies. Further OPIC has started to develop programs to share some of the organizational and legal costs involved in completing documentation for OPIC loans. In conjunction with officers from the Export-Import Bank, U.S. Department of Commerce, and Small Business Administration, since March 1978 OPIC personnel have visited more than 50 cities around the United States to explain how OPIC services can benefit small businesses. Accordingly, it is safe to assume that further emphasis will be directed toward this segment over the next several years.

For business of all sizes, OPIC has stepped up the pace of investment-mission tours, which visit one or a few nations to explore business development opportunities for direct investment. These tours generally cost several thousand dollars per person with participants paying their own expenses and involve around two dozen persons. OPIC, through its close working connections with other government units and especially U.S. embassies, is able to provide numerous appropriate introductions and extremely effective use of time. Since spring 1979 OPIC has arranged missions to eight countries and more events are planned.

During fiscal 1979 OPIC made its second loan and grant to a private voluntary organization, the Witherspoon Development Corporation, an affiliate of the Presbyterian Church. Funds were used to aid small business projects in the Caribbean area. The first loan/grant of this type was made in fiscal 1978 to the Institute for International Development, Inc. for small business and farming projects in Kenya, Colombia, Indonesia, and Honduras. Based upon the success of these programs, OPIC may expand its efforts to work with private voluntary organizations engaged in helping small businesses in less developed lands.[38]

With U.S.-government aid cut backs, the need for U.S. exports to earn foreign exchange and continued shortages of energy and key raw materials, OPIC programs may assume increased importance for U.S. financial institutions, businesses of all sizes, and even private foundations and charities operating abroad. OPIC's insurance programs still are relatively unique, although a few private insurers are slowly increasing their foreign political-risk insurance activities. While OPIC's direct loan portfolio is somewhat small, its loan-guaranty program can often be useful to U.S. international bankers and all OPIC programs and information sources bear periodic monitoring for detection of innovative ideas and indications of possible future trends in international finance.

[38] *1979 Annual Report*, p. 4.

30
The World Bank Group

JAMES L. KAMMERT
Executive Vice President
Equibank

INTRODUCTION

The World Bank Group is composed of three international financial institutions, the World Bank itself (officially called the International Bank for Reconstruction and Development), the International Development Association (IDA), and the International Finance Corporation (IFC). The World Bank was established at the end of World War II along with a companion organization, the International Monetary Fund (IMF). IFC was formed in 1956 and IDA in 1960. Both IDA and IFC are referred to as affiliates of the World Bank or members of the World Bank Group, although each of the three entities has a separate legal existence with slightly different ownership.

All three World Bank Group entities and the IMF, which are headquartered in Washington, D.C., were created by individual treaties referred to as Articles of Agreement. Each organization is owned by member nations which are parties to the treaties. According to the World Bank Articles of Agreement, only members of the IMF are eligible to become World Bank members, and membership in the World Bank is a prerequisite to joining either IDA or IFC. The IMF and the three units of the World Bank Group each fulfill distinct functions and were designed to complement each other's efforts. Hence, these organizations cooperate fully and coordinate their activities closely in order for the IMF to improve the world monetary system and for the World Bank Group to assist developing member nations.

The author wishes to thank members of the World Bank staff, including Peter C. Muncie, Publications Department, and Elizabeth Wetzel-Apitz, Legal Department, as well as Colbert I. King of the Riggs National Bank and former U.S. Executive Director of the World Bank, for their comments and suggestions on the material used in this chapter. However, all contents and errors, if any, are solely the responsibility of the author.

This chapter first examines the history and purpose of the World Bank Group entities in the context of the IMF. Then it discusses World Bank and IDA organization and operating methods and certain World Bank external relations functions which help to improve the overall climate for international lending and investment among other activities. Exploration of external relations and international coordination activities is followed by detailed examination of a specialized form of World Bank lending known as co-financing with emphasis on how the World Bank works with private financial institutions. The chapter next deals with the considerable body of research generated by the World Bank Group. While most international bankers may have a more immediate interest in income-producing opportunities from the Bank's co-financing program, much of the Bank's research is published and readily available. This material contains many suggestions for short-term business development leads, as well as long-range planning ideas for the observant international banker. Finally, the chapter reviews how the World Bank markets its own debt obligations and carries out its treasury functions and concludes with some brief comments on likely future trends in World Bank Group activities.

Due to its specialized role and increasing importance, the subsequent chapter of this Handbook deals separately with IFC.

HISTORY AND PURPOSE

Before the end of World War II experts from the Allied Nations began to identify and consider solutions for postwar economic problems. These problems included not only reconstructing war-torn nations but also revising the world monetary system and providing financing for developing nations. At the same time planning started for a body to cope with political issues (which later became the United Nations), it was determined that new and separate institutions would be required to deal with international monetary and financial matters on an ongoing basis. Accordingly, during the summer of 1944 representatives of the Allied Nations met in Bretton Woods, New Hampshire, to prepare separate treaties for two new international institutions, the IMF and the World Bank.

The purpose of the IMF is to assist member nations facing economic problems, especially balance of payments difficulties, in making the adjustment process. Thus, the IMF was designed according to its Articles of Agreement to provide funding to nations with temporary balance-of-payments deficits and to encourage the elimination of exchange restrictions and the observance of accepted rules of international financial conduct. The purpose of the International Bank for Reconstruction and Development (World Bank) is to help finance reconstruction and development of its member nations. With the rapid reconstruction of war-torn industrialized nations during the immediate postwar years, the World Bank quickly shifted its focus to assisting the development process and today works exclusively in developing countries. Accordingly, the World Bank's central purpose now is to promote economic and social progress in developing nations by helping to increase productivity so that their people may live a better and fuller life. In carrying out its purpose the World Bank provides more development assistance than any other agency, multilateral or bilateral, in the world.

The Articles of Agreement of the World Bank were formally accepted by a majority of the participants in the Bretton Woods Conference on December 27, 1945. Six months later, on June 25, 1946, the Bank opened for business and received capital subscriptions from its member nations. The Articles establish the Bank as an intergovernmental institution, corporate in form, with all of its capital stock being owned by its member nations which totalled 135, as of June 30, 1980. From an initial $10 billion in capital the Bank has grown to total assets of almost $45 billion with approximately $43 billion in capital at the end of fiscal 1982 (June 30, 1982).[1]

Of total capital at this date only about $4 billion is actually paid in. When the Bank was formed it was recognized that private capital would be insufficient to rebuild destroyed nations and increase productivity and living standards in underdeveloped nations without some type of governmental guaranty. Thus, the formula devised at Bretton Woods provided for member nations to share risks roughly in accordance with their relative economic strengths. Wealthier nations, for example, subscribed to more bank capital than the less wealthy. However, by plan only a fraction of all the capital was initially paid in by the member nations.[2]

The Bank was designed so that outside borrowings from governments and private capital markets could supplement the paid-in capital. Borrowing from governments or other investors would be readily available at favorable rates, because the Bank could call for the balance of subscribed capital as needed. Thus the financial strength of all member nations but particularly, the wealthy, industrialized ones stands behind the Bank. For this reason each subscriber nation is committed independently to pay when its subscription is called regardless of the action or non-action of others.[3]

From time to time over the years member nations have agreed to increase authorized capital and capital subscriptions. However, until

---

[1] World Bank, 1982 *Annual Report*, IBRD, Appendix A–Balance Sheet, June 30, 1981 and 1982 (Washington, D.C. 1982, pp. 146–47.

[2] World Bank, *The World Bank* (Washington, D.C.: 1981), p. 53.

[3] World Bank, *Articles of Agreement of the International Bank for Reconstruction and Development*, Article II (Washington, D.C.: 1976), (hereinafter *Articles of Agreement*) pp. 1–3.

increased subscriptions are agreed upon by the member nations, each nation, of course, is legally liable only to pay the total amount of its then current subscription level. Although the Bank has never had to call subscriptions to capital, investors who provide funds to the Bank are reassured by the large pool of resources available solely for the purpose of protecting them by this method. To date the Bank has suffered no loan losses, and delays in payments of loan service charges have been insignificant. With this record and the subscription obligations of its member nations, the Bank enjoys the highest credit rating, Triple A, accorded to debt issuers by the two principal bond rating services in the United States.

Before preparing the Bank's Articles of Agreement the Bretton Woods participants carefully studied past mistakes in international finance, especially the record of international loan and bond defaults during the 1930s. In too many of these cases debt had been raised for nonproductive purposes and without adequate consideration of the ability of borrowers to service and ultimately repay new and existing foreign debt. Accordingly, by its Articles the Bank was designed to provide financing to well-defined, carefully prepared, thoroughly appraised, and closely supervised projects. The Bank studies in detail the nations, activities or industries (referred to as sectors), and individual projects to which it lends, and from 1946 to 1981 the World Bank, including IDA, lent a cumulative total of over $80 billion for more than 2,800 projects in almost 100 countries.[4]

To assure quality loan assets the Bank's Articles of Agreement require that its lending be for high priority and productive purposes, generally be used for the foreign exchange component of specific projects, and be made directly to a member government or else guaranteed by the member government in whose territory the project is located. Furthermore, the Articles require that the Bank act prudently in making loans, give due regard to the borrower's or guarantor's ability to meet its obligations, ensure that loan proceeds are used only for the purposes for which the loan was granted, and pay attention to economy and efficiency.[5]

While the World Bank generally lends for up to 20 years with a grace period of up to five years at a fixed "rate which is somewhat lower than but related to market rates," the Articles also require that the Bank be satisfied that the borrower would be unable to obtain the loan from other sources on reasonable terms, and specify that the Bank cannot impose conditions for spending loan proceeds in particular countries, and that the Bank should not be influenced by the political

---

[4] World Bank, *1980 Annual Report*, Appendix 1. Bank and IDA Cumulative Operations, by Major Purpose and Region, June 30, 1980, (Washington, D.C.: 1980) (hereinafter *1980 Annual Report*) pp. 180–181.

[5] World Bank, *Articles of Agreement*, Article III, pp. 3–4.

character of members, nor should the Bank or its officers interfere in members' political affairs.[6] Thus, the Bank does not lend in support of military or political objectives.

During the 1950s considerable debate occurred in international financial circles and the U.S. Congress about the need for exceptionally favorable loan terms for certain less developed nations, which although able to utilize foreign loans, did not have the current capacity to pay interest close to market rates and repay loans within the periods prescribed for World Bank loans. As a result of this discussion, Articles of Agreement, which became effective by September 1960, were prepared to create the International Development Association (IDA), as an affiliate of the World Bank.[7]

By the terms of its Articles of Agreement, IDA is a separate legal entity and financially distinct from the Bank. However, only World Bank members are eligible to become members of IDA, and World Bank and IDA staff are identical. From IDA funds obtained from IDA members (and a few nonmembers which volunteered to make special contributions), World Bank/IDA staff prepare and act upon applications for *credits* (a term carefully used to distinguish IDA's lending from World Bank *loans*). IDA credits are handled and granted on the same basis as World Bank loans except that generally there is no interest charged and repayment terms are 50 years, including a 10-year grace period. However, a service charge of ¾ of 1 percent per annum is charged on the disbursed portion of IDA credits.[8]

As of June 30, 1982, IDA had almost $25 billion in assets, including credits of almost $26 billion of which approximately $11 billion were undisbursed. Subscriptions and supplementary resources amounted to $24 billion, and 130 of the 142 World Bank members belonged to IDA as of June 30, 1982.[9] Of the total IDA membership on June 30, 1981, there were only 40 borrowing countries, although about 70 nations met the criteria of annual per capita gross national product of less than $680 (measured in 1979 dollars). Additional fundings from members for IDA are referred to as general replenishments, although since its formation, IDA also has received special contributions from richer members and transfers from the net earnings of the World Bank, which the Bank pays out to IDA from time to time in lieu of dividends to World Bank members.

International Finance Corporation (IFC) was established as an affili-

---

[6] Ibid., p. 4.

[7] World Bank, *The World Bank*, p. 7.

[8] Ibid., p. 10.

[9] World Bank, *1982 Annual Report*, p. 3, and IDA Appendix A–Statement of Condition, June 30, 1981 and 1982, pp. 164–65. Also see World Bank, IDA in Retrospect, New York: Oxford University Press, 1982, for a comprehensive history of IDA's first 20 years of operations.

ate of the World Bank in 1956 to promote private investment and assist individual enterprises in developing member countries. IFC has its own Articles of Agreement, legal existence, and separate membership, although only World Bank members are eligible to join IFC. IFC maintains its own separate staff, but also utilizes some World Bank employees for certain administrative functions. A more complete discussion follows in this Handbook's subsequent chapter which deals separately with IFC.

ORGANIZATION

Subscriptions to capital stock by World Bank member nations are roughly based on each members' participation quota in the IMF, and the IMF quota system is based upon each country's relative economic strength. Member voting rights are related to shareholdings, and the Bank Articles provide with certain exceptions that all Bank matters are decided by a majority of votes cast. Each member has 250 votes plus one additional vote for each share of capital subscribed. Similar methods govern IDA and IFC except that subscriptions and voting are based on the proportion of World Bank ownership.

All powers in the World Bank, IDA, and IFC are vested in the Board of Governors with one governor appointed by each member country. Typically, a governor is his country's finance minister, central bank governor, or a minister or official of similar rank. Governors of the bank serve ex officio as governors of IDA and IFC. The Articles of Agreement permit the Board of Governors to delegate some of its authority, but certain powers are reserved to the board. Only the board may admit or suspend members, increase or decrease capital stock, decide appeals resulting from interpretations of the Articles of Agreement by the executive directors, enter into formal arrangements with other international organizations, suspend operations and distribute assets, determine distribution of net income, and approve amendments to the Articles of Agreement.

Except for these reserved powers the board of governors of each entity has delegated most of its authority to 21 executive directors, whose chairman is the president of the bank. In addition to delegated powers, the Articles of Agreement provide that executive directors have responsibility for interpreting the Articles subject to appeal to the board of governors and for conducting general operations. Accordingly, proposals for loans and other financing, borrowing, major technical assistance operations, budgets, various reports, and certain policy recommendations are submitted by the president to the executive directors for their consideration and decision.[10]

---

[10] World Bank, *The World Bank*, p. 71.

Based upon the ownership and voting system the five largest shareholders (France, the Federal Republic of Germany, Japan, the United
Kingdom, and the United States) each appoint a single executive director with the other 16 executive directors being elected for two-year
terms by governors from other members with each governor casting
the total number of votes to which his country is entitled. Except
for China, these other executive directors represent several or a group
of member nations rather than only one nation. Executive directors
of the bank serve ex officio as directors of IDA and IFC, and each
governor and each director appoints his own alternate. The combined
effect of the Articles of Agreement and practice is to make the bank
president, who is selected by the executive directors, the chairman
of the executive directors, and president of IDA and IFC. The president
votes only in case of an equal division, and the duty of the president,
officers and staff is to the bank and to no other authority.[11]

The World Bank and IDA are organized internally on a fairly decentralized basis mainly by regions of the world. Six regional offices headed
by regional vice presidents (for Latin America and the Caribbean;
Europe, Middle East, and North America; South Asia; East Asia and
Pacific; Western Africa; and Eastern Africa) and the vice president,
Central Projects Staff, report to the senior vice president, Operations,
who reports to the president. Also reporting to the president is the
senior vice president, Finance, who has responsibility for financial matters, advising the president on financial policies for the bank, leading
IDA replenishment negotiations, and for liaison with member countries
on matters related to sources of funds. Reporting to the senior vice
president, Finance, are the vice president and treasurer, the vice president and controller, the vice president, Programming and Budgeting,
the Financial Policy and Analysis Department, the Internal Auditing
Department, and the Tokyo office.

In addition to the Operations and Finance areas functional departments headed by vice presidents have responsibility for administration,
conducting business of the board of governors and executive directors
(vice president and secretary), external relations, legal matters (vice
president and general counsel), and policy (the vice president of the
Development Policy staff). These five vice presidents report to the
president along with the two senior vice presidents.

Within each of the six regional offices there are Country Program
Departments staffed by financial analysts, economists and loan officers
with responsibility by individual nations, and Projects Departments
with specialists in various sectors such as agriculture, development
finance, education, public utilities, and transportation. There are also
small offices in New York, Paris, Geneva, and Tokyo for maintaining

---

[11] Ibid., pp. 71 and 74.

contact with financial communities, governments, and international organizations in those locations. More than two dozen World Bank offices or missions are located around the globe. These missions administer programs in individual nations or regional groups of nations and report to the headquarter's regional offices in Washington, D.C. Policy formulation, quality control and technical innovation are functions of each regional office, but support is provided by specialists in the two broad staff departments, Central Projects Staff and Development Policy Staff.[12]

The Central Project Staff Department is composed of specialists for different functions, including industry, population, health, nutrition, petroleum, and telecommunications, who are assigned mainly to the geographical regions. The Development Policy Staff deals with global, country, and sector policies which tend to cut across national boundaries, coordinates policy work throughout the bank, maintains and improves the quality of the bank's economic work, including economic data and projections systems, and helps regional offices establish priorities on economic work in their area countries. The Development Policy Staff also reviews economic analysis supporting country lending programs, provides specialist resources for country economic work in the regional offices, and manages the Bank's research programs.[13]

Based upon the work of the decentralized regional offices with support and coordination from the central staff departments, lending proposals are developed and presented to a Loan Committee consisting of the senior vice president, Operations; senior vice president, Finance; vice president and general counsel; vice president, Projects Staff; and the regional vice president responsible for the loan being considered. Besides assuring that each loan is financially sound, the Loan Committee is responsible for determining that the loan has been prepared in accordance with the bank's policies and procedures.

Separate from the work of the internal auditing staff, which reports to the senior vice president, Finance, after loans are approved and funded the Operations Evaluation Department reviews and independently evaluates the effectiveness of bank operations. The director-general of the Operations Evaluation Department has a rank equivalent to a vice president, and is appointed by and reports directly to the executive directors as well as the president.

OPERATING METHOD

With knowledge of World Bank/IDA organizational structure it is now appropriate to examine the way a bank or IDA project is created

---

[12] Ibid., pp. 74–77.
[13] Ibid., p. 77.

and implemented. This process is referred to as the "project cycle" or stages of the project cycle in World Bank Group literature. It involves identification, preparation, appraisal, negotiation, supervision, and evaluation. Understanding the project cycle is important for bankers involved with the co-financing program and for anyone evaluating and using the results of World Bank efforts from its international relations and coordination function or from its research activities.

In a sense much of the Bank's external relations and coordination work may be considered as part of its preparation for lending activities, and publications and research may be considered as by-products of its lending activities. The project cycle as the method for focusing all of these activities, not only raises the quality of individual World Bank lending decisions, but actually tests each lending decision and feeds the results back into the process for the next practical application by means of the evaluation process. Furthermore, through its connection with the IMF and other international organizations, the World Bank perhaps more than any other international lender has the ability to create the conditions necessary to insure the success of its own lending.

The World Bank project cycle starts with its information base and accumulated staff experience as a backdrop for a detailed economic examination of each borrowing country. Periodically an economic mission composed of perhaps five to 10 specialists will visit each country. The mission investigates a nation's macroeconomics profile, creditworthiness, overall development plan, and sectoral plans. The work of the mission forms a basis for an evaluation of national and sectoral policies and problems and for discussions between the Bank and the country on an appropriate development strategy for the entire national economy and its main sectors. Then, individual projects are defined and selected based upon their high economic or financial rates of return for a multiyear lending program that becomes the basis for the Bank's future work in the country. Projects may result not only from current missions, but also from government proposals, work of previous missions, outgrowth of existing projects, and suggestions by private sponsors, such as mining enterprises seeking to develop new resources. If a series of projects related to each other is being considered, all projects must be studied and pass a prima facie test of feasibility before starting preparation work on the first project of the series.

After a project has been identified, defined, and included in the Bank's lending program for a nation, project preparation starts. Preparation is the responsibility of the borrower and requires feasibility studies. These studies establish preliminary designs of technical and institutional alternatives for implementing projects along with cost and benefit analysis. Assistance in various forms, including use of outside consultants, may be necessary to accomplish this work. The World

Bank will assist borrowers in preparing terms of reference for using consultants and assuring that consultants selected are qualified. However, borrowers select their consultants.

When preparatory studies are almost finished, World Bank staff visit the borrowing country again for a detailed appraisal of the economic, technical, organizational, managerial, operational, and financial aspects of the project. Appraisal is solely the Bank's responsibility. A project's benefits and rate of return must justify its costs, technical processes must be feasible, and the borrower must be able to manage the project upon completion and meet the financial conditions for efficient operations. Marketing, training needs, and social and environmental implications of projects are some of the detailed aspects which are examined.

In some projects an economic justification might include calculating an expected economic rate of return to the country and taking into account who will receive the benefits from the project and who will bear the costs, as well as what impact there will be on employment, the nation's fiscal situation, and its balance of payments. Likely behavior of the project's beneficiaries also is important, and a sound financial plan and sufficient operating funds must be available after project completion. In some cases it may be necessary to develop or improve the organization, management, staffing, policies, and procedures for the entity undertaking the project or even government policies. The bank also stresses planning, monitoring, financial management, and evaluation techniques at the appraisal stage.

After appraisal, a bank loan is negotiated with the usual terms for amount, rate, and repayment embodied in a loan agreement along with covenants to assure successful implementation. Typical covenants deal with management, rates of return, and tariffs for utilities and similar projects and borrowing limitations. Other clauses provide that the bank is entitled to obtain certain information and to inspect the project. Before negotiation the Loan Committee reviews proposed projects and authorizes the staff to negotiate terms according to approved guidelines. After agreement is reached on all terms and conditions the loan agreement is signed.

Although the borrower implements the project, the bank is responsible for supervising implementation by reviewing progress reports from the borrower and making periodic on-site visits. The bank's role at this stage is basically to help the borrower identify and solve problems arising during implementation. Problems are treated as matters of joint concern. The bank routinely shares its experience gained from similar projects and in its supervisory role provides valuable technical assistance. Borrowers and others involved in implementing World Bank projects benefit significantly from this experience and recognize the usefulness of the bank's role.

Finally, after project completion World Bank personnel independent from those involved with developing and administering the project, Operations Evaluation Department staff, review the work of the World Bank and look for ways to minimize future problems and further improve World Bank procedures. To help disseminate its own experience from the evaluation process, since 1977 the World Bank has published an "Annual Review of Project Peformance Audit Results." Results to date indicate that over 90 percent of investments in bank projects were clearly worthwhile as measured by achieving their major objectives and that the great majority of projects involving calculation of economic rates of return achieved satisfactory results. Moreover, independent project evaluation has caused greater emphasis to be placed on sociocultural factors and ways to increase the effectiveness of institutions, especially with regard to project related training and the use of monitoring systems.[14]

INTERNATIONAL RELATIONS AND COORDINATION

In addition to the internal discipline of its own project-cycle process the World Bank Group has the opportunity to maximize the chances for success of its lending activities through various functions which involve contact with numerous international organizations and groups. Some contacts provide information on trends and developments which lead to better decision making for selecting priorities or improved methods for conducting its lending programs. Other entities actually provide specialized technical assistance to various World Bank and IDA projects. Through other associations the World Bank participates actively with lending nations and financial entities in planning and coordinating bilateral and multilateral aid to certain nations. Specific cases will better illustrate some of these functions and the advantages which they provide for World Bank and IDA lending activities.

Through its close association with the International Monetary Fund (IMF), for example, the World Bank Group gains valuable perspective on international monetary conditions and related matters which bear directly on the development process. The IMF and World Bank were not only created simultaneously, but continue to meet together for their annual meetings during September or October of each year. Traditionally, the IMF-World Bank Group annual meetings are held for two years in Washington, D.C. and every third year in a different member country. At these meetings of governors, executive directors, their alternates, and invited guests, the World Bank management and staff not only gather information and renew personal contacts, but also have the opportunity to influence opinion and shape actions of borrowing members and members whose policies effect borrowers.

---

[14] Ibid., pp. 14–22. Also see Warren C. Baum, *The Project Cycle,* The World Bank, (Washington, D.C. 1982).

Agreements between the president of the World Bank and the IMF managing director on collaboration, missions, policy, and similar matters are embodied in official documents referred to as joint memoranda.

As a specialized agency within the meaning of Article 57 of the Charter of the United Nations (UN), the World Bank maintains close relations with key UN organs and units. Formal agreements between the UN and each individual member of the World Bank Group govern such matters as reciprocal representation, consultation, and exchange of other than confidential information. A liaison committee composed of the secretary-general of the UN, the president of the bank, and the administrator of the UN Development Program (UNDP) meets from time to time for consultations and exchange of information.

The Bank also works closely with UNDP on a direct basis. The president of the bank is a member of the Inter-Agency Consultative Board which advises the UNDP Administrator on policy matters and reviews programs to be presented to the UNDP Governing Council. One of UNDP's functions is to finance the foreign exchange costs of preinvestment studies on a grant basis. However, since UNDP itself does not conduct these studies but relies on the UN and the specialized agencies for this purpose, the World Bank has frequently acted as the executing agency for preinvestment studies.

Bank representatives also participate in the meetings of the UN General Assembly, the Economic and Social Council (ECOSOC), and the UN Conference on Trade and Development (UNCTAD). Further, the Bank has entered into cooperative program agreements with the UN Food and Agricultural Organization (FAO), the UN Education, Scientific, and Cultural Organization (UNESCO), the World Health Organization (WHO), and the UN Industrial Development Organization (UNIDO). Under these agreements assistance is provided to governments in indentifying and preparing projects for Bank financing. The agencies also supply technical staff for bank sectoral studies and Bank missions for economic studies and appraisal and supervision of specific projects.

Contact on an ad hoc basis is maintained with ILO (the International Labor Office), the International Telecommunications Union, UNFPA (the United Nations Fund for Population Activities and UNICEF (the United Nations Children's Fund). Also the bank works closely with regional development banks, such as the Interamerican Development Bank, the African Development Bank, and the Asian Development Bank, as well as the Commission of the European Communities (EC), the European Investment Bank, and the Development Assistance Council of the OECD (Organization for Economic Cooperation and Development).[15]

---

[15] Ibid., pp. 63–69.

As a further illustration of its international coordination function, in May 1971 the World Bank, FAO, and UNDP sponsored establishment of a Consultative Group on International Agricultural Research (CGIAR). Membership in CGIAR includes not only nations, but the Ford, Kellogg, and Rockefeller Foundations, regional development banks, and other entities. CGIAR was formed to mobilize financial support for international agricultural research in order to increase world food supplies. Since its formation CGIAR has helped synchronize national and international agricultural research efforts and encourage application of international research in national agricultural programs.

With support from a Technical Advisory Committee CGIAR has implemented numerous research programs at leading world agricultural centers, including the International Maize and Wheat Improvement Center (CIMMYT) in El Bataan, Mexico, the International Center of Tropical Agriculture (CIAT) in Cali, Colombia, the International Potato Center (CIP) in Lima, Peru, the International Board for Plant Genetic Resources (IBPGR) in Rome, Italy, the International Center for Agricultural Research in Dry Areas (ICARDA) in Beirut, Lebanon and Aleppo, Syria, the International Crops Research Institute for the Semi-Arid Tropics (ICRISAT) in Hyderabad, India, the International Institute of Tropical Agriculture (IITA) in Ibadan, Nigeria, and the International Rice Research Institute (IRRI) in Los Banos, Philippines. CIMMYT and IRRI date back to efforts begun in the 1940s and are well known for research which was the basis for the "Green Revolution," involving improved crop strains, including high-yielding wheat and rice. CGIAR also supports cattle and swine research and animal disease studies in Addis Ababa, Ethiopia and Nairobi, Kenya and programs of the West African Rice Development Association (WARDA) based in Monrovia, Liberia.[16]

Early in its history the bank recognized that coordination of multilateral and bilateral assistance to developing nations is necessary in order to help assure that donors are supporting consistent development goals and that financial and technical aid from various sources is applied efficiently to priority projects. Accordingly, the bank has taken the lead in forming and leading groups to coordinate aid flows and exchange information and views about aid programs and development problems in member countries. Active aid coordinating groups chaired by the World Bank as of June 30, 1981 included those for Bangladesh, Bolivia, Burma, the Caribbean, Colombia, Egypt, India, East Africa (Kenya, Tanzania and Uganda), Korea, Mauritius, Nepal, Pakistan, Philippines, Sri Lanka, Sudan, Thailand, Zaire, and Zambia. In 1978 the World Bank helped start the Caribbean Group for Cooperation in Economic Development. The bank also participates in the meetings of

---

[16] Ibid., p. 68.

the aid groups for Indonesia (chaired by the Netherlands) and Turkey (chaired by the Organization for Economic Cooperation and Development).

Through such contacts and activities the World Bank variously diffuses knowledge and information, minimizes instances of "reinventing the wheel," coordinates aid and development efforts, establishes realistic national economic priorities, improves national development plans, and ultimately implements its own project lending in the most efficient and beneficial manner. At the same time, especially during the last 5–10 years, the bank has undertaken project lending through co-financing activities, which involve private international financial institutions, as well as government programs and public lending agencies. Through co-financing private institutions indirectly can obtain the advantages of World Bank international coordination and cooperative efforts, share in the group's information and research base, and benefit from the project-cycle process.

CO-FINANCING PROGRAM

Although the World Bank and IDA have lent over $80 billion since formulation, emphasis always has been not so much on the amounts which the bank could lend directly, but rather on the concept of the bank as a safe bridge over which private capital could move internationally. For years the World Bank has joined with other nations and regional development institutions in lending to the same borrowers. National and multinational lenders with which the World Bank has worked include Sweden, Canada, the United States, Germany, Japan, Norway, the United Kingdom, the European Investment Bank, and regional development banks. Typical projects in the past with multiple lenders are the Volta River power and aluminum project in Ghana, the Las Truchas steel project in Mexico, and dams in Nigeria and Sudan. In fiscal 1980, the bank joined with nine official national and multilateral agencies in funding a $500 million project to develop iron ore mining in Mauritania.

More recently, the World Bank and national and multilateral institutions formed by the Middle East members of the Organization of Petroleum Exporting Countries (OPEC) have been working together closely. These institutions include the Abu Dhabi Fund for Arab Economic Development (ADFAED), the Arab Fund for Economic and Social Development (AFESD), the Kuwait Fund for Arab Economic Development (KFAED), the OPEC Fund for International Development (OPECFID), the Saudi Fund for Development (SFD), the Islamic Development Bank (ISDB), and the Banque Arabe pour le Dèveloppement Èconomique en Africa (BADEA). In fiscal year 1980 alone these aid agencies together with the World Bank provided about $1.5 billion for 25 projects for power, water supply, railways, industry, and agriculture.

Official sources constitute, however, only one of the three main categories of co-financing partners.

In recent years, *export credits* have become an important source of co-financing, particularly for larger projects in the industrial, public utility, and transportation sectors. As official aid agencies have turned more attention and funds to other sectors and have cut their programs in the medium- to higher-income countries among the bank's borrowers, the export credit market has often been called on to fill the void. Under competitive conditions, borrowers have found the terms of export credits quite attractive.

The World Bank has also encouraged co-financing with *private investors* since the early days of its operations. In the 1950s and 1960s, World Bank financing was occasionally linked to public issues by the borrowing countries, and, from time to time, bank lending has been coordinated with private placements by institutional investors. For over six years the bank has pursued a specific program to increase the participation of the private sector in its operations by entering into formal arrangements with them. In these co-financing operations, the World Bank and private financial institutions, especially commercial banks, enter into separate loan agreements with the borrower.

The bank in placing greater emphasis on co-financing with private financial institutions is taking a number of measures to expand its association with private lenders, including a more active promotional program vis-a-vis the private banking community and new techniques which could make co-financing more attractive to some borrowers and private lenders. The bank's co-financing program aims to encourage private financial institutions to direct their lending in developing countries to high-priority projects, to introduce new lenders to developing countries, to bring new entities in borrowing countries to the market, and more generally, to encourage the bank's borrowers to broaden their sources of external finance and diversify the instruments of borrowing.

For many years the World Bank offered to sell participations in its loan portfolio to private banks. These loans were either negotiated or both negotiated and funded by the bank. For some private lenders, especially for some international commercial banks during the postwar years when interest rates tended to be relatively stable, purchase of World Bank loan participations was an attractive alternative to seeking out and arranging their own loans. However, with the unstable and generally rising interest rate environment during the last several years, fixed-rate loans have limited resale possibilities. Furthermore, the size of projects, which the World Bank has financed in recent years, has become so large that increasingly it is necessary to obtain financing from numerous sources and different financial markets.[17]

The World Bank's role as a catalyst in attracting development finance for high-priority programs in the developing countries through co-financing has increased significantly in recent years. Over the five years from fiscal years 1977 to 1981, co-financing reached a yearly average of nearly $3.7 billion in around 90 projects per year. Co-financing has been a feature in about 37 percent of Bank/IDA operations, and the volume of funds mobilized from other sources external to borrowing countries has been equivalent to more than 36 percent of the total volume of bank group lending. Historically, the major source of co-financing has been official bilateral and multilateral aid agencies. However, in fiscal year 1981, co-financing with private banks became the single most important source for the first time, contributing about $1.7 billion to project financing for 18 operations. (See Table 1.)

Most projects with private co-financing have been in the industrial and power sectors. However, recently private co-lenders have been involved in agricultural and urban development projects, as well as projects supporting tourism, transportation, and mining. Private co-financing opportunities are expected to grow significantly during the coming years, especially for energy and mining projects.

Identification of co-financing opportunities begins at the stage when a financial plan emerges from the World Bank project-cycle process, and gaps or shortfalls in financing from long-term, fixed-rate sources appear. Understandably, borrowers first maximize the use of these sources, which in addition to the World Bank, include regional development banks, various other related bilateral and multilateral sources, and official export credit agencies. For the shortfall or gap it is necessary to turn to commercial institutions and pay market rates. In a few recent cases private co-financing also has been used to finance specific sub-projects within a larger World Bank investment program.

Under the World Bank's co-financing program with private financial institutions, the borrower is ultimately responsible for selecting the lending bank. At the request of the borrowers, the World Bank has assisted in making co-financing opportunities widely known to potential private lenders and has often provided borrowers with the names of private institutions which have shown an interest in co-financing. In some cases when requested by its brrowers, the bank has taken the initiative to establish contact with prospective borrowers. From the borrower's viewpoint, in addition to filling financial gaps, it may be possible that co-lenders for World Bank projects are willing to lend

---

[17] World Bank, *Co-Financing: A Review of World Bank Co-Financing with Private Financial Institutions* (World Bank: Washington, D.C., 1980), (hereinafter *Co-Financing*), pp. 1–4.

Table 1
World Bank Co-Financing Operations (for fiscal years 1977–1981)

	FY 77	FY 78	FY 79	FY 80	FY 81*	Total FY 77–81
Total bank group lending†						
IBRD	5,759.3	6,097.7	6,989.0	7,644.2	8,808.9	35,299.1
IDA	1,307.5	2,313.3	3,021.5	3,837.5	3,482.1	13,961.9
Total	7,066.8	8,411.0	10,010.5	11,481.7	12,291.0	49,261.0
Number of operations						
IBRD	161	137	142	144	140	724
IDA	67	99	105	103	106	480
Total	228	236	247	247	246	1,204
Co-financing						
Amount†	2,289.1	2,426.4	3,149.4	6,516.3	4,038.0	18,419.2
Percent IBRD/IDA lending	32%	29%	31%	57%	33%	37%
Number of operations	81	81	109	93	79	443
Percent of IBRD/IDA operations	36%	34%	44%	37%	32%	37%
Co-financing by source‡						
Co-financing						
Official	1,541.7	1,757.2	1,976.3	2,458.6	1,569.7	9,303.5
Export credit	197.5	539.3	659.2	2,282.3	734.1	4,412.4
Private	549.9	129.9	513.9	1,775.4	1,734.2	4,703.3
Total	2,289.1	2,426.4	3,149.4	6,516.3	4,038.0	18,419.2
Local	5,063.2	6,432.0	6,715.9	10,221.1	12,742.0	41,174.2
Bank group	2,564.2	2,440.8	4,139.5	4,798.1	4,614.0	18,556.6
Total project Financing	9,916.5	11,299.2	14,004.8	21,535.5	21,394.0	78,150.0

Percent of contribution					
Co-financing	23	21	22	30	18.9	23.6
Local	51	57	48	48	59.5	52.7
Bank group	26	22	30	22	21.6	23.7
Total	100	100	100	100	100.0	100.0
Memo number of operations with co-financing					
Official	72	71	88	68	66	365
Export credit	9	15	16	23	7	70
Private	9	7	13	21	18	68
Total‡	81	81	109	93	79	443

* Fiscal Year 1981 data is based on information extracted from the President's and Appraisal Reports.
† In millions of dollars (U.S.).
‡ The number of individual operations with co-financing by source is greater than the total amount since there are projects co-financed from more than one source.

on longer terms, at lower rates, or with less security than for similar
projects without World Bank involvement, although this is difficult
to demonstrate. Also, the World Bank, in certain situations, may skew
its own amortization tables towards the later maturities in order to
accommodate funds from private sources.[18]

After the borrower selects a private lender or lending group, separate negotiations are conducted with the private lenders and the World
Bank. However, the World Bank reserves the right to comment on
the private loan and on specific clauses in the private loan documentation that affect the bank's rights, such as the cross-default clause.

Reciprocal cross-default clauses and other cross references in the
World Bank-borrower and private lender-borrower loan agreements,
along with a memorandum of agreement between the World Bank
and the private lenders, are the main characteristics of World Bank
co-financing documentation. World Bank loan agreements typically
provide that the Bank has the option to suspend disbursements on
its loans if, for good cause, a loan from a private bank is suspended
or cancelled, or if repayments are accelerated. (Default in service payments by the borrower is one example of "good cause.") If repayment
of the private loan is accelerated because of the borrower's default,
the World Bank also has the option to accelerate payments on its loan.
The private lender-borrower loan agreement contains reciprocal wording. However, neither the bank nor the private lender is obligated
to suspend disbursements or accelerate. Each has the right to exercise
or not exercise its remedies at its own discretion. Other cross-refer-
ences, which private lenders generally include in their agreements
with the borrower, cover the normal commitments by the borrower
with regard to project implementation, management, and operations
of the borrower and the typical financial covenants.[19]

In a separate agreement between the private lender and the World
Bank, called a memorandum of agreement, the parties undertake to
exchange information and consult with each other about matters that
affect the borrower's implementation of the project or ability to repay.
By this agreement private lenders have greater than normal access
to country and project information (in a readily usable format) which
the World Bank has gathered and analyzed. Each party retains the
right to withhold confidential information, however. In addition the
memorandum of agreement may contain provisions for the World Bank
to serve as billing agent for the private lender and to instruct the
borrower to make payment directly to the private bank.[20]

---

[18] Ibid., pp. 9–10.

[19] Ibid., pp. 5–6. Also see Richard F. Janssen, "Business Role Abroad," *The Wall
Street Journal*, April 14, 1981, p. 56.

[20] World Bank, *Co-Financing*, p. 4–6.

RESEARCH AND INFORMATION SERVICES

In addition to items specifically relating to co-financing opportunities for potential lenders, the *Catalog of World Bank Publications* provides other selected materials of interest to international bankers. This catalog is a basic reference document for inclusion in international banking libraries. It may be obtained from the World Bank, Publications Distribution Unit, 1818 H. Street, N.W., Washington, D.C. 20433, U.S.A.

Information about specific World Bank projects may be obtained from the World Bank's *Monthly Operational Summary* which in 1981 cost $60 per year (Baltimore and London: The Johns Hopkins Press, Journals Division, Baltimore, Maryland, 21218, U.S.A.). Goods and work to be procured by international competitive bidding are advertised as General Procurement Notices in *Development Forum Business Edition* which is issued 24 times per year and in 1981 cost $250 per year, including a subscription to the *Monthly Operational Summary* at no additional cost. Requests for subscriptions and sample copies of *Development Forum Business Edition* (including the *Monthly Operation Summary*) may be addressed to: Development Forum Business Edition, Subscription Department, United Nations, CH–1211, Geneva 10, Switzerland or to the World Bank, Room E–1035, 1818 H Street, N.W., Washington, D.C. 20433, U.S.A.

For general background and information on current developments on world monetary and development finance issues the International Monetary Fund and the World Bank jointly publish a quarterly magazine entitled *Finance & Development*. In addition to timely articles this publication summarizes quarterly IMF and World Bank activities in a few pages, announces new World Bank and IMF materials, and publishes short book reviews. Subscribers should write to *Finance & Development*, International Monetary Fund Building, Washington, D.C. 20431, U.S.A.

For use in connection with country analysis and international economic research the *Catalog of World Bank Publications* currently lists some 17 topics such as Agriculture and Rural Development, Country Studies, Finance and Debt, Industry, Trade, Urban Development, and World Bank (Institutional). Indexes also cross reference all publications included by author and title.

Under the Finance and Debt listing, for example, appears the *World Debt Tables*. This document may be used in conjunction with the *International Financial Statistics* (*IFS*) series from the IMF and is indisposable for institutions which undertake serious country analysis as a basis for lending decisions. While the *International Financial Statistics* series is ordered from the IMF, *World Debt Tables* which includes only public debt, must be ordered from the World Bank. Under the World Bank (Institutional) listing, topics include summaries of the

World Bank Group annual meetings, addresses by the President of
the World Bank, Articles of Agreement and By-Laws of the group
members, guidelines for Procurement under World Bank loans and
IDA credits, booklets describing World Bank policies and operations,
the project cycle, uses of consultants by the Bank and its borrowers,
and abstracts of current World Bank research programs.

Other representative publications for sale include extremely thorough country studies, easy-to-use compounding and discounting tables
for project evaluation and an extensive collection of investment laws
of the world compiled and classified by the International Centre for
Settlement of Investment Disputes (ICSID). ICSID, associated with
the World Bank Group, is an autonomous institution established under
World Bank auspices to provide a forum for conciliation and arbitration
of international investment disputes between nations and foreign
investors.[21]

The research and publications mentioned in this section are meant
only to be representative of materials available from the World Bank
and barely scratch the surface of the wealth of information which
could be useful to the international banker. Additional useful publications are cited in the footnotes to this chapter. Annual reports, the
June 1981 booklet of 84 pages entitled "The World Bank" and the
small pamphlet on co-financing are also available from the bank.

TREASURY FUNCTIONS AND FUTURE TRENDS

In considering the asset/liability management aspect of the bank's
treasury function, the World Bank under its Articles of Agreement
cannot allow outstanding loans to exceed the total of subscribed capital,
reserves, and surplus. The articles, however, do not limit the amount
which the bank may borrow from others by issuing its own obligations.[22]
Historically, bank borrowings have not exceeded the sum of subscribed
capital, reserves and surplus, which is referred to in some past writings
about the bank as a "gearing" ratio of 1:1. Thus, by a policy decision
the bank could increase its ability to lend significantly by increasing
its gearing ratio. Examining this situation from another perspective
with total paid-in capital, reserves, and income of almost $7.5 billion
and outstanding debt of almost $30 billion as of June 30, 1980 the
bank's debt to paid-in equity ratio was 4:1. By either measure of debt
to capital the bank is quite conservative. Many commercial banks,
for example, typically have comparative ratios in ranges of from 15:1
to 20:1. From time to time proposals have been made to increase

---

[21] World Bank, *Catalog of World Bank Publications*, (Washington, D.C.: 1979) pp.
3–10. Also see World Bank, *The Research Program of the World Bank* (Washington,
D.C.: 1981) and *World Bank Abstract of Current Studies* for further details of World
Bank research projects.

[22] World Bank, *Articles of Agreement*, Article III, Section 3, p. 4.

the bank's rate of borrowing and thus provide more funds for World Bank lending by increased borrowing. To date this has not been done.[23]

Most of the World Bank's borrowing comes from private capital markets around the world. Of total outstanding bank debt of almost $30 billion at June 30, 1980, almost $10 billion represented U.S. dollar obligations, approximately $9 billion was deutsche mark debt, about $5.5 billion was in Swiss francs, and over $4 billion in Japanese yen. However, the bank has borrowed in about 20 currencies and constantly seeks to broaden its funding sources. In virtually all countries where its debt issues are sold the World Bank is the largest nonresident borrower.[24]

The bank pays market rates for its funds, receives the highest rating (Triple A) from the leading U.S. bond rating services and issues both public offerings and makes private placements. All securities issued by the bank are its direct obligations. None is secured by a pledge of specific assets, and World Bank securities state that they are not obligations of any government. However, as detailed above in this chapter member governments are obligated to make payments on their uncalled capital, if required by the bank in order for it to meet its obligations on borrowings. Thus, the uncalled capital effectively provides strong backing for the bank's securities. Further, the bank's articles provide for a special reserve which is invested in liquid assets and may be used only to meet bank obligations arising out of its borrowings or guarantees. At June 30, 1980 this special reserve stood at $292 million where it has remained since the mid-1960s. In accordance with the bank's articles, during the first 10 years of operations, a commission of 1 percent was charged on the outstanding portion of all loans made by the bank out of borrowed funds and on all loans guaranteed by the bank in order to build up this special reserve.[25]

The average life of outstanding bank loans is approximately 9.4 years, while the average life of the bank's entire debt is 6.05 years. The average life of public debt is 7.02 years. Borrowings from governments bring the overall debt to a shorter maturity. However, for more than 20 years the central banks in Germany, Japan and Switzerland among others have been consistent providers of funds year after year and in practice these official borrowings may not be short term, although they are denominated as such. Thus, while the bank is a relatively

---

[23] Leonard Silk, "McNamara Warns U.S. of Perils in Reducing Aid to World's Poor," *New York Times,* June 21, 1981, p. 46.

[24] World Bank, *1980 Annual Report,* Financial Statements, Appendix E, Summary Statement of Borrowings, p. 157. Also see World Bank, *The World Bank's Borrowing Program: Some Questions and Answers* by Eugene H. Rotberg, Vice President and Treasurer, World Bank (Washington, D.C.: 1979) pp. 1–5.

[25] World Bank, *Articles of Agreement,* Article IV, pp. 6–7. For an independent evaluation of the *World Bank's* credit quality monthly from an investor's standpoint also see Kidder, Peabody and Co. Incorporated, *Multilateral Development Banks Analysis and Outlook* (New York, 1982).

long term lender at fixed rate, it has a good match with debt of similar maturity. Capital accounts of over $7 billion provide resources of "infinite maturity" and the rate spread has provided continued income for pay out to IDA and continuous annual increases in retained earnings.[26]

With regard to managing the difference between cost of funds and price of loans, as of June 30, 1980, the average cost of almost $30 billion in total bank borrowings was 7.28 percent. Including capital accounts the average cost of total resources was 6.00 percent. These percentages had increased from 7.06 and 4.96, respectively, as of June 30, 1975. The weighted average cost of funds borrowed during fiscal year 1980 was 8.24 percent, and the cost of new borrowings is reflected directly in the bank's charges on new loans. At least once a year and more often if necessary, the bank adjusts its lending rate to achieve a spread of approximately 0.5 of 1 percent above its cost of borrowing. At June 30, 1980 the loan rate was 9.25 percent per annum, and on January 1, 1981 the rate was increased to 9.60 percent.[27]

Short-term liquid assets of the bank amount to almost $10 billion and represent one of the largest pools of such funds outside OPEC (the Organization of Petroleum Exporting Countries). In addition to maintaining liquid funds to offset the Special Reserve account the bank deliberately maintains large liquid reserves in order to fund disbursements on previously committed loans without heavy reliance on world capital markets in times of high interest rates. The flexibility provided by the bank's policy regarding liquidity is demonstrated by the fact that the bank did not borrow at all in the U.S. market in 1969, 1973, 1974 and the three-and-a-half years after August 1977.[28]

To manage its pool of liquidity funds the bank has assembled a special group of securities traders and economists, who undergo extensive training in a bank-run program. The bank's trading policy prohibits assuming currency risk, although bank borrowers, of course, must assume that risk. Accordingly, all bank borrowings are matched either by loans or securities in the same currency. Furthermore, the bank by policy decision avoids high-interest credit risks in its securities purchases and instead relies on correctly forecasting major moves in interest rates for periods as long as three months in advance.[29]

[26] World Bank, *The World Bank*, p. 51.

[27] On loans negotiated after July 1, 1982 the bank charges a variable rate that will be adjusted semi-annually. It will amount to 0.50% more than the weighted average cost in the past six months of a pool of the bank's borrowings. For loans negotiated after January 5, 1982 a frontend fee is payable when the loan becomes effective. This fee was initially set at 1.50% of the principal amount of the loan but was reduced to 0.75% for loans negotiated after December 7, 1982. The bank also imposes a commitment charge (0.75% per year) on the undisbursed portion of loans.

[28] Ibid., pp. 55–56.

[29] Daniel Hertzberg, "Specialized Breed of Traders Manages World Bank's Huge Pool of Assets," *The Wall Street Journal*, March 30, 1981, p. 25.

In addition to its borrowings, capital, surplus, and special reserve, the bank, of course, is supported in its operations by interest earnings, loan repayments, and sales of loan participations. As of mid-year 1981 the sixth replenishment for IDA and a further increase in the bank's authorized capital were being considered. However, as the United States and other industrialized member nations periodically reevaluate their bilateral and multilateral foreign aid contributions, the importance of the bank's co-financing program with private lenders and the role of private commercial banks and other private international lenders acting alone undoubtedly will continue to increase. For instance, total commercial bank lending for international development finance has increased from an average of $4 billion in the 1970–72 period to an estimated $23 billion in 1979.[30]

With commercial banks increasing their international lending, especially to the more industrialized, less developed countries, the World Bank at its annual meeting in 1981 selected agriculture and rural development and sub-Saharan Africa as sectoral and geographical target areas. The possibility of a radical transformation for India, Indonesia, Pakistan, and Bangladesh could result in agricultural self-sufficiency. At least this goal now seems to be coming into sight. While the bank will continue to work with all members needing help, greater emphasis will be placed on sub-Saharan African nations among those needing the most help. The bank will encourage government policies which provide adequate prices for agricultural producers, increased research, new feeder roads to farm areas, and adequate extension services. Also, the bank in its own programs will continue to stress agricultural research, new tools, techniques, and seeds for increasing productivity.[31]

With the significant increase in the price of oil and other forms of energy since the mid-1970s more developing nations now are engaged in exploring for and producing oil, gas, and other energy sources. The energy sector also will be a priority sector for World Bank effort. Various proposals have been put forth to more heavily involve the World Bank in the energy sector, including creation of a special fund or entity parallel to IDA or IFC exclusively for financing energy-related projects. It now appears that such activities will be conducted within the World Bank itself and increasingly by IFC, whose role is expanding significantly as larger flows of private capital move into development finance.[32] Accordingly, it is appropriate to undertake more detailed study of the international finance corporation in the next chapter.

---

[30] World Bank, *1980 Annual Report*, p. 69.

[31] World Bank, *Address to the Board of Governors* by A. W. Clausen, President, World Bank (Washington, D.C.: September 29, 1981) pp. 8–9 and World Bank, *Address to the Board of Governors* by A. W. Clausen, President, World Bank, Toronto, Canada, September 6, 1982, pp. 7–11.

[32] Ibid., pp. 9–10. Also see Art Pine, "Clausen Moves with Caution to World Bank," *The Wall Street Journal*, June 30, 1981, p. 47.

31
International Finance Corporation

JAMES L. KAMMERT
Executive Vice President
Equibank

INTRODUCTION

The International Finance Corporation (IFC) is an international organization formed in 1956 by treaty among its member nations, which numbered 122 as of June 30, 1982. IFC was established to promote private investment and assist individual enterprises in developing member countries. To carry out these tasks IFC provides both equity and loan funds and a growing range of technical and finance related services. In the course of conducting these activities IFC works closely with international bankers, as well as their customers. Participations in IFC loans by international banks, for example, have been increasing rapidly during recent years. Accordingly, it is important for international bankers to understand the functions of the IFC and how to work with this growing institution.

As an affiliate of the International Bank for Reconstruction and Development (the World Bank), IFC is headquartered in Washington, D.C. and is referred to as a member of the World Bank Group. The preceding chapter describes the activities of the group (which consists of the World Bank and the International Development Association, as well as IFC), with emphasis on the role of the World Bank. The World Bank itself as the oldest unit of the group is now the largest and most prominent of the three entities. Some analysts predict, how-

In connection with writing this chapter the author wishes to acknowledge with thanks the comments and suggestions of Monique Amaudry and Carl T. Bell from the IFC Information Office, Rolk Th. Lundberg, IFC Director of Syndications, Miles Carlisle, IFC Manager of Syndications, and Colbert I. King of The Riggs National Bank and former U.S. Director of IFC. However, all contents, including any errors are the sole responsibility of the author.

ever, that during its second quarter of a century IFC may become the fastest growing organization within the group.[1] For this reason a separate chapter is being devoted to IFC in this Handbook, although until now most financial writing has dealt with IFC only as a part of the World Bank Group.

For commercial and investment bankers, their customers, and others who might work with IFC staff during the coming years it is important to understand the basic distinctions between IFC and the other two units of the World Bank Group. These differences and the aims of the three entities are not inconsistent with one another. In fact the three organizations were designed and operate to complement each other. As shown in the preceding chapter, the World Bank and the International Development Association work at the national government or public level. IFC focuses on the private sector by financing projects and providing services which encourage the flow of domestic and international capital into developing-member countries.

The objectives of IFC are stated in Article One of its Articles of Agreement, the treaty which forms the legal basis for IFC, as follows:

> The purpose of the Corporation is to further economic development by encouraging the growth of productive private enterprise in member countries, particularly in the less developed areas, thus supplementing the activities of the International Bank for Reconstruction and Development . . . In carrying out this purpose, the Corporation shall:
>
> i. In association with private investors, assist in financing the establishment, improvement, and expansion of productive private enterprises which would contribute to the development of its member countries by making investments, without guarantee of repayment by the member government concerned, in cases where sufficient private capital is not available on reasonable terms;
> ii. seek to bring together investment opportunities, domestic and foreign private capital, and experienced management; and
> iii. seek to stimulate, and to help create conditions conductive to the flow of private capital, domestic and foreign, into productive investment in member countries.
>
> The Corporation shall be guided in all its decisions by the provisions of this Article.[2]

Analysis of how IFC has carried out its objectives during its first 25 years gives valuable insight and direction for using IFC's resources and services in the future. Although it is an important international source of equity and loan funds for various types of projects in develop-

---

[1] Richard F. Janssen, "Business Role Abroad," *The Wall Street Journal*, April 14, 1981, p. 56.

[2] International Finance Corporation, *International Finance Corporation Articles of Agreement*, Article One.

ing nations, IFC provides more than money. In addition to supplying funds, IFC undertakes various specialized activities to improve the investment climate and raise investor confidence in the countries where it operates. Moreover, IFC generally provides expertise and experience and brings different institutions, organizations, and people together in projects which promote development. Activities or projects designed to fulfil simultaneously more than one of these objectives and lead to the creation of mechanisms for bringing about continuing development are obviously of most interest to IFC. For this reason, IFC's role as a catalyst for development is often singled out for emphasis, although its commitments now total over $2 billion and IFC has the ability to grow substantially beyond this level based on its existing borrowing capacity.

To explain how to work effectively with IFC and use its services efficiently this chapter analyzes IFC's financial resources, scope of operations, organization, management, and staff. Then IFC's investment policies, its role as a catalyst, and IFC's technical assistance and various financial services are examined. Finally, mention is made of how future trends might influence IFC's activities and how to contact IFC to obtain further information or use its resources.

FINANCIAL RESOURCES AND OPERATIONAL SCOPE

At the close of its June 30, 1981 fiscal year, IFC had 119 member nations from around the world and authorized capital of $650 million. Each member nation is a capital subscriber. At June 30, 1982 paid-in capital amounted to $497 million and accumulated earnings equaled an additional $181 million for a total of $551 million in capital and accumulated earnings. Also IFC has a steady flow of loan repayments and can sell equity and loan assets to supplement its resources. During the fiscal year ending June 30, 1981 repayments of loans and recoveries amounted to $98 million, and $6.8 million of equity investments were sold.[3]

Total borrowings of $917 million, all but $35 million of which were obtained from the World Bank, brought total liabilities and capital to almost $1,234 million. IFC is permitted by its Articles of Agreement to borrow up to four times the amount of its unimpaired subscribed capital and IFC may borrow from member nations and world capital markets, as well as from the World Bank. Of total assets of almost $1,085 million loan and equity investment net of undisbursed amounts and a reserve against losses amounted to $1,050 million as of June 30, 1981. Net income for each of the last three years has been around

---

[3] International Finance Corporation, *1982 Annual Report* (hereinafter *1982 Annual Report*), pp. 4, 16–17, and *Financial Statements*, Exhibit A, "Balance Sheet," p. 48.

$20 million and the reserve against losses totalled $61 million, equal to 5.5 percent of the total disbursed portfolio on June 30, 1981.[4]

This brief financial analysis indicates that IFC has substantial resources and the financial capacity to increase its activities significantly beyond its current levels. In fact for the last several years IFC has been growing faster than during its first two decades. In accordance with its five-year program, continued expansion is planned. Authorized capital has been increased from $110 million to $650 million. Paid-in capital increased from $108 million at fiscal year-end 1977 to $144 million at year-end 1978, to $229 million in 1979, $307 million by 1980, and 392 million at year-end 1981, while borrowing remained essentially constant at around the $450 to $500 million level and accumulated earnings increased steadily. Because IFC can borrow up to four times its unimpaired capital and surplus, IFC's potential resource base is currently about $2,600 million and is expected to increase to over $3,000 million within the next few years.[5]

This expanding capital base supports growing investments which increasingly are being directed to enterprises in lower-income member countries in the world's least developed regions. At the same time, operations are being expanded steadily to more countries and the sectoral composition of IFC investments is being broadened, particularly into natural resources projects. For example, the number of countries in which IFC operates has increased from an average of 20 in the early 1970s to 34 in fiscal 1981. During each of the last several years IFC has undertaken first-time investments in at least one member country.[6]

With this volume of growth both the number of projects and number of investments also have increased rapidly. During fiscal 1981 for example, $811 million went into 56 different projects compared to $681 million for 55 projects for fiscal year 1980 and $425 million for 48 projects the year before. After three years of planning and promotion, projects undertaken in smaller and least developed countries have increased. Twenty-nine of the 56 projects during fiscal 1981 were initiated in nations where gross national product per capita amounted to less than $626 per year.

Most of the 56 projects in fiscal 1981 were, as in past years, in the manufacturing sector. IFC provided technical assistance and financing for seven cement plants, three steel operations, four pulp and paper mills, and two fertilizer plants. Agroindustry projects figured more prominently in 1981 investment activity, while manufacturing projects

---

[4] *1981 Annual Report*, pp. 16–17 and *Financial Statements*, Exhibit B, "Statement of Income," p. 40.

[5] *1981 Annual Report*, pp. 39–40 and *1980 International Finance Corporation Annual Report* (hereinafter *1980 Annual Report*).

[6] *1981 Annual Report*, p. 5.

dropped below 50 percent of the total for the first time in IFC's history. The 10 agroindustry projects with a total cost of $208 million included flour milling, rice growing, rubber and palm oil production, and two storage terminal operations. Of other investments, six were for fuel and mineral projects, six for hotels, and nine for various kinds of financial institutions.[7]

IFC works to tailor its investments to the individual needs and circumstances of projects in each member nation. In this regard IFC works closely with various economic and other experts at the World Bank to insure that IFC-supported activities and projects coincide with other efforts by the World Bank Group. Furthermore, while IFC to some extent can promote various sectors and even specific types of projects, in the final analysis it is dealing with private investors. Hence, it must be flexible and recognize the results of their decision-making processes. For this reason much of IFC's work involves efforts to improve the climate for private investment and the perception of this climate and business opportunities by private investors, both foreign and domestic.

ORGANIZATION, MANAGEMENT, AND STAFF

While IFC's impressive parentage and strong financial resources make it a significant factor in the field of international development finance, IFC's greatest resource is without doubt its staff. Although only 388 in number at June 30, 1981 with 221 higher-level staff among the total, IFC's employees represent some 60 different nationalities and a unique blend of skills and experience.[8] Besides the lending, operations, treasury, and support functions expected in any large international financial organization, IFC staff include experienced investment bankers, financial analysts with an equity orientation, legal experts, engineers, and specialists in marketing, management consulting, and other fields, as well as some economists, country and area experts for virtually every corner of the globe.

In addition, IFC can rely for support upon the various technical experts in related fields at the World Bank. This permits IFC staff to concentrate on their particular tasks with a singleness of purpose once a project or activity has been identified and targeted for implementation. Often large projects take several years to develop even to the stage of starting construction. Persistence and patience are required by IFC staff to bring and keep together parties not only of different nationalities, but also with diverse investment and economic objectives. Equity investors, whether large or small corporations or even individu-

---

[7] *1981 Annual Report*, p. 15.

[8] *1981 Annual Report*, p. 32.

als, long-term lenders, short-term lenders, contractors, suppliers, managers, customers, and government bodies among many others must work together in order to implement large greenfield projects or significant expansions of existing enterprises. The fact that IFC has many repeat customers testifies to the quality and effectiveness of its staff.

IFC derives its authority and status as an international entity from the international agreement among its member nations. This treaty called the Articles of Agreement provides that all World Bank members may become members of IFC. All the powers of IFC are vested in its Board of Governors who are also governors of the World Bank. Each member nation of the World Bank appoints one governor and one alternate.[9] This body normally meets once a year at the time of the annual meeting of the International Monetary Fund-World Bank Group. As a rule this meeting is held for two years in Washington, D.C. and in a different country every third year.

Responsibility for the conduct of IFC's general operations is vested in its board of directors which generally meets weekly and consists of the 21 executive directors of the World Bank. The president of the World Bank is chairman *ex officio* of the IFC Board of Directors, which appoints him president of IFC. Several other officials for specialized functions such as administrative services, internal auditing, programming and budgeting, operations evaluation, compensation, personnel, and the secretary also serve in dual capacities with both IFC and the World Bank in order to provide economies of scale and consistency of policy.[10]

Besides the governors and Board of Directors, IFC has an International Advisory Panel composed of six leading international bankers who provide guidance on special matters when requested. With the president effectively occupied with heading the World Bank and setting broad policies for IFC, responsibility for the day-to-day administration of IFC rests mainly with the executive vice president, who has a handful of vice presidents and other key aides reporting to him.

In addition to the vice president and general counsel, vice president–Engineering and Technical Assistance, vice president–Administration and Finance, and the director–Finance and Management, vice presidents for Africa, for Latin America and the Caribbean and for Asia, Europe, and Middle East report to the executive vice president. Directors for Departments of Investments in these geographical areas report to the three regional vice presidents. Personnel in the geographic units have responsibility for both loans and equity investment in the countries within their respective areas. Other directors are responsible for

---

[9] International Finance Corporation, *IFC/General Policies*, Washington, D.C., September 1979 (hereinafter *General Policies*), p. 1.

[10] *1981 Annual Report*, p. 3.

corporate planning, the capital markets department, and syndications (previously called marketing), and in addition there are senior advisors for portfolio and technical matters and the Chief of the Information Office. Special representatives and regional mission heads are in charge of IFC's various offices and locations outside its Washington, D.C. headquarters.

IFC maintains small offices in New York, London, Paris, and Manila, Nairobi, Cairo, New Delhi, and Abidjan. The New York office deals mainly with financial market activities, as do the London and Paris offices, although the last three also are important contact points for coordinating various projects and dealing with member governments, project participants, sponsors, and others. The Manila, Nairobi, Cairo, New Delhi, and Abidjan offices administer and coordinate projects in developing member countries within their regions.[11]

INVESTMENT POLICIES

The greatest part of IFC's work now and for the immediate future consists of investing in specific projects in developing countries. Thus, most staff are occupied with investment-related activities, although other staff provide various specialized services including technical assistance and advice and planning for developing local capital markets. Accordingly, it is important for potential users of IFC financing services to understand IFC investment policies as applied by the staff with regard to projects. Simply stated, these policies involve investing in eligible enterprises based upon certain criteria. When these criteria are met the amount, terms, and conditions of IFC financing are quite flexible, although there are a few basic ground rules.

Eligible Enterprise. Generally, IFC will invest in almost any type of private enterprise in developing member nations provided its other criteria are met. In its earlier years IFC investments were concentrated mainly in manufacturing industries, especially various basic industries. More recently, while continuing to invest in manufacturing projects IFC has broadened its activities to cover energy, mining, utilities, agriculture, financial institutions, and projects in service industries, such as hotels, which promote tourism.

A more complicated situation in connection with eligibility arises when a government owns part or all of an enterprise which is otherwise eligible for IFC financing. IFC has adopted the posture that government ownership does not necessarily preclude IFC investment. Rather IFC will look at each project on a case-by-case basis considering such factors as the extent of government ownership and control, the nature of the enterprise, the efficiency of management, and the possibility of increasing the extent of private ownership in the future.

---

[11] *1981 Annual Report,* p. 3.

For example, in some nations only government institutions or government-controlled corporations might have sufficient financial resources to invest with foreign owners in large projects. In other nations some types of enterprises are traditionally owned by the government, although in many nations the activities conducted by these units would fall into the private sector. Utilities, mining, and energy projects are examples. Accordingly, IFC supports projects varying from purely private to mixed public/private ventures and even to wholly owned government enterprises where they act as channels for assistance to the private sector.

Profit and Economic Benefit. After dealing with the eligible enterprise issue, IFC considers whether the project will benefit the economy of the host country and earn a profit. This two-part test is necessary in order to gain government support in the host nation and attract both foreign and local private investors.

Adequate Private Capital. Next, IFC will not invest alone in a project. In fact IFC expects to mobilize and supplement private capital. Its goal is to stimulate other investment not to replace it. Thus, IFC places great emphasis on the amount of capital mobilized and especially the extent of the sponsor's participation in the total equity of the project. IFC will never be a majority shareholder and seldom provides more than 25 percent of total equity. Accordingly, IFC will invest only in projects where sufficient private capital can be obtained on reasonable terms.

Sufficient Local Participation. IFC also requires that local and foreign resources be combined. It will invest only where there is provision for immediate or eventual local participation. For example, if necessary, IFC in appropriate cases will join underwriting or other arrangements to make equity ownership available to local investors either immediately or in the future.

Host-Government Agreement. IFC does not require nor may it accept government guarantees for repayment. However, it will not invest in projects when the government objects. In fact in most nations specific government approvals, authorizations, or permits of various government units are necessary for any project. In addition as is normally the case for other international investors, IFC requires that appropriate arrangements be made for repatriation of its investments and earnings.

Because IFC seeks to mobilize private capital from many different sources to supplement its own resources, in theory there is no limit to the size of the projects it is prepared to consider and for which it will attempt to arrange financing. However, traditionally IFC has invested between $1 million and $30 million per project for its own account. In some cases it may invest less than its normal $1 million lower limit, especially in ventures in the smaller and least developed countries, in pilot operations, and in promotional companies.

IFC has no particular requirements for the proportion of equity and loan investment it will undertake for each project. Each project must be examined based upon its cash flow, individual risks, and estimated return on investment. IFC may make either loan or equity investments, but as a practical matter for many enterprises it makes both types of investments, since this is often necessary in order to assemble an acceptable financial package.

IFC loans usually are granted at fixed rates on commercial terms for periods ranging from 7 to 12 years. Interest rates vary with market conditions based upon IFC's cost of funds, which are obtained mainly from the World Bank. During 1981–82 this formula placed IFC rates in the 13–14 percent range. However, rates may vary for some projects, usually based upon the repayment period. Longer loan maturities may be granted, for instance, in certain projects where necessary for prudent and successful project implementation. In some cases, loans with an equity feature (convertible loans) have been granted. After an agreed upon grace period loans are usually repayable in semi-annual payments with interest payable on the same dates. A commitment fee of 1 percent per annum is payable on the undisbursed portion of IFC loans.

In situations where IFC syndicates loans to private investors, including commercial banks, merchant banks, and insurance companies, market interest rates are based on the London interbank offered rate (LIBOR). In many cases IFC has granted loans in two portions, one at a fixed rate to be held in IFC's portfolio and another at floating rates based on LIBOR to be participated totally to private institutions.

While loans generally are expressed in U.S. dollars, other major convertible currencies may be used to denominate loans. Equity investments, of course, are denominated in the local currency of enterprise's host country in accordance with local legal requirements.

IFC will provide standby or underwriting arrangements to support public offerings or private placements of equity shares, debentures, and other corporate securities. Also, IFC may serve either as the sole underwriter, or as a member of an underwriting group. However, IFC does not engage in the direct sale of securities to the general public. Beyond its own underwriting capacity, it is important to note that over the years IFC has helped establish numerous investment and development banking institutions in developing member nations. The close ties between IFC and these entities, some of which even may take up equity shares outside their home countries, enable efficient underwriting groups to be formed and operated. In many cases close personnel ties of many years standing exist between IFC staff and the staffs of these other regional or local institutions, and this further increases the effectiveness of the underwriting process in developing nations with relatively new capital markets.

IFC seeks to establish permanent relationships and in fact has financed the repeated expansions of numerous enterprises. However, consistent with its goal of mobilizing private capital and encouraging the growth of markets for the types of securities in which it invests, IFC will sell both its loan and equity investments at appropriate times to private local investors and other institutions when satisfactory terms can be arranged. Generally, IFC will not sell its equity investments until projects are well underway and deemed successful as evidenced by good earnings and sufficient cash flow to repay loans. Then IFC prefers to sell its share to private investors in the country in which the enterprise is located in a manner which does not cause severe price fluctuations. Accordingly, IFC usually disinvests gradually over a period of years. In privately negotiated sales IFC will not sell its shares to investors to whom its investment partners object for valid reasons.

IFC funds, whether from equity or loan investments, may be used by enterprises for foreign exchange or local currency expenditures, to acquire fixed assets or for working capital requirements. IFC funds are not tied to the purchase of specific equipment, materials, and services nor limited to any specific country.

Although IFC may hold an important equity interest in an enterprise, it expects its investment partners to provide management, since IFC as a general rule does not participate in management responsibilities. Nor is IFC usually even represented on the board of directors of the firms in which it invests. However, should a purpose be served by IFC's active participation or if it becomes necessary, IFC will become involved and exercise its rights as a shareholder. Over the years such situations have not been frequent.

In most cases IFC follows the progress of its investments through regular reporting requirements based on copies of the usual information necessary to properly manage any enterprise. In this regard, IFC investment agreements require annual financial statements, audited by independent public accountants and various other routine accounting and financial reports. IFC personnel also make periodic on-site visits, confer regularly with management and project participants, and have established a supervision program involving preparation of evaluations covering technical, economic, and financial assessments of all IFC investments.[12]

Although IFC levies no fee in connection with monitoring its investments, its efforts in this regard almost always serve to benefit the project participants and management of the enterprise being financed. IFC's experience, broad range of contacts, and neutral position give its staff perspective from which to analyze developments, identify and define

---

[12] *General Policies*, pp. 2–5.

potential difficulties, and often propose solutions before problems get out of control.

IFC's follow-up process probably ranks in importance only behind IFC's role in developing and promoting projects and clearly ahead of its function in supplying investment funds. Numerous international institutions can supply funds, but few can match IFC in the depth of its management skills, experience, and ability to help organize successful projects which encourage the economic development process in member countries.

IFC'S CATALYTIC ROLE

The special ability of IFC to assist in organizing projects from their earliest stages often is referred to as IFC's catalytic role. Several aspects of this function require explanation in order to convey a more complete understanding of IFC's workings.

First, IFC takes an active role in identifying and promoting projects which have a reasonable prospect of eventually becoming suitable for financing. From its position as an affiliate of the World Bank, IFC often identifies well in advance of other institutions and private investors the need for private enterprises to fill in the gaps of developing national economies. With this in-house early intelligence system IFC is able to take responsibility either alone or with others for developing projects from inception through the stages of feasibility studies, detailed engineering and marketing investigations, finding technical and financial partners and creating financial plans.

Second, even after the opportunity for a new enterprise is perceived by private investors, foreign sponsors may feel more comfortable in having an international organization in the project. These sponsors realize, for example, that the IFC frequently can deal with developing-nation host governments more effectively than they can. Furthermore IFC's participations in a project may be useful if local conditions in the host country change. While economic systems and political alliances often must respond to immediate social and related pressures, developing nations generally realize that it is to their advantage to stay in good standing with the World Bank family, whose 35-year record stands as public testimony to its avowed purpose of assisting these nations.

Third, IFC's presence in a venture also may make a project more attractive to the government of a developing nation. On the one hand IFC participation helps lessen dependence on investors of a single foreign nationality or even one large multinational corporation. At the same time, IFC's reputation for independent and professional project appraisals helps raise both host-government and private-investor confidence. Often neither of these parties alone is in a position to put all the pieces into place for sound decision making. Large sums may be required for preliminary project studies and prefeasibility investigations. However, when IFC is able to marshall complete information, some of which may be of an intangible nature, the entire investment process can be speeded up.

Fourth, from its neutral stance IFC may be able to help facilitate the process by which private investors and host governments can reach mutually satisfactory agreements. Often IFC is invited to participate in projects which face unusual problems. Using its experience, standing, and prestige IFC is able to exert its considerable influence under these circumstances towards finding reasonable and practical solutions to these problems. Sometimes these solutions are used as precedents to ease the way for future investors in a developing country, and helpful ideas also can be spread from one country to another. Although IFC enjoys various special immunities, its general approach when problems arise is to seek solutions which all private investors can accept rather than to invoke those immunities.

Finally, in addition to its affiliation with the World Bank and its own independent personnel and financial resources, IFC over the years has developed close relationships with numerous other organizations which share its objectives. These include multilateral agencies, bilateral agencies, government and quasi-government corporations, development finance companies operating in single nations or in regions of the world, investment and commercial banks, investment banks, other financial institutions, individual business enterprises, and accounting, consulting, and law firms, which are interested and experienced in the conduct of international activities. Thus, should it be necessary IFC may be in position to suggest other qualified participants, who are required to help carry out a project.

TECHNICAL ASSISTANCE AND FINANCIAL SERVICES

From its investment activities, including the sale of its equity holdings, IFC has acquired valuable experience which it utilizes to supply various forms of technical assistance and specialized finance-related services. In discussing IFC's investment functions, the project-related services of project identification and project promotion have been examined. IFC's other or nonproject related services, include:

1. Helping to establish, finance and improve privately owned development finance companies and other institutions which assist development of the private sector.
2. Encouraging the growth of capital markets, including stock exchanges, in developing countries.
3. Creating in the capital-exporting countries interest in portfolio investments in enterprises located in the developing countries.

4.   Giving advice and counsel to less developed member countries
     on measures which will create a climate conducive to the growth
     of private investment.

Assistance to development finance companies and other similar institutions also could be considered as another form of investment activity,
since IFC generally puts its own funds into such ventures. Some additional comments are appropriate here, however, since more than mere
investment is involved. Along with identifying the need for these institutions and planning their creation, IFC often is able to share its experiences from other nations with regard to government policy level and
legal issues. In many developing nations it is necessary to assist the
host government in formulating financial-sector plans and the regulatory framework, as well as the legal environment for new types of
institutions. In some circumstances new types of financial instruments
must be created as well.

IFC's Capital Markets Department has been increasing its activities
during the last several years and has handled projects such as starting
a housing bank in Senegal, advising Egypt's Capital Market Authority
on a long-term program to strengthen capital market development,
assisting Nigeria in studies related to securities-market supervision and
the development of unit trust operations. In Chile help is being provided to reorganize the stock exchange and similar assistance is being
provided in Uruguay and Colombia.

In Korea advice is being provided for improving the commercial
banking system, and a feasibility study was undertaken for establishing
a discount house in Lebanon. For the Caribbean region IFC serves
as the Secretariat for the Task Force on Private-Sector Activities, which
is the first such group to examine the problems and opportunities for
private investment in the Caribbean. Increasingly, in addition to its
financing projects IFC is becoming an international policy-planning
and management consultant to governments and regional groupings.[13]

Since its formation in 1971 the IFC capital-markets program has
supported over 35 concerns in 19 developing countries, provided technical assistance in various forms to more than 60 countries, and undertaken more than 160 individual technical assistance projects. To illustrate this work by one example, during fiscal year 1981, IFC under
its capital markets program made an initial $1.5 million in equity investment in a $11.5 million financing for SPI, a Portuguese development
finance company. SPI in turn will provide loans, equity, and related
services to domestic enterprises in Portugal. SPI will help finance projects that contribute to increased exports and substitute for imports,

---

[13] *1980 Annual Report*, p. 27. Also see International Finance Corporation, *Capital
Markets—Mobilizing Resources for Development*, Washington, D.C.: 1981, for a summary of IFC's activities involving its Capital Markets Department during the last 10
years.

assist in the expansion of private investment in that country, contribute
to the revival of capital markets, broaden share ownership among local
residents, and encourage joint ventures with foreign investors resulting
in the channeling of technical expertise, management assistance, and
foreign capital to Portugal.[14]

FUTURE TRENDS

The most significant trend for IFC's future is its accelerating growth.
Planned capital subscriptions and permitted borrowings increases
alone would allow IFC to more than double in size before the end
of the 1980s. At fiscal year-end 1981 net investments amounted to
$1,050 million or approximately $184 million more than at the preceding year-end. Moreover, gross investments before undisbursed, disbursed, and outstanding investment and reserves against losses
amounted to $1,647 million or $243 million more than the comparable
figure the year before.[15]

Estimates of IFC's future investment volume growth must take into
account not only IFC's own capital and borrowing resources, but also
its capacity to syndicate financings which it arranges. In this regard
it is noteworthy that 52 financial institutions participated in IFC financings during fiscal year 1981 compared to only 20 institutions the preceding year. During fiscal year 1981 IFC arranged its largest syndication
to date—$110 million for the expansion of a Brazilian cement company.
During fiscal 1980 a $101 million facility for a Mexican glass manufac-
turer was syndicated. Of the 52 financial institutions taking participations during fiscal 1981, 23 had not previously participated. Participants
included commercial banks, development banks and special funds, investment banks, finance companies, and an insurance company from
the Middle East, Europe, Asia, and the western hemisphere.[16]

In reviewing the size of the commercial banks involved in IFC participations total assets of these institutions ranged from less than $3
billion to over $100 million with, money center, as well as regional
banks from Europe, Canada, and the United States well represented.
Newer participants are increasingly from the Middle East, Latin America, and Asia. Obviously, even from this brief examination it is safe
to conclude that most of the world's commercial banks with international activities have not worked with IFC to say nothing of insurance

---

[14] Carl T. Bell, "Promoting Private Investment: The Role of the International Finance
Corporation," *Finance and Development*, September 1981, pp. 8–9.

[15] *1981 Annual Report*, p. 38.

[16] *1981 Annual Report*, pp. 30–31. Also see International Finance Corporation, *Cooperation with Commercial Banks—The IFC Experience*, by Miles Carlisle, Manager Syndications, Dubai, United Arab Emirates, February 23–24, 1982, for additional information
for participants in IFC syndication.

companies and pension funds, whose investment portfolios are rapidly becoming more diversified internationally.

With increased investment capability coupled to its enviable lending record and World Bank Group affiliation, more financial institutions than ever before will be working with IFC during the 1980s. While successful international project finance requires long lead times, IFC by remaining relatively small in asset size and staff for its first decades in order to perfect its skills and build its record, is well poised for significant increases in the dollar volume of its activities during the 1980s. IFC has a well-established record within its developing member countries and will be able to expand its activities without huge staff increases. Some staff increase probably will be required, however, for IFC's syndications and financial institutions liaison functions in order to cope with the projected growth in business volume. This development in turn could help increase the number of institutions working with IFC in the participation area.

Beyond growth in volumes and working partners, it appears that IFC also will expand the range of its activities along at least two dimensions. First, during recent years IFC seems to have broadened its definition of private enterprise to cover various selected functions and roles in certain national economies, which previously might have been considered totally public in the sense of government controlled. Perhaps, however, it is not completely accurate to ascribe such changes to IFC criteria alone. During recent years changes within various national economies have blurred substantially the distinction between public, private, and mixed enterprises and introduced in varying degrees elements of response to market forces along with modern management methods for resource allocation and decision making.

Second, as already mentioned IFC has moved into new industrial sectors. Since IFC has started only quite recently to invest or increase investments in projects in energy, mining, agrobusiness, and services, this trend is by no means spent. With continued energy, raw material, and food needs, less developed countries with the resources for these activities but shortages of capital and related skills for project development will be turning increasingly to IFC at the same time international investors seek new outlets for their capital. Energy and other natural resources projects especially seem to be the focus of increased emphasis.

In diversifying away from its previously heavier reliance on basic manufacturing into natural resources and service industries IFC will be moving with trends in economic development involving stages of growth from primary agriculture and natural resources and secondary industry to tertiary service activities. Simultaneously, IFC will be using its more sophisticated technical and consulting services gained as an outgrowth of its investment functions to help developing nations overcome bottlenecks in economic development. Through its connections with financial institutions of all types and nationalities, IFC thus could become an even more important conduit for more rapid transmission of the developed world's most advanced financial services and techniques to less developed nations.

CONTACTING IFC

The first step in dealing with IFC for most international bankers and others should be contact with the Information Office, International Finance Corporation, 1818 H Street, N.W., Washington, D.C. 20433, U.S.A., telex ITT 440098, RCA 248423, or WU 64145, telephone number (202)676-0391 or 676-1234, which is the World Bank's main number, or with other local offices or regional missions mentioned earlier in this chapter. Much time can be saved for all parties concerned when inquiries in person are preceded by requests for IFC's literature and preparation for a call or visit by study of these materials. While this chapter attempts to prepare potential users of IFC services, an additional hour spent with IFC's latest annual report, the booklet entitled *IFC/General Policy* and brochure called *IFC Preliminary Project Information Required* will provide up-to-date information on services, as well as officer's names. Although IFC personnel welcome direct inquiries, corporate international personnel not experienced in dealing with bankers will probably obtain faster results by introducing themselves through their own corporation's treasury staff or their international commercial or investment bankers.

Most financial institutions maintain their IFC contacts through the Syndications Department, whose director and staff have responsibility for liaison with institutions around the world which are interested in loan participations. Both the Information Office and the Syndications Department are prepared to arrange introductions to the geographical and other specialized line departments and offices. In the absence of well-developed personal contacts on a continuous basis with line staff it is preferable to route inquiries through the Information or Syndications Departments, since persons in those areas travel less internationally and thus are more likely to be available. Yet, they have relatively detailed knowledge of all current activities and developments throughout the organization due to the broad nature of their jobs and the comparatively small size of the IFC organization.

For those who have determined through preliminary inquiry or experience that an application to IFC for project financing is appropriate, no special format is required. Materials used for internal corporation presentations or dealing with potential project participants are often quite adequate for preliminary reviews by IFC staff. In addition to a brief description of the project, such material should include information on project sponsorship, management, and technical assistance. In many cases corporate annual reports, general descriptive information, or product descriptions are useful in this regard. Market and sales information should be tailor-made for the project in question. Market studies or surveys with projected volumes, sales objectives, market shares, present and potential suppliers, and other factors such as tariff or other import restrictions are needed.

Technical feasibility studies, including manpower and raw material or supply resources should describe any technical process involved, equipment details, infrastructure requirements, project location, size and sources, costs and quality of materials, supplies or services required. With regard to financial details IFC needs proposed costs broken down by land, construction, equipment, and working capital, the proposed financing plan with estimated sources, costs, and other terms of debt and equity, the type and amount IFC financing requested and projected cash flow statements. Finally, information is needed on the time scale required for the project, including preparation, construction, and start up, as well as government support and regulations, including taxes, other charges, any government incentives, and exchange regulations.[17]

IFC's anticipated further increase in resources and projects probably will not be matched in the near future by significant staff additions. IFC also is working in more countries than ever before and increasingly in countries with lower per capita gross national product and less experience in the private sector. IFC's projects in some of the nations are relatively small. Yet during each of the last few years IFC also has broken previous year records for the size of projects undertaken. Thus, financings of $100 million and more are not uncommon, and these large financings are becoming more complex. From 1980 to 1981 the number of financial institutions involved in IFC participations has increased from 20 to 53, and participation volumes also are expected to grow. Obviously, under these circumstances the international bankers who are the best prepared or most experienced with regard to IFC activities will be the most effective in dealing with IFC staff. This experience and preparation will benefit not only the IFC staff, but also international bankers, their customers, and all participants related to IFC projects and syndications.

---

[17] International Finance Corporation, *Preliminary Project Information Required*, Washington, D.C., September 1980. See also James L. Kammert, *International Commercial Bank Management*, American Management Association, New York, 1981, pp. 216–20 and 337–38 for further information on dealing with IFC personnel and for ideas for specialized documentation in project finance.

32

Inter-American Development Bank

JOSE D. EPSTEIN
Manager
Plans and Programs Department
Inter-American Development Bank

INTRODUCTION

The Inter-American Development Bank is a multilateral financial institution established in 1959 to accelerate the economic and social development of Latin America.

Its membership, originally comprising 19 Latin America Republics and the United States, has been broadened since 1976 to include a group of nonregional members—most of the countries of Western Europe, as well as Japan, Yugoslavia, and Israel. The regional membership also has expanded with the additions of Canada, four English-speaking Caribbean countries, and Surinam. As of 1981 the bank had 43 member countries—27 regional and 16 nonregional.

The growth in membership has not altered the bank's original design. The Latin American countries as a group are the majority shareholders, with about 55 percent of the voting power. The United States, with about 35 percent, remains the largest single shareholder. The United States, along with Canada and the 16 nonregional members, contribute to the bank but do not borrow from it. The Latin American members are both contributors and borrowers.

The subscribed capital and other funds at the bank's disposal have increased steadily over the years, from $1 billion in 1960 to $24 billion by the end of 1980. Its leading operations have also expanded, now nearing $2.5 billion per year. With a cumulative lending volume of $18 billion as of the end of 1980, the bank is the most important single source of public external financing for the majority of the Latin American countries.

The diversified and continuing involvement by the bank in the re-

503

gion's development has transformed the bank into a leading international counsel on economic and social issues of importance to the area. It also has become a major financial intermediary for capital transfers to Latin America, via borrowings in the international capital markets and co-financing operations with private commercial banks and other international lending institutions. The bank's accomplishments as the oldest multilateral financial agency focusing on a single developing region of the world helped pave the way for the establishment of similar institutions in Asia and Africa: the Asian Development Bank and the African Development Bank.

ORIGINS

A Multipurpose Approach

The Inter-American Development Bank came of age in 1980, when it celebrated its 21st anniversary; its ancestry, however, dates back to the end of the last century. An early specific proposal for an inter-American banking agency—a goal long-sought by Latin America—was advanced by the United States at the First Inter-American Conference held in Washington, D.C., in 1890, where the Pan American Union—the forerunner of the Organization of American States (OAS)—was born. At that conference, the United States proposed the establishment of a hemispheric customs union which would give all the members substantial trade advantages, complemented by a private regional banking network and a regional monetary unit to settle commercial transactions. Although the proposal did not prosper, it illustrates the long-standing concern with hemispheric commerce, the clearing of payments, and stimulation of investment in Latin America that has marked inter-American relations for the past hundred years.

Similar aspirations were rekindled at various times in the early 1900s but did not command major support until the 1930s, when world events began to test the fabric of the Pan American system. The Great Depression of the early 1930s saw a proposal advanced at the Seventh Inter-American Conference to establish a hemispheric institution along the lines of a central bank that would help regulate credit and investment flows and encourage monetary stability. While at the time it did not progress beyond discussion stage, by 1939 the idea had been refined to the point where the foreign ministers of the hemisphere requested a specific proposal that could be submitted to their governments. By early 1940, the text of a charter for an Inter-American Bank which would have the attributes of a hemispheric central bank, a commercial bank, and an investment bank, received the backing of most of the hemisphere's governments. President Roosevelt gave it strong support as part of his "good neighbor" policy, but the enabling U.S. legislation failed to command the support of the Congress.

A Bank for Inter-American Development

At the end of World War II, the Bretton Woods Agreements which led to the establishment of the International Bank for Reconstruction and Development (World Bank) and the International Monetary Fund, foreclosed immediate prospects for creating a separate inter-American financial agency. The primary concern of the international economic system then was European reconstruction, an effort whose magnitude made necessary the transfer of additional financial resources through the Marshall Plan, launched in 1947.

The 1950s witnessed the beginnings of the contemporary debate in the OAS, the United Nations, and in other international fora, of issues relating to underdevelopment and bilateral development assistance. In Latin America, by the middle of that decade, most countries had begun to face serious problems as the reserves accumulated during World War II and the Korean conflict began to dwindle, and the prices of their exports plummeted. Although the World Bank and the United States through its bilateral program had been supporting development projects in Latin America, the need for additional external cooperation within a framework that would permit the participation of the recipient countries in the decision-making process was increasingly noted in the region. The core issue of economic development, manifested in the widening gap in income levels and living standards between the industrialized countries and Latin America, became the dominant theme of inter-American relations.

A study prepared in 1954 under the leadership of Raul Prebisch, the distinguished Argentine economist who was then the executive secretary of the U.N. Economic Commission for Latin America, defined Latin America's position. Ascribing the region's sluggish development to insufficient internal savings and investment combined with a slow growth rate of export revenues due to excessive dependence on a few basic commodities subject to wide price fluctuations in the world market, it proposed a $1 billion annual increase in foreign investment in the region, $300 million to come from the private sector and $700 million from public sources. It also recommended the creation of a fund to promote agricultural development and industry, to be subscribed in equal parts by the United States and Latin America. Moreover, the report prescribed the adoption by the region of an industrialization policy based on import substitution supplemented by international commodity stabilization agreements.

At a meeting of the hemisphere's finance ministers at Quitandinha, Brazil, in November 1954, where the report was discussed, the United States noted that it was willing to expand the facilities of the U.S. Export-Import Bank and to support the creation of an International Finance Corporation as subsidiary of the World Bank to promote private investment in the developing countries. From the U.S. standpoint, the creation of an additional agency to support the development of the hemisphere was likely to result in a duplication of effort. The Ministers, nevertheless, established a commission composed of representatives of the central banks, to draw up a plan for a regional development financing agency. The commission's report, advocating the establishment of an Inter-American Economic Development Bank, gained the support of only nine countries.

In the next few years, as the economic situation of many Latin American countries worsened, tensions in inter-American relations escalated. In May 1958, Brazilian President Juscelino Kubitschek urged President Eisenhower to join in a reassessment of hemispheric relations in the light of Latin America's development requirements. President Eisenhower suggested that both governments consult promptly with the other Republics on possible measures to promote common interests and improve the region's general welfare. In response, President Kutbitschek proposed a plan for a multilateral drive against underdevelopment in the hemisphere, termed *Operación Panamericana,* which called for a series of collective measures in such fields as international public financing, private investment, technical cooperation, and trade in primary commodities. For its part, the United States, at a Special Meeting of the Economic and Social Council of the OAS, expressed its readiness to consider the establishment of a regional development agency if all the countries of the region supported the idea.

By 1959, a negotiating commission was at work on the draft of the Agreement Establishing the Inter-American Development Bank. Later that year, President Eisenhower submitted to the U.S. Congress a legislative proposal authorizing United States participation in the bank. In supporting the bank's creation, President Eisenhower cited three considerations: (*a*) The special relationship, historical, political, and economic, between the United States and Latin America; (*b*) the pressing economic and social problems in the area; and (*c*) the desirability of an institution which would specialize in the needs of Latin America, which would be supported in large part by Latin American resources, and which would give the Latin American members a major responsibility in determining priorities and authorizing loans.

The proposed institution became a reality on December 30, 1959, when the requisite number of countries formally ratified the Agreement Establishing the Bank.

MEMBERSHIP, PURPOSE, AND ORGANIZATION

Membership

The bank's charter originally restricted membership in the institution to the member countries of the Organization of American States

(OAS). At the time of the bank's founding, the OAS comprised the then 20 Latin American Republics and the United States. Canada did not belong to it, nor did the English-speaking Caribbean islands. The United States and 19 Latin American Republics ratified the charter; Cuba did not do so, although it had participated in its negotiation.

One of the bank's immediate efforts after opening its doors for business in October 1960 was to enlist the cooperation of the capital-exporting countries of Europe as a source of convertible currencies for its lending operations. As early as 1961, bank missions visited Europe to discuss possible formulas for cooperation, particularly the opening up of its capital markets to bank bond placements. This effort, soon extended to Canada and Japan, enabled the Bank to raise $471 million in nonmember countries during the 1960s.

By the end of that decade, the bank's leading operations and Latin America's development drive began to play an important part in the international competition for capital and goods needed for development projects, making desirable a more structured relationship between the bank, the European countries, and Japan. In 1970, the bank's Board of Governors designated a special committee to explore the alternatives to assure an increased flow of resources to the institution from these countries.

During 1971, the management of the bank undertook a series of parallel consultations with the European governments and Japan. Meanwhile, Canada had expressed the desire to join the bank and, to this end, negotiations also began. The charter was amended to permit the admission of Canada, as well as of other countries outside the western hemisphere who might wish to do so without meeting the original requirement of OAS membership. On May 3, 1972, Canada joined the bank as a contributing but a nonborrowing member.

The discussions and negotiations held with nonregional countries in the ensuing two years culminated in a meeting in Madrid in December 1974, where 12 industrialized countries pledged to take the necessary legal steps to become full-fledged members. Three others did so at a later date. During 1976 and 1977, the bank welcomed as new partners: Austria, Belgium, Denmark, Finland, France, the Federal Republic of Germany, Italy, Israel, Japan, the Netherlands, Spain, Sweden, Switzerland, the United Kingdom, and Yugoslavia. Portugal joined in 1980.

The admission of nonregional members has substantially strengthened the multilateral base and resource mobilization capacity of the bank, but has not changed its regional character. The nonregional countries participate with the regional members in all decisions affecting bank resources, policies, and operations. Similarly, suppliers in the nonregional member countries bid on equal terms with those of the regional members on opportunities to furnish goods and services for projects financed with bank loans. Furthermore, in joining the bank, the nonregional members expanded the multilateral dimension of their many ties with Latin America, opening up a new avenue for greater cooperation in the development of a region of major economic importance to their economies.

Purpose and Functions

As defined in its charter, the bank's purpose is "to contribute to the acceleration of the process of economic and social development of the regional developing countries, individually and collectively." To this end, the charter assigns to it a broad role as promoter of investment of public and private capital for development purposes in Latin America, in addition to the use of its own resources and borrowings in the world's capital markets. It also mandates the bank to cooperate with the member countries to orient their development policies toward a better utilization of their resources, to contribute to making their economies more complementary, and to foster the orderly growth of their foreign trade. Finally, it authorizes the bank to provide technical cooperation for the preparation, financing, and implementation of development plans and projects, including the study of priorities and the formulation of specific project proposals.

The bank has translated these functions into action in many ways. A prime example has been its success in mobilizing resources in the United States, Europe, and Japan, where it has raised almost $5 billion through long- and short-term borrowings. The increasing use of cofinancing techniques whereby private commercial banks and other international financial institutions cooperate with the bank in financing projects in Latin America is another example. Its wide-ranging efforts in support of the region's private sector is still another: it lends directly to local private enterprises engaged in such basic industries as petrochemicals, steel, and cement, and finances industrial and agricultural credit programs through local financial institutions for the benefit of small- and medium-sized enterprises, farmers, and farm cooperatives. Furthermore, its lending for infrastructure facilities—to expand the supply of energy and improve transportation and communications networks—has induced an increase in domestic private investment as well as direct foreign investment. In the latter regard, the bank has performed unceasing missionary work in the United States, Canada, Europe, and Japan to point out investment opportunities in Latin America, particularly through joint ventures.

In the field of technical cooperation, the bank has helped to build institutions and train manpower involved in development, has strengthened the countries' planning processes, especially in the less developed ones, and has helped to relieve one of the early bottlenecks to greater external financing in Latin America—the availability of sound investment project proposals.

Levels of Authority

The bank has three levels of authority: The Board of Governors, the Board of Executive Directors, and the president and executive vice president.

The Board of Governors, in which all member countries are represented, is the nexus between the governments and the institution. The fact that governors are usually their countries' Ministers of Finance or Economy (in the case of the United States, it is the Secretary of the Treasury), ensures close coordination between their decisions affecting the Bank and the national economic policies and development programs of their own countries. Decisions are adopted by vote, with the voting power of each governor linked to his country's subscriptions to the bank's capital. The governors meet once a year to review the bank's performance and to make major policy decisions. A 12-member Committee of Governors handles issues in the interim, for submission to the full board.

The Board of Executive Directors is composed of 12 members who are named or elected by the member countries for three-year terms. The board, which performs its duties on a full-time basis at the bank's headquarters in Washington, D.C., is responsible for the approval of loans, the setting of interest rates, the sanctioning of operational policies and borrowings in the capital markets, and the approval of the administrative budget. Of the 12 directors, the United States appoints one, one is elected by Canada, two by the nonregional members and eight by the Latin American members. Each titular designates an alternate who has full power to act in his absence. Board decisions are made by vote on the same basis as in the Board of Governors. The board relies on a system independent of management—the External Review and Evaluation Office—to assess the results and effectiveness of the bank's operations and to ensure that the bank is fulfilling its purpose.

The president and the executive vice president manage the bank's day-to-day operations. The president, who is elected by the Board of Governors for a term of five years, conducts the bank's ordinary business, serves as its legal representative, and is the head of its staff. He presides at meetings of the Board of Executive Directors, but votes only when needed to break a tie. The executive vice president is appointed by the board of executive directors on the recommendation of the president of the bank.

The bank's operations are handled through eight departments and two offices: Operations, Finance, Economic and Social Development,

Project Analysis, Legal, Plans and Programs, Administrative, and Secretariat Departments, and the Offices of the Controller and of the External Relations Advisor. The bank has field offices in its Latin American
member countries whose staffs help to identify and prepare projects,
administer loans, and supervise the execution of projects. Offices in
Paris and London facilitate contacts with the nonregional members
offices, international agencies, and with the financial markets outside
the western hemisphere.

Institutional Features

The common objective of accelerating the economic and social development of Latin America makes possible the conciliation of views
of the membership in the decision-making process. The bank's charter,
the decisions and guidelines of the Board of Governors, and a modus
operandi developed over the years by the Board of Directors and the
Management to bridge the diversity of interests, cultures, and languages, are designed to facilitate consensus.

The dual role of the president as the chief of the bank's international
professional and administrative staff and as the chairman of the Board
of Executive Directors—which represents the member countries at
the bank's headquarters—guarantees the independence of the process
of technical, financial, and economic evaluation of projects submitted
for bank financing. It also reinforces the charter's provision to the
effect that "the Bank, its officers, and employees shall not interfere
in the political affairs of any member, nor shall they be influenced
in their decisions by the political character of the member or members
concerned. Only economic considerations shall be relevant to their
decisions, and these considerations shall be weighed impartially in order to achieve the purpose and functions of the Bank."

Development Role

Because of its purpose, the bank is much more than a focal point
for the transfer of external financial resources for brick-and-mortar
investments in Latin America. While the hydroelectric projects it supports, involving billions of dollars in construction and equipment, have
the immediate purpose of generating power, the final objective is to
reach industry and people. While its agricultural credit loans finance
the purchase of equipment, fertilizer, and seed, their ultimate goal
is helping the farmer raise his income, expand domestic food supplies,
and increase agricultural exports. When the bank supports industrial
credit programs for small- and medium-size private enterprises, it aims
not only at aiding firms to increase their efficiency and profitability
for their own sake, but also to help modernize national industry, expand

employment, and encourage diversification of production and of exports. As the bank supports educational projects, including advanced vocational and technical training, it is broadening the opportunities for people as well as expanding the supply of engineers, agronomists, business managers, and skilled craftsmen who benefit the society as a whole.

In sum, the bank's financing aims at cooperating with the Latin American countries in increasing production, productivity, and employment, raising living standards, and strengthening international trade. Its mandate, in the final analysis, is to support the region in its drive to become a self-sustaining and a stronger contributing partner in an increasingly interdependent world. This is why in evaluating loan applications, the bank complements the conventional financial analysis with an economic cost-benefit analysis. The latter is a means for quantifying the anticipated effects of an investment project on the recipient country's economy. In the past three years, the bank has gone one step further, seeking to identify the distribution impact of its lending, particularly on the lower-income groups.

This evaluation procedure enables the bank to make judicious decisions on the merits of a given project in terms of (1) its financial soundness as an investment, that is, its capacity to generate a financial rate of return sufficient to make it self-financing; (2) its developmental impact as shown by its economic rate of return—the benefits and costs to the economy as a whole; and (3) its technical and managerial feasibility, as shown by the appropriateness of the technology and the availability of the expertise necessary to carry it out successfully.

Latin America's Economic Integration

Another special feature of the bank's operations is the continuous support it has given to the process of Latin American economic integration. This role stems from the charter's mandate that it contribute to the development of the Latin American countries "individually and collectively." It is hard to think of an undertaking by the Latin American countries to foster their integration in which the bank has not participated. In Central America, it has supported integration with loans and technical cooperation to the Central American Bank for Economic Integration. The Secretariat for Central American Economic Integration and other specialized agencies have received continuing assistance under the bank's technical cooperation program. The Caribbean Development Bank, the development financing agency of the Caribbean Economic Community, has received the bank's financial and technical cooperation. The bank has lent its support, as well, to the Latin American Free Trade Association (today known as the Latin American Integration Association) and the Andean Group by extending its technical cooperation. In addition, the bank has been instrumental in the preparation and financing of development projects benefiting more than one country, particularly in the field of hydroelectric power. Several transportation and communications projects of regional significance also have been financed by the bank. More than 10 percent of the bank's lending has been for projects whose benefits extend to two or more countries.

RESOURCES

The bank was established with two separate sets of resources: the capital resources, consisting of shares subscribed by all the member countries, and a Fund for Special Operations, funded by separate contributions from the same countries.

The Capital Resources

As of December 31, 1980, after periodic increases by the membership, the bank's subscribed capital amounted to $15.1 billion. Only 11 percent of this amount—$1.67 billion—has been paid in by the member countries. The balance, representing callable shares valued at $13.4 billion, has not involved any cash outlays on the part of the bank's membership. It is subject to call only if the bank should become unable to meet its obligations arising from borrowings in the capital markets. This has never occurred in the bank's history. The callable capital constitutes, therefore, a guarantee of the securities placed by the bank in the international capital markets to raise funds for its capital lending operations. Since 1961, the bank has borrowed a total of $4.5 billion. The funded debt outstanding on December 31, 1980 amounted to $3 billion. During 1980, even as the bank repaid $211 million in borrowings maturing that year, it raised $372.5 million through new long-term placements in the United States, West Germany, Switzerland, and The Netherlands and $87.2 million in new short-term borrowings from member countries.

In its capital-raising operations, the bank has followed a conservative policy in order to safeguard its standing in the international capital markets. The ratio of its funded debt outstanding to its authorized callable capital was only 22 percent as of December 31, 1980.

In lending from its pool of available capital—the paid-in shares, borrowings in the world financial markets, and loan repayments—the bank sets interest rates that reflect the cost to it of the borrowings as well as the desired level of reserve formation. The terms of the capital loans vary between 15 and 30 years. The loans not extended directly to governments have to be appropriately guaranteed.

The Fund for Special Operations

The Fund for Special Operations represented an innovation in public international financing. Its purpose was to enable the bank to make concessional loans to meet special needs arising in specific countries or with regard to specific projects. The member countries' initial contributions to the fund amounted to $146 million. Periodic replenishments have raised total contributions to $7.7 billion, as of December 31, 1980. This fund has been instrumental in enabling the bank to provide special support for the economic and social development of the less developed countries of Latin America. Since 1979, the region's more developed countries—Argentina, Brazil, Mexico, and Venezuela—have joined the ranks of the industrialized members as contributors of convertible currencies to the fund. In 1980, the fund's loans went primarily for projects in Central America and the Caribbean member countries.

Interest rates on loans from this concessional fund vary between 1 and 4 percent, depending on the stage of development of the beneficiary country and the nature of the project. The terms range between 20 and 40 years.

Other Funds

The bank also administers a series of trust funds placed under its administration by various members. Loans from these funds are made under terms and conditions agreed to with the donor countries. All told, these funds amount to $1.2 billion and include:

A $525 million Social Progress Trust Fund established by the United States in 1961 to promote social development in Latin America.

A $500 million Venezuelan Trust Fund established by that country in 1975 to help finance projects involving development of nonrenewable resources in the less developed countries of Latin America. The fund has also been used by the Bank to help finance a program of equity financing of enterprises in Latin America.

Several other funds totaling $150 million, established by Argentina, Canada, the United Kingdom, Sweden, Switzerland, Norway, and the Vatican.

Mobilization of Other Resources

Latin America's requirements for external financing and the fiscal constraints imposed upon the governments of the industrial countries by recent trends in the world economy have caused the bank to search for new ways to transfer external development capital to the region. The bank's role as a financial intermediary has been strengthened by the realization in the industrialized countries that Latin America, in comparison with other developing regions, has achieved a stage of economic growth which permits many of the region's countries to make more frequent and intensive use of conventional sources of external financing. The bank's operations in this area fall under the heading of co-financing activities, through which it not only contributes its own resources for project financing, but also arranges for the participation of other funding sources. These operations can be classified as follows:

Joint Financing. Under this arrangement, the bank and other participating institutions, such as the OPEC Fund, agencies of the European Economic Community, and the International Fund for Agricultural Development grant separate loans for a given project. However, by agreement among the participating institutions, the bank is responsible for evaluating the project, monitoring its execution, and for administering its own and the other institutions' loans.

Parallel Financing. As part of its coordination activities, the bank engages in periodic consultations with other multilateral sources, particularly the World Bank, and with bilateral aid agencies. When specific projects are identified which are of interest to the other institutions as well, the bank and other participating institutions, such as the World Bank, grant separate loans to help finance a given project. Each institution may conduct its own project evaluation and administer its own financing, but both act in coordination.

Export Credit. Under this arrangement, the bank's role is to provide resources for the financing of exports of manufactured, semi-manufactured and capital goods and of services, both within and outside the region, and also to promote export credit financing mechanisms in Latin America, such as the Panama-based Latin American Export Bank, BLADEX. The bank also provides the borrower with guidance and assistance in obtaining export credits from specialized national agencies in the major industrial countries. These credits are generally "tied" to procurement in those countries.

Complementary Financing. This program, instituted in 1976, aims at helping the Latin American countries obtain resources in the international capital markets for specific development projects. The objective is threefold: first, to assist borrowing countries in gaining access to the capital markets or to improve or diversify the forms and scope of such access; second, to reduce the risk factor in credit operations and thus improve the terms and conditions of such financing; and, third, to enhance the economic effectiveness and the financial soundness of the external borrowing programs of the Latin American countries.

The complementary financing program has attracted the participation of a wide spectrum of financial intermediaries and lenders, particularly commercial banks operating in international credit markets. Numerous banks in Canada, Japan, the United States, and various

European countries have participated in it to date, and many others have submitted offers to do so. Some institutional investors, such as insurance companies and pension funds, have also expressed interest in the program. The form of financing used thus far has involved loans in Eurodollars, syndicated by a group of banks and granted with a floating rate of interest related to the London interbank offered rate (LIBOR). Nevertheless, resources can also be mobilized in other convertible currencies and at fixed interest rates. The bank is constantly seeking to expand such funding operations through diversification of the financial instrument used and participation by various sectors of the international financial community. Since 1976, complementary financing mobilized by the bank under this program has exceeded $500 million. The projects involved represent a total investment of $4 billion.

Two-Way Benefits

The fact that the bank counts in its ranks the world's leading capital-exporting countries as contributing but nonborrowing members does not mean that it represents merely another channel for the transfer of some of their resources to Latin America. In reality, in financing projects the bank generates a circular flow whereby financial resources return to the contributing countries in the form of procurement of goods and services needed to carry out the projects. In addition, as development enlarges the Latin American region's import capacity, it exerts important long-term effects on the economies of the industrialized countries. A major one is an increasing level of these countries' general exports to Latin America which, in turn, have an effect on the industrial economies similar to a rise in the level of domestic investment. Furthermore, as development in the region brings about greater efficiency and diversification in the production of goods and raw materials, the industrial countries benefit from the expansion and improved productivity of their international sources of supply. And as the domestic markets expand in Latin America and as overhead capital facilities—electricity, roads, communication—and trained manpower are improved through the development process, the economic environment become more propitious for direct foreign investment.

THE BANK'S LENDING

Latin America is a heterogeneous area whose countries exhibit sharp contrasts in size, resource endowments, and levels of economic and social development. The bank, therefore, regards each country as a particular case insofar as its economic and social structure and financing needs are concerned.

In programming its lending activities, the bank plans over a five-year horizon with the objective of maintaining a current project inventory or "loan pipeline." The inventory is updated regularly with the help of programming missions that the bank sends periodically to the Latin American countries. Together with local authorities, these missions review the country's development plans and investment programs, help to identify priority projects which may be appropriate for bank financing, update each country's loan pipeline, and report back to the bank management. Individual loan applications flow from this process of consultation and analysis. At the request of prospective borrowers, the bank may provide technical cooperation for feasibility studies and for the preparation of loan projects.

Once a loan application has been reviewed for policy considerations, the bank subjects the proposal to detailed institutional, technical, socioeconomic, financial, and legal analysis. Since 1980, the bank also has been making a distributive analysis of most of the loan proposals in order to determine their impact on low-income groups, in line with a Board of Governors directive providing that one half of the bank's lending during the 1979–82 period should directly benefit such groups.

After the Board of Executive Directors acts on a loan application, a detailed loan contract is entered into with the borrower. The loan proceeds, however, are not disbursed in a lump sum. Instead, the bank disburses the loan over a period of time, as the project progresses and actual expenses are incurred by the borrower. Each disbursement request must be properly documented and its consistency with the contract verified by the bank.

Project Supervision

The bank monitors the execution of each of the projects it helps to finance on a continuous basis. The bank's field offices in Latin America are staffed by specialists who, in addition to supervising the administration and disbursement of loans, follow closely the day-to-day progress of each project. The loan contract requires that the borrower provide the Bank with a schedule of the investment expenditures of the project prior to the first disbursement and maintain a complete accounting of the costs and services acquired, as well as of the use to which they are put. In addition, the borrower is required to supply to the bank periodic reports, including financial statements and physical progress reports. The bank also performs ex post evaluations of selected projects as part of a continuous effort to test the effectiveness and relevance of its policies and criteria.

Procurement

Bank procurement policies stress the principle of competition in order to achieve maximum economy and efficiency in the execution of projects. Procurement for public-sector projects must be effected through international public bidding when the value of goods and services exceeds $100,000. For private-sector projects, the bank requires a competitive bidding system.

In the hiring of professional and technical services, the borrower is responsible for the selection and contracting of a qualified firm or individual, subject to the requirements established in the contract with the bank and to the latter's approval of the selection.

Achievements

Through the end of 1980, the bank has lent approximately $18 billion to help finance projects worth an estimated $66 billion. Its financing has helped to meet a broad range of Latin America's development needs, such as the expansion of its economic infrastructure—hydroelectric plants, roads, and communication systems—and improvement of its productive capacity in agriculture, industry, and mining. It has also worked towards improving living conditions by financing clean water and sanitation systems, hospitals and health clinics, by strengthening savings and loan systems and housing institutions and by helping to develop human resources through education projects designed to meet the economic and social requirements of the region.

A top priority of the bank in recent years has been the development of Latin America's energy resources. During its first 13 years of operations, from 1961–74, the bank provided $1.6 billion for energy projects, particularly hydroelectric generation, transmission, and distribution. Because most Latin American countries are heavily dependent on oil imports, after the 1973–74 oil crisis the bank stepped up its financing in this sector. Since 1975, it has nearly tripled its lending for energy investments, bringing its cumulative lending in this sector to $4.4 billion for projects worth $24 billion.

Half of the bank's energy lending has been for hydroelectric projects with a combined generating capacity of 27 million kilowatts. Comparatively, in 1960, the region's installed capacity was about 20 million kilowatts. In addition to hydroelectric projects, the Bank has financed gas pipelines, oil refineries, and rural electrification projects. Since 1980, the bank has broadened the scope of its energy lending to include the exploration of oil and natural gas and the utilization of nonconventional renewable resources.

Financing for agricultural and rural development has aimed at expanding food production, increasing farm employment, and improving rural living standards. Lending for the agricultural sector totalled $4.3 billion through 1980 for projects worth $10 billion. In addition to irrigation projects, soil and water conservation, flood control, agro-industrial projects, land settlement, and fisheries projects, the bank has given

priority to integrated rural development and agricultural credit programs. Through these projects 32 million acres of land have been
brought into production, including 5.5 million acres of irrigated land.
Fisheries projects have increased the region's annual catch by 2.5 million tons. And loans channeled through local-development financing
institutions have made available 1.4 million individual credits to farmers.

In the industrial and mining sector, the bank has provided $2.7
billion for specific projects as well as credit programs undertaken by
local financial institutions that channel resources to private enterprises.
The total investment in these projects and programs exceeds $18 bil-
lion. The direct loans are helping to build, improve, or expand 91
industrial plants. Financing granted to local credit institutions have
funded over 10,000 credits to small- and medium-size enterprises. The
bank has also provided funds for equity financing of manufacturing
enterprises. Furthermore, it has extended to export financing agencies
in many Latin American countries lines of credit totaling $346 million
to help finance exports of capital goods and services and nontraditional
exports from the region. And, since 1978, the bank also has authorized
over $18 million under its Small Projects Program, that provides financ-
ing for productive projects in such fields as handicrafts and food processing. These resources are channelled to low-income entrepreneurs
through nonprofit intermediary institutions such as cooperatives and
foundations.

Support for energy, agricultural, industrial, and mining development
has been accompanied by $2.6 billion in loans to help improve or
expand the region's transportation and communications systems. The
projects financed, which involve a total investment of $6.4 billion,
are helping to build or improve 16,500 kilometers of main roads and
42,000 kilometers of secondary roads. The bank has also helped to
finance the construction of four major bridges and over 900 smaller
ones. Ports, canals, and grain elevators have also been financed in
various countries.

In helping to develop Latin America's productive capacity, the bank
has not ignored the need to upgrade the quality of life in the region's
urban centers and rural areas. It has lent over $3 billion to build or
improve almost 6,000 clean water systems and 350 sewage systems,
1,800 public health facilities from hospitals to rural health clinics, and
400,000 housing units. In the field of education, 2,400 learning centers,
including universities, research centers, vocational and technical
schools with an enrollment of 1.8 million persons have been built or
modernized to help the region expand its pool of skilled labor as well
as professional talent.

The bank's role in the development of Latin America has also included the transfer of skills and knowledge through technical coopera-

tion. This effort has contributed to the creation or strengthening of a wide range of development institutions, to training local personnel in development planning and to the identification and preparation of priority projects. As of the end of 1980, the bank had authorized $427 million for technical cooperation projects.

OUTLOOK FOR THE 1980s

The development challenges facing Latin America in this decade point to the need for an intensified international cooperation effort because of the magnitude of financial resources required. For example, in the agricultural sector, the Food and Agriculture Organization of the United Nations estimates that Latin America will need $500 billion in investments between now and the year 2000; bank estimates in the field of energy place investment requirements to the end of this century on the order of $240 to $280 billion.

Within this cooperative effort, the bank proposes to continue searching for ways to broaden its scope as intermediary between the private international financial community and the Latin American countries. With more than 20 years of experience behind it in project financing in Latin America, the bank is uniquely suited for this role, having accumulated considerable expertise in the financial, economic, administrative, and legal aspects of development financing in the region. Its focus will continue to be on high priority, sound development projects, particularly in the fields of energy, nonfuel mineral development, and food production.

Energy. The challenge in energy for Latin America is to explore and produce more—for the region itself and for exporting. By the end of the 1970s, oil represented 70 percent of Latin America's energy consumption, compared to 45 percent for the world as a whole, and 50 percent for the developed countries. In 13 Latin American countries oil provides over 90 percent of energy requirements. This dependence on oil is creating a heavy burden for the region; oil imports have added significantly to the external debt of those countries that are importers.

Fortunately, most of the Latin American countries have substantial undeveloped energy reserves. Current proved reserves of oil are estimated at 74 billion barrels. The region also has large deposits of natural gas. And the potential for production based on heavy oils and bituminous shales is believed to be at least three times the level of conventional oil. Furthermore, hydroelectric potential is conservatively estimated at the equivalent of 50 billion barrels of oil. To date, only 10 percent of this resource has been harnessed. The region also has important reserves of coal, uranium, and thorium.

In addition to these conventional forms of energy, Latin America should take advantage of its nonconventional, renewable energy resources. Solar and geothermal power represent reliable and efficient forms of energy. And the use of biomass could play an important role in the production of ethanol and methanol to replace oil-based fuels. It is not inconceivable that Latin America, with all of these energy resources, could in the next 10 years double its current energy production.

Food Production. Latin America has to increase food production. The magnitude of this challenge is underscored by the fact that in order to increase per capita consumption by only 10 percent during this decade, the region's food supply will have to be increased by 45 percent. Increasing food production requires more than cultivating new lands. It is also necessary to expand the use of advanced agricultural techniques such as fertilizer and hybrid seeds, as well as machinery, and to strengthen the agricultural infrastructure—irrigation and flood control systems, farm-to-market roads, refrigeration facilities, agro-industrial enterprises, and rural electrification.

Industry. Latin America's industrial development has expanded less rapidly in recent years than the region's economy as a whole for a variety of reasons. The shortage of domestically produced raw materials, the sluggish growth of external markets for Latin American manufactures, insufficient financing, a shortage of skilled workers and qualified managers, as well as technological constraints, have dampened growth of manufacturing. But industry can play a key role in contributing to the region's foreign exchange needs in the 1980s if the bottlenecks are relieved.

Nonfuel Minerals. Latin America has the potential to be a major supplier of nonfuel minerals to the world. It provides 10 percent of the world demand for iron, ore, copper, lead, zinc, and tin; and over 30 percent for bauxite, nickel, and silver. However, mining currently contributes less than 3 percent of the regional GDP. Greater knowledge of the region's reserves, closer integration of the sector with the rest of the national economies, expansion of capital investment in mining operations, and more trained manpower are among the challenges that face the development of the mining industry.

Social Concerns. The social concerns of the 1980s are associated with three related trends: the continuation of the rapid population growth, the migration from the rural areas to the cities, and the increasing size of the labor force. The basic challenge is to create jobs—approximately 4 million a year between now and the year 2000—and to extend social services such as clean water, sanitation, health care, housing, and education in both urban and rural areas.

SUMMARY

Latin America has experienced tremendous change in the past 20 years. This has brought a measured degree of progress to the people of the region. But the task of development is far from over. The magnitude of the investment necessary to achieve self-sustaining growth in the region underscores the importance of developing innovative financial recycling mechanisms to mobilize the required resources. The Inter-American Development Bank expects to participate actively in that undertaking and to expand its role as a channel of external funds for the region. The bank is prepared to make available to its member countries its experience and capacity for evaluating specific investment projects that can, because of their satisfactory rate of return, attract financing from the international capital markets and to serve the cause of the region's development in other ways deemed suitable by its member governments.

33
Regional Development Agencies

KEIGO TATSUMI
Deputy President
The Sanwa Bank Limited

Important in international investment and finance are numerous public and quasi-public institutions. Some of these organizations interact regularly with private banks, and others interact only peripherally. This chapter will survey the activities of a number of the nonprivate institutions which are not covered in individual chapters in this book. The group of institutions reviewed in this chapter does not include all such activities, but does cover important representative institutions that play a major role in world finance and illustrates the forms of organization, objectives, and operating methods of agencies.

ASIAN DEVELOPMENT BANK—ADB
MANILA, THE PHILIPPINES

History

The Asian Development Bank (ADB) was established in August 1966 and began operations in December of the same year. Its objective is to assist in economic growth and economic cooperation in the Asian and Far Eastern regions, including the Southern Pacific area, and to contribute to the economic development of emerging nations within these regions. At the time of the founding of the ADB, the World Bank Group was already in existence, but the ADB was created with the mission of providing development finance closely tailored to the requirements and conditions prevailing in the Asian region. Since its founding, the scope of activities has been steadily expanded and the size of the ADB has grown as shown below. Although there are some regional development finance institutions which have emphasized the regional nature of their activities and not permitted membership by nations outside their respective areas of operation, the ADB has adopted the policy that such exclusivity would lead to difficulty in obtaining sufficient development funds to meet requirements of its region and therefore has allowed nations outside the Asian region to have member status since its founding. However, the ADB has set a rule that regional members nations must hold 60 percent or more of the subscribed capital resources and that the governor of the ADB must be a national of one of the member nations in the region.

Membership

At the end of 1980, 29 countries within the Asian region were members of the ADB and 14 countries outside the region held membership status. Of this total of 43 member countries, 26 were classified as developing nations and 17 were industrialized. The major member nations, their subscribed capital resources and voting power are shown in the accompanying table.

Subscribed Capital Resources and Voting Power of Principal ADB Member Countries (U.S. dollars in millions)

Name of Country	Subscribed Capital Resources	Voting Power (Percent)
ADB region		
Japan	1,498.6	14.0
India	696.8	6.8
Australia	636.9	6.2
Indonesia	599.4	5.9
Republic of Korea	554.5	5.5
Malaysia	299.7	3.2
Philippines	262.3	2.8
Pakistan	239.8	2.6
New Zealand	169.0	2.0
Thailand	149.9	1.8
Others	610.1	14.5
Total regional	5,717.0	65.3
Other areas		
United States	1,183.5	11.2
Canada	575.8	5.7
F.R. Germany	476.2	4.8
United Kingdom	224.8	2.5
France	187.3	2.2
Italy	149.9	1.8
Netherlands	82.4	1.2
Others	231.2	5.3
Total nonregional	3,111.1	34.7
Grand total	**8,828.1**	**100.0**

Source: ADB Annual Report 1980.

Sources of Funds

Regular Sources. At the end of 1980, ordinary capital resources amounted to US$8,828 million, including callable shares of US$7,084 million and paid-in shares of US$1,774 million. Borrowings amounted to US$1,870 million, and other regular sources included reserves.

Special Funding Sources. The special funding source of the ADB is called the Asian Development Fund and its resources are made available for lending on softer terms and for technical assistance activities. The principal source of these funds is contributions from various nations. At the end of December 1980 this fund stood at US$2,747 million.

Activities

The ADB is engaged in a range of activities, including lending, provision of guarantees, investments and technical assistance, but its principal activities are development finance and technical assistance. The latter activity consists of loans or grants or a combination of the two. These various forms of assistance are provided to member governments, their organizations, public or private organizations or firms, and international or regional organizations which have a relationship to economic development in the Asian region. Finance of the ADB in principle is provided for specific projects in such areas as agriculture and agro-industry, energy, industry and nonfuel minerals, development banks, transportation and communications, water supply, urban development, health, multiprojects, and other uses. However, under some special circumstances, program loans (or nonproject loans) are possible.

The terms and conditions of loans made from regular funds sources provide for a repayment period ranging from 10 to 30 years, with grace periods of between two and seven years. However, for those developing countries with relatively high levels of per capita income, repayment periods are kept under 15 years, with a grace period of three years or less. Interest rates are fixed, but rates are changed from time to time, according to rate movements in international financial markets. During the first half of 1980 the rate was 8.1 percent per annum and during the latter half it was raised to 9.0 percent per annum. For loans which have been approved, but not disbursed, a commitment charge is levied. For loans funded from special sources, a service charge of 1 percent p.a. is collected and the payback period is 40 years, including a grace period of 10 years. For program lending, a rate of interest or service charge is determined according to the source of funds. Terms of program lending are limited to 15 years, including a grace period of three years, for those loans from regular funding sources. For program loans from special funding sources, terms are limited to 15 years, including a grace period of eight years.

Record of Accomplishments

As of the end of 1980, total loans approved on an accumulated basis amounted to US$8,093 million. The breakdown of loans by country and by source of funds is shown in the following table.

Cumulative ADB Loans Approved by Country and Source of Funds (U.S. dollars in millions)

Country	Ordinary Capital Resources	Special Funds	Total	Percent
Indonesia	1,069.0	162.3	1,231.3	15.2
Republic of Korea	1,168.3	3.7	1,172.0	14.5
Philippines	1,067.1	64.3	1,131.4	14.0
Pakistan	479.4	526.0	1,005.4	12.4
Thailand	795.2	57.1	852.3	10.5
Bangladesh	11.4	619.9	631.3	7.8
Malaysia	590.0	3.3	593.3	7.3
Burma	6.6	284.0	290.6	3.6
Sri Lanka	14.1	210.1	224.2	2.8
Nepal	2.0	217.7	219.7	2.7
Others	449.6	292.2	741.8	9.2
Total	**5,652.7**	**2,440.6**	**8,093.3**	**100.0**

Source: ADB Annual Report 1980.

Cumulative ADB Loans Approved by Industrial Sector (U.S. dollars in millions)

Sector	Amount	Percent
Agriculture and agro-industry	2,264.4	28.0
Energy	1,963.3	24.3
Industry and non-fuel minerals	362.2	4.5
Development banks	1,106.1	13.6
Transport and communications	1,283.6	15.9
Water supply	705.8	8.7
Urban development, education and health	407.9	5.0
Total	**8,093.3**	**100.0**

Source: ADB Annual Report 1980.

AFRICAN DEVELOPMENT BANK—AfDB
ABIDJAN, IVORY COAST

History

The plan for establishment of the African Development Bank (AfDB) was presented to the second All-African People's Conference in 1960. This plan was adopted by the second United Nations Economic Commission for Africa during the following year. AfDB was founded in November 1964, three years later, and its operations began in July

1966. The purpose of the AfDB was to promote the social and economic development of the countries of Africa. The establishment of the AfDB had been strongly requested by the newly emerging countries of this region, which had gained their independence during the post-World War II period. Although these African nations had obtained their political independence, in actuality they were obliged to rely on their previous governing nations economically, receiving large sums in assistance and investment funds. Consequently, for the African nations a regional development financial organization capable of dealing with the problems of African countries from an African point of view was needed, quite apart from the assistance provided on a bilateral basis to individual African countries.

The AfDB began with 33 member nations, but in subsequent years the number of members has increased and the scope of activities has expanded. However, since membership has been limited to independent African nations, it has been difficult to overcome the problem of a shortage of funds. The bank therefore, has decided to open membership to countries outside the African region, strengthening the funding capabilities of the AfDB.

Membership

During 1980 two additional countries joined the AfDB, bringing the total number of members nations to 50 at the end of 1980. All member nations are independent African countries, but for the reasons noted above, 22 other nations outside the African region, including the United States and Japan, are scheduled to become members in the near future. The shares of capital and voting percentage of member nations are shown in the table on page 527.

Sources of Funds

Total capital subscribed of the AfDB amounted to 1,270 million U.A. at the end of 1980, including paid-in capital of 277.4 million U.A. Borrowings amounted to 323.6 million U.A., special funds to 91.5 million U.A., and other funds included trust funds and reserves.

Activities

Regular activities of the AfDB include loans to governments, governmental agencies of member nations, loans to development banks in the African region, investments through the purchase of stock, guarantees of credits, and provision of technical assistance. Special activities include finance from Special Funds and Trust Funds. Funds are made available for projects promoting the economic and social development

Subscriptions to Capital Stock and Voting Power of AfDB Member Nations as of December 31, 1980

Member Countries	Subscriptions (number of shares)	Voting Power (Percent)
Algeria	11,772	8.28
Angola	1,908	1.69
Benin	420	0.70
Botswana	420	0.70
Burundi	716	0.89
Cameroon	2,832	2.31
Cape Verde	200	0.55
Central African Rep.	300	0.57
Chad	612	0.63
Comoros	200	0.55
Congo	1,044	0.88
Djibouti	200	0.55
Egypt	8,440	6.05
Equatorial Guinea	200	0.55
Ethiopia	3,072	2.47
Gabon	1,992	1.55
Gambia	300	0.62
Ghana	4,708	3.50
Guinea	984	1.07
Guinea-Bissau	300	0.62
Ivory Coast	4,700	2.93
Kenya	3,132	2.51
Lesotho	328	0.64
Liberia	1,576	1.47
Libya	10,000	7.09
Madagascar	1,400	1.35
Malawi	776	0.94
Mali	688	0.72
Mauritania	508	0.72
Mauritius	1,392	1.28
Morocco	5,548	4.12
Mozambique	2,000	1.75
Niger	1,076	1.14
Nigeria	16,900	11.69
Rwanda	360	0.66
São Tome & Principe	200	0.55
Senegal	2,236	1.61
Seychelles	200	0.55
Sierra Leone	864	0.82
Somalia	812	0.96
Sudan	3,760	2.14
Swaziland	716	0.90
Tanzania	2,832	2.31
Togo	596	0.81
Tunisia	3,012	2.43
Uganda	1,672	1.35
Upper Volta	388	0.64
Zaire	8,940	3.84
Zambia	4,768	3.60
Zimbabwe	5,000	3.75
Total	**127,000**	**100.00**

Note: The par value of one share is equal to 10,000 units of account (U.A.). One U.A. is defined as the equivalent of one SDR and was equal to US$1.27541 as of the end of 1980.

Source: African Development Bank Annual Report 1980.

of member nations. Particular emphasis is placed on inter-African projects involving two or more African countries.

Rates on regular loans are 7 percent p.a., with terms of between 12 and 20 years, including a grace period ranging from 2 to 5 years. A statutory commission of 1 percent p.a. and a commitment charge of 0.75 percent p.a. for undisbursed loans are levied. Projects which are inappropriate to fund from regular sources are funded from special funds, in which case softer terms and conditions apply.

Record of Accomplishments

Cumulative loan approvals by industrial sector and country are shown in the accompanying tables.

Cumulative Loan Approvals by Sector (1977–1980)

Sector	Amount	Percent
Agriculture	166.23	15.64
Transport	261.56	24.61
Public utilities	361.28	34.00
Industry and development banks	255.64	24.06
Education and health	18.00	1.69
Total	**1,062.71**	**100.00**

Unit: Million U.A. (units of account).
Source: AfDB Annual Report 1980.

Summary of Statement of Loans (as of December 31, 1980)

Country	Loans Approved Less Cancellation	Amount Disbursed	Outstanding Balance
Congo	48.31	17.99	15.82
Egypt	48.00	18.83	17.79
Ghana	42.90	15.03	14.68
Ivory Coast	45.38	19.37	17.28
Kenya	57.62	21.57	18.93
Morrocco	52.31	26.14	22.14
Senegal	45.55	17.95	16.88
Tanzania	40.66	11.79	8.48
Tunisia	54.14	24.75	20.19
Uganda	52.26	16.30	14.67
Zaire	51.39	18.50	16.82
Multinational	38.35	25.13	20.16
Others	485.71	212.28	191.71
Total	**1,062.58**	**445.63**	**395.55**

Unit: Million U.A. (unit of account).
Source: AfDB Annual Report 1980.

AFRICAN DEVELOPMENT FUND—AfDF
ABIDJAN, IVORY COAST

History

The African Development Fund was established in 1973 as an international institution to assist the African Development Bank in contributing to the economic and social development of the bank's members and to promote cooperation and increased international trade, particularly among the bank's members and to promote finance on concessional terms for such purposes.

While the African Development Bank has limited membership to countries in the region, in contrast the AfDF was set up with 13 member nations, principally industrialized nations, outside of the African region. Receiving contributions from nations outside the region, the AfDF has been able to provide loans on soft terms and has contributed greatly to the improvement of the financial capabilities of the African Development Bank Group. However, 50 percent of the voting rights of the AfDF are held by the African Development Bank and, from an organizational point of view, not only does the president of the bank head the AfDF, but there is also overlap in personnel.

Membership

At the end of 1980, members of the AfDF included 22 countries and one international organization. The list of members and their respective voting percentages is shown in the table on page 530.

Sources of Funds

The principal sources of funds at the end of 1980 included subscriptions of 1,134.02 million units of account and profits, but subscriptions are the major source.

Activities

The major activities of the AfDF are provision of funding for projects involving one country or several countries in the region and funding for project-related surveys. For regular loans, the payback period is 50 years, including a grace period of 10 years. In the case of loans for pre-investment studies, the amortization period is 10 years including a grace period of three years. For regular loans, interest rates from the 11th year to the 20th year are 1.0 percent p.a. and 3.0 percent p.a. thereafter, however, a service charge of 0.75 percent p.a. is levied.

Subscriptions to Capital and Voting Power of AfDF Members (as of December 31, 1980)

Participants	Subscriptions	Voting Power (Percent)
ADB	21.50	50.00
Argentina	2.00	0.13
Belgium	21.00	1.07
Brazil	15.00	0.70
Canada	135.14	6.98
Denmark	42.00	1.59
Finland	14.00	0.67
France	29.08	1.42
F.R. Germany	111.00	5.42
Italy	60.00	3.14
Japan	177.94	9.17
Republic of Korea	15.00	0.78
Kuwait	14.40	0.72
Netherlands	18.00	1.13
Norway	52.50	2.56
Saudi Arabia	36.00	1.52
Spain	19.00	0.77
Sweden	69.00	2.57
Switzerland	50.57	2.39
United Arab Emirates	9.00	0.47
United Kingdom	52.39	2.01
U.S.A.	157.50	4.23
Yugoslavia	12.00	0.56
Total	**1,134.02**	**100.00**

Unit: Million units of account.
Note: One unit of account was equivalent to SDR 0.921052 or US$1.174719, as of the end of 1980.
Source: AfDF Annual Report 1980.

For loans to finance preinvestment studies, interest rates are zero with a service charge of 0.75 percent p.a.

Record of Accomplishments

The accumulated lending totals of the AfDF (1977–1980) by sector are shown in the accompanying table.

Sectoral Distribution of Cumulative Lending 1977–1980

Sector	Amount	Share (Percent)
Agriculture	351.17	39.00
Transport	245.27	27.24
Public utilities	147.38	16.36
Industry and development banks	31.00	3.44
Education and health	125.72	13.96
Total	**900.54**	**100.00**

Unit: Million units of account.
Source: African Development Fund Annual Report 1980.

EUROPEAN INVESTMENT BANK—EIB LUXEMBOURG

History

The European Investment Bank was created by the Treaty of Rome, which came into force on January 1, 1958 establishing the European Economic Community. An independent public institution within the European Community, the bank's function under the treaty is to contribute, on a nonprofit-making basis, to financing investment which assists the balanced development of the community.

The bank's operations were initially confined to the territory of the member states, but since 1963 these activities have been extended gradually outside this area to include financing for development projects in nations bordering the Mediterranean Sea, and African, Caribbean, and Pacific (ACP) States.

Membership

The member nations of EIB are the 10 members of the European Community, namely Belgium, F.R. Germany, France, Italy, Luxembourg, the Netherlands, Denmark, Ireland, the United Kingdom and since 1981, Greece. The capital structure of the EIB is shown in the accompanying table.

Capital Structure (as of December 31, 1980)

Name of Country	Subscribed Capital	Total Paid in and to Be Paid in	Percent
F.R. Germany	1,575.00	202.50	22.22
France	1,575.00	202.50	22.22
United Kingdom	1,575.00	202.50	22.22
Italy	1,260.00	162.00	17.78
Belgium	414.75	53.325	5.85
Netherlands	414.75	53.325	5.85
Denmark	210.00	27.00	2.96
Ireland	52.50	6.75	0.74
Luxembourg	10.50	1.35	0.15
Total	7,087.50	911.25	100.00

Unit: Million units of account.
Source: European Development Bank Annual Report 1980.

Sources of Funds

At the end of 1980, the paid-in capital of the EIB was 911.25 million units of account (U.A.), with subscribed capital of 7,087.5 million U.A. and uncalled capital of 6.176.25 million U.A. Borrowings, which include bonds, notes and medium- and long-term borrowings, amounted to

10,598.26 million U.A. and reserves were 785.15 million U.A. One unit of account at the end of 1980 was equal to US$1.30963.

Activities

Regular Activities. The form assumed by the operations of the EIB is provision of the bank's funds for lending and supplying of guarantees. These services are provided for members of the European Community and nations in the Mediterranean area as well as for African, Caribbean, and Pacific States, and Overseas Countries and Territories (OCT). Recipients of finance in these areas are governments, public and private corporations, and financial institutions. The term of loans provided for industrial projects is usually from 10 to 12 years and about 15 years for infrastructure projects. Interest rates are set with reference to market rates, but only represent a margin above funding costs sufficient to cover administrative expenses and to build up enough reserves and provisions for EIB operations. However, for loans provided to nations of ACP, the Mediterranean area, and OCT, interest-rate subsidies are supplied from the Economic Development Fund or the budget of the European Community.

Special Operations. The EIB also acts as agent for lending within the region involving the use of the New Community Instrument for borrowing and lending (NCI) and for lending outside of the region from funds made available from the Economic Development Fund and budget of the European Community. The NCI system was set up to substantially increase promotion of investment in projects which are of common benefit to members of the European Community in such fields as energy, infrastructure, and industrial development. Un-

Financing Provided from 1958 to 1980

	Number	Amount	Percent
Loans from EIB owned resources and guarantees			
within the Community:	1,023	14,407.7	83.5
of which guarantees	14	242.4	1.4
outside the Community	179	1,537.2	8.9
Total	1,202	15,944.9	92.4
Special section operations			
within the Community, from the resources of			
the New Community Instrument for borrowing			
and lending	20	474.6	2.7
outside the Community from Member States			
or Community resources	173	844.1	4.9
Total	193	1,318.7	7.6
Grand Total	1,395	17,263.6	100.0
of which—within the Community	1,043	14,882.3	86.2
—outside the Community	352	2,381.3	13.8

Unit: Million units of account.
Source: EIB Annual Report 1980.

der this system the Committee of the European Community raises funds in domestic and international capital markets, and these are then lent based on the decisions of the Committee. The EIB also provides funding for capital and outlays to finance risk capital assistance from Economic Development Fund resources.

Record of Accomplishments

Data on financing provided by EIB are shown in the accompanying table.

EUROPEAN DEVELOPMENT FUND—EDF BRUSSELS, BELGIUM

History

The Treaty of Rome, which went into effect in January created the European Economic Community (EEC). At the same time an agreement was signed between the allied nations and the EEC with the objective of promoting trade and providing economic assistance to those nations. This agreement also created the European Development Fund (EDF), with the purpose of supplying development assistance to those nations with close ties to the EEC.

The latter agreement has been renewed approximately every five years (first and second Yaounde Convention). In 1976 the First Rome Convention between the EEC and the African, Caribbean, and Pacific (ACP) States went into effect, and in 1979 the second Rome Convention was signed and went into effect on January 1, 1981. At present the EDF operates under the latter Convention.

Membership

The membership of the EDF consists of the nations of the EEC.

Sources of Funds

The source of funds for the EDF is contributions from the member nations of the EEC. During the fourth period for collection of contributions, from 1976 to 1980, a total of 3,074 million units of account (one unit of account at the end of 1980 equaled US$1.30963) were obtained. By country, the largest contributions have been provided by F.R. Germany and France.

Activities

The EDF provides capital and technical assistance in the form of grants, loans on special terms, and interest subsidies to nations in Africa and other nations and areas having a special relationship with the EEC. Interest subsidies are provided for loans made by the European Investment Bank. At present the maximum subsidy is 3.0 percent p.a., and these are paid to the EIB from grant assistance funds. The longest term for EDF loans is 40 years, including a maximum grace period of 10 years. Interest rates range from 1.0 to 3.0 percent p.a. Loans are made for projects in such areas as agricultural development, industrialization, energy, mining, and economic-social infrastructure. Loans are also made for such activities as technical cooperation, market surveys and stabilization of export income.

ISLAMIC DEVELOPMENT BANK—JEDDA, SAUDI ARABIA

History

The Islamic Development Bank (IDB) was established in October 1975, based upon a decision of the Conference of Finance Ministers of Muslim Countries in December 1973. The objective of IDB is to foster the economic development and social progress of the Islamic nations and Muslim communities.

Membership

As of November 8, 1980, 40 nations were members of the IDB. The subscriptions and voting percentages of the member nations are shown in the table on page 535.

Sources of Funds

The subscribed capital of IDB was Islamic dinar (ID) 790 million as of November 8, 1980, and paid-up capital was ID 760.38 million. Others sources include reserves and the Special Assistance Account as of November 8, 1980. (One ID is equivalent to one SDR).

Activities

Activities of the IDB include provision of loans, equity participation, foreign trade finance, leasing, technical assistance, and application of specific funds. These forms of finance are provided for member nations. A fee of 2.5 percent p.a. is charged and the term for repayment is set at a maximum of 40 years, including a maximum grace period of 10 years.

Member Countries' Subscriptions and Voting Power

		Total Subscription in Islamic Dinars		Voting Power	
	Member	Amount in Million	Percent of Total	Number of Votes	Percent of Total
1.	Republic of Afghanistan	2.5	0.32	750	0.76
2.	Democratic and Popular Republic of Algeria	25.0	3.16	3,000	3.03
3.	State of Bahrain	5.0	0.63	1,000	1.01
4.	People's Republic of Bangladesh	10.0	1.26	1,500	1.51
5.	United Republic of Cameroon	2.5	0.32	750	0.76
6.	Republic of Chad	2.5	0.32	750	0.76
7.	Federal Islamic Republic of Comoro Islands	2.5	0.32	750	0.76
8.	Republic of Djibouti	2.5	0.32	750	0.76
9.	Arab Republic of Egypt	25.0	3.6	3,000	3.03
10.	Republic of Gambia	2.5	0.32	750	0.76
11.	Republic of Guinea	2.5	0.32	750	0.76
12.	Republic of Guinea Bissau	2.5	0.32	750	0.76
13.	Republic of Indonesia	25.0	3.16	3,000	3.03
14.	Republic of Iraq	10.0	1.26	1,500	1.51
15.	Hashemite Kingdom of Jordan	4.0	0.50	900	0.90
16.	State of Kuwait	100.0	12.65	10,500	10.60
17.	Republic of Lebanon	2.5	0.32	750	0.76
18.	Socialist People's Libyan Arab Jamahiriyah	125.0	15.82	13,000	13.13
19.	Malaysia	16.0	2.02	2,100	2.12
20.	Republic of Maldives	2.5	0.32	750	0.76
21.	Republic of Mali	2.5	0.32	750	0.76
22.	Islamic Republic of Mauritania	2.5	0.32	750	0.76
23.	Kingdom of Morocco	5.0	0.63	1,000	1.01
24.	Republic of Niger	2.5	0.32	750	0.76
25.	Sultanate of Oman	5.0	0.63	1,000	1.01
26.	Islamic Republic of Pakistan	25.0	3.16	3,000	3.03
27.	Palestine	2.5	0.32	750	0.76
28.	State of Qatar	25.0	3.16	3,000	3.03
29.	Kingdom of Saudi Arabia	200.0	25.32	20,500	20.70
30.	Republic of Senegal	2.5	0.32	750	0.76
31.	Somali Democratic Republic	2.5	0.32	750	0.76
32.	Democratic Republic of Sudan	10.0	1.26	1,500	1.51
33.	Syrian Arab Republic	2.5	0.32	750	0.76
34.	Republic of Tunisia	2.5	0.32	750	0.76
35.	Republic of Turkey	10.0	1.26	1,500	1.51
36.	Republic of Uganda	2.5	0.32	750	0.76
37.	United Arab Emirates	110.0	13.92	11,500	11.61
38.	Republic of Upper Volta	2.5	0.32	750	0.76
39.	Yemen Arab Republic	2.5	0.32	750	0.76
40.	People's Democratic Republic of Yemen	2.5	0.32	750	0.76
	Total 40 members	**790.0**	**100.00**	**99,000**	**100.00**

Source: IDB Annual Report 1979–1980.

Record of Accomplishments

The IDB approved a total of ID 131.58 million for project finance, including technical assistance, for the Islamic year 1,400 (1979–80). Cumulative loans approved since the founding of IDB, by type of finance and by sector, are shown in the accompanying tables and amount to ID 445.43 million.

Project Finance Approved Since the Founding of IDB (Islamic dinars in millions)

Type of Finance	Number	Amount
Financing of projects		
Loans	33	179.78
Equity	32	163.77
Leasing	12	90.74
Profit sharing	1	4.27
Subtotal	78	438.56
Technical assistance	17	6.87
Total	95	445.43

Source: IDB Annual Report 1979–1980

Sectoral Distribution of Project Financing (Islamic dinars in millions)

Sector	Amount
Industry & mining	189.56
Agriculture & agrobased industry	52.05
Transportation & communication	115.70
Public utility	57.46
Social services	23.34
Others	7.32
Total	445.43

Source: IDB Annual Report 1979–1980.

Total trade financing since the founding of IDB amounts to ID 798.24 million. Total operations approved since the inception of the bank's activities amount to ID 1,248.68 million in 36 of the member countries.

PRIVATE INVESTMENT COMPANY FOR ASIA (PICA) S.A.
REGISTERED HEAD OFFICE—PANAMA CITY, PANAMA
OPERATING HEADQUARTERS: SINGAPORE

History

The Private Investment Company for Asia (PICA) is the only private company among the regional development agencies introduced in this chapter. The objective of PICA is to contribute to fostering the development of private companies in Asia. PICA is an investment company and was originally set up in February 1969. The operating headquarters of PICA is located in Singapore, and representative offices are maintained in Tokyo, Seoul, Manila, Jakarta, Bangkok, Kuala Lumpur, Hong Kong, and New York. PICA accepts the risks of its investments, and its activities are characterized by close involvement in the establishment, expansion, and restructuring of companies. Since its establishment, PICA has invested in and assisted in the development of about 100 companies.

Shareholders

Capital for PICA is provided by private companies and banks in Japan, Europe, and the U.S. Taiwan became a new shareholder early in 1981, bringing the total number of shareholders to 228, having their base of operations in more than 20 nations. By country, shareholders include 103 Japanese companies, 44 U.S. companies, 20 from Australia, and 11 from Canada. The shareholders are divided by countries in terms of percentage of capital held as follows: Japan holds 29.1 percent; the U.S., 23.8 percent; Australia, 14.5 percent; Canada, 6.1 percent; the United Kingdom, 4.9 percent; and other nations 21.6 percent.

Sources of Funds

The principal sources of funds at the end of 1980 were paid-in capital, which amounted to US$42.87 million and borrowings of US$115.47 million, plus retained earnings.

Activities

PICA offers a wide range of services, including provision of investment funds, loans, project development, and advisory and consultation services. These services are supplied to new and existing enterprises, located in developing Asian nations, which are profitable and operate in industries contributing to economic development.

Conditions for investment are that PICA participate in management as a minority shareholder. Loans are supplied on a commercial basis, and terms are about the same as those offered by commercial banks. Repayment periods range up to about seven years. Rates are set by adding a spread to funding costs in the London and Singapore financial markets.

Record of Accomplishments

At the end of 1980 loans outstanding amounted to US$127.99 million and equity investments to US$23.89 million. PICA combines its investments in companies and loans together in one total called operational investment. That total is disclosed at US$86.2 million. A breakdown of operational investment by industry and by country is shown in the accompanying tables.

Operational Investment by Industry
(U.S. dollars in millions)

Industry	Amount
Shipping	3.0
Palm oil	3.5
Cement and other construction materials	4.2
Metal products	6.0
Chemicals and petro chemicals	6.4
Glass containers	7.4
Electrical products	7.9
Estate development	8.0
Textiles	9.5
Finance	10.3
Others	20.0
Total committed	**86.2**

Source: PICA Annual Report 1980

Operational Investment by Country
(U.S. dollars in millions)

Country	Amount
Papua New Guinea	1.3
Thailand	3.1
Singapore	3.3
Hong Kong	3.9
Taiwan	5.5
Korea	9.8
Malaysia	11.0
Indonesia	22.4
Philippines	25.9
Total committed	**86.2**

Source: PICA Annual Report 1980

EXPORT-IMPORT BANK OF JAPAN—TOKYO, JAPAN

History

The Export-Import Bank of Japan (EIBJ) was founded with the objective of supplementing and encouraging the financing of trade and investment overseas by private financial institutions, through the provision of financial assistance, and thereby promoting economic interchange, particularly in the area of trade, between Japan and other nations. The EIBJ was originally founded in December 1950 as the Export Bank of Japan, with all capital provided by the Japanese government. Its original objective was to promote the export of heavy machinery and industrial plants, including ships and rolling stock, through the provision of export finance. In April 1952, activities were expanded to include imports and the bank was renamed the Export-Import Bank of Japan. In subsequent years the scope of the bank's activities have been expanded, in response to the needs of the times both in Japan and overseas. Today, the EIBJ makes a major contribution to the promotion of economic interchange between Japan and other nations.

Sources of Funds

The bank's capital is provided by the Industrial Special Account of the Japanese government and is authorized to borrow from the government's Trust Fund as well as foreign financial institutions and foreign capital markets.

Activities

Activities of the EIBJ can be divided into three major areas: finance provided in Japan, that provided to borrowers overseas, and guarantees. The major types of lending, by domestic and external, together with terms and conditions are explained in the following paragraphs.

1. Loans to Domestic Borrowers

a. Export Finance. The EIBJ provides long-term loans, or suppliers' credits, to exporters or manufacturers in Japan to finance the export of equipment, parts, or other items which have been manufactured in Japan.

b. Technical Service Credits. Long-term loans are provided to the suppliers of technical assistance in such projects as the construction of factories, dams, and other projects overseas.

c. Import Finance. Long-term credits are provided either to the importer or user of imported items (including equipment) which are judged to be of an urgent or very important nature for economic development.

d. Overseas Investment Finance. The EIBJ provides long-term loans required by Japanese investors in overseas projects. These may take several forms, including funds to Japanese companies for investment in overseas corporations, loans to foreign investors in overseas joint ventures with Japanese corporations, and so on.

e. Funding for Overseas Ventures. Loans are provided to Japanese companies which do not set up companies overseas but operate projects, such as resource development activities directly from Japan.

2. Direct Loans to Foreign Governments, Banks, and Corporations

a. Tied Loans. The EIBJ provides loans to foreign governments and their agencies, as well as foreign corporations for financing imports of machinery, equipment, and technology from Japan.

b. Investment Finance. Loans are supplied to foreign governments and other entities to provide capital to foreign corporations investing in ventures together with Japanese corporations.

c. Untied Loans.   Loans are also provided to foreign governments,
their agencies and foreign financial institutions to provide long-term
finance for ventures located overseas or imports of goods (including
equipment) and technology into overseas countries.

3. Terms and Conditions

With the exception of government-to-government loans, interest
rates range from 6 percent to 9 percent p.a. Payback periods vary
by type of finance, but for export finance for industrial plants they
range from two to 10 years, and run a maximum of seven years for
ships. Import finance is for terms ranging from five to 10 years, while
overseas investment finance is for seven years or less. Terms for direct
loans to overseas buyers are set on a case-by-case basis. With the exception of government-to-government loans, all loans in principle are
made on a joint basis with private financial institutions.

Record of Accomplishments

Cumulative credit commitments by type and by region over the
five-year period from 1975 to 1979 are shown in the accompanying
tables.

Credit Commitments by Type
(yen in billions)

Type	Amount
Export finance	2,316.9
Import finance	1,216.0
Investment credits	562.5
Direct credits	1,036.9
Total	**5,132.3**

Note: Direct Credits include government-to-government loans, buyers'
credits and bank loans.

Credit Commitments by Region
(yen in billions)

Region	Amount
East Asia	465.9
Southeast Asia	765.1
Middle East	518.5
North America	516.9
Central and South America	825.4
Europe	1,019.4
Africa	822.7
Oceania	151.8
International organizations	46.6
Total	**5,132.3**

Source: The Export-Import Bank of Japan.

EXPORT DEVELOPMENT CORPORATION—EDC
OTTAWA, CANADA

History

The Export Development Corporation (EDC) was set up in October 1969 to replace and expand upon the activities of the Export Credit Insurance Corporation which had existed previously. EDC is an enterprise of the Canadian government, having the objective of promoting and enlarging Canada's export trade through the provision of a range of financial services.

Sources of Funds

Paid-in capital amounted to 310.00 million Canadian dollars as of the end of 1980, and loans payable, including short- and long-term borrowings amounted to C$3,188.29 million. Other sources included retained earnings.

Activities

Export Credits Insurance. Insurance is provided to cover up to a maximum of 90 percent of the value of exports in the following circumstances: insolvency of the foreign buyer, default, blockage of funds, or transfer difficulties which prevent the Canadian exporter from receiving payment, war or revolution in the buyer's country, and similar circumstances.

Loan. EDC provides long-term loans to finance exports of capital goods and services from Canada. These are generally for a term of five years or more. EDC also provides lines of credit and is engaged in note purchases.

Foreign Investment Guarantees. Three broad political risks, namely inconvertibility or inability to repatriate earnings or capital, expropriation, and war, revolution, and insurrection, are covered by EDC guarantees. Fees are 0.6 percent p.a. or less. The period of guarantees extends normally for 15 years, and the portion of the risk borne by EDC is normally 85 percent.

Surety Insurance. EDC issues performance-type bonds to insure Canadian exporters, financial institutions, and other entities.

Record of Accomplishments

Loans made in 1979 amounted to C$1,448.3 million (including C$61.27 million government-account loans) and those in 1980 were C$851.36 million (including C$20.3 million government-account loans).

Exports insured in 1979 amounted to C$1,654.47 million, and those in 1980 to C$2,539.60 million. Loans receivable as of December 31, 1980 amounted to C$3,172.30 million.

EXPORT CREDITS GUARANTEE DEPARTMENT—ECGD LONDON, UNITED KINGDOM

History

Following World War I, the U.K. government embarked on a policy of encouraging exports. As part of this activity, the Export Credits Department was set up within the government. In 1926 the name of this department was changed to the Export Credits Guarantee Department (ECGD), and it was set up as a separate department of the government in 1930, but remained under the jurisdiction of the minister of the Department of Trade. At the time of its founding, the ECGD was primarily engaged in providing export credits, but at present the principal activities are provision of export insurance and guarantees for exports.

Sources of Funds

Insurance and guarantee activities are accounted for on an independent basis. Funding for refinance and certain other activities is provided from government accounts.

Activities

1. Export Insurance

a. Comprehensive Short-Term Guarantees. These guarantees may be used to cover continuing exports of consumer goods for a period of six months or less after loading aboard ship. For cases where the shipment takes place within 12 months from the time of the contract, risks can be covered upon request.

Risks which are covered are the following: insolvency of the buyer, the buyer's failure to pay within six months of the due date for goods which he has accepted, the buyer's failure to take up goods which have been despatched to him, a general moratorium on external debt decreed by the government of the buyer's country or of a third country through payment must be made; political events, economic difficulties, legislative or administrative measures arising outside the U.K. which prevent or delay the transfer of payments or deposits made in respect of the contract; war and certain other events preventing performance of the contract, provided that the event is not one normally insurable with conventional insurers, and certain other cases.

The extent of coverage depends on the type of risk, but normally ranges from 90–95 percent.

b. The Supplemental Extended Terms Guarantee. This type of guarantee provides for insurance coverage which in effect extends the period of coverage described in (*a*) above. It is applied to exports of such items as commercial vehicles, machine tools, and engineering goods. The period for insurance extends from the time of contract, prior to shipment, to within about two years, or five years following shipment. Insurable risk and extent of coverage are the same as for comprehensive short-term guarantees, but insurance rates are higher.

c. Specific Guarantees. This type of guarantee is applied to shipments of consumer goods which are not conducted on a continuing basis and to transactions involving capital goods or projects. The period of coverage is from the time of manufacture, prior to shipment, up to five years after the time of shipment. For exceptionally large projects, coverage for periods of more than five years is possible. Insurable risk is virtually the same as for comprehensive short-term credit guarantees, and extent of coverage is 90 percent.

d. Other Types of Export Insurance. These include supplementary stocks guarantees, external trade guarantees and construction work guarantees. Insurance of invisible exports, such as technical or professional assistance is also possible.

2. Guarantees for Supplier Credit Financing

These guarantees provide for 100 percent payments by ECGD to banks providing export finance to exporting companies.

a. Financing Shorter-Term Credits. (*i*) Comprehensive bill guarantees: These are provided for promissory notes or bills of exchange with maturities of up to two years issued to finance exports of goods or services. (*ii*) Comprehensive open-account guarantees: These guarantees apply to amounts provided to finance trade on an open-account basis using unsupported bills or notes. Terms are limited to six months or less.

b. Financing Medium-Term Supplier Credit. This applies to bank finance for capital goods on a medium- to long-term basis and involves the issuance of specific guarantees to banks providing the finance. In this case, each contract is considered, documented, and rated separately.

c. Guarantees for Buyer Credit Financing. These guarantees are supplied to banks providing buyers' credits for contracts of £1 million or more. Guarantees are provided for 100 percent of the value of the contract. A special case of this type of insurance provides coverage for lines of credit.

d. Insurance for Overseas Investors. This type of insurance covers the political risks (expropriation, war damage, and restriction on remittances) of companies carrying on business in the United Kingdom and

their overseas subsidiaries. Equity investment, loans, and other exposures are covered. The term of coverage is normally 15 years. The
premium is set at 1 percent p.a. of the current insured amount, plus
an additional commitment premium of 0.5 percent p.a.

 e. Other Types.   Other types of sophisticated insurance are also
available, including cost-escalation insurance, performance bond insurance, and consortium insurance, but a description of these is omitted
here. In addition, in the past, the ECGD has also provided refinancing
of export credits, but beginning in 1980 this activity was suspended,
except in special cases.

Record of Accomplishment

The accompanying table shows the business declared and the percentage of U.K. exports covered by the ECGD insurance in recent
years.

Progress of Business 1977/78–1979/80 (pounds in millions)

Financial Year	Business Declared	Percentage of Total U.K. Exports
1977/78	12,940	33.3
1978/79	14,515	33.0
1979/80	16,235	30.5

Source: ECGD Trading Results 1979/1980.

SECTION 6
Approaches to World Financial Markets

34
Correspondent Banking

ALBERT F. NAVEJA
Vice President
Harris Trust and Savings Bank

The evolution of world money markets has been led by the world banking industry. The steady progression of events that has led to the present global economy has created new and interesting opportunities for banks to expand their international activities. Expansion both abroad and at home was a natural phenomena for major banks, and in the expansionary era since World War II, most bankers have found that the use of correspondent banks located in other cities has proved a natural and efficient way of transacting and expanding business.

Decisions by banks as to how to approach foreign markets are influenced by a number of variables, such as overall financial resources, volume of international business, and the strategic plans of the bank, as well as the banking structure of the foreign countries in which business is done. The range of opportunities to accomplish the transaction of international business includes branching, agencies, local bank acquisitions, joint ventures, and merchant banks. However, until the volume of business in another country is substantial, a bank will usually choose to rely on traditional correspondent bank relationships to handle its needs in that country. Banks choosing the correspondent route do not incur the significant and ever present costs of operating abroad, but can still enjoy the benefits derived from having multiple sources of business given and received, as well as referrals of local banking opportunities. Mutually beneficial service arrangements abound and are only limited by legal restraints, available flexibility, and size and scope of banking operations.

In evaluating the different opportunities for a bank to get into foreign markets, a bank must consider the obvious and major advantage of using the correspondent route. Direct overseas correspondent networks do not pose a threat to local bankers as do branches, foreign affiliates, or agencies. Normally local banks welcome the correspondent relationship and will work to maintain and enhance that arrangement. These business relationships can develop into mutually dependent and profitable ones.

A correspondent bank, by its broadest definition, is a bank located in any other city, state, or country that provides a service for another bank. That service can be purely depositary, credit related, or otherwise. Often, a main ingredient provided by the usual correspondent relationship is that of providing a credit facility. In the past, since much of the world's trade has been denominated in dollars, U.S. banks have generally been the source of U.S.-dollar lines of credit to the foreign correspondents. In turn, U.S. banks without branches abroad have relied on their foreign correspondents to help finance their multinational corporate customer's local foreign subsidiaries that require local currency funding. Those mutual and beneficial arrangements contributed to stronger correspondent relationships particularly during the 1960s and 70s.

The 1980s have brought an era of major reassessment of the international activities of many U.S. banks. The operation of a costly global branch system in the inflationary, high-interest climate of the 1980s has created economic pressures resulting from lower spreads and reduced profitability. Some banks are finding that the expansion of correspondent networks can develop a greater customer base and can be the basis for strategic area marketing decisions. Since national branch banking systems exist in most countries of the world today, an overseas correspondent generally can provide countrywide capability. When two banks agree to act as correspondents, they usually exact an agreement, such as the exhibit at the end of this chapter, outlining the services to be provided and the terms and conditions.

REIMBURSEMENT BANKS

While it is common for banks to develop and organize their own correspondent networks both here and abroad, it is obviously impossible to have a depository relationship with every bank everywhere. When for various reasons, whether they be organizational, political, economic, and so on, a direct depository relationship does not exist or is unwarranted because of the volume of activity between institutions, a third bank is then chosen as the common denominator in which to settle specific transactions. This bank, called the reimbursement bank, may be a bank that is a mutual correspondent, or one that is simply located in the city or country in which the transaction is to be consummated. In essence, the bank issuing the instrument, be it a letter of credit, collection payment instructions, foreign remittance via draft or transfer, etc. authorizes that reimbursement or legal claim for payment of the instrument can be made on the designated third party or reimbursement bank. This claim is honored by the reimbursement bank based upon receiving an authorization directly from the original issuing bank. The transaction is completed when the claim for funds is made via letter, telex, and so forth, and the reimbursement bank debits the issuing bank's account and pays, via a credit, check, or transfer, the bank requesting reimbursement for the transaction in question.

CREDIT RELATED CORRESPONDENT RELATIONSHIPS

International banking relations often rely on credit provided to overseas correspondents, often referred to as "normal international transactions": confirmation of letters of credit, creation of the U.S.-dollar acceptances, clean advances, and overdrafts.

Letters of Credit

Letters of credit are a major correspondent service. A U.S. bank might originate a letter of credit on behalf of a domestic importer and will depend upon its foreign correspondent to confirm that credit to the exporter, or merely to advise the credit and negotiate the arrangements for payments under the letter. Conversely, if the foreign correspondent opens a credit for its importer, a U.S. correspondent will be expected, depending upon the terms, to confirm that credit to the U.S. exporter, or to advise the credit and negotiate the documents involved. Thus, correspondent banks provide a conduit by which letters of credit are operationally and functionally delivered to a beneficiary. When an advising bank adds its confirmation to the letter of credit, regardless of the origin of the credit, that request is considered an extension of credit to the issuing bank by the confirming bank.

The many details involved in the issuances, confirmation, advising, and negotiating under the provisions of a letter of credit require continuous and extensive communications between correspondent banks. Such transactions provide the basis for other kinds of banking relationships that can be to the advantage of both banks.

Acceptances

Letters of credit are one of the basic building blocks of international trade, and acceptance financing is the other. Acceptances are a natural result of a time letter of credit. Once a bank accepts the beneficiary's draft calling for payment in a certain number of days, a banker's acceptance has been created. That traditional manner of creating acceptances continues to exist today, but has clearly been surpassed by wholesale bank-to-bank financing of trade with bankers' acceptances. Foreign correspondent bankers rely heavily today on U.S.-dollar acceptance facilities to provide funds in the United States for their branches and agencies. In addition, this method of credit extension is used to provide dollars for their home office or overseas branch locations to finance U.S.-dollar denominated assets.

Money Market Credits

As overseas correspondent banks have entered the U.S. markets, there has been a need to provide short-term credit facilities for them through money market lines of credit for local liquidity.

Special-Purpose Letters of Credit

For many years stand-by letters of credit have been used by major U.S. banks to support the local borrowings of good U.S. corporate customers for their overseas subsidiaries. These letters of credit are usually payable to the local foreign correspondent bank which uses them to support local currency borrowing required by the subsidiary of the U.S. corporation. While special-purpose letters of credit continue to be used for the support of local subsidiaries, there have developed many new uses. Special-purpose letters of credit may be used to support bid and performance bonds that are now commonplace. Further, a variety of financing arrangements related to governmental and self-policing agencies, as well as central-bank regulatory requirements, are being met by the use of special-purpose letters of credit. Correspondent banks have a heavy involvement in these instruments as issuers, beneficiaries, and sometime negotiators of the credit. In some areas of the world, local custom or statute allow only certain authorized banks to issue such credit. In these cases the local correspondent is required to reissue a U.S. letter of credit so that it becomes legally acceptable. In other circumstances only advising and negotiating of the credit need be accomplished by the overseas correspondent.

NONCREDIT SERVICES

Normally one bank will act as the local correspondent bank for another bank to handle most of its transactional requirements. These transactions include, but may not necessarily be limited to the following types of items that do not require an extension of credit. These services are normally paid for either by fees or balances required, based on an earnings allowance, or a combination of both.

Payments

Payments include the free payments of funds in either U.S. dollars or a local currency. These transactions will take the form of drafts or checks drawn by one bank on its account with the local correspondent bank or under the protection of a mutual correspondent. Further, funds can be transmitted by mail or by tested telex instructions from the U.S. bank to the local bank authorizing such payment. Check cashing accommodations are also usually provided by the local bank for good customers of the overseas correspondent who are travelling in that country.

Clearings

Local banks will provide clearing services to facilitate the settlement of local currency payments, foreign exchange contracts denominated in the local currency, or Eurocurrencies, as well as local check-clearing services.

Collection

Through agency agreements the correspondent can act on behalf of another bank by preparing and presenting negotiable instruments and related documents to drawees or buyers. Such collections will cover the settlement of terms of contracts, sales of merchandise, as well as the purchase or sale of securities. Security delivery and receipt services are normally provided to facilitate both bank and customer dealings in securities, along with dividend receipts and coupon collections. As a convenience, local safekeeping facilities are also provided to correspondents for the secured storage of such items as stocks, bonds, and precious metals.

Foreign Exchange Services

Foreign exchange trading has always been and continues to be one of the most significant of the correspondent bank relationships. Expansion of the activities of the customers of major banks and the bank overseas expansion itself have increased the need for foreign exchange services.

Documentation of the Correspondent Relationship

Specific arrangements between international correspondents are based upon an understanding as to whether or not an account is to be maintained and an agreement as to the types of services that are to be provided. How the services are priced and the terms covering the range of correspondent relationships will vary considerably among banks. A sample of a "Terms and Conditions Statement" for foreign correspondent relationships is included at the end of this chapter.

TRADE DEVELOPMENT AND BUSINESS REFERRALS

Correspondent banks may provide one another the opportunity to serve each other's commercial customers and prospects for trade development or other business activities. Such opportunities occur regularly. A bank might contact its correspondent on behalf of a commercial customer to obtain names of companies in given lines of business who might either be a source of supply or sales outlet. It might also seek such names as possibilities for a joint venture. The banker will often be able to accommodate the request with reliable names. With the added interest of foreign investment in the United States today, many U.S. bankers are substantially engaged in referral opportunities.

Bankers also look to their correspondents to provide local credit information for the bank's own use or use by the bank's customers. In addition, a bank also looks to its correspondents for insight into local economic and political conditions. Assistance in helping to interpret local business and banking regulations is also an essential correspondence service. Further, the use of a local correspondent's help and its expertise in the processing of applications does help insure that the foreign bank and its clients will be in compliance with local regulations.

CONCLUSION

A good correspondent relationship is built upon mutual needs and the ability to fill those needs. Opportunities can arise for correspondents as a result of changing customer needs that can be met most effectively through the correspondent relationship. Today all banks are being forced to review more closely the profitability of traditional correspondent banking arrangements. The old theory that the honored overall relationship is *all* that is important is being questioned seriously. As the world financial markets continue to expand and converge into a true world money market, there will be continued pressure for banks to go abroad to service those markets. However, the need for effective correspondent bank relationships will also continue to grow. Funding and liquidity will become more important as asset/liability management requirements become more precise. Traditional noncredit and credit services will become increasingly important. Here, as always, the key will be the *quality of timely service*. Bankers should take note that automated communications systems which link the world via satellites with real-time computer capabilities are clearly evolving and will influence the future nature of the traditional correspondent banking relationship.

Schedule of
TERMS AND CONDITIONS
For the Account of

These terms and conditions replace and supersede all those previously issued.

	Commission	Value
Interest		
Current Account	Under the terms of the Banking Act of 1933 no interest can be paid on demand deposits.	
Time deposits	Rates on application	
Temporary debit balances	Subject to arrangement	
Statements	Rendered monthly unless otherwise arranged	
Drawings		
U.S. dollars on us	Free	Date of payment
Foreign currency (Payable at our buying rate on date of payment)	Free	
Remittances (credited on receipt subject to *final* payment)		
Checks		
On ourselves	Free	Date of receipt
On New York banks which are members of the New York Clearing House Association when item is received in time for clearings	Free	Date of receipt
On other New York banks and Clearing House items received after clearings	Free	Next business day
On other cities	Free, plus actual charges to us, if any	According to number of days required to collect
On banks outside the U.S.A.	Free	Date of receipt of proceeds
Payments of third parties for your credit	Free	Date of receipt of proceeds
Transfers to and from New York (wire transfers transmitted over our private wire are free of wire costs)		
Collections (credited or remitted after payment with advise)		
On New York		
Clean items on banks or bankers	Free	Date of receipt of proceeds
Clean items on others	$15	Date of receipt of proceeds

	Commission	*Value*
Documentary items on banks	Free	Date of receipt of proceeds
Documentary items on others	$20	Date of receipt of proceeds
On others, same as on New York plus correspondent charges, if any		Date of receipt of proceeds
All items payable in a currency other than U.S. dollar	We attempt to collect at rates which will allow us to remit free of commission.	
(If payment is tendered by draft in foreign currency issued by another bank, it will be accepted on your behalf without responsibility to us.)	If we cannot, rates for U.S. dollar items will apply.	
Items returned unpaid	$1.00 each	
Items unpaid or unaccepted on first presentation	$2.50 each additional presentation	
Items requiring more than ordinary handling	Charges will be made proportionate to the work involved	
Coupons and called or matured bonds	By arrangement	

Note: We cannot assume responsibility for the authenticity of signature of acceptance.

All items received for collection shall be subject to the Uniform Rules for the Collection of Commercial Paper fixed by the International Chamber of Commerce and set forth in Brochure No. 254 thereof.

Clean Payments

U.S. dollars

To banks for your own account	Free	Date of payment
To accounts on our books	Free	Date of payment
To individuals, corporations, or commercial firms	$5.00	Date of payment
To banks for account of individuals, corporations, or commercial firms	$5.00	Date of payment

Note: All U.S.-dollar payments will be made in Clearinghouse funds unless otherwise instructed; and charges, if any, are for beneficiaries account unless otherwise indicated by you.

	Commission	*Value*
Foreign Currency Payments:		
In New York	Same as above except that payments that exceed U.S. dollar equivalent of $5,000 are free	
Other cities (payable at our buying rate on date of payment)	Same as above plus correspondent's charges, if any	
Payments against Documents*		
New York	$15.00	Date of payment
Other cities	Same as above plus correspondent's charges if any	Date of receipt of execution

* This bank and/or its correspondents do not assume any liability either as principal or agent, for the genuineness of any documents received, nor for the title to, quantity, quality, condition, or delivery of any goods purporting to be represented thereby.

Commercial Letters of Credit†		
Advising your letter of credit without our confirmation	Our form $20 Your form $10	Date of receipt
Confirmation of your letters of credit	$\frac{1}{20}$ percent minimum $25 for each 3-month period or fraction thereof	Date of confirmation
Amendments:		
Increase or extension of confirmed letters of credit	$15 plus $\frac{1}{20}$ percent minimum for each 3-month period or fraction thereof	Date of receipt
Other amendments	$15 each	Date of receipt
Payments:		
Clean or documentary sight payments debited to your account	$\frac{1}{10}$ percent minimum $20 per payment	Date of payment
Payment claimed from other banks	$\frac{1}{10}$ percent minimum $25	Date of payment
Acceptance letters of credit	$\frac{1}{8}$ percent for each 30 days, minimum $30 per acceptance	Date of acceptance
Reimbursement of sight letters of credit	$15 per drawing	Date of payment
Acceptance financing	By arrangement, minimum $25 per item	Date of acceptance
Ineligible acceptances	$\frac{1}{8}$ percent for each 30 days, minimum $30 per item plus incremental percentage to compensate for required reserve	Date of acceptance
Letters of credit requiring special handling	By arrangement, minimum $50 per credit	Date of receipt
Issuance of our letters of credit	$20.00 unconfirmed $25.00 confirmed	Date of issuance Date of issuance
All letters of credit transactions are subject to cor-		

	Commission	*Value*

respondent bank charges in addition to our own when the letters of credit are made payable at or advised through another bank.

All letters of credit negotiated or issued by this bank shall be subject to the Uniform Customs and Practice for Documentary Credits (1974 Rev.) fixed by the International Chamber of Commerce and set forth in Publication 290 thereof.

† This bank and/or its correspondents do not assume any liability, either as principal or agent, for the genuineness of any documents received, nor for the title to, quantity, quality, condition or delivery of any goods purporting to be represented thereby.

Foreign Exchange

All orders effected at our best rate at time order received   Free

Securities

Delivering or receiving with or without payment   By arrangement

Stock and bond orders, for your account through brokers   Tariff on application

Safekeeping   Tariff on application

Registered and air mail postage, insurance, telegrams, and other direct out-of-pocket expenses are to your debit except as may otherwise be noted herein. Ordinary postage, free.

_____ Bank

New York _____   By _____
                                                                                   Authorized Signature

Subject to Change

35
Foreign Branches

DONALD R. MARSH
Senior Vice President
Rainier National Bank

INTRODUCTION

The phenomenal growth of international banking in the past two decades has consisted, in part, of the equally remarkable expansion of overseas branching by banks. Prior to 1960 only seven U.S. banks maintained a total of 132 branches abroad. By 1964 the number of banks had grown to 11, and their foreign branches totaled 180. But the next decade brought an explosive expansion in overseas branching—by 1974, 125 U.S. banks were operating 732 branches in foreign locations. At the end of 1979 the numbers had grown more moderately to 130 banks with just under 800 foreign branches.[1]

Major banks from Europe, Canada, and Japan have also joined the bandwagon, although their accelerated expansion has taken place only in more recent years. For some of the European banks it has meant extending beyond old colonial branch systems. The major Japanese banks have been building their overseas branch systems fairly steadily since the late 1950s, but the past decade has seen numerous regional Japanese banks also entering the fray. Canadian banks' expansion abroad would undoubtedly be even more extensive were it not for the reaction of foreign governments to the only recently lifted Canadian prohibition of foreign banks operating in Canada.

REASONS FOR ESTABLISHING BRANCHES

What has caused this massive proliferation of overseas branching by banks? Why do not only large multinational banks, with assets measuring in the tens of billions of dollars, but also regional banks much

---

[1] *Economic Review*, Federal Reserve Bank of Kansas City, November 1980.

smaller in size extend their operations so far afield from their local indigenous markets? The reasons are several.

First, there is the "We follow our customers abroad" syndrome. With corporations expanding their operations around the globe, many banks felt the need to be able to serve those corporations with local banking capabilities in foreign markets. Related to this is the competitive factor: "If bank A is going to be in Germany to serve our mutual customer X, then we've got to be there too."

Undoubtedly this feeling of a need to serve head-office customers abroad provided the initial impetus for many banks expanding overseas, and it still serves as a rationale for some banks justifying at least some of their overseas operations. Yet upon examining the customer composition of foreign bank branches, one finds that usually only a minor share of the business is with head-office customers. Increasingly the business of overseas bank branches has consisted of providing services to purely local, indigenous business enterprises of the host country (although some of them also may be multinational corporations). This has led to a growing multinationality of banks, not only in the geographic dispersion of their operations, but also in their customer base. So when a large U.S. bank today says it needs overseas branches to serve its customers, it may well have in mind being able to accommodate Mitsubishi Heavy Industries in West Germany as much as Coca-Cola.

There are two reasons for this growth in the importance of local companies in the customer base. First, banks soon found that the business of head-office customers alone wasn't sufficient to support a branch in a foreign country. Secondly, business with purely local companies was proving to be profitable in itself.

And this leads us to the second reason for having branches abroad: the direct contribution to bank earnings the branches provide, completely aside from any indirect contribution through enhancement or protection of head-office customer relationships or financing trade with the economic region that is the bank's market back home. In fact, some of the most profitable banking that can be found today is in the operation of branches in certain markets abroad. This is particularly so in less developed countries with less sophisticated banking markets, where competition is not as keen as it is in the banking industries of the more industrial countries of the United States, Europe, and Japan. There are some markets in which the banks, often under government auspices, get together and determine what interest rates are to be paid for deposits and what rates will be charged on loans. As can be expected, the spread between the two is usually substantial. Foreign banks, accustomed to more competition and with a greater emphasis on cost control and bottom-line earnings, are often able to enter such markets and enjoy comparatively high profitability. Over time they may contribute significantly to a greater efficiency in the banking system of a less developed country, although this of course can lead to an erosion of the high profit environment they have been enjoying.

Overseas branch profits not only add quantitatively to bank earnings, they also provide a more diversified earnings base. The moderating effect of this diversification on swings in total bank earnings has been of considerable value to banks who in recent years have experienced substantial fluctuations in domestic earnings.

A third reason for having foreign branches is the access they provide to overseas money markets. This could be called the "funding" reason or purpose. But it should be noted that participation in an overseas money market can also be useful on the asset side of the balance sheet, that is, it can at times be used to lay off surplus liquidity more profitably than can be done in a bank's own domestic money markets. Placing money sourced from domestic money markets in the Euro or Asia currency market has been used to particular advantage by U.S. banks when market conditions have been conducive to doing so at a profit.

Certainly large international banks with earning assets in their international operations amounting to several, or several tens of billions of dollars have a need for branches located in international money markets abroad for the purpose of funding those international assets. Many medium-size banks with lesser volumes of international assets have seen fit to do likewise, often establishing branches in London, the center of the Eurocurrency market, primarily for that purpose. To have an active, physical presence in that market, with traders, bookkeepers, accountants, money transfer, and other operations personnel all located right there on the spot, in close proximity to their counterparts in the other banks making up the bulk of the market obviously has its advantages.

However, smaller banks, particularly those with international assets amounting to only a few hundred million dollars or less, may find their requirements insufficient to warrant the establishment and expense of maintaining an actual, active presence in an overseas money market locale. Yet such banks may still want to rely on the Eurocurrency market for funding their international asset portfolios because of limited funding capacity domestically, an unwillingness to employ domestically sourced funds abroad or, at times, government controls on international capital flows. While they are able to do the trading from their offices in the United States, in order to quote competitive interest rates for deposits in the Eurocurrency markets, they still need an overseas branch to escape the Federal Reserve reserve requirements and interest-rate limitations that are applicable to deposits accepted by banks in the United States but not at their overseas branches.[2]

This need gave rise to the offshore "shell" or "post office box" branch, most of which have been established by U.S. banks in the Caribbean at Nassau in the Bahamas or Georgetown in the Cayman Islands. The local registration and servicing, including the maintenance of liability and asset ledgers, for such shell branches are handled by a local agent engaged for that purpose by the bank's head office. In this way a U.S. bank whose international assets are not of sufficient size to warrant the cost of maintaining an actual presence in an overseas money market can have access to the Euro/Asia currency markets by booking the deposits and loans or interbank placements in an offshore shell branch and thereby avoid reserve requirements and interest-rate limits, while conducting the trading from its head office or perhaps a U.S.-based Edge Act office.

It should be noted, however, that the largest U.S. banks also maintain branches in the Caribbean in addition to their branches in London and other overseas money centers. This is done in order to take advantage of the absence of local taxes[3] as well as provide a booking office for Eurocurrency trading conducted by their head offices in the United States. Some large banks actually maintain trading operations and backup staff with their own people on the spot in their Caribbean branches.

Another reason for having a branch abroad is to provide a base in financial centers like London, New York, Hong Kong, and Singapore for conducting activities somewhat peripheral to traditional commercial banking such as loan syndication management, leasing, project financing, international money management, and investment advisory services. Not only does a branch facilitate the providing of such services, but the rationale goes, "If we're going to incur all the staff, premises, and other expenses to conduct such operations, why not have a branch engaged in regular commercial banking as well?" Many banks have established merchant banking subsidiaries in London in conjunction with their London branches. While in most cases the branch preceded the merchant bank, a number of banks today are finding the merchant

---

[2] It is, of course, the exemption from Federal Reserve reserve requirements and interest-rate limitations on deposits in overseas branches of U.S. banks that is the essential reason for the existence of the Eurodollar market as a separate market from the market for dollar deposits in the United States. The differential in rates paid for deposits of like tenor between the two markets, with the higher rate being paid in the Euromarket, simply reflects the absence of the cost of reserves having to be set aside against deposits in the overseas branches of U.S. banks.

[3] Conducting banking business through a branch in an overseas locale with few or no local taxes does not, of course, in itself avoid U.S. income taxes. However it can help build up an aggregate of foreign-sourced income, the U.S. tax liability for which may be offset by foreign taxes paid as a result of business conducted in other foreign countries.

bank the more profitable of the two, to the point where they might even consider closing or scaling down the branch operation; yet they continue it largely as an adjunct to the merchant bank. This kind of situation could become increasingly common in the future in certain markets.

ACTIVITIES OF FOREIGN BRANCHES

In reviewing the reasons for establishing and maintaining foreign branches, some of the kinds of business engaged in by branches have been covered. However, it will be worthwhile to examine their scope in greater detail.

The principal service offered by foreign bank branches, as with commercial banking anywhere, is the extension of credit, primarily in the form of lending money as distinct from issuing guarantees, letters of credit, and acceptances, although any of these services can be important in some markets. Lending by foreign branches can be divided into two categories: (1) truly international, that is, cross-border lending and (2) local lending in the country in which the branch is located. Local lending may be conducted in either local or a foreign currency, most commonly the U.S. dollar, although a number of hard currencies of the major industrial countries are also used.

The major part of the lending done by branches in important international money centers such as London and Singapore, and virtually all the lending done by Caribbean branches, is international lending. It is not so much that the local markets are small—although this is a factor in the cases of Singapore and obviously the Caribbean—as it is that those locations are the major trading and booking centers for the Euro/Asia currency markets. It is the vast pool of liquidity represented by this worldwide money market that is the principal funding source for the international lending that is done today. With the deposits used to fund so much of this lending being taken in by the London, Caribbean, and Singapore branches of international banks, the asset sides of the balance sheets of those branches are consequently heavily laden with international loans.

Most of the lending in the Euro/Asia currency markets is of a term nature, with final maturities running out as far as 10 years and beyond. Interest rates are normally designed to float at a fixed spread over the cost of funding the loan through the purchase of one-, three- or six-month time deposits in the market. Borrowers are typically multinational corporations, usually from industrialized countries, and banks and foreign governments or government agencies, these latter usually from less developed countries. A substantial part of international term lending is in the form of large syndicated loans, occasionally running up to as much as $1 billion in amount, with anywhere from several to over one hundred banks participating in a loan. The purposes of the loans cover a broad range, but will commonly be for financing large industrial projects, general economic development, or balance-of-payments deficits. Bankers sometimes like to say they do not finance balance-of-payments deficits, but the line between economic development and balance-of-payments deficit financing can often be a thin one.

For many banks most of the business development, credit assessment, and decision making in international lending is done by head office personnel, although some larger banks who have decentralized their international management structures are increasingly performing those functions in regional headquarters abroad. But regardless of where the preliminary work and decision making are done, and regardless of whether there is a direct relationship with the borrower or a loan is merely a participation in a large syndicated credit, international term lending from overseas branches accounts for a very substantial share of today's international banking business. Yet it should be noted that, with the advent in recent years of increasing numbers of banks from Europe, Canada, Japan, and elsewhere into the international lending business, profit margins have been declining to the point where more and more banks are looking with increasing skepticism on this kind of business as a worthwhile source of earnings.

Direct lending to borrowers is not the only involvement of banks in the Euro/Asia currency markets. The placing of money in time deposits with other banks, commonly known as interbank "placements" or "redeposits," also represents a substantial part of the business of branches in both major and sometimes lesser international money market locations. This is a money market activity conducted by traders rather than lending officers. It is usually combined with the branch's foreign exchange operation and may be more under the direction of global treasury management at head office than the local branch manager.

This interbank redepositing is a high-volume, low-margin business done at spreads of often no more than a few basis points. Consequently many banks, particularly those with more worthwhile opportunities to employ their resources and with little leeway in their capital-to-asset ratios, endeavor to minimize this international money market activity. Yet for those banks dependent on the Euro/Asia markets for funding their international loan portfolios, there is the adage that you can't be just on one side of the market, you've got to put some money back into it too. The attitudes and practices of dealers on the trading desks tend to enforce this condition. Hence some Euro/Asia currency trading is engaged in by virtually all foreign bank branches located in international money market centers.

Foreign exchange trading is an important source of earnings for many branches. Some banks engage in purely interbank trading for a profit in addition to meeting the foreign exchange needs of their customers. In money market centers like London, Hong Kong, and Singapore, exchange trading may be combined with money market activity as banks borrow one currency and invest it in another on a short-term basis.

Short-term financing of international trade can also be important business for a branch. Some trade financing takes place through the medium of interbank deposit placements discussed earlier, with large banks from industrial, capital rich countries placing hard currencies with banks from less developed countries who in turn use the funds for financing trade. Branches with exporting customers are in a position to finance exports by extending credit to either the exporters or their foreign customers. The former, of course, is not cross-border financing in itself. Similarly, import financing extended to a local importer may not be international per se, but it enables a foreign exporter to receive cash for goods shipped, whereas the exporter would otherwise have had to sell on deferred payment terms; hence there is an international element to the financing.

Import financing is an important business for many foreign branches in less developed countries that are short of hard currency. In fact, the governments of such countries often expect the branches of foreign banks to provide import financing to local commerce and industry. Their capacity to finance imports can be an inducement to a government to allow foreign banks to operate within its country and to permit them to bring in hard currency without restriction.

This leads us to local lending in the branch's indigenous market. As suggested earlier, this can be one of the most lucrative businesses a bank can engage in today. As the profit margins of real international lending have declined, many banks are increasingly measuring the success of their international strategies by their ability to get into and conduct a commercial banking business in foreign markets, especially in those countries with less competitive and developed banking industries. However, the opportunities are not what they once were and may continue to diminish. Banking industries in developing countries are becoming increasingly competitive and technically advanced. As countries become less dependent on foreign capital, and those that remain so dependent are able to adequately meet their needs in the international credit markets, governments become less willing to permit foreign banks to enjoy anything beyond a reasonable profitability. Simply having a lot of money to lend does not guarantee high profits any more for a branch abroad. There do remain a few locales where exceptionally good profitability is enjoyed by foreign banks, but they are becoming fewer and the long-established branches have a decided advantage over newcomers.

The degree to which foreign bank branches engage in local lending depends on the opportunities available to them, which vary greatly from country to country. In some developing countries private business enterprises are not considered to be of sufficient financial strength to warrant credit from branches of foreign banks, so that most lending is done to local banks, to a private company with a local bank guarantee, or to the government. Some countries so restrict the extent to which foreign banks may do business with local residents that the bulk of foreign bank branch business is international or offshore. In the more industrialized countries, the more attractive business may be so dominated by major indigenous banks, sometimes through their strong shareholding and directorship ties with local industry, that foreign branches find it difficult to penetrate the market.

The kinds of lending done will tend to conform much more to local practice than to practices in a bank's home country. It should be noted that for most, if not all, other countries of the world, commercial bank credit plays a much more important role in financing their economies than it does in the United States. Other private sources of capital— the public equity and bond markets, nonbank financial institutions, other institutional investors—do not begin to have the capacity they do in the United States. And generally, the less developed the country, the greater the reliance on bank credit. Moreover, most of the credit is short term, with 90-day "evergreen" loans being rolled over endlessly to finance fixed plant and equipment as well as working capital.

What this means is that where they are not precluded by government restriction or local bank dominance of the market, foreign bank branches, like local banks, can face an almost insatiable demand for credit. Again, the less developed the country, the more this tends to be so. Doing business often means just turning on the spigot!

It should also be noted that consumer credit does not exist in other countries to the extent that it does in the United States. It is beginning to take hold in some of the more industrially advanced countries, and some U.S. banks have ventured into consumer financing abroad, but it remains the exception more than the rule. Additionally, the absence of an extensive branch network within a country handicaps a foreign bank from getting into consumer financing. Wholesale banking is the mainstay of the business of overseas branches, although this does not mean the customer base may not include small- and medium-sized enterprises as well as large corporations.

As would be expected, therefore, the most common form of local lending by foreign bank branches is making short-term loans to industrial and commercial enterprises. In addition to promissory notes, overdraft financing and discounting of domestic trade bills with recourse are common in many countries. The loans may be in local or foreign currency and may be secured or unsecured, depending on local practice. As mentioned earlier, much of the lending may not be for any specifically identified purpose; the proceeds end up in the borrower's general pool of funding and may be used for financing fixed assets as well as for inventory and receivables.

Other, more specialized kinds of lending are found and will vary from country to country. Foreign branches may be eligible to participate in government programs designed to support particular industries through subsidized financing. Probably the most common form of such support is central bank rediscounting of export paper at low interest rates to enable commercial banks to offer low-cost financing to export industries. The purchase of export bills generally is a common practice for banks in many countries and is usually categorized in financial reporting as part of their foreign exchange business since the bills are usually denominated in U.S. dollars or some other foreign currency.

Longer fixed-term lending may be done, most commonly secured by real estate. However, this can be risky for foreign branches which usually do not have the more stable base of deposits or other long-term funding sources indigenous banks are likely to have.

Despite the major role played by bank credit, the variety of kinds of lending and what might be called more "sophisticated" structuring of financing do not exist in most countries to the degree they do in the United States. Large international banks who have tried to introduce such techniques as production payment financing, construction financing with a firm takeout, and the "three-year revolver convertible into a four-year term loan" type of facility have met with considerable resistance. "Why bother with all this rigmarole and attendant documentation and legal fees when the 90-day note or overdraft has served us so well in the past?" Each country has its own ways of financing its economy, but lending money is generally done more simply in other countries than it is in the United States.

Credit assessment can present special problems in the operation of foreign branches. With short-term bank lending playing such an important role in the financing of business, balance sheets tend to reflect liquidity and capital ratios that would be unacceptable in the United States. Large manufacturing, as well as commercial concerns, may have outstanding debt equivalent to many times equity and current liabilities equivalent to or even exceeding current assets. Financial analysis standards commonly used in the United States can be of limited value in such circumstances. A solution to this dilemma must be found if a foreign branch is to take advantage of opportunities to extend credit to local private business enterprises.

The most common remedy is a guarantee, either by a local bank, the borrower's owner or an affiliated company. Since the local subsidiaries of U.S. and other foreign companies are also likely to be undercapitalized, a guarantee of a foreign parent is often obtained.

But guarantees are not always available, nor are they necessarily appropriate for ongoing successful firms. What has to be really looked at are those institutional characteristics in the business environments of other countries which compensate for what appear on the surface to be precarious corporate financial structures.

It should be noted first of all that much of the short-term bank borrowing, while technically short-term as 90-day notes, overdrafts, or discounted trade paper, is much more permanent in reality in that it is endlessly rolled over. This reflects the closer ties that exist between banks and customers; their relationships are much less "arms length" than is customary in the United States. In some countries a company's principal bank will be expected to, and will, bear a disproportionate share of the loss in the event of bankruptcy, relieving marginal lenders at least to some extent, if not entirely, of their share of the burden.

Secondly, the relative standing of a company in its industry and the importance of that industry in a country can determine how much support it will receive from outside elements in the society. These can include the firm's banks, shareholders, suppliers, customers, government, and even other members of the same industry. Instances have been known in which, under government direction, "antirecession cartels" are formed whereby prices, production quotas, and capital expenditures are set for each member of an industry. This can provide a degree of resiliency to adverse business conditions not found in a country that is more dependent instead on stronger equity positions in its business enterprises.

Another consideration is the need and intention of many countries, especially those dependent on heavy foreign borrowing for financing balance-of-payments deficits and economic development, to avoid default on any external indebtedness, public or private. Any default could make it substantially more difficult or costly, if not impossible, to meet future foreign exchange requirements through borrowing. Consequently it is assumed that the governments of such countries will take whatever measures are necessary to ensure the prompt payment of all external debt. The behavior of national governments has borne out the validity of that assumption in many instances, and a substantial amount of international lending is done on the basis of an anticipated continuation of that behavior. The significance of this for the foreign branch is that, while such government efforts might not be expected to apply to local lending by a foreign branch, they often do anyway, as a result of the government's desire to maintain an impeccable record with respect to all credit extended by large international banks with whom the government wants to maintain good relations for future borrowing purposes.

Additionally, social mores and cultural attitudes toward indebtedness can justify a more debt-structured economy in some countries than others. If going into bankruptcy and defaulting on indebtedness bears a high social stigma, proprietors and managers can be expected to make greater efforts to continue operations successfully and fulfill obligations to creditors who have "honored" them by supporting their businesses. A nation's very perception of business and individual business enterprises, their roles and responsibilities in society and society's responsibilities to them, can create a degree of interdependence and resultant stability not found in the more sink or swim atmospheres of Western-cultured nations.

Perceptions of the roles and responsibilities of individual business enterprises toward each other and toward society in general can impart qualities to an entire economy. The foreigner, upon observing the heavy debt structure and apparent illiquidity of businesses in a country, is likely to perceive the whole economy as exceptionally vulnerable to the slightest downturn and such expressions as "This place is a house of cards!" are heard. One of the objectives of the emphasis on personal obligation and "honorable" conduct in business dealings found in some countries is a high level of stability and harmony, the avoidance of disruptive and troublesome events. The protective blanket this affords for individual business firms and industries is also transmitted in some respects to the entire economy, often providing deterrence particularly to the snowballing effect of adverse internal forces. The close paternalistic employer-employee relationship provides an example of how a strong recognition of interdependence at the micro level can affect the macro economy, as exemplified by how the reluctance to lay off workers during a business downturn deters high levels of nationwide unemployment and the propelling effect that it has on an overall business recession.

It is very important that caution is exercised in not overestimating or misinterpreting these cultural differences in making credit and other business decisions. Nor should snap value judgments be made about some of the cultural qualities noted. Stability and harmony are usually purchased at a price of inefficiency, misallocated resources, lack of innovation, and less growth, and, notably, some loss of freedom.

Yet such cultural differences must be recognized in conducting business abroad. In assessing credit worthiness, information about the borrower in addition to the calibre of management and what appears in financial statements must be obtained and evaluated. That additional information will particularly relate to the kinds of outside support the borrower can expect to enjoy. How is the company really looked upon by its principal bankers? How is it looked upon by the government? Its suppliers? Its customers? How important is the company in the entire economy? If it is especially close to the present government, what are the prospects of that government being replaced by one not so friendly to the company?

Reliable information of this kind may not be easy to develop. Dependable sources must be established and branch management must consist of the type of people who can do this. Failure to recognize that lending can still be done in a country, despite sometimes horrendous-looking balance sheets, can mean lost opportunities for very worthwhile business. Misinterpreting cultural differences, overcompensating for them, or failure to develop supplemental information needed to make good credit decisions can be even more costly.

We have given considerable attention to the subject of lending because of its importance and because of the differences that prevail among countries in the assessment and extending of credit. Other services, of course, are also important to the business of foreign bank branches. Some of them contribute more to profitability than lending in some markets.

The acceptance of deposits—the holding of customers' money—provides the basic raw material of any banking operation. Customer deposits are the cheapest money, including shareholders', with which a bank can generate earning assets, and generally the more its assets are funded with customer deposits, the greater the profit margins the bank will enjoy.

This is as true for foreign bank branches as it is for banks in their home markets. However, deposit gathering can be particularly difficult for branches of a foreign bank, for several reasons. Foreign banks usually do not have a network of branches to provide close proximity to customers throughout the country. It is easy to lend to a customer from a remote branch, but for both the individual and corporate customer to get all the conveniences of keeping deposit accounts with you, the customer must be closer to you. In some cases the scope of a foreign bank's operations simply does not warrant an extensive branch network; in others government restrictions may preclude more than one, or a few, branches by a foreign bank.

Government restrictions of various kinds may also apply directly to the acceptance of deposits per se. Some governments have established a category of foreign bank branch which is prohibited from accepting deposits from (or, for that matter, conducting any business with) residents, giving rise to the offshore branch which does business only with nonresidents of the country. Or foreign branches may be allowed to accept time, but not demand, deposits; they may be allowed to accept interbank money market deposits but not deposits from nonbank parties. Or there may be combinations of these or similar restrictions.

The explanation for such restrictions can range from pressure from local banks, who wish to protect their market while yet allowing foreign banks to help finance economic development, to a genuine desire on the part of banking authorities to avoid disrupting influences of foreign banks on the domestic banking system or monetary policy. One ministry of finance is known to have said, in prohibiting the acceptance of deposits from individuals, that it did not want foreign banks engaging in "deposit warfare" (obviously a translation) with local banks for the savings of the general public.

The structure of deposits varies considerably among banking systems. In no country is the individual checking account as prevalent as it is in the United States. Moreover, as mentioned earlier, the business of foreign bank branches tends to be more wholesale than retail, further limiting the ability of foreign banks to generate deposits from the general public, traditionally the cheapest of deposits regardless of whether they are time or checking. In most countries interest is paid on a high percentage of all deposits, including those of very short maturity such as "at notice" accounts which are close to being demand deposits. Corporations in those countries usually keep the bulk of their bank deposits in interest-bearing accounts.

There is also the preference to keep money in a bank of one's own country. This was not always so, particularly in less developed countries where European colonial or American banks were at one time perceived as safer repositories for one's money. However, more advanced stages of economic development and resultant stronger banking systems, combined with growing national pride, have largely eliminated this advantaged position foreign banks once enjoyed. In fact, whereas at one time it may have been a matter of prestige to have a deposit with a foreign bank, today bank depositors, both corporations and the wealthy individual, are just as likely to take pride in keeping their money with a local bank.

Notwithstanding the handicaps, foreign banks do compete aggressively for deposits, with their principal source being the customers to whom they extend credit. Compensating balances for credit extended are found in some countries, although the formal arrangement common in the United States is more the exception than the rule. Central banks and other government agencies are sources of hard currency deposits representing a portion of their countries' foreign exchange reserves. Such deposits usually command top money market interest rates. Money market deposits generally, usually from other financial institutions, are a major source for foreign banks in many markets; in some markets they are the predominant source.

Other bread-and-butter type services are provided by foreign banks in most markets. The traditional international banking services—letters of credit, foreign drafts and collections, international money transfers, foreign exchange—represent a significant business for most foreign bank branches. Other services can include domestic money transfers, custody of securities, safe deposit boxes, credit investigations, credit cards, regular payment of bills, and a variety of savings plans.

Managing large, syndicated Eurocurrency loans has become an important activity for banks located in international financial centers such as London, Hong Kong, and Singapore. The fee income accruing to managers provides an added inducement to participating in such loans. Manager positions, while there might be several in a loan, in the past were usually limited to large banks able to take a substantial portion, say several tens of millions of dollars, of the loan. However, with the continuing narrowing of spreads in international lending noted earlier, in order to induce smaller banks to participate in loans management, fees are being shared with banks taking participations as small as $1 million or $2 million. Many large banks have separate "merchant bank" subsidiaries located in London or Hong Kong to handle loan syndication management, although some still do the work in their overseas branches or at the head office.

International money management is a service for the multinational corporation that has been developed in recent years by a number of large banks. It is offered most effectively by banks with worldwide branch networks. The service has its origins in domestic cash management, but on an international scale it encompasses considerably more. In addition to facilitating the flow and concentration of cash, it can include advising and assisting in the cross-border investment of short-term surplus funds, taking into account such factors as comparative interest rate levels, the cost of hedging exchange risk, government exchange controls, and tax effects. Hence the term *money* rather than just *cash* management. Banks providing this service will have a team of experts located at the head office or London branch, but who will either travel to or have associates located in other major industrial countries, marketing international money management services with the bank's branch network assisting in providing the service. A large international airline, involved in collecting and disbursing funds in many locations around the world, would be a typical customer of this service.

Personnel in an overseas branch, especially those in countries attracting foreign investment, can spend very substantial amounts of time and effort in advising and assisting foreign companies on how to do business in that country. The variety of help that can be provided is almost limitless. Aiding in finding a joint venture partner, structuring a financial package with local banks for the company's local affiliate, conducting market research, introductions to government officials and other influential persons, the selection of lawyers and accountants, helping find a local manager, providing information on foreign investment laws and exchange controls, counseling on the subtleties of working in the local culture—these are but a few examples. Working with companies on problems of these kinds results in the development of a body of knowledge and expertise that becomes increasingly useful to future customers in need of similar assistance.

Much of this kind of service is provided without direct, indentifiable compensation. The incentive in offering it is enhancement of the bank's overall relationship with the company, getting the business of the company not only in that particular country but elsewhere around the world. Providing real help to a customer, existing or potential, with his business abroad can be one of the most effective ways of making a unique impression that will force him to distinguish your bank from the rest of the crowd. A branch manager looks awfully good when the chairman of a large corporate customer goes back to the head office and tells the bank's chief executive officer, "Of all the people I met on my recent extended trip to South America, your man in Santiago was by far the most outstanding and helpful!" But the manager must also guard against expending too much time on a customer without his bank somehow getting paid for it.

An increasing number of noncommercial banking activities are being located in overseas branches, especially by larger banks. Corporate mergers and acquisitions, while not yet as common as in the United States and Britain, are becoming increasingly familiar to the businessmen of other countries. To a considerable degree investment banks and the financial services departments of commercial banks are responsible for this, and the latter are positioning people in their banks' branches in major industrial countries. Much of the acquisitions work done to date has been in connection with foreigners purchasing positions in U.S. companies. The arrangement of nonbank financing is also a service provided by these units. All this kind of work of course is done on a fee basis.

Trust departments investing in foreign stocks have for some years been locating securities analysts in their banks' foreign branches to conduct more on-the-spot analytical work. Trust banking per se, as it is known in the United States, with its distinctive fiduciary responsibility, is not common abroad, and U.S. banks generally do not provide trust services in their overseas branches.[4]

Banks are locating economists in selected branches around the world to provide economic reporting on their respective regions. A branch's staff may also include specialists in certain types of financing, ship and real estate financing and leasing being examples. A team of specialists may be sent to a branch for a period of weeks or months to work on a project, for example, a production-payment credit facility for the development of an offshore oil field.

---

[4] Banks in a number of countries may have the word *trust* in their names, but the activity engaged in is usually significantly different from that of trust departments in U.S. banks.

With the trend toward more decentralized organization, some banks are establishing regional headquarters in places like London, Sao Paulo, and Hong Kong or Tokyo. This usually entails additional supporting staff which may be a part of the branch organization but more often is organized separately and frequently occupies other premises in the city.

PROBLEMS

Overseas branching presents its own set of problems that bank managements and branch managers must confront. We use the word *problems* because it is more descriptive; however, in approaching them, *challenges* could be considered a better word to use.

Government restrictions pose a major problem for overseas branching operations in many countries. Some countries completely prohibit foreign banks from operating branches within their borders while others allow branches but impose varying degrees of control on their activities. The pattern of controls among countries is very mixed and difficult to explain or attribute to common characteristics such as level of economic development, geographic location, or cultural heritage. Some highly developed, industrialized countries provide ready access for foreign bank branches while in others the door is completely closed, and the same mixed pattern can be found among less developed countries. Similarly, in controlling the activities of existing branches there is a broad range of the severity of control with, except for Caribbean-type offshore banking centers, no discernible pattern among different types of countries. In some countries foreign banks are subject only to those controls applicable to domestic banks.

Nor is there any broad trend toward greater liberalization. Some less developed countries, as their banking systems develop and become stronger, will open their doors more to foreign banks and allow them to operate more freely; others appear to conclude that, becoming less dependent on foreign banks for credit, they can further restrict foreign banking operations in their countries. Among more developed countries the same mixed trend can be observed, some imposing further restrictions as time goes on, others permitting a greater scope of activity.

One pattern that can be discerned is that the monetary authorities in smaller countries often express concern about the number of foreign banks operating in their country and will either close the door completely from time to time or admit only a very few additional banks each year.

Persistent efforts can often be successful in bringing about some degree of liberalization of restrictions. However it is much better to pursue this as an organized group of banks rather than bank by bank, for obvious reasons. In addressing the matter of government restrictions, distinction should be made between *discrimination* and *reciprocity*. Bankers are using *discrimination* to refer to foreign banks being discriminated against vis-a-vis indigenous banks within a country, while *reciprocity* refers to the degree to which a bank is treated in a foreign country in a manner comparable to the way banks of that country are treated in the bank's own country. Obtaining relief from discrimination is usually easier than achieving reciprocity.

Restraints on the acceptance of deposits are the most common form of government restriction. The various kinds of restrictions on deposits were reviewed in our earlier discussion of deposit taking, but it is important to note here that such restrictions can aggravate the single most prevalent and difficult challenge confronting foreign branches: obtaining adequate local currency funding. As was noted earlier, local currency lending usually represents the most lucrative form of business for foreign bank branches, but this potential is limited by the ability to generate local currency. With the high interest-rate environments experienced in recent years, disintermediation has taken place abroad too, forcing foreign bank branches as well as local banks to have to rely increasingly on high-cost money market sources of funds.

In addition to the general scarcity of local currency, those sources that are open to foreign banks may be less stable during a period of tight money than sources available to indigenous banks. Foreign banks often do not have access to the central bank rediscount window, and corporate customers may be more likely to withdraw money from foreign than local banks during a money crunch, especially considering that foreign banks are often only marginal lenders to local companies. These factors, too, can make foreign banks more dependent on money market sources, which tend to become still more expensive or even dry up in tight money periods.

Providing that exchange controls permit, local currency can be generated by converting (swapping) foreign currency into local currency. This is normally done on a hedged basis to eliminate exchange risk. If the money and foreign exchange markets are operating freely, interest-rate arbitraging will eliminate any significant cost advantage to such swapping. However banking authorities, in order to curtail the inflow of money this activity produces, have been known to limit the amount of foreign currency conversion each bank may have outstanding at any one time. While this serves to limit this source of funding, the artificially imposed limits can also prevent arbitrage from taking place with the result that phenomenally high profits can occasionally be realized through the swap process. However this cannot be considered a reliable source of continuing earnings.

Another method of reducing vulnerability to tight-money periods is to obtain a standby commitment from a local bank to provide local currency for a specified period of time. A variation of this is the parallel facility arrangement, whereby two banks, each with a branch in the other's country, agree to provide each other's currency to the other bank on demand for a specified period of time. However, the value of the facility may not be the same to each bank, so that agreement on any commitment fees and the bases for interest rates to be charged is not always easy. The potential for such arrangements has probably not been fully realized.

Staffing can be a problem in any market; it can be especially so in certain foreign markets. A good personnel complement can be developed over time. But for the newcomer it is essential to fill key lending, operations, and administrative positions at the outset with able, experienced people who are thoroughly familiar with local practices in their respective areas. Those persons must be able to read and write the language of the head office, and, unless the branch manager is a native, they must be conversationally bilingual too.

The importance of selecting the right manager, whether it be an expatriate or local person, cannot be overemphasized. The merits of having a native vis-a-vis an expatriate are the subject of endless debate. The important thing is getting the right person, regardless of nationality. A local person's nationality may help provide him or her with some of the qualifications to be the right person, but it is those qualifications which should be the reason for that person's selection, not the nationality per se. There is a too often unrecognized distinction between these two characteristics that can be of vital significance in making the right selection.

Notwithstanding these considerations, the high cost of maintaining expatriates abroad is causing banks to give increasing emphasis to employing local people to the extent possible. But at the same time, as wage levels rise more rapidly abroad than in the United States, U.S. banks are finding that the differential between expatriates and local personnel is not as great as it used to be.

If a native of the country is the manager, he or she not only must be a good banker of unquestioned character, but one who, in addition to possessing a high degree of fluency with the head-office language, has as much familiarity as possible with banking practices and the general culture of the country of the head office. An expatriate, too, must not only be an exceptional banker and manager, but also have a genuine interest in working and living in the country in which the branch is located. It is important that the person's spouse, too, have a positive attitude toward the assignment. For banks, as with industrial concerns, the record is strewn with employers who have sent the wrong kind of person to a foreign country.

Some countries limit the number of visas they will issue for expatriates to work for a foreign firm, making it more difficult to optimally staff a branch if there is a shortage of good local people. It should also be noted that foreign banks have to pay a slight salary premium in some countries due to perceived less job security and, in some cases, a slight social stigma attached to working for a foreign employer.

Establishing a branch in a foreign country constitutes an investment in that country, with all the risks attendant to foreign investments. A minimum investment in premises and fixtures is needed, and most foreign authorities require an additional capital investment beyond that. This investment is subject to the risk of normal business failure of the branch through operating or loan losses. But it is also subject to the concept and reality of country risk—the risks of war, revolution, expropriation, availability of foreign exchange—that is given so much consideration in international lending. If the bank makes additional investments in the form of deposits or advances from the head office or other branches to meet the branch's funding requirements, these are exposed to country risk as well. The bank may choose not to consider as country exposure an amount of the branch's assets equivalent to its liabilities in local currency, since the exchange convertibility risk isn't there, or assets funded by liabilities to residents, since those liabilities might not have to be met in the event of loss of the branch through war, expropriation, or some other force majeure occurrence.

But in any event, a bank must be prepared to take on sufficient country exposure and do enough overall lending in whatever countries the branch is likely to be lending to, to enable the branch to become of sufficient size to more than cover minimum overhead costs and make an adequate return on assets. This matter should be given serious consideration by any smaller bank contemplating establishing an overseas branch.

There is also the exchange rate, as distinct from convertibility; risk on invested capital denominated in local currency assets. Large swings in foreign exchange rates have produced substantial losses, and sometimes profits, on the valuation of investments in branches. Accounting rules in recent years have required such losses or profits to be accounted for in a bank's income statement. A change in accounting rules effective in 1982 will permit these entries to be made directly to the bank's capital accounts, but that of course does not eliminate the loss or profit. The risk can be hedged in the forward exchange market, but usually at a cost, provided there is an adequate forward market in the respective currencies. The risk can also be reduced by adjusting the composition of assets and liabilities funded with local and head-office currencies, but here again there is likely to be a cost in the form of sacrificed yield on earning assets.

Another factor to be considered in determining whether to open a branch in a country is the effect on existing correspondent relationships with banks in that country. Experience has shown that anticipated adverse effects have usually been exaggerated and, in fact, the overall results have probably been more beneficial than harmful to correspondent relationships. Foreign bank branches are usually not perceived as that much of a competitive threat to local banks. The business of a branch may displace some correspondent bank business in the form of letters of credit, collections, money transfers, and foreign exchange, but the financing of trade done with correspondents through acceptances, advances, and deposit placements is not likely to be adversely affected at all. In fact a branch may actually increase the volume of business done through increased contact provided by the branch with the other bank. The circumstance under which opening a branch is most likely to result in lost correspondent business is that in which other banks in your home market have not established branches in the foreign country, prompting banks of that country to send correspondent banking business to those other banks rather than to you.

In our review of credit practices and assessment, some institutional characteristics of the business environments in other countries were mentioned that enable U.S. banks to extend credit to financial structures that would not be considered viable in the United States. Interdependence and the responsibilities of certain elements in a society were cited. However, it is important for bankers to realize that these qualities are subject to change. A degree of interdependence and support that existed in the past may not be here now. International lenders are already finding that they are not getting bailed out of some credits they thought they would. The pace of economic development, combined with increased exposure to other cultures stemming from vastly expanded world travel and communications, is accelerating change in attitudes and the way people do things. Banks doing business in other countries must be aware of these changes as they take place, even anticipate them to the extent possible. Failure to do so can be costly in lost credit extended, as well as in lost opportunities.

THE FUTURE

We have seen the rapid growth of foreign bank branching over the years. Some reasons for the growth have been examined, and we have reviewed the principal activities that branches engage in. What does the future hold? Will the growth continue? If so why, and in what directions? Will the business done by overseas branches in the future be the same as it is today?

In attempting to answer these questions it is worthwhile to look back to the reasons for opening branches and also to identify several trends and developments that are taking place. The applicability of these considerations in indicating what banks are likely to do in the future will vary among banks, depending on a bank's size and customer composition and on what part of the world it is from.

We have seen that American banks have substantially slowed down their opening of branches abroad. The largest money center banks will continue to open an occasional branch as new markets open up or become more viable than they had been. These banks number among their customers the largest and most widespread multinational corporations in the world, and there is a need to be where those customers are. They are still to a degree following the We-follow-our-customers-abroad syndrome, even though the customer base of those remote branches may prove to be more local than multinational. Moreover, the largest banks have the resources, financial and human, to maintain such worldwide networks.

Regional U.S. banks, on the other hand, do not have that compelling need to blanket the world. The customer of a regional bank that actually conducts operations abroad, as distinct from merely buying and selling abroad, and will therefore have need for banking services in foreign markets, is likely to be also a customer of the large money center bank. That customer will normally turn to that larger bank for its international banking requirements. Rare will be the regional bank that will have enough of its own captive customers from its own head-office market with sufficient actual operations overseas to warrant the bank's establishing branches overseas. The following-our-customers-abroad reason no longer exists for the average U.S. regional bank.

Nor is the need to have an actual, physical presence in overseas money markets as strong as it once was for regional banks with more modest Euro/Asia currency requirements. With trading being conducted by more banks in more locations around the world and with more money brokers opening offices in western U.S. cities, regional banks are increasingly finding that they can meet their international money needs by conducting trading from their head office or perhaps an Edge Act office in the United States. The time zone disadvantage has far from disappeared entirely, but just as banks located in the western United States have always conducted their domestic money market activities and done substantial foreign exchange trading from their head offices, they are finding they can do likewise in the Euro/Asia currency markets. The world's money markets are becoming more widely dispersed. Increasingly, the trading can be conducted from anywhere, and the booking can be done just about anywhere.

The advent of the IBF should substantially accelerate this process. Beginning December 3, 1981, the Federal Reserve authorized U.S. banks to accept deposits from and make deposits with and loans to nonresidents of the United States, free of reserve requirements and interest-rate limitations, in "international banking facilities" located in their offices in the United States. This enables U.S. banks not only to trade, but to actually book Euro/Asia currency transactions in the United States, something that heretofore required an overseas branch, even if it was only a shell branch in the Caribbean. Led by New York, many states have exempted IBF operations from local taxes to enable banks to conduct their Euro/Asia currency trading operations more competitively from the United States. It is reported that within three weeks of the authorized opening 254 IBFs had been opened with $47 billion in assets on their books.

Money center banks in the United States will continue their very substantial Euro/Asia trading operations in such markets as London and Singapore, and the larger regionals can be expected to do the same. However, for smaller regional banks the decision is likely to become increasingly less clear cut. To realize a reasonable return in high-cost international money centers, a substantial book of what are generally very low yielding assets must be built up. Under normal times many, probably most, regionals find that they can employ the resources consumed more profitably elsewhere. So with the expanding ability to participate in the international money markets from the United States, combined with the new authorization to book the trans- actions at home as well, a growing number of U.S. regional banks with relatively modest Euro/Asia currency portfolios can be expected to forego incurring the expense of an overseas branch just for the funding or money market purpose. That reason for branching abroad is diminishing.

This leaves the direct earnings contribution as the remaining pri- mary reason for regional banks in the United States to establish new and continue to operate existing branches abroad. Banks can be ex- pected to open a foreign branch solely for the same reason they open a domestic branch, simply to make more money by directly getting into the commercial banking business in the market the branch can serve. The potential for good profitability and the contribution to earn- ings diversification are the attractions.

For non-U.S. banks, the perspective is different. Among even the largest European banks there is still some catching up to do with U.S. banks. Foreign banks from the major industrial countries of the world will continue to follow their customers overseas, as will some banks from some not so industrialized countries. Some banks will continue to perceive a need to be in the money market centers of London or New York, and this will include some relatively smaller banks from the many countries that do not have active trading communities.

Joining the herd will be a driving force for many banks from all around the world with respect to both the money market function and the following-the-customer-abroad motivation. But for non-U.S. banks too, the direct profit motive will ultimately be the real and most valid reason for moving into new markets, and the expansion of branch banking worldwide can be expected to continue.

But where does it all end? A bank in Kuala Lumpur or Sao Paulo perceives a need to have branches in London and New York. Next in Tokyo and Frankfurt. Then come Los Angeles and Singapore. Next Bahrain and Santiago? Houston? Madrid and Kansas City? Do we see hundreds of banks operating branches in hundreds of cities all around the world?

Obviously not. But where is the line? That can't be answered at this point in time. But one thing we can be sure of is a growing selectivity. We have already seen the beginnings of a watershed among U.S. banks with the closing or sale of several branches in response to changing market conditions. This has not been due to failures of those units as much as it has to realization that the resources could be employed in a more worthwhile way elsewhere.

New opportunities are appearing, old ones diminishing. With the growing dispersion of the money markets around the world and with the realization that only a handful of banks have a need to blanket the world, bank managements will be challenged to identify those markets that present worthwhile branch opportunities from those that don't. Increasing selectivity and specialization, as to both products offered and markets, are going to be necessary if the world's banking resources are to be employed most effectively for the benefit of all.

36
Foreign Affiliates and Subsidiaries

STEWART E. SUTIN
Vice President
The First National Bank of Boston

Banks considering establishing equity vehicles overseas may choose
from investment options that vary from complex multibranch operations on one extreme to representative offices on the other. In between,
one may find single unit money center operations of the type frequently found in London or Panama, as well as leasing, finance, and
factoring companies. Customarily, representative offices, whether they
are one-man shops or full-blown loan production centers in the way
they function, commonly do not require the investment of a minimum
capital base as a legal prerequisite to conduct operations. Nor do these
facilities customarily provide direct financial services, other than an
assortment of liason, marketing, evaluative, and documentary maintenance activities. To the extent that capital flows into the country from
head office, it is usually earmarked for fixed-asset acquisitions associated
with the local office, and occasionally living quarters for top staff. In
other words, a representative facility is often looked upon as a marketing or sales office, whereas the full-fledged equity vehicle has its own
capital base, or has call on the capital of its parent company and engages
in specific financial services for its own accounts.

Classification and definition of such investments may be found in
Section 211.2 of Regulation K of the Federal Reserve Board which
became effective on June 14, 1979. This section distinguishes between
affiliates, subsidiaries, foreign branches, portfolio investments, and joint
ventures. From this regulatory viewpoint, the foreign branch is an
extension of a banking office to an overseas location. A subsidiary is
an organization that is more than 50 percent owned (i.e., possession
of voting stock) directly or indirectly by the investing entity or which
is effectively controlled by the investor and/or its affiliates. A joint
venture is an entity 20 percent or more owned directly or indirectly

by the investor. Portfolio investments are holdings of equity at levels below 20 percent. An affiliate, on the other hand, implies ownership by the holding company of a bank or one of its subsidiaries. Each of the above vehicles has legal and regulatory implications, both in the United States and the country in which the investment is made, as well as accounting and tax components, and management strategy features.

The choice of location and type of investment vehicle selected presupposes that the senior management of an institution has fully assessed political, economic, legal, financial, and other strategically defined variables in arriving at its investment decision. Other sections of this book explore a number of these factors in detail. Consequently, the principal objective of this chapter is to highlight those considerations in the context of equity investment, and to offer additional ideas for those readers who are unfamiliar with the processes in which those decisions are reached. Particular attention will be devoted to affiliates and subsidiaries, the joint venture, and considerations in managing a foreign operation.

PRE-INVESTMENT CONSIDERATIONS

Strategic Planning

The establishment and management of overseas equity vehicles are highly complicated and demanding procedures. In an ideal setting, management of institutions engaged in this activity will work from a medium-term plan that identifies such objectives as the general form of overseas network that is desired, assigns priorities to preestablished goals, clarifies marketing plans, estimates equity that may be allocated to this function, outlines budget and control systems to monitor progress, incorporates quantitative and qualitative projections, addresses staffing implications, and identifies procedures for assessment and hedging of risk to capital on an ongoing basis. Even relatively comprehensive and sophisticated strategies should be sufficiently flexible in the implementation stage to permit adjustments for unanticipated circumstances that affect the risk/opportunity mix. Nevertheless, a general structure and investment orientation from which specific overseas equity placement decisions are made is a prudent methodology, given the cost of capital and the alternative investment opportunities that a bank may find attractive in its own country. In the United States, for example, we have witnessed the proliferation of Edge Act banking operations in recent years, as well as an expansion of factoring, leasing, trust, and other forms of financial service subsidiaries. In addition, several large banks have already made investments in financial institutions in other states which may be a precursor to the much publicized move toward nationwide banking. It is probable that this trend toward increased, domestic investments in the United States will intensify in years ahead, thereby demanding even more stringent planning requirements regarding overseas equity placements.

Feasibility Study

Function.   A feasibility study is customarily provided to senior management as a part of the decision-making process, and it often provides the basis for supporting documentation that accompanies an application for overseas investment that is sent to the Federal Reserve Board for its approval. Depending upon the dynamics for decision making by a given institution, the study and recommendations provided by the zone manager responsible for the region in which the investment would be made may comprise virtually the sole basis upon which senior management reaches a conclusion. On the other hand, senior management is frequently sensitive to a variety of factors that may not be fully addressed in feasibility studies. Predispositions are derived through years of experience and are usually based upon a sound knowledge of market competition and/or inherent risk factors. For example, there might be a propensity to approve investments in a country in which other foreign banks have operated with success, while there may be a reluctance to either enter a virgin market or embark upon a venture in a geographical region known to be traditionally unstable or hostile to foreigners.

Regardless of the decision-making forum or style of a particular institution, feasibility studies can be particularly valuable instruments in pre- and post-investment stages if they incorporate a well-conceived and comprehensive marketing plan, as well as proposed strategies for protection against such contingencies as foreign exchange losses through specific hedging mechanisms. By devoting careful attention to these factors before the investment decision is reached, managers charged with responsibility for assuring the successful operation of the new venture will have a clear idea of their marching orders. Pro forma feasibility studies lacking this extra dimension not only deny senior management an opportunity fully to assess the potential of the investment, but tend to prolong the start-up phase of operations, for the overseas manager would have to devote valuable time to piecing together his game plan on location after the capital is invested. As a result, this type of investment is more prone to have a delayed break-even point, and other desired collateral benefits may not be forthcoming. In brief, the feasibility study should not be looked upon as an end in itself, but rather as a means to enable senior management to evaluate an investment proposal and as an instrument by which overseas managers fully understand the principal objectives of the unit they will administer.

In order to realize these goals, there must be effective communications linkage between senior management and persons charged with the responsibility for preparing the study. A preset format should: (1) Identify all major variables worthy of consideration, (2) provide a topical outline, and (3) prescribe maximum length. This process should insure that the document has utility as a working paper and does not become a weighty tome of seemingly limitless scope, yet dubious functional value.

Scope. Each institution inevitably defines its own approach to evaluating foreign investment possibilities based upon accrued experience and independent criteria. The following comments are introductory in nature and are intended as an orientation for those unfamiliar with investments studies. The order in which these points are made does not imply an assignment of priorities, nor that the scope of the report should be limited to those sections noted below.

First, one might expect to read a well-thought-out and cogent analysis of political risk in the country in which the investment is proposed. This section would assess, among other things, the potential for political events to bring about either the unwillingness or inability of the government to permit the repatriation of dividends or equity, should the decision ultimately be reached to divest. In the aftermath of the chaos surrounding the post-Shah political fabric of Iran, banks more than ever are devoting considerable attention to this consideration. Within this framework, it is more essential to evaluate the prospects for continued political stability and the degree of antiforeign sentiment that may be discernible than to dwell upon such surface issues that any reasonable almanac can cover, such as the type of government in power, the identities of national leaders, and the names of the major political parties should a democratic form of government prevail.

Since equity can only be protected in the event that insurance policies are available through the Overseas Private Investment Corporation or an equivalent entity, senior management must feel reasonably comfortable with the long-term investment outlook for a country prior to placing capital there. Parent institutions often place sizable credit facilities at the disposition of their equity investments, and risk may exceed by multiples the size of capital actually invested. The latter form of exposure is customarily uninsured, which further underscores the need for political risk analysis. Admittedly, this type of evaluation is perhaps more art than science, but objectivity and access to appropriate and diverse sources of information are essential.

Second, attention should be given to economic realities and forecasts of the country in general and foreign exchange risk in particular.

Among the issues to be considered in this regard are prospects for remittance of foreign currency obligations, including dividends, in a full and timely fashion, as well as the potential for devaluation and options available to protect or hedge against inherent foreign exchange losses. Two basic elements of this section are an assessment of how well the economy is traditionally managed, and the balance-of-payments situation. A well-managed economy is more apt to weather difficult periods without precipitating excessive uncertainty in the business sector and the population at large. Similarly, a country's ability to sustain adequate levels of international reserves will impact directly upon its capacity to provide foreign exchange in a timely manner for remittance overseas. During the past few years, long-term economic analysis has been especially problematic due to the ebbs and flows of petroleum prices, the tendencies toward precipitous variations in prices for other commodities, and the changing value of the dollar against other major currencies. Nevertheless, a country with a reasonably diversified export base and ability to control imports can cope with troubled times in a manner superior to those unfortunate nations that have to import substantial amounts of petroleum and are dependent upon one or two principal export items as sources of foreign exchange. Thus, a medium-term balance-of-payments projection and an elaboration of primary assumptions is a worthwhile but difficult exercise.

Third, one should be familiar with the foreign investment laws and the interpretation of these codes in the host country. For example, while the law may not prohibit a foreign bank from opening a branch or wholly owned subsidiary, the monetary authorities may nevertheless choose to limit foreign banks to the acquisition of equity positions in existing local banks or to minority ownership in a joint venture. Discussions with local counsel, regulatory authorities, bankers, and businessmen should clarify such issues as the capital requirements to establish operations, policies, and practices pertaining to remittance of dividends, and the types of legally permissible financial services a bank may offer. Some countries do not allow leasing, factoring, or trust activities, among other services. An effort should be made to assess the soundness, integrity, and independence of the local legal system, for this will significantly impact upon the day-to-day operations of any financial entity. For example, one should know the rules of the game for obtaining and effecting judgments. It is also important to become familiar with local labor laws.

Fourth, the study should carefully explore the pros and cons of all investment options in a particular country, and conclude with an intelligently stated case as to why one equity vehicle in particular is preferable to others. This section should include an analysis of current market competition, and the near-term prospects for increased competition. Medium-term financial statement projections for the proposed entity, inclusive of all pertinent assumptions, are invaluable. Indeed senior management might wish to have this section reviewed and commented upon by an accounting firm of international stature that has an office in the country in question. Since devaluations and hedging mechanisms adopted to protect against possible foreign exchange losses would affect the financial statements of the local operation, it is fitting to comment upon those alternatives available to management and the estimated cost of sustaining the hedge. In brief, a review of investment options should include a reasonable commentary on financial data.

Finally, the study should contain the type of marketing plan mentioned previously. The analysis should strive for a realistic appraisal of the marketplace in terms of funding sources, prospective clients, and the types of profit-generating activities in which the unit intends to specialize. Apart from generation of earnings, there should be a clear statement of the types of collateral benefits the unit is expected to provide to the parent organization and its member units. This is particularly important in that field managers are frequently evaluated in terms of profit-center performance and, therefore, may perceive their function as being limited to the generation of earnings for their own unit. This section of the study should not terminate without a statement regarding the prospects for growth and the type of management style and operating philosophy desired during the formative years.

If, for instance, a unit is being established with the intention that it initially serves as a low key window on the market, with minimum staff and profit expectations, the study should so state. On the other hand, if market share, growth to a multibranch operation, aggressive marketing of multinationals, or expansion to such services as consumer finance, factoring, leasing, and so on provide the basis for senior management approval, the unit manager should be aware of his broader level of responsibilities. Should a proposal be made for a joint venture, a full background discussion and critique of the prospective partner(s) are mandatory. This particular type of equity vehicle will be commented upon in some detail later in the chapter.

Equity Investment Options

Most institutions seeking a banking presence in a particular foreign marketplace ordinarily prefer a branch or wholly owned subsidiary rather than a joint venture or portfolio investments. The reasons are obvious in that, in a branch or wholly owned subsidiary, the parent organization has unilateral control over such critical areas as credit policy, personnel, market targets, and designation of priorities. Many multinational banks are usually reluctant to absorb disproportionately large measures of responsibility and risk relative to the share of profits that may be derived from a joint venture. Nevertheless, there are a number of countries that simply do not permit the opening of even majority-owned joint ventures, much less branches or wholly owned subsidiaries.

From a practical standpoint, there are certain funding or regulatory benefits that a branch may enjoy. For example, even though case law in the United States regarding the legal liabilities of a parent bank toward one of its foreign branches is less than well developed, the public, nevertheless, in many so-called third world countries often tends to feel that deposits placed with branches of foreign entities are relatively more secure than with local institutions. In some countries local branches of foreign banks are considered to have call upon the capital of their parent institutions, and, therefore, are not subject to the legal lending limits that apply to subsidiaries, joint ventures, or local banks. On the other hand, a joint venture with well-positioned local partners may give a newcomer to a relatively mature market access to a local client base that might otherwise have been difficult to obtain.

The portfolio investment has tended to lose favor among a number of major U.S. banks in recent years. Drawbacks often include lack of collateral benefits, relatively low return on investment, having to account for the investment on a cash basis for financial reporting purposes, management time required to monitor the investments, and lack of effective influence or control over the quality of the loan portfolio or other activities in which the company is engaged. Not infrequently, entities in which portfolio investments are made tend to expect substantial lines of credit at favorable terms. In certain cases, banks have adopted programs whereby only strategic equity holdings are retained while portfolio investments have been sold off. This represents sensitivity to prudent use of capital and to a perceived imbalance between risk and management time expended, on one hand, and benefits on the other. This is a departure from a propensity particularly common in Latin America in the 1960s for large U.S. banks to sprinkle token investments in a number of fledgling financial entities in efforts to achieve improved market penetration. Experience has largely shown that market penetration was not a consistently realistic objective.

Apart from legal, management, and market implications of an overseas operation, there are also tax and financial reporting considerations to keep in mind. Favorable tax treatment and ability to sustain confidentiality of information has lead a number of banks to establish branches or wholly owned subsidiaries in Nassau, Cayman, Luxemburg, and Panama for the purpose of offering a variety of investment and trust services. In a consolidated U.S. income tax return, earnings or losses of a foreign branch impact immediately on the U.S. tax liability of the parent bank or holding company. Similarly, the tax benefit of currency devaluations against an overseas branch capital loss may be utilized immediately. On the other hand, devaluation or operating losses relating to a subsidiary are not applicable until liquidation or divestiture. Similarly, income from a subsidiary is taxable in the U.S. subsequent to remittance of dividends. From a financial reporting standpoint, the impact of devaluations and earned income may generally be accounted for on an equity basis for an entity in which the parent bank or holding company owns 20 percent or more of the voting shares. This accounting method means that income or devaluation losses impact almost immediately on an equity basis, whereas such gains or losses are only reported upon divestiture or upon receipt of dividends when the cash method is utilized.

Should a bank desire to evaluate a subsidiary as opposed to a branch as an investment alternative, it would be advisable to have properly trained staff or outside consultants examine whatever tax advantages are obtainable through local incentives, favorable tax treaties between the host country and the nation in which the investing entity is legally constituted, and such variables as an ability to utilize foreign tax credits at appropriate times. Further, close examination may reveal that certain foreign countries do not tax branches and subsidiaries in an identical manner. Apart from income tax, one should examine whether withholding taxes may be applied to the remittance of dividends.

A joint venture is commonly regarded by U.S. bankers as an alternative way into a foreign market when regulatory or other constraints mitigate against the possibility of establishing a branch or a wholly owned subsidiary. Sole ownership permits, by definition, exclusivity over profits, design and implementation of a game plan intended to satisfy the corporate objectives, and adoption of controls and a management style consistent with the parent institution's desires. Yet joint ventures, where the foreign bank has a strong presence in the senior management of the affiliate, can hold substantial potential. Three key ingredients, however, must be addressed at the outset:

1. Choice of partners.
2. Role in management assigned to major shareholders.
3. Role and composition of the board of directors.

In a manner similar to any successful marriage, the selection of one's partner is of paramount importance. Open, candid, and detailed discussions of several issues should occur before the marriage is consummated. Among the subjects that require agreement are:

1. Definition of what each partner will contribute to the relationship in terms of capital, management, and setting of policies.
2. Identity of the primary and secondary marketing objectives.
3. Clarification of medium-term growth plans.

4. The functions of the board of directors in credit policy and approvals, planning, and day-to-day management.
5. A predetermined selection process for all senior managers of the company, plus clear delineation of responsibilities.
6. The desirability of a management contract whereby the foreign bank designates the managers of the local operation.
7. The contents of the statutes governing the unit. It is advisable to clarify in writing as many issues as possible in order to avoid confusion among partners later on.

In summary, while a joint venture offers the potential of market penetration that might not be possible otherwise, it is no place for a casual management or ownership style. Failure to define the nature of the relationship and to maintain open communication with local partners at the outset significantly increases the prospect for shareholder difficulties later on. Structured the right way, however, it is possible for a multinational bank and local partners to substantially satisfy their respective objectives for having made the mutual investment in the first place.

MANAGING FOREIGN INVESTMENT VEHICLES

The components of managing foreign equity vehicles include, but are not limited to design of management information systems, financial planning, implementation of a viable form of budget and financial analysis programs, designation of general policies and procedures relative to credit administration and liability management, policies on hedging capital, formulation of adequate personnel manuals and programs, tax planning, establishment of sound policies governing operations, maintenance of an independent role for internal and external auditors, incorporation of computerized and other forms of automated systems as necessary, formulation of a broad public relations program, determination of the appropriate analytical and procedural formats for ongoing evaluation of political and foreign exchange risk, clarification of criteria by which the managers of foreign units are evaluated.

Unless evaluated with some measure of frequency, a management information system (MIS) can readily evolve into a nonproductive activity. A cumbersome system may be redundant in certain areas and shallow in others, not to mention the relatively high cost that accompanies the preparation, distribution, and review of these reports. By establishing a centralized group charged with responsibility to sustain a viable MIS program, these pitfalls can either be avoided or substantially reduced. Perhaps most important is the contribution that senior management can render by a periodic reexamination of the types of reports needed, the appropriate format for the reports, and the frequency with which they should be produced. In addition, a mechanism should be established by which the MIS group can measure the cost of producing each report. For instance, a "nice to know" but nonessential report for senior management may require many man-hours to produce at overseas locations. Sensitivity to the cost/benefit features of each reporting package can become an invaluable management tool. Reports that are designed so that worthwhile information is received in a concise, easy-to-read fashion, while containing all necessary substantive data, are essential to the successful operation of any business.

Financial planning, inclusive of establishing clear objectives, budget preparation, and analysis of operating results, should be a fully integrated program. When done properly, budgets will become the media through which senior management and field managers jointly establish targets, while responsibility for attaining those goals reside with a unit management. A viable budgeting system will also require substantive input from persons designated with responsibility for managing various functions within each unit. Whether an organization opts for a pure profit/cost center or another approach to budgeting is less important than the extent to which it is established as a viable means to assure realistic goal setting, control, and accountability. If, for example, a manager claims that a 20 percent increase in staff is required in order to arrive at certain preset objectives, a sound system will provide measurement with objective criteria to measure the added benefits relative to the costs involved, and the manager will be keenly aware that his of her performance will be evaluated in this context.

The budgeting approaches that are as uniform as possible for all overseas units have the advantage of providing head office with common criteria by which to evaluate the success of those entities. Conversely, head-office reporting requirements do not necessarily serve the local needs of all foreign units to the same extent. A relatively small unit within the system may find that an unduly detailed budgeting system, or one that requires complete quarterly revisions, tends to involve a high level of cost, in terms of man-hours and management time, relative to the benefit derived locally. On the other hand, a streamlined or overly simplified system may be almost useless to managers of sophisticated multibranch foreign operations who will then have to devise their own local system to supplement head-office requirements. Without seeking to belabor this point, it is imperative to insure that budgets and plans intended to assure the successful operations of foreign units do not become end products in themselves or tasks to be endured as a means of "playing the game." Both head office and field management must truly believe in the functional utility of the system in operation in order to make this a worthwhile exercise.

Sound programs, policies, and procedures relative to liability management, credit approval, and credit administration are essential to the prudent functioning of any unit. General guidelines should be supplied by the parent organization in the form of written policy manuals. Liability memoranda or manuals should, among other things, clarify the policy of matching the maturities and rates of funding sources to the tenors of loans. Lending limits, credit approval authorities, and documentation requirements must be in written form in order to sustain operating control and permit examination by persons charged with responsibilities for credit administration, loan review, and audit. Credit policy manuals may be comprehensive to the point of designating lending activities in which overseas units may not engage without first requesting a head-office review of their capacities to evaluate the risks associated with such areas as the financing of commodity exports, construction loans, ship or project financing, consumer lending, leasing, agriculture loans, or the factoring of accounts receivable. Field units should provide their head office with comprehensive reports of their lending activities. Parent organizations should send loan-review teams periodically to inspect foreign units in order to evaluate the quality of the loan portfolio, adequacy of information in the credit files, and the soundness of credit approval and review systems utilized by the local unit.

Reference has been made previously to the existence of foreign exchange or devaluation risks associated with the investment of capital in foreign markets. This risk is inherent with the exception of those few instances whereby the currency of that locality is identical to that in which the parent institution is domiciled. For example, there is obviously no devaluation risk associated with the equity investments by U.S. banks in such commonwealths or territories as Puerto Rico, Guam, or the U.S. Virgin Islands. Parent institutions customarily set global policies regarding the protection of their capital invested overseas. Not uncommonly, the policy is to establish a hedge wherever and whenever possible, regardless of the opportunity cost involved. For those persons not familiar with this problem, a relatively simple illustration of the dynamics of cost/risk/benefits analysis may be found in the following, perhaps oversimplified, illustration.

Suppose that country X is expected to devaluate its currency 30 percent per annum against the dollar (currency of the parent institution). Failure to protect the capital through the hedge mechanism could precipitate a substantial foreign exchange loss to the parent institution. Should that country have dollar-denominated local bonds, at perhaps a yield of 30 percent per annum, the local unit could hedge its capital by investing 100 percent of its capital in those bonds. Let us further suppose that the inflation rate of that country is 65 percent per annum and that local currency government bonds or notes offer an annual effective compounded yield of 90 percent. The local unit, if it is certain about its ability to predict acceleration of the devaluation rate, might argue for an investment in higher-yielding local currency bonds, particularly should there be a sufficient secondary market to insure timely convertibility of the local currency bonds for dollar-denominated bonds. The rationale is that risk would be limited, and profitability can be improved. This scenario provides but one glance at the multifaceted process in which hedging decisions and policies are set.

Without a doubt, the key to the success of any operation is the staff. Yet some managers may place so much emphasis on immediate bottom-line results that important human-resource programs are neglected. The subissues involved in the personnel area are many. The range of issues include pension plans, employee loan policy, training, upward mobility, health and insurance, vacations, and educational assistance. There must be unequivocal support by a parent institution and its overseas managers for a program sufficiently comprehensive in scope to take hold. Overseas units should have personnel managers with strength of personality, creativity, sensitivity to employee needs, and integrity to head up this important function. There is no substitute for a well-motivated, high-quality staff to improve quantitative and qualitative performance.

There are an assortment of substantive issues relating to the maintenance of international staff overseas. Decisions have to be made regarding compensation programs, designation of staff hired overseas to fill management jobs, U.S. and foreign tax implications, pension, and health insurance programs. The scope of issues which are certainly not limited to the few areas mentioned above require definition in personnel manuals so that official and nonofficial staff are aware of rights and obligations alike. An overseas staff manual is necessary to assure uniform treatment of employees relocating to foreign units and full knowledge of benefits available to this staff on an ongoing basis. This will also assure relatively equal treatment within foreign units and a degree of conformity between those units. While labor laws vary from country to country, such normally discretionary programs as pension or bonus programs for locally hired staff should be matters of global policy. A core personnel manual, authored by the personnel department of the parent institution and adapted to local needs as necessary, can insure a reasonably similar treatment of staff employed overseas.

A sound operations department administered by a capable operations manager is the backbone to the successful functioning of a unit. For one thing, there can be security implications of a system that is inadequate or where supervisory vigilance is inconsistent. Going beyond downside risk, one need only perceive of banking as essentially a service industry to recognize that the lack of a quality operations area will inevitably impact upon customer relationships. On the other

hand, prompt, courteous, and effective handling of operational matters
will substantially support the marketing efforts of account officers. At
larger units, the cornerstone for a successful operations area largely
depends upon an ability to dominate, rather than become captives
of, computers and automated systems.

A viable audit function, both internal and external, is an integral
feature of virtually any business. Each organization and manager may
perceive stylistic differences to handling this role, but the need for
this group to have unrestricted access to information and to be recognized as an integral feature of management is rarely disputed. From
an organizational viewpoint, the auditors need direct access to senior
management, as well as support in fulfilling their responsibilities. For
example, the board of directors for a joint venture may wish to establish
an audit committee in much the same way that the boards of major
banking institutions tend to prefer unobstructed access to the auditors.
Apart from assuring senior management and the board that operating,
credit, and other systems are satisfactory, auditors can provide valuable
forward thinking as to how an institution may improve its operations
since internal and external auditors have functional independence and
access to a vast and diversified body of information.

A full-fledged public relations program at overseas units covers a
broad range of issues, ranging from advertising to a variety of public
service functions. Control over these programs may be centralized,
with control over basic programs sustained by the parent institution
in order to assure a reasonable degree of continuity between units.
In contrast, a parent institution may offer general guidelines or suggestions with delegation of decision-making authority to local management. As with any other program, management should carefully analyze the objectives of a public relations program. Certain managers
may wish to deemphasize this function as one that carries potentially
high cost with minimal direct and immediate benefits. For those who
embark upon advertising, most countries have reasonably capable local
firms that are equipped to design programs and advise on the selection
of media. Use of an advertising firm does not, however, relieve management of the responsibility to define the objectives of the program and
the style of approach desired. Indeed, many advertising firms appreciate input from management so that a program conforms to the tastes
and goals of the client.

Beyond the use of media to accomplish objectives ranging from
improvement of image to the selling of specific banking services, institutions operating in foreign markets, especially third-world countries,
are well advised to consider ways and means to sponsor programs
consistent with being a good corporate citizen. Programs can be established compatible with virtually any budgetary allocation. Scholarships
can be funded. Contributions of time and/or money can be made to

any number of local charitable organizations. Seminars can be organized around worthwhile economic or cultural topics. Public schools
in neighborhoods serving the poorer classes often lack adequate libraries, equipment for science laboratories, and uniforms for their sports
program. The list of alternatives is endless. Yet, sufficient provision
for these activities has a way of becoming known and appreciated
by the people in countries in which one has a presence.

This chapter makes no pretense at having been definitive in either
the scope of issues addressed or the discussion of those subjects. The
decision to invest, the selection of type of investment vehicle, the
choice of location, and the administration of the equity vehicle requires
careful and prolonged study. Identification of the right questions to
ask is in itself difficult. In the final analysis, each banking institution
must develop its own modus operandi regarding an overseas investment program based upon an assessment of its priorities regarding
capital and manpower allocations.

37
Representative Offices

MILTON E. BERGLUND, JR.
Vice President
Mellon Bank, N.A.

For a commercial bank, representative offices provide one of the most common forms of establishing a physical presence in international markets. This chapter will examine the characteristics of representative offices in the context of a management decision to open such an office and then to implement that decision.

DEFINITION

At the most basic level, representative offices are simply another vehicle for generating profit through the development of international loan assets, bankers' acceptances, deposits, and fee-generating services. Representative offices facilitate international banking, serving in essence as foreign loan production offices able to negotiate efficiently various business transactions. They do not provide on-site operating services or have deposit-taking and independent funding capabilities. The assets and liabilities attributable to a representative office are booked elsewhere in the parent bank's system. Operational activity is similarly performed elsewhere. Such offices are regarded as excellent listening posts for information on the economic, political, and social conditions of a market where the parent bank has cross-border risk exposure and, therefore, a reason to monitor its risk closely.

BASIC RATIONALE

Representative offices may be a useful instrument when one or more of the following characteristics are present:

1. The expected business volume in a particular market is considered too small to justify a major investment in the form of a branch or a subsidiary.

2. There is a perceived need to accomplish further market penetration with modest incremental expense ultimately to determine the feasibility of opening a branch or making a future investment.

3. The local regulatory environment is such that other forms of bank investment are not permitted, and representative offices are the only practical vehicle of establishing market coverage for general banking purposes in a desirable location; Mexico, Brazil, and Australia are outstanding examples of such markets.

4. There is a strong local demand for foreign currency loans in a banking market characterized by:

   a. An underdeveloped local currency market incapable of sustaining the local funding of a branch.

   b. An insufficient local savings rate in the private sector.

   Both these conditions are nearly always associated with high sustained demand for foreign loans and therefore provide an excellent market for business negotiated by representative offices. In such circumstances, representative offices do not require more extensive facilities to maximize the profit opportunity.

5. There is an otherwise attractive market but the contingent political risks of possible expropriation or similar difficulties preclude the investment risk associated with a branch or subsidiary; in such environment it may be considered appropriate to maintain a low profile.

Representative offices may be contrasted briefly with several alternative methods of establishing activity in a foreign market. Travel from the parent bank's head office is the most common method and still the most cost effective when the business volume is not only small but likely to remain so either by market limitations or by policy intent. The frequent disadvantages of this method are superficial market penetration, high travel cost, and above all, lack of the private information sources which are best cultivated by a local presence. In a worthwhile market, these difficulties soon outweigh the apparent cost advantages of travel from head office. This situation happens most often when business development objectives result in an increase in cross-border risk exposure beyond a certain limit. Some banks have a policy to establish a local presence when the loan portfolio exceeds or is expected to exceed a particular target—$50 to $75 million for example.

When the target is reached, a representative office may be the next step considered. The decision usually involves a trade-off between a representative office and a full branch. Where the five characteristics listed above are not present or significant, full service branches have considerable capacity to leverage the parent bank's resources in a local market. When the conditions are right—high market demand; permissive regulatory and tax environment; local funding capability; political, economic, and social stability—branches are more cost effective than representative offices. However, the practical observation is that the suitable conditions for local branching are not all that common outside the advanced countries or the significant entrepot markets such as Hong Kong, Singapore, and Luxembourg. Representative offices provide a compromise solution when the available business is considered too large to manage from head office but not yet suitable for a branch. The trade-off is sometimes difficult to resolve in the countries considered to be newly industrializing such as Korea and Taiwan.

Investments in subsidiaries and joint ventures tend to be done for special purposes and not for general banking—leasing, real estate, merchant banks for syndications, consumer finance offices among others. Yet another alternative is for the parent bank to take a minority interest in a local bank. The results of such investments have proven to be mixed over the last several years. This is especially true in cases where the investing bank does not really have a strong role in the management. Representative offices, of course, are compatible with other investment interests of the parent bank, and personnel in representative offices can often monitor an investment interest better and maximize participation in the management thereof.

CONDITIONS PRECEDENT TO OPENING

Firstly, the concept of using representative offices at all must conform to the strategic plan and general objectives of the parent bank. Representative offices may not fit a particular bank's overall concept of how it wishes to manage its international banking activity. Usually, however, representative offices are included in the mix of methods by which banks establish themselves internationally. This is especially the case in the early phases of growth.

Secondly, the specific business development plan of a particular representative office must conform to the credit policy objectives of the parent bank. The country-risk profile of the host country to a representative office and the customer credit characteristics of the local market must be evaluated.

Since credit policy issues must be settled in advance of considering whether to open a representative office, extensive data must be gathered and analyzed. The bank's country review process for assessing economic, political, and social risk must be invoked. Market data on likely customers must be refined into a business development strategy in the context of the local competitive situation.

The next step is to analyze the regulatory environment to be sure that the various policies and procedures of the host country's central bank, banking supervisors, and ministries of finance and trade, among others, do not excessively circumscribe the business prospects.

Although not necessarily a purely regulatory problem, the prickly issue of withholding taxes must be faced squarely where relevant. In countries where the withholding taxes are high, for example over 10 percent, absorption of local withholding taxes on loans is frequently a competitive feature of the marketplace. Therefore, a bank considering whether or not to open a representative office should marshall the facts on its capacity to absorb taxes. It must have a clear policy both on the limits for absorbing taxes in a particular location and on the minimum compensation necessary for so doing. A forecast of withholding tax absorption capability is very difficult to achieve at most banks, especially beyond one year. Representative offices need consistent policy guidelines on withholding tax issues.

Certainly some level of business development activity should precede the opening of a representative office. Banks newly engaged in a particular market usually find lending to the government sector either directly or through syndicated loans the quickest avenue of building a modest book of loans in advance of opening any form of local representation, even if such loans carry only a modest profit margin.

Traditionally, correspondent relations with local banks is the cornerstone of international lending. Short-term lines of credit for trade financing are usually extended to several banks in the target markets. The bank relationships may be further enhanced by reciprocal clearing and paying accounts and active foreign exchange trading. For bankers traveling from the head office, correspondent bank relationships are usually the most effective and profitable method of getting established in a market. Local banks can provide information relevant to credit risk evaluation. They can be especially helpful in assisting when a representative office is opened. Since representative offices frequently expedite correspondent banking relations at the practical operational level, such offices are not necessarily considered a competitive threat to local banks. By contrast branches making local currency loans are considered less neutral competitively.

Once government and correspondent bank lending is underway, the private sector is usually the next target for local business development. Some banks follow the policy that local representation by the bank's own officers must precede any significant volume of private-sector risk. The parent bank may wish to service the local subsidiaries of its traditional head office customers and to establish business relations with the leading local businesses. In contrast with government-sector loans and some short-term interbank loans, private-sector lending may be more profitable and lead to more extensive ancillary business and service fees. In fact, once a base of government and correspondent bank loans is built, a main justification for setting up representative offices is to develop more extensive business in connections with the private sector.

In this context, it is also argued that a representative office enhances not only the credit management of the portfolio but also the administrative control necessary to service customers properly. In some countries, the mail and overseas telephone/telex systems are unreliable. This condition not only hinders timely receipt of loan documentation and financial statements but also makes cash management services for correspondent banks and corporate customers difficult to provide.

Against the background of a preestablished business base, the officers responsible for a target market are ready to develop a proposal to management to open a representative office. If the market is considered lucrative enough, such a proposal may even precede a significant local business base. The common argument is that if prospects are good enough, a satisfactory volume of business can be quickly created once a representative office is opened.

For a decision, management expects to receive statistics on the market situation and credit environment as part of a feasibility study. The study may present balance-sheet and income projections, along with a detailed expense analysis. This information is intended to make the case that the "full-measurement cost" of entry through a representative office is covered by the profit potential. Full-measurement cost includes data to show that a representative office can earn enough profit to cover all associated direct expenses and contribute to:

a.   The parent bank's loan loss reserve, appropriate for the assumed higher level of risk expected to be undertaken by the representative office.

b.   The parent bank's return on capital and return on asset ratios.

Representative offices are not regarded as particularly capital intensive when compared with branches or other forms of bank investments. They do represent an investment of human resources, funding resources, and at least some capital for office fixtures or purchased premises. Full-measurement cost analysis implies that the cost of a particular representative office must be within certain limits, and the parent bank's objectives on rates of return or internal "hurdle rates" on allocation of its scarce resources must be met.

The statistical analysis may be supplemented by a presentation of the incremental or opportunity costs of establishing a representative office over the present method of covering a market, usually through travel from head office. Incremental costs are typically high when the associated personnel expenses are itemized. These expenses included the extra costs of expatriate personnel for cost of living adjustments, foreign service premium, housing, tax equalization, education for children, and in some cases club memberships and a car with driver. These incremental expenses, when added to rental of office space and local staff requirements, result in a cost projection which must be more than adequately covered by the expected volume of incremental earnings to be derived from the commitment to open a representative office.

Along with a presentation on the full measurement cost of entry and an incremental cost evaluation, the feasibility study for opening a representative office may then be supplemented further by detailed portfolio and customer activity projections. The latter elements require that there be a business strategy for the representative office.

SETTING OUT A DEFINED BUSINESS STRATEGY

Assuming there exists already a business base in the local market, the program for further business development involves projections by customer name of performance targets for the representative office staff. The projections show the planned mix of customer assets and deposit liabilities by sector: public and private; bank and nonbank; government direct and related (such as government enterprises); private corporate, large and small, or multinational and indigenous—and so on. In some representative offices, leasing customers and candidates for syndicated loans are considered separate and important market segments.

For each market segment, the specific business development strategy includes:

a. The types of loans to be offered, with appropriate pricing objectives.
b. Fee-producing services to be developed.
c. The deposit potential.

From the mix of business, the expected profile for diversification of risk is revealed.

Representative offices are intended to enhance the parent bank's capacity to control the credit risk of the market. The officer in charge of the representative office usually is given a major role in setting the country limit for the market. The representative office generates much of the basic information relevant for the country review process. In fact, the representative office normally structures the initial recommendation on the amount of cross-border risk exposure to be undertaken, the mix of business, diversification objectives, and the like. With respect to customer credit analysis, some of the larger representative offices are staffed with local credit analysts as opposed to sending the basic information back to head office for analysis.

Lastly, the business development strategy usually includes a mission statement about protecting the parent bank's existing market share. If a market is considered by many competitors to be attractive and entry is generally free, representative offices are expected to be effec-

tive in mounting the calling effort to maintain position in the distribution of customer business against increased competition.

NORMAL ACTIVITIES AND RESPONSIBILITIES
OF THE REPRESENTATIVE

From the foregoing the main activities of the representative and
his staff are easily defined:

1. Formulate the corporate business development program of the
   representative office and manage it.
2. Maintain contracts with and generate business from the local government and its various agencies or enterprises, the central bank,
   multilateral lending institutions, and their various missions.
3. Enhance correspondent bank relationships.
4. Provide country intelligence on economic, political, and social factors.
5. Serve as a liaison when required for the parent bank's management
   and customers when local intermediaries are desired.
6. Manage the office personnel, providing the requisite staff training,
   expense control, and administrative leadership.

VARIATION—A REGIONAL REPRESENTATIVE OFFICE

Up to this point we have presented the characteristics of a representative office in the context of a market without necessarily defining
the geographical focus too precisely. Typically, the larger countries
offer enough business to occupy the full attention of a representative
office. However, a regional representative office covering more than
one market is also very common. This is the case where the individual
country markets in a region may be too small to merit a representative
office of their own. When two or more countries are considered as a
whole, a regional representative office may be justified. For example,
the Andean countries in Latin America, the Central American and
Caribbean area, and the Middle East are frequently covered in this
manner. Earlier Beirut and now Athens are the best examples in the
Middle East.

Because London, Frankfurt, Zürich, Hong Kong, Singapore, and
Bahrain are money markets and funding centers in their own right,
banks tend to have branches or investments in such centers. Even
there, representative offices may be present, especially as a prelude
to a branch or a more extensive regional commitment by the parent
bank.

SELECTION OF THE REPRESENTATIVE OFFICE PERSONNEL

The key individual is the representative himself. In most banks he is an officer with at least four to five years lending experience and can be trusted to act independently far from head office. Rarely is the representative hired locally unless he has been given extensive head-office experience prior to posting. Depending on the role representative offices play in the parent bank's organization overseas, the representative may be the senior man in a territory and kept on location for some years. In the larger banks with overseas branches, the assignment as representative may be an intermediate training ground for future branch managers or for management personnel elsewhere.

The rest of the staff may be hired locally or be composed of a few junior officers sent from the parent bank for initial overseas posting. Representative offices are regarded as suitable training posts for junior personnel and may be good sources of future officers among indigenous staff with transfer potential elsewhere. A branch usually has more independent local authority, but a representative office with its loan assets booked elsewhere may be subject to more central control and guidance. Consequently, representative offices can be useful in building staff resources under controlled circumstances.

REPRESENTATIVE OFFICES—AN INTERPRETIVE EVALUATION

At one time, especially prior to the middle 1960s, only a few of the larger international banks operated extensive networks of branches overseas. Representative offices were a common form of overseas representation by commercial banks. More recently, however, most banks engaged in international lending have found it convenient to have offshore funding capability through branch offices in at least the major financial centers and largest countries of the world. Earlier practices of pursuing an international banking overseas generally through correspondent banks have been relaxed, as has been the reluctance to disturb correspondent bank relations through local branching. For these and other reasons, representative offices are not the predominant form of marketing vehicle they once were considered to be.

The continued future usefulness of representative offices, however, seems assured in the context of the much greater volume of international lending now pursued by so many international banks. Trends of increasing political and economic risk argue for more local representation to manage complex lending environments. Increasing nationalism and local regulations are not conducive to branching everywhere.

If the basic trends of increasing political risk and undiminished international lending activity continue, representative offices will still be among the most cost-effective methods of establishing a presence in desirable overseas banking markets and managing the associated risk. As with any other form of activity, the locations chosen and business plans for them must be consistent with the overall strategic plan of the parent bank for pursuing international banking activity.

The evaluation of the actual contribution of a representative office to the overall banking activity is often difficult to measure since these offices create no strict financial accounting for that entity. It is important that disciplined routines be developed to plan and control time allocations for various purposes such as calling, transactions, and customer relations (i.e., tourist courtesies) that are provided for the head office. In so far as possible accurate records should be maintained on loans, income, and other business generated by the representative office. Only with such controls and records will it be feasible to evaluate the contribution of the representative office to the total banking activity and the effectiveness of the representative office operation.

38
Edge Act and Agreement Corporations

E. C. STONE
Executive Vice President
First American Bank, N.A.

In 1919, Senator Walter E. Edge of New Jersey sponsored a bill to amend the Federal Reserve Act by enacting Section 25A. The bill permitted national banks to incorporate subsidiaries for international banking and investment. Unlike many bills proposed by new senators, his bill was passed in the year introduced, and the resulting legislation still carries Senator Edge's name. The resulting subsidiary corporations are usually called "Edge Acts." The Edge Act itself provided the vehicle for banks to establish deposit-taking, on-site offices across state lines, subject to strict controls. As banks position themselves for deregulation and possible changes in the McFadden Act, they are using this legal means of interstate banking as an important part of their expansion strategy.

The impact on domestic banking at the time the bill was passed was minimal. Several Edge Act corporations were established, but few remained active a decade after the enabling legislation. This legal mechanism for limited interstate banking remained nearly dormant for another two decades until the use of the Edge Act corporation began reviving after World War II. By the early 1970s, Edge Acts were commonplace among money center and major regional banks, though their full potential was limited by strict capital constraints and the inability to branch. Most banks established Edge Acts in New York, Miami, or other major markets with enough international business to support the required commitment of capital, staff, and other resources. Although not legally restricted to large markets, the practical restraints of capital, staff, and other were barriers to Edge Act expansion. This barrier to fully using Edge Acts was overcome with the amendments to Regulation K of the Federal Reserve Act in June 1979, allowing

603

for branching of Edge Acts. Since June 1979, the Edge Act corporation and branch of the Edge Act corporation have rivaled the loan production office in giving money center and major regional banks on-site access to otherwise restricted markets. The initial act allows banks to cross state lines and conduct business subject to specific limitations. The 1979 amendment permitting branching enables banks to establish branches of Edge Acts in markets without sufficient volume to justify the capital and staffing of a full Edge Act corporation. The intent of Senator Edge's legislation was to enhance international banking and investment with the thought that this would be beneficial to international trade in general and the United States in particular. The practical constraints of the original legislation limited the use of Edge Acts even though the law did not. Rather than enhancing international trade, the Edge Act was near dormant until market-driven forces revived it.

As growth of world trade in the United States grew in the early 1960s and expanded exponentially throughout the 1970s, the Edge Act became a familiar banking operation, and the growth of Edge Acts paralleled that of international banking in general. Federal Reserve statistics show that foreign activity in commercial banks rose almost three times the rate of domestic business in the decade of the 1960s. Since New York was the financial center of the United States, the Edge Acts were usually in New York to provide non-New York banks a vehicle for tapping this lucrative and growing international market.

By the mid-1970s the larger U.S. banks with headquarters outside New York were maintaining Edge Act corporations with hundreds of employees. Aggressive regional banks were using this vehicle equally effectively though on a smaller scale. Profitable Edge Acts with capital from $2 million to $5 million and fewer than 50 employees were commonplace, though major Chicago and New York banks had Edge Act corporations with deposits in the billions. California-based Bank of America's Edge Act in New York is larger than many regional banks themselves. In addition to profitably serving their own markets, these Edge Act corporations provide a strong link to other corporate business served by the parent bank.

The ties to corporate business with affinity to parent companies were only a first step for aggressive regional banks as they expanded into the money centers via the Edge Act subsidiary. Smaller staffs, more personalized service, and a large network of foreign correspondents made the lucrative clearing business a natural target for regional banks and their Edge Acts. Foreign commercial and central bank clearings generated volume and prestige for smaller Edge operations and regional banks. Many hoped these ties would lead to other business in time. Money center banks frequently relied on their own worldwide branch network for operational service. Regional banks were slower to expand their foreign branch system and tended to rely on correspondents. With the establishment of a regional bank Edge Act in New York, these close correspondent ties were avenues to solicit clearing accounts. When the indigenous New York banks developed operational problems in the early and mid-1970s, the Edge Act subsidiaries exploited their New York locations and smaller, more personalized operational staffs. Aggressive competition for clearing business fostered the expansion of the popular call account, enabling depositors to earn interest on the balances in excess of the amounts needed to service the account.

Corporate business—import, export, and capital investment flowing both to and from the United States—is natural for an Edge Act subsidiary. Correspondent banking, including private and government or central bank activity, is another traditional major market for Edge Act subsidiaries. A third and growing segment of the market is individual accounts. U.S. citizens living outside the United States and foreign citizens wanting their deposits in New York, Miami, or elsewhere represent an expanding market and source of attractive, relatively low-cost deposits. Some Miami Edge Act subsidiaries are thought to be almost exclusively oriented to individual accounts, particularly wealthy Central and South American depositors. Though Edge Acts may not openly acknowledge a solicitation of "flight capital" deposits, it is generally acknowledged that individual deposits from any particular country tend to grow in inverse proportion to the political stability and in proportion to the perceived likelihood of currency-exchange restrictions and devaluation in that country. On March 10, 1982, the Federal Reserve Board expanded the permissible activities of Edge Act corporations which will make accounts for wealthy individuals outside the United States even more attractive. The revised regulations enable an Edge Act bank to provide counseling similar to that offered by most trust departments.

In a press release dated March 12, 1982, the Federal Reserve Board announced the adoption of an amendment to Regulation K enabling an Edge (or Edge branch) to provide economic and investment advisory management services to both foreign customers and foreign assets of U.S. customers. Under the broad phrase, "incidental to an Edge corporation's business," an Edge may offer:

1. Investment or financial advice by providing portfolio investment advice and portfolio management with respect to securities, other financial instruments, real property interests, and other investment assets.

2. General economic information and advice, general economic statistical forecasting services, and industry studies.[1]

The Edge has always been a method for banks to make equity investments. The law requires that they be foreign; that is, out of the United States. In many cases they have been foreign in the sense that they were unusual or strange as well. Edge Acts have made investments in oil and gas properties, gold mines, soft drink bottling companies, and at least one cemetery. For a while, a cocktail hour topic among New York Edge Act bankers was the alleged investment of an Edge in an exclusive European brothel. The permissible approach related to corporate investments may carry over to individuals. J. Charles Partee, a member of the Fed board, is quoted in the March 11, 1982, *American Banker* as saying that while old master paintings would be included as responsible investments, bottle cap collections probably would not.[2]

Corporate financial officers surveyed typically rank international banking alongside cash management as the important banking services they will need in the next decade. Every corporate bank and corporate banker should understand the potential and the restrictions of the Edge Act—both as a tool for expansion and in recognition of the methods competitors will use to seek business in formerly protected markets.

Section A, Regulation K, of the International Banking Act of 1978, effective June 14, 1979, is the rule book for Edge Act and Agreement corporations. The highlights of Regulation K are:

Organization. An Edge Act corporation must be approved by the Board of Governors of the Federal Reserve System upon proper application. The name of an Edge Act corporation shall include the words, *International, Foreign, Overseas,* or a similar word.

Ownership. Ownership and transfer of ownership is restricted and subject to the approval process. In practice, most Edge Acts are wholly owned subsidiaries of a single national bank; however, in 1979 Regulation K was modified to allow foreign majority ownership and these are joint ventures.

Branches. In June 1979, the Federal Reserve Board revised Regulation K to allow branching. The significance of this revision will be discussed later in the article as it may be the vehicle for the most effective use of an Edge Act since the enabling legislation in 1919.

Reserve Requirements and Interest Rate Limitations. An Edge Act corporation is regulated as if it were a member bank.

Permissible Activities in the United States. An Edge Act corpora-

---

[1] The Federal Reserve System Press Release, Federal Reserve Bank of Atlanta, Atlanta, Georgia, Circular Letter 517–82, March 12, 1982.

[2] Linda W. McCormick, "Fed Approves Expanded Activities for Edge Firms, Holding Companies," *American Banker,* March 11, 1982, p. 18.

tion may accept deposits, make loans, and transact business "incidental to international or foreign business." In practice, this limits an Edge Act corporation to foreign customers and international activity of domestic customers. Regulation K provides a lengthy list of permissible activities; however, the intent strictly limits an Edge to international business. For example, an Edge Act corporation may not maintain a payroll account for its own employees. However, Edge Acts have engaged in numerous activities beyond the scope of the original legislation.

Various proposals have come forth from time to time suggesting that regulations be amended to enable an Edge to accept deposits, make loans, and other for corporations or persons whose businesses meet some percentage (66⅔ percent to 75 percent) of foreign business or some other tests. The Bankers' Association for Foreign Trade proposed that Edge banks be allowed to handle banking requirements of international companies such as export management companies and Domestic International Sales Companies (DISC). To date, the interpretation of "incidental to international and foreign business" has been restrictive, and the burden of proof is on an Edge Act bank to show that deposits, loans, or other business transacted is *directly* related to foreign or international business in compliance with the intent of the legislation. It is argued that to allow otherwise would be acting against the prohibition of interstate banking, and to allow percentage tests or other encroachments would cause the regulatory process to become too subjective and interpretative.

Agreement Corporations.   A bank may invest in a federally or state-chartered corporation which agrees not to exercise any power not permissible for an Edge Act corporation.

Under Section 211.5, an Edge Act is allowed investments in other organizations subject to the "high standards of banking or financial prudence, having due regard for diversification of risk, suitable liquidity, and adequacy of capital," and other limitations. An Edge Act corporation is given broad authority to invest in equities as well as debt instruments. Many of the so-called investment Edges were formed for the specific purpose of owning and holding equities in companies not engaged in business in the United States. Under the regulations, an Edge Act corporation is granted general consent for equity investment up to the lesser of 5 percent of the Edge Act corporation's capital or $2 million. In the case of an Edge Act corporation not engaged in banking (an investment Edge) the 5 percent limitation is raised to 25 percent. Effectively, an Edge Act corporation is thus given the power to acquire and hold equity investments in foreign corporations while its parent U.S. bank is denied similar powers in the United States.

Capital restrictions on Edge Act banks are monitored closely. An Edge Act corporation engaged in banking is required to maintain capital-to-risk assets of at least 7 percent. The 5 percent/$2 million restriction and the 7 percent capital-to-risk assets restriction effectively placed limitations on the use of Edge Acts. There were practical and marketplace limitations resulting from these legal restrictions. Until branching was allowed in 1979, only major markets, such as New York or Miami, generated the volume justifying the commitment of capital and resources, including the internal resources. For smaller or limited markets, the cost/benefit equation did not make it practical for major money center or regional banks to consider using an Edge Act as a vehicle of expansion. With the amendments to Regulation K in June 1979 allowing the branching of Edge Acts, this practical limitation no longer applied.

With the capability of branching, several Edge Acts could be consolidated into a single parent Edge with numerous branches. This gave immediate benefit in consolidating the capital and increasing the lending limits of the consolidated Edge branches to a figure based on the sum of all their previous capital. Additionally, it made it possible to put an Edge with only a few people in a relatively small market without committing capital or other resources. The impact of this regulation is probably best measured by the number of applications to form Edges or Edge branches approved by the Federal Reserve rather than merely the numbers of Edges as many have been consolidated since June 1979. In less than two years, the Board approved nearly 70 new Edge offices, including new corporations and branch offices. This compares with an approval rate of three to four Edge Act approvals per year in the several years immediately preceding 1979. At the end of first quarter 1981, 57 banks were actively engaged in Edge Act banking, and several applications were pending. New York continued to be the leader with 21 active Edge Act facilities, either branches or corporations, followed closely by Miami with 17. In order, Los Angeles, Chicago, Houston, and San Francisco were next in line. It appears likely that the candidates for the next wave of Edge Act banking will be regional business centers that may or may not be port cities.

Edge Act subsidiaries have particular appeal to foreign banks in specialized situations. Most banks would prefer a full-service branch to a restricted subsidiary such as an Edge Act—whether the bank is foreign or domestic. In the case of domestic banks, inability to cross state lines means that an Edge is frequently the next best alternative. An Edge branch has substantially more capability than a loan production office. An Edge can accept deposits, make loans, and conduct business to a limited degree but requires only a few more people than a loan production office. A loan production office with an Edge branch in the same market enables a bank to solicit business for the parent and provides limited local service.

In the case of a foreign bank, a branch may be subject to the regulations of the state. Individual states have different laws regarding foreign branches and some are prohibitive. An Edge Act corporation is not subject to state laws, and this vehicle provides a method for bypassing restrictive state regulatory procedures if a foreign bank is anxious enough to gain a presence in an attractive market. To date, the foreign-owned Edges are in the minority, and most are located in Florida.

Some business strategists have compared the current banking environment in the United States to maneuvers on a large chess board. In anticipation of less restrictive banking laws and perhaps eventual repeal of the McFadden Act, corporate banks are trying to position themselves aggressively in their perceived growth markets. Much like the chess strategist trying to maneuver specific pieces into their most advantageous position on the board, banks are limited in that each piece is restricted in its ability to move. The various pieces available to banks are numerous—including acquisitions, grandfathered operations, trust companies, loan production offices, various subsidiaries, and others. Clearly, the Edge Act has emerged as one of the most versatile players on the banking chess board. Since June of 1979, this piece has had the ability to make moves that were impractical before. Banks are using this versatile legal vehicle to gain on-site representation and to generate limited deposit, loan, and other banking activity with major corporate customers. At worst, a bank can enhance its marketing effort in an attractive market. At best, if and when the McFadden Act is altered, it will be easy to expand from an existing Edge into a full-service branch. All of the essential people and facilities would be in place serving a customer base with attractive potential for other banking services.

Banking Edges and Agreements—Locations and Total Assets as of September 1981

City	Edge Name	Assets (000s)
Atlanta	Citibank International—Atlanta Branch	213
Beverly Hills	Citibank International—Beverly Hills Branch	0
Boston	Citibank International—Boston Branch	7
Boston	First Chicago International—Boston Branch	18,800
Cayman	Bank of Boston International—Cayman Islands Branch	179,850
Chicago	Bank of Boston International—Chicago Branch	73
Chicago	Crocker Bank International—Chicago Branch	16,615
Chicago	Security Pacific International Bank—Chicago Branch	13,353
Chicago	Chase Bank International—Chicago Branch	26,296
Chicago	Citibank International—Chicago Branch	129,570
Chicago	Manufacturers Hanover International—Chicago Branch	23,342
Chicago	Bankers Trust International (MDW) Corporation	18,714
Chicago	Chemical Bank International—Chicago	34,716
Chicago	European-American Corporation	412
Chicago	Continental Bank International	94,406
Chicago	Algemene Bank Nederland International U.S.A.	5,000
Chicago	First Chicago International	47,109
Chicago	Banco Real International Inc.	2,686

Banking Edges and Agreements (*continued*)

City	Edge Name	Assets (000s)
Chicago	Bank of America International—Chicago Branch	304,536
Cleveland	Citibank International—Cleveland Branch	4,010
Cleveland	Bank of America—Cleveland Branch	2,587
Dallas	Bank of Boston International South—Dallas Branch	0
Dallas	Citibank International—Dallas Branch	14,885
Dallas	Bank of America—Dallas Branch	525
Houston	Security Pacific International—Houston Branch	51,797
Houston	First Interstate International of California—Houston Branch	4,674
Houston	Chase Bank International—Houston Branch	47,667
Houston	Citibank International—Houston Branch	137,762
Houston	Morgan Guaranty International Bank—Houston Branch	165,438
Houston	Continental Bank International—Houston Branch	9,711
Houston	ABN—Houston Branch	2,055
Houston	First Chicago International—Houston Branch	34,284
Houston	Banco Real International Inc.—Houston Branch	245
Houston	Bankers Trust International (SW) Corporation	27,034
Houston	Tokyo Bancorp International (Houston)	7,520
Houston	BNQ de Paris et des Int. Co.	5,108
Houston	Bank of America International—Houston Branch	150,077
Houston	Standrd Chrtrd International	0
London	Allied Bank International—London Branch	217,151
Los Angeles	First Interstate International of California	263,486
Los Angeles	Chase Bank International—Los Angeles Branch	83,447
Los Angeles	Citibank International—Los Angeles Branch	420,000
Los Angeles	Morgan Guaranty International Bank—Los Angeles Branch	0
Los Angeles	Manufacturers Hanover International Banking Corp.— Los Angeles Branch	159,493
Los Angeles	Continental Bank International—Los Angeles Branch	21,147
Los Angeles	First Chicago International—Los Angeles Branch	93,565
Los Angeles	Bankers Trust International (PAC) Corp.	71,542
Los Angeles	Bank of Boston International—LA	20,795
Los Angeles	Chemical Bank International of California— Los Angeles Branch	76,416
Los Angeles	Irving Trust Co International—Pacific	13,337
Los Angeles	Rainier International Bank	26,248
Los Angeles	European-American Bank International	12,687
Los Angeles	Republic ITL Bank of New York (California)	7,972
Miami	New England MRCH Bank International	7,951
Miami	Wells Fargo Bank International—Miami Branch	46,047
Miami	Security Pacific International Bank—Miami Branch	11,099
Miami	First Interstate International of California—Miami Branch	3,060
Miami	Chase Bank International—Miami Branch	297,550
Miami	Marine Midland INTERAM Bank	68,733
Miami	Irving Trust Company International/Miami	114,426
Miami	Citizens & Southern International Bank	163,436
Miami	Bank of Boston International South	121,665
Miami	Citibank International	373,249
Miami	Bankers Trust International (Miami) Corp.	42,964
Miami	Wells Fargo INTERAM Office	5,749
Miami	Northern IR INTERAMERICAN Bank	48,829
Miami	Morgan Guaranty International Bank	503,198
Miami	Manufacturers Hanover International Banking Corp.	139,352
Miami	Chemical Bank International of Miami	78,409
Miami	Republic International Bank of New York	55,897
Miami	Banco de Santander International, Inc.	65,850

Banking Edges and Agreements (*concluded*)

City	Edge Name	Assets (000s)
Miami	J. Henry Schroder International Bank	12,746
Miami	American Security Bank International	2,694
Miami	Shawmut BSTN International Banking Corp.	4,640
Miami	Continental Bank International—Miami Branch	52,323
Miami	Bank of America International—Miami Branch	182,724
Miami	Banco de Bogota International Corporation	5,621
Minneapolis	Citibank International—Minneapolis Branch	1,026
Minneapolis	Bank of America International—Minneapolis Branch	0
Nassau	Allied Bank International—Nassau Branch	388,196
Nassau	Bank of America International—Nassau Branch	0
Newark	Chase Bank International	119,790
New Orleans	Citizens & Southern International Bank	32,308
New York	Allied Bank International	276,970
New York	State Street Bank Boston International	97,028
New York	Bank of Boston International	211,848
New York	Connecticut Bank International	12,417
New York	Mellon Bank International	257,291
New York	North Carolina National Bank International Banking Group	253,592
New York	Wachovia International Banking Corp.	43,723
New York	Fidelity International Bank	63,016
New York	Philadelphia International Bank	316,716
New York	Wells Fargo International—New York Branch	0
New York	Crocker Bank International	492,431
New York	Northern Trust International Banking Corp.	172,947
New York	Girard International Bank	71,010
New York	Security Pacific International Bank	342,925
New York	First Bank Minn. International	47,814
New York	Harris Bank International Corp.	212,883
New York	First Wisconsin International Bank	83,201
New York	Central Cleveland International Bank	288,097
New York	Bank of California International—New York Branch	86,917
New York	Industrial International Bank	32,922
New York	First Dallas International Corp.	125,176
New York	Skan Enskld Banken Int. Corp.	0
New York	Consolidado International Bank	2,685
New York	Pittsburgh International Bank—New York Branch	245,084
New York	Continental Bank International—New York Branch	1,583,600
New York	First Chicago International—New York Branch	575,831
New York	Bank of America International—New York Branch	3,154,030
Pittsburgh	Pittsburgh International Bank	7,542
St. Louis	Citibank International—St. Louis Branch	227
San Francisco	Wells Fargo Bank International	47,776
San Francisco	Bank of California International	7,118
San Francisco	Citibank International—San Francisco Branch	358,779
San Francisco	Morgan Guaranty International—San Francisco Branch	407,950
San Francisco	First Chicago International—San Francisco Branch	82,189
San Francisco	Chemical Bank International of California	72,451
San Francisco	Bank of America	405,372
Seattle	Citibank International—Seattle Branch	35,271
Seattle	Bank of America International—Seattle Branch	6,032
Seattle	NBA International Banking Corp.	0
Total		$16,498,756

Source: Federal Reserve, Washington, D.C.

SECTION 7
Managing International Banking Activities

39

Internal Organization and Personnel

CHARLES F. TURNER
Senior Vice President
Comerica Bank–Detroit

INTRODUCTION

As we emerged from World War II, international banking and what it connotes today was virtually nonexistent. With the exception of off-shore branch systems, reflecting the colonial ties of some countries, such as England, and short-term trade finance, commercial banks in the United States and other leading developed nations had not engaged to a meaningful degree in this field. In fact, it was not until the late 1950s that major money center banks started their growth internationally. In the 1960s this was reinforced by the continued growth in world trade and investment along with the birth of the Eurocurrency markets. These trends have continued with the result that, by 1980, regional and smaller banks in many countries of the world had international departments with varying degrees of sophistication. In those earlier times, the Foreign Departments, as they were often called, were simply organized, and the major requirements for staffing seemed to be some knowledge of a foreign language and the ability to process letters of credit and other routine services.

Present-day sophistication in the international sector, however, has spawned an equally sophisticated organization and staffing structure. The nature of that structure is the function of several considerations. Size and duration of time in the international arena have greatly influenced the organization chart. The resources in terms of both people and capital that can be brought to bear are clearly as diverse as the size of institutions. The stage of development of an institution, usually measured in terms of time, again suggests a wide variation in structure. Modifying these considerations are the objectives of an institution internationally. What markets are to be segmented and how are the various business units to be organized to pursue these markets? Some institutions, particularly large ones, perceive themselves as being all things to all people, while in regional or specialized banks there is a tendency to exploit specific niches in various markets. Moreover, a smaller bank might well organize itself for "defensive purposes" to protect against incursion into its customer base and geographic area rather than seeking a course of aggressive exploitation. Whatever the structure and staffing, as in any business, it should not be irrevocable. The dynamics of the market and evolution of a bank necessitate constant review to ensure that the structure and the people are optimal for providing the chosen services to clients on an *effective* and *profitable* basis.

TRADITIONAL STRUCTURE

Certain factors have combined to produce a fairly standard structure in international banking departments. First, there is a historical pattern for geographic distinctions in the domestic lending areas of most banks, and it is not unusual to see that reflected on the international side. Secondly, most departments have evolved quite distinctly from the domestic activities of the institution. Frequently the start of an international function provided for lending and some documentary services, and these were usually established separately from domestic activities. As one might expect, the impetus for the broadening of services, penetration of other markets, and the beginnings of the corollary staff functions came from within the department. This segregation was probably reinforced by the fact that the unproven contribution and perceived risk involved combined to provide less support than might be expected from existing areas of the bank. The result is that the bank-within-a-bank concept with geographic specialization has become widespread, particularly in the United States. That is, the entire support structure exists within the international department despite the fact that, in many cases, it duplicates functions that are in place for the domestic banking functions. This type of organization is depicted in Exhibit 1 below.

In the illustration, the Head of the International Department would typically report to the executive in charge of the wholesale or commercial area of the bank, or in some cases to the Chief Executive Officer. This bank-within-a-bank concept is largely a self-contained unit. The staff functions of credit and economics play virtually the same role as on the domestic side but involve the added ingredients and the risk decision that go with the peculiarities of foreign entities and the environments in which they operate. The operations section as portrayed provides the back office necessary for both the lending and money market activities, the maintenance of the necessary "due to"

Exhibit 1

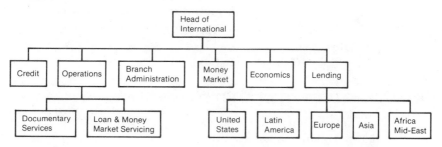

and "due from" accounts, and documentary services which would include letters of credit, collections, remittances, and bankers' acceptances. In addition, this section is responsible for the compilation of statistics vital to management, such as reciprocity, loan quality and yields, noninterest income figures, and so forth. Clearly these functions could be configured differently, perhaps even separately, depending upon their importance. Branch administration would typically be a separate section when the network becomes sufficiently large to realize economies of scale. Another variation is also possible. In this case, offshore branches report directly on a line basis to the heads of the various lending areas.

As previously mentioned, it is also typical to find the geographic breakdown for lending as is usually the case on the domestic side of the bank. The chart also illustrates a U.S. group that would cover commercial transactions that bear local risk. The money market section is responsible for deposit placement, foreign exchange trading, and liability management.

By carrying the self-containment philosophy further, a bank may well opt for the inclusion of a personnel function that addresses the needs of the department. Many banks have also felt that it was necessary to have a separate group for the product planning and business development functions, since experiences have been less than satisfactory in penetrating local markets for international services by relying on a business development group outside of the department.

The foregoing self-contained structure has some very real advantages. First the accounting function can clearly capture the necessary information to produce the equivalent of both a balance sheet and a profit-and-loss statement for the area. Questions of cost allocations or quality of performance of sections outside of the department do not have to be addressed. Secondly, the authorities and responsibilities are clearly delineated again without the blurring effect of having reporting lines outside the department. Thus, the accountability for performance can be clearly affixed. The separate nature can also be a double-edged sword. It provides an environment where strong leadership can build team effort and esprit de corps which are obviously inimical to the institution's interest. The primary disadvantage of the structure is that it duplicates many functions that are conducted in other parts of the bank and therefore raises questions of efficiency in terms of staff, capital, and equipment.

FUNCTIONALLY INTEGRATED STRUCTURE

The functional approach appears to be gaining support in the United States and has been traditionally more common in other countries such as Japan. Philosophically, it is, in many ways, the antithesis of the stand-alone organization. It seeks to address areas that are particularly troublesome in that type of organization, and this would be true of money market activities, corporate lending, and credit, to mention some of the areas. Also, the continued growth in institutions and increased emphasis on efficiencies and economies of scale have given rise to an organization chart similar to Exhibit 2. Interestingly, this type of organization seems to be utilized in both major international banks and also much smaller banks.

Certain duplications noted previously have been shifted and report on a line basis outside of the department. Some of the more striking differences are separate areas beyond direct control of international that relate to corporate or multinational lending, funds management, loan servicing, credit, and economics. The lending function in this case pursues sovereign risk, correspondent banking, and export financing, but corporate relationships for major international companies is conducted in a separate area as a corporate or multinational group. Loan servicing, credit, and economics which exist for other sections of the bank are provided by centralized areas external to the department. The merging of the foreign exchange and deposit/liability management into the funds management or bank investment function is very appealing. The interplay of interest rates and foreign exchange rates suggests that a close physical proximity and working relationship reporting to a single controlling officer is extremely important. The merging of these two areas increases the range of alternatives for gathering or placing funds to balance appropriately the bank's position.

When these areas exist separately as in Exhibit 1, there is the risk of poor communication and missed opportunities at best, and, at worst, outright rivalry could produce negative effects. Loan servicing, which is usually a highly systemized process, does not deserve separation as a general rule, and this back-office function can benefit from the pooling of both personnel and system expertise. Corollary arguments can be advanced for the credit function, and although international department personnel may resist because of the perceived peculiarities of international credit, that can be overcome by education. The question of a corporate or multinational group located between a purely domestic commercial group and an international commercial group is a difficult one. Numerous institutions have chosen this path, and many more have it under consideration. An important consideration in that decision is the size and sophistication of the corporate base at present or as projected.

The department depicted in Exhibit 2 is greatly streamlined, particularly in two key areas. These are the generation of risk assets in the lending function and the generation of income through documentary services. Departmental managerial attention can then be focused more closely on these crucial items with the expectation that better results could be obtained. The process can be applied further still to the branch administration section by merging them with counterpart operations on the domestic side. In essence, many banks organize themselves as in Exhibit 2 nearly completely contrary to the bank-within-a-bank

Exhibit 2

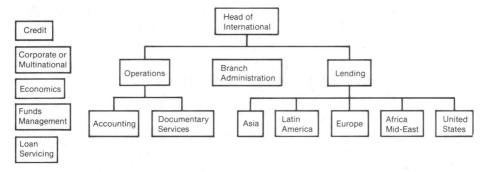

theory. Interestingly, many of the advantages and disadvantages of this form of organization are the reciprocal of those in Exhibit 1. Here the economies of scale that go with merging of the nearly duplicate functions is the major advantage. The organization chart is much more cluttered with dotted lines. The diffusion of responsibility outside of the department results in the aforementioned measurement of performance and accountability which is less clear.

CHOOSING THE APPROPRIATE STRUCTURE

In view of some of the conflicting characteristics of both types of organization, the choice of the appropriate configuration is quite difficult. There are several factors which influence this choice. One of these which should not be ignored is the historical precedent. As a department is initiated and evolved, it gains a momentum which can continue for some time and is not easily changed. People acquire per-

ceived, vested interests, and thus this structure could continue for
some time.

Secondly, personnel available for staffing is a critical factor. Organization charts are not theoretical exercises but in fact reflect management's ability to fill particular assignments. A strong management team
enjoying the confidence of senior management would tend to have a
structure with a wider range of direct responsibilities as depicted in
Exhibit 1.

The choice as to the appropriate structure is a difficult one. Rarely
does senior management have the luxury of a start-up situation; usually
they must deal with an existing structure and decide whether to modify
it and in what direction. In fact, most organizations today represent
a combination of the two example charts, and for the moment there
appears to be no clear-cut optimum way to organize the department.
Whatever the structure, however, an institution must periodically conduct an objective reexamination of itself to ensure that the existing
structure is appropriate for its departmental objectives. This would
include weighing the advantages and disadvantages previously recited
and not merely continuing on with the structure that exists largely
for historical and perhaps invalid reasons.

STAFFING THE INTERNATIONAL FUNCTION

In view of the importance of personnel in determining structure
and performance, the requisite characteristics for an international officer should be examined. Obviously, a language ability or aptitude, a
willingness to travel along distances for extended periods, and a degree
of sophistication in representing the institution in international circles
are important. Beyond that, however, there is little in the way of other
qualities that are different than those needed in other parts of the
bank for similar positions. Basic characteristics of good judgment, willingness to expand knowledge in a chosen professional area, and motivation to succeed are still the most important. The perception continues,
however, that there is a certain mystique to international banking
business, and to some extent this is fostered by international department personnel.

The selection of nonofficer staff appears to differ even less from
other areas in the bank than at the officer level. The staffing of the
necessary support functions should be no more difficult than on the
domestic side of the bank, since the work involved is only different
and not necessarily more difficult than other nonofficer positions in
the bank. Clearly, if someone possesses a language ability or some
other special skill, that would facilitate the development of that person,
but such characteristics or skills are not requisite. There is also a caveat
which should be emphasized in relation to the selection of officer and

nonofficer staff. There is a glamour associated with international work that, for the most part, is a perception of people outside of the department. Neither the traveling contact officer nor the nonofficer in the head office will support this perception, and the idea should be corrected if that appears to be a major motivation for entering into international work.

Undoubtedly there are additional qualities that would be appropriate for persons who are stationed abroad. In this instance, the ability of the individual and family unit to withstand the cultural shock of living in a different society must be examined closely. Many institutions use a mobility interviewing technique involving outside assistance. This psychological interview with adult members of the family, and sometimes the children to be transferred, could well be an excellent investment. The stresses of offshore living are different on various members of the family, and unhappiness by one or more can drastically impair the efficiency of an officer. The posting of personnel offshore has its own peculiar set of problems. Some people clearly enjoy it and are content to move from one offshore location to another, as long as their position stays roughly in tune with their professional expectations. Others will accept offshore posting, as it is perceived as a way to advance, but in fact depart already anticipating their return to the head office.

To modify the disruptive effect of this posting, the benefits package associated with an offshore assignment should be competitive. This should include consideration of tax equalization, housing, cost-of-living differentials (including currency fluctuations), appropriate schooling for children, home leave, a hardship allowance, and a plan for maintenance of the residence in the head-office city. Not all of these considerations are applicable, as the hardships of living abroad vary greatly from one country to another. It is appropriate, however, to have the policy for these matters clearly defined at the outset to avoid misunderstanding and subsequent bitterness. Many banks have utilized outside services that provide lengthy detailed bases for the treatment of each of these areas. These agencies provide tables that are adjusted periodically for changes in inflation and currency fluctuations and serve as an objective basis for the administration of personnel matters. The total cost of the financial package is significant enough to suggest that a minimization of head-office people posted abroad is appropriate. One can significantly reduce costs by staffing to a maximum degree with local people despite the difficulties of hiring and training. In most major banking centers of the world this option is generally available.

Offshore posting should also involve, at the outset, an agreement for return to head office at an approximate date. This of course can be modified with the mutual consent of employer and employee. Without such an initial agreement, however, considerable resentment may result either because of return to head office much sooner or later than desired. In addition, the problems of reentry into the head-office environment can be painful. The view from an offshore entity is considerably different and most likely involves status higher than had been the case at home. It is important, therefore, to "tune in" people periodically to what is happening in head office, and when possible to foresee the assignment position available upon return. Head-office visits and home leaves are particularly helpful in this regard.

Additionally, by choosing high potential people for offshore assignments, there is a strong possibility that upon their return they can be placed in positions of higher responsibility. The reinforcement of this pattern by example would increase the attractiveness of those options to younger people, thus facilitating the initial selection procedure. Since the purpose of offshore posting is twofold (namely the efficient performance of the assigned task and the further development of the officer involved), by failing to take into account some of the foregoing considerations, both purposes are greatly endangered.

In many institutions with large or rapidly expanding international departments, an assignment in that area for an entire career can be challenging. Opportunities for upward mobility are plentiful, and the problem of being stalled is less. As the growth curve slows, however, and international operations mature, career paths diminish. As a result, rotation of personnel between domestic and international departments becomes more important.

As was the case with offshore people, the selection of good people for international can be greatly enhanced by the demonstrated mobility of achievers from the international department into other areas of the bank. Most officers would prefer that their opportunities not be limited to the international arena, and periodic demonstrations of this policy are beneficial both to the individual and the institution.

The training function, in contrast to selection, does differ somewhat from the domestic part of the bank. This is particularly true in smaller institutions where the staff is required to perform a variety of tasks rather than specialize. Perhaps the best training device, particularly in the nonofficer section, is a consistent job rotation. One should keep in mind that rotation does bring with it some inefficiencies but that the longer-term overall effect is highly beneficial to the organization.

The peculiarities associated with dealing with as many as 75 or more distinct cultures around the world presents difficult problems on both the officer and nonofficer level. Thus the rotation of personnel will assure greater depth in the organization and flexibility to meet changes, and there seems no substitute for this process. In-house training programs have been particularly effective at all levels of staff. In the more highly specialized areas of foreign language training, foreign exchange, and letters of credit, increased usage of outside training sponsored by banking and private organizations is becoming more prevalent.

On the surface these peculiarities of international personnel and training matters would appear to require a specialized personnel function. In fact, in many institutions this is the case. There is usually a person in the branch administration section who deals with the personnel function for the entire department, both ashore and abroad. Again, despite some differences with the domestic personnel function, the basic ingredients are still the same. Thus it could be argued again that this staff function could be more efficiently performed in conjunction with the bank personnel department, freeing the international staff for achievement of its basic objectives.

SUMMARY

The organization of international departments has evolved significantly over the last approximately 30 years and continues to do so. Much of what exists today had its basis in tradition and should be reexamined periodically to ensure that the current organization structure serves its purpose. There is an increasing tendency to depart from the bank-within-a-bank philosophy to achieve economies of scale and a clearer basis for measurement of achievement of business plans. Aside from this, the chosen method of organization must also reflect the characteristics of the institution and the personnel available to manage and staff the department. If these factors change, departmental organization should eventually reflect the change.

The staffing of an international department, which on the surface appears to be quite different from the rest of the bank, upon close examination is remarkably similar. Thus, the principles of personnel management, except for some specific differences described above, should again reflect the character and policies of the total institution.

40
Marketing International Services

AIDAN H. F. HARLAND
Darien Consulting Group

It was only in the late 1960s and early 1970s that international departments of banks changed from a passive approach to selling their services to an active one. After World War II, major banks in the United
States and elsewhere had a precious commodity to sell—credit. Even
well-developed, industrialized nations were in need of that product,
and the best approach to marketing was merely to say "no" occasionally. The way a bank's international business developed was more the
result of personalities and happenstance. As more and more banks
became active internationally and as the need for external credit diminished in the developed countries, international departments became
more competitive, the range of products offered increased substantially, and geographic markets spread to the developing nations. By
the 70s the number of banks active beyond their own country's borders
had multiplied many times over, and it became clear that banks would
have to specialize to be sure of a worthwhile share of the market at
an acceptable return on capital.

It was no longer rewarding merely to reach for the telephone and
pursue those pieces of international business that happened to beat
a path to the bank's door. The resources, both financial and human,
that are needed to be all things to everybody are tremendous, and
only a few banks worldwide could expect to cover the whole world
geographically with a full range of products. Even those banks, to
be effective, realized they must apply their resources with forethought
if they were to have the optimum return. It was at this point that
international departments started to focus on marketing plans and
appointed marketing officers. Marketing, however, goes far beyond
the official "marketing officer." Effective marketing requires the realization that every lending officer, foreign exchange trader, product
manager, or anyone else in contact with the client is a marketer of
the bank's services. Effective marketing is no more, and no less, than

effective selling. However, effective selling requires forethought and the marshalling of resources and energies. Hence the need to start with planning.

Marketing plans are logical extensions of departmental planning. Whereas departmental plans describe broad objectives, marketing plans zero in on the best way to accomplish those objectives, and they are heavily weighted by considerations of availability of resources, client need for particular products, salability and profitability. They help chart the shortest, easiest path for the bank to the objectives described in the departmental plan. This is not to say, however, that marketing only has short-term objectives.

Marketing plans for an international department should be broken down into as many parts as the department has selling groups. For a small regional bank with only two or three international-division selling officers, this might be only one unit. For a good-sized regional bank or for a major international bank, marketing plans are likely to be broken down into territories, or even countries. In some cases, marketing plans might be developed for a particular set of products, such as Foreign Exchange Services or Cash Management Services, or even Ship Loans. It is important, however, to note that marketing plans are not broken down into too many units, for fear that they become merely a compendium of what everybody is presently doing. It is intended that they focus on best utilization of resources, and for this reason a larger grouping of territories and services will ensure the play-off of one market possibility against another or the choice of use of a resource in one way or another.

For the purpose of this chapter it is best to assume that the bank is a medium- to large-sized U.S. regional bank whose selling officers are parts of territorial teams, supported by a few product specialists who cover all the world for their particular product.

It is useless to start developing marketing plans unless the bank already has an international departmental plan. The departmental plan will give guidance on the bank's tolerance for risk and credit exposure. Credit is almost certain to be the most important product. There is no point planning effective marketing of the credit product in countries to which the bank does not wish to lend. Effective selling, being a focusing of energies, becomes more and more the elimination of useless activity. The very best thing the bank can first do in developing marketing plans is to see how little time and effort it can apply to those markets to which it is not willing to extend credit. Can it avoid traveling to that country entirely, or perhaps once a year to be ready for the turn around? Having established the least effort required in certain areas, the bank is now free to review the required objectives of its departmental plan, count its remaining resources, and look for the most effective way to reach the objectives.

Departmental short- or long-range plans are presumed already to have taken into account, in a general manner, the size of markets, desirability of extension of credit, and the availability of human and financial resources. Nevertheless, these will be in broad terms. A review of the territory was presumably done at the time of the departmental plan. Another look should be taken when planning marketing efforts. Indeed marketing plans will always be changing as prices, economies, people, and other circumstances change. The country or territorial officer should be responsible for developing his or her own marketing plan. From this will follow individual account or prospect plans. These latter, however, are merely coordination plans, so that different people impacting on a different account know exactly what they have to do, and when. The marketing plan is the link between individual accounts and departmental objectives.

DEVELOPING MARKETING PLANS

Before developing marketing plans, a territorial officer will make the broad decisions dictated by the departmental plan. It has already been noted that the territorial officer should ignore some of the countries in his or her area entirely if credit is off limits or so small that it is not worthwhile. To make decisions that are less obvious the territorial officer will need some guidance, and market research is the first order of business. An international department should be suited to the bank's overall objectives, and if nationwide banking with companies heavily involved in the bank's own region is a bankwide objective, then the territorial officer should review his or her area and see what domestic clients or prospects are located with subsidiaries or sell through dealers in the various countries for which he or she has the responsibility.

This information is available from a variety of sources: Chamber of Commerce directories; Dun & Bradstreet reports; annual reports of the National Division's "Client and Prospect List"; Journal of Commerce Exporting List; Department of Commerce listings; and so on. If this information has not been gathered previously including good listings prepared for each country, then this is the time to do it, and if the department has appointed a marketing officer, his or her first order of priority should be to review the worldwide implications of the domestic account/prospect list. It is easy to identify which of the major clients and prospects of a bank have international potential; the middle market or occasional importers and exporters are harder to find. "Dun's Marketing Identifiers" or other sources can be used to identify importers and exporters, and then the marketing officer can develop a questionnaire on each name to be completed by the account officer after contacting the company, indicating in which countries the company is doing business. In this manner, the territorial officer can be assisted in deciding which countries need more coverage to satisfy potential domestic customer demand.

The territorial officer cannot build a satisfactory mix of business in a foreign country based only on U.S. subsidiaries or trade. To handle trade business effectively, the bank must have an active involvement with the "financial mainstream" in each country it does business. But how extensive should the financial mainstream be considered? And to what extent is business outside the financial mainstream worthwhile?

It is necessary, therefore, for the territorial manager to review the different types of actual or potential customers in his or her market countries, such as correspondent banks, other financial institutions, capital goods importers, multinationals, individuals, and whatever other category of clients makes sense. Next it is necessary to put some sort of dimension on those groups of clients to see how important each type is in each country. There is no point in putting great effort into obtaining private-sector business with capital goods importers if there are very few in the country in question, and none are creditworthy. On the other hand, if there are a large number of subsidiaries of U.S. companies headquartered in the manager's domestic market, then the country needs further attention.

It is not sufficient, however, only to analyze the clients or potential clients. It is also necessary to analyze the services they can potentially buy. A good marketing officer will supply the territorial managers with continuing product information. In addition, the departmental plan will have provided input on which services to emphasize and which to deemphasize. ("Courier Services to enhance check collection and cash letter business are to be emphasized in the coming year. This is to help increase our deposit liabilities which are expected to be at a premium in the coming high interest rate environment.") The country manager should be aware of the bank's abilities on each service. He or she will naturally wish to provide those services that are both profitable and well executed by the bank and will ignore those services that are unprofitable or incapable of being handled properly.

The profitability of each service is important, and a review of a market potential should bear in mind the competitive factor. Is the bank going to make a worthwhile profit on the business? A small market making use of only limited services, but at good profitability, is far better than a large market making use of only those services the bank has to sell at a loss or break even. It soon becomes clear in doing a market analysis of this sort that all the bank's products can be sold to a small extent in each market. This is all well and good if the product needs little expertise. However, for a sophisticated product such as "Foreign Exchange Exposure Management," can sending specialists on a one- or two-day call trip to one country be justified? Also, when the geographic breakdown (by city) of all potential clients is reviewed, can three or four trips a year to a city where there are only two worthwhile prospective clients be justified?—even if they are profitable clients? To utilize human resources effectively, the country manager must make some hard choices at this point.

In making these choices the country manager can be assisted significantly by using a matrix approach and obtaining the input of all the traveling officers and product specialists in the area concerned. This is done by listing the types of clients on one axis and the product categories on the other axis, and then obtaining a concensus of opinion using a rating scale of 1 to 5, with 5 scoring high.

A typical matrix is shown below:

	Letters of credit	Collection	Foreign exchange	Drafts and remittances	Money market	Credit
Correspondent banks						
Non-bank financials						
Capital goods importers						
Private sector manufacturers						
U.S. client subsidiaries						
Trading companies						
Multinationals						

The breakdown of client types and service types should be according to the logical needs of the bank and the country being reviewed. When this matrix is being completed, the scoring should reflect not only the size of a potential market for that product, but also the profitability and salability. If it is well known that another bank already has the market sewn up at rates one might be willing to match or even improve upon, but that the two largest prospects are tied to the other bank by similarity of shareholders, then it is probably unsellable. Taking all these factors into account, the overall score entered in each box is a measure of desirability. It is far from scientific, but it does provide the country manager and his or her selling staff with an opportunity to review markets and products and make some basic decisions. With such a matrix the country manager can describe the key markets and missions and subsequently review one country against another to see where to put the emphasis.

After this has been done, the territorial manager should be in a position to put a marketing plan on paper. He or she should identify client types and products that can be eliminated entirely. Here again, the best way to give direction is to narrow the field as much as possible. The territorial manager should be able to advise product specialists on what the potential is in each market and agree on what time might be available for product specialist trips, with or without the country traveling officers. It is even possible at this point that a country manager, rather than being a credit specialist, as is normal, might be a product specialist. If it is well identified that the only business the bank expects to do in Switzerland is foreign exchange and money market business with financial institutions, then a foreign exchange specialist might be given responsibility for the country and be the only person traveling there.

The country marketing plan should give firm goals: the amount of credit to be extended—short-term or medium-term; number of new accounts to be obtained; establishment of an airline pick-up system; development of a local currency lending alternative; and so on. These goals should add up to the objective defined in the departmental plan, but they should be decided upon by the actual marketing/selling staff. Since time is the usual limiting factor for most organizations, they should spell out the coming year's travel expectations by city and person. Each account officer should have a copy of his or her territorial marketing plan and should feel part of it. However, neither the officer nor his or her superiors should leave it there. It is now necessary to develop individual account plans. By *account* is meant either present or future client. It is not really appropriate to separate a market into "accounts" and "prospects." It is quite possible that the best prospect for further business is an existing account. It is also possible that an existing account be of no particular consequence. All of them are to be viewed with the same approach.

DEVELOPING ACCOUNT PLANS

From all that has been written so far, the reader might begin to
get the idea that a lending or selling officer traveling internationally
for a bank is going to find little time to travel with all the "planning"
to be done. This is a danger. The international scene is too fluid to
plan precisely. Opportunity, when it presents itself, should not be overlooked. However, it would be equally wrong to rely only on opportunity
in developing business. A little planning will help the marketer of
services be in the right place at the right time to meet the opportunity.
The need for account plans is essentially one of coordination. A single
person needs to be appointed responsible for developing a particular
relationship. This does not mean that he or she should be the only
person to call on that relationship. Effective account responsibility
means having product and other marketing officers call on the account
if that would be more productive. An account officer should, therefore,
be looked on as the orchestrator of selling efforts, rather than the
sole provider of that effort.

The specialists need to be told and to agree on whom to call and
when. This coordinated approach needs to be taken for all the major
accounts. In some cases, however, plans might not be prepared by
individual account but by customer type. If, for instance, it had been
decided that all insurance companies in Caracas were prospects for
check collection services, the Venezuelan country officer might ask
that a cash management product specialist visit Caracas and provide
the person with a list of names and addresses for initial calls. It is
not necessary to develop lots of complicated account plans for those
insurance companies. Common sense must prevail! In the case of a
large manufacturing-cum-financial group in Mexico, on the other hand,
the relationship might already include direct credit, export loans, trust
services to senior executives, check collection services, letter of credit,
and foreign exchange services. In this case, a number of specialists
might be required to make a visit. It would be most undesirable for
them all to turn up at roughly the same time without knowledge of
each other's calls. Maybe some of them could have saved others a
visit. Orchestration is obviously needed, and specific action plans should
be prepared. These plans are the responsibility of the account officer
to prepare and to keep current. A typical form for writing up a plan
is shown below:

Client/Prospect:	Compania Ultramar, S.A.
Address:	155 Naucalpan
	Mexico 3, D.F., Mexico
Contacts:	Jorge Gonzalez M., Treasurer
	Telephone: (905) 31–47–59
Account Officer:	J. Ryan
Our Relationship:	A/C since 1972, $1.5 million

	U/S Line, active usage		
	LIBOR + 1¼ percent, net of taxes		
	Balances: 1979—$81,000; 1980—		
Type of Company:	Manufacturing steel stampings.		

Action	By Whom	When	Completed
J. R. visit to review fin'ls Push for higher balances.	J. R.	Q1	2/80—J. R. $150,000 Balance promised immediately.
Call to propose a collection computerization study.	Systems Dept.	Q2	
Present for approval line increase if balances O.K.	J. R.	Q2	
Executive call on M. Tonez, Pres., and J. Gonzalez.	President and J. R.	Q3	

In this manner the need for senior officer trips, product specialist trips, and so on, are all foreseen and can be appropriately planned.

These action plans must be upstreamed to the territorial head who then advises the different product team where they will be needed and when. The territorial head will also see if the senior level trips can be made and adjusts the action plans accordingly. Obviously account officers, once they have accepted the system, will want all available specialists to call on all of their prospects and clients. It is up to the territorial head to weigh the merits and recommend appropriately. Once the territorial head has seen the combined need for a particular trip by a team of specialists, he or she will then include this in a marketing plan and confirm the action plans of those that can be covered, altering those that cannot. This is when the desired decisions on best use of resources should be made.

As soon as rough account plans have been developed for the territory and the territorial manager has given rough approval, the territorial manager will want to get together with the other people to be involved with his or her names. A coordination meeting or sales meeting is called for. An agenda should be provided in advance, listing the names of accounts or prospects that will be discussed. The most recent action plans, updated for completion of prior requested actions, should be sent to attendees. Attending a typical sales meeting will be:

Department head, occasionally.

Territorial head.

Country heads of those countries being covered.

Credit department analyst.

FX and money market representative.

International operations representative.

Trust department coordinator.

Others, as needed.

Each name will be quickly reviewed and a new action plan agreed upon. This gives the department head a chance to review whether actions are being completed on schedule and which product specialists are getting out and doing the job when needed. It also gives the chance to review profitability, new product possibilities, and so forth.

These meetings are best held prior to a trip by the country head, or just after a trip when there is plenty of information to pass to and fro to the various people involved in the relationship solicitation.

One of the things that these meetings tend to bring out is the frequent lack of product knowledge in marketing officers. This is best corrected by organizing courses, seminars, workshops, or even just talks given by the product specialist or an individual who has had recent success with that particular product. Often such a sales promotion effort can be combined with a sales meeting at which action plans are being coordinated. A territorial manager covering five countries in Latin America might arrange for three country heads, their subordinates, the export finance specialist, and half a dozen other interested parties to spend two days in the bank's conference center coordinating action plans. At the same time, the country head might arrange for half of the specialist attendees to give presentations on their own fields, and the department head might arrange for all junior officers to attend those presentations as well.

Never mind how big a bank is or how competent its international staff, the bank is sure to have a large number of domestic clients who have occasional international department needs. The larger names can be covered by a special international department specialist assigned to call on smaller domestic names; but there will be thousands of other clients that it just does not make sense to send an international department specialist to see. The domestic officer has to be given some brief training to be able to spot potential international business and to know the nature of the services the international department provides.

Courses for domestic officers are called for. These should be held every few months, and 16–20 domestic calling officers should spend four to eight hours learning the different ways a company can be involved abroad, what services those involvements are likely to require, and in what manner the bank can assist.

A typical outline for such a course is shown in the appendix to this chapter. This is designed as a marketing course, with emphasis on selling techniques rather than just a training program.

TRIP ORGANIZATION

It is inevitable that much of a bank's marketing efforts will be organized around trips. The selling officer has to visit the customer because the customer is not likely to visit the bank frequently enough. Since effective utilization of human assets is usually the first priority, it is wise to organize trips effectively. It is the territorial head's responsibility to see that the traveling staff is going to be in the right places, with the appropriate frequency, and in a properly organized manner. An effective trip requires preparation, follow-up, and, least important of all, the actual trip itself. A two-week trip is a seven-week affair: two full weeks of preparation, two weeks on the calls, and three weeks of intensive follow-up. So often an international calling officer has been heard to say "I'm going on my six-monthly maintenance trip to the Far East and will make a courtesy call on all our line clients, covering seven countries in four weeks." This is about the worst thing a traveling officer could do. A "Maintenance" trip means the officer has not bothered preparing properly and, therefore, does not have much specifically to talk about but hopes that something will come up as the trip goes along. The officer is only calling on "line clients" because the lack of preparation has provided no new prospects. The officer is covering seven countries, if a hop, skip and a jump can be called coverage. No way can seven economies be assimilated effectively in a four-week trip. Maybe the officer will be lucky and come up with a great piece of new business in the first week out; but even if this happens, the momentum will be lost and the business dead if the officer does not return back to base for another three weeks to work on it.

Economy, travel budgets, and the like are no reasons for organizing ineffective trips. The best trip is likely to be only one week long, well prepared, and with definite objectives, and upon returning the account officer has to follow through immediately. Preparation has already been partly covered in describing the formation of marketing plans and account action plans. Organization helps the preparation tremendously. A good way of organizing an overseas sales territory is to keep a three-ring binder with a sheet for each of the accounts or prospects in each country—the "Country Trip Book." If the account is one that has been put on the account plan list, then that sheet will be included. Otherwise, the sheet should have the name, address, and logistics of each account/prospect, together with a diary of visits and a brief synopsis of other information on the development of the name. Prior to each trip abroad, the traveling officer should type in on the sheet any "call objectives." In this manner, just before going in to visit the company, it is easy to quickly review what to talk about, offer, or ask. It is easy to do this in advance but hard to do while visiting the prospect. Thinking about it and writing it down in advance also helps to decide whether the call is really necessary; there is nothing more undesirable than calling on a prospect and having nothing worthwhile to offer or ask.

Having called on the company, it is necessary to prepare a "Report of Visit" or "Call Report." Some people dictate these into a machine right after the visit. Others make brief notes after the visit, sufficient to help them recall the conversation and dictate call reports on returning to home base. Immediately dictated reports tend to be long winded, but it is a matter of personal preference. Irrespective of the method of recalling the conversations, it is a good idea to prepare a "Trip Follow-up Sheet" at the end of the trip. This will specify actions that need to be taken on each name, and makes note of who should take them. A typical Trip Follow-up Sheet might look as follows:

Quimica Norte:	1.	Send 1980 statement to Credit Department for analysis—J. R.
	2.	Write Chavez reminding him of his repayment offer, 30 percent now, 30 percent six months, and 40 percent 12 months—J. R.
	3.	Submit tax receipts to Accounting—J. R.
Banco Oeste:	1.	Send our documentation—J. R.
	2.	Write Belanger re offering 180 day acceptance line at B/A's + 1¼ percent—S. M. P.
	3.	Have Operations write re Courier System—Operations.
Banco del Rio:	1.	Have S. M. P. write Moreno re American Bankers Association Convention—S. M. P.
	2.	Get Operations to send all Area 2 collections to this bank—Operations.
	3.	Write thank you letter and promise to revert on T/L—J. R.
	4.	Process $3MM T/L for their client ASMASA with Banco del Rio guarantee, 5 years, 10 semi's. Discuss improving rate with S. M. P. and J. F. L.

In addition, if the country in question is only visited two or three times a year, it is well to write a "Trip Report" for review by the territory head and/or department head. This is a good opportunity to reevaluate the effort in that country, to review the economic and political situations, and to suggest finetuning to the departmental plan as a result. Of course, for a country being visited six or more times a year, this only need be done occasionally and probably after the trip on which the country head takes along the international economics/country-risk officer.

SELLING TECHNIQUES—PERSONAL LEVEL

There are good sales people and poor sales people, and it is widely held that a poor one was made that way and cannot be changed. The truth is different. A person with a natural sales flair can fall far short of his or her real potential if badly organized; while a person with only moderate sales ability can perform reasonably if well organized.

Since credit is the largest product most banks have for sale, it is the area requiring most organization. It is not reasonable to expect every traveling officer to be a superb credit officer with the highest authority in a bank's credit approval system. On the other hand, the traveling officer can do a lot of prior work to obtain approvals before visiting a client and then be able to act with authority on the spot. The client wishes to deal with the decision maker. The calling officer can act as the decision maker if given the necessary prior approvals.

In the same way that the client wishes to work with the decision maker, the selling officer should make sure he or she is dealing with the client's decision maker. This should be decided as early as possible in developing a relationship or going after a particular piece of business. If in doubt, start a little too high in the client's organization. It is easier to slide down from one person to a junior one than it is to climb up. Many people do not like to humiliate themselves by admitting that it is their boss that will make the decision. In the other direction, however, a subordinate might read a superior's willingness to deal with the selling officer if he or she was referred to them by a superior.

Pricing knowledge and ability to quote prices are also essential and often overlooked by international bank selling officers. It is no good to say "Deal with us because we give good service" and then reveal that one is not aware of the bank's terms and conditions. It is most effective, on the other hand, to come right out and offer a particular service for a specific price and indicate how it compares to the competition. In this manner, not only is the client given a good reason for dealing with the bank, but has been given the correct impression that he or she is dealing with a decision maker. Since credit is such an important product, the officer should be able to price it on the spot. Compare the following sales pitches:

1. "We would like to consider offering you a line of credit."
2. "We have approved for you a $1 million line of credit."
3. "At LIBOR + ¾ percent per annum we could offer you a $1 million line."
4. "I could lend you $1 million, value the day after tomorrow, at $13^{15}/_{16}$ percent per annum, under a $1 million line I have approved for you, if it is of interest."

The last one is the best attention getter and gives the client the best indication of how good your offer is.

Continuity is important. It used to be possible to obtain international business by continuity alone. Frequent courtesy calls developed a friendship that eventually caused business to follow. Subsequently, it became clear that it was necessary to have something to offer, solve a problem, or price a product to get business. The better the marketing person became at selling his or her wares, the more he or she was promoted up the line. Continuity was lost altogether. A combination of the two is important. The multiple-effect, action-plan coordination method can alleviate this problem by having the same face show up again occasionally at a client's office. However, a territorial manager or departmental marketing officer must keep in mind the benefits of continuity and foster it the best way possible.

Flexibility and adaptability are also key personal selling techniques. When in Rome, do as the Romans do. This means being sensitive to the local ways and adjusting to them where appropriate. This applies most of all with eating habits. It is best in Mexico to adjust one's schedule to the local one and not expect prospects to look favorably upon a luncheon at noon when they usually eat at 3 P.M. It is best to accept some of the local delicacies, especially if the host went to great length to prepare them. If this advice is taken too far, however, it can have the opposite results. There is the story of the vice president of a large New York bank who traveled the United Kingdom before every bank had a branch there. He used to keep a bowler hat and pin-striped trousers at the hotel to wear on his visits to the banks. He looked the very British banker to the tee, but the British bankers all felt they were being ridiculed, as can well be understood.

Specificity helps. Offering a specific service gives the client a decision to make. Offering general services can be met with a polite thank you. Persistence helps, too, but rudeness has to be avoided. Knowing the difference between the two is an art that cannot be explained here.

WITHHOLDING TAX POLICY

One of the keys to new business in the 1980s is a thorough understanding of the bank's position on foreign withholding taxes. As the reader will no doubt be aware, many countries require those remitting interest payments to foreigners to withhold a certain percentage of the gross interest payment and remit it to the local tax authorities on behalf of the foreign lender as a tax payment on business done in the country. These withheld taxes can often be taken as a credit against a bank's U.S. tax bill. Often the size of the withheld tax is far greater than the profit spread on a loan. It is a key element in the pricing of a loan. It is absolutely essential for an international lending officer to understand his or her bank's tax position fully. Whether a bank has, or has not, the ability to absorb foreign withheld taxes must be made known to the lending officers, and rules of thumb or other direction must be given to them to enable them to compete effectively and price their loans profitably. A bank that advises its lending officers, "We cannot absorb foreign withholding taxes, therefore, do not accept any withholding" is deficient. In some cases, the level of withholding might be lower than the tax burden the loan itself creates, in which event, on a marginal basis, the bank might still be better off to make the loan. Foreign tax credits have a carry back and carry forward ability. It is possible that with good management some business might be acceptable without unduly mortgaging the bank's future tax position. And just the fact that a bank found itself in a position where it did not expect to pay taxes for a few years may not be cause to eliminate all lending in a particular country in the meantime. A more flexible rule is needed; and lending officers must be aware of the extra benefit accruing in a deal that creates foreign-source income but does not cause withheld taxes. The territorial manager should get a ruling on the amount of withholding his or her territory can endure and then manage that asset effectively.

DIRECT MAIL AND ADVERTISING ASSISTANCE

From a selling point of view, banking is a one-on-one affair. A lending officer identifies prospective borrowers, goes and calls on them, and tries to solve their financial problems. The banker is selling ingenuity and personal attention. Even the newer bank services, involving computerized account and payment information and foreign exchange information services, are appropriate for only a small, well-defined prospect list. This makes media advertising ineffective. Nevertheless, there is some help that can be obtained, not only from media advertising, but also from direct-mail campaigns.

Where a small, readily identifiable market exists for a product, direct mail is of great assistance. A regional bank wishing to introduce a new direct collection system might develop a list of all foreign credit managers in corporations in a 200-mile radius and mail them descriptive literature. This is best done in combination with a one-on-one visit. It is important that the mailing piece be sufficiently attractive that the recipient does not care to throw it away, and it remains on the desk as a reminder of the product or visit.

Advertising in newspapers and magazines is of best value in the personal banking market. Since there are few banks involved in retail banking on a worldwide basis, there is limited use to which medium advertising can be put. There is some value though. In specialty magazines focusing on capital goods industries, export financing can be advertised. In foreign Chamber of Commerce bulletins or area financial magazines or newspapers, advertisements directed at correspondent banks can be placed. Manuals and directories (*Polk's, Bankers' Almanac*, etc.) make excellent places to put ads aimed at attracting the attention of a foreign bank clerk wondering which bank to send a particular collection or remittance.

Each territorial manager, while on trips abroad, should build up knowledge of magazines, newspapers, bulletins, and so on, that might be suitable places for an advertisement. Fortunately, this sort of advertising is fairly inexpensive as opposed to national newspaper advertising. Much international banking advertising falls into the image category. While this might be good for correspondent banking, image can best be obtained by selling a product at the same time. Publication of the bank's annual report should be considered as merely another alternative, rather than the corner piece of international advertising.

Media advertising for international products is often done in the bank's own country, focusing on international services to domestic clients. This has a twofold intention. Not only does it hopefully attract business from domestic exporters and such, but it also gives a general image of overall ability to other domestic clients who might never actually handle international business. Indeed the ability to handle international transfers and foreign exchange remittances might have a most beneficial effect on the bank's savings accounts. Alas, this is impossible to measure.

All users of international banking services, be they corporate treasurers, foreign credit managers, accountants, correspondent bankers, or whoever, are often in need of a handbook reminding them how to handle a transaction. Many of the larger banks have invested in the production of a how-to manual. This has been a most effective advertising tool and one that many smaller banks could copy, albeit in a more limited manner.

SALES TRAINING

The most effective key to successful sales is training. A bank typically gives its sales/traveling officers one year's credit training, little product training, and no sales training. Some banks send their sales staff on courses to improve sales effectiveness. This is most desirable. Even more desirable, however, is to institute a continuing sales training program. A program should be organized in a formal but flexible manner, with a person appointed to track the coverage of all people in the department according to their needs.

The most obvious sales training is the on-the-job junior/senior method. A new, new-business officer is sent on a trip with a superior and subsequently left to go on his or her own. There is nothing wrong with this, but again it should be done in an organized manner. A new business officer should be accompanied by the department head, the economics officer, a money market specialist, a cash management specialist, and others, on different trips, and a record should be kept to see that each person has the benefit of a joint experience with each special area.

In-house courses should be organized for the promotion of product knowledge. Certain key people will need to be sent on outside courses and should be given the opportunity to pass on the outside knowledge in subsequent in-house groups.

Language efficiency is an obvious benefit to new business development abroad, although a poor linguist and good banker is better in any situation than a good linguist and bad banker. A bank should promote language courses and encourage even those with good ability to join in-house programs to help the development of language abilities. Small groups of officers might get together for biweekly luncheons at which only the foreign language is spoken. If such a get together includes people from different departments, such as foreign exchange, operations, and international platform, useful esprit de corp is generated at the same time.

Sales training pays huge dividends, and if an international department is large enough to warrant a full-time marketing officer, it is probably appropriate that one third of that time be spent on planning/sales coordination, and one third on sales training.

This leaves one third for new product development. International bankers are product driven. There is only a limited amount to offer, and there is a tremendous unbounded market out there. A good new product is a sure road to success. During the 60s and 70s the banking community came upon courier systems, direct collections, computerized foreign exchange exposure simulators, Eurobonds, Eurodollars, zerobalance accounts, automatic investment of excess funds, and many exotic ideas. Isn't it worth investing one third of the time of one person keeping up to date, and hopefully developing a product variation which will give a bank's traveling staff a chance to get worthwhile attention?

APPENDIX—WORKSHOP ON INTERNATIONAL MARKETING FOR DOMESTIC OFFICERS

    I. Introduction.
        A. Why it is good to do foreign business with your customers?
            1. Profitable.
            2. Expands their sales; is profitable for them.
            3. Do not want them to go to another bank.
            4. Are usually very grateful for assistance.

        B. What sorts of companies do foreign business?
            1. Smaller manufacturing companies, exporters.
            2. Trading companies.
            3. Capital goods manufacturers.

   4. Importers for resale.

   5. Manufacturing companies, small and large, that import some component.

   6. Multinationals with sales offices, joint ventures, and subsidiaries abroad.

  C. Typical terms of sale, dependent on risk.

   1. Confirmed letter of credit (L/C).

   2. Unconfirmed L/C.

   3. Collection.

   4. Open account.

 II. International banking services.

  A. Confirmed export L/Cs, typical example.

   1. Diagramatic explanation of how they work.

   2. What they accomplish for the exporter.

    a. Credit risk elimination.

    b. Assurance of proper paperwork.

   3. What our bank's services are.

    a. Negotiating, confirming, immediate payment.

    b. Time L/C discounting.

   4. Sometimes difficult to get foreign company to send L/C to us directly.

   5. Our selling points.

    a. Personal service.

    b. Correspondent network.

  B. Unconfirmed export L/Cs.

   1. Exporter takes foreign bank risk.

   2. Same selling points.

  C. Import L/Cs, typical application.

   1. Credit risk.

   2. Pricing.

   3. Refinancing.

   4. Performance L/Cs.

  D. Acceptances, typical draft.

   1. Requirements—simply.

  E. Collections.

   1. Documentary.

   2. Clean.

   3. Direct collection system.

   4. Our selling points (computerization of aging).

  F. Forms of credit.

   1. Time L/Cs.

   2. Loans versus collections.

  G. Export finance.

   1. Short term.

    a. Financing customers receivables.

    b. FCIA.

           c. Buyer credit limits.
       2. Medium term.
           a. EXIM/FCIA
           b. Recourse/without recourse (very brief attention).
    H. Loans to foreign subsidiaries, US dollars and foreign currency.
    I. Other services.
       1. Drafts and remittances.
       2. Telegraphic transfers.
       3. Trade information.
       4. Credit inquiries.
       5. Foreign bank notes.
       6. Spot and forward foreign exchange (very brief on forwards).
III. Services international department provides in the money market.
    A. Liability service to own bank.
    B. Explanation of Eurodollars (demystification, rather than indepth discussion).
    C. Short-term investment in Eurodollar market.
    D. Purchase of acceptances by doctors, etc.
IV. What types of companies use which services.

(Develop a matrix on the board.)

	Middle market manufacturing companies	Capital goods manufacturers	Individuals	Correspondent banks	Foreign-owned companies	MNC's	Domestic construction companies	Other
L/C								
Collection								
FX								
Drafts and remittances								
Money market								
Credit								

(Discuss each as entering in the boxes.)

(Include some categories chosen by the audience.)

  V. How to develop a prospect list.
      A. Various sources.
          1. Duns.
          2. Journal of Commerce.
          3. Dunn & Bradstreet $1MM Directory.
          4. Others.
 VI. Use of a questionnaire (provide typical one).
      A. To develop marketing information.
          1. Which countries need correspondents in.
          2. Level of attention from travel staff.
          3. Likely need for country limits.
          4. Need for operational services.
      B. To give account officers ideas for potential business.
      C. To assure correct questions are asked by domestic officers,
          help them in selling.

(Go over questionnaire and explain how and why.)

VII. Discussion of some pricing techniques.
      A. Collections for free?
      B. Does the L/C fee cover the credit risk?
      C. Should the "weekly rate" be applied on less than $2,500
          FX items, or less than $10,000?
VIII. Examples of success cases in selling international to domestic
       clients.
      A. Company with small Mexican affiliate.
      B. MNC who used B/As for subsidiary purchases.
      C. MNC who was borrowing from New York bank on advances
          against collections.
      D. Company that borrowed Swiss francs and did not cover.
      E. Leads from foreign banks sending L/Cs.
 IX. Q. and A.
      A. Heavy on asking for live cases.
      B. Ideas on what to ask, or offer.

This should be followed or preceded by an explanation of the organization chart of the bank's international department, together with pertinent statistics.

The people in the international department who should be approached by the domestic calling people on different matters should be physically introduced.

Domestic/International liaison staff should be present during entire presentation.

International Survey Questionnaire

Company Name: _____

Sales: _____

Type of Company (Product): _____

Does the Company have an account with the Bank? _____

What Bank does the Company use for International Services? _____

What International Banking Services does the Company require?
Credit?
Foreign Exchange?
Letter of Credit/Collection?
Drafts/Remittances?
Other? (Please specify)

IF THE COMPANY IS AN EXPORTER,
What is the size of a typical export sale?

What is the volume of the Company's annual export sales?

What are the terms of sale? _____

What countries are sold to on a consistent basis? _____

Is credit granted to buyers, or is credit requested by customers? _____

Does the Company maintain an FCIA Master Policy? _____

Does the Company maintain a Domestic International Sales Company?

IF THE COMPANY IS AN IMPORTER,
What is the size of the Company's annual imports?

What type of products are imported? _____

From what countries does the Company import? _____

What terms of sale are granted on imports? _____

IF THE COMPANY IS A MANUFACTURER,
Does the Company have any manufacturing facilities abroad? _____

Does the Company have any joint ventures or affiliates overseas? _____

41
Managing International Funding and Liquidity

PAUL H. AUSTIN
Senior Vice President
Citibank, N.A.

International banks perform their financial intermediation function by taking and lending funds in many currencies in many geographical markets. They must generate a satisfactory rate of return from these activities for their shareholders. In order to preserve their ability to continue functioning as an ongoing concern, they must obviously remain liquid, meet contractual day to day obligations, and be able to react to unexpected market developments.

This chapter focuses on the key role of liquidity management in determining the viability of an international bank's overseas operations. It starts with a discussion of funding alternatives in domestic and offshore markets and how options are affected by the economic and regulatory environments. This leads into the broader area of liquidity (asset/liability) management, the critical importance of access to money markets at all times and the profit and interest-rate and liquidity-risk dynamics of mismatching the maturities of assets and liabilities. Finally, a system for monitoring and controlling the liquidity and interest-rate risks will be discussed. Before we proceed, let us examine the flow of funds in the global financial system.

INTERNATIONAL FLOW OF FUNDS

The technological advances of the 20th century have made the world smaller. Through a network of sophisticated communication channels, the market has essentially become one global financial system where conditions in different geographical areas affect another's liquidity.

In local and foreign markets, banks access pools of funds in areas of liquidity and interest-rate opportunity and channel them to other

644

markets. This process of recycling money is continuous, since money, regardless of its use, never leaves the financial system except through certain actions of central banks.

Figure 1 illustrates the relationship among the participants in world financial markets. For instance, take a purchase of goods by a U.S. company from abroad. Funds to pay for the goods would be withdrawn from a bank in the United States for remittance to the exporter's account with his bank abroad. While this remittance means a change in ownership of funds, there would be no actual change in the liquidity of the global financial system. In fact, dollars never physically leave the United States in this transaction, since the remittance is simply the crediting of the account of the U.S. correspondent of the foreign bank which the exporter traditionally uses.

The exporter can use the U.S. dollar receipts in a number of ways, depending on exchange regulations that exist in his country. In one instance, the dollars can be exchanged for local currency at banks; eventually, they would end up with the central bank. In another in-

Figure 1
International Flow of Funds

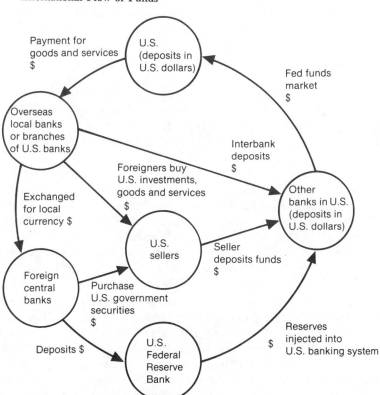

stance, the exporter can use the U.S. dollar proceeds to purchase U.S. commercial or government securities, or goods and services, again, depending on regulations. Payments for these would be credited to a bank account in the United States. Finally, the exporter may retain the dollars on deposit with his bank abroad. The bank would most likely relend the funds to customers or place them in either the inter-bank domestic or Euromarket.

In all cases, ownership of the U.S. dollar funds changes hands domes-tically and overseas, but liquidity never leaves the dollar system except when the dollars are deposited at the U.S. Federal Reserve and are not reinjected into the banking system.

MULTICURRENCY FUNDING

The funding activities of an international U.S. bank involve not only accessing domestic and international sources of dollars but also tapping other currency sources to fund a multicurrency asset portfolio. Thus, the funding objective of an international bank is to access all pools of liquidity wherever they appear in the global financial system.

In order to manage its funding task, a bank should diversify its sources of funds by depositor, funding instrument, maturity, geographi-cal location, and currency. Such a diversification program precludes overconcentration in any segment of the market and enables a funds manager to tap sources wherever available and thus reduce liquidity risk.

Should other than local currency be considered as a funding source, exchange regulations, sovereign risk, and exchange-rate risk would have to be evaluated by the bank.

The ability to fund with local currency in any country is affected by the regulatory environment and the degree of development of the economy and financial markets. In an open economy, where a foreign bank is allowed to compete freely with local banks, an array of funding alternatives may be available from traditional demand, sav-ings and time deposits to sophisticated money market instruments. On the other hand, in a highly regulated market, the foreign bank may find itself at a significant competitive disadvantage because of restrictive regulations pertaining only to foreign banks.

To fund the local currency asset portfolio, one alternative that is occasionally available to international banks is cross-currency funding, that is, borrowing one currency and converting it to the local currency. A case in point would be a country with a developing money market and high interest rates. It may be attractive to borrow lower-cost for-eign funds, convert them to local currency, and relend the local cur-rency at more attractive rates.

However, in such instances where there is no forward exchange market because of central-bank regulatory restrictions, this would not be prudent since the bank exposes itself to an exchange risk. At the time of repayment of the foreign funds borrowed, the local currency may have devalued, resulting in a loss that exceeds the interest gains on the cross-currency transaction. Where there is an unrestricted foreign exchange market, it may be possible to hedge the exchange risk through a forward exchange contract. In this way, the total cost of generating local currency can be fixed, inasmuch as overall cost factors, such as hedge and interest costs, are finalized.

Generally speaking, however, lending in any currency should be supported by funding in the same currency because of sovereign and exchange-rate risks. It follows that the growth of local currency assets should not exceed the ability to fund those assets in the same currency. Therefore, it is important for a bank to develop a variety of funding instruments and sources in order to be able to access the local market.

While cross-currency funding might be attractive in terms of profits, limits should be imposed to prevent overreliance which could result in losses if, in the future, the exchange market for the local currency dries up, a devaluation occurs, or restrictive regulations are enacted.

DOMESTIC AND OFFSHORE MARKETS

For some currencies with international demand, an offshore money market usually exists in addition to the domestic market. This market operates beyond the boundaries and jurisdiction of the country. The best example of such an offshore market is the Eurodollar market. The term *Euro* has been used loosely to indicate the geographical area where the offshore currency market exists. In the case of the U.S. dollar, the offshore market was Europe, hence Eurodollars. With the development of financial centers around the world, such as Hong Kong, Singapore, and Bahrain, such terms as *Asian Dollar* have been coined. The words *Eurodollar* and *Eurocurrency* continue to be used generically to describe offshore currency held anywhere in the world.

Historically, the offshore dollar market developed in the years after World War II because of the reluctance of Eastern Bloc countries to keep their reserves of hard currency U.S. dollars in the United States for political and jurisdictional reasons. These funds were placed on deposit in Europe, usually in London. Additionally, U.S. banking regulations spurred the development of the Eurodollar market. Regulation D imposed reserve requirements on deposits with U.S. banks, increasing the banks' cost of borrowing and reducing the nominal rates of interest they were willing to pay for funds. Regulation Q imposed interest-rate ceilings on deposits in the United States.

These regulations, among others, resulted in a shift of funds to the unregulated Eurodollar market where depositors get better returns for their funds and where banks can borrow without bearing the incremental cost of reserves and deposit insurance. Also, other borrowers could realize this cost advantage, further increasing the market size. However, over time, regulation differentials have disappeared, but rate differences still exist because of reserve requirements on domestic (U.S.) instruments.

International banks access the Eurocurrency markets through correspondents or by setting up operations in major offshore centers such as Hong Kong, Singapore, Bahrain, London, or Nassau. In addition to having such characteristics as good communications and political stability, these places do not have significant regulations governing foreign currency transactions. Funds generated in these centers can be channeled to areas of demand, supplementing local currency funding in countries where the free flow of funds is allowed among offshore centers and domestic markets.

LIQUIDITY

The management of liquidity goes beyond the development of funding sources. It also involves managing the relationships among the maturities of assets and liabilities in each currency and in all currencies and, importantly, the maturity structure of the liability portfolio as a whole.

The maturity of deposits and borrowings of a bank rarely match the maturity of its assets, mainly loans. For example, five-year loans may be funded by a combination of demand and savings accounts and short-term borrowings. One of the fundamentals of banking is borrowing short and lending long as opportunities occur, assuming that, on average, the yield curve is positively sloped and stable. As financial intermediaries, banks provide an economic value to society by pooling and then recycling funds, a function that necessitates the undertaking of a liquidity risk for which banks are compensated.

Liquidity means the ability to meet any financial commitment when due, whether it be a checking account withdrawal, a maturing Eurodollar deposit, or a maturing issue of commercial paper. Historically, this has meant the careful structuring of assets and the maintenance of liquid reserves especially in the form of government securities that could be readily sold for cash. However, for most banks, government securities do not provide liquidity because they may be temporarily loaned under repurchase agreements or pledged to secure certain types of deposits. Today, in order for large money center banks to meet their liquidity requirements, they must be able to access money markets at all times in order to manage their maturing liabilities' net cash outflows.

Given the degree of development in world financial markets, international currencies can be assessed as readily in Hong Kong, Singapore, or Bahrain as in New York or London, provided a bank has earned a reputation that gives it access to global money markets. If the market concludes that a bank is an historically well-managed, ongoing business, that institution is able to borrow funds to meet its maturing obligations at the prevailing market price.

Banks must manage both assets and liabilities, but the core of liquidity management for large international banks is liability management. Banks have more flexibility to manage liquidity on the liability side inasmuch as assets tend to be determined by customer requirements and market terms. For instance, liquidity can be improved on the asset side by increasing holdings of cash and securities; however, there are carrying-cost factors involved as well as market size limitations. Liquidity can also be improved by shortening the maturities of loans or by not rolling over loans as they mature; but the drawback could be the inability to fully satisfy customer needs.

RISKS ASSOCIATED WITH GAPPING

A gap is a mismatch between the maturities of assets and liabilities. When longer-term assets are funded by shorter-term liabilities, we say there is a negative gap. When the reverse is true, we say there is a positive gap. When there is no gap, we say that maturities are matched.

There are two types of risk which should be considered; the first is liquidity which is the risk that obligations may not be met as they mature because of the inability to raise sufficient funds. The second risk is interst rate which implies the potential of loss in a mismatched book if interest rates change. Both types of risk relate to gapping activity but must be managed separately.

MANAGING THE INTEREST-RATE RISK UNDER GAPPING

A simplistic approach to funding management is to match all asset and liability maturities. However, the strategic funding policy of a bank is traditionally one that allows liabilities to mature before assets. A bank's financial intermediation function is hampered if it constantly takes only those liabilities that match its asset maturities. While the bank does not assume much risk, neither does it add much economic value in the process, and in its matching objective, it may be forced to quote off-market rates which, in turn, would oblige its customers to look elsewhere. It may also be much less profitable to match all assets and liabilities because longer-term funds tend to be more expensive, and banks can take advantage of lower-cost funds with shorter tenors if they are willing to gap under an acceptable economic scenario and when the interest-rate yield curve is normal and stable.

Interest yield curves are normally upward sloping, that is, interest rates for longer tenors tend to be higher because the market pays a premium for longer availability, or conversely, depositors demand a higher rate for committing their funds for a longer period of time. For example, banks pay lower rates for ordinary savings accounts than for time deposits since savings accounts can be withdrawn at any time. In such an environment, it is frequently desirable to maintain a negative gap in order to take advantage of lower-cost, short-term funds. The expectation is that as liabilities mature prior to assets, they can be rolled over at a rate no higher than the rate at which the matching funds could have been obtained. Gapping is a profitable strategy if interest rates are expected to decline. By lending a fixed tenor, say three months, but funding only one month, incremental profits can be generated as interest rates drop. The liability can be rolled over at the then prevailing lower rate.

Let us take a hypothetical example in which a bank lends to a customer for three months at 12.75 percent. The yield curve at that time is:

Tenor	Money Market	Lending Rate
1 month	12.000%	12.500%
2 months	12.250%	12.625%
3 months	12.500%	12.750%
4 months	12.750%	12.875%
5 months	13.000%	14.000%
6 months	13.250%	14.125%

If the bank were to match its loan by borrowing three months at 12.50 percent, then it would lock in its lending spread with an incremental gain of 25 basis points. If the bank were to gap by borrowing one month at a time and interest rates remained constant, then the average funding cost of 12.00 percent would mean an incremental spread of 75 basis points on the loan.[1]

If the bank expects interest rates to drop by half a percent at the end of one month, it would gap by borrowing for one month at 12.00 percent. At the end of the month, if its forecast were correct, the bank could now close its gap and lock in its spread by borrowing for two months at 11.75 percent, or it could continue to gap by borrowing one month again. Assuming the bank decides to close the gap, then the average funding cost would be 11.833 percent, or an incremental 67 basis point spread against the three-month funding cost of 12.50 percent.

---

[1] The effect of compounding on interest rates is ignored in the example.

A gapped position will generate a loss if interest rates move opposite to expectations. In our example, if interest rates moved up instead of down by 125 basis points at the end of the first month, the bank would be confronted with a possible loss. At this point, the bank could close its gap by borrowing for two months at 13.50 percent, bringing its average funding cost to 13.00 percent; the gap would result in an average loss of 25 basis points. On the other hand, the bank can continue to gap by borrowing for another month at 13.00 percent bringing its average funding cost to 12.50 percent for the first two months. If the one-month interest rate drops back to 12.75 percent or lower by the end of the second month, a loss will be avoided. However, if interest rates continue to rise, then a larger loss will occur. Whether a bank decides to close an unfavorable position or continue to gap, depends on its outlook for interest rates and its ability to bear further possible losses.

When interest rates are forecast upward, a bank can open a positive gap provided assets are expected to be rolled over. In the example, if the forecast is for a 125-basis point increase in interest rates and, currently, six-month funds can be borrowed at 13.250 percent, then after three months, when the asset is rolled over at a spread over the new three-month rate of 14.00 percent, the bank's funding cost will continue to be 13.250 percent. Therefore, by borrowing six-month funds, the bank initially funds at an incremental cost of 50 basis points, but recovers this cost in the next three months when it makes an incremental gain of 75 basis points. The net result is a gain of 25 basis points.

A positive gap is also profitable when the yield curve is inverted; that is, when short-term interest rates are higher than long-term interest rates. When a positive gap is taken in this case, the expectation is that interest-rate levels will not decline.

It is evident from these examples that the decision to match or gap depends on expectations of interest-rate movements. While matching will eliminate uncertainty and possible losses, as we have said previously, it may not maximize earnings. In a changing rate environment, a matching strategy will either be a good asset-rate decision or a good liability-rate decision, but it could not be both at the same time.

MANAGING LIQUIDITY RISK UNDER GAPPING

Liquidity risk implies a risk in which the bank's ability to continue operating as an ongoing concern is at stake. While it can be argued that there is no such thing as liquidity risk for creditworthy borrowers because funds can always be acquired at a price (i.e., there is only an interest-rate risk), yet under extraordinary conditions, the price may be so high as to be totally impractical.

Liquidity risk, as well as interest-rate risk, can be measured and controlled through analysis of cumulative cash inflows and outflows. To illustrate this, suppose that a bank has assets of 100 million in a particular currency which have the following maturities: 20 million each in overnight, 3-month, 6-month, 12-month, and 2-year loans. Suppose that these loans are funded by borrowings of 30 million overnight, 40 million three months, and 30 million six months. Period by period, these maturities will create net inflows and outflows as detailed in Table 1.

Table 1
Maturity Analysis (in millions of currency units)*

Maturity	Assets	Liabilities	Net Cash Flow	Net Cumulative Cash Flow
Overnight	20	30	−10	−10
During months 1–3	20	40	−20	−30
During months 4–6	20	30	−10	−40
During months 7–12	20	0	+20	−20
During year 2	20	0	+20	0
Total	100	100		

* In this discussion, we do not include forward exchange contracts which, like deposits and loans, cause fund inflows and outflows as they mature. In an actual operating environment, exchange contracts should be taken into account in managing liquidity.

The analysis in Table 1 takes existing assets and liabilities and spreads them according to a maturity schedule. Assets generate fund inflows as loans are collected. The assumption here is that loans will be paid at maturity and will not be replaced by new assets. Similarly, liabilities represent outflows of funds when they mature. The net cash flow column indicates for the maturity period the amount of net inflow (+) or outflow (−) that is expected to occur; finally, the net cumulative column is the accumulation of these figures.

In Table 1, the bank's liquidity risk on day one is 10 million. This is the amount that has to be raised in the market that day to cover the net outflow of 10 million. Assuming the overnight funds market is used constantly, then this borrowing will have to be rolled over from day to day for three months. At the end of the third month, 20 million in assets and 40 million in liabilities mature, producing an incremental net outflow of 20 million. This increases to 30 million the amount that has to be raised in the overnight market. At the end of the sixth month, the liquidity risk reaches a peak, since the net cumulative outflow hits 40 million. Therefore, the liquidity risk declines as more assets than liabilities mature at the end of year one.

This analysis provides management with a useful profile of liquidity risk. It shows the maximum amount of risk to the current structure of the balance sheet or maximum cumulative outflow (MCO), when it occurs, and how long it will last.

The bank's interest-rate risk in the above example is also reflected in Table 1. The fixed/floating-rate characteristics of both assets and liabilities are considered here but are treated in a subsequent section; (see Table 4). During the first three months, earnings are subject to interest fluctuations on the 10 million that has to be funded. Thus, interest-rate risk is on 30 million at the end of the third month, but then increases to a maximum of 40 million at the end of the sixth month.

This analysis can be used to estimate earnings sensitivity to interest-rate fluctuations. In the example, if rates go up or down by one percentage point on a basis perceived to be permanent, earnings will be impacted by 300,000 in the first year and 200,000 in the second year. This is computed in Table 2.

Table 2
Impact of 1 Percent Interest Fluctuation on Earnings

Period	Size of MCO	Impact of 1 Percent Annualized
First 3 months	10 million	25,000
Next 3 months	30 million	75,000
Next 6 months	40 million	200,000
Next 12 months	20 million	200,000

An interest-rate sensitivity analysis of a bank's portfolio can be made by using this methodology, applying various assumptions to the interest-rate forecast and the size and structure of the gap.

By managing asset and liability variables, liquidity and interest-rate risk can be controlled. For example, to reduce its liquidity risk, suppose the bank decides to change its liability structure by offering one- and two-year certificates of deposit, and it successfully sells 10 million of each to current holders of three-month CD's. The maturity profile of the balance sheet will now be as shown in Table 3.

Table 3
Maturity Profile (in millions of currency units)

Maturity	Assets	Liabilities	Cash Flow	Net Cumulative Cash Flow
Overnight	20	30	−10	−10
During months 1–3	20	20	0	−10
During months 4–6	20	30	−10	−20
During months 7–12	20	10	+10	−10
During year 2	20	10	+10	0
Total	100	100		

Note that the maximum cumulative outflow has dropped from −40 million to −20 million. By stretching the maturity of its liabilities, a bank reduces its liquidity risk. Interest-rate risk is also reduced if the original position is a negative gap.

Another consideration in analyzing liquidity/interest-rate risks would be the contractual repricing opportunities on assets or liabilities before their final maturity dates. For example, a bank could issue floating-rate two-year CDs that are repriced every six months. If 10 million of these are sold to holders of six-month CDs in Table 3, then the maturity profile from a final maturity or liquidity point of view, would look like Table 4.

Table 4
Maturity Profile (in millions of currency units)

Maturity	Assets	Liabilities	Cash Flow	Net Cumulative Cash Flow
Overnight	20	30	−10	−10
During months 1–3	20	20	0	−10
During months 4–6	20	20	0	−10
During months 7–12	20	10	+10	0
During year 2	20	20	0	0
Total	100	100		

The maturity profile indicates a shift of 10 million from "During months 4–6" to "During year 2," representing the lengthening of the time period during which the bank has possession of the funds. Consequently, the maximum cumulative outflow (MCO) drops further to 10 million. From an interest-risk standpoint, however, the maturity schedule remains unchanged because the six-month repricing provision implies that the interest rate on these two year CDs will be subject to the same market fluctuations as regular six-month CDs. The interest risk, therefore, remains unchanged with an MCO of 20 million; however, liquidity risk is reduced.

Liquidity risk can be controlled by setting a limit on the maximum cumulative outflows that may exist at any time. The most critical day from the point of view of liquidity is *today*, because, if maturing obligations are not met today, then the ability to continue business tomorrow is in doubt. The next most critical day is *tomorrow*, and, as the days go further out into the future, the cash flows become relatively less important. Sublimits should be imposed for very short tenors, say one or two weeks, because cumulative outflows in later months can always be managed down, by shifting the strategy to borrowing long-term funds, since few funding alternatives may be available to meet this week's requirements if market conditions happen to be unfavorable.

Interest-rate risk can be controlled similarly by setting limits on the maximum cumulative outflows and *inflows*. The limit on inflows is needed to control positive gapping. In the case of interest-rate risk, sublimits should be imposed on long-term gaps (i.e., over one year). The risk to earnings increases as gaps lengthen in maturity because of uncertain interest-rate levels which are affected by future economic, political, and regulatory developments.

Limits for liquidity and interest-rate risk should be established for each currency in which a bank has transactions. In addition, while the bank sets limits for the maximum risk it will bear in each currency, it may not want to be subject to the maximum risk in all these currencies at the same time. Therefore, an override or total limit for the aggregate of all currencies should be set.

In practice, a bank will vary the amounts and maturities of its borrowings depending on its interest-rate forecast and market condition expectations. For instance, borrowings will be taken to mature beyond periods of seasonal market tightness in order to avoid funding difficulties and to take advantage of lower interest rates at roll over. The shortening and lengthening of maturities will reflect the bank's strategy as it responds to changing market conditions.

The reduction of liquidity risk by lengthening the maturity of liabilities implies less profitability because long-term funds tend to be more expensive than short-term funds. It also implies fewer earning opportunities from negative gapping. The appropriate balance between liquidity and profitability is determined by senior management's assessment of the bank's capacity to bear these risks.

CONCLUSION

The proper management of liquidity is vital; it involves continuity and profitability. It means skillful management of funding to tap many sources in many markets through a variety of instruments at a cost commensurate with asset pricing. It means the development of an impeccable market reputation that assures access to money markets wherever liquidity is available, and it means the ability to successfully support asset growth and meet all obligations that mature. Liquidity management ensures that the bank will continue to operate tomorrow to service its customers' needs and to generate a satisfactory return for its shareholders.

42
Accounting and Internal Controls

M. C. NELSON
Partner
Ernst and Whinney

Accounting is the international language of business. However, in many respects foreign accounting and reporting practices differ from those used in the United States. Foreign banking customs and practices understandably also may not correspond to those in the United States and may directly influence the accounting and reporting requirements. Some foreign accounting and reporting practices are prescribed by law even to the extent that a foreign operation may be required to maintain, in a prescribed form, certain accounting books and records. Tax legislation and regulations have had great effect on foreign accounting requirements as foreign governments have frequently used financial reporting as a vehicle to foster programs for economic, social, and other development. A number of foreign countries require conformity between their tax, regulatory, and financial reporting. Managements of foreign operations and their accountants have to devise accounting and control methods that satisfy their foreign country needs as well as those of their U.S. parents and their regulatory authorities. It may not be possible for one set of rigid reporting requirements to meet all those various needs.

Many U.S. banks use similar accounting and control systems for both foreign and domestic operations. A common complaint among managers of overseas business units and international divisions is that the top management of the U.S. parent company does not fully appreciate the influence of the overseas environmental factors on overseas operations, and the U.S. parent company control system is not responsive enough to the particular overseas environmental factors.

The author expresses his appreciation to colleagues in Ernst & Whinney who made major contributions to the substance of this chapter. These were: J. Frank Drapalik, Managing Partner, Ernst & Whinney Grand Cayman Office, and Jack Behrens, Manager, Ernst & Whinney Chicago Office.

656

It is important for U.S. bankers to be aware of foreign environmental factors external to the company that must be considered in establishing controls to minimize risks and to insure international business success. Although these factors are unique to each foreign location, examples are: devaluation of currencies, changing price levels, multiplicity of tax practices, political instability, import-export controls, exchange controls, and experience and educational levels of the nationals in the overseas operations. These factors do exist, and their effects on management objectives and controls need to be recognized.

In almost all cases it is not practical to maintain accounting records only in the United States for foreign operations. Overseas operating, regulatory, tax, and secrecy requirements usually require that the overseas unit maintain its own accounting records and system of internal control under the direction of on-site overseas personnel.

Good internal control and bookkeeping are universal in importance for the preparation of basic foreign financial statements, even though the presentation of the financial statements may differ from that in the United States. It is not practical in this chapter to describe all the numerous differences between foreign and domestic bank accounting and reporting practices. Instead, the remainder of the chapter will deal with some of the more common accounting, reporting, and internal control considerations in international banking operations.

INTERNATIONAL BANKING OPERATIONS

International operations of domestic banks may be domiciled in the United States or in a foreign country. In the United States they may take the form of a department or branch of the domestic commercial bank or of an incorporated subsidiary. An international banking facility (IBF) may be a department, a branch, a subsidiary, or simply a function within one of those units. Many domestic banks have established operations in a foreign country in recent years. These operations usually have taken the form of an unincorporated branch or a corporation.

Foreign operations can be classified as either a limited offshore facility or a full-service banking facility.

Limited offshore facilities (a branch or an incorporated entity) provide a means of expanding into international banking with limited foreign regulatory and tax implications while at the same time minimizing those restrictions in the United States. The Bahamas, Bermuda, and the Cayman Islands are presently popular sites for limited offshore facilities. Many foreign banks on these islands have licenses that allow them to do business only off the island although some have licenses that enable them to offer full service banking locally. A limited offshore facility generally acts as collection and disbursement agent for the

parent institution, and most of its transactions are initiated and accounted for at the direction of the home office. Its accounting and
internal control procedures are, as a general rule, those used by the
domestic bank for similar transactions. In the early stages of a limited
offshore facility, it may be practical to have parallel sets of accounting
records, one in the United States and the other in the foreign country.

A *full-service banking facility* in a foreign country (a branch or
an incorporated entity) usually can conduct all types of banking in
its country of domicile as well as in the international marketplace.
The facility usually is subject to all of the banking laws and reporting
requirements of the country in which it operates. Every effort should
be made to understand the legal and reporting requirements of the
host country before the facility becomes operational. The accounting
system in a full-service foreign banking facility should be tailored to
accommodate both the foreign reporting requirements and those of
the domestic parent. It should provide the home office with management and financial information on a timely basis in a form compatible
with that being generated by the U.S. operations.

The internal control system in the foreign facility should be based
on the same types of control objectives as are appropriate for its domestic parent. Policies and procedures should be in place to insure that
transactions are not only recorded but properly authorized. The control
system should provide a mechanism enabling the home office and not
just the foreign management to monitor and evaluate the unit's operation. Management reports should be designed with internal control
in mind. Internal audit staff can play a valuable role in the overall
monitoring of internal control. Through its field audits at the foreign
location, an internal audit staff independent of the management of
the foreign facility can provide the home office with assurance that
authorized policies and procedures are being followed.

INTERNAL CONTROL

The Statements on Auditing Standards of the American Institute
of Certified Public Accountants define internal control as follows:

> Internal control comprises the plan of organization and all of the coordi-
> nate methods and measures adopted within a business to safeguard its
> assets, check the accuracy and reliability of its accounting data, promote
> operational efficiency, and encourage adherence to prescribed manage-
> rial policies.
>
> Internal control in the broad sense includes . . . controls which can
> be characterized as either accounting or administrative as follows:
>
> a. Accounting controls comprise the plan of organization and all meth-
>   ods and procedures that are concerned mainly with, and relate di-
>   rectly to, the safeguarding of assets and the reliability of the financial
>   records. They generally include such controls as the systems of au-

thorization and approval, separation of duties concerned with operations or asset custody, physical controls over assets, and internal auditing.

   b. Administrative controls comprise the plan of organization and all methods and procedures that are concerned mainly with operational efficiency and adherence to managerial policies and usually relate only indirectly to the financial records. They generally include such controls as statistical analyses, time and motion studies, performance reports, employee training programs, and quality controls.

Each of the factors and concepts in the above definition should be present in a sound system of internal control, whether the operation is foreign or domestic. Accomplishing these goals within realistic cost/benefit constraints calls for strict coordination in accounting and internal control-system development. Each system will have to be designed to deal with both the physical distance and the particular nuances of the international market being served.

A sound system of internal control over the process of making loans is a good example of the parallel requirements of foreign and domestic operations. From an accounting system standpoint, either modification of the existing domestic loan system or design of a completely new system, compatible with the domestic system, must be performed in order to deal with the new consideration found in the international sector. For example, in order to insure that appropriate rates of interest are being charged to customers, the monitoring of foreign interest rates must be incorporated into the foreign system of internal control. Likewise information regarding foreign tax liabilities and their resulting effect on U.S. income taxes must be taken into consideration. New regulatory reports (i.e., Country Exposure Reports), both foreign and domestic, may be required thus necessitating a mechanism within the system to accumulate appropriate information. Delinquency information and country limit reports will need to be generated. And since Uniform Commercial Code forms are not universally accepted and foreign bankruptcy laws are seldom similar to U.S. laws, procedures for perfecting collateral liens will have to be modified.

Reference lists for internal control-system evaluation for international lending and foreign currency transactions are included as Exhibit 1.

CASH AND DUE FROM BANKS

A correspondent account due from a foreign bank is sometimes referred to as a "nostro" account. Deposits in U.S. banks that are due to foreign banks are sometimes referred to as "vostro" accounts. These accounts are used in three basic ways to make international payments through international correspondent banking. They are listed below.

Mail Remittance. The foreign bank sends a letter to the domestic bank, authorizing it to charge the foreign bank's correspondent account (either a due-to or a due-from account) and pay the customer (for example, an exporter) named in the letter. Before doing this, the domestic bank must be sure that the letter from the foreign bank is issued under proper authority. The correspondent banking relationship provides an exchange of authorized signatures between the corresponding foreign and domestic banks, and the banks inform each other as to the number and officer classification of required signatures in transfer letters.

Cable Remittance. To speed the transfer of funds, the foreign bank might communicate this same request to the domestic bank by cable or telephone. In such a situation, signatures cannot be verified, so the foreign bank and domestic bank have preestablished codes or "test keys," known only to each other, that must be present in the telegram or communicated over the telephone before the request is honored.

Foreign Draft. This is a common draft, drawn by the foreign bank on the domestic correspondent, used when the foreign customer (for example, a foreign importer) desires a negotiable instrument for forwarding to the domestic bank's customer. The domestic bank's customer must receive the draft and present it for payment at the domestic bank before the funds are transferred.

Many domestic banks maintain dual currency subsidiary ledgers for correspondent accounts. This means that the transactions and balances are recorded in both foreign currency denominations and U.S. dollar equivalents, enabling the international department to better monitor its international money position.

The internal control considerations for foreign bank accounts generally mirror those for domestic bank accounts. Deposits and withdrawals should be properly authorized and the system's controls should ensure that the transactions are properly recorded as to account, amount, and period. One of the best controls is the timely reconciliation of bank statements to book balances by an individual who is independent from the initiation or recording of transactions. These reconciliations, once completed, should be reviewed and approved by a responsible managerial employee on a regular basis. Exposure in individual foreign currencies also should be monitored. Minimum and maximum balances for each account and/or currency should be specified. The minimum and maximum parameters should be frequently challenged for adequacy, and overexposures in individual currencies should be identified and remedied on a timely basis.

LENDING

Two basic instruments involved in international lending are letters of credit and bankers' acceptances.

A letter of credit is an instrument issued by a bank on behalf of one of its customers authorizing a third party to draw drafts on the issuing bank, or on one of its correspondents for its account, under conditions stipulated in the letter.

There are various types of letters of credit. One type, usually called a "clean sight letter of credit," generates an accounting entry when issued. The accounting entry charges the individual or corporation acquiring the letter and credits a liability account to reflect the amount of credit available. The issuing domestic bank usually informs the foreign bank that it will be asked by the beneficiary of the credit to honor drafts drawn against it. As drafts are drawn against the credit, the foreign bank informs the domestic bank, and an entry is made that reduces the liability for the credit granted and credits the foreign bank that honored the draft.

Bankers' acceptances usually are closely related to letters of credit. An international department of a domestic bank usually creates a banker's acceptance in connection with a letter of credit granted by a foreign bank. These often are referred to by domestic banks as "export letters of credit."

When a draft is drawn against an export letter of credit, the domestic bank, after verifying that all documents are in order, usually accepts the draft. On acceptance, the domestic bank makes an entry debiting customers' acceptance liabilities and crediting acceptances outstanding. When the acceptance matures, this entry is reversed. The domestic bank then charges the foreign bank which issued the letter of credit and credits its customer's demand deposit account (or disburses the funds to the customer).

The domestic importer might want the cash proceeds of a time draft immediately, in which case the bank discounts the acceptance. This involves establishing an asset account for the discount, a credit to the domestic importer's demand deposit account (or a credit for cash disbursed to that importer), and a credit to unearned income for the discount charged by the domestic bank.

Customers' acceptance liabilities and acceptances outstanding are given separate asset and liability presentation in a bank statement of condition. If these amounts are not material they are sometimes grouped with other assets and liabilities.

When an acceptance outstanding is discounted, the resulting discount becomes a part of loans in a bank's statement of condition. If the offsetting acceptance liability and acceptance outstanding remain in the bank's general ledger, they should be netted against each other and not reflected separately in the bank's statement of condition.

A great potential for loss due to inadequate internal controls is in the lending area. One of the most important elements of control in the foreign lending area is the establishment of a formal loan policy which includes review procedures and documentation standards.

Also included in the loan policy should be standards for loan authorization and approval. The system used varies from bank to bank. Some banks permit senior lending officers to approve loans up to the bank's legal lending limits. Ideally, no loans should be granted without approval by someone other than the individual officer processing the loan application. For smaller loans, this approval often is granted after loan proceeds are disbursed. For loans of larger dollar amounts, many banks require several approvals before loan proceeds are disbursed.

Credit review and credit examination functions may be significant control elements of foreign lending operations. These functions vary widely from bank to bank but for our purpose they can be defined as follows:

> *Credit Review*—A department or activity, either separately organized or part of the loan administration function, which usually is responsible for a variety of activities, such as:
>
> Maintaining current status of selected credit files.
>
> Grading the quality of selected loans on a periodic basis.
>
> Assisting with structuring of larger, more complicated credit arrangements.
>
> Assisting with workout situations.
>
> *Credit Examination*—A department or activity responsible for periodic, independent examination and "classification" of selected credits. Usually this activity will report to senior management or the board of directors.

Other considerations which should be carefully analyzed and reviewed and their effect incorporated into the system of accounting and internal control for foreign lending include the following:

> The availability of audited financial statements or other reliable financial information on borrowers.
>
> Regulatory control on business in foreign countries often differs from that in the United States.
>
> Local independent credit checks may not be available or may not meet domestic standards.
>
> Methods of credit extension and problems of using them may differ greatly in other countries. For example, overdraft facilities, standby letters of credit, and other types of bank guarantees are widely used foreign methods for granting short-term loans and other credits.
>
> Professional qualifications and standards of auditors and other external consultants may not be the same as those in the United States.

The above lending controls apply to all types of lending, including letters of credit. The most common type of credit in a domestic bank's international department is the import letter of credit. The credit standing of the individual or business applying for an import letter of credit should be investigated, and the bank should be satisfied that the applicant has the ability to repay the drafts drawn against the letter of credit. A formal application for the credit should be obtained, and the bank's various credit review procedures should be performed before the credit is issued.

An import letter of credit specifies the documents that are required before drafts drawn against the credit will be honored. These documents vary, depending on the location of the foreign exporter and numerous other considerations, but three that are almost always required are:

A special customs invoice.

A full set of on-board ocean bills of lading evidencing shipment.

A commercial invoice stating the specific goods sold.

Other documents often required are insurance certificates, packing lists, and certificates of origin, inspection, weight, etc.

In general, the system of accounting and internal control for foreign loans should afford assurance that the following control objectives are achieved:

Proper review is performed and authorization obtained before monies are disbursed.

Transactions are recorded properly as to account, amount, and period.

Problem accounts are identified on a timely basis and appropriate action is taken.

Country exposure limits are established, maintained, and monitored.

FOREIGN EXCHANGE TRADING

As a bank becomes more sophisticated in international banking, its involvement in foreign exchange trading may expand.

Foreign exchange trading is the activity in international bank operations which is least like any of those in the domestic bank departments. In some ways it is similar to the securities trading function. Foreign exchange trading may be either spot or futures and either for the account of customers or for the bank's own account. The typical sequence of the principal trading operations and related accounting functions of a foreign trading operation are summarized in the following paragraphs.

A trader obtains current quotations from possible counterparties (another bank, a foreign exchange broker, etc.) almost always via telephone or telex, selects one of these, and indicates acceptance. Although no formal paperwork has been processed at this time, it should be recognized that from a practical point of view the foreign exchange contract now has been made. The trader immediately should prepare a trading slip showing transaction date, settlement date, rates, amounts, counterparty, etc. If it is a spot transaction, settlement instructions indicating the paying and receiving correspondent banks also might be given to the counterparty at this time. The trader enters the transaction on "position sheets." These sheets usually are maintained separately for each currency, each type of transaction (spot or future; short or long) and each future settlement period (month or half-month). This memorandum record serves to keep the trader up to date at all times on the gross and net positions in each currency and to maintain these in line with established trading and position limits.

In the optimum system, where there is a complete segregation of duties, the trader's direct involvement in the recording and control process now is complete, and the trading slip is passed to the control unit outside the foreign exchange trading section for further processing and review.

A formal contract/confirmation is prepared from the trading slip information, reviewed, and approved by an authorized executive. The original is sent to the counterparty. The bank also will receive a like confirmation prepared by the counterparty. If the counterparty is a customer (not another bank or foreign exchange broker), the bank usually must send an extra copy of the contract/confirmation to be acknowledged and returned by the customer.

Ledgers, by currency, by type of transaction, and by future settlement period, are posted daily from the contracts/confirmations (or from the trading slips). A daily position summary or "exposure report" is prepared and usually is available at the beginning of the next business day. It is reviewed by designated executives and by the traders who compare it to their position sheets.

About a week or 10 days prior to the maturity date of each future contract, settlement instructions are exchanged between the bank and its counterparty and given, as necessary, to the paying and receiving correspondent banks.

Periodically (usually at least twice a month) a "maturity schedule" or "gap report" is prepared from the currency ledgers to summarize for management the short and long positions by currency and by future settlement periods. The report also is used by the traders for comparison to their position sheets.

Customer, currency, or maturity-period exposure should be carefully reviewed and any excesses should be reduced to the established limit at the earliest possible date. By adequately monitoring the open positions, the bank will be able to minimize the potential for loss.

All foreign currency positions should be revalued on a monthly basis using rates generally recognized in banking. Finally, the trading, recordkeeping, and reconciliation functions should be segregated and reviewed frequently by an independent party.

FOREIGN CURRENCY TRANSLATION

The most pertinent and frequently encountered accounting issue in international operations is accounting for foreign currency translation. Frequently, translations of foreign currency accounts are made at a date other than month end, usually to expedite financial reporting by the U.S. parent.

Financial Accounting Standards Board (FASB) Statement No. 52, "Foreign Currency Translation," prescribes the required accounting for translation of foreign currency financial statements and foreign currency transactions. The Statement adopts the functional currency approach to translation. Each entity's financial statements are *measured* in its functional currency before translating to U.S. dollars.

The functional currency should be determined for each entity included in the financial statements. It is the currency of the primary economic environment in which the entity operates. If an entity's operations are relatively self-contained and integrated within a particular country, the functional currency generally would be the currency of that country. The entity's financial statements would be translated to U.S. dollars using the current rate method and resulting translation adjustments would be made directly to a separate component of stockholders' equity.

If the foreign entity is primarily an integral component or extension of the U.S. parent, its functional currency might be the U.S. dollar. If so, its financial statements would be translated using a monetary–nonmonetary approach and resulting translation adjustments would be made to income.

If the foreign country's cumulative three-year inflation rate is approximately 100% or more, the U.S. dollar should be used as if it were the functional currency. Thus, the resulting translation adjustment would be made to income.

The Statement defines foreign currency transactions as transactions that are denominated in other than an entity's functional currency— for example, a U.S. bank's loan that is payable in Swiss francs. For an entity with a foreign functional currency, these would include any intercompany and other accounts denominated in U.S. dollars. Resulting translation adjustments (now referred to as transaction gains or losses) should be made to income in the period the exchange rate changes unless the gain or loss relates to certain hedging transactions or to certain intercompany accounts of a long-term investment nature.

Forward exchange contracts are grouped under two classifications:

hedging contracts and speculative contracts. Hedging contracts are revalued at the balance sheet date to current spot rates. If the contract hedges an exposed net asset or liability position, accounting for the revaluation adjustment depends upon the nature of the hedged position. If the contract hedges a foreign currency commitment, the revaluation adjustment is deferred and becomes part of the accounting for the hedged commitment.

In general, a U.S. bank is not authorized to hold a speculative position in forward exchange contracts solely in anticipation of realizing a gain from a change in currency value. U.S. banks are authorized to hold forward exchange positions for the business purpose of servicing the needs of their customers. Those positions should be accounted for as speculative contracts, i.e., revalued at the balance sheet date to current forward rates. Revaluation adjustments are made to income.

INCOME TAXES

Foreign income and other taxes are as complex as those in the United States. It is not unusual for local purposes that taxes are recorded on the cash basis. The U.S. practice of recording taxes on the accrual basis (current and deferred) has met with resistance in some countries. For domestic financial reporting purposes, foreign income taxes should be accrued as well as the appropriate U.S. income tax on the foreign income. For U.S. income tax purposes, a determination should be made regarding the treatment of foreign income taxes. Presently they may be treated either as a deduction in the calculation of taxable income or as a direct credit against the U.S. tax liability due (subject to certain limitations). Adequate records (i.e., tax receipts) are necessary if the Internal Revenue Service is to approve of the deductions/credits. Current U.S. accounting literature provides that under certain circumstances U.S. income tax need not be provided. Before a final decision is made on providing for foreign and U.S. taxes on overseas income, a competent tax and accounting advisor should be consulted.

FOREIGN CORRUPT PRACTICES ACT OF 1977

In closing, some reference should be made to the legal aspect of internal control in international banking. The Foreign Corrupt Practices Act of 1977 requires registrants under the Securities Exchange Act of 1934 to "devise and maintain a system of internal accounting controls sufficient to provide reasonable assurances that . . . transactions are executed in accordance with management's general or specific authorization, properly recorded, that access to assets is properly authorized, and that the system is able to identify accounting record differences." While amendments to the Act have been proposed, it still presents serious ramifications concerning the legal liability of a corporation's officers and directors. It is evident that the concept of good internal control is a foremost issue for domestic banks that venture into the area of international banking.

OTHER REFERENCE

Pertinent rules of the U.S. Comptroller of the Currency and other regulators should be consulted by the U.S. bank entering into international banking. The *Comptroller's Manual for National Banks* and the *Comptroller's Handbook for National Bank Examiners* can be especially helpful.

Exhibit 1
Reference List for System of Internal Control

Lending Arrangements Require Authorization of Credit and Terms (Authorization)

System Attributes to Consider

All loan categories:
Independent credit department and/or loan review department reviews adherence to formal loan policies and documentation standards
Credit check performed for each new loan applicant
Separate credit file maintained for each loan independently reviewed for completeness
Adjustments to loans approved by independent loan officers
Lending limits established and monitored
Loans in excess of established limit approved by Board of Directors/Loan Committee
Renewals and extensions authorized by independent loan officers
Adherence to established policies for loans to officers and directors determined by Board of Directors/Loan Committee

Commercial loans (including letters of credit and acceptances):
Credit file regularly updated and reviewed; current financial statements obtained
Country concentration and maturity reports reviewed by Board of Directors/Loan Committee
Maximum country risk limits established based on evaluation of economic and political risk exposure and regularly reviewed

Mortgage loans:
Written appraisals independent of lending officer obtained and reviewed
Periodic independent reappraisals performed
Construction loan disbursements made only after review of evidence of completed work (e.g., architects' certificates, periodic inspections)
Take-out commitments on construction loans reviewed before loan disbursements
Checklists used to monitor completeness of credit file documentation independently reviewed

What Can Go Wrong

Errors:
Loans granted do not conform to loan policy
Loan losses arising from unauthorized credit risks
Overconcentration of assets in geographical locations, types of loans, or maturities
Loans exceed legal lending limits

Irregularities:
Unauthorized loans made for personal benefit of management, directors, employees, or third parties

Exhibit 1 (*continued*)

Fictitious loans
Loans to related parties violate regulations

Accounts affected:
Loans (all categories)
Allowance/provision for loan losses
Customers' acceptance liability
Bankers' acceptances outstanding
Interest and fee income
Unearned income

Lending Arrangements Are Recorded Correctly as to Account, Amount, and Period (Recording)

System Attributes to Consider

All loan categories:
Clerical accuracy of notes independently checked
Notes or subsidiary records and liability ledgers balanced at least monthly to general ledger
Notes marked if paid off or renewed
Subsidiary records posted by employee independent of note tellers
Restructured debt identified by loan officers and reviewed for appropriate accounting treatment by financial officers
Charged-off loans segregated and maintained under separate accounting control
Rejected payments require follow-up by employee independent of cash handling function
Daily summary of loan transactions compared to general ledger entries
Inquiries about loan balances received and investigated by employee independent of cash handling function
Participations purchased and sold maintained in separate ledgers or memorandum accounts; outstanding agreements periodically reconciled

Commercial loans:
Liability ledger maintained for individual commitments and in total; periodically reconciled to notes
Tickler systems used to monitor maturity and interest due
Sequence of prenumbered letters of credit independently checked
Separate general ledger control maintained for letters of credit and acceptances; outstanding commitments periodically reconciled to control account

Mortgage loans:
Detail statement of account balance and activity mailed to mortgagors at least annually; exceptions handled by an employee who is denied access to loans
Detail of commitments to prospective borrowers or sellers of loans reconciled periodically to total
Warehoused loans held for sale separately identified and recorded at the lower of cost or market; valuation periodically reviewed by someone who is independent of mortgage banking operations

What Can Go Wrong

Errors:
Loans not recorded or recorded at wrong amounts, in wrong accounts, or in wrong period

Irregularities:
Misappropriation of loan proceeds or payments
Suppression of uncollectible or delinquent loans through rollover, renewal, or extension

Accounts affected:
Loans (all categories)
Customers' acceptance liability

Exhibit 1 (*continued*)

Bankers' acceptance outstanding
Unearned income
Other real estate

Potentially Uncollectible Accounts Are Promptly Identified, Evaluated, and Provided for (Valuation), and Known Uncollectible Accounts Are Charged Off with Proper Authorization (Authorization, Recording)

System Attributes to Consider

Past-due listing independently prepared and checked for accuracy
Problem loans reviewed by Board of Directors/Loan Committee
Credit files independently reviewed by credit department
Supervisory examination results reviewed and action taken as appropriate
Concentrations in portfolio monitored (e.g., purchased loans, troubled industries, related borrowers)
Charged-off notes segregated from active files; regularly reviewed for possible realization
Adequacy of allowance for loan losses regularly reviewed
Charge-offs reviewed by Board of Directors/Loan Committee
Collateral periodically reviewed and priced to determine adequacy
Collateral reports regularly reviewed to ensure against excessive concentration in types of collateral or industries
Reports indicating extensions, renewals, or other factors which result in a change in status of customer accounts regularly reviewed
Construction loan disbursements reviewed for compliance with disbursement policy

What Can Go Wrong

Errors:
Interest income overstated
Uncollectible accounts not identified or provided for
Irregularities:
Uncollectible accounts (e.g., resulting from fictitious loans or used in lapping scheme) suppressed to prevent charge-off or reversing of recorded interest income
Collectible accounts charged off for the benefit of management, employees, or third parties
Collections on charged-off loans misappropriated or misapplied to loan balances to suppress delinquency problems or charge-offs
Accounts affected:
Loans (all categories)
Allowance/provision for loan losses
Interest income
Accrued interest receivable
Unearned income
Other assets-repossessions

Transactions Involving Real Estate and Other Repossessed Property Are Authorized, Evaluated, and Recorded Correctly as to Account, Amount, and Period (Authorization, Recording, Valuation)

System Attributes to Consider

Independent appraisals obtained from qualified appraisers upon acquisition of title, annually thereafter; appropriate writedowns or additional loss provisions recorded
Disposals handled or approved independent of loan officer
Gains or losses from disposal reviewed by management
Rental income and related expenses approved and recorded in appropriate accounts; accountability for collection of income assigned to responsible employee
Additional investments related to real estate held for resale require senior management approval

Exhibit 1 (*continued*)

What Can Go Wrong

Errors:
  Foreclosed or repossessed assets not reclassified from loans
  Losses on loans, gains/losses on disposal of real estate or other repossessed property
    misclassified, not recorded, or recorded in the wrong period or at the wrong amount
  Rental income not received, not recorded, or recorded at wrong amount or in the
    wrong period
  Rental expenses incurred without authorization
  Loss in value not monitored; not reflected in accounting records

Irregularities:
  Real estate or other repossessed property misappropriated or sold for benefit of man-
    agement, employees, or third parties
  Rental or other income misappropriated
  Foreclosures and repossessions not reported, not reflected in accounting records;
    known losses suppressed

Accounts affected:
  Other real estate and related allowance for loss
  Loans
  Allowance for loan losses
  Gain or loss on sale
  Other income/expense
  Other assets

Interest, Loan Fees, and Other Charges Are Billed to Customers in the Correct Amount (Authorization, Recording)

System Attributes to Consider

Tickler files or similar system by due date used to monitor interest, fee billings
Interest rate changes approved by appropriate committee or loan officer; changes com-
  municated to employees responsible for billings
Payment books, maturity advices, etc. used to control billings
Independent officer approval required for interest rates and/or adjustments on employee
  loans
Clerical accuracy of amounts billed independently checked
Adjustments and credits documented, require officer approval

What Can Go Wrong

Errors:
  Adjustments misclassified, not recorded, or recorded at wrong amounts
  Unbilled or miscalculated interest, fees, or charges
  Incorrect pricing; misstated income

Irregularities:
  Management, employees, or third parties not charged loan fees or receive loans at
    unauthorized reduced rates
  Shortages or misappropriations concealed by adjustments

Accounts affected:
  Interest income
  Loan fee income
  Late charge income
  Accrued interest receivable/other assets
  Unearned income

Interest, Loan Fees, and Other Charges Are Recorded Correctly as to Account, Amount, and Period (Recording)

System Attributes to Consider

Record-keeping independent of billing
Loan fees, interest charges, and billings reconciled to general ledger posting

Exhibit 1 (*continued*)

Prompt processing of billings
Periodic inventories of accrued interest (e.g., accrual proofs)
Budget fluctuations analyzed and investigated
Accrued interest cut-off reviewed by responsible employee
Listing of nonaccrual loans independently reviewed for conformity to bank's nonaccrual
   loan policy
Changes to/from nonaccrual status reviewed by responsible officer

What Can Go Wrong

Errors:
   Revenues misclassified; accrued interest receivable/unearned income or other assets
      not properly stated
   Revenues recorded at wrong amount or in wrong period
Irregularities:
   Billings recorded at less than full amount; customer remits in full and difference
      misappropriated
   Revenue recorded in wrong period to smooth earnings
Accounts affected:
   Interest/other income
   Accrued interest receivable/other assets
   Unearned income

Physical Loss or Misuse of Loan Documents, Collateral, and Repossessed Items Is Prevented or Promptly Detected (Safeguarding, Reconciliation)

System Attributes to Consider

Loans:
   Access to notes restricted to note tellers and accountability established
   Notes for charged-off loans physically controlled independent of note tellers
   Unissued letters of credit physically controlled
   Accounting records maintained independent of note teller
Collateral:
   Collateral register maintained and periodically reviewed
   Negotiable collateral under dual control
   Acceptance/release of collateral receipted; collateral returned promptly to borrower
   Collateral receipts prenumbered; sequence independently checked
   Release or substitution of collateral requires officer approval
   Insurance coverage on real or personal property pledged as collateral regularly re-
      viewed
   Responsible employee follows up nonreceipt of collateral being forwarded to bank
Repossessed items:
   Assets adequately secured, protected against deterioration and other damage
   Assets held by others regularly inspected and inventoried

What Can Go Wrong

Errors:
   Notes, collateral, or repossessed items lost
   Loans outstanding not supported by notes
   Loan and repossession transactions not recorded
Irregularities:
   Management, employees, or third parties able to obtain or alter notes, collateral, or
      repossessed items for personal use or sale
Accounts affected:
   Loans
   Other real estate
   Repossessions
   Other expense (loss of repossessed items or collateral—nonbook item)

Exhibit 1 (*continued*)

Loan Disbursements Are Properly Authorized (Authorization)

System Attributes to Consider

Checks or funds transfer advices prepared and/or reviewed and approved independent of loan officers
Lending limits independently verified before disbursement of proceeds
Loan proceeds not disbursed in cash
Signatures on notes compared to corporate resolutions before disbursement of proceeds
Employees disbursing loan proceeds prohibited from posting and/or reconciling subsidiary records; denied access to general ledger
Delinquency listings regularly prepared by employee independent of disbursing or accepting payments
Disbursements from escrow accounts supported by tax bills, premium notices, etc.; reviewed before issuance

What Can Go Wrong

Errors:
   Disbursement of loan proceeds not authorized or exceeds loan officer's authorized lending limit
   Notes signed by someone other than approved signatory
   Disbursements from escrow accounts exceed authorized amount or cause overdrawn condition
Irregularities:
   Disbursement of proceeds for fictitious loans for benefit of management, employees, or thir parties
   Loan approval procedures intentionally circumvented for the benefit of management, employees, or third parties
   Escrow account funds misappropriated for benefit of management, employees, or third parties
Accounts affected:
   Cash
   Loans
   Deposits
   Other liabilities

Foreign Currency Transactions and Foreign Exchange Futures Contracts Are Authorized and Recorded Correctly as to Account, Amount, and Period, and Timely revaluations Are Made Using Appropriate Rates (Authorization, Recording, Valuation)

System Attributes to Consider

Prenumbered trading slips and contracts used and accounted for
Limits by customer (settlement and total), currency, and maturity periods established and independently reviewed
Excessive customer, currency, or maturity period exposure monitored
Adherence to limits monitored during and at close of trading day; reviewed on test basis by executive independent of trading function
Counterparty confirmation follow-up performed promptly
Independent sources of market rates used for revaluations
Timely calculations made of combined foreign exchange position if more than one trading unit
Exposure of unhedged spot positions or commitments monitored
Rates on cross-currency transactions established and monitored

What Can Go Wrong

Errors:
   Foreign exchange contract not recorded on a timely basis
   Foreign exchange contract or foreign deposit transaction recorded with error in value,

Exhibit 1 (*concluded*)

date, foreign currency amount, or local currency amount; not recorded or recorded in wrong period

Failure to pay on maturity

Failure to note, on a timely basis, counterparty nonperformance of foreign exchange settlement or deposit transaction

Contract posted to wrong customer or currency record

Monthly revaluation not performed, entry not recorded, or recorded at wrong amount

Failure to post local currency equivalent of foreign currency transaction or vice versa

Irregularities:

Speculative positions concealed

Trading for own account

Wrong rates, extensions, etc., used in monthly revaluation to conceal losses

Loss contracts intentionally excluded from monthly revaluations

Local currency equivalent of foreign currency transaction not recorded, or vice versa, to conceal losses or irregularities

Accounts affected:

Foreign currency futures—purchased and sold (and spot if memo accounts are used)

Foreign exchange trading gains and losses

Interest income and interest expense

Revaluation contra accounts

Due-to/due-from accounts in foreign banks and/or foreign currencies

Time deposits received and placed—foreign banks and/or foreign currencies

Other assets and liabilities in foreign currencies

Foreign loan commitments (nonbook item)

43

Fundamental U.S. Taxation of International Banking Operations

JOHN PATRICK CASEY
LEONARD A. LIPSON
Peat, Marwick, Mitchell & Co.

OVERVIEW

International transactions, whether through cross-border loans made by the international department of a U.S. bank's home office or by an Edge Act subsidiary or through loans made by foreign subsidiaries of domestic banks, have taken on more and more importance to U.S. banks in recent years. As this trend is expected to continue on into the future, the international aspects of U.S. taxation assume a greater role in overall tax planning.

Perhaps the single most important area of concern is the U.S. foreign tax-credit mechanism, which generally enables a bank to obtain offsetting relief, dollar for dollar, from its U.S. income tax liability for paid or accrued foreign income taxes. Full utilization of foreign tax credits is important in that a bank must pay, in effect, the higher of the U.S. or foreign income taxes incurred on its foreign-source income. To the extent that a foreign tax payment cannot be used as a credit against U.S. taxes, it represents an additional tax cost, sometimes duplicating taxes paid to the United States on the same item of income.

Assuming that the foreign taxes in question constitute creditable foreign income taxes, the foreign tax-credit mechanism involves a three-step process beginning with identification of the sources of a bank's gross income, followed by allocation and apportionment of expenses to arrive at foreign source taxable income, and ending with computation of the foreign tax-credit limitation. This chapter first describes the foreign tax-credit provisions and then examines the elements making up the limitation rules. It then goes on to comment on other areas of interest, including blocked income, branch translations, controlled foreign corporations, the minimum tax, and employees working abroad.

THE FOREIGN TAX CREDIT

Direct Foreign Tax Credit

In order to alleviate double taxation arising from the taxation of income in two separate countries, the U.S. taxation system contains the foreign tax-credit mechanism.[1] A U.S. bank can claim a foreign tax credit by calculating its U.S. tax liability on total income, domestic plus foreign, and then crediting against the U.S. tax liability, any foreign income taxes it has incurred, subject to certain limitations. Generally, the calculation of the maximum foreign tax credit available in a tax year uses the following formula:[2]

$$\frac{\text{Foreign-source taxable income}}{\text{Entire taxable income}} \times \frac{\text{U.S. tax liability}}{\text{on total income}} = \frac{\text{Foreign tax}}{\text{credit limitation}}$$

This formula is applied on a worldwide income basis rather than by considering individual countries separately.

Foreign income taxes incurred on foreign source income may be higher than the U.S. taxes on this foreign income. Thus, if there were no limitation, the foreign tax credit would be able to offset not only U.S. tax on foreign-source income, but also U.S. tax on domestic-source income. Section 904 prevents this spillover generally by limiting the credit in any one year to a proportion of the total U.S. tax liability as reflected by the formula above. Foreign income taxes paid or accrued in excess of the limitation may be carried back two years and forward five years, subject to the appropriate limitation in each year.[3] Under no circumstances may the credit exceed the amount of foreign income taxes paid or accrued.[4]

The amount of foreign income taxes which may be taken as a credit may differ depending on the bank's method of accounting for foreign income taxes. A bank using the cash receipts and disbursements method of accounting would translate its foreign taxes paid into U.S. dollars at the rate of exchange in effect at the time it actually pays its foreign tax liability. An accrual basis bank, on the other hand, would use the rate in effect on the last day of its taxable year. While this initial determination may produce differing amounts of foreign tax

---

[1] IRC §§901 through 908.

[2] IRC §904(a).

[3] IRC §904(c).

[4] *H. H. Robertson, Inc.* v. *Commissioner,* 59 TC 53 (1972), *aff'd without opinion,* 500 F.2d 1399 (3rd Cir. 1974).

credits depending on the method of accounting used, an accrual basis bank must notify the commissioner if the rate of exchange at the time of actual payment differs from the rate on the accrual date.[5] Pursuant to Section 905(c), the commissioner then redetermines the allowable amount of creditable foreign taxes and adjusts the bank's tax liability accordingly.[6] The regulations provide a cash method bank with the ability to elect to treat its foreign taxes paid on an accrual basis for foreign tax-credit purposes.[7]

A bank's first steps are identifying foreign-source taxable income and computing its foreign tax-credit limitation. Its next step is to identify those foreign taxes which it has paid that qualify for credit. Not all foreign taxes are creditable. Generally, only those foreign taxes that are considered income taxes are available for foreign tax-credit relief.[8] The exception to this general rule is that certain foreign taxes which are imposed "in lieu" of foreign income taxes are also creditable.[9] Those foreign taxes which are not creditable may be deducted by the bank.[10] If a bank chooses to take a foreign tax credit for its foreign income taxes paid or accrued, it may not, in that same year, use as a credit only a part of its creditable foreign income taxes and deduct a part. The creditable foreign income taxes must either all be used as a foreign tax credit or all be used as a deduction.[11]

Indirect Foreign Tax Credit

In situations where loans are made by a U.S. bank through a foreign subsidiary, the foreign tax-credit mechanism works in an indirect manner. Foreign taxes paid by a foreign subsidiary may be used as a credit by its U.S. parent bank upon the repatriation of the subsidiary's profits in the form of a dividend.[12] The U.S. bank may treat as a foreign tax paid by itself, an amount computed according to the following formula:[13]

$$\frac{\text{Dividends}}{\text{Earnings and profits}} \times \frac{\text{Subsidiary's foreign}}{\text{taxes paid or accrued}} = \frac{\text{Indirect foreign taxes}}{\text{deemed paid by U.S. parent}}$$

---

[5] IRC §905(c).

[6] See also IRC §6689 providing the possibility of a civil penalty for failure to make the required notification.

[7] IRC §905(a).

[8] IRC §901(a).

[9] IRC §903.

[10] IRC §164.

[11] IRC §275(a)(4).

[12] IRC §902.

[13] IRC §902(a).

This computation is performed on a year-by-year basis, with the most recently accumulated earnings and profits deemed to have been paid out as dividends first.[14] The foreign taxes deemed paid in the hands of the U.S. bank are then subject, along with the U.S. bank's directly paid foreign taxes, to the foreign tax credit limitation of Section 904. The foreign taxes which are subject to these deemed paid rules must also qualify as creditable foreign income taxes or "in lieu" foreign taxes. In addition, the foreign taxes deemed paid by the U.S. parent corporation are treated as an additional dividend paid to the U.S. corporation by its subsidiary.[15]

Creditable Foreign Income Taxes

The question of what foreign income taxes are creditable has received considerable attention in recent years, culminating with the Treasury Department's release of temporary and proposed regulations in November 1980.[16] These regulations provide that the requirements which must be satisfied in order for a foreign charge to be considered as an income tax, creditable dollar for dollar against U.S. income tax liability, include that the charge: (1) not be compensation for a specific economic benefit; (2) be based on realized net income; and (3) follow reasonable rules of taxing jurisdiction.[17]

Economic Benefit. Generally, a foreign charge is not compensation for a specific economic benefit if the payor or a related party receives no specific economic benefit in return for payment of the charge.[18] The charge is presumed to be compensation for a specific economic benefit if any such benefit is received.[19] This presumption may be rebutted if the same charge is paid by persons not receiving benefits, the recipient of the benefit pays only an amount which is similar in amount to an income tax paid by persons not receiving benefits, or a factual showing is made that no significant part of the charge is for an economic benefit.[20]

Realized Net Income. The realized net income requirement includes the following three items: (1) realization; (2) imposition on gross receipts; and (3) imposition on net income.[21] Each concept attempts to reconcile substantially different tax systems with the Internal Revenue Code. The realization requirement is generally satisfied by a for-

---

[14] IRC §902(c).

[15] IRC §78.

[16] Treasury Decision 7739, November 12, 1980.

[17] Temp. Reg. §4.901–2(a)(1).

[18] Temp. Reg. §4.901–2(a)(1).

[19] Temp. Reg. §4.901–2(b)(1).

[20] Temp. Reg. §4.901–2(b)(2).

[21] Temp. Reg. §4.901–2(c).

eign charge that is imposed upon the occurrence of an event which would also result in the realization of income under the Code, or on the occurrence of any subsequent event.[22] The gross receipts requirement generally is met if the foreign charge is imposed on the basis of actual gross receipts.[23] In cases where gross receipts may not be clearly reflected, a formulary base is permitted if it is designed to produce, and does in fact produce, an amount approximately equal to or less than the fair market value of actual gross receipts. The net income requirement is generally met when gross receipts are reduced by actual costs and capital expenditures attributable under reasonable principles to the gross receipts. In cases where costs may not otherwise be clearly reflected, a formulary method, designed to approximate or exceed actual costs and capital expenditures, is permitted.[24]

The regulations also incorporate a special rule permitting persons, subject to the net income tax of a foreign country, to periodically elect to compute a portion of their tax base under a formulary method and still have the charge meet the gross receipts and net income requirements.[25] This election is particularly relevant in the case of negotiated tax arrangements applied to headquarters and management companies in certain foreign countries and is presumably based on the theory that a person would always elect to pay the lesser of the normal tax on net income or the formulary substitute. Special rules governing the payment or accrual of foreign taxes protect the U.S. government in the situation where a taxpayer chooses to pay the higher of the two amounts.[26]

Of particular interest to banks is the regulation's exception from the net income requirement for foreign charges on items of gross income that generally constitute fixed or determinable annual or periodical income under Sections 871(a) and 881(a), provided that the foreign law makes a reasonable distinction between income taxed on a gross basis and income taxed on a net basis. The reasonable distinction must be based upon a standard which looks to the contacts of the income recipient with the foreign country or looks at the connection between the activities or assets generating the income and the foreign country.[27] Thus, certain income, such as interest, may be taxed on a gross basis by a foreign country and not be disqualified as a creditable income tax, depending upon the basis the foreign country utilizes to differentiate between gross and net taxation.

---

[22] Temp. Reg. §4.901–2(c)(2).
[23] Temp. Reg. §4.901–2(c)(3).
[24] Temp. Reg. §4.901–2(c)(4)(i).
[25] Temp. Reg. §4.901–2(c)(4)(ii).
[26] Temp. Reg. §4.901–2(f).
[27] Temp. Reg. §4.901–2(c)(4)(iii).

Taxing Jurisdiction. The final element of a creditable foreign income tax is that the foreign country, in imposing its tax, uses reasonable rules of taxing jurisdiction. This concept is defined in the regulations in a negative rather than in a positive manner. The regulations note that a "soak-up tax," which is a foreign charge imposed only with relation to the availability of a tax credit in the taxpayer's home country for the charge, is not viewed as a foreign charge based on reasonable rules of taxing jurisdiction.[28]

"In Lieu" Foreign Taxes

"In lieu" taxes are those foreign taxes, generally not satisfying the above requirements, which are treated as having been paid instead of creditable foreign income taxes.[29] In order to qualify as an "in lieu" tax, the following conditions must be satisfied: (1) the charge must not be compensation for a specific economic benefit; (2) the charge must be in substitution for a generally imposed income tax; (3) the charge must be comparable in amount to the income tax otherwise generally imposed; and (4) the charge must follow reasonable rules of taxing jurisdiction.[30] The first and last elements are identical to those applicable to the definition of a creditable foreign income tax. The substitution requirement is generally met if the charge was clearly intended as a substitute for a generally imposed income tax and, in fact, operates as such.[31] A bank may be subject to both a creditable income tax and a qualifying "in lieu" charge as long as the income subject to each charge does not overlap. The comparability requirement is met unless it is reasonably clear that foreign law is structured or operates to cause the "in lieu" charge to be significantly greater over time than the otherwise applicable income tax.[32] A key to this element of qualification is measurement over time rather than on a year-by-year basis.

Limitations on Use

While the foreign tax credit is generally allowed on an overall income basis, rather than on a country-by-country basis, limitations are applied separately to certain distinct classes of income. There are three such classes to which the rule of Section 904(a) is applied.[33] Class number (1) is interest income other than interest: (*a*) derived in a transaction

---

[28] Temp. Reg. §4.901–2(a)(1)(iii).

[29] IRC §903.

[30] Temp. Reg. §4.903–1(a).

[31] Temp. Reg. §4.903–1(b).

[32] Temp. Reg. §4.903–1(c).

[33] IRC §904(d).

directly related to the active conduct of a business in a foreign country or U.S. possession; (*b*) derived in the conduct of a banking, financing, or similar business; (*c*) received from a corporation in which a 10 percent direct or indirect ownership position is maintained; or (*d*) received on obligations acquired from the disposition of a business actively conducted in a foreign country or U.S. possession or on obligations of a corporation in which the stock ownership position was at least 10 percent.[34]

Class number (2) includes dividends from a DISC (Domestic International Sales Corporation) or former DISC to the extent treated as foreign source income.[35] Class number (3) is composed of all income other than that described in Classes (1) and (2).[36]

An additional type of limitation is imposed in conjunction with the international boycott rules. To the extent that a bank or a member of the bank's controlled group (as defined) participates in or cooperates with an international boycott, the allowable foreign tax credit is reduced by an appropriate factor.[37] Other rules exist dealing with the computation of foreign-source taxable income in the case of capital gains income,[38] with the conversion of foreign-source income into U.S.-source income where years of overall foreign losses are followed by years of profitable operations,[39] and with similar conversion on certain sales of personal proberty.[40]

SOURCE OF INCOME

The starting point in determining the foreign tax-credit limitation is the source of income rules, which are found in Sections 861 through 863. The most important application of these rules is in the determination of a bank's foreign tax-credit limitation.[41] Another major use of these rules for a bank concerns its liability to withhold U.S. tax on payments of U.S.-source income to nonresident alien individuals and foreign corporations.[42]

The source rules are definitional in nature and rely on operative sections of the Code, such as Section 904, in order to have an impact on a bank's tax liability. An understanding of the statutory construction of the three relevant sections is helpful in organizing the body of regula-

---

[34] IRC §§904(d)(1)(A) and (d)(2).
[35] IRC §904(d)(1)(B).
[36] IRC §904(d)(1)(C).
[37] IRC §§908 and 999.
[38] IRC §904(b).
[39] IRC §904(f).
[40] IRC §904(b).
[41] IRC §904.
[42] IRC §§1441 and 1442.

tions, rulings, and case law in this area. In the lead section (Section 861), seven common types of income are identified, and the circumstances under which each of these items are considered to have a U.S. source are detailed. The companion section (Section 862) identifies the same seven types of income and uses a "mirror" approach, in that if the item of income is not considered to have a U.S. source by the lead section, it automatically is considered to have a foreign source. Substantive regulations dealing with both of these sections are promulgated under the lead section only.[43] Authority to issue regulations defining the source of all other types of income, other than the seven items covered in Sections 861 and 862, was given to the IRS by Section 863. Rather than issuing extensive regulations on other items of gross income, the IRS has generally taken the approach of issuing rulings on an ad hoc basis. The discussion below first covers the seven types of income identified in Sections 861 and 862, and then items treated by Section 863, rulings and case law applicable to certain other types of income which are important to banks, such as letter-of-credit commissions and guarantee fees.

Interest Income

Interest income from a resident of the United States on a bond, note, or other interest-bearing obligation is treated as U.S.-source income.[44] All other interest income is generally considered to have a foreign source.[45] (See below for a series of specific exceptions to this general rule.) The first key to the general definition is the residence of the obligor. The term *resident of the United States* is defined broadly for this purpose as including U.S. corporations, individuals who had a U.S. residence at the time the interest was paid, partnerships (U.S. and foreign), and foreign corporations which at any time during their taxable year are engaged in trade or business in the United States.[46] Thus, by use of a broad definition, the category of U.S. residents is larger than one would initially anticipate. Although the following entities are not technically defined as U.S. residents, interest income received from them also has a U.S. source: the United States or any agency or instrumentality thereof (other than a possession of the United States), a state or any political subdivision thereof, and the District of Columbia.[47] Another key to understanding the general definition is that it is the residence of the obligor that is controlling and not

---

[43] Reg. §§1.861–1 through 1.861–9.

[44] IRC §861(a)(1).

[45] IRC §862(a)(1).

[46] Reg §1.861–2(a)(2).

[47] Reg. §1.861–2(a)(1).

that of the payor of the interest. For example, if interest is paid on an obligation of a U.S. resident by a nonresident in his capacity as a guarantor, the interest is treated as U.S.-source income.[48] The method by which, or the place where, payment of the interest is made is also immaterial in determining the source of interest income.

Interest paid on deposits by persons carrying on a U.S. banking business, received by a nonresident alien individual or a foreign corporation, is considered foreign-source income if the interest is not effectively connected with the conduct of a U.S. trade or business by the recipient.[49] This first exception to the general source rule was designed to attract funds to the United States for balance-of-payment purposes, and provides a special advantage to banks and certain other financial organizations (savings and loan institutions or other similar associations and insurance companies) in that, currently, they are the only U.S. entities that have access to this source of funds and that can pay interest to foreign persons free of U.S. withholding tax (with the exception of certain domestic corporations discussed below and certain entities involved in a transaction governed by an income tax treaty between the United States and a foreign country). This exemption from U.S. withholding tax, derived from the foreign-source characterization of the interest, makes these deposits attractive to foreign investors. Congress has been reviewing recently the withholding tax provisions for all types of interest obligations, as well as for other types of investments, but has not as yet reached a comprehensive conclusion regarding U.S. tax policy affecting these types of investments. The U.S. withholding tax is currently imposed at the rate of 30 percent on the gross amount of U.S.-source interest (and certain other types of passive income) paid to nonresident alien individuals (Section 871(a)) and foreign corporations (Section 881(a)). The obligation to withhold U.S. tax is imposed on the payor (e.g., a U.S. bank) of the income to the foreign person (Sections 1441 and 1442). It should be noted that the U.S. withholding tax may be reduced or eliminated by a number of tax treaties to which the United States is a party.[50] The approach of the sourcing provisions of the Code in those instances where it has been determined to exempt a particular type of income (e.g., interest) from withholding tax, which would be classified as U.S.-source income under the general rule, is to reclassify that income as foreign source. The U.S. withholding tax applies only to U.S.-source income.[51] This approach has made the source rules more cumbersome than they would otherwise be if a direct ex-

---

[48] Reg. §1.861–2(a)(5).
[49] IRC §861(a)(1)(A).
[50] IRC §894(a); e.g., U.S.:-U.K. Income Tax Convention, Article 11.
[51] IRC §§1441 and 1442.

emption were granted to the foreign investors, similar to the approach taken in several income tax treaties.[52]

Interest income received from a U.S. corporation, which derived less than 20 percent of its gross income from U.S. sources, is considered to have a foreign source.[53] Corporations covered by this second exception to the general source rule are commonly referred to as "80/20 corporations." A typical use of these special entity corporations is to raise funds from foreign persons and to relend or contribute these funds to the capital of the taxpayer's foreign affiliates. Corporations used for this purpose are also known as "International Finance Subsidiaries." Since their income consists principally of foreign-source interest and dividends from their foreign affiliates, they meet the requirements of this exception and are able to pay interest income to their foreign creditors free of any U.S. withholding tax. This exception also applies to interest received from a resident alien individual who derived less than 20 percent of his gross income from U.S. sources. For purposes of determining whether a corporation or individual meets the "less than 20 percent" gross income test, the relevant period is the three taxable years (or part thereof) preceding the year of the interest payment. If the corporation or individual had no gross income during this test period, then the determination is made with respect to the current taxable year (i.e., the year of payment of the interest).[54]

Foreign corporations which at any time during their taxable year are engaged in trade or business in the United States are considered U.S. residents, and thus, under the general source rule, interest paid by these foreign corporations is treated as U.S. source income subject to U.S. withholding tax when paid to foreign persons. In order to alleviate the broad impact of the general rule, especially in de minimus situations, another exception has been introduced into the statute. If a foreign corporation, which has otherwise been classified as a U.S. resident, has less than 50 percent of its gross income effectively connected with the conduct of a trade or business within the United States, then interest paid by the foreign corporation is treated as foreign-source income.[55] For purposes of determining whether the "less than 50 percent" test has been met, the same time period used for 80/20 corporations, discussed above, are used. If the foreign corporation has 50 percent or more of its gross income effectively connected with its U.S. trade or business, then a proportionate part of the interest which it pays is considered U.S. source and the balance is foreign source.[56]

---

[52] E.g., U.S.-Netherlands Income Tax Convention, as extended to the Netherlands Antilles, Article VIII.

[53] IRC §861(a)(1)(B).

[54] IRC §861(d).

[55] IRC §861(a)(1)(C).

[56] IRC §861(a)(1)(D).

The proportionate part which is considered U.S. source is based on the ratio of the foreign corporation's gross income effectively connected to its U.S. trade or business to its worldwide gross income. It should be noted that this exception to the source rule for foreign corporations does not apply to interest paid by U.S. banking branches of foreign corporations. The rationale for excluding foreign banks from this exception is to keep these banks in parity with U.S. banks under similar circumstances.

Another exception peculiar to the banking industry is that interest paid on deposits with a foreign branch of a U.S. bank or savings and loan association is considered foreign-source income.[57] This exception applies regardless of the status of the recipient and is also designed to help U.S. banks maintain parity with foreign banks under similar circumstances.

Dividends

Dividends received from a domestic corporation are treated under the general rule as U.S.-source income.[58] There are a series of exceptions to the general rule which are similar in purpose to the exceptions under the interest rule. The first exception relates to dividends received from 80/20 corporations (i.e., U.S. corporations which derive less than 20 percent of their gross income from U.S. sources) and characterizes these dividends as foreign source.[59] A closely related exception applies to dividends received from "possessions corporations" (i.e., U.S. corporations engaged in business within a possession of the U.S. and which have an election in effect under Section 936), which are also characterized as foreign source.[60] Another special type of U.S. corporation whose dividends (both deemed and actual) are generally treated as foreign source income (with limited exceptions not discussed here) is a Domestic International Sales Corporation.[61]

Dividends received from a foreign corporation are considered foreign source income provided that less than 50 percent of the foreign corporation's gross income was effectively connected with the conduct of a U.S. trade or business.[62] This exception is identical to the exception for interest paid by a foreign corporation and also provides that a proportionate part of dividends paid by a foreign corporation is considered to have a U.S. source in those instances where 50 percent or more of the foreign corporation's gross income is effectively connected

---

[57] IRC §861(a)(1)(F).

[58] IRC §861(a)(2)(A).

[59] Reg. §1.861–3(a)(2).

[60] IRC §861(a)(2)(A).

[61] IRC §861(a)(2)(D).

[62] IRC §861(a)(2)(B).

to its U.S. trade or business. The ratio used to determine the amount of U.S.-source dividend income is the ratio of gross income effectively connected to a U.S. trade or business to gross income from all sources. Dividends which are characterized as having a U.S. source generally are eligible for the dividends received deductions under Section 245.

Personal-Services Income

Personal-services income takes on the source of the location where the services are performed. Thus, compensation for services performed in the United States has a domestic source.[63] The statute contains a de minimus rule for nonresident alien individuals temporarily present in the U.S. in that if they are not present in the United States for more than 90 days during the taxable year, their compensation for the U.S. services does not exceed $3,000, and they are working for a foreign person not engaged in a U.S. trade or business or for a foreign business office of a U.S. person, then their compensation is considered foreign-source income.[64]

Rental and Royalty Income

Rental and royalty income takes on the source of the location of the property or, in the case of intangible property (e.g., patents, copyrights, trademarks, etc.), the location of the use or right to use the property.[65] A special rule applies to rental income derived from the lease of a craft (i.e., vessel, aircraft, or spacecraft) under which the income is treated as U.S. source if the craft qualifies for the investment tax credit, the craft is leased to a U.S. person, and the craft is manufactured or constructed in the United States.[66] Once this rule applies to a craft, it applies in all subsequent years in which the taxpayer owns the craft, even if it is leased to a foreign person.[67] All income or loss, including gains from the sale of the craft is also U.S. source.[68] Another special rule applies to rental income from the rental of rolling stock to railroads.[69] The rental income is considered to be U.S. source if the rolling stock is not used outside the United States, except on a temporary basis not expected to exceed 90 days. The de minimus rule is applicable only to rolling stock and does not have wider application.

[63] IRC §861(a)(3).
[64] IRC §861(a)(3)(A), (B), and (C).
[65] IRC §861(a)(4).
[66] IRC §861(e).
[67] Reg. §1.861–9(d).
[68] Reg. §1.861–9(d).
[69] IRC §861(f).

Gain from the sale of the rolling stock is also treated as having a U.S. source.

Gain from the Disposition of a U.S. Real Property Interest

Gain from the disposition of a U.S. real property interest results in U.S.-source income.[70] A U.S. real property interest includes any interest in real property located in the United States or the Virgin Islands, as well as any interest, other than solely as a creditor, in any U.S. corporation that qualifies as a "United States real property holding corporation."[71] The location of real property determines the source of income resulting from its sale.

Gains from the Sale or Exchange of Personal Property

Gains from the sale or exchange of personal property which has been purchased outside the United States and sold within the United States are considered U.S.-source income.[72] The country in which the personal property is sold determines the source of the income.[73] For this purpose, the place where title passes to the buyer generally determines the country in which the property is sold.[74] This source rule is limited to transactions involving a purchase and sale and does not apply to situations involving the sale of property manufactured by the seller.[75]

Underwriting Income

Underwriting income derived from the insurance of U.S. risks is considered U.S. source-income.[76] A U.S. risk includes property in the United States or liability arising out of activity in connection with the lives or health of residents in the United States.[77] The location of the risk determines the source of income.

Other

The seven types of income discussed above are the only items of income which have been assigned a source by the Code. To date,

---

[70] IRC §861(a)(5).
[71] IRC §897(c).
[72] IRC §861(a)(6).
[73] Reg. §1.861–7(a).
[74] Reg. §1.861–7(c).
[75] Reg. §1.861–7(d).
[76] IRC §861(a)(7).
[77] IRC §953(a).

the Service has issued regulations under the authority of Section 863(a) only for income derived from natural resources. No other regulations have been issued pursuant to the authority given to the secretary under Section 863(a). Section 863(b) provides special rules dealing with three specific activities (manufacturing, transportation and other services, and purchase of personal property within a possession and its sale within the United States) which are considered to result in income partly from sources within and partly from sources without the United States and provides rules for the attribution of the taxable income from these activities to U.S. and foreign sources.

Apart from the specific items of income identified by the statute and regulations, a body of case law and rulings have dealt with the source of other items of income on an ad hoc basis. A common element of these decisions has been the effort to equate the item of income under consideration with one of the items specifically covered by the statute. For example, guarantee fees earned by a domestic corporation from guaranteeing loans obtained by its foreign subsidiaries were held to be similar to compensation for services, and the services were deemed to have been performed at the location of the guarantee, thus giving rise to foreign-source income.[78] Also, confirmation and acceptance commissions related to export letters of credit were sourced by analogy to interest and were held to be foreign source where the obligors were foreign banks.[79] Negotiation commissions related to letters of credit are sourced under the rules for personal services income.[80] Other examples include decisions on the source of alimony payments,[81] puzzle contest prizes,[82] insurance proceeds,[83] and income from a covenant not to compete.[84]

ALLOCATION AND APPORTIONMENT OF DEDUCTIONS

The foreign tax burden of U.S. banks has increased significantly in recent years and the need to use the foreign tax credit system effectively has accordingly become more urgent. As explained in greater detail in a separate section, the foreign tax credit allows U.S. banks to absorb foreign income taxes by offsetting U.S. income tax dollar for dollar. However, this offset is limited to the extent to which the bank incurred U.S. income tax on its foreign-source taxable income. Thus, a key feature in determining the availability of foreign income

---

[78] LTR 7822005.
[79] *Bank of America* v. *United States*, No. 402–71 (Ct.Cl. June 2, 1982).
[80] *Bank of America* v. *United States*, No. 402–71 (Ct.Cl. June 2, 1982).
[81] *Trust of Welsh* v *Commissioner*, 16 TC 1398 (1951).
[82] Rev. Rul. 66–291, 1966–2 CB 279.
[83] Rev. Rul. 70–304, 1970–1 CB 163.
[84] *Korfund Co., Inc.* v. *Commissioner*, 1 TC 1180 (1944).

taxes as a credit against U.S. income taxes is the determination of foreign-source taxable income.

General Concepts

For taxable years beginning on or after January 1, 1977, the regulations provide rules for allocation and apportionment of deductions to gross income in order to determine taxable income from sources within and without the United States.[85] The expenses, losses, and other deductions of a bank are considered as part of a two-step procedure. The first step is to allocate all deductions, which effectively is the identification of each deduction with a particular class of gross income. The second step, the apportionment of the deduction as allocated, is to determine whether the deductions within each class relate to foreign-source or U.S.-source gross income.

The regulation generally requires that a factual relationship between deductions and income be relied upon and that only when this is not possible should mechanical formulas be applied in allocating and apportioning deductions.[86] Determining the "class of gross income" is the first step in the two-step allocation/apportionment procedure used to identify a deduction with income. A class of gross income does not necessarily mean an item of gross income, as defined in Section 61.[87] On the contrary, a class of gross income generally includes a number of items listed in Section 61. A class of gross income can consist of all income from a particular line of business of a bank where that line of business gives rise to a cluster of individual items of gross income as defined in Section 61. For example, a class of gross income can include only interest received by the bank as a result of its investments. However, that class of gross income can include not only interest but in addition, include gains from the sale or exchange of securities which gave rise to that interest, recognizing the relationship between these two types of income and the particular line of business in which the bank is engaged.

As contrasted with the definition of the class of gross income, the "statutory" and "residual" groupings are definitions whose meaning is more readily understood.[88] For purposes of this chapter, the residual and statutory groupings are the terms used to refer to U.S.-source gross income and foreign-source gross income, respectively. In determining the foreign tax-credit limitation, these definitions relate to each class of gross income. Once a class of gross income is determined and an allocation of deductions to each class has been made, the next step

---

[85] Reg. §1.861–8.
[86] Reg. §1.861–8(b)(1).
[87] Reg. §1.861–8(a)(3).
[88] Reg. §1.861–8(a)(4).

is to apportion the allocated deductions between the statutory grouping and the residual grouping within that particular class.

In connection with allocation of deductions to a class of gross income, even though the factual relationship determines whether or not a deduction is allocable to a certain class of income, there may in fact be no items of gross income in the class.[89] The regulation intends that though a deduction may be related to certain activities of the taxpayer (and, therefore, related to a class of gross income), those activities in fact may not have given rise to an actual item of gross income in a particular taxable year. Furthermore, a class of gross income may include excluded income such that after the allocation, a negative amount may be created by the excess of the deduction allocated over the excluded income.

A related rule of allocation is that a deduction is allocated to the class of gross income to which it relates without regard to the taxable year in which it is received or accrued.[90] Deductions in the current taxable year can be allocated to a class of gross income, even though the actual gross income was not generated from that class in the current year if it has been received from that class in a prior year or could be expected to be received in the future. A deduction is considered related to a class of gross income (and allocable thereto) if it is incurred as a result of an activity, or in connection with property, from which the class of gross income is derived.[91] Essentially, the allocation is a two-step procedure itself, identifying (*a*) expenses with activity or property and (*b*) activity or property with the income involved.

In apportioning a deduction, which has previously been allocated to a class of gross income, to particular items of gross income in the statutory grouping, the regulation sets out a series of bases which should be considered.[92] These include:

Comparison of units sold attributable to the statutory and residual grouping.

Comparison of the amount of gross sales and receipts.

Comparison of assets.

Comparison of profit contribution.

Comparison of expenses incurred, salary paid, space utilized, or time spent attributable to the activities or property giving rise to the class of gross income.

Comparison of the amount of gross income in the statutory grouping with the amount in the residual grouping.

---

[89] Reg. §1.861–8(d).
[90] Reg. §1.861–8(b)(1).
[91] Reg. §1.861–8(b)(2).
[92] Reg. §1.861–8(c)(1).

Many of the bases, such as the asset method, do not require that there be any gross income from the particular class in order for an apportionment to be made. The regulation intends that if a more precise method for apportionment is not presented by the taxpayer, then a formula approach should be used.[93]

The general methods of allocation and apportionment prescribed by the regulation are designed to give the bank flexibility in selecting the most reasonable method of matching items of expense with related income. However, with respect to certain items of expense, the regulation prescribes specific rules of allocation and apportionment that limits the bank's discretion. For banks, the most important of the expenses for which specific guidance is given is interest. The specific rules of the regulation as they apply to interest and certain other expenses that are important to banks are commented on below.

Interest Expense

Because interest represents such a significant deduction in the tax return of banks claiming foreign tax credits, special rules have been written regarding allocation and apportionment of interest expense deductions in the calculation of the foreign tax-credit limitation. The method of allocation and apportionment of interest expense is based on the theory that money is fungible (i.e., that all activities and property require funds and that management has a great deal of flexibility as to the source and use of funds) and that interest expense is attributable to all activities and properties regardless of any specific purpose for incurring an obligation on which interest is paid.[94]

The general rule is that interest is considered to be related to all income-producing activities and properties of the taxpayer.[95] Thus, it is allocable to all gross income which the activities and properties of the taxpayer presently generate, have generated, or could reasonably expect to generate. This general rule uses the concept of a span of taxable years, as opposed to allocation rules relating to only the current taxable year. Generally, the regulations provide that interest cannot be specifically identified with particular classes of gross income, and therefore is to be related to all classes of income.[96] Due to the simplicity of the allocation rules, more detailed rules are provided with regard to apportionment of the interest expense deduction.

Together with the underlying concept that money is fungible, the regulations are very strict in permitting interest expense to be allocable only to specific property. Essentially, the regulations provide that an

---

[93] Reg. §1.861–8(c)(1).
[94] Reg. §1.861–8(e)(2)(i).
[95] Reg. §1.861–8(e)(2)(i).
[96] Reg. §1.861–8(e)(2)(ii).

interest deduction is considered related solely to a class of gross income which the specific property generates if all of the following requirements are met:[97]

The indebtedness on which the interest was paid was specifically incurred for the purpose of purchasing or maintaining the specific property.

The proceeds of the borrowing were actually applied to the specified property.

The creditor can look only to the specific property (or any lease or other interest therein) as security for payment for the principal and interest of the loan.

It may be reasonably assumed that the return (cash flow) from the property will be sufficient to fulfill the terms and conditions of the loan agreement with respect to the amount and timing of payment of principal and interest.

There are restrictions in the loan agreement on a disposal or use of the property consistent with assumptions described above.

The regulations go on to state that the above facts and circumstances must be present in substance as well as in form. Taxpayers are not permitted to make a specific allocation of interest expense to particular property where the motive for structuring a transaction is without economic significance.[98]

The regulations indicate that an asset method is generally used for apportioning the interest deduction among items of foreign and U.S.-source gross income.[99] Interest expense is considered to relate more closely to the amount of capital utilized in an activity (property) than to the gross income generated from the activity or property. Indebtedness permits the taxpayer to acquire or retain different types of assets which may produce substantially different yields of gross income in relation to their value. For that reason, an apportionment of the interest deduction solely on a gross income basis is considered unreasonable by the regulations.

The apportionment of interest expense must initially be calculated using the "asset method." Should it be decided that an optional gross income method is preferable, then a bank may use the preferred method, subject to certain limitations.[100] The formula used for apportioning interest expense under the asset method is as follows:[101]

---

[97] Reg. §1.861–8(e)(2)(iv).

[98] Reg. §1.861–8(e)(2)(iv).

[99] Reg. §1.861–8(e)(2)(v).

[100] Reg. §1.861–8(e)(2)(vi).

[101] Reg. §1.861–8(g) Ex. (1).

$$\frac{\text{Average value of foreign assets}}{\text{Average value of total assets}} \times \text{Interest expense}$$

To determine the amount of interest which is to be apportioned to foreign-source gross income, a determination has to be made as to which of the bank's assets are related to foreign and which to U.S. operations. In this determination, the bank is to utilize only the assets on its balance sheet. On a consolidated tax return, the separate balance sheets of each company are to be used and not the aggregate of all of the assets of the consolidated return.[102] The "source" of assets for this purpose is to be determined by looking to the source of the income which the assets might normally be expected to generate.[103]

The apportionment of the interest deduction is generally done on the basis of "tax book value."[104] While the regulations indicate that the bank can use the fair market value of assets, very few banks wish to go through the time and expense of asset valuations and rely basically on tax book value. The term *tax book value* is defined as "original cost for tax purposes less depreciation allowed for tax purposes."[105] The determination of U.S. and foreign assets for interest expense apportionment must be made by using an average of those assets at the beginning and end of the taxable year. A simple average of these two numbers will suffice except where substantial distortion of asset values follows from using one of these dates. In cases where a substantial distortion would result, an appropriate method satisfactory to the commissioner must be used.[106] One possible satisfactory method may be a monthly weighted average of the assets rather than the simple average described above. Assuming that a simple average of the beginning- and end-of-year assets can be used, these asset balances are segregated between foreign and domestic assets, using the source of the income which those assets normally generate as the basis for segregation.

An optional method for apportioning interest expense based on gross income provided by the regulations utilizes the following formula:[107]

$$\frac{\text{Gross foreign-source income}}{\text{Gross worldwide income}} \times \text{Interest expense}$$

The election to use the optional gross income method can be made for any taxable year. That is, if it provides a better result in 1981, that method may be used. If the asset method produces a better result in 1982, a bank is not required to use the optional gross income method

102 Rev. Rul. 72–281, 1972–1 CB 285.

103 Reg. §§1.861–8(b)(2); 1.861–8(e)(2)(iv).

104 Reg. §1.861–8(e)(2)(v).

105 Reg. §1.861–8(e)(2)(v).

106 Reg. §1.861–8(e)(2)(v).

107 Reg. §1.861–8(e)(2)(vi).

that year. The most important condition for using the optional gross income method is that it produce an apportionment of interest expense to foreign-source gross income which is at least 50 percent of the amount that would have been apportioned using the asset method.[108] Thus, while the optional gross income method may give some relief, the best relief it can give can only be an amount equal to half of the interest expense apportionment that the asset method would have generated. Where a consolidated tax return is filed, if one member decides to use the optional gross income method, then all members in the consolidated return must use that method.[109]

Where the optional gross income method does not produce an apportionment equal to 50 percent of the asset method, the bank may still use the optional gross income providing it increases the allocation to the 50 percent number.[110] Thus, if the optional gross income method apportions only $500,000 of interest expense, whereas the asset method would apportion $2 million, the optional gross income method may still be used, but the amount apportioned must be increased from $500,000 to $1 million.

The regulations provide a transition rule with regard to apportionment of interest on obligations incurred before January 1, 1977.[111] The transition rule provides that interest paid on those obligations may be apportioned using the rules in effect in the regulations promulgated in 1957, as amended on September 29, 1975. However, with regard to post-1976 indebtedness, where the transition rule is taken advantage of, a bank must apportion interest using the asset method and may not use the optional gross income method. Once a bank has elected to use the optional gross income method, however, it is not permitted for that year or any following year to use the relief provisions for pre-1977 indebtedness.[112] Consequently, from a bank's standpoint, it seems appropriate to attempt to use the 1957 regulations with regard to pre-1977 indebtedness even where the post-1976 indebtedness must use the asset method. A bank can shift to the optional gross income method when the benefits of the special rules on pre-1977 indebtedness no longer outweigh sacrifice of the optional gross income method.

Research and Experimental Expenditures

While the regulations provide detailed rules pertaining to the allocation and apportionment of research and experimental expenditures, the Economic Recovery Tax Act of 1981 suspended these rules tempo-

---

[108] Reg. §1.861–8(e)(2)(vi)(A).
[109] Reg. §1.861–8(e)(2)(vi).
[110] Reg. §1.861–8(e)(2)(vi)(B).
[111] Reg. §1.861–8(e)(2)(vii).
[112] Reg. §1.861–8(e)(2)(vii).

rarily. In a taxpayer's first two years beginning within two years after enactment of ERTA, all research and experimental expenditures as defined in Section 174 paid or incurred for research activities conducted in the United States are to be allocated and apportioned to U.S.-source gross income.[113]

Stewardship and Other Service Expenses

The regulations require the allocation and apportionment of all deductions, including those normally considered general and administrative (G&A), or overhead type expenses.[114] The various rules in this area are grouped under the general heading of "service-oriented expenses," a term that does not appear in the regulations. This term encompasses the allocation and apportionment rules relating to: (1) expenses properly chargeable under Section 482; (2) supportive expenses; (3) expenses of a supervisory department not classifiable as stewardship, supportive, or Section 482 expenses; and (4) stewardship expenses.

The rules require an allocation and apportionment of service-oriented expenses to foreign-source gross income in general and, in the case of stewardship expenses, to foreign dividend income in particular, even though these expenses may not be incurred in material part as a result of foreign activity.[115] Marginal or incremental costing is not allowed, and, as in the case of other expenses, the annual accounting period is ignored in effecting any allocation and apportionment.[116]

A bank's internal cost accounting allocation system should be used wherever possible, since the regulations indicate that the basic allocations and apportionments are to be made on the basis of cause and effect relationships between the cost and the income.[117] This is an overriding consideration in the regulations which banks, as a practical matter, have to rely upon in order to comply with the regulations and avoid the rigid formulas provided.

The first step in properly applying the regulations to service-oriented expenses is to divide these expenses into one of the four categories above. A bank may be able to allocate and apportion certain expenses in alternative ways; thus providing some flexibility to otherwise rigid rules. The basic definitions provided in the regulations are as follows: (1) Section 482 expenses are direct and indirect expenses incurred in providing marketing, administrative, technical, management, and

---

[113] P.L. 97–34, §223(a).
[114] Reg. §1.861–8(e)(4).
[115] Reg. §1.861–8(e)(4).
[116] Reg. §1.861–8(b)(1).
[117] Reg. §1.861–8(b)(2).

other services for the benefit of or on behalf of a related party for which a charge must be made;[118] (2) supportive expenses, such as overhead, G&A, and supervisory expenses, are deductions that are "supportive in nature." This term does not include providing assistance to foreign (or domestic) subsidiary activity, but rather, these expenses must be supportive of the income of the U.S. bank;[119] (3) other expenses of a supervisory department are defined as expenses incurred by an administrative department which are not related to stewardship activities, and (4) stewardship expenses are defined as expenses incurred as a result of, or incident to, a corporate stockholder's equity investment in a related corporation.[120] These expenses are intended to be "overseeing" in nature.

Expenses chargeable under Section 482 are considered definitely related to the income generated by those charges and allocated accordingly.[121] For example, if a U.S. bank incurs $100,000 of expense rendering managerial services that benefit a foreign subsidiary, the expense is directly allocable to the amount of income received from the subsidiary for the services. The amount of Section 482 expenses allocated to foreign-source income under this rule depends on the source of the underlying income which, in turn, depends on where the services generating the income were performed. Services performed in the United States generate U.S.-source income, while services performed outside the United States generate foreign-source income. In sourcing this type of income, the status (foreign or domestic) of the related party is irrelevant. Activity performed in the United States on behalf of a foreign subsidiary does not generate foreign-source income.

Alternative allocation and apportionment rules provide for supportive expenses. The language of the regulations indicates that a bank has the option of which alternative should be used.[122] Because of the indirect nature of supportive expenses, the regulations provide that they may relate to other deductions and may be allocated or apportioned along with these other deductions. For example, the supportive expense may relate to interest expense or stewardship expense and be allocated and apportioned in the same manner as these related expenses. Alternatively, the regulations provide that it would be "equally acceptable" to allocate and apportion supportive expenses to all gross income (or a broad class of gross income) using some reasonable basis. For example, it would appear to be acceptable to allocate

---

[118] Reg. §1.861–8(b)(1).
[119] Reg. §1.861–8(b)(3).
[120] Reg. §1.861–8(e)(4).
[121] Reg. §1.861–8(e)(4).
[122] Reg. §1.861–8(b)(3).

and apportion supportive expenses using a gross income ratio, where this approach is supported by the circumstances.

If a corporation has a separate supervisory department which performs other than stewardship or Section 482 activities, then the expenses incurred in performing these other activities are considered directly allocable to income generated from those activities. For example, if some of the activities of a supervisory department relate to finalizing syndication arrangements (and thereby generating fee income), the expense of these activities is allocable to the fee income. A bank need not have a formal department for these kinds of expenses to exist. The amount of these other supervisory expenses allocable to foreign-source gross income depends on the source of any underlying income which may be generated. In any event, the generally detrimental allocation and apportionment rules relating to stewardship expenses do not apply to these expenses.

The regulations provide a separate definition of stewardship expenses, thus clearly recognizing a distinction from supportive expenses.[123] Although the definitions illustrating these distinctions are somewhat unclear, these are two separate terms having different allocation and apportionment rules. Narrowly defined, stewardship expenses are only those expenses incurred by a bank in connection with an equity investment (not in connection with a creditor relationship) in a related corporation. Thus, the stewardship expenses are essentially duplicative in nature; that is, they are expenses incurred in performing services at the corporate shareholder level which have already been performed at the subsidiary corporation level. For example, to protect its investment position, a corporate shareholder incurs $50,000 of expenses reviewing a proposed business transaction that its subsidiary is about to enter into. The subsidiary also incurs expenses in arranging and reviewing this business transaction. Another area that should be considered in this context is the treatment of foreign exchange hedging costs, where this activity takes place at the parent-company level in connection with its investment in foreign subsidiaries. This should be distinguished from foreign exchange hedging at the subsidiary level.

The regulation provides that stewardship expenses are directly related to dividend income received or to be received.[124] By disregarding the annual accounting concept (i.e., requiring an allocation even in situations where there is no current dividend income), the regulations allow for the possibility of negative dividend income.[125] If the class of dividend income includes both domestic and foreign-source dividends (by virtue of the existence of domestic and foreign subsidiaries),

---

[123] Reg. §1.861–8(e)(4).
[124] Reg. §1.861–8(e)(4).
[125] Reg. §1.861–8(d)(1).

an apportionment of stewardship expenses among domestic and foreign sources is required. Two permissible apportionment methods are covered in the regulations. If a bank maintains adequate supportive documents, an apportionment can be effected by comparing the time spent "overseeing" domestic and foreign corporations.[126] This method may be preferable and is likely to minimize the apportionment of stewardship expenses to foreign-source income. However, detailed supporting records are needed to justify its use.[127] If records are not maintained, the regulations provide for the use of a so-called look through apportionment method.[128] The look through approach rejects an apportionment using current dividend income. Rather, an apportionment must be made by looking through to the various subsidiaries benefiting from the stewardship activities and comparing the gross receipts, gross income, or sales of these subsidiaries. This apportionment goes through to multiple tiers of subsidiaries. This procedure stops with consideration of the above items. General and administrative expenses undertaken by the subsidiaries themselves are disregarded, and these expenses cannot be offset against any apportionment computed under the regulations.

Legal and Accounting Fees

As with other deductions, all legal and accounting fees are to be allocated and apportioned. The regulations recognize that some of the expenses, such as those relating to specific projects, may be related to certain classes of gross income, whereas other fee amounts are related to gross income as a whole.[129] With regard to this latter type, gross income ratios may be used for apportionment although it would be preferable to request a bank's professional advisor to provide a description of such services so as to aid the allocation among domestic and foreign-source income.

Income Taxes

The deduction for state, local, and foreign taxes allowed by Section 164 is stated in the regulations as being definitely related and allocable to the gross income with respect to which these taxes are imposed.[130] Although the tax systems of most states are designed to tax only income arising from within their borders, the regulations require an apportionment to foreign-source income unless a state statute specifically ex-

---

[126] Reg. §1.861–8(e)(4).

[127] Reg. §1.861–8(f)(5).

[128] Reg. §1.861–8(g) Ex. (18).

[129] Reg. §1.861–8(e)(5).

[130] Reg. §1.861–8(e)(6).

cludes foreign-source income from state taxation. Apportionment is accomplished using the ratio of foreign-source income taxed by the state to total income taxed by the state.

A simplified example of the type of apportionment envisaged by the regulations is the following situation where a bank has federal taxable income of $1 million of which $700,000 is domestic and $300,000 is foreign. Assume that the bank is subject to taxation in a state, which does not have a specific statutory exclusion for taxation of foreign source income. If after state modifications and apportionments, the aggregate amount of taxable income for state purposes is $700,000, then that amount is deemed to consist entirely of the domestic income which amounted to $700,000. Should the aggregate of the state taxable income exceed this domestic income amount, then the excess would be attributable to foreign-source income.[131]

Net Operating Loss Deduction

In order to allocate and apportion a net operating loss deduction, a bank must look at the circumstances surrounding the loss, that is, the activity or property which generated the loss and the taxable year in which such loss occurred.[132] It is important to remember that for apportionment, the ratio of foreign-source income to total income in the year in which the loss is to be used is irrelevant.

To illustrate the rules involved, consider a bank with taxable income amounting to $5,000 before a net operating loss deduction. Losses available for the deduction are $2,000 from year 1 and $3,000 from year 2, of which $1,000 of losses in each year was attributable to foreign sources. The full $5,000 of available losses can be used, and current taxable income is zero as a result. The apportionment of the loss deduction ignores the current year's ratio of domestic to foreign-source gross income but looks instead to the ratios in the years the losses arose. Consequently, the loss deduction apportioned to the statutory grouping of foreign-source gross income is $2,000, and the balance of the loss deduction, $3,000, is apportioned to the residual grouping of domestic-source gross income.

Losses from Property Transactions

The allocation of losses arising from disposition of a capital asset is based on the type of income to which the property ordinarily gives rise.[133] Where the nature of that income generated has changed over

---

[131] Reg. §1.861–8(g) Ex. (25) and (26).

[132] Reg. §1.861–8(e)(8).

[133] Reg. §1.861–8(e)(7)(i).

the years, the regulations suggest that a bank refer to the income generated from the property during the taxable year or years immediately preceding the sale.[134] The place of sale and the foreign tax treatment are irrelevant in this allocation procedure.

The principles of allocation of these losses do not follow the principles contained in the source of income rules with respect to gains from the sale of property. Hence, it is possible for a bank to be in the anomalous situation of having a gain on the sale of an asset treated as U.S.-source income for foreign tax credit limitation purposes, while a loss on the sale of the same asset would have been allocated against foreign-source income. Any necessary apportionment is carried out using a gross income ratio approach.[135]

Other Deductions

The allocation and apportionment of deductions other than those previously discussed, which includes deductions considered not related to any class of gross income, are generally accomplished using a gross income ratio. Deductions which generally are not considered related to any class of gross income include certain nonbusiness interest expense, real estate taxes on personal residences, sales tax on the purchase of items for personal use, medical expenses, alimony, and charitable contributions.[136] The use of the term *generally* seems to allow for the possibility of specific allocation to gross income if the taxpayer develops sufficient documentation. Certain special deductions to which some banks may be entitled, such as the deductions for partially tax-exempt income (e.g., the 85 percent corporate dividends-received deduction), are directly allocated to the class of gross income which gives rise to the deduction.[137]

BLOCKED FOREIGN INCOME

Situations can arise in which a cross-border loan made by the head office of a U.S. bank or by one of its foreign branches results in the receipt of income which cannot effectively be repatriated to the United States, perhaps due to currency restrictions present in a foreign country. The Internal Revenue Service has provided rules for this type of situation in Revenue Ruling 74–351[138] and Revenue Ruling 81–290.[139]

Section 446 provides the general rule that taxable income is com-

---

[134] Reg. §1.861–8(e)(7)(i).
[135] Reg. §1.861–8(e)(7)(ii).
[136] Reg. §1.861–8(e)(9).
[137] Reg. §1.861–8(e)(10).
[138] 1974–2 CB 144.
[139] 1981–50 IRB 10.

puted under the method of accounting on the basis of which a bank regularly computes its income in keeping its books. The regulations generally provide the commissioner with the authority to ensure that the method of accounting on which taxable income is based clearly reflects the income of the taxpayer.[140] Under this authority, Revenue Rulings 74–351 and 81–290 present a series of questions and answers explaining the circumstances under which a bank can defer the reporting of blocked foreign income on its U.S. tax return.

Deferrable income is defined to include income received by, credited to the account of, or accrued to a taxpayer that, owing to monetary, exchange or other restrictions imposed by a foreign country, is not readily convertible into U.S. dollars or into other money or property which is readily convertible into U.S. dollars. A bank may elect to use a method of accounting which defers the reporting of deferrable income until the income ceases to be deferrable or becomes unblocked. The election is made by filing an information return showing the amounts of income deferred. Losses incurred in the production of deferred income as well as expenses paid or accrued in a foreign country in which there is deferrable income are treated in a manner similar to the treatment of the deferrable income itself. A proportionate part of the expenses attributable to deferred income is deductible as the deferred income becomes includable in gross income and reportable on the bank's U.S. income tax return in future years.[141] In addition, foreign income taxes paid or accrued with respect to deferred income may not be currently used by a bank as a foreign tax credit. Use as a credit must be deferred to the time when the income itself is reported.

The election to use the deferred income method may be made in the first year in which blocked foreign income is received or in a later year. If the election is made in the first year in which blocked foreign income is received, the commissioner's consent is not required to make the election. A change in a later year to a nondeferred method of accounting for such blocked income will require the consent of the commissioner.[142] Where blocked foreign income has been previously reported under a nondeferred method of accounting, a change to a deferred method of accounting for the income also requires the consent of the commissioner.

Pursuant to Revenue Ruling 74–351, income ceases to be deferrable income when the money or property in the foreign country becomes readily convertible into U.S. dollars or into money or property which is readily convertible into U.S. dollars, when a conversion into U.S.

---

[140] Reg. §1.446–1(a).
[141] Rev. Rul. 57–379, 1957–2 CB 299.
[142] Rev. Rul. 81–290, 1981–50 IRB 10.

dollars or into other money or property which is convertible into U.S. dollars is made (notwithstanding applicable foreign law), or when the blocked income is used for nondeductible personal expenses, is disposed of by way of gift, request, devise, inheritance, or by dividend or other distribution.

FOREIGN BRANCH TRANSLATIONS

Domestic banks operating in the international markets have a choice of several methods for translating foreign currency transactions into U.S. dollars. Overseas branches of U.S. banks generally keep their books in the currency of the country where they operate and translate the collective operating results by the branch profit and loss statement or by the branch balance sheet. Two alternative methods described as the profit and loss (P&L) method and the net worth (or balance sheet) method are usually considered for the foreign branch translations. The P&L method is the translation method used most commonly by banks, although in areas of regular and rapid devaluation of currency, the net worth method may be preferable. For foreign branches with an excess of assets over liabilities, translating a devaluing currency on the net worth basis is preferred, because the net worth basis is calculated by taking the difference between the net worth at the beginning and end of the period, a calculation which decreases tax liability.

The P&L method is authorized by Revenue Ruling 75–107[143] and incorporates the following procedures:

Net profits are computed in the foreign currency.

Profits remitted to the home office during the year are converted into U.S. dollars at the exchange rate prevailing at time of remittance.

Balance of profits shown in foreign currency are translated at the year-end rate of exchange.

The amount remitted plus the amount converted are recorded as income or loss for the branch on the bank's U.S. tax return.

Under the P&L method, unrealized exchange gains (and losses) are not recognized. This method may be illustrated as follows:

		1981
(1)	Determining profit to be converted at year-end:	
	Net profit of London branch stated in U.K. pounds	10,000
	Less:	
	Remittance on June 30, 1981 stated in U.K. pounds	1,000
	Unremitted net profits at December 31, 1981 stated in U.K. pounds	9,000

---

[143] 1975–1 CB 32.

	1981
(2) Conversion into dollars:	
Remittance of 1,000 pounds on June 30, 1981 at exchange rate of 1 pound = $2.25	$ 2,250
Unremitted profits at December 31, 1981, to be valued at exchange rate on December 31, 1981, of 1 pound = $2.00	18,000
Net profit as converted	$20,250

The net worth (or balance sheet) method is authorized by Revenue Ruling 75–106.[144] Under this method, balance sheets at the beginning and end of the year are prepared in foreign currency. The branch profit or loss for U.S. tax purposes is the sum of the remittances during the year, plus the difference between the net worth at the beginning of the year and the net worth at the end of the year, that is, after the balance sheets have been converted into U.S. dollars. These accounts are converted into U.S. dollars under the following rules:

Year-end exchange rates are used for current assets and current liabilities.

Historical rates are used for fixed assets and long-term liabilities.

Remittances during the year are converted at the exchange rate prevailing on the date of the remittance.

Under the net worth method, unrealized gains or losses on net current assets or liabilities due to foreign currency fluctuations are recognized. This method may be illustrated as follows:

	1/1/81	*12/31/81*
(1) Dollar value of the excess of current assets over current liabilities at:		
January 1, 1981 (100,000 pounds at 1 pound = $2.25)	$225,000	
December 31, 1981 (130,000 pounds at 1 pound = $2.00		$260,000
Add		
(2) Adjusted basis of the noncurrent assets, computed at the currency exchange rates prevailing, respectively, when each asset was acquired	100,000	90,000
(3) Branch net worth in U.S. dollars	$325,000	$350,000
(4) Increase in dollar value of net worth for the taxable year		$ 25,000
Add		
(5) Dollar value of remittance of 1,000 pounds on June 30, 1981, at exchange rate of 1 pound = $2.25		2,250
(6) Branch net profit in U.S. dollars		$ 27,250

---

[144] 1975–1 CB 31. See also Rev. Rul. 75–105, 1975–1 CB 29.

In summary, when engaging in foreign branch operations, the preferable method of accounting, that is, the method that gives the greatest deferral of taxable income (exchange gains) or the greatest acceleration of deductible losses (exchange losses), should be sought. The decision is based on the foreseeable branch asset-liability position and the anticipated fluctuations, if any, of the local currency-U.S. dollar relationship.

CONTROLLED FOREIGN CORPORATIONS

Taxation of Operations

U.S. stockholders of foreign corporations which are controlled foreign corporations (CFCs) for an uninterrupted 30-day period during a taxable year must include in their gross income a ratable share of the subpart F income of the CFC and of certain other amounts.[145] U.S. shareholders include domestic corporations, citizens, and resident aliens who own at least 10 percent of the total combined voting power of the foreign corporation.[146] A CFC is a foreign corporation more than 50 percent of whose combined voting power is owned or considered as being owned by U.S. shareholders.[147]

The most important category of subpart F income for banks is foreign personal holding company income, which includes interest, dividends, and nondealer gains from the sale or exchange of stocks and securities.[148] These three items, however, are excluded from the definition of foreign personal holding company income for subpart F purposes if derived in the conduct of a banking, financing or similar business and received from a person who is not a related person.[149] Interest income received from a related person is also excluded if both parties are engaged in the conduct of this type of business predominantly with unrelated parties.[150]

General exclusions from the category of subpart F income exist where such income constitutes less than 10 percent of total gross income,[151] and where the CFC was not created or organized, and the income-producing transaction was not effected, with a significant purpose being a substantial reduction of income taxes.[152] Subpart F income

---

[145] IRC §951(a).
[146] IRC §951(b).
[147] IRC §957(a).
[148] IRC §954(c).
[149] IRC §954(c)(3)(B).
[150] IRC §954(c)(4)(B).
[151] IRC §954(b)(3).
[152] IRC §954(b)(4).

is a net income concept,[153] and is further limited by the earnings and profits of the CFC.[154]

Investments by a CFC in certain U.S. property, including obligations of U.S. persons, can also result in income inclusions by U.S. shareholders.[155] Both "U.S. property" and subpart F income inclusions are accompanied by an indirect foreign tax credit similar to that described earlier.[156]

Dispositions

The sale or exchange by a 10 percent or more U.S. shareholder of a CFC (or of any foreign corporation which has been a CFC during the 5-year period ending on the date of the sale or exchange) results in dividend treatment of a part of the gain proportionate to the earnings and profits of the foreign corporation attributable to the stock sold.[157] The remainder of the gain is treated as gain from the sale of a capital asset. Several exclusions from the earnings and profits of a CFC are statutorily mandated as are certain exceptions from the application of the general rule (generally, ordinary income-producing situations).[158] Certain nonrecognition transactions under Sections 311, 336, and 337 are also overridden by Section 1248.[159] Dividend treatment under Section 1248 does qualify for indirect foreign tax credit purposes as described earlier under Section 902.[160]

MINIMUM TAX FOR TAX PREFERENCES

In addition to the regular corporation income tax, a minimum tax applies to corporate taxpayers.[161] The base on which the tax is calculated is the total of certain "tax preference" items. The major tax preference item for banks has been the amount by which the bad debt deduction computed under the reserve method exceeds the amount allowable if the bank had computed the bad debt deduction on the basis of actual bad debt experience.

In the context of its international transactions, where a domestic bank has foreign-source tax preference items, the general rule, found

---

[153] IRC §954(b)(5).

[154] IRC §952(c).

[155] IRC §§951(a)(1)(B) and 956.

[156] IRC §960.

[157] IRC §1248(a).

[158] IRC §§1248 (g) and (d).

[159] IRC §1248(f).

[160] Reg. §1.1248–1(d).

[161] IRC §56(a).

in Section 58(g), is that the minimum tax is imposed only on those tax preference items from sources within the United States. Preference items which are attributable to sources within any foreign country or within any U.S. possession are added to domestic-source preference items only to the extent that they reduce income from domestic sources. For this purpose, foreign tax preferences are deemed to reduce domestic income before other foreign items. This may be illustrated by a situation in which a bank's foreign-source tax preference items cause foreign losses, which, in turn, offset taxable income from sources within the United States.

U.S. EMPLOYEES WORKING ABROAD

The Economic Recovery Tax Act of 1981 significantly altered and simplified the provisions dealing with the taxation of foreign earned income for taxable years beginning after 1981.

Bank employees, whose tax home is in a foreign country and who are either U.S. citizens establishing bona fide residence in a foreign country or U.S. citizens or residents present outside the United States for period of 330 days in a consecutive 12-month period, may elect to exclude earned income attributable to services performed overseas from their gross income.[162] The maximum annual exclusion for 1982 is set at $75,000, prorated daily and increasing $5,000 per year until 1986, when the maximum exclusion will be $95,000.[163] In the case of a married couple, the exemption is computed separately for each qualifying individual. The income which is not excluded is to be taxed as if it were the first income earned. In this way, taxable income is taxed through all the relevant tax brackets without losing the benefit of the lowest marginal tax rates.

In addition to the exclusion described above, an expatriate may separately elect to exclude a portion of his income or deduct an amount for housing for which the employee himself paid.[164] This exclusion or deduction is equal to the excess of the taxpayer's reasonable "housing expenses" over a "base housing amount." Housing expenses are reasonable expenses when paid or incurred during the taxable year by, or on behalf of, the individual for housing the taxpayer and the taxpayer's family if they reside with him in a foreign country.[165] These expenses include the cost of insurance, utilities, and similar expenses but not expenses which are separately deductible, such as taxes and interest. The "base housing amount" is 16 percent of the salary paid to a U.S.

---

[162] IRC §§911(d) and 911(a).

[163] IRC §911(b)(2).

[164] IRC §§911(a)(2) and (c)(3).

[165] IRC §911(c)(2).

government employee at the GS 14, Step 1 level.[166] Sixteen percent of the salary in mid-1981 amounted to just over $6,000.

Expatriates, maintaining a second household outside the United States for a spouse and dependents who do not reside with him because of adverse living conditions, may exclude also the housing expenses of the second household.[167] However, deductions and credits attributable to excluded income, such as those for moving expenses and foreign income tax, are eliminated.[168]

Both the exclusion of foreign earned income and the exclusion based on excess housing costs are elective. These elections apply until revoked, although a revocation precludes a new election for five years after the year of revocation, except with the consent of the secretary of the treasury.[169]

The act retains with certain modifications the present rule that lodging and meals furnished in a camp located in a foreign country by the taxpayer's employer are excludable from gross income.[170] The main difference from earlier legislation is that the camp no longer need be in a hardship area and need not constitute substandard lodging.

TRANSACTIONS IN FOREIGN CURRENCY

General Rules

The basic principles for transactions in foreign currency for U.S. tax purposes can generally be segregated into four topics. These topics include: (1) recognition; (2) valuation; (3) character; and (4) source.

Recognition.   The general rule requiring recognition of gain or loss requires a closed transaction.[171] This generally means that with respect to the receipt of income involving a foreign currency, a realization event under U.S. tax principles is required before the gain or loss can be determined. For example, the receipt of an interest payment by the head office of a U.S. bank in foreign currency constitutes the receipt of income in a closed transaction. At the point of receipt, gain is realized and recognized by the U.S. bank. Exceptions do exist to this closed transaction rule. For example, the accrual of an interest receipt in a foreign currency which is not convertible into U.S. dollars may present an example of blocked foreign income whose recognition may be deferred until such time as the conversion restriction is

---

[166] IRC §911(c)(1)(B).

[167] IRC §911(c)(2)(B).

[168] IRC §911(d)(6).

[169] IRC §911(e).

[170] IRC §911(c).

[171] Rev. Rul. 75-108, 1975-1 CB 69.

removed.[172] Another example involves dealers in foreign currency who may choose to inventory their holding of such foreign currency.[173] Since their inventory must be valued at the end of their taxable year, in U.S. dollars, gain or loss due to foreign currency fluctuations may be recognized currently.

As a consequence of the closed transaction rule, the general approach followed by the Internal Revenue Service and by the courts has been to follow a separate transaction approach. The emphasis under this approach is on separately cognizable realization events, with gain or loss recognizable at each point in a series of transactions where a realization event for U.S. purposes has occurred.[174] Under this approach for example, the receipt of interest by a bank's U.S. head office in foreign currency constitutes a realization event such that at the time of receipt the interest must be valued at the rate of exchange in effect at the time of receipt. A conversion of the foreign currency received into U.S. dollars is not a prerequisite of realization and recognition of income for U.S. tax purposes. Should the rate of exchange between U.S. dollars and the particular foreign currency change between the time the foreign currency is received as an interest receipt and is converted into U.S. dollars, such conversion would constitute a separately taxable transaction to the bank.

Valuation. As a general matter, the prevailing rate of exchange between U.S. dollars and a particular foreign currency is the rate used to translate the foreign currency. This prevailing rate is not necessarily the official exchange rate in the foreign country.[175] In situations other than the purchase or sale of property, for example, upon the receipt of rental or interest income, the date of receipt or accrual of the income item (depending upon the method of accounting employed by the recipient) is the date on which to apply the appropriate exchange rate and convert the currency into U.S. dollars.[176] In the case of the purchase and sale of property, exchange rate determinations at several dates may be relevant in order to determine gain or loss on the transaction. This is a direct result of the separate transaction approach employed in determining gain or loss.

Character. The nature of a transaction underlying the exposure to foreign currency fluctuations is generally determinative of the character of the gain or loss as a result of currency fluctuations. For example, if a U.S. manufacturing corporation hedges the exposure of a foreign subsidiary in terms of the inventory maintained by the subsidiary, the

---

[172] Rev. Rul. 74–351, 1974–2 CB 144.
[173] Rev. Rul. 75–104, 1975–1 CB 18.
[174] Rev. Rul. 74–379, 1974–2 CB 18.
[175] *Ternovsky* v. *Commissioner*, 66 TC 695 (1976).
[176] Rev. Rul. 74–222, 1974–1 CB 21.

exposure of the parent is treated as related to the value of the parent's investment in its subsidiary. Since the value of the parent's investment in the subsidiary is determined with relation to the value of its stock-holding, such hedging exposure generally is treated as resulting in either capital gain or loss.[177] On the other hand, hedging the exposure of a foreign branch with respect to its inventory is generally treated as resulting in ordinary gain or loss since the property hedged would have resulted to the U.S. parent in ordinary gain or loss when disposed of.[178] The Internal Revenue Service appears to take the position that banks are "special" in that money in all forms represents their basic business. As such, foreign currency gain or loss of a bank will be treated as ordinary income or loss in almost all cases.[179]

The rules are unsettled as to whether the method of performance of a forward exchange contact affects the character of the gain or loss. The closing out of a forward exchange contract prior to maturity through sale may depend on whether the transferee is viewed as the agent of the taxpayer or the transferee is not viewed as the agent of the taxpayer. It is also possible that the character of the gain is not affected by whether the transferee is considered the agent of the tax-payer or not.[180] Prior to 1981, it was generally the rule that capital gain or loss treatment could only be obtained if a sale or exchange of the contract occurred, as opposed to holding the contract to maturity.[181] Exceptions to this rule however, were not infrequent.[182] After the passage of the Economic Recovery Tax Act of 1981, gain or loss could assume the character of a capital gain or loss where a right to personal property was terminated, if disposition of the property underlying the forward exchange contract was a capital asset.[183]

Much as the character of gain or loss in a hedging transaction de-pends upon the character of the underlying asset, so too, the collection of foreign currency receivables generally depends upon the transaction which generated the receivable. For example, the extension of credit in the ordinary course of business, where such credit was in the form of a foreign currency, generates ordinary income on both the interest element of the extension of credit and on any gain due to a change in rates between the time of the extension of credit and the time of repayment.[184] So too, a foreign currency borrowing used to invest in

---

[177] *Hoover Co., Inc.* v. *Commissioner*, 72 TC 206 (1979).

[178] *Wool Distributing Co.* v. *Commissioner*, 34 TC 323 (1960).

[179] Rev. Rul. 78–396, 1978–2 CB 114; PLR 7847004.

[180] *La Grange* v. *Commissioner*, 26 TC 191 (1956); *U.S.* v. *American Home Products Corp.*, 79–2 USTC ¶9418 (1979); PLR 8016004.

[181] *United States* v. *Starr Brothers*, 53–1 USTC ¶9410 (1953).

[182] *United States* v. *Ferrer*, 62–2 USTC ¶9518 (1962).

[183] IRC §1234A. See also IRC §1256.

[184] *Foundation Co.,* v. *Commissioner*, 14 TC 1333 (1950).

a capital asset will generally result in capital gain or loss with respect to gain or loss incurred as a result of currency fluctuations.[185] The repayment of foreign currency borrowings generally follow the same rule as the receipt of foreign currency receivables.

Source. The source of foreign exchange gains and losses is primarily important for foreign tax credit purposes but it is an area that has been given little attention by the Internal Revenue Service and Congress. The foreign exchange gain or loss here should be differentiated from gain or loss upon the sale of foreign currency itself. Foreign currency as property comes under the source rule involving the sale or exchange of personal property. It is the element of the overall gain or loss on a foreign currency transaction attributable to exchange-rate fluctuations which is here at issue. Just as the character of a foreign exchange gain or loss may be determined generally from the transaction underlying such gain or loss, the source of the gain or loss may also be related back to the gain or loss on the sale of the underlying asset. While it has been suggested that most foreign currency dealings will result in foreign source income or loss, the legal requirements of a transaction may override the fact that the transaction has a foreign currency element.[186] For example, the conversion of convertible debentures issued by a domestic corporation into stock of such corporation through a U.S. exchange agent was held to result in U.S. source gain in Revenue Ruling 75–263.[187] The fact that the transaction occurred in the United States, and therefore came under the rule for the sourcing of gain from the sale or exchange of personal property, overrode any considerations with respect to the foreign aspects of the transaction. If the underlying nature of the transaction is recognized as determinative of the source of income attributable to a currency fluctuation vis-a-vis the U.S. dollar, the foreign currency gain or loss element (as distinguished from the interest element) of the receipt of a loan installment should perhaps be treated as foreign-source income or loss, if the terms of the loan require that payment may only be made at a specific location outside of the United States, for example, at the office of the bank's foreign branch.

---

[185] *Columbia Sand and Gravel Co.* v. *Commissioner*, 11 TCM 794 (1952).

[186] Campbell and O'Connor, "Taxation of Foreign Exchange Activities of Commercial Banks," *The Tax Adviser*, September 1976.

[187] 1975–2 CB 287.

44
Audits and Examinations

STEPHEN C. EYRE
Senior Vice President—Secretary
Citibank, N.A.
and
DANIEL T. JACOBSEN
Chief Auditor
Citibank, N.A.

The principal safeguard of a banking institution's soundness is its system of internal controls. This is the body of policies, accountabilities, and standard operating procedures established by management for extensions of credit, transaction processing, accounting, and each of its other business activities.

Audits and examinations provide independent measures of assurance for directors, managers, depositors, investors, and regulators that internal control systems are adequate, that irregularities are identified and resolved promptly, and that operations are well run.

Until recent years the banking business evolved gradually, and time-tested management controls were fine-tuned as required. Successful bankers today must keep in step with rapid changes in a highly competitive financial services marketplace: advances in technology, more sophisticated services, escalating transaction volumes and velocities, the impact of deregulation, and geographical expansion in the U.S. and overseas. The principal challenge for bank management in this environment is managing the process of change to maintain soundness and quality as well as profitability.

While delegating overall responsibility for operations to management, the board of directors itself continues to be accountable for the health of the organization. In all but the smallest banks, the board—through its examining or audit committee—delegates the day-to-day monitoring, testing, and evaluating of internal controls to a chief auditing officer and his staff. Public accounting firms may also provide independent auditing services for the board, ranging from basic directors' audits to full certification of financial statements.

Government agencies examine individual banks to determine that depositors, investors, and the public are protected. They also monitor the overall health of the banking system.

The auditing and examination of international banking activities are extensions of the process of independent review and evaluation familiar to domestic bankers.

INTERNAL AUDITS

In 1977 the Audit Commission of the Bank Administration Institute (BAI) issued a revised *Statement of Principle and Standards for Internal Auditing in the Banking Industry* which brought the organizational and professional standards for auditing into line with the revolutionary changes taking place in the banking and bank-related financial services industry. The statement makes a clear distinction between internal controls and internal audits.

The control systems themselves, established and maintained by management, are comprised of

the plan of organization and all methods and measures designed to:

1. Provide reasonable assurance that assets are safeguarded, information (financial and other) is timely and reliable, and errors and irregularities are discovered and corrected promptly;
2. Promote operational efficiency;
3. Encourage compliance with managerial policies, laws, regulations, and sound fiduciary principles.

On the other hand, internal auditing is defined as "that management function which independently evaluates the adequacy, effectiveness, and efficiency of the systems of control within an organization and the quality of . . . all activities involved in the conduct of the organization's business."

Independence

The essential element in an effective internal audit program is independence—the ability to act with integrity and objectivity. The BAI statement of principle concludes: "The internal auditor is accountable to the board of directors and executive management. This accountability precludes the auditor from organizational relationships that may conflict with the need for independence." In addition, the institution must maintain an environment in which the auditor can operate freely at all levels, allocate sufficient resources to perform the audit function, and require management to respond to adverse audit findings and take appropriate corrective action.

The Bank Administration Institute audit standards state that

> Only the board of directors can protect the auditor's need for independence; consequently, the board should be the final judge of the auditor's performance. . . . Both the auditor and executive management have received a delegation of authority from the board—management to design and maintain systems of control; the auditor to evaluate these systems of control. Because the evaluation process exists to serve the design and maintenance responsibility, the auditor must also be accountable to executive management. This accountability, however, does not create the usual corollary right of the executive to directly apply sanctions or to otherwise restrict the auditor's functional independence. Such action, if necessary, must be decided by the board.

Monitoring Controls

The auditing staff conducts continuous reviews and periodically evaluates all facets of the bank's business and administration—including not only credit, transaction processing, accounting, safekeeping, trading, and trust operations, but also personnel practices and premises safety. Auditors must also test systems for compliance with government regulations ranging from reserve ratios to "Truth in Lending." Control procedures for each segment of the business are tested for adequacy, effectiveness, and efficiency—that is, are they appropriate, do they work as intended, and are they cost effective.

Where errors or irregularities are found, auditors monitor management's corrective action program, reporting on serious problems and corrective action results to the appropriate levels of management as well as to the board of directors.

When new services are introduced or when processing systems are modified, auditors evaluate the adequacy of the controls before implementation. This is particularly critical in computer operations. To be most effective, auditors become involved in the early stages of automated-system design, well before the system is to be put into use. Where advisable the audit department designs auditing software as an integral part of new systems. Once an automated system is up and running it can be very expensive to go back and build in the proper controls.

Reporting

In reporting their findings, auditors comment on the status of controls, call attention to any shortcomings, and include management's responses to and comments on the report. Audit reports may include recommendations for improving the efficiency of operations. Auditors may also comment on the adequacy of staff and management, in terms of experience, competence, numbers, and continuity. Problems which may present significant exposure to loss are referred to higher levels of management and reported to the examining or audit committee of the board of directors. Managers of substandard operations are required to submit plans for corrective action which the auditors monitor to see that targets are met.

While the internal auditor's primary responsibility is to the board of directors, audit findings and recommendations at the same time provide management at each level of the institution with independent evaluations of how well risks are managed, early warnings of actual or potential problems, and recommendations for improving efficiency and quality. An auditor who inspects a number of related units in the course of his assignment frequently can offer suggestions for improved operations that have proved effective elsewhere.

Organization and Staffing

Bank holding companies and larger independent banks typically have a chief auditing officer who reports directly to the audit or examining committee of the board of directors. An independent credit review function may be part of the chief auditor's responsibilities. The more closely the parallel functions of auditing and credit review work together, the more effective they can be.

Demands upon internal auditors have grown in step with the changing nature of the banking industry. Contrary to traditional practice, banks now recruit a significant percentage of their management trainees from graduate schools, and they go outside the institution for professionals in production, marketing, accounting, data processing, communications, law, and other fields. The increasing "professionalization" of banks with highly trained and experienced managers, controllers, and operations and lending officers requires equally well qualified staff in internal auditing.

Today a typical audit staff has inspectors proficient in accounting, electronic data processing, and operations. A growing number of bank internal auditors have qualified, or are in the process of qualifying, as certified public accountants (CPAs), chartered bank auditors (CBAs), certified internal auditors (CIAs), and certified information systems auditors (CISAs).

Banks may supplement their career-auditor staff with experienced officers "borrowed" from line and staff departments for two to five years. Such career development assignments give the individuals involved a broader view of the organization and give the audit function the benefit of up-to-date familiarity with business developments.

A strong audit program is risk sensitive, achieving cost effectiveness by apportioning its professional resources to give appropriate attention to activities with greater risk potential. It establishes "early warning" monitoring systems to identify problem situations before they get out of hand. If significant deficiencies do surface, the audit function becomes closely involved with monitoring remedial action plans and progress.

Maintaining a professional audit function in an environment of change requires a well-structured continuing program of technical training and on-the-job development of skills and judgment. It also requires that the auditor keep pace with technical advances in audit techniques and that he keep in close touch with the constantly changing business and regulatory environment.

Credit Review

The principle of having an independent credit, or risk-asset review function that parallels the financial and operational audit program has not been fully established by the banking industry because individual institutions have developed their own extension-of-credit and loan-review processes over the years to meet their particular circumstances.

A growing number of banks have, however, established independent review programs under the direction of the chief auditor or another senior official designated by the board of directors to examine and evaluate individual credits and loan portfolios. More sophisticated review programs also critically evaluate the lending process in such categories as credit initiation, loan administration, documentation and disbursement, and adherence to policy.

Lending officers and managers have the primary responsibility for identifying and evaluating credit problems and initiating corrective action. The classification of loans according to the degree of risk associated with their collectibility is a longstanding banking practice, employed along common lines by bankers and regulators. The National Bank Examiners use a five-category rating system ranging from "current" to "loss." The categories may be summarized briefly as:

Current—no collection problems foreseen.

OLEM (Other Loans Especially Mentioned)—collectibility could be affected by evidence of borrower weakness or lack of credit information.

Substandard—collection probable but only under restructured terms and extended maturity.

Doubtful—probability of some loss but amount and timing not clear.

Loss—outstandings which are to be reserved or written off.

It is the function of internal reviewers to see that individual credits are properly classified and, in the case of a problem, that a detailed corrective-action program is put in place. Credit reviewers evaluate individual credits and classifications, and in problem situations monitor the remedial steps to conclusion—repayment or workout.

Taken together, the evaluations of individual credits form the basis for rating the loan portfolio. They may also be the basis for a credit reviewer's comments on the adequacy of loan-loss reserves.

External Auditors

External auditors are not usually engaged to perform basic auditing tasks in the larger banks which have their own internal auditing staffs. But when the shares of the institution are publicly traded, a public accounting firm must certify the accuracy of financial statements to meet regulatory requirements.

Since audits by qualified independent public accountants must comply with the accounting profession's generally accepted auditing standards, their reports and opinions give bank management, directors, stockholders, and other interested parties a standard measure of a bank's condition.

External auditors examine the internal auditing and credit review programs closely. They assess the adequacy of these activities in providing reasonable protection for the bank and determine the extent to which they can rely on the internal audit and review work in evaluating the institution's accounting systems, records, and assets.

The greater the reliability of the internal systems, the less detailed work the public accountant will need to do to be able to express an unqualified opinion on the institution's financial statements.

Supervisory Examinations

Finally, government agencies—which may include the Federal Reserve System, the Office of the Comptroller of the Currency (National Bank Examiners), and the Federal Deposit Insurance Corporation, as well as state banking commissions—examine banks under their jurisdictions. The agencies have statutory responsibility for supervising a broad range of regulations governing bank operations, including securities-related activities and consumer matters.

The agencies, led by the Comptroller's Office, have modernized their approach to bank examinations since the mid-70s, basing their revised procedures on public accounting practice. Examinations now focus on the management process and are system oriented, rather than transaction oriented. Examiners hold management and boards of directors more closely accountable for the adequacy of the institution's control systems and its internal auditing and credit review programs. They evaluate the competence, independence, adequacy, and effectiveness of internal auditors. If satisfied with the effectiveness of the internal audit program, they can avoid duplicating its work.

Examiners have become more analytical. They test to see that significant exposures and risks get proper attention. They are expected to identify weaknesses in a bank's management policies and operating systems and to make recommendations based on a broad understanding of the institution's particular objectives and strategies.

Regulators look more closely at the formulation of credit, investment, and trading policies, and—where internal controls prove effective—expend less of their efforts on detailed reviews of transactions and individual credits. In today's high-volume, high-velocity environment, supervisory authorities expect bankers to be alert to potential risks and to manage problem situations promptly and effectively.

AUDITING INTERNATIONAL BANKING ACTIVITIES

When banks go abroad, the fundamentals of auditing and examination do not change. However, these functions take on new dimensions: U.S. regulation of overseas activities as well as host-country regulations, business practices, and currencies. A critical appreciation of country-by-country differences in banking and commercial practices, and the application of regulations are key ingredients of international auditing.

Scope of Overseas Business

The scope of an individual bank's overseas auditing and credit review functions will depend upon whether the institution has one branch overseas, a global multibusiness network, or something in between. Even a single overseas branch today is likely to be engaged in ever-broader activities—for example, foreign-exchange and money-market trading, and syndicated Eurodollar lending. A U.S. bank may also be involved overseas in merchant banking, consumer finance, investment management and leasing through subsidiaries or affiliates.

An overseas branch is typically a microcosm of head office with its own general ledger and individual units that correspond to the divisions and departments of the parent. Since an auditing team overseas cannot always call upon the range of specialists—electronic data processing (EDP), financial, operations, trust—available at head office, it requires a staff of broadly experienced professionals.

Regulation and Accounting Practices

U.S. laws and regulations governing the international activities of American banks include not only the specific banking and securities regulations issued by the Federal Reserve and the Comptroller of the Currency, but also statutes that apply generally to the conduct of business abroad by U.S. companies—for example, the Federal Anti-Boycott Law and the Foreign Corrupt Practices Act.

In addition, the international auditor may assess compliance with local statutes. These vary widely from country to country, depending upon history, the stage of economic development and degree of political maturity. Each country has its special view of how banking should serve the national interest, the part foreign banks should play, and how banking should be supervised. Exchange controls, credit controls, social welfare, and consumer credit, for example, may be highly regulated or virtually ignored in a particular country.

Few countries have accounting standards as detailed and specific as the United States. On the other hand, local laws may require certified audits of every subsidiary in a country. Branch or subsidiary bookkeeping must conform to local requirements and to head office accounting standards. The reporting demands of host-country authorities, and both financial and management-information system reports to head office each require that the basic data be organized somewhat differently. The auditor must determine that these parallel reporting systems are properly reconciled as well as accurate.

Auditors must also be acquainted with host-country regulation of general commercial activities, labor relations, electronic data processing, telecommunications, privacy protection, and premises safety and fire-prevention standards.

Auditors must necessarily rely on the opinions of locally qualified legal and accounting counsel for compliance with host-country regulation and commercial practice.

Host-Country Cultures

International auditors and credit reviewers must also take into account the host country's particular political and economic environment and its banking, commercial and legal customs and practices. Chronic double-digit inflation, unusual legal systems, and unpredictable labor relations are among the special situations auditors may encounter. Unreliable power supplies and erratic telecommunications—aggravating but not critical in pre-computer times—now pose special risks for electronic data processing and international funds transfer systems.

Although English is the international commercial language in most of the world and at least the key people in overseas branches must be fluent in English, auditors need a working knowledge of local languages, such as Spanish and Portuguese in Latin America.

Investment Banking

American banks may engage in certain activities overseas, through subsidiaries or affiliates, which are not permitted at home—securities underwriting and equity investment, for example. The same processes of analyzing risk and testing controls apply in the auditing and credit review of these businesses.

Automation

Until the 1970s, banking overseas—like much of American banking—was still largely a paper-based business that followed traditional procedures. Computerized local operations and satellite-relay communications networks that enable branch and head-office computers to "talk" to each other are rapidly changing the operational side of international banking. In certain areas the reliability of vendor servicing, back-up availability, and potential physical-security risks present special problems. With the internationalization of electronic banking, it has become essential that overseas audit teams—as well as their domestic colleagues—have EDP expertise.

ORGANIZATION OF OVERSEAS AUDITING

Banks with broad overseas operations have large professional audit staffs directed from head office, giving the audit staff in the field a direct reporting line up through the chief auditor to the board of directors. Typically, a large international staff has resident auditors in key countries who also cover neighboring countries, plus a cadre of traveling inspectors with special expertise—in EDP, merchant banking, treasury, and trust auditing, for example.

A bank whose overseas presence is limited may choose to handle its auditing requirements through periodic visits by auditors from head office. In countries where a bank has a limited operation and where competent public accounting services are available, a bank may choose to rely on local accountants for basic audit coverage.

EXTERNAL AUDITING AND EXAMINATION OVERSEAS

In the overseas system of checks and balances, local public accountants and regulators are added to the audit-examination interplay.

Outside Auditors

Overseas units of American banks typically require the services of a firm of locally certified accountants to meet the requirements of host-country statutes and accounting standards. A bank's U.S. public accounting firm may also audit overseas offices to determine that control systems are in place and that income and condition reports sent to head office meet U.S. accounting standards.

In major overseas centers where the large American public accounting firms have offices, host-country and U.S. domestic external auditing requirements can be met by a single firm.

Regulatory Examinations

The Federal Reserve, the Comptroller of the Currency, and state banking supervisors inspect overseas offices of banks and their subsidiaries on a selective basis in the course of their examinations. In addition to checking compliance with U.S. regulations on overseas banking, they also examine key operations in selected offices and test the work of the internal auditing staff.

Host-country regulators of banks—or banking activities—also examine for conformity with their own statutes.

CONCLUSION

To be fully effective, the auditing function requires a firm base of management controls, independent accountability to the board of directors, and well-trained and experienced auditors and audit managers who keep abreast of the latest developments in the banking business and in their profession.

The organization of the auditing program varies widely from bank to bank depending upon the institution's size, the extent of its domestic and overseas business, its management style, and other factors. However organized, auditing activities require experienced professionals who can operate independently and effectively in all kinds of environments.

Auditing, credit review, and government-agency examinations of bank activities do not differ in any fundamental respect when banks go overseas. But each country presents a somewhat different set of circumstances which the international auditing program must recognize and deal with.

The auditing of international banking activities cannot be considered in isolation; it is an extension of the overall audit function which is, in turn, an integral part of a bank's overall system of organizational checks and balances.

SECTION 8
Legal and Regulatory Framework for International Banking

45
Legal Constraints within the United States

CLARK H. HUTTON III
Simpson Thacher & Bartlett

INTRODUCTION

Legal constraints on the conduct of international banking activities can be divided roughly into two categories. The first category, and generally the first to occur to a person asked to consider the nature of legal constraints on international banking, is comprised of the inherent difficulties for the lender in enforcing an international credit transaction. These difficulties arise in such familiar legal areas as governing law, jurisdiction, sovereign immunity, available remedies, arbitration, foreign taxes, and foreign exchange availability and control.

The second category of legal constraints, of equal or greater concern to the banking institution doing business in the United States, is comprised of those legal constraints that specify directly within what limits a bank must conduct its international banking business or that directly or indirectly affect the cost of conducting that business. These constraints, well-known to any banker engaged in international lending but generally unfamiliar to the wider business community, include the effect and application of reserve requirements, the effect of domestic taxes and foreign tax credits, limitations on the activities of foreign subsidiaries and Edge Act subsidiaries in the United States, competitive differences between foreign banks and domestic banks doing business in the United States, and limitations on credit transactions generally that are peculiar to the United States banking system. This chapter will discuss some of the major considerations in the second category that should be taken into account in the conduct of international banking business within the United States.

Before commencing a discussion of the legal restraints on international banking activities in the United States, two of the chief vehicles through which such activities are conducted should be described first as constant reference will be made to them in the remainder of this chapter. These facilities are Edge Act corporations and international banking facilities (IBFs). Edge corporations have been an important part of international banking for many years and, with the amendments to Regulation K of the Board of Governors of the Federal Reserve System (Board of Governors) that resulted from the International Banking Act of 1978, Edge corporations promise to become even more useful and widespread in the future. IBFs are little over a year old at this writing as the regulations adopted by the Board of Governors that permit their formation became effective on December 3, 1981. The full impact of the IBF regulations has yet to be felt, but it is already clear that IBFs will take over a significant portion of international bank financing heretofore conducted through offshore branches.

Edge Corporations. Edge corporations are federally chartered companies formed with the permission of the Board of Governors. The purpose of Edge corporations is to engage, from offices located in the United States, in international banking activities. Edge corporations are barred from doing any business domestically except such as may be incidental to their foreign banking business. Generally Edge corporations may accept only deposits from foreign persons and make loans only to finance international transactions. These limitations impose particular restraints on Edge corporations that limit their usefulness; however, the ability of banks to own Edge corporations located outside the bank's home state and, since 1979, the added ability of Edge corporations to open branches in yet other states is a powerful incentive to their use. Distinctions will occasionally be made in this chapter between an "Edge corporation engaged in banking," which is simply an Edge corporation that ordinarily accepts deposits in the United States from third parties, and other Edge corporations that make investments in foreign organizations.

International Banking Facilities. IBFs are the product of amendments to Regulations D and Q of the Board of Governors, local tax legislation adopted or proposed now in several states, and amendments to federal law covering deposit insurance. Briefly put, IBFs may engage in international banking activities on virtually the same basis as foreign branches except that they may accept deposits from and make loans to non-U.S. residents only, and their deposits are subject to a two-day minimum maturity and a minimum deposit or withdrawal amount of $100,000. Their earnings are subject to no or reduced local taxes (depending on the particular state), their deposits are generally not subject to reserve requirements, and they may pay interest on their deposits without restriction. In addition, their deposits are not subject to FDIC insurance assessments. An added convenience of IBFs is that they are not branches or subsidiaries of a bank or Edge corporation and need not necessarily even have a separate office, but may have no more physical presence than a set of books. IBFs are subject to restrictions, however, that will be discussed later in this chapter.

LEGAL CONSTRAINTS AFFECTING COSTS TO BANKS

Withholding Taxes and Foreign Tax Credits. The effect of foreign withholding taxes and U.S. foreign tax credits against such taxes on the net yield on an international loan is a complex subject far beyond the scope of this chapter. However, there are some basic points that should always be kept in mind in international lending. One important rule is not to focus too narrowly on individual loan transactions. Unless careful attention is paid to the overall tax position of the lending bank as well as the nature of the tax indemnities and "gross-ups" for withholding taxes in the related loan documentation, a loan that on its face has a positive spread may in fact result in a net loss to the lending bank.

For instance, a loan transaction in which a bank agrees to absorb withholding tax on the theory that it can recoup by utilizing the resultant foreign tax credit can result in a loan made at below-cost rates. If the bank's foreign tax credits exceed its current tax liability or are curtailed by its foreign tax credit limitation fraction, the bank will have excess foreign tax credits that will not offset its required tax payments until a later year. Even if the foreign tax credit will be used to offset the current year's taxes, the bank's estimated tax payments are always made slightly in arrears so there will be some "cost to carry" the tax credits being absorbed. These factors will prove especially costly if a loan made at a small margin will produce an inordinately large foreign tax credit—which will sometimes be the case if the foreign jurisdiction's withholding tax on gross interest payments is imposed at a high rate. Though theoretically profitable, such a tax credit-intensive loan will eliminate a disproportionate part of the bank's overall tax base, which could be more profitably exploited through alternative means.

A related (and somewhat ministerial appearing) matter in an international lending transaction that is actually quite critical to establishing a bank's tax position is ensuring that tax receipts with respect to foreign withholding taxes are obtained by the bank. This action is often overlooked or ignored as mere paperwork on top of the apparently more important issue of ensuring that the borrower actually pays the withholding tax. However, the Internal Revenue Service is in the fortunate position of being entitled on the one hand to presume that, if the contract rate of interest is received by a bank on a loan made in country X (country X being known to have a withholding tax) then the interest rate was actually grossed-up (to a higher rate such that after payment of withholding tax on the interest, the bank received the contract rate net of the tax), thereby increasing the income to such bank. On the other hand, the Service is also entitled to demand proof of payment of such taxes for the bank's account in the form of a tax receipt as a condition to allowing the resultant foreign tax credit. To prevent the unfortunate result of having increased income without an off-setting tax credit, loan documentation should always provide explicitly that the necessary tax receipts (or certified copies) are furnished to the bank. If there is an exemption from withholding taxes for a specific loan transaction, an opinion of counsel or a governmental certificate as to such exemption should be obtained.

Local Taxes.   The effects of local taxation are usually far more obvious than those of the foreign withholding tax problems discussed above and can have an equally severe impact on earnings as well as create competitive inequalities among banks in the United States. Banks have long recognized the utility of using offshore branches in making international loans to mitigate or eliminate the effect of local taxes, but this can be offset by taxes imposed by the jurisdiction where the branch is located and is often a cumbersome way to do business. Recent developments with respect to Edge corporations and IBFs, however, have increased the ability of banks to continue to do certain international business in the United States while avoiding or minimizing local taxes imposed by the jurisdiction where the bank is located.

The first of these developments was the substantial revision of Regulation K of the Board of Governors in June of 1979. Among other things, revised Regulation K permits Edge corporations engaged in banking to have domestic branches in different states whereas prior to the revisions an Edge corporation was limited to one state. The advantage of this revision is that it enables Edge corporations to operate with a broader capital base (an important factor in lending limits discussed later) while spreading their income in accordance with careful local tax planning.

The second and more important development in the area of local taxation is the approval by the Board of Governors of the establishment of IBFs by banks and their affiliates. As noted earlier the IBF regulations are designed to permit banks to engage in international lending activities in the United States free of reserve requirements and interest ceilings on deposits. In an attempt to encourage the use of IBF's by local banks, several states, including Connecticut, Florida, Georgia, Maryland, and New York, have passed tax legislation that eliminates or substantially reduces local taxes on IBF income. Similar legislation is pending in several other states.

Reserve Requirements.   Reserve requirements imposed by the Board of Governors under Regulation D have become increasingly difficult to deal with and increasingly more important in international banking transactions which in turn have grown more complex. Several years ago loans by United States banks to their foreign customers were almost uniformly made by foreign branches and pricing was based on the London interbank Eurodollar offering rate (LIBOR) while loans to domestic customers were made by domestic branches with pricing based on the prime rate. In the first instance reserve requirements did not apply, and in the second, the prime rate presumably took into account current reserve requirements.

In the last three to five years, however, two developments have occurred. Once the old reserve rate against Eurodollar loans (reserves are imposed on deposits but in this case the deposits are measured by the supposedly corresponding loans) made by a foreign branch of a U.S. bank to U.S. residents was reduced to zero, sophisticated domestic customers began to ask for a LIBOR pricing option in their domestic loan facilities. As this became more prevalent their foreign counterparts began to seek a prime rate pricing option in their facilities. In the midst of these developments the Board of Governors revised Regulation D substantially in 1980, once more imposing reserve requirements on so-called "Eurocurrency liabilities." It is beyond the scope of this chapter to dissect the intricacies of Regulation D, its phase-in requirements, and its application to various classes of deposits. Nonetheless there are certain considerations which should not be overlooked in a loan transaction that features either Eurodollar loans by a U.S. bank to a domestic borrower or foreign banks lending at prime to domestic or foreign customers. Loans extended by a foreign branch of a U.S. bank to a domestic borrower are (subject to some exceptions) included in "Eurocurrency liabilities" under Regulation D and as such are subject to reserve requirements. Because this development occurred after the prime/LIBOR option loan had become fairly well established, banks have tended to respond by adjusting their return on Eurodollar loans rather than by eliminating the option. Some banks have determined that they will rely on a modified version of the standard "Increased Costs" section found in most Eurodollar loan agreements and bill their customers for any costs of maintaining the required reserves. Other banks have adopted the approach of quoting a LIBOR rate with a built-in reserve requirement factor. Thus the quoted rate (QR) would be determined by the formula QR = LIBOR divided by (1.0 − RR) where RR equals the then current reserve requirement expressed as a decimal fraction. The problem with both approaches, which has yet to be resolved to the mutual satisfaction of borrower and bank, is that the Eurocurrency liability reserve requirements relating to loans to U.S. residents are not imposed on a transaction-by-transaction basis but on an overall netting basis with other categories of Eurocurrency liabilities and other deposits. The result may be at a particular time a reduced or negative Eurocurrency liability balance

even though there are loans outstanding that, in and of themselves,
qualify as Eurocurrency liabilities. In this circumstance a borrower
may argue that the bank is not entitled to what amounts to a windfall
increase in its effective yield. From the bank's point of view, however,
the administrative nightmare of attempting to monitor reserve costs
for thousands of loans, the impracticability of an equitable allocation
of those costs, and the already thin margins in the Eurodollar loan
market are strong counter-considerations.

The other situation that may arise does not affect domestic banks
directly but may be a factor when attempting to put together a syndicate of foreign and domestic banks in a prime/LIBOR option loan
agreement. If a foreign bank does not fund its prime-based loans
through a sufficiently large U.S.-based pool of funds, the prevailing
money center prime rate may not be reflective of the foreign bank's
true cost of funds, that is, the prime rate may be too low. To counter
this threat to the profit margin as well as a fear that the prime rate
may be held artificially low through governmental intervention, foreign banks have begun to ask that the domestic price quote be made
as the higher of prime or a spread over the three-week moving average
of secondary market certificates of deposit (CD Rate). Thus, the certificate of deposit market mechanism is used as a domestic equivalent
of the London interbank market and assumes that a loan is matched
by a deposit obtained in the certificate of deposit market. Since the
real cost of such a deposit to a bank is a function of the interest rate
paid, reserves required to be maintained, and FDIC insurance assessments, the banker should consider whether the CD Rate should be
adjusted for reserve requirements in a manner similar to that stated
above for LIBOR quotes as well as for FDIC costs.

One further restriction that should be noted in the area of reserve
requirements is in connection with IBFs. At present, IBF deposits are
not subject to reserve requirements; however, as noted earlier IBFs
are not permitted to accept deposits of less than two days' maturity.
Since overnight deposits form a significant part of international funding
transactions, until (and unless) this restriction is lifted many observers
feel that IBFs will not be able to challenge London and other offshore
international banking centers on an equal footing. The fact that they
cannot offer a significant banking function will not only eliminate that
segment of the deposit market but also through linkage (or lack thereof)
discourage other types of deposits.

Interest on Deposits.   One of the major differences between domestic banking and offshore banking is the rate of interest that banks
are permitted to pay on deposits. Regulation Q of the Board of Governors prohibits the payment of interest on demand deposits in the U.S.
banking system and limits severely the rates on time deposits of less
than 14 days' duration and $100,000 in amount. On the other hand,

there are few if any restrictions on the interest rate that may be paid by offshore branches on deposits that are payable only outside the United States. Deposits of Edge corporations are subject to the interest-rate limitations of legislation, and the nature of the deposits they are permitted to accept is limited to deposits by foreign customers in connection with international transactions. IBFs provide more flexibility in this area as their permitted deposits are exempt from Regulation Q. As noted above, however, IBFs are limited in that permitted deposits are restricted to obligations with a maturity (after notice or creation) of at least two days.

Section 23A of the Federal Reserve Act. The funding restraints imposed on a bank holding company system by Section 23A of the Federal Reserve Act are not limited to the international lending area. Simply put, Section 23A prohibits any member bank of the Federal Reserve System (as well as any nonmember FDIC insured bank) from extending credit to any non-bank affiliate (other than a direct or indirect subsidiary of the bank) unless the credit is secured. The level of security required is such as to make the practical effect of Section 23A a virtual prohibition on loans to affiliates by banks. Since the bank or banks in a holding company system tend to be able to acquire funds more cheaply than the other members, Section 23A is a major consideration in determining whether to structure an international lending facility through a bank and/or its subsidiaries or through a nonbanking subsidiary of the holding company. The latter alternative may be attractive for many reasons—tax, management structure, segregation of risk, less regulatory restrictions on activities, avoidance of lending limits, and so on—but the loss of funding availability from the affiliated bank or banks in the holding company system may outweigh all these considerations.

LEGAL CONSTRAINTS AFFECTING THE ACTIVITIES OF BANKS

Lending Limits. Both state and federal law impose limits on the aggregate amount that a domestic bank may lend to a single person or in some cases a group of related persons. Because state and federal law vary in their application, it is not practical in this chapter to be very specific about the various limits imposed. However, as a general rule unsecured loans by national banks to any one person are limited in aggregate amount to 15 percent of capital and surplus of the bank. Many states follow this rule. Lending limits may vary depending on the nature of the borrower (governmental entity, local authority, private corporation, etc.), the type of obligation (banker's acceptance, loan, letter of credit, etc.), the amount and type of security for the obligation, and the rules pertaining to aggregation of loans to related borrowers.

Loans by a foreign branch of a bank and by an IBF set up by a bank are subject to the overall lending limits of the bank. In the case of Edge corporations, an Edge corporation engaged in banking has a lending limit of 10 percent of its capital and surplus; however, under the 1979 revisions to Regulation K, all loans by an Edge corporation and any of its majority-owned subsidiaries to the same person must be aggregated for purposes of the lending limit. Revised Regulation K has also added a new general lending limit that requires that the aggregate of all loans to one person by member banks, their Edge corporation subsidiaries, their foreign banking subsidiaries, and the subsidiaries of both their Edge corporation and foreign banking subsidiaries not exceed the member bank's lending limit. Since many banks own the stock of their foreign banking subsidiaries through their Edge corporations, these aggregation requirements can limit severely the loans by an Edge corporation engaged in banking that also owns the stock of the foreign banking subsidiaries. The partial solution that many banks have adopted is to remove their Edge corporations engaged in banking from owning any stock of foreign banking subsidiaries.

The aggregation rules for determining what constitutes loans to a single "person" must be watched carefully. Under the National Banking Act and related regulations, for instance, loans to a corporation and its subsidiaries are treated as loans to a single person while under the New York Banking Law, loans to related corporations are aggregated only if loans to one corporation are "for the benefit of" another corporation in the group. When lending to governments or quasi-governmental entities the rules become less clear. Generally speaking an agency of a foreign government that can be demonstrated to stand alone, having its own assets and revenue base, may be regarded as an entity apart from the government itself for lending limit purposes while agencies that derive their current funds from general tax revenues will be counted as part of the government. In any event, each situation must be evaluated in light of its own facts and applicable law.

Gurantees; Letters of Credit. One of the peculiar distinctions between the U.S. banking system and that of the rest of the world is the lack of power of U.S. banks to issue guarantees of the obligations of third parties. In other parts of the world banks have traditionally backed up their customers' obligations with guarantees in the nature of guarantees of payment. In recognition of this, and in order not to put domestic banks at a competitive disadvantage, U.S. banking law permits foreign branches of U.S. banks to issue guarantees to the extent that local banks can and customarily do so, so long as the guarantee specifies a maximum liability and is payable only upon readily ascertainable events.

The domestic counterpart of the bank guarantee is the so-called stand-by letter of credit. A letter of credit can provide much the same comfort that a bank guarantee does, and domestic banks are increasingly asked to issue them in a variety of transactions. This can lead to unforeseen difficulties and some embarrassment if the parties to a transaction are not familiar with the limitations on letters of credit. The problem usually arises in the context that the party seeking the letter of credit is a foreign entity who is accustomed to bank guarantees and who expects the letter of credit to conform to the usual bank guarantee. However, a letter of credit is, most fundamentally, not a guarantee and has several characteristics that distinguish it from a bank guarantee. These include a definite expiry date, a definite maximum amount of liability, and payment against presentation of conforming documents, with no involvement in the underlying transaction. In addition, the bank should evaluate the credit of the account party and issue the letter of credit only if it would be willing to lend the account party a similar amount. Since many international transactions where bank guarantees are customarily sought do not lend themselves to the timing and quantification requirements of a letter of credit, the banker must determine in advance whether a letter of credit can be tailored to the transaction to the satisfaction of all parties.

Regulation U. Regulation U of the Board of Governors restricts the amount of loans made by banks the proceeds of which are used to acquire "margin" stock. Margin stock is, generally, any stock registered on a national securities exchange or traded in sufficient volume in the over-the-counter market. Effective March 31, 1982, a loan made to purchase margin stock that is secured directly or indirectly by margin stock is a regulated loan under Regulation U and the amount thereof may not exceed the maximum loan value (generally 50 percent of fair market value) of the margin stock held as security. A loan may be deemed indirectly secured when a bank has no more than an ordinary negative pledge or restriction on sales of assets with respect to the borrower's assets if more than 25 percent of those assets, after giving effect to the contemplated loan and acquisition of margin stock, consist of margin stock.

Regulation U should always be considered in the making of a loan that may be used to acquire margin stock because the penalty for failure to comply with the margin rules is that the loan may be declared void. In addition to the margin requirements of Regulation U, the regulation also requires, effective March 31, 1982, that a bank making any loan secured by margin stock, regardless of purpose, must obtain from the borrower a purpose statement on Form U-1 of the Board of Governors.

Regulation U is no longer as burdensome as it was prior to March 31, 1982 when it applied to loans for the purpose of acquiring margin stock secured by *any* stock (including the stock of wholly-owned subsidiaries) and when the definition of "indirectly secured" was less clear; however, the extreme penalty for violations of the margin rules should dictate extreme caution on the part of a bank lender. In particular, when a loan for the purchase of ostensibly foreign corporation stock is considered, the bank should determine whether the target stock falls within the definition of margin stock. Loans for unspecified purposes to foreign borrowers who may be unfamiliar with U.S. margin requirements (which under Regulation X also apply to borrowers) and may be subject to such requirements should likewise be scrutinized for possible margin rule problems.

Johnson Act. The Johnson (Debt Default) Act makes it an offense in the United States to make loans to governments (or their political subdivisions) that are in default in payment of their obligations to the United States, unless the country of the government in question is a member of both the International Monetary Fund and the International Bank for Reconstruction and Development or unless the Export-Import Bank of the United States participates in the loan transaction. Several opinions of the Attorney General of the United States have somewhat narrowed the apparent broad scope of the Johnson Act prohibition. The thrust of the opinions has been to the effect that the Johnson Act was intended to prohibit general purpose loans to the affected governments but not to restrict loans that are made "in the ordinary course of trade and normally move exclusively within the restricted channels of banking and commercial credit." In addition, it is generally felt that loans by foreign branches of U.S. banks would not violate the Johnson Act as long as the loans are for commercial purposes and the foreign branch is not merely a conduit for available loan funds in the United States. Nevertheless, the Johnson Act is a criminal statute providing for both fines and imprisonment for violations of its provisions and, accordingly, counsel should be consulted in connection with any loans to a foreign government (or subdivision thereof) that is on the proscribed list under the Johnson Act.

CONCLUSION

The foregoing discussion of legal constraints on international banking in the United States has only touched upon some of the more important and currently active areas in U.S. banking law and regulation. Other equally important areas such as restrictions on foreign banks doing business in the United States and the entire subject of the Glass-Steagall restrictions on banks' securities-related activities have not been discussed at all, but should not on that account be overlooked. In any event international banking in the United States is subject to such a variety of restrictions either directly related to international banking or to banking in general that it is one of the most legally intensive areas in commercial finance. Despite this complex system of laws and regulations, however, the United States remains one of the best environments for banking, and international banking in particular, in the world. The U.S. system imposes less control over banks' general lending policies and practices and affords more equal opportunities to foreign banks entering the system than virtually any other country. As the process of deregulation of banking now in progress continues, this situation can only improve.

46
Legal and Regulatory Constraints within Other Countries

WILLIAM J. KORSVIK
Senior Vice President (Retired)
The First National Bank of Chicago

INTRODUCTION

The International Banking Act of 1978 had as its primary objective the establishment of a federal regulatory framework governing entry and operations of foreign banks. Moreover, it was intended that it would be nondiscriminatory in its effect on domestic and foreign banks and that it would afford foreign banks equality of competitive opportunity vis-a-vis domestic institutions in similar circumstances. In this spirit, the Congress included a provision in the Act which directed the Department of the Treasury to determine the treatment of U.S. banks by foreign governments. Accordingly, the Treasury, responding to this Congressional mandate, produced a thorough study of contemporary conditions facing U.S. banks overseas. The preparation of this report, covering 140 nations, included a survey of all U.S. banks having branch, subsidiary, or affiliate operations abroad, consultation with knowledgeable government experts and regulators in a wide variety of agencies, and solicitation of information from American diplomatic posts in every foreign nation which the United States recognizes.

The resulting study, *Report to Congress on Foreign Government Treatment of U.S. Commercial Banking Organizations*[1] was submitted to Congress on September 17, 1979. It is the most comprehensive and definitive review of the general subject of this Chapter that is available. The material in this Chapter summarizes much of the material in that excellent Report.

---

[1] *Report to Congress on Foreign Government Treatment of U.S. Commercial Banking Organizations* (Washington, D.C.: U.S. Government Printing Office, 1979).

CLASSIFICATION OF RESTRICTIONS

Official constraints on foreign banks take the form of entry restrictions and restraints on the operations of banks already established in the host country's market. Restrictions on foreign banks' entry, whether by law or by administrative policy or practice, range from total prohibition of foreign bank presence within a country to various limitations on the organizational form allowed. Particular forms of entry—such as establishment of branches or a subsidiary bank or acquisition of equity interest in an existing bank—may be specifically restricted. Or, foreign bank presence may be limited only to representative offices which do not engage in any direct banking transactions.

Regulations affecting the operations of foreign banks already established in a country may be categorized for simplicity into two types according to their economic impact on the banks' operations. Most restrictions on bank operations increase their cost and thus have effects that are equivalent to the imposition of a tax. When a "taxlike" restriction is imposed, it costs a bank more to extend credit (or provide any other bank service), and the bank will generally charge higher rates and extend less credit as a result. An example of a taxlike regulation is reserve requirements. Banks that are subject to higher effective reserve requirements than domestic banks suffer a competitive disadvantage identical in effect to the imposition of a differentially higher tax.

The second category of regulations affecting bank operations is restrictions that are equivalent in effect to quotas. Quotalike restrictions on banks set absolute limits on the amount of credit or services that banks may offer. Faced with quotas, banks are restricted in the amount of credit or services they can offer, which is detrimental to both them and their customers. Quotalike restrictions may directly limit the competitive opportunity of foreign banks. For example, foreign bank operations may be effectively restrained by absolute limits on the amount of capital they are allowed to dedicate to their operations within a foreign country.

Although official restraints on foreign bank operations take many different forms in practice, they can all be viewed, conceptually, as having either taxlike or quotalike effects. Examples of both types of restraints are given in the table on page 736.

ENTRY RESTRICTIONS

Entry policies toward foreign banks range across a spectrum from prohibitions against any foreign banking presence to admission of foreign banks in any institutional form the bank prefers. Very few countries have policies lying at either of these two extremes. Some limita-

Example of Taxlike and Quotalike Restrictions on Foreign Banks

Taxlike restrictions*
  Differential reserve requirements
  Prohibitions against accepting retail deposits
  Prohibitions against foreign exchange transactions
  No access to rediscount facilities
  No access to subsidized funds for export finance
Quotalike restrictions
  Credit/lending ceilings
  Specified loan and investment portfolio structures
  Swap limits
  Required capital to asset ratios combined with
    capitalization limits
  Ceilings on loans in domestic currency
  Ceilings on loans in foreign currencies
  Prohibition or limitation on branching

*Most of these restrictions effectively increase funding or other costs.

tions on foreign banks' choices of how entry can be accomplished are imposed by nearly all countries.

Entry restrictions are frequently not clear-cut. Policies also are subject to change, and even at a given time, other ambiguities with respect to entry conditions arise.

Certainly there are cases where laws are very explicit; prohibitions of certain types of foreign bank entry are a good example. Nevertheless, there are numerous instances where restrictions are not imposed by laws or formal policy declarations, but are accomplished through administrative practice. Where this occurs, entry policy becomes clearly defined only by test cases of banks seeking entry. Several countries' policies on foreign acquisition of domestic banks are of this uncertain nature. And, finally, the interpretation of existing entry criteria may be particularly difficult when one of the criteria is some form of reciprocity.

To help understand the difficulties surrounding the interpretation of entry policies, key elements of the present restrictions on entry are outlined below.

Time Horizon. The clearest form of discrimination is complete exclusion from the market. In practice, very few countries deny foreign banks any presence, and those are countries in which U.S. banks have, for the most part, expressed little interest.

Ambiguity. Many countries' entry policies, especially those relating to acquisition of domestic banks, are ambiguous. Even where laws or regulations exist, there is often a difference between the letter of the law and effective policy. Therefore, the operational effect of stated entry policies of many countries can only be determined through the experience of banks making actual attempts at entry. Policy may vary according to the size of the bank applying for entry or according to the size of the bank being sought for acquisition.

Attempt to assess the ability of U.S. banks to enter foreign markets by acquisition illustrates many of these complications. As of mid-1979, 50 countries were believed to prohibit all acquisition of domestic banks by foreign banks and an additional 29 countries did not allow acquisition of controlling interest in their domestic banks by foreign banks.

Moreover, past experience may be a misleading basis for assessing present policies because their application may vary over time or be dependent upon the size of the foreign bank, or, even more importantly, the size of the domestic bank which is subject to acquisition. For example, it is likely that the acquisition of a large bank would be unacceptable to most foreign governments, even where there is no explicit prohibition, except, perhaps, when a large bank is failing and no domestic banks are willing or able to assume its obligations. Due to those uncertainties, any appraisal of restraints on U.S. banks' ability to make acquisitions abroad must be tentative.

Reciprocity.   Reciprocity applied to foreign bank entry reduces, in its simplest form, to one country admitting banks from a second country only if the second country also grants entry to the first country's banks. Reciprocity as a condition of bank entry tends to limit entry opportunities and is often ambiguous and complex. Very few countries apply a narrow defintion of reciprocity in considering foreign banks' applications for entry, although many countries include reciprocity among the other factors considered.

Nevertheless, there are some instances in which a narrowly defined reciprocity test is currently in use. Brazil's central bank defends its prohibition of entry of additional U.S. bank branches by applying a one-for-one interpretation of the reciprocity concept.

When countries apply the reciprocity principle to subnational political units, such as the various states of the United States, the effect of a reciprocity criterion becomes very complicated.

Other Effective Barriers

Assessment of entry restrictions is further complicated because some restrictions effectively deter the entry of all but a certain class of foreign banks. Countries may impede foreign bank entry by imposing high capitalization requirements, which particularly affect relatively small banks. Spain, for example, imposes capital requirements on foreign branches of approximately $10 million and twice that amount for foreign subsidiaries. While both domestic and foreign banks in Spain are subject to similar requirements, such high capitalization clearly precludes entry by all but large foreign banks.

Other countries limit more directly the entry of all but large foreign banks, presumably in the belief that there is little likelihood of those banks failing. The United Kingdom, for example, requires that a foreign bank have an established international reputation and clientele prior to its admission. The banking authorities in Hong Kong require that the parent of an applicant bank have assets (not including contra items) of greater than $3 billion and, in assessing applications, take into consideration the adequacy of the home country's supervision. Recent actions taken by the People's Republic of China indicate that they may have preference to large U.S. banks since they have recognized only a few of the very largest banks in handling documentary business.

Summary.   Restrictions on the entry of U.S. banks into domestic markets of other countries take many forms. Some countries prohibit foreign banks from entering their markets altogether, while others limit the institutional forms available to foreign banks. Some countries require that their banks receive reciprocal treatment in a foreign bank's home country in order for a foreign bank to be granted permission to enter their markets. U.S. banks may be adversely affected by narrow definitions of reciprocity referring to the treatment accorded foreign banks in the U.S. banks' home state.

Indirect exclusion or limitation of foreign bank entry is sometimes affected by imposing high capitalization requirements or by requiring the parent organization to be a certain size or international stature.

None of the highly developed, industrial countries completely excludes foreign commercial banking presence, and most of them have liberal entry policies. Restrictions do not follow geographic patterns and do not correspond to level of development of either the countries or their banking systems.

Entry restrictions are often defended on the grounds that they protect local banks from foreign competition, prevent local markets from becoming overbanked, or allow countries to maintain national control over their domestic banking system. The particular circumstances of each country should be considered in assessing the degree of restrictiveness of the country's policy toward foreign bank entry.

In 1979, the Treasury Department's report to the Congress on the treatment of U.S. commercial banks by foreign governments included a number of tables distributing countries that limited the entry of foreign banks into their respective countries.

Each country appears in the most restrictive of the categories considered in which it belongs and is not repeated in subsequent, less restrictive categories.

The countries listed in Table 1 totally deny competitive opportunity to foreign banks by prohibiting their presence in any form. All of those countries have wholly nationalized banking systems and, thus,

Table 1
Countries Whose Laws Prohibit
Foreign Banking Presence in
Any Form

Afghanistan	Iraq
Bulgaria	Laos
Cuba	Libya
Czechoslovakia	Madagascar
Ethiopia	Somalia
Guinea	Nepal

prohibit both domestic and foreign privately owned banking operations.

By specifically prohibiting new entry, but not necessarily the presence of foreign banks in any form, the countries in Table 2 also impose severe restrictions. Because Guyana and the United Arab Emirates (UAE) previously permitted foreign banks to enter their markets in various institutional forms, the severity of this policy causes a disparity between the interests of established banks and potential new entrants. The governments of those two countries decided that the number of foreign banks already present was sufficient for the size of their respective banking markets and stopped admitting new foreign banks. Concern about the possibility of becoming "overbanked" arose in the UAE after the failure of two foreign banks there in 1977.

The countries listed in Table 3, which do allow entry by representative offices of foreign banks are, in fact, limiting entry in a manner that is only slightly less restrictive than the entry policies of the first two groups of countries. Representative offices cannot, by definition, engage in any type of banking business and are frequently constrained from advertising the services of their parent bank. Again, many of these countries have grandfathered foreign bank branches and/or subsidiaries and affiliates. This group of countries spans the globe and includes some highly developed countries, such as Sweden and Norway, as well as less developed countries, such as India and Columbia.

For the majority of foreign banks which do not have a grandfathered

Table 2
Countries Whose Current Policies or Licensing
Practices Prohibit Foreign Bank Entry in
Any Form*

Benin	Surinam
Guyana	Tanzania
Kuwait	United Arab Emirates
Netherlands Antilles	

* In addition to the countries listed in Table 1.

Table 3
**Countries Prohibiting All Forms of Foreign Banking Entry
Except Representative Offices by Law, Policy or
Administrative Practice***

Prohibition Imposed by Law	
Algeria	Sweden
Burma	Syria
Colombia	USSR
Portugal	Yugoslavia
	Venezuela

Prohibition Imposed by Policy or Administrative Practice	
People's Republic of China	Poland
El Salvador	Saudi Arabia
German Democractic Republic	Trinidad and Tobago
Guatemala	Turkey
India	Mexico
Indonesia	New Zealand
	Norway

* Countries in Table 1 and 2 do not permit representative offices.

facility, a representative office is some improvement over complete exclusion. Although representative offices cannot take deposits or make loans, they can sometimes solicit loans for their parent and establish banking relationships with local firms.

Several of these countries permit affiliated banks. Again, no particu-

Table 4
**Countries Prohibiting Foreign Banks from Entering Their
Markets via Branches by Law, Policy, or
Administrative Practice***

Prohibition Imposed by Law	
Bermuda	Ghana
Cameroon	Hungary
Canada	Iceland
People's Republic of the Congo	Niger
Costa Rica	Peru
Finland	Philippines
The Gambia	South Africa
	Uruguay

Prohibition Imposed by Policy or Administrative Practice	
Bahrain	Netherlands Antilles
Botswana	Nigeria
Dominican Republic	Oman
Ecuador	Qatar
Haiti	Singapore
Jordan	Solomon Islands
Republic of Korea	Surinam
Malaysia	Thailand
Malta	Tunisia
Morocco	Zaire

* In addition to those listed in Tables 1, 2, and 3.

lar pattern, geographic or by stage of development, characterizes these countries. The importance of prohibitions on foreign branches can scarcely be overemphasized. Not only is the branch the vehicle which most U.S. banks prefer, but it is in fact the form through which most of the worldwide expansion in banking has taken place over the last two decades. Prohibitions against foreign branching are generally defended on the grounds of protecting local banks from foreign competition or preventing a country's banking markets from becoming overbanked. Elimination of the branch choice may completely deter any entry by some banks which find other forms either inadequate, such as representative offices, or too expensive or unwieldly, such as subsidiaries or affiliates.

Table 5
Countries Prohibiting Foreign Banks from Purchasing Any Interest in Indigenous Banks By Law, Policy, or Administrative Practice*

Bangladesh	Papua New Guinea
Costa Rica	Surinam
Pakistan	

*In addition to those listed in Tables 1, 2, and 3.

In many countries, the purpose of such restrictions is to maintain national control over the banking system. Some countries, notably Nigeria, Morocco, Saudi Arabia, and Venezuela, have recently required foreign banks to divest their interests in local banks to less than majority control in an effort to indigenize their banking systems. Nationalistic feelings, fear of foreign dominance of the vital banking sector, and a belief that the government can exert more control over domestic banks than it can over foreign-owned banks play a role in the establishment of such policies. Other countries, such as the People's Republic of the Congo, Gambia, Japan, Republic of Korea, and Canada prohibit both domestic and foreign banks from acquiring controlling interest in established, indigenous banks to maintain competition in their banking markets. Entry by acquisition provides a foreign bank with an already established market share, clientele, staff and facilities. However, prohibitions against acquisition are relatively less injurious to foreign banks if entry via branch or de novo subsidiary, the two more preferred forms, is possible.

OPERATING RESTRAINTS

Given its economic and social importance, banking is traditionally one of the most heavily regulated and supervised industries. Virtually all restraints on bank operations exist for purposes of prudential regula-

Table 6
Countries Which Limit Foreign Banks to Acquiring Less than
Controlling Interest in Indigenous Banks by Law, Policy, or
Administrative Practice*

Australia	10%
Bermuda	40%
Canada	10%†
People's Republic of the Congo	49%
Denmark	30%‡
Ecuador	20%§
Finland	20%
The Gambia	20%
Japan	5%
Nigeria	40%
Philippines	30%‖
Republic of Korea	10%
Upper Volta	49%

Specific Maximum Foreign Participation Allowed in Practice

Bahrain	49%
Dominican Republic	30%
Greece	49%
Iceland	49%
Morocco	50%
Oman	49%
Qatar	49%
Singapore	20%
South Africa	50%
U.K.	15%

No Majority Control; No Specific Maximum

Central African Empire	Netherlands
Cyprus	Oman
Egypt	Qatar
Iceland	Trinidad and Tobago
Malaysia	Tunisia
Malta	

* In addition to those listed in Tables 1, 2, and 3.

† Canada permits an individual foreign party to own up to 10 percent of
a bank, and up to 25 percent of any bank may be foreign owned.

‡ Denmark requires a merger if any party, foreign or domestic, acquires
30 percent or more of a bank.

§ For non-Andean Pact nations.

‖ 40 percent with Presidential approval.

tion—promoting the safety and soundness of the system—and for purposes of implementing national monetary policy and promoting other
governmental objectives.

However, some countries use these and other regulations and administrative practices to discriminate against foreign banks. Less obviously,
operating restraints or national economic policy measures applied
equally to foreign and domestic banks sometimes have a differential
competitive impact on foreign banks because of the nature of their
operations. Some governments have deliberately reduced competitive
inequities by flexible application of regulatory requirements to foreign

banks or by granting them privileges not extended to domestic banks in order to compensate for the differential impact of restrictive regulations.

However, as a practical matter, most U.S. bankers are not greatly concerned about obtaining competitive equality across all segments of foreign financial markets. Obtaining permission to establish operations in a given country is more often a problem for U.S. banks than conducting successful operations once entry has been accomplished. Many U.S. banks have indicated a desire to enter certain countries where foreign bank entry is presently prohibited or severely limited, even though operations of established foreign banks are subject to substantial restraints. Operating restraints are not often an overriding concern to U.S. banks that perceive sound business opportunities in a foreign market. Their typical strategy is to assess the environment in which they must operate, and if the business prospects appear favorable, they then cope with the restrictions.

Operating restraints that differentially affect foreign banks may impede their ability to compete with domestic banks in several ways. Most importantly, such restrictions may increase their cost of funds or their general operating costs, relative to domestic competitors, or constrain expansion of their operations within the country.

Explicitly Discriminatory Regulations. Most countries with regulations which intentionally constrain the operations of foreign banks are developing nations. Their regulations are designed to limit foreign bank operations to certain segments of the financial market, while preserving other segments entirely for domestic banks. A small number of developed countries also impose restrictions applying only to foreign banking operations.

Among the most prevalent intentionally discriminatory regulations are those prohibiting or limiting foreign bank solicitation of various kinds of deposits. Deposits are usually one of a bank's lowest cost sources of funds. To the extent that deposit-taking limitations force foreign banks to use more expensive sources of funds, they constitute a significant competitive disadvantage to foreign banks.

Another common and important restraint on foreign bank operations is their inability to expand existing branch networks. Very few countries limit foreign branches by law, as does Spain, but nearly 30 countries effectively limit, by administrative practice, the number of branches foreign banks can establish. Some countries prohibit any additional branching by both foreign and domestic banks out of concern that the nation is "overbanked." Foreign banks are usually more adversely affected than are domestic banks, however, since they typically have fewer established branches. In some cases, a prohibition on additional branches is one of many constraints imposed on grandfathered foreign banks.

Table 7
Current Restrictions on Foreign Commercial Bank Entry

Country	No Foreign Presence	No New Foreign Commercial Bank Entry	No Foreign Commercial Banking Except Representative Offices	No Foreign Commercial Bank Branches	No Equity Interest in Indigenous Commercial Banks	No Controlling Interest in Indigenous Commercial Banks	No Restrictions Found	Restrictions Indeterminate
1. Afghanistan	X	X		X	X	X		
2. Algeria				X	X	X		
3. Argentina							X	
4. Australia			X	X		X		
5. Austria							X	
6. Bahamas							X	
7. Bahrain				X		X		
8. Bangladesh					X			
9. Barbados							X	
10. Belgium							X	
11. Belize								
12. Benin		X		X	X	X		
13. Bermuda				X		X		
14. Botswana							X	
15. Bolivia								
16. Brazil				X	X	X		
17. Bulgaria	X	X		X	X	X		
18. Burma			X		X	X		
19. Burundi								X
20. Cameroon				X		X		
21. Canada				X				
22. Republic of Cape Verde							X	
23. Cayman Islands							X	
24. Central African Empire						X		X
25. Chad							*	
26. Chile			X	X	X	X		
27. China, Peoples Republic			X	X	X	X		
28. Colombia				X		X		
29. Congo, Peoples Republic				X		X		
30. Costa Rica				X	X	X		
31. Cuba	X	X			X	X		
32. Cyprus				X		X		
33. Czechoslovakia	X	X		X	X	X		

#	Country	1	2	3	4	5	6	7	8
34.	Denmark								
35.	Republic of Djibouti			*					
36.	Dominican Republic		X	X		X			
37.	Ecuador			X		X			
38.	Egypt			X					
39.	El Salvador				X				
40.	Ethiopia			X	X	X	X		X
41.	Federal Republic of Germany		X					X	
42.	Fiji		X						
43.	Finland			X					
44.	France		X			X			
45.	Gabon		X						
46.	The Gambia								
47.	German Democratic Rep.			X	X	X	X		
48.	Ghana			X		X			
49.	Greece				X				
50.	Guatemala			X	X	X	X		
51.	Guinea	X		X		X		X	X
52.	Guinea-Bissau								X
53.	Guyana		*	X	X	X		X	X
54.	Haiti				*	X			
55.	Honduras			X	X	X			
56.	Hong Kong			X	X	X	X		
57.	Hungary			X	X	X			
58.	Iceland					X			
59.	India	X		X			X		
60.	Indonesia					X	X		
61.	Iran								
62.	Iraq		X	X	X	X		X	
63.	Republic of Ireland		X	X	X	X			X
64.	Israel		X						
65.	Italy								
66.	Ivory Coast								
67.	Jamaica		X						
68.	Japan			X					
69.	Jordan								
70.	Kenya				X	X			
71.	Republic of Korea	X	X	X	X	X			
72.	Kuwait			X	X	X		X	
73.	Laos								X
74.	Lebanon								X
75.	Lesotho								

Table 7 (concluded)

Country	No Foreign Presence	No New Foreign Commercial Bank Entry	No Foreign Commercial Banking Except Representative Offices	No Foreign Commercial Bank Branches	No Equity Interest in Indigenous Commercial Banks	No Controlling Interest in Indigenous Commercial Banks	No Restrictions Found	Restrictions Indeterminate
76. Liberia	X			X	X	(X)		
77. Libya	X	X		X	X	X	X	
78. Luxembourg	X	X				X		
79. Madagascar				X		(X)		
80. Malawi						X		
81. Malaysia				X		X	X	
82. Mali				X		X		
83. Malta							X	
84. Mauritania							X	
85. Mauritius			X	X		X		
86. Mexico				X	X	X		
87. Morocco							X	
88. Mozambique	X			X	X	X		
89. Nepal		X		X	X	X		
90. Netherlands Antilles		X		X		(X)		
91. Netherlands						X		
92. New Zealand			X	X	X	X		X
93. Nicaragua								
94. Niger				X		X		
95. Nigeria				X	X	X		
96. Norway			X	X	X	X		
97. Oman				X	X	X		
98. Pakistan							X	
99. Panama					X	X		
100. Papua New Guinea							X	
101. Paraguay				X	X	X		
102. Peru				X		X		
103. Philippines			X	X	X	X		
104. Poland			X	X	X	X		
105. Portugal				X	X	X		
106. Qatar								
107. Romania					X	X		

No.	Country	1	2	3	4	5	6
108.	Rwanda						
109.	Saudi Arabia		X	X	X	X	X
110.	Senegal			X	X	X	X
111.	Seychelles						X
112.	Sierra Leone						X
113.	Singapore			X	X	X	
114.	Somalia	X			X	X	
115.	Solomon Islands	X		X		X	
116.	South Africa			X	X	X	
117.	Spain					X	
118.	Sri Lanka						X
119.	Sudan		(X)	(X)	X		X
120.	Surinam	X	X	(X)	X	X	
121.	Swaziland	X		(X)	(X)	(X)	
122.	Sweden		X	X	X	X	
123.	Switzerland						X
124.	Syria	X	X	X	X	X	
125.	Taiwan					X	
126.	Tanzania	X	X	X	X	X	
127.	Thailand	X		X		X	
128.	Togo						X
129.	Trinidad & Tobago	X	X	X	X	X	
130.	Tunisia		X	X	X	X	
131.	Turkey	X	X	X	X	X	
132.	U.S.S.R.	X	X	X	X	X	
133.	United Arab Emirates	X		X	X	X	
134.	United Kingdom			X	X	X	
135.	Upper Volta					X	
136.	Uruguay						
137.	Venezuela	X	X	X	X	X	
138.	Yemen Arab Republic		(X)	(X)	(X)	(X)	
139.	Yugoslavia	X	X	X	X	X	
140.	Zaire	X		X	X		
141.	Zambia						X

*

* Chile: Either a representative office or a branch is permitted, but not both. Denmark: *De novo* subsidiaries are permitted. Haiti: Equity participation is unclear. Honduras: No representative offices are permitted. Taiwan: Branch and representative offices are permitted; equity participation is unclear.

Notes: (X) Indication that the situation is unclear but entry might be possible. This table presents an overview of restrictions on foreign bank entry in countries recognized by the United States plus Taiwan and the Cayman Islands. The classifications are based on current practices (August 1979), not statutes. In most cases where restrictions were found to be indeterminate, foreign banks have not attempted those specific forms of entry, so that clear conclusions about current practices cannot be drawn. Other instances represent cases where government practices are unclear or not defined.

Denial of foreign bank access to central bank discount facilities is another prevalent specifically discriminatory policy that places foreign banks at a disadvantage in meeting liquidity needs in a timely and inexpensive manner, forcing them to hold a larger proportion of their assets in lower-yielding secondary reserves.

While the policies described above are fairly common, other unusual discriminatory operational restrictions constitute an important restriction to the foreign banks operating in particular countries. Restrictions on the services which foreign banks can offer make it difficult for them to expand their market share because they cannot offer the "full line of services" permitted domestic banks.

Sources of Unintended Differential Effects. Foreign banks rarely mirror domestic banks, either in organization and structure, or in the relative emphasis they give to various banking operations. For example, a bank just entering a foreign country tends to concentrate on securing the business of multinational corporations of their own nationality. Thus, trade financing and other foreign currency activities are likely to account for a substantial proportion of its activity. Subsequently, the foreign bank may move into more extensive wholesale banking operations related to international finance or to domestic corporate business. It is usually only later, if at all, that the importance of a foreign bank's retail operation will even approach that of domestic banks.

One problem which affects the operations of U.S. banks in over 65 countries emanates from maximum permissible asset/capital ratios and limits on the size of loans to individual borrowers which are imposed by most countries for prudential reasons.

For domestic banks, the calculation of capital-based limits is generally based on the capital of the parent organization. Many nations, again for prudential reasons, treat a foreign bank's operations in the host country as an independent entity. Thus, they calculate asset/capital ratios and individual lending limits only on the capital of the foreign bank's entity, which is typically a small fraction of the total capital of the foreign bank's parent organization or of the capital of large domestic banks. Thus, the permissible extent of a foreign bank's total activity in those countries and its maximum individual loan size are much less than those of domestic banks.

Foreign banks are thus constrained in competing directly for large commercial loans through their local branch or subsidiary. The problem is exacerbated when such restrictions occur in combination with limits on importation of foreign branch capital.

Credit ceilings are often imposed on both foreign and domestic banks for purposes of domestic monetary policy. Such policies can have a greater impact on foreign banks than on domestic banks by limiting their ability to expand their lending volume. France, for example, controls domestic credit by levying supplementary reserve requirements on any bank whose loan growth exceeds a specified limit beyond a total loan base at a certain point in time. Those controls are imposed on both foreign and domestic banks. However, the fact that foreign banks are among the latest entrants into the French market and therefore have not built up their domestic loan portfolios has constrained them from increasing their share of the loan market. That constraint is significant because such growth is necessary for them to establish a viable foothold in the market. French authorities have been sensitive to the problems of new foreign entrants, however, and have generally been flexible in their interpretation of the loan-growth limits. They have allowed foreign banks to use their capitalization as a base for credit expansion.

The United Kingdom has imposed similar credit controls by levying a reserve requirement on banks whose liability growth exceeds a specific limit beyond their sterling deposits as of a certain base period. Because foreign banks tend to have a smaller proportion of sterling deposits to total liabilities than domestic banks, those controls differentially restrain their ability to expand loan volume. Lending ceilings based on domestic deposit liabilities may be particularly detrimental when branching by foreign banks is prohibited or limited in comparison with domestic banks.

General economic and balance-of-payments policy measures, though not directed at the banking sector, sometimes affect foreign more than domestic banks. Limitations on foreign exchange transactions, for example, will have a harsher impact on foreign banks because of the international orientation of their business, even though they are applied evenhandedly to all banks. In another instance, capital controls and limitations on foreign currency deposits tend to be more restrictive on foreign banks, since they fund operations by borrowing from their parent institution and often rely heavily on borrowing in the interbank market.

The need to obtain alien work permits provides an example of differential effects on foreign banks caused by a measure totally divorced from the banking sector. Foreign enterprises are hampered more severely by such regulations because they may desire, at least initially, a staff of their own nationality, while such considerations have little impact on domestic banks. Similarly, restrictions on the repatriation of funds or profits affect only foreign institutions.

Differential Advantages.   Not all operating restraints have a differentially adverse impact on foreign banks. On the contrary, some have a favorable impact on foreign banks, although they were not designed for this purpose. One important example of this kind is differential reserve requirements on foreign and domestic currency deposits, which are often lower on foreign deposits. This gives an advantage to foreign banks because they hold a greater proportion of foreign currency liabilities. While those policies are not instituted to favor foreign banks, they do so because of the composition of foreign banks' portfolios and mix of activities.

In some developing countries, foreign banks are not required to make loans to the priority sectors targeted in the government's development plans. Foreign banks in other countries frequently are excused from obligations imposed on domestic banks to support government bond issues. On a less formal basis, governments rarely require foreign banks to participate in "rescue" operations of failing firms. Foreign banks are sometimes granted access to currency swap facilities that are not available to domestic banks. This may be done as administrative compensation for differential restraints elsewhere.

Operating restraints may have differentially adverse or, differentially beneficial, impact on foreign banks. In practice, the injurious impacts outweigh the beneficial ones. But on the whole, the effects of these operational restraints have not been severe enough to deter U.S. banks from entering most countries.

47

The Federal Reserve System and Regulation of International Banking

C. KEEFE HURLEY, JR.*
Vice President and General Counsel
Shawmut Corporation

From its establishment in 1913, the Federal Reserve System has played a significant role in the regulation of international banking. Central banks are traditionally concerned with the international positions of their currencies and carry out a variety of functions in the international financial arena. In addition, the Federal Reserve, as a result of its responsibilities with respect to member banks and bank holding companies, occupies a unique regulatory and supervisory position astride the dual banking system of the United States. These central bank and supervisory functions have been recognized by Congress over the years and have resulted in the Federal Reserve playing a key role regulating and supervising both international activities of U.S. banking organizations and, more recently, the U.S. activities of foreign banks.

To varying degrees, the Federal Reserve has regulatory and supervisory jurisdiction over the following kinds of financial institutions: (1) member banks of the Federal Reserve System (including national banks and state chartered banks); (2) Edge and agreement corporations; (3) domestic and foreign bank holding companies; and (4) U.S. branches and agencies of foreign banks licensed by either federal or state authorities. In addition, the tools that the Federal Reserve uses in regulating the supply of money and credit are brought to bear on all "depository institutions."[1] In this connection the Board's recent authorization of

* Vice President and General Counsel, Shawmut Corporation, Boston, Massachusetts; formerly Assistant General Counsel, Board of Governors of the Federal Reserve System. The views expressed in this chapter do not necessarily reflect those of the Shawmut Corporation or the Federal Reserve.

[1] The term *depository institution* as used in the Monetary Control Act of 1980 (Pub. L. 96–221) includes a bank, savings bank, credit union, or savings and loan association that is insured or eligible to apply for insurance. It does not include money market funds many of which have characteristics similar to depository institutions.

depository institutions to operate International Banking Facilities reflects the integration of international banking markets.

This chapter provides an overview of the relationships that exist
between the Federal Reserve and each of the institutions listed above
with regard to international banking. The legal and regulatory constraints on some of these institutions are discussed in other chapters
at greater length. References to those chapters are made where appropriate.

MEMBER BANKS

Foreign Branches

By far the largest share of the foreign operations of U.S. banks is
accounted for by foreign branches. As of December 31, 1981, U.S.
banks operated 799 foreign branches in over 100 foreign countries.
Those branches had total assets of approximately $416 billion. A branch
does not enjoy separate corporate status, and is therefore supervised
and regulated by the agency primarily responsible for the bank—either
the Comptroller of the Currency or the state banking authority. The
Federal Reserve performs functions critical to the operations of foreign
branches.

Prior to the establishment of a branch a member bank must receive
the approval of the Board of Governors. For member banks with existing foreign branches, this process may simply involve giving notice
to the Board after the branch has been set up. The application process
for member banks that do not have foreign branches is also streamlined.
It is rare in the extreme for the Board to deny an application to establish
a foreign branch.[2] Nevertheless, the Board on occasion uses the application process as a means of expressing concern regarding the rate of
expansion or the capital position of a member bank. This may be accomplished by attaching conditions to the Board's approval of the foreign
branch or through formal or informal communication to the member
bank's senior management.

Once established, the branch generally must operate within the
powers and limitations of its governing charter. However, Congress
recognized that some of the limitations on the banking powers of U.S.
banks, while appropriate in the United States, cannot be imposed when
those banks operate in a foreign environment without placing U.S.
banks at a competitive disadvantage. Therefore, under the law the
Board is given authority to permit foreign branches of member banks

---

[2] Under section 25 of the Federal Reserve Act (12 U.S.C. 601), the board may deny
an application if for any reason approval is deemed "inexpedient." Application procedures are set forth in section 211.3(a) of Regulation K (12 CFR 211.3(a)).

to engage in additional activities that are usual in connection with the business of banking abroad. The board has authorized several activities such as the issuance of certain guarantees and acting as insurance agent or broker.[3] If a member bank believes a particular banking practice that is impermissible in the United States is, nevertheless, generally engaged in by banks abroad or by banks in a certain country, the member bank can petition the Board for permission to engage in the activity.[4]

Although not separate entities, branches enjoy preferred status so far as reserve requirements and interest-rate limitations are concerned. Under the Federal Reserve Act, a deposit that is payable only outside the United States is not subject to basic reserve requirements, interest-rate limitations, or to the prohibition against the payment of interest on demand deposits.[5] From the customer's perspective, the foreign payability feature requires that he assume the risks that payment may be impeded.[6] Thus, a guarantee by the member bank that it will pay foreign branch deposits will result in the loss of the exemptions.[7] These exemptions, like the additional activities, allow foreign branches of member banks to compete more effectively with local institutions.

Bankers' Acceptances[8]

The use of bankers' acceptances to finance international trade has increased markedly in recent years. At June 30, 1982, there was approximately $72.6 billion in acceptances created by banks in the United States outstanding. A credit in the form of an "eligible" acceptance is functionally equivalent to a loan funded by a certificate of deposit. The attractiveness of the acceptance form of financing is that, whereas a domestic certificate of deposit is subject to reserve requirements, an "eligible" bankers' acceptance is not.

The Board's responsibilities with respect to bankers' acceptances

---

[3] The permissible activities are listed in section 211.3(b) of Regulation K (12 CFR 211.3(b)). For a state member bank, the list of additional activities has the effect of removing any impediment that may exist in federal law to the bank performing the activity. The list does not override any prohibition against the activities that may exist in state law. In contrast, for a national bank, the list grants additional banking powers not contemplated by its charter. The debt for this arcane distinction is owed to the dual banking system.

[4] Activities the board is *not* empowered to authorize are underwriting, selling or distributing securities, and the buying or selling of goods, wares, or merchandise.

[5] 12 U.S.C. 461(b) (6), 37(b), and 371a.

[6] For a discussion of the consequences of payability at a foreign branch being impeded see, Heininger, "Liability of U.S. Banks for Deposits Placed in Their Foreign Branches," 11 L. and Pol'y in Int'l Bus. 903 (1979).

[7] 12 CFR 204.112.

[8] For a more detailed discussion of bankers' acceptances, see Chapter 20.

are traceable to the original Federal Reserve Act[9] which expressly authorized member banks to accept drafts and bills of exchange growing out of transactions involving the importation and exportation of goods.[10] The Act, as amended, contains limitations as to the acceptances that a member bank may have outstanding at any time to one person and the total amount of acceptances outstanding.

The recently enacted Bank Export Services Act (Pub. L. 97–290) extended the statutory limitation on bankers' acceptances to U.S. branches and agencies of foreign banks maintaining reserves as a result of the International Banking Act of 1978. The per customer and total acceptance limits are based on a percentage of the institutions capital and surplus. With respect to a U.S. branch or agency of a foreign bank, its capital and surplus is calculated as the dollar equivalent of the capital and surplus of the parent foreign bank as determined by the Board.

Generally, an institution may not issue acceptances to one person in an amount more than 10 percent of the institution's capital and surplus (unless the acceptance is secured by attached documents or some other form of actual security). Total acceptances are limited to 150 percent of capital and surplus with a possible increase of the ceiling to 200 percent of capital and surplus upon approval by the Board.

Investments in Foreign Banks

One of the few exceptions to the general prohibition against a member bank acquiring for its own account shares of stock of a corporation is that provision of section 25 of the Federal Reserve Act with respect to the acquisition of voting stock of foreign banks with prior Board approval. Some countries prohibit foreign banks from establishing branches making the acquisition of an interest in a local institution the only means of entry. Because ownership of a local bank serves as a substitute for a branch and in order to allow the member bank to operate through the local bank with flexibility similar to a branch,

---

[9] Bankers' Acceptances are "eligible" for exemption from reserve requirements if they meet criteria in Section 13 of the Federal Reserve Act including requirements that the acceptance grow out of a trade transaction involving exporting, importing or domestic shipment and storage of goods and have a maturity of less than six months.

[10] In 1963, the Comptroller of the Currency ruled that financing through bankers' acceptances is an essential part of banking permissible not only under authority of the Federal Reserve Act but as an "incidental power" under the seventh paragraph of 12 U.S.C. 24 as well.

[11] Authority to issue bankers' acceptances arising out of the domestic shipment of goods was granted subsequently; however, the inclusion of a requirement that the accepting bank obtain title to the goods has inhibited the use of the instrument in domestic commerce. Currently, only about $2 billion of the total acceptances issued are associated with domestic storage and shipment of goods.

[12] 12 CFR 211.3(b) (2) (1981).

the law exempts a member bank's extensions of credit to its foreign bank affiliate from the amount and collateral limitations of federal law that otherwise apply to loans to affiliates.[13]

In order that member banks not use this authority to invest in other than commercial banks, the board has defined the term *foreign bank*. To be eligible for investment the foreign institution must: (1) engage in the business of banking; (2) be recognized as a bank by the local supervisory authority; (3) have the power to accept demand deposits; and (4) receive deposits to a substantial extent in the regular course of its business. The Board has not offered guidance as to what constitutes receiving deposits to a "substantial extent."

A foreign bank owned in whole or in part by a member bank is not limited in its activities to those that would be permissible for the member bank. However, the foreign bank may not engage directly or indirectly in any activity in the United States except as the Board determines is incidental to the foreign bank's international or foreign business. The Board has ruled that in certain circumstances a member bank may make a noncontrolling investment in a foreign bank that engages in business in the U.S.[14] In this connection, it is Board policy that a foreign bank subsidiary of a member bank should not lend to U.S. residents where the loan is to be used for domestic purposes.

EDGE AND AGREEMENT CORPORATIONS[15]

An Edge corporation is a financial institution chartered, regulated, and supervised by the Federal Reserve either to engage in international banking business or to serve as a holding vehicle for foreign investment. By law, an Edge corporation is limited to international or foreign financial operations. An Agreement corporation is similar functionally to an Edge corporation. Usually it is a state chartered corporation that enters into an agreement with the Board to limit its activities to those of an Edge corporation and, by virtue of the agreement, its shares become eligible for purchase by member banks.[16]

In recent years, the so-called banking Edge corporations[17] have undergone dramatic growth both with respect to the total number of

---

[13] Section 23A of the Federal Reserve Act (12 U.S.C. 371(c)).

[14] 12 CFR 211.602(1981).

[15] See Chapter 42 for further discussion of Edge corporations.

[16] Agreement corporations, first authorized by amendments to the Federal Reserve Act in 1916, are something of an anachronism in light of the 1919 Edge Act and subsequent amendments. Currently there are only seven agreement corporations in operation.

[17] An Edge corporation that ordinarily accepts deposits in the United States from nonaffiliated persons is regarded as a banking Edge corporation, section 211.2(d) of Regulation K (12 CFR 211.2(d)).

Edge corporation offices and the number of cities served by such offices. The impetus for this growth was the International Banking Act of 1978. That Act directed the Board to overhaul its regulations governing Edge corporations to make those institutions more competitive particularly in the area of financing international trade. Also, the Act provided for the first time that foreign banks could acquire Edge corporations.

The major change in the Board's regulations in response to the directive allowed Edge corporations with the approval of the Board to establish and operate branches in the United States. Edge corporations and their domestic parents have taken advantage of this new authority by consolidating networks of separately chartered corporations into one "master" Edge corporation with a branch system. Thus, the Edge corporation has been added to a growing list of vehicles for conducting an interstate banking business. As discussed below, it is primarily through the New York branches of Edge corporations that non-New York banks hope to compete in the recently authorized International Banking Facility market.

Besides the branching authority, the revisions to the Board's regulations liberalized the funding and lending powers of Edge corporations. In addition, the Board proposed allowing Edge corporations to do a complete banking business (i.e., domestic as well as international) with companies whose business consists predominantly of international trade. In this connection, the Board has urged that Congress consider allowing Edge corporations to engage in domestic commercial lending activities.[18] Progress on either of these initiatives would enhance the competitiveness of Edge corporations.

DOMESTIC AND FOREIGN BANK HOLDING COMPANIES

The fundamental policy of the United States that banking and commerce should be conducted separately is embodied in the Glass-Steagall Act (12 U.S.C. 24, 78, 377, 378) and the Bank Holding Company Act (12 U.S.C. 1841 *et seq.*). That policy was extended by the International Banking Act of 1978 to cover not only domestic banks and the foreign and domestic companies that control those banks but the growing number of foreign banks that engage in banking in the United States directly through branches or agencies.[19] The Federal Reserve has the task of implementing that policy as it relates to both categories of institutions.

---

[18] Testimony of then Vice Chairman Schultz before the Senate Banking Committee, April 28, 1981.

[19] The IBA applies also to foreign banks that own or control "commercial lending companies" organized under Article XII of the New York Banking Code.

Although the principle of separation of banking and commerce is believed to have served the United States well, promoting economic competition and a strong banking system, other nations have pursued a different philosophy. The financial systems that prevail in many foreign countries authorize, and in some instances encourage, participation by banks in a range of nonfinancial activities that would not generally be permissible for U.S. banking organizations. In view of this, the law makes two general exceptions. First, U.S. banking organizations are permitted to engage in a limited but wider range of activities abroad than in the United States; and second, foreign banks are permitted to engage abroad in the full range of nonbanking activities sanctioned in their home countries and, within certain limitations, to extend those nonbanking activities to the United States.

Foreign Activities of U.S. Banking Organizations

As discussed, some Edge corporations serve as a means of investing in foreign firms on behalf of the corporation's parent bank or bank holding company.[20] Under the Edge Act, the Board may approve an Edge corporation's purchase of stock in "any other corporation organized . . . under the laws of any foreign country." The Act places limits on the amount which may be invested in foreign corporations and on the activities that such corporations may engage in in the United States, but there are no limits set forth in the law on the kinds of activities that a corporation whose shares are held by an Edge corporation may engage in abroad.

On its face, the provision would appear to grant broad investment powers to Edge corporations. The Board, however, in administering the statute has tended to stress the purpose of Edge corporations of serving as a means of engaging in "banking" and "financial" operations abroad.[21] Thus, the Board's Regulation K is designed to ensure that the investment powers of Edge corporations are not used as a means of engaging indirectly in nonfinancially related foreign activities. In keeping with that purpose, the scope of the nonbanking companies that Edge corporations are permitted to invest in is inversely related to the extent of Edge corporation ownership; that is, passive minority

---

[20] Like the banking Edge corporations, most investment Edge corporations are held by member banks rather than holding companies. One reason for this is that a member bank's loans to an Edge corporation subsidiary of the member bank and wholly owned subsidiaries of the Edge corporation are exempt from the amount and collateral requirements on loans to affiliates; however, the exemption is not available when the Edge Corporation is placed under the holding company, section 23A of the Federal Reserve Act (12 U.S.C. 371c).

[21] See *Bankers' International Corporation*, New York, New York; *Citibank Overseas Investment Corporation*, 67 Federal Reserve Bulletin 364, 366 (1981).

investments are permitted in a wider range of companies than are controlling investments.

Regulation K establishes three categories of Edge corporation investments—portfolio, joint venture, and subsidiary. In general, the nature of an investment is determined by the percentage of voting stock held by the Edge corporation (portfolio, up to 20 percent; joint venture, 20–50 percent; and subsidiary, 50–100 percent). The procedures to be followed in obtaining the Board's consent for each type of investment are set out in detail in Regulation K (section 211.5(c)).

There are no restrictions in the regulation as to the kinds of foreign nonbanking companies in which an Edge corporation can make *portfolio* investments.[22] The regulation does, however, limit the *total* amount of portfolio investments that may be made in nonfinancial companies. Section 211.5(b) (iii) provides that the total direct and indirect portfolio investments in organizations that are engaged in activities that would not be permissible for joint ventures (see discussion below) may not exceed the investor's capital and surplus. While the Board permits relatively small portfolio investments to be made without its specific consent, any portfolio investment that exceeds either $2 million or 25 percent of the Edge corporation's capital and surplus can only be made after application to and specific approval by the Board. The Board's regulations with respect to portfolio investments are designed to afford Edge corporations a degree of flexibility in their foreign operations particularly in instances where small equity acquisitions may be a part of a financing transaction. At the same time, the limits imposed ensure that Edge corporations do not serve solely as holding companies for investments in commercial enterprises.

With regard to *joint ventures,* the Board's regulation is more restrictive as to the kinds of activities that may be conducted. Section 211.5(b) (1) (ii) provides that, unless otherwise permitted by the Board, a joint venture in which an Edge corporation is a participant may not have more than 10 percent of its business (as measured by consolidated assets or revenues) attributable to activities that are not on the list of permissible activities for subsidiaries (see discussion of subsidiary powers below). The authority for joint ventures to engage in a limited amount of nonfinancial activities is considered necessary in view of the inability of the Edge corporation to control their activities. Imposition of rigid limits on their activities would hinder the competitive position of such companies and would make Edge corporations undesirable coventurors. Nevertheless, because of the increased managerial and financial involvement associated with joint ventures as opposed

---

[22] An Edge corporation may not, however, make an investment in any foreign company that buys and sells goods, wares, merchandise, or commodities in the United States or that engages in any activities in the United States that are not incidental to its international or foreign business.

to portfolio investments, the Board considered it necessary to impose activity limits.

In instances where the Edge corporation owns a majority of the voting stock or otherwise controls a foreign company, the Edge corporation is considered to be engaged indirectly in the foreign company's activities. Regulation K lists the permissible activities that an Edge Corporation may engage in through a *subsidiary* abroad. In addition to commercial banking and activities that the Board has determined under section 4(c) (8) of the BHCA as being closely related to banking, the list includes management consulting, data processing, general insurance brokerage and underwriting, distributing, and dealing in securities (subject to specific limits). The regulation also invites Edge corporation investors that are of the view that other activities are usual in connection with the transaction of banking or other financial operations abroad to apply to the Board for a determination that such activities are permissible. A subsidiary that engages in any activity not on the list of permissible activities must be disposed of promptly unless the Board authorizes its retention.

Besides investing in foreign firms through an Edge corporation, the bank holding company itself can make such investments. The 1970 Amendments to the Bank Holding Company Act authorized the Board to permit by regulation or order the holding by a bank holding company of shares of a nonbanking company that does no business in the United States except as an incident to its international or foreign business. In implementing this section, the Board is required to determine whether, under the circumstances and subject to conditions that the Board may impose, the exemption from the nonbanking prohibition is substantially at variance with the purposes of the BHCA and in the public interest. In general, the same investment powers and procedures that apply to Edge corporations apply as well to bank holding companies.

Foreign Banks and Foreign Bank Holding Companies

As discussed, both foreign companies that own or control U.S. banks and foreign banks that operate branches or agencies in the United States are subject to the provisions of the Bank Holding Company Act that separate banking from commerce. At the same time, it has not been the intention of Congress or the Board to impose U.S. ideas of banking on foreign countries. To do so not only would deprive the United States of the benefits of foreign involvement, but might invite retaliation against U.S. banks operating abroad. Accordingly, the law allows some flexibility as to the nonbanking prohibitions as applied to foreign institutions doing a banking business in the United States.

In implementing the exemptive provisions for foreign institutions, the Board has sought to achieve three basic purposes: first, to ensure that foreign institutions that do a banking business in the United States whether directly or indirectly are, in terms of the nature, scope and location of their business, *bona fide* foreign commercial banks; second, to afford such institutions a maximum amount of flexibility in conducting their foreign operations; and third, to allow certain commercial activities to be conducted in the United States where those activities stem from similar activities conducted abroad.[23]

In addition to its responsibilities with respect to the BHCA, the Board has varying degrees of supervisory and regulatory responsibility for all foreign bank operations in the United States. Congress recognized, when it enacted the International Banking Act, that one foreign bank could operate a combination of federal or state licensed offices, insured or uninsured branches, and a network of interstate offices. The Board, therefore, was viewed as the most appropriate body to be given residual responsibility for bringing together at the federal level supervision and regulation of foreign bank operations.

One step taken by the Board in carrying out that responsibility has been the issuance of regulations limiting the interstate expansion of foreign banks.[24] Prior to the International Banking Act foreign banks, unlike their U.S. competitors, were permitted to establish branches in any of the several states that would license such offices. Regulations issued by the Board pursuant to the Act restrict the future expansion of the interstate domestic deposit taking capability of foreign banks by requiring each foreign bank that takes domestic deposits to select a "home state."[25] The foreign bank may not thereafter establish a domestic deposit-taking office in another state without incurring certain penalties. The foreign bank may, however, establish in other states new offices that take credit balances, internationally related deposits, and make domestic loans.

In furtherance of its residual supervisory responsibility with respect to foreign banks in the United States, the Board requires the submission of detailed reports within four months of the end of the foreign banks' fiscal year.[26] The reports must be submitted by all foreign bank holding

---

[23] See Board regulations implementing sections 2(h) (2) and 4(c) (9) of the Bank Holding Company Act, section 211.23 of Regulation K (12 CFR 211.23).

[24] See Board regulations implementing section 5 of the International Banking Act, section 211.22 of Regulation K (12 CFR 211.22).

[25] Foreign banks were required to select a "home state" by March 31, 1981. Of the 112 foreign banks selecting, 79 chose New York; 27, California; two, Florida; two, Illinois; one, Massachusetts, and one, the District of Columbia. Foreign banks that had nondeposit-taking agencies in the United States and no branches were not required to select a home state. In the future, a foreign bank's home state will be that in which it establishes its initial domestic deposit-taking office. A mechanism is provided for changing a foreign bank's home state.

[26] Reports F.R. Y-7, Annual Report of Foreign Banking Organizations; and F.R. 2068, Foreign Banking Organization Confidential Report of Operations.

companies and, with certain limited exceptions, by foreign banks that operate one or more branches or agencies in the United States. The information required frequently exceeds that which is made public in the foreign bank's country of origin and is more detailed than that required by the Securities and Exchange Commission for registration of an initial public offering under the Securities Exchange Act of 1934. The difference between the reports and the SEC's registration requirements is that, whereas registration is a disclosure vehicle, the Board's reports are primarily a supervisory tool. Thus, much of the sensitive information in the reports can be submitted in confidence to the Board and where appropriate the Board will make every effort to maintain that confidentiality.

INTERNATIONAL BANKING FACILITIES

Because of the regulatory and tax environment in the United States, many domestic banks conduct their international operations through offshore branches. Frequently, these offices are simply "shell" operations used solely for booking purposes.[27] By taking advantage of foreign offices, considerable state and local taxes are avoided. In addition, deposits placed at foreign branches, as discussed, are free of basic reserve requirements and interest-rate ceilings that would apply if the deposits were placed in the United States.

In response to this condition, the New York Clearing House Association in 1978 urged the Board to amend its regulations to enable U.S. banks to conduct more of their international banking business in the United States. In essence, the proposal was to permit depository institutions to accept deposits in the United States from foreigners free from the reserve requirements of Regulation D and the interest-rate ceilings of Regulation Q and to lend such funds to foreigners and to similar facilities at other depository institutions. The groundwork for the proposal had already been accomplished in New York with the passage of legislation freeing such facilities from state and local taxes.

After proposing the matter for public comment on two occasions, the Board has issued final regulations (effective December 31, 1981) permitting the establishment of International Banking Facilities (IBFs). An IBF is not a facility in a physical sense but rather is a recordkeeping technique not unlike an offshore shell branch. No application is required to establish an IBF. All a bank need do prior to establishing an IBF is notify the local Federal Reserve Bank 14 days prior to the first reserve computation period in which it intends to operate the

---

[27] In a series of communications known as the "Martin-Burns Letters," the Board expressed the view that foreign branch operations are to be conducted ". . . for the purpose of developing new international business, and not as a means of shifting deposits to such branches from offices in the United States or of obtaining deposits that would otherwise be placed in the United States." Letter of June 3, 1969, to all member banks.

IBF and agree to abide by any conditions the Board may impose on the operation of an IBF.

Generally, an IBF may accept deposits only from non-U.S. residents. The IBF may also obtain funds from foreign offices of other U.S. depository institutions or foreign banks, from other IBFs, and from offices of the same institution. An IBF may not accept demand deposits; however, the time deposits that it accepts may have shorter maturities than would be permissible for other types of time deposits under Regulation Q.[28] The instrument evidencing the time deposits may not be in negotiable form, and such deposits when received from nonbank foreign residents must be subject to an agreement prohibiting deposits or withdrawals of less than $100,000.

As is the case with shell branches, the Board is concerned that IBFs could be used as a means of circumventing interest-rate restrictions or reserve requirements. Accordingly, the following model statement was adopted by the Board for communication to each nonbank deposit and loan customer:

> It is the policy of the Board of Governors of the Federal Reserve System that, with respect to nonbank customers, deposits received by international banking facilities may be used only to support the non-U.S. operations of a depositor (or its foreign affiliates) located outside the United States and that extensions of credit by international banking facilities may be used only to finance the non-U.S. operations of a customer (or its foreign affiliates) located outside the U.S.

For nonbank customers that are affiliates of U.S. companies, an acknowledgement of this policy must be executed prior to the opening of an account.

Although several other states have initiated tax legislation to authorize IBFs, it is believed that New York will be the principal market for IBF activity. For non-New York banks, direct participation in this market is prohibited by the McFadden Act limitation on interstate branching. Indirect participation is, however, made possible through the use of an Edge corporation subsidiary or its branches. By early 1983, almost 450 institutions had created IBFs. As expected, more are located in New York than any other state although California and Florida have a substantial number of IBFs as well. As of early 1983, 156 foreign banks with offices in the U.S. had established IBFs. Assets of over $163 billion had been booked in IBFs as of February 9, 1983.

---

[28] Permissible maturity of time deposits is related to the nature of the customer. For nonbank foreign residents the minimum maturity or notice period is two business days. For other depositors, the maturity may be on an overnight basis.

EXPORT TRADING COMPANIES

In an effort to promote the export of U.S. goods and services, Congress enacted the Bank Export Services Act of 1982 (Pub. L. 97–290). That Act authorizes banking organizations (primarily bank holding companies) to invest in and operate export trading companies. Export trading companies under the Act are companies organized and operated principally for the purpose of exporting goods and services produced in the United States or facilitating the export of such goods and services. An export trading company subsidiary of a bank holding company can engage in a wide range of commerical activities hitherto prohibited by the Glass Steagall and Bank Holding Company Acts.

The Board is charged with regulating and supervising the relationship between bank holding companies and export trading companies. That relationship is guided by a number of requirements. First, a bank holding company investment in an export trading company may only be made after the Board has been given 60 days' prior notice. Second, a bank holding company may only invest up to 5 percent of its consolidated capital and surplus in an export trading company. Third, total extensions of credit by the bank holding company and its affiliates to the export trading company, may not exceed 10 percent of the bank holding company's consolidated capital and· surplus. The Board has published other regulations for comment governing export trading companies and those regulations would be part of the Board's Regulation K (12 C.F.R. 211).

CONCLUSION

In the not very distant past, a handful of U.S. banks accounted for almost all of this country's international banking business. In recent years, many other U.S. banks have recognized the opportunity and the necessity of participating in international banking. While domestic banks have become more active in the international arena, foreign banks have come to be recognized as a significant force in the domestic banking market. The responsibility for adapting to this integrative process falls to the Federal Reserve Board. Through close consultation with other agencies of the government; through dialogue with the regulated institutions; and through participation in international organizations, such as the Bank for International Settlements, the Board is able to fashion its policies to promote a sound and efficient financial system.

48

The Prudential Framework for International Banking

ROBERT R. BENCH
Deputy Comptroller of the Currency
for International Banking

INTRODUCTION

Prudential supervision of banks is a key aspect of public policy related to international banking practices and structure. The purpose of this chapter is to discuss the prudential supervision national authorities exercise over the various elements of international banking practice as well as the international banking system. The chapter also is intended to provide specific sources of summary and reference information about the international bank supervisory process in response to growing interest from bankers, other market participants, academics, and the public.

The prudential supervisory process is discussed in this chapter primarily in the context of how the supervisory authorities in the United States implement the U.S. legal and regulatory framework for international banking. However, as the major banks of the world become more dependent on each other, the mutual interests of the various national bank supervisors intensify and converge. Therefore, the chapter also covers the evolving efforts of multilateral bodies to establish an international system of bank supervisory coordination and cooperation.

PURPOSES OF BANK SUPERVISION

Banks, as depositories of the public's assets and primary allocators of credit, play a central role in the functioning of most economies

The views expressed in this chapter are those of the author and do not necessarily represent the view of the Office of the Comptroller of the Currency. The technical edits by W. B. Glidden, Senior Attorney at OCC and L. S. Tarrant, National Bank Examiner are greatly appreciated.

and consequently in the socio-political stability of nations. Therefore, governments establish public policy goals for banking, such as financial structure and credit allocation.

The fundamental reason for bank supervision in all countries is to support the vital lender of last resort function every government must exercise when financial instability threatens or occurs in an economy. The function of a lender of last resort is to maintain public confidence which forms the base of all financial intermediation. Any known or potential insolvency or illiquidity of a sizable credit institution can reduce public confidence in the overall financial process and spark panic behavior among those who control financial assets. The degree of systemic disruption depends on how quickly and deeply market linkages transmit a confidence problem. Transmission of a financial market problem can be instantaneous through highly efficient networks of global telecommunications, interbank transfers, and bank technology.

The depth in the loss of confidence depends on the public's perception of whether or not there is an institution in the credit chain with the capacity, financial integrity, and knowledge of the extent of a problem to provide the necessary action; that is, the right amount of liquidity and/or capital to restore confidence.

If the public does not perceive that a capable institution is available in the financial markets, then instability remains until the government, as the ultimate lender of last resort, acts on the problem.

But as the lender of last resort, the government's actions must be quick, precise, and effective. The lender of last resort must know and understand the problem so its actions appropriately respond to the market's needs. Any insufficient or excessive response can exacerbate market confidence domestically, and could pose serious shocks abroad if the disrupted markets were actively linked to the Euromarkets or other national financial systems.

Banking authorities critically influence and support the lender of last resort function with ongoing and emergency supervisory programs. The ongoing programs are intended to prevent or minimize the development of systemic financial instability. This preventive maintenance includes setting guidelines for industry structure (entry, competition, products) as well as establishing specific operating parameters for capital adequacy, lending limits, liquidity, interest rates, and so on.[1]

A vital supervisory support program in an ongoing and emergency context consist of regular prudential evaluations of the condition of banks through on-site inspections coupled with remote examination/ analysis of operating reports that banks submit periodically to their

---

[1] Comptroller of the Currency, *Comptroller's Manual for National Banks*, (Washington, D.C.: Comptroller of the Currency, 1981). Also see 12 U.S.C. 1, *et seq.*

authorities. The examinations are superior supervisory tools for detecting difficulties early in an individual bank or systemically and for either correcting them, or, if uncorrectible, preparing for the consequences.[2]

The examinations, especially on-site, permit bank supervisors to be knowledgeable on a current basis about banking transactions, conditions, and banking management. Examinations also create a supervisory shadow on the "street" as well as permit a documentation process to track a bank's performance.

The dynamic volume of foreign activities in U.S. banks requires the U.S. banking authorities to "internationalize" their traditional domestic supervisory approach and programs. U.S. regulators extend their consolidated supervisory perspective to a bank's international subsidiaries, branches, and affiliates. The U.S. banking agencies operate multinational supervisory divisions. The Comptroller of the Currency and the Superintendent of Banks in New York maintain supervisory offices in London. Annually, more than a hundred U.S. bank examiners travel to more than 20 countries to conduct prudential examinations of U.S. banks' offshore activities. Modified traditional U.S. bank supervisory programs address country risk, foreign commercial credit, foreign exchange, interbank dealing, and international operating systems. Overall, the U.S. bank supervisory performance evaluations and CAMEL composite ratings include agencies' conclusions about a bank's global activities.

Supervisory Framework for International Activities of U.S. Banks

U.S. commercial banks can choose to be chartered either under state or federal laws. The state banking authority is the primary regulator (legal) and supervisor (prudential) over the affairs of a state-chartered bank. The Office of the Comptroller of the Currency is the primary regulator and supervisor of federally chartered (national) banks. Practically all the largest state and national banks are members of the Federal Reserve System. U.S. laws give the Federal Reserve primary regulatory and supervisory authority over the activities of U.S. bank holding companies, Edge Act Corporations, and overseas affiliates of U.S. banks. The Federal Reserve also has primary statutory authority over the foreign branches of U.S. member banks. There are some U.S. state-chartered banks that operate internationally but are not member banks. Their primary regulator and supervisor is the licensing state government. The Federal Deposit Insurance Corporation statutorily is a significant party at interest in the affairs of all banks it insures,

---

[2] Comptroller of the Currency, *Comptroller's Manual for National Bank Examiners*, (Englewood Cliffs, N.J.: Prentice-Hall, 1981).

and, in addition to supervising the international activities of nonmember banks, plays an advisory role to the other agencies in the regulation and supervision of U.S. banks' international activities.

Administratively, the Comptroller of the Currency and the state authorities centralize policy and operations for international regulation and supervision. The Comptroller of the Currency operates a Multinational Banking Division in Washington for this purpose, and the state of New York has established a Deputy Superintendent for Multinational Banking. The Federal Reserve's international regulatory and supervisory policies emanate from the Board of Governors in Washington and are implemented by the 12 Federal Reserve Banks. While the Federal Reserve System promulgates the legal parameters under which member banks may conduct specific holding company or international activities, in practice the Federal Reserve consults the chartering authority of the main banking unit. For instance, the Federal Reserve processes and reviews applications for international activities from national banks in consultation with the Comptroller of the Currency whose opinions effectively represent the deciding factors on approving or disapproving an application.

The agencies also share the supervisory responsibilities for international banking. The Comptroller of the Currency conducts prudential examinations covering all the international activities of national banks while the Federal Reserve Banks also examine Edge Act Corporations of national banks. The international activities of state member banks are examined jointly by state governments and the Federal Reserve.

Examination of U.S. Banks' International Activities

The U.S. banking agencies employ the same supervisory tools for U.S. banks' international activities that the supervisors use for domestic banking operations. The agencies extend their policies, practices and procedures internationally through remote and on-site examinations. The examinations are carried out to the extent necessary to permit supervisory conclusions about the impact of a bank's international operations on the consolidated safety and soundness of the banking organization. The agencies tend to enjoy greater flexibility designing the scope of their examination process for the major U.S. international banks because these institutions generally operate sophisticated systems of internal control, credit review, and management information on which the banking authorities can rely.

The banking agencies gear their examination of U.S. banks' international operations to the dynamics of each bank and its operating environment. The degree to which the agencies use on-site or remote examination techniques depends on the quality of a bank's systems for self-supervision, the way a bank structures and manages itself inter-

nationally, and bank examiners' perceptions about their information
needs to achieve their examination objectives. Supervisory cost is also
a factor in deciding whether on-site overseas examinations will be conducted. Sending cadres of bank examiners abroad is expensive. However, on-site prudential examinations overseas are mutually beneficial
to the banks and bank supervisors. International on-site examinations
provide examiners with broader perspectives, additional specialized
technical knowledge, and the opportunity to verify and learn a bank's
overseas systems.

Overall, the U.S. banking agencies use five combinations of on-site
and remote examinations to supervise the international activities of
U.S. banks. The examinations monitor and evaluate: a bank's systems
of internal and external controls; asset quality and loan portfolio management; funding and dealing operations; compliance with applicable
laws; and overall performance vis-a-vis a bank's plans and objectives.
The five international examination methods are:

Examination of Offshore Units on a Remote Basis from Head Office.
Most U.S. banks which conduct international activities do so through
limited branch or affiliate booking centers located offshore because
of exemptions in U.S. tax laws or deposit reserve requirements. Generally, the primary records for these "shell" offshore operations are maintained at a bank's head office where all banking decisions for the shell
unit are made, and U.S. bank examiners can evaluate offshore operations from the records at head office.

**On-Site Examination of Major Offshore Units in Coordination and
Concurrently with Examinations at Head Office.** The larger U.S.
banks maintain at their head office key management information about
the activities in their major overseas branches or affiliates. The banks
do not send to head office detailed data and information because of
cost reasons. However, the banks make available at locations accessible
to examiners, the information necessary for examiners to make supervisory conclusions about the banks' operations at their major overseas
locations. The examiners travel to these offshore locations and perform
on-site the same examination procedures used at head office. U.S. federal and state banking authorities have reduced some of this travel
requirement by stationing examining personnel in London.

On-Site and Remote Examination at Regional Centers. The largest
U.S. multinational banks decentralize a great deal of their global banking activities. These major banks establish policy and operating parameters at head office and establish regional credit, operations, and funding
centers around the world with executive authorities to implement the
policies within those operating parameters. These regional management centers cover the banks' activities in a number of countries and
maintain practically all the information examiners need to validate
and evaluate the consolidated management reports at head office.

Therefore, teams of examiners travel to the regional centers where they conduct on-site examinations on the banks' activities. The examiners also conduct remote examinations of the banking units reporting to these centers using the internal reports those units submit to the center.

On-Site Supplemental Examinations.   Throughout the year, and not necessarily concurrent with any head office examination, the U.S. banking agencies send federal examiners to conduct on-site examinations of U.S. banks' lesser size overseas units located in national financial markets. The main purpose of these examinations is to verify the timeliness and accuracy of management reports these units submit to regional management centers or head office. The examinations also provide the agencies and their examiners with perspective and knowledge about national credit and money markets.

Remote Examinations Based on Data Filed with U.S. Banking Authorities.   The major U.S. banks quarterly must report detailed balance-sheet and income data to U.S. banking authorities. The banking agencies have computerized systems which analyze the international components of this data on an institutional and peer group basis. In addition, U.S. banks with international operations must report on a consolidated basis to their regulators their foreign exchange positions (monthly), country exposures (semi-annually) and foreign branch balance sheets by country (annually). This data also is computerized and analyzed on an institutional and peer group basis. Whenever these remote analyses indicate sudden shifts or an accelerating trend in a bank's international activities, the banking agencies conduct supervisory inquiries. As a regular operating program, the Comptroller of the Currency's Multinational Banking Division quarterly visits the chief financial officers of the largest U.S. banks for supervisory discussions which include those banks' international asset portfolios, offshore funding, and overall international earnings.

Finally, U.S. bank examiners develop, through their various international examination methods, supervisory conclusions about how a bank's international operations impact the consolidated condition of the bank. The examiners present their international supervisory conclusions in their consolidated *Report of Examination* to a bank's board of directors.

The U.S. Supervisory Approaches for Evaluating Country Risk and Banks' Country Exposure Management Systems

U.S. bank supervisory evaluations include analyses of the social, economic, and political risks associated with a bank's asset exposures. Domestically, the U.S. banking agencies consider how these risks impact the repayment abilities of a bank's municipal, commercial, and retail

borrowers. The agencies also are concerned with how these risks may
disrupt other areas of a bank, such as fixed asset management or transactional operations because of social disturbances, political instability,
renewal/eminent domain programs, or demographic shifts in primary
market areas.

Internationally, U.S. banking authorities also must weigh national
environmental risks to banks. Overseas asset exposures in U.S. banks
exceed $200 billion, comprise a significant portion of individual bank's
assets, and establish country risk as an important interest of U.S. bank
supervisors. The U.S. banking agencies consider country risk encompassing the whole spectrum of risks that arise from the social, economic,
legal, and political conditions in a foreign country. The agencies perceive that these conditions can have favorable or adverse consequences
for U.S. banks. Political or social instabilities, nationalization, expropriation, or exchange controls can interrupt payments on external debts
and create frozen, nonperforming assets for all U.S. banks. These supervisory perspectives cover many countries, categories of countries, or
regions in the world, such as LDCs, the Caribbean region, or Eastern
Europe.

U.S. bank examiners use two supervisory approaches to deal with
the challenge of developing prudential conclusions about country risks.
One approach categorizes international social-economic-political risks
into traditional U.S. supervisory classifications for asset quality. The
second approach quantifies and evaluates a bank's country-exposure
management system.

Supervisory Evaluations of Country Risks.   The U.S. banking authorities recognize that countries do not disappear, and foreign public-
sector borrowers from U.S. banks generally have a record of ultimate
repayment. However, banks and governments can become insolvent
and disappear. Furthermore, high levels of foreign exposures in U.S.
banks are a relatively recent phenomena. Therefore, the U.S. banking
agencies have a prudential responsibility to evaluate these exposures,
not only for loss potential to banks, but also in a dynamic sense to
detect earlier repayment difficulties which can result in illiquid, nonperforming assets in U.S. banks.

In 1974, the Comptroller of the Currency established a structured
approach for assessing foreign government loans in national banks portfolios. The Comptroller formed a Foreign Public Sector Credit Review
Committee which evaluated the credit facilities national banks made
available to foreign governments, their agencies, or their instrumentalities.[3] During 1979, the Federal Reserve and the Federal Deposit
Insurance Corporation joined the Comptroller in expanding the Com-

---

[3] For a full discussion of the Comptroller's approach and why it was necessary to
establish it, see Robert R. Bench "How the Comptroller of the Currency Analyzes the
Country Risk," *Euromoney*, August 1977.

mittee and revising its scope. It now is known as the Interagency Country Exposure Review Committee (ICERC), and its supervisory focus has shifted from classifying only banks' specific foreign public-sector borrowers to evaluating transfer risk.[4]

The ICERC is comprised of nine federal bank examiners who form their assessments and classifications from a wide assortment of data and information. First, the ICERC receives detailed country studies prepared by the Federal Reserve Bank of New York (FRB-N.Y.). The studies discuss economic, social, and political risk factors in a country as well as provide statistical information about a country's external debt, balance of payments, and general economic conditions. Second, FRB-N.Y. also prepares and sends the ICERC a list of countries statistically ranked by ability to service external obligations. The rankings are based on five basic ratios: current account deficit/exports; cumulative current account/exports; net external interest payments/exports; net external interest payments/international reserves; and total current debt service requirements/receipts from exports of goods and services. The committee uses these rankings as an initial, *very rough screen* for categorizing countries as to their strong, moderately strong, or weak abilities to service external debts.

Third, the ICERC members visit U.S. money center banks to review the banks' country files as well as to discuss country conditions with the banks' senior international officers. The examiners seek the banks' statistical analyses of countries and their perceptions about the quality of a country's economic and political management. The ICERC also explores bankers' attitudes about additional lending and lending terms to countries. Finally, the examiners access U.S. government information about countries. The U.S. government input to the ICERC generally is used to confirm or reconcile other information the ICERC has received. U.S. government sources also can indicate to the ICERC any bilateral or multilateral financial assistance that may be in progress for a country.

The ICERC meets three times a year in Washington to assess country risk. Using the FRB-N.Y. country rankings as a beginning screen, the ICERC evaluates the various quantitative and qualitative information they have gathered and categorize countries on the basis of the degree to which economic (primarily), social, and political conditions in a country affect the country's flow of foreign exchange necessary to repay U.S. banks' cross-border exposures in that country. The ICERC may determine that one category may apply to all U.S. bank loans in a country or that several categories apply depending on the type of facilities and maturities of cross-border exposures U.S. banks have in a country. The ICERC distributes its country evaluations to the federal

---

[4] For a full discussion of the supervisory philosophy and need for the ICERC see: "A New Supervisory Approach to Foreign Lending," *FRBNY Quarterly Review,* 1978.

bank examiners who regularly examine the international activities of
U.S. banks. General guidelines of ICERC country categorizations are:

1. *Strong.* The country does not experience social, economic, or politi-
    cal problems which could interrupt repayment of external debt.
2. *Moderately Strong.* The country experiences a limited number
    of identifiable economic, social, or political problems which do not
    presently threaten orderly repayment of external debt.
3. *Weak.* The country experiences a number of economic, social, or
    political problems which if not reversed, could threaten orderly
    repayment of external debt.
4. *Substandard.* An interruption in a country's repayment of external
    debt has occurred or is perceived as occurring within six months.
5. *Doubtful.* Interest due on a country's external debt is delinquent
    regularly and the country evidences no definite prospects for gen-
    erating sufficient foreign exchange to restore orderly repayments
    of external debt.
6. *Loss.* A country has formally repudiated on its external debt.

**Supervisory Evaluations of Banks' Country Exposure Management
Systems.** The ICERC assessments of country risk do not stand alone
as a supervisory tool. The assessments are used within the overall U.S.
supervisory objective of determining the safety and soundness of a
bank's policies, practices, and procedures for country risk. This includes
risks per se, but overall supervisory conclusions also consider a bank
management's policies for diversifying risks and the bank's capacities
or systems for analyzing risks.

The ICERC categorizations of substandard, doubtful, and loss are
traditional U.S. supervisory classifications for problem assets. U.S. supervisory policies require bank examiners to criticize all nonperforming
assets in their *Report of Examination* to bank directors. However, if
the exposures the ICERC categorizes as weak, or moderately strong
respectively exceed 10–15 percent of a bank's capital funds, then the
examiners discuss the exposures in detail in their *Report of Examination.* In other words, nonclassified, performing country exposures are
categorized in three levels of risk, but only scheduled and discussed
in a *Report of Examination* when certain concentrations of risk exists.
The examiners criticize performing exposures only when they conclude
the levels of concentration are immoderate per se, cause insufficient
portfolio diversification, or are managed inadequately.

In addition to the above, U.S. bank examiners look across a bank's
portfolio at various country exposures and individual assets to determine whether there are groups of country or borrower exposures at
risk because of common economic, social, or political factors. For instance, the cash flow of a diverse group of borrowers may be dependent
on the world market conditions for the same commodity, such as copper

demand, shipping services, or steel production. As another example, regional political or economic uncertainties or instabilities can ripple across the borders of a number of countries in a geographical region and disrupt the orderly repayment of external debt of a number of individual countries in that region.

Therefore, when federal bank examiners determine a group of a bank's assets is reliant on the same essential repayment factor, and when the total of those assets in the group exceeds 25 percent of a bank's capital funds, the examiners consider the group exposure a concentration of risk and detail the concentration in their *Report of Examination*. The 25 percent threshold is only a trigger for inclusion in an examiner's report; albeit mere inclusion usually catches the attention of directors. However, the 25 percent inclusion is not necessarily a trigger for examiner criticism. Any criticism of a group concentration depends on the subjective opinions of the bank examiner on the spot as to whether a bank's concentration is immoderate or unwarranted. The examiner forms a prudential opinion by reviewing a bank's traditional relationship with the concentration, the level of bank management's expertise, and the quality of a bank's supervision over the concentration, such as credit file analysis and the depth of calling programs to the areas or borrowers.[5]

In order for U.S. bank examiners to determine the degree of diversification in country exposures, the examiners first must quantify a bank's gross exposure in a country and then disaggregate the exposure for risk analysis. Disaggregation includes reviewing the variety of borrowers, the portfolio maturities, the currencies of the exposures, the ultimate reliance for repayment such as a guarantor in another country, and the amount of contingent versus actual commitments a bank has made to a country.

Most of the necessary quantification and disaggregation of country exposure is done semiannually in an interagency country lending survey. The supervisory survey requires all U.S. insured banks with at least one foreign branch and foreign assets exceeding $20 million to report their foreign assets on a global consolidated basis and by broad categories to their federal banking supervisory. The banking agencies publish the survey data in aggregate form. The banking agencies computerize and analyze the data by bank and by peer groups of banks for confidential prudential purposes, including use by bank examiners.

In order for U.S. bank examiners to establish supervisory conclusions about the adequacy of a bank's management of country exposures, U.S. bank examiners evaluate during their on-site examinations a bank's international credit administration process. The specific primary objec-

---

[5] For a more complete discussion see: *Comptroller's Handbook for National Bank Examiners*, Sections 205–219, and Sections 805–809.

tives of an examiners' evaluations are: (1) to determine if policies, practices, procedures, and internal controls for country-risk management are adequate and prudent; (2) to determine if bank officers are operating in conformance with the guidelines the bank has established for country-risk administration; (3) to determine the impact of country risk on the overall quality of the international loan portfolio; (4) to initiate corrective action when policies, practices, procedures, and internal controls are deficient; (5) to prepare narrative commentary on the bank's country-risk management system; and, (6) to prepare appropriate criticisms in a *Report of Examination* when deficiencies exist in a bank's country-risk management system.

The bank examiners expect to see three basic components in every bank's country-risk management system: (1) evaluation of economic trends and political or social trends in countries where the bank has asset exposures; (2) country exposure limits established by executive bank management; and (3) current, accurate, and complete internal reporting systems to monitor and control country risk. Finally, the examiners inspect a bank's reports, committee minutes, and other records to determine the quality and frequency of a bank's country evaluations, the quality of internal country exposure reporting, and the bank's compliance with its own internal country limits.

Legal Lending Limits. U.S. public policies do not establish country exposure limits for U.S. banks. However, federal and state laws do limit a bank's loans to one person. The federal statute, 12 USC 84, limits national banks' loans to one person at 10 percent of the bank's capital funds. In 1979, the Comptroller of the Currency interpreted foreign governments and their related entities as "persons" under 12 USC 84. The Comptroller also ruled that a national bank's loans to foreign government agencies and instrumentalities should be combined with loans to the central government and considered one person for lending limit purposes unless: (1) the borrower has resources or revenue of its own sufficient over time to service its debt obligations (means test); and, (2) the loan is obtained for a purpose consistent with the borrower's general business (purpose test). This does not preclude converting the loan proceeds into local currency prior to use by the borrowing entity. The Comptroller's ruling requires the purpose and means test be applied at the time each loan is made to a foreign public-sector entity. The ruling also establishes minimum documentation a bank must retain in its files.[6]

Funds Management

Funds management in U.S. banks is a principal area of supervisory interest to U.S. banking authorities.[7] The banking agencies view funds

[6] See 12 U.S.C. 84, 12 CFR 7.1330 and *Federal Register,* April 17, 1979, page 22712; Comptroller of the Currency Banking Circular No. 123 dated April 12, 1979.

[7] See *Comptroller's Handbook for National Bank Examiners,* Section 405 et al.

management in a bank as the management of assets and liabilities to provide prudent sources of liquidity for anticipated needs as well as the management of interest-rate sensitivity between assets and liabilities to provide for adequate net interest earnings. The larger U.S. banks are dependent on money market sources of funds, and their liquidity and net interest earnings are exposed to fragile market confidence and volatile market interest rates. This can be especially true in the U.S. international banks where funds management represents a complex matrix of managing liquidity and net interest margins in various national markets or currencies as well as on a global institutional basis.

The federal banking agencies insist U.S. banks establish comprehensive policies, operating parameters, and management information systems to supervise their funds management activities. First, funds management policies should emphasize forward planning which considers the unique operating dynamics inherent in every large bank. This includes a bank's composition of assets and liabilities, earnings, and interest margins. The plan also should address a bank's future funding needs and thoroughly assess the liability products and money markets which can be used to meet those needs.

Second, the policies should include the formation of an asset/liability management committee of executive officers. The committee should have responsibility for implementing and supervising a bank's funds management policies and programs. This includes making global institutional funds management decisions and coordinating these decisions among different areas of the bank. The asset/liability management committee also should establish and supervise formal operating guidelines for funds management activities, including parameters for: consolidated loans to deposit ratio, loans to capital ratio, and total assets to capital ratio; the ratio of interest-rate sensitive assets to interest-rate sensitive liabilities; the ratio of rate-sensitive assets less sensitive liabilities to total assets and to total capital; degrees of reliance on any funding source or liability product; matching of asset and liability maturities; and minimum acceptable interest-rate differentials between asset yields and liability costs.

Third, a comprehensive management information system is critical to safe and sound funds management decisions in a bank. The system must generate sufficient current and accurate information to permit a bank's directors and asset/liability management committee to properly supervise the bank's funds management activities worldwide. As a minimum, a funds management information system should generate data about economic conditions, interest-rate projections, deviations from the funding plan, exceptions to policy guidelines or operating parameters, gaps between assets and liabilities, and the amounts of rate-sensitive assets and liabilities.

The U.S. banking agencies supervise U.S. bank's funds management policies and programs through on-site and remote examinations. The agencies' computerized data bases, such as the Comptroller of the Currency's National Bank Surveillance System and Performance Analysis Reports, are designed to analyze and highlight a U.S. bank's composition of assets and liabilities, dependence on money market funds, and net interest margin trends.

These remote examinations often prompt supervisory inquiries about a bank's funds management practices and are used by the banking agencies in planning regular on-site prudential examinations. The Comptroller's Multinational Banking Division visits quarterly with the chief financial officers of the largest U.S. banks to review funds management performance. During their regularly scheduled on-site examinations, federal bank examiners establish supervisory conclusions about the safety and soundness of U.S. banks' policies, practices, and procedures for funds management activities.

The examiners first determine whether or not a bank is planning adequately for anticipated funding needs. The examiners develop their perspectives by reviewing planning reports which a bank internally generates and by reviewing examination data and conclusions of various departments in the bank. Second, the examiners conduct interest-rate sensitivity analyses. The examiners consider: a bank's interest-rate sensitive position in its assets and liabilities; that position's impact on present bank earnings; the bank's ability to adjust the rate-sensitive position; and, the impact on future earnings should interest-rate scenarios occur differently than bank management anticipates.

Third, the examiners evaluate a bank's net interest margins historically against bank management's plans and peer group banks. The examiners also consider the present and projected stability for interest margins. Finally, throughout their review of funds management activities, the examiners inspect the components of a bank's management information to determine whether the bank's directors and officers receive current, accurate, and sufficient information to make sound funds management decisions.

Foreign Exchange and Interbank Deposit Activity

The U.S. banking agencies exercise a high degree of supervisory interest and surveillance toward the foreign exchange and interbank deposit areas in U.S. international banks. These dealing activities are critical elements of the banks' consolidated credit administration and funds management programs. The fluctuating values of foreign exchange positions also pose additional risks to the banks' capital and earnings. Systemically, the interbank deposit and exchange markets are the credit and transactional linkages vital to the efficient intermediation of international capital movements.

The Federal Financial Institutions Examination Council (FFIEC) advocates that U.S. international banks develop written documents establishing the banks' goals and policies for dealing activities. The FFIEC advises U.S. banks to describe: the scope of the dealing activity they authorize; the delegation of authorities and responsibilities; the types of dealing services offered; reporting requirements; internal accounting requirements; and dealing limits. More specifically, U.S. supervisors expect U.S. banks' dealing policies to limit aggregate volume, overnight positions, maturity distributions in positions, and exposures to individual customers.

The banking agencies also expect that U.S. banks' dealing guidelines cover: (1) credit approval procedures for delivery or settlement risks; as well as (2) reporting procedures which adequately inform executive bank management about dealing activities and readily detect any exceptions to dealing policies. The U.S. banking authorities also have issued guidelines to U.S. international banks which set forth minimum internal control and audit standards for dealing activities.

Finally, U.S. bank examiners regularly conduct on-site examinations of the major dealing offices of U.S. banks.[8] The examiners form supervisory conclusions about: the adequacy of a bank's policies, practices, procedures, and internal controls for dealing activities. The examiners also determine whether: bank personnel operate within established dealing guidelines; the extent of risk to a bank's consolidated capital and earnings because of its net open exchange positions, maturity gaps, or counterparty credit weaknesses; and the scope and adequacy of a bank's internal audit function for dealing activities.

MULTILATERAL SUPERVISION OF INTERNATIONAL BANKING

The preceding individual sections in this Handbook discuss the various forms of specialized financial services which comprise international banking practice. Collectively, the sections reflect the breadth and depth of the transactional, environmental, and philosophical aspects of international banking. Collectively, the Handbook demonstrates the interdependence of international financial intermediation. The major banks of the world increasingly have become reliant on their international activities for growth, diversification, and earnings. In that process, banks have become more dependent on each other because of the vital linkages they have developed through Euromarket syndication and interbank activities as well as through their expansion into local currency markets of other countries.

Governments establish a banking structure and bank supervisory function to support their national political and economic policies. The

---

[8] For a detailed discussion of foreign exchange examinations see *Comptroller's Handbook for National Bank Examiners,* Sections 809, 813, and 814.

development and implementation of policies occur within traditional forms of governance and address domestic needs. In the United States, banking and bank supervision is fragmented and geographically disbursed among some 60 federal and state government authorities and some 40,000 depository institutions statutorily limited to specific markets and products. In many other countries, the governments prefer and allow concentration and centralization of banking and state resources, including state ownership control of banks.

Public policies toward international banking also have been formulated in a national context. That is, specific policies toward international banking practices or structure generally represent amendment or interpretation by individual governments of their domestic banking regulations in response to a perceived national interest. For instance, the U.S. banking authorities generated several international supervisory initiatives during 1965–79 in response to the dynamic international growth of U.S. banks during that period. All of these initiatives were logical extensions of the U.S. supervisory structure to the geographical spread of U.S. banks' activities.

However, the deepening interdependence of international banking activities creates a multinational regime of banking structure and practice involving mutual reliances and vulnerabilities among financial institutions of the world. This interdependence inherently requires that nations' policymakers consider the mutual public interests across borders of nation-states and establish a multilateral policy development process which addresses prudential supervision of multinational banking activities.

Multilateral Coordination and Cooperation Among Bank Supervisors

The need to establish a framework of multilateral bank supervision was recognized by the governors of the Bank For International Settlements (BIS) in Basle in December 1974. The governors formed the Committee on Banking Regulations and Supervisory Practices comprised of foreign exchange and supervisory officials from Belgium, Canada, France, Germany, Italy, Japan, Luxembourg, the Netherlands, Sweden, Switzerland, the United Kingdom, and the United States.

> The committee is a standing committee whose object is to promote discussion and cooperation among those responsible for the supervision of banks and of foreign exchange markets in the Group of Ten Countries, Luxembourg, and Switzerland. The Committee does not attempt far-reaching harmonization of member countries' supervisory techniques. Rather, it aims to establish broad principles, with which different national supervisory systems might conform in establishing their own detailed arrangements; it attempts to identify gaps in the supervisory coverage

of international banking and to recommend corrective action; and it provides an opportunity for the supervisors who attend its meetings to learn of each others techniques and profit from each other's experiences.[9]

This committee established a framework to deal with the banking and jurisdictional issues posed by the growth in international banking. The committee established principles of cooperation, known as the Concordat. Kennett reports the committee agreed as follows:

1. No foreign banking establishment should escape supervision.
2. In the case of joint ventures involving parent institutions in more than one country, supervision must be by the host authorities.
3. The supervision should be adequate, judged by the standards of both host and parent authorities.
4. The achievement of these objectives calls for contact and cooperation between host and parent authorities.
5. While it is difficult, if not impossible, to determine clear-cut lines of responsibility for supervision, a number of general guidelines were agreed to: (a) Responsibility for supervising liquidity must rest first with the local authorities. It is also recognized that, in the case of branches, liquidity cannot be judged in isolation from the whole bank to which it belongs. (b) Supervision for solvency must rest primarily with the host authority for foreign subsidiaries and joint ventures, but parent authorities must take into account the exposure of their domestic banks' foreign subsidiaries and joint ventures in view of the parent banks' moral commitment to such foreign establishments. In the case of branches, solvency is indistinguishable from that of the parent bank and consequently the parent bank supervisory authority is principally responsible. (c) The division of responsibility described in (b) above also pertains to the supervision of foreign exchange positions for prudential reasons.

Finally, this important statement encouraged action in the following areas to facilitate cooperation among supervisory authorities: (a) provide for the possibility of the direct transfer of information between supervisory authorities; (b) facilitate inspections by parent authorities of their banks' foreign establishment; and (c) where direct inspection is not allowed, the host authority should be prepared to carry out an inspection at the request of the parent authority and report its findings.[10]

Multinational banking extends beyond the Group of 10 Countries, however. Other official groups also have been formed to strengthen

---

[9] From *Record of Proceedings*, International Conference of Banking Supervisors, London, July 5, 1979.

[10] W. A. Kennett, "International Banking's Challenge For Supervisory Authorities," *Canadian Banker and ICB Review* 88, no. 3 (June 1981).

understanding, cooperation, and coordination of international bank supervisory issues. The Organization for Cooperation and Development in Paris has formed the Export Banking Group comprised of bank regulatory and supervisory officials from the 24 industrialized countries. The Center For Monetary Studies in Latin America (Mexico City) has expanded its bank supervisory services to all countries in Latin America. The Central Banking Department at the International Monetary Fund increasingly provides developing countries support in their efforts to strengthen their bank supervision programs. The Groupe d'Contact promotes cooperation and coordination among banking authorities in the European Economic Community. Finally, the banking supervisors of offshore financial centers, such as Bahrain, Panama, the Bahamas, Hong Kong, and so on, have established regular contact among each other and with the authorities in national financial centers to coordinate and harmonize prudential programs of supervision. Private and semiofficial groups also are working on harmonizing traditional commercial banking practices of many countries to strengthen the efficiency and prudential controls in international banking. The Group of Thirty, a New York-based study group of internationally prominent bankers and government officials, explores the basic problems multinational banking presents to the functioning of the international economic system. The international accounting associations are developing more standardized accounting, audit, and disclosure principles and practices for multinational banking. The international legal profession continually seeks ways to strengthen lending agreements in an international setting.

The International Supervisory Agenda

A fundamental premise of official bank supervision is that the banks establish the systems, internal controls, and operating systems necessary to monitor and supervise their interests, and when the banks cannot agree on a self-imposed system of supervision or fail to impose a system, then official action is required. Generally, the development of an interdependent, multinational banking system has caused the world's largest banks and bank supervisors to become mutually vulnerable. This vulnerability stimulates the parties at interest to develop a level playing field and uniform, or at least harmonized, rules of the game.

For instance, banks and their supervisors have agreed on minimum standards of control and confirmation of foreign exchange activities. General international agreement is developing on the need for all world-class banks to report their activities on a global consolidated accounting basis, albeit the precise forms of consolidation and the degrees of disclosure for inner or secret reserves have not been settled.

The international banks now report to their bank supervisors more consolidated data and information about liquidity, foreign exchange positions, and country exposures.

There remains much more to do in gearing the supervisory programs of banks and authorities to the modern, integrated international banking system. The future agenda includes establishing international prudential perspectives about banks' maturity transformation, capital adequacy, lending limits, bad debt allocations, and nonperforming loans. Overall, the trend is clear. The growth in multinational banking exposures requries banks to strengthen their internal system of supervision as well as to know more about the affairs of their counterparty banks. Since bank supervisors, with their lender-of-last-resort responsibilities, underwrite the confidence of multinational banking transactions, they must ensure that the world's financial markets function with adequate prudential data, information, and controls.

SECTION 9
The Future of International Banking

49

Expansion of Foreign Banks in the United States

JAMES B. SOMMERS
Executive Vice President
North Carolina National Bank

EARLY HISTORY

The expansion of foreign banks into the United States is not a new phenomena. Foreign banking agencies have been established and operating in New York since the end of the Civil War. By 1880, two British banks had established operations in California. They held 15 percent of all deposits in California and ranked third and fourth in the state. Before the close of the century, California also had banks from Japan, Canada, and Hong Kong.

After the liberalization of New York banking laws in 1911, 19 foreign banks established agencies in the state, and by 1925 the number had swelled to 33. Then, as it is now, the geographic diversity was great. The first subsidiary trust company banking operations set up in New York included banks from the United Kingdom, Greece, Italy, and Portugal.[1]

This move by foreign banks into the United States was accompanied by the expansion abroad of U.S. banks and trust companies. In 1887, the old Guaranty Trust Company opened its London Office. Utilizing the additional powers granted by passage of the Edge Act, Section 25(a) of the Federal Reserve Act, U.S. banks began their expansion abroad in earnest, and by 1926, 12 U.S. banks had established 154 foreign branches around the world.[2] The vehicles used for expansion

The author wishes to thank Gary Welsh of Prather Seeger Dolittle & Fanner, Washington, D.C., for his review and helpful suggestions for this chapter.

[1] Diane Page and Neal M. Soss, "Some Evidence of Transnational Banking Structure," *Comptroller of the Currency Staff Paper*, September 1980, pp. 7–8.

[2] Ibid., pp. 9–10.

by both the U.S. and foreign banks were as varied as they are today, that is, agencies, branches, subsidiaries, and consortiums.

POSTWAR HISTORY

The postwar history of the expansion of foreign banks into the United States is one of accelerating growth of agencies, branches, representative offices, and subsidiaries. In addition, major acquisitions of U.S. banks took place in the late 70s and early 80s. This growth was a natural result of the substantial increase in world trade, the emergence of the multinational corporation, the increasing interdependency of the world economy, and rapid technological advances in communication and transportation.

There are several motivations which led to the substantial increase in the presence of foreign banks in the United States. First was the basic motivation of following a domestic customer base as they traded and expanded abroad. This motivation has led banks into foreign countries since the days of the Pharaoh. Second, the size and growth potential of the U.S. market has been a powerful attraction. This point was particularly important to a number of banks whose indigenous markets were relatively small compared to the United States and whose growth potential was much more limited. Third, the emergence of the dollar as a reserve currency after World War II, coupled with the explosive growth of dollar-denominated trade, necessitated the establishment of a dollar-based funding source. Fourth, a number of major foreign banks perceived the advantages which were available to foreign banks because of the anomaly of our dual banking system and the lack of any federal constraints in the establishment of multistate banking operations. In addition, there were clear cost advantages for foreign banks relative to reserve requirements and the option of not paying insurance premiums to the FDIC, which is a practical requirement for all U.S. banks. These clear advantages over domestic banks could not be expected to last forever so a number of banks took advantage of the opportunities while they lasted. Last, but not least, is the perception that the United States is the last bastion of free enterprise. Thus, for those pursuing an asset diversification policy, the U.S. is viewed as a "safe haven." As Hans Brinckmann so aptly stated in a recent article in the *American Banker*, "Here [the United States] he feels his hard-earned money will be safe from bureaucratic red tape, hyperinflation, theft, confiscation, or mere social disdain. Here, money still equals success, and success is respected.[3]

---

[3] Hans Brinckmann, "Bastion of Free Enterprise Image Draws Banks to the U.S.," *American Banker* 146, no. 55, March 20, 1981, p. 27.

EXPANSION

With the exception of the striking decline of the branch/agency network of the European colonial powers in their former colonies in Africa and Asia, the expansion of the transnational banking networks is one of accelerating growth which reached massive proportions by the end of the 70s. This expansion can be broken down into four major categories: (1) banks which maintain worldwide networks of banking offices in various forms; (2) banks which maintain branches/agencies/rep offices in the major financial centers of London and New York; (3) those banks which maintain branches in the traditional offshore centers of Nassau, Grand Cayman, Panama, Hong Kong, Singapore, and Bahrain; (4) banks which expand within their own geographic region.

The majority of the expansion took place in the decade of the 70s and was a phenomenon experienced by all the major European countries, the United States, and Japan. However, the United Kingdom and the United States were clearly the leaders in terms of the number of foreign banks establishing new branches and agencies on their shores.

In the United States the growth rate was dramatic. "Between 1972 and 1980, the number of foreign bank agencies in the United States more than tripled, branches quintupled, and banking subsidiaries more than doubled. . . . New York, California, Illinois, and Florida—account for 98 percent of all foreign banks' agencies in the United States, 84 percent of all branches, and 93 percent of all banking subsidiaries."[4] As of March 1980, there were at least 345 foreign bank presences in the United States representing at least 153 different parent banking organizations from over 34 foreign countries. These foreign banking organizations operate 164 agencies, 134 branches, 47 subsidiary commercial banks, six investment companies, and two agreement corporations in the United States.[5] These numbers do not include certain securities affiliates and bank-related activities such as leasing and factoring. There is a very close correlation between the states in which foreign banks have a presence and the states whose banks have a presence abroad. This follows for the states listed above with the exception of Florida.

Foreign bank penetration of the domestic market has increased substantially in the last several years as strong marketing programs aimed predominantly at the commercial and industrial loan market have begun to take effect. This thrust, coupled with a number of major acquisitions, has provided the foreign banks with a significant base of operation

---

[4] Page and Neal, "Transnational Banking," pp. 62–63.

[5] Ibid., pp. 60–61.

in the United States. There were 14 foreign banks which had $1 billion or more in commercial loans on their books as of June 30, 1981. These foreign banks' commercial portfolios would easily rival a number of the large regional wholesale banks in the country, and foreign banks now own 11 of the top 100 banks in the United States.[6] A large portion of the portfolios of many of the foreign banks is comprised of loans to the U.S. subsidiaries of companies from their home country. This is particularly true for the Japanese banks.

The combined assets of the agencies, branches, and subsidiaries of foreign banks operating in the United States now represent approximately $171.6 billion, or roughly 12 percent of the total U.S. banking system.[7] Most of these assets are concentrated in branches and agencies. A recent study by the Comptroller of the Currency found that the assets of U.S. banks acquired by foreign banks were less than 5 percent of all U.S. commercial bank assets.[8] However, the true penetration of foreign banks is very difficult to measure because the reported loan figures do not include loans which foreign banks book overseas.

Foreign bank assets in the United States have grown over 500 percent since 1972, as compared to a growth of 92 percent for growth for domestic assets of all U.S. commercial banks.[9] Even so, it should be kept in mind that the assets and operations of U.S. banks abroad remain substantially greater than those of foreign banks' operations in the United States.

As of December 1980, there were 151 U.S. banks operating over 800 foreign branches and agencies with assets in excess of $375 billion.[10] According to Federal Reserve figures, the location of these foreign branches of U.S. banks was as follows: 212 in Latin American nations; 154 in the Far East; 150 in the Bahamas and Cayman Islands; 108 in continental European countries; 64 in the United Kingdom; 51 in U.S. overseas-area trust territories; 50 in the Near East and Africa.

FORM AND STRUCTURE

The main vehicles used by the foreign banks to expand into the United States are as follows:

1. Agency—as defined by the International Banking Act of 1978 (IBA) "any office or any place of business of a foreign bank located

---

[6] "Foreign Banks with over $1 Billion in Business Loans Outstanding at U.S. Agencies and Branches," *American Banker*, March 20, 1980, p. 51.

[7] Thomas J. Stuhldreher and James C. Baker, "Bankers' Attitudes Toward U.S. Foreign Bank Regulation," *American Banker* 146, no. 55 (March 20, 1981), p. 43.

[8] Gaynor, R. L., "U.S. Regulations No Longer Favor Foreign Banks," *American Banker*, March 20, 1981, p. 22.

[9] Stuhldreher and Baker, "Bankers' Attitudes," p. 43.

[10] Page and Soss, "Some Evidence," p. 53.

in any state in the United States at which credit balances are maintained
incidental to or arising out of the exercise of banking powers, checks
are paid, or money is lent, but at which deposits may not be accepted
from citizens or residents of the United States." Agencies are thus
limited to raising money from the bank-to-bank market or their parents. Agencies have been one of the most frequently used vehicles
for foreign bank activities in the United States from the following
countries: Argentina, Australia, Brazil, Canada, Colombia, France, Germany, India, Iran, Israel, Italy, Japan, Korea, Malaysia, Mexico, Netherlands, New Zealand, Philippines, Portugal, Scotland, Singapore, Switzerland, Thailand, the United Kingdom, Venezuela, and Yugoslavia.

   2. Branch—as defined by the IBA, "an office or any place of business
of a foreign bank located in the state of the United States at which
deposits are received." Branches are empowered to offer a full range
of banking services relating to lending and deposit-taking activities.
In March of 1980 there were 134 branches representing 23 countries
and 39 banks operating in the United States. The foreign banks having
branches in the United States are from the following countries: Argentina, Belgium, Brazil, Canada, Denmark, France, Germany, Greece,
Hong Kong, India, Ireland, Israel, Italy, Japan, Korea, Netherlands,
New Zealand, Pakistan, Philippines, Puerto Rico, Switzerland, Taiwan,
and the United Kingdom. These branches are located in the following
cities: Boston, Chicago, New York, Philadelphia, Pittsburgh, Portland,
San Francisco, Seattle, and Washington, D.C.

   3. Subsidiaries—subsidiaries fall into three basic categories:

a.   Banking subsidiaries—partially or wholly owned banks which are
     state or nationally chartered and offer a full range of both wholesale
     and retail services. Foreign banks most often utilized the state
     charter because, until the passage of the International Banking
     Act of 1978, the National Banking Act required that all of the
     members of the board of directors of a national bank had to be
     U.S. citizens. In early 1980 there were 47 banking subsidiaries
     owned by foreign banks with operations centered in New York
     and California with most of the acquired assets being centered
     in banks from the United Kingdom, Japan, and Hong Kong.

b.   Securities affiliates—very similar to a domestic securities house
     which executes purchases and sales of securities, bonds, and gov-
     ernment obligations on behalf of both foreign and domestic cus-
     tomers. In addition, some of these affiliates participate in under-
     writing and distribution activities. There were eight securities
     affiliates of foreign banks operating in the United States in March
     1980, with operations centered in New York.

c.   New York Investment Companies—"operate only in New York
     as permitted by New York State Banking Law. These companies

are permitted to deal in securities to a certain extent, and they provide direct financing and advice to firms establishing marketing networks for their products in foreign countries."[11]

4. Representative offices—liaison offices which have no legal capabilities with regard to either taking deposits and/or booking loans. The primary purpose of such offices is to facilitate business with the home office through direct marketing efforts, stimulate trade with their home country, and gather information for their parent bank and its customers. As of March 30, 1980 there were 148 representative offices in the United States. Many foreign banks begin their initial operations in the United States with a representative office and later upgrade to an agency, branch and/or subsidiary.

FOREIGN BANK OPERATIONS IN THE UNITED STATES

In the *Analysis of Current Operations of Foreign-Owned U.S. Banks,*[12] foreign-owned U.S. banks, when compared to U.S. peer banks, were found to have: lower returns, higher equity to asset ratios, more commercial loans as a proportion of total loans, fewer residential mortgages as a proportion of total loans, fewer municipal securities as a proportion of total securities, and more large certificates of deposit as a percentage of total assets.

Another *Comptroller's Staff Paper*[13] found that American banks which have been acquired have tended to be less profitable than their peers before acquisition. Earnings improved after acquisition but remained below average. The improvement has been accompanied by a decline in the securities portfolio, especially municipals, and an increase in time deposits. The paper found little evidence that the acquired banks turned away from their local markets. In addition, foreign-owned U.S. banks have a lower proportion of checking and small savings accounts than domestic banks and a higher proportion of purchased funds, such as large certificates of deposit and security repurchase agreements.

With regard to capital, there has been considerable concern that foreign banks are allowed by their indigenous regulators to operate on lower levels of capital than their U.S. counterparts. A lower level of capital would allow the foreign banks to earn a reasonable return on equity, even though they may be charging lower rates which would be unsatisfactory for an American bank. This comparison is more true

---

[11] Stuhldreher and Baker, "Bankers' Attitudes," p. 43.

[12] Ellen S. Goldberg, "Analysis of Current Operations of Foreign-Owned U.S. Banks," *Comptroller of the Currency Staff Paper.*

[13] Blair B. Hodgkins and Ellen S. Goldberg, "Effect of Foreign Acquisitions on the Balance Sheet Structure and Earnings Performance of American Banks," *Comptroller of the Currency Staff Paper.*

for regional banks in the United States than for money center banks whose capital ratios are more comparable with their foreign counterparts. However, there are a number of foreign banks, particularly government owned and/or supported banks, whose leverage is substantially higher than U.S. money center banks. This disparity clearly puts the American banks at a pricing disadvantage, which is often exacerbated by the foreign bank having lower target ratios for return on assets and equity.

INTERNATIONAL BANKING ACT OF 1978 AND COMPETITION

The accelerating growth in the size, number, and scope of the foreign banks operating in the United States necessitated a review of the need for a federal presence in their activities in the United States. With the exception of subsidiaries, the federal government of the United States had no control in the admission and regulation of foreign banks in the United States. This condition existed in the largest banking market in the world because of the historic development of our dual banking system and its separation of federal and state powers. No other federal authorities in the world left such important powers to be solely administered by states, provinces and/or other local authorities.

This peculiar situation led to competitive advantages for foreign banks. This was due to the uneven treatment between U.S. banks and foreign banks with respect to activities such as the ease of entry into the U.S. market, reserve requirements, deposit insurance, securities operations, multistate banking, and the acquisition of U.S. banks. It is important to stress that the foreign banks were not doing anything illegal or unethical. They were simply taking advantage of what was available to them, but not to U.S. banks, under the dual banking system. Thus, foreign banks became aggressive competitors in the U.S. banking market and in the process caused concerns in a number of areas. These concerns were manifested in the fact that the "playing field was not level;" that is, the foreign banks had a number of basic and structural advantages over U.S. banks.

There were two basic approaches to solving the inherent discrepancies caused by our dual banking system: the McFadden Act (prohibiting interstate branching), and the Glass-Stegall Act (separating commercial banking from securities activities). The first approach was to liberalize the current U.S. laws in an effort to allow American banks to have, in essence, the same privileges in the country which were accorded foreign banks. Many of the largest banking institutions in the country supported this view as a way to increase their own competitive position in the United States by eliminating a number of anarchistic statutes which were artificially limiting legitimate banking competition. In addition, these banks had large foreign operations, and they were concerned with the possibility of retaliation by foreign governments.

The second approach was to directly address each of the competitive advantages which foreign banks had in the United States in an effort to "level the playing field" and put both U.S. and foreign banks' operations on the same basis in the United States, and to grandfather all of the foreign banks' current activities in the country as a matter of simple justice. This second approach was manifested in the International Banking Act of 1978 (IBA). The legislation was first introduced at the request of the Federal Reserve on March 5, 1975, as the Foreign Bank Act of 1975–S. 958. It took four years and six Congressional hearings before the passage of the International Banking Act of 1978 on September 17, 1978. A section-by-section summary of this legislation is seen in Exhibit 1.

The major provisions of the Act, which helped establish the concept of competitive equality between U.S. and foreign banks, are as follows:

1. Section 2—Directors of National Banks—The Comptroller of the Currency was given authority to waive the requirement that all directors of national banks be U.S. citizens.

2. Section 3—Edge Act Corporations—Provisions of the Edge Act which discriminate against foreign-owned banks were eliminated or modified. For the first time, foreign banks were allowed to acquire the majority of the stock of an Edge Corporation, and the requirement that all directors be U.S. citizens was eliminated.

3. Section 4—Federal Branches and Agencies—For the first time, foreign banks were given the option of either a federal or state charter for branches and agencies, so long as it is not prohibited by state law. The branching restrictions of McFadden were made applicable as well as the provisions of the National Bank Act.

4. Section 5—Interstate Banking—Foreign banks were prohibited from establishing full-service branches or banking subsidiaries outside of a designated "home state" of operations. As of April 1978, 63 foreign banks had banking facilities in more than one state, with 31 of these institutions operating in three or more states. According to Federal Reserve statistics, of the 112 foreign banking organizations operating in the United States as of June 5, 1981, New York led as a home state with 79 banks, followed by 27 in California, two in Florida, two in Illinois, one in Massachusetts, and one in the District of Columbia. Any federal or state branches outside of a designated home state were limited by the International Banking Act to taking deposits permissible for Edge Act corporations; that is, deposits from foreign sources and deposits incidental to certain foreign and international banking activities. In addition, foreign banks were prohibited by the IBA from acquiring any bank located outside their designated home state. Foreign banks were not prohibited from establishing agencies or New York

Investment Companies outside their home state because these offices do not accept domestic deposits. The foreign bank branches or subsidiaries which were applied for before July 26, 1978 were grandfathered.

5. Section 6—Insurance of Deposits in Branches—Foreign banks were given the option of deposit insurance for their branches; however, branches were required to insure deposits if they accepted deposits of less than $100,000.

6. Section 7—Authority of the Federal Reserve System—The Federal Reserve was given the power to impose on foreign bank branches and agencies the reporting, reserve, and examination requirements which are applicable to member banks.

7. Section 8—Nonbanking Activities—Applied the restrictions of the Bank Holding Company Act to the nonbanking activities of foreign banks in the United States and grandfathered those activities which were in operation before July 26, 1978.

8. Section 10—Representative Offices—Required foreign banks to register any representative office in the United States with the Secretary of the Treasury.

Thus the basic intent of the International Banking Act of competitive equality was addressed in a comprehensive and yet fair manner. The multistate banking operations of the foreign banks were grandfathered, as well as their securities affiliates and other nonbanking subsidiaries. But in the future, the foreign banks would have the same limitations as those imposed on domestic banks through McFadden, the Bank Holding Act, and the Glass-Stegall Act on their ability to expand out of their home state and also on their ability to acquire nonbanking subsidiaries. In addition, their cost of operations was put on the same relative basis as their domestic counterparts with the imposition of reserve requirements.

In addition, the IBA mandated two studies: one on the applicability of the McFadden Act on the current economic and banking environment, and a second study on the treatment of U.S. banks abroad.

The *Treatment of U.S. Banks Abroad* study has been completed, and in its conclusions and recommendations it outlines the basic criteria for competitive equality. "Extension of essential equality of competitive opportunity requires that the host country provide adequate opportunities for entry, choice of organizational forms, and subsequent expansion within the host country's banking markets, as well as equitable application of rules and regulations to establish U.S. banks, vis-à-vis comparably situated domestic situations." It is clear that in a number of both industrialized and third-world countries all of these basic criteria are often not available to U.S. banks in their market. Yet these criteria for competitive equality are available to foreign banks from those countries coming into the United States. The best opportunity to rectify these situations will be through the negotiations in the services sector which were mandated by the Trade Act of 1979, and which gives the United States the authority to expand opportunities for U.S. banking services abroad through negotiations to be carried on by our Special Trade Representative.

FUTURE

As part of the IBA, foreign banks were grandfathered certain competitive advantages in their multistate operations and securities affiliates. The Comptroller's study, *The Competitive Balance Between Domestic and Foreign Banks,* was released in September of 1980, approximately two years after the IBA was enacted. The Study found that "Recent developments with the United States and anecdotal evidence suggest that the competitive balance between domestic and foreign banks, however imperfect, is not seriously out of line."[14] However, there was, and still is, a considerable amount of concern surrounding a number of large acquisitions of U.S. banks by foreign interests. In the spring of 1980, a moratorium on foreign bank acquisitions was enacted by Congress. The moratorium expired July 1, 1980, and has not been revived. This issue, as well as the one of open access to the U.S. market on a basis of full competitive equality, is related to the whole question of equal national treatment of U.S. banks abroad.

In any case, the foreign banks are now an important part of our domestic banking system. They have contributed capital, stimulated trade, strengthened management, and increased competition. The number of new entrants is forecast to diminish because most of the large foreign banks are already operating in the United States. Many foresee increased competition on all fronts: corporate, retail, middle market, and financial related services such as leasing, factoring, and commercial finance.

Exhibit 1*
Report of the Committee on Banking, Housing, and Urban Affairs, United States Senate

SECTION-BY-SECTION ANALYSIS
SECTION 1. SHORT TITLE; DEFINITIONS AND RULES OF CONSTRUCTION

This section provides that the act may be cited as the "International Banking Act of 1978," and defines certain terms used in the act. Principal among these are "agency," "branch," "bank" and "commercial lending company," the four primary means by which a "foreign bank" does business in the United States.

SECTION 2. DIRECTORS OF NATIONAL BANKS

This section amends the National Banking Act to allow the Comptroller of the Currency, at his discretion, to waive the requirement that all directors of national banks be U.S. citizens, in effect permitting not more than a minority of directors of national banks to be non-U.S. citizens.

[14] Steven J. Weiss, "The Competitive Balance Between Domestic and Foreign Banks in the U.S.," *Comptroller of the Currency Staff Paper,* September 1980, p. 43.

Exhibit 1 (*continued*)

SECTION 3. EDGE ACT CORPORATIONS

Subsection (a) of section 3 states the three principal objectives of the section: Elimination or modification of provisions in the Edge Act which discriminate against foreign-owned banking institutions, which disadvantage or unnecessarily restrict or limit Edge Act corporations in competing with foreign-owned banking institutions in the United States and abroad, or which impede the attainment of congressional purposes of the Edge Act as amended by subsection (b). The Federal Reserve Board is required to revise its regulations to eliminate or modify any regulatory restrictions, not required by the statute, which discriminate against foreign-owned institutions, disadvantage or unnecessarily restrict or limit Edge Act corporations in competing with foreign-owned institutions, or impede the attainment of the policy objectives set forth in the Edge Act as amended by subsection (b). The Board is required to issue its revised regulations within 150 days after date of enactment, and to adopt final regulations to be effective not later than 120 days after they are first issued.

Subsection (b) amends the Edge Act to include a declaration of Congressional policy which is to serve as guidance to future regulatory actions and interpretations of the Edge Act by the Board. The purposes set forth recognize the importance of establishing international banking facilities throughout the country in promoting international trade, especially U.S. exports; the need to foster Edge Act ownership by regional and smaller banks, in particular to bring trade financing opportunities to small farms and businesses; to stimulate export opportunities and competition in international finance; the need to maintain competitive equality between Edge Act corporations and similar foreign-owned banking institutions in the United States and abroad; and the need to interpret the act in the light of changing economic conditions and banking environments, with a requirement that regulations be reviewed at least once every 5 years.

Subsection (d) eliminates two separate provisions in the Edge Act which prevent such corporations from having liabilities outstanding at any one time upon their debentures, bonds, or promissory notes in excess of ten times their paid-in capital and surplus.

Subsection (e) would eliminate a mandatory 10-percent reserve requirement imposed on Edge Act corporation deposits and provide instead that Edge Act corporations be subject to the same requirements that apply to member banks.

Subsection (f) would modify the Edge Act to permit foreign-owned banking institutions to acquire majority stock control of such corporations.

Subsection (g) requires the Federal Reserve Board to report to the Congress not later than 270 days after the date of enactment of this bill on its recommendations with respect to permitting Edge Act corporations, and their sister State corporations operating under section 25 of the Federal Reserve Act, to become member banks.

Subsection (h) requires the Board in its annual report to the Congress under the Federal Reserve Act, to include its assessment of the effects of the amendments made by this bill on the capitalization and activities of Edge Act corporations, similar State corporations operating under section 25 of the Federal Reserve Act, and on commercial banks and the banking system.

SECTION 4. FEDERAL BRANCHES AND AGENCIES

For the first time, foreign banks may, with the approval of and subject to the supervision of the Comptroller of the Currency, establish one or more Federal branches or agencies in any State in which it is not operating a State branch or agency and where the establishment of a branch or agency by a foreign bank is not prohibited by State law. No foreign bank may maintain both a Federal branch and a Federal agency in the same State. With certain exceptions, statutory or regulatory, the activities of a Federal branch or agency shall be conducted in the same manner as a national bank.

SECTION 5. INTERSTATE BRANCHING

Subsection (a) of section 5 provides that, except as grandfathered by subsection (b), no foreign bank may directly or indirectly establish and operate either a Federal or State branch outside of its home State unless the foreign bank enters into an agreement or undertaking with the Federal Reserve Board to accept only such deposits at such Federal or State branch as would be permissible for a corporation organized under

Exhibit 1 (*continued*)

section 25(a) of the Federal Reserve Act (an "Edge Act corporation"). The existing deposit limitations on Edge Act corporations are set forth in the sixth paragraph of section 25(a) of the Federal Reserve Act (12 U.S.C. 615(a)) and section 211.7(c) of the Board's Regulation K [12 CFR 211.7(c)]. In addition, neither Federal branches nor Federal agencies can be established and operated outside of a foreign bank's home State unless the receiving State expressly permits entry; State branches and agencies can be established and operated outside of a foreign bank's home State only if approved by the bank regulatory authority of the receiving State. It should be noted that this latter requirement confers no authority on State bank regulatory officials to approve foreign bank offices; that authority must derive from appropriate State law. Finally, no foreign bank could acquire any interest in a bank located outside of its home State if such a transaction would be prohibited by section 3(d) of the Bank Holding Company Act of 1956, as amended, (12 U.S.C. 1842(d)) if the foreign bank were a bank holding company the operation of whose banking subsidiaries are principally conducted in the foreign bank's home State. The last sentence of the subsection provides that notwithstanding any provision of Federal or State law, any branch receiving deposits subject to the limitations of an agreement imposed under this subsection shall not be subject to any mandatory Federal deposit insurance on such deposits. This insures competitive equality with Edge Act corporations, which are not required to obtain insurance on their deposits.

Subsection (b) grandfathers from the limitations or restrictions of subsection (a), any foreign bank branch, agency, or bank or commercial lending company subsidiary which lawfully commenced operation or for which an application to commence business had been lawfully filed on or before July 26, 1978, the day the bill was ordered reported by the committee.

Subsection (c) provides that for purposes of section 5, the home State of a foreign bank that has branches, agencies, subsidiary commercial lending companies, or subsidiary banks, or any combination thereof, in more than one State is whichever of such States is so determined by election of the foreign bank, or in default of such election by the Board.

SECTION 6. INSURANCE OF DEPOSITS IN BRANCHES

Under section 6, all branches of foreign banks have the option of applying for deposit insurance; however, Federal branches and State branches of foreign banks in states in which deposits of a State bank are required to be insured, must obtain deposit insurance if they accept deposits of less than $100,000. This section contains numerous technical amendments to the Federal Deposit Insurance Act which are necessary to enable the FIDC to deal with the special problems involved in the insurance and supervision of branches operated in the United States by foreign banks.

SECTION 7. AUTHORITY OF THE FEDERAL RESERVE SYSTEM

This section imposes on Federal branches and agencies the reporting, reserve, and examination requirements applicable to member banks, and authorizes the Federal Reserve Board to impose on any branch or agency subject to the bill any reserve requirement the Board has authority to impose on Federal branches and agencies. The Board is required to exercise the latter authority "after consultation and in cooperation with the State bank supervisory authorities," with respect to State-licensed institutions controlled by foreign banks. Since these institutions are State licensed and supervised, it was felt entirely appropriate and reasonable for State authorities to have some input into the setting of reasonable reserve requirements, recognizing the ultimate authority of the Federal Reserve to determine reasonable reserve requirements. If the cooperation on the part of the State banking authorities were not forthcoming in any instance, that would in no way diminish the power conferred on the Board to impose reasonable reserve requirements, or the legal obligation imposed on the branches and agencies to comply therewith.

The Federal Reserve Board has residual authority to examine any foreign bank branch, agency, commercial lending company, or bank subsidiary. In doing so the Board should make maximum use of reports by the Comptroller, FDIC, and State bank supervisory authorities.

Exhibit 1 (*continued*)

Within 2 years after the enactment of this bill, the Board shall submit a report concerning the implementation of the act, and any recommendations for change.

SECTION 8. NONBANKING ACTIVITIES

Subsection (a) of this section in general applies the restrictions of the Bank Holding Company Act to the nonbanking activities of foreign banks and foreign companies carrying on banking activities in the United States, even though the banking activities may be conducted through commercial lending companies or agencies rather than branches or subsidiary banks.

Subsection (b) grandfathers, until December 31, 1985, nonbanking activities engaged in on the date of enactment of this bill by a foreign bank or company, either directly or indirectly, in the United States.

Subsection (c) permanently grandfathers, after December 31, 1985, a foreign bank's or foreign company's nonbanking activities in the United States, if such activities were lawfully engaged in, or such bank or company had applied to be engaged in, on or before July 26, 1978. This grandfather provision is subject to the Federal Reserve deeming it necessary to issue a termination order regarding such activities, if that action is necessary to prevent unsound banking practices or for other specified reasons.

Subsection (a) and (d) specify that a foreign branch, agency, or commercial lending company will be subject to the antitying provisions of the Bank Holding Company Act, as well as eligible for certain statutory exemptions from the restrictions on nonbanking activities included in section 4(c) of that act.

Subsection (e) clarifies the Congressional intent that the prohibitions of the Bank Holding Company Act on nonbanking activities of bank holding companies should not be applied extraterritorially to foreign banking organizations whose principal banking activities are conducted outside the United States.

SECTION 9. STUDY ON TREATMENT OF U.S. BANKS ABROAD

The Secretary of the Treasury, in conjunction with the Secretary of State, the Federal Reserve, the Comptroller of the Currency and the Federal Deposit Insurance Corporation are directed to conduct a study of the extent to which American banks operating overseas are denied national treatment; the effects of such discrimination on U.S. exports; and recommendations for elimination of such foreign laws or practices.

SECTION 10. REPRESENTATIVE OFFICES

This section requires foreign banks maintaining offices in the United States other than branches or agencies to register with the Secretary of the Treasury in accordance with rules prescribed by him.

SECTION 11. CEASE-AND-DESIST ORDERS

Federal bank regulatory agencies are empowered to issue cease-and-desist orders, under the Federal Deposit Insurance Act, to any foreign bank or holding company to which subsection (a) of section 8 applies and to any nonbank subsidiary of such bank or company.

SECTION 12. AMENDMENT TO THE BANKING ACT OF 1933

This section constitutes a conforming amendment to the Glass-Steagall Act to make it consistent with the policies set forth in section 4.

SECTION 13. REGULATIONS AND ENFORCEMENT

The Comptroller, the Board, and the FDIC are authorized and empowered to issue such rules, regulations, and orders as are necessary to carry out the duties and responsibilities conferred on them under this bill.

SECTION 14. REPORT ON McFADDEN ACT

The President, in consultation with the Attorney General, the Secretary of the Treasury, the Board, the Comptroller, and the Federal Deposit Insurance Corporation, shall transmit a report to the Congress containing his recommendations concerning the appli-

Exhibit 1 (*concluded*)

cability of the McFadden Act to the present financial, banking, and economic environment, including an analysis of the effects of any proposed changes to the act on the structure of the banking industry and on the financial and economic environment in general. The report is to be submitted within 1 year after the enactment of this bill.

FISCAL IMPACT STATEMENT

In accordance with section 252(a) of the Legislative Reorganization Act of 1970, the committee estimates the bill will result in no additional outlays. This concurs with the estimate prepared by the Congressional Budget Office.

CONGRESSIONAL BUDGET OFFICE—COST ESTIMATE

U.S. CONGRESS,
CONGRESSIONAL BUDGET OFFICE,
Washington, D.C., August 1, 1978.

Hon. WILLIAM PROXMIRE,
Chairman, Committee on Banking, Housing and Urban Affairs, U.S. Senate, Washington, D.C.

DEAR MR. CHAIRMAN: Pursuant to section 403 of the Congressional Budget Act of 1974, the Congressional Budget Office has reviewed H.R. 10899, as amended, the International Banking Act of 1978, as ordered reported by the Senate Committee on Banking, Housing and Urban Affairs, July 26, 1978. This bill would provide for Federal regulation of the activities of foreign banks in U.S. financial markets.

Based on this review, it appears that no significant additional cost to the Government would be incurred as a result of enactment of this bill.

Sincerely,

ALICE M. RIVLIN, *Director.*

CHANGES IN EXISTING LAW

In the opinion of the committee, it is necessary to dispense with the requirements of paragraph 4 of rule XXIX of the Standing Rules of the Senate in order to expedite the business of the Senate.

REGULATORY IMPACT STATEMENT

(RULE XXIX, PARAGRAPH 5)

The extent to which foreign banks will establish operations in the United States under the jurisdiction of the Comptroller is a matter which cannot be precisely defined. It does not appear that the impact of this legislation on the Comptroller's office will be substantial.

This legislation mandates FDIC insurance only for branches of foreign banks if they accept deposits of less than $100,000. The FDIC projects the establishment of few insured branches of foreign banks under the legislation. The regulatory impact of the deposit insurance provisions of the legislation, therefore, should be negligible, according to the FDIC.

The legislation gives the Federal Reserve residual examination and supervisory authority over the domestic operations of foreign banks. The Federal Reserve is to the maximum extent possible to make use of the reports of the Comptroller, the FDIC, and the relevant State regulatory bodies. Branches and agencies of foreign banks principally fall within the regulatory purview of State authorities. Coordination with the State authorities should insure that the role of the Federal Reserve under this legislation does not substantially increase the volume of regulation. The Federal Reserve should be able to implement its reserve setting requirements without a significant impact on its operations.

The 1980s promise to be an interesting and challenging period for commercial banks in the United States. The possibilities of liberalization of the laws restricting interstate branching and the amalgamation of finance-related industries will be opportunities which will be available to all banks in the country, regardless of whether they are U.S. or foreign owned.

50
The Future Role of U.S. Banks in
the World Economy

ALFRED F. MIOSSI
Executive Vice President
Continental Illinois National Bank and Trust Company

INTRODUCTION*

Faced with dramatic changes in the shape of the world economy, the external debt problems of many developing and developed countries, rising competition from bank and nonbank financial institutions, and regulatory change in the United States and abroad, major American banks are modifying their approaches to international markets. Increasingly, the United States itself is becoming the focal point of international finance. To compete profitably and effectively both at home and abroad, banks are emerging as global "financial supermarkets," in which traditional commercial banking services are only a few of many important financial activities.

Specific aspects of international banking, including department operations, strategies, and goals have been covered in this Handbook. There is, however, another area of equal concern to anyone interested in international finance: the future. For it is the future world environment that will determine where banks will operate, what strategies they will employ, and how they will formulate and achieve their goals.

In spite of the vast amount of economic, financial, and political information available today, or perhaps because of it, prognostication has become a difficult and risky undertaking. But the advent of the 1980s has sharpened American bankers' awareness of the need to forecast the future and reassess international activities accordingly. The fundamental global restructuring underway since the early 1970s has brought shifting patterns of growth, trade, and investment, along with unprecedented market volatility, tremendous political uncertainty,

---

* This text was prepared in 1981 with minor revisions in early 1983.

and massive capital flows. These changes have forced U.S. bankers to come face to face with the question of their role in the world economy in the years ahead.

Specifically, bankers are evaluating which markets have the greatest long-term growth potential, the services those markets are most likely to need, and the best organizational structures to deliver those services. Those questions all play a central role in the planning processes of all international departments, and all will receive attention in the following discussion.

The principal purpose of this chapter, however, is not to provide specific answers to those questions (which can come only from individual institutions in light of individual capabilities) but to provide a general framework for answering them, emphasizing broad trends affecting all organizations—and involving two basic questions. First, what is *international* banking? Does the term apply solely to the overseas activities of U.S. banks, or can the domestic operations of American bankers be "international" as well? Beyond that, what is *banking?* Or, more important, what is banking becoming?

Simply raising these questions implies changes in traditional definitions. The direction and importance of these changes can best be understood by reviewing the major developments of the past two decades, the processes which have been set in motion in the United States and abroad, and the implications these developments carry for the future.

SETTING THE STAGE: AN OVERVIEW OF GROWTH

Earlier chapters and several recent articles have outlined the major forces behind the dramatic expansion of American banks and bank holding companies overseas in the 1960s and early 1970s, including:

The expansion of international trade and investment following the post-World War II reconstruction and the return to convertibility in 1958.

The rise of the American multinational corporation and the resulting growth in demand for international financial services.

The existence of domestic regulatory restraints on bank branching and acquisition activities, which encouraged banks to seek international avenues for expansion.

The imposition of capital controls in the United States, which gave rise to the Eurocurrency markets and made overseas financing more cost-competitive than that available domestically.

The series of energy-related events which created ballooning OPEC capital surpluses and simultaneously skyrocketing loan demand among oil-importing countries which brought U.S. banks into the petrodollar recycling business.

These factors and other changes occurring from 1967 to 1974 set off explosive international growth for American banks. While statistics cannot tell the whole story, they can tell us something—and in this case what they tell is astonishing.

In 1967, 15 major U.S. banks operated 295 overseas branches with total assets of about $15 billion. By the end of 1974, 125 banks operated 734 branches overseas, with assets totaling $152 billion—more than 10 times the amount only seven years before.[1]

During the same period, the contribution of international earnings to total bank earnings rose from approximately 10 percent to almost 38 percent for major banks, while more than 35 percent of all international bank claims in major countries were held by banks chartered in the United States.[2] In less than a decade, the role of American banks on the international financial stage had changed from member of the supporting cast to leading actor.

The apparently unlimited prospects for international growth naturally began to color the attitudes of U.S. bankers toward their overseas activities. While many of the risks involved in international lending were recognized, overseas loan-loss records were, and still are, significantly better than those domestically. Management tended to focus on earnings alone, rather than on the asset and capital bases necessary to generate those earnings. Gradually, international operations came to be viewed as distinct from domestic operations. Many bankers viewed international activities as virtually independent entities, whose goals and strategies need not necessarily coincide with those of the organization as a whole.

THE SCENE BEGINS TO SHIFT

Between 1974 and 1976, the international situation began to change, and the march overseas by American banks slowed markedly. The number of banks with overseas branches increased during this period by only two, to 127, while the number of overseas branches in operation actually declined to 731. Despite this slowing of activities, the total assets held by those branches continued to rise, reaching almost $220 billion at the end of 1976, representing a peak level of 38 percent of all international bank claims.[3]

---

[1] Christopher M. Korth, "The Evolving Role of U.S. Banks in International Finance," *Banker's Magazine*, July–August, 1980, p. 69.

[2] Ibid.

[3] Arturo P. Porzencanski, "The International Financial Role of U.S. Commercial Banks," *Journal of Banking and Finance* 5 (1981), p. 7.

Since 1976, the scene has shifted further. The international assets of U.S.-chartered banks have continued to rise to record levels, and today those assets represent 30 percent of total international bank claims. However, U.S. banks suffered a 10 percent decline in market share in only four years and statistics compiled by the Bank of International Settlements (BIS) show that international lending by U.S. banks has been growing at only half the average annual rate for all reporting institutions.[4] Beginning in 1981 foreign bank activity began to slow down as concern over creditworthiness grew.

A number of factors have to be taken in to account when evaluating those shifting statistics. For example, advances in technology, a field of continuing American leadership, have made physical, on-site facilities less important today than they were even five years ago. At the same time, loan volume or market share statistics tell us less about international operations than profitability figures, which, according to a Salomon Brothers study, rose by almost 20 percent in 1980 at the 10 largest U.S. banks.[5] Nonetheless, those statistics do demonstrate that the circumstances that supported the dramatic growth of U.S. banks overseas have changed radically in the past few years as international profitability rose by only 9 percent in 1981. The era of apparently unbounded global economic growth is fast drawing to a close, replaced by an age of international volatility and uncertainty.

RISING ENERGY COSTS: TODAY'S SITUATION

At the top of the list of challenges facing American banks today on the world level are the soaring energy prices that have diminished the share of the world's wealth available for productive investment, contributed to pernicious and pervasive global inflation and accompanying high interest rates, and helped slow real GNP growth worldwide from an average annual rate of 5 or 6 percent before 1973 to about 2 or 3 percent today.

The sudden accumulation of huge trade and current account surpluses by OPEC nations has placed increasing demands on the private banking system. In 1973, private sources accounted for some 39 percent of total capital flows to developing countries: today that figures exceeds 60 percent.[6] American banks, by far the most important participants in the petrodollar recycling effort, increasingly are reaching internally imposed lending limits to some countries and are facing

---

[4] Arturo P. Porzencanski, "The International Financial Role of U.S. Commercial Banks," *Journal of Banking and Finance* 5 (1981), p. 7.

[5] Cited in "1980: A World Banking Essay," *Euromoney*, May, 1981, p. 10.

[6] Continental Bank, Economic Research. See also F. John Mathis, ed., *Offshore Banking* (Chicago: Continental Bank, 1981), fig. 1–10.

the choice of limiting lending to certain areas or confronting mounting exposure risks.

Those risks, along with the growing volatility of international financial and currency markets, have stimulated new governmental efforts to bring the international banking system under closer control and supervision. Governments in many major industrial countries are reviewing offshore exposures, and in the United States, specific capital guidelines already are being used to control the concentration of bank lending abroad. Pressures also are mounting to regulate the Euromarkets, and although no specific action has been taken yet, the imposition of reserve requirements on Eurocurrency deposits (as suggested by the Federal Reserve) or of exchange of capital controls on Eurocurrency transactions (as suggested by European central bankers) would have a severe effect on the lending and funding operations of all American banks.

FOREIGN EXCHANGE VOLATILITY

Linked to the problems of inflation and market volatility is the managed floating of key currencies which replaced the fixed-rate foreign exchange system that once pegged national currencies to the dollar and the dollar to gold. So far, however, the world has seen few signs of the financial discipline and restraint on the part of national fiscal and monetary authorities that the system requires if it is to operate efficiently. Not only have most major industrialized nations pursued economic and political policies that today make moves toward disciplined restraint difficult and painful for individuals and industries alike, but even in those countries where attempts have been made to contain domestic inflation through so-called supply-side or tight money policies, the moves have been greeted more with alarm than welcome internationally. The higher interest rates available on assets denominated in the currencies of tight money countries attract investors worldwide and can result in dramatic and perhaps inconvenient depreciations of the currencies of other countries. Depreciation of a country's currency can, of course, have the positive effect of stimulating exports and, perhaps, GNP. The international consequences of domestic moves to control inflation pose serious problems, and attempts to establish currency blocs like the European Monetary System (EMS) may alleviate but will not solve them.

INCREASED ECONOMIC CONFLICT

These long-term adjustment problems faced by all nations are heightened by the different degrees of success individual countries have had in adjusting in the short term. Optimistically, the noticeable and continuing shift in economic advantage toward the rapidly industrializing, export-oriented economies throughout Latin America and the Pacific should open new opportunities for the United States and its international banks to expand their involvement in trade and investment and to help other nations reach their full economic potential. Realistically, as worldwide economic growth has slowed and current account deficits have deteriorated under pressures from imported energy costs, the potential for economic and political conflict among nations has increased.

In Africa, Latin America, the Middle East, and Southeast Asia, nations have emerged to assert their role on the world stage and challenge their traditional terms of trade with developed countries. Confronted by a mutually diminishing ability to absorb imports and a mutually increasing need to export to sustain domestic economic growth, the fabric of cooperative support among industrialized countries also is being tested. While the prospect of retaliation may serve to hold outright trade restraints to a minimum, as rising protectionist pressures in the United States and abroad demonstrate, the fabric is beginning to fray.

Most notably, the freezing of Iranian assets by the U.S. government in 1979 and the subsequent offsetting of deposits by U.S. banks against the possibility of loan default sent tremors through the entire international banking system and raised a serious question for the future: will governments engage freely in financial warfare in the years ahead, using assets in the international banking system as weapons? Although the initial shock of the events in Iran has begun to fade with the stop-gap resolution of the crisis, the essential question is far from resolved and, coupled with recent events in Afghanistan, Poland, and other areas, suggests that the international banking system has been politicized to an unsettling degree.

The issue of free trade is particularly complicated in the U.S., which is one of the few nations in the world to view trade policies as convenient political tools. That view was particularly apparent in the '70s, as trade was repeatedly used as a weapon. And a very expensive one at that. In the long run, cutting off U.S. supplies to other nations takes its heaviest toll on the U.S.—through lost business, lost income, and lost confidence in our reliability as an exporter. The soybean, grain, and pipeline embargoes are clear cases of the ease with which other suppliers can be found to fill the void—cutting into U.S. market share. Clearly, our best weapon against other nations remains a strong economy in the U.S.

Unencumbered trade will result in benefits to all—with growth industries compensating declining industries. The arguments advanced by protectionists for trade restrictions—upholding the national defense, assisting in the development of new industries, or aiding traditional but slumping industries—ask for a reallocation of wealth between portions of the economy. And that costs the consumer, who should, in a free society, have the freedom to decide which products and industries to support.

EVOLVING POSITION OF THE UNITED STATES

Finally, as a result of the factors mentioned above and others as well, the relative position of the United States in world affairs, particularly financial affairs, continues to change. No longer are the United States and its dollar the acknowledged guarantors of world economic stability. While there are many ways to evaluate this change, one observation is particularly telling. In 1970, seven American banks ranked among the world's 10 largest in asset size; today, only two U.S.-chartered banks grace that list, largely as the result of the broad, prolonged depreciation of the dollar against other major currencies over the past decade.

SLOWER OVERSEAS GROWTH AND NEW INTERNATIONAL OPPORTUNITIES

The factors described above suggest that the overseas growth of American banks will proceed much more slowly and cautiously in the 1980s than it did in previous years. The exuberance which characterized the boom period of the 1960s and 70s today must be tempered by the closer analyses of earnings, margins, and risks.

By focusing on global trends alone, however, several equally important changes in the structure of international banking itself can be overlooked. These changes suggest that, while the overseas role of American banks may be smaller in the future, their overall international contribution may be stronger and more vital than ever before.

INTERNATIONALIZATION: ACHIEVEMENT AND CHALLENGE

U.S. banks led the explosion in offshore banking operations. However, they have since been joined by banks from a number of other countries. No longer is the international financial system dominated by the institutions of one country or a select group of countries: world class banks today are found not just in New York or London but in a growing number of financial centers around the world. These institutions form a highly complex and integrated network, and the fact that this system has been able to respond to tremendous global changes without major disruptions testifies to its strength, flexibility, and innovative capacity.

Banking's internationalization is a significant achievement. It has greatly improved capital mobility, reduced the costs of funds and services to customers, and made the allocation of resources among countries much more efficient. However, although the international banking system is highly integrated, it is also extremely competitive. Unlike many other industries in which a handful of companies clearly dominate a field, fully 50 international banks compose the industry's top tier, with another 50 close behind.

COMPETITION AND CAPITAL

The increasingly competitive environment in which financial institutions operate worldwide has had dramatic effects on the banking business, the most notable, or at least the most highly publicized, of which has been a significant reduction in interest spreads on international loans. Since 1976, the margin over the London interbank offered rate (LIBOR) charged by commercial banks on international loans declined from roughly 1.5 percent to only .68 percent in 1982.[7] At the same time, maturities on loans rose from 5 to 6 years to almost 10 years. While there has been a noticeable reduction in average maturities recently as banks have become more acutely aware of interest-rate risk and the perils of a negatively sloped yield curve, margins have widened only slightly. Competition has indeed made international lending a borrowers market.

Combined with competition, the oversupply of dollars in world financial markets, caused by large U.S. current and capital account deficits from 1976 to 1979, also played a role in depressing margins. This situation has begun to change recently: the current account has now moved into balance, and the high interest rates recently available in the United States have attracted sufficient investment to create a capital account surplus in 1980 and 1981. Assuming that the demand for dollars will continue to exceed the liquidity created by an anticipated deterioration in the current account, lending terms should begin to improve.

But that improvement lies in the future and, at current margins, the continuing profitability of some international lending operations has become a source of real concern. Returns sometimes are not sufficient to support the risk and expense of individual loans themselves, to say nothing of supporting further loan expansion. Consequently, banks have become more conservative lenders.

Reduced loan earnings have become even more of a problem as international lending adds to the pressures of domestic inflation on banks' equity-to-assets ratios. From 1976 to mid 1982, the international

---

[7] Organization for Economic Cooperation and Development, *Financial Market Trends* (various issues), Paris.

assets of major American banks grew at roughly an 18 percent average annual rate. When combined with an average of about 12 percent growth rate in domestic assets, the result has been a gradual decline in capital ratios at major banks from around 4 percent in 1976 to about 3.7 percent today.[8]

While those ratios may compare well with the capital ratios of many major foreign institutions, there is no cause for celebration. A study by a London-based analysis firm showed that of the world's 98 largest banks, only 38 (and only four of the top 10 U.S. banks) were showing a real return on capital against inflation.[9] Declining capital ratios increasingly are worrying bank managers, stockholders, investors, and regulators alike. While bankers often disagree with regulators on precisely what constitutes capital adequacy, there is no disagreement that capital generation, to support growth and insure continuing access to world funding markets, will be one of the key challenges facing banks in the 1980s. Capital has, in fact, become a precious resource, one to be allocated carefully to the most effective uses. For many banks, accustomed to trying to be all things to all customers in all markets, hard strategic choices lie ahead about where and how they can best compete.

WHERE TO COMPETE: U.S. OPPORTUNITIES

Those allocation decisions are becoming even more important in light of an ongoing shift in the focus of international operations. For most American bankers, the term *international banking* traditionally has connoted offshore operations almost exclusively. During the 1950s and 60s, U.S. industry rose to dominate the international horizon, and where U.S. industry expanded, U.S. banks followed. Both American firms and their banks were willing and able to invest strongly in overseas economies. Foreign institutions, however, were less inclined to invest in America. Not only had past conflicts disrupted economies abroad, but even after economic worldwide strength and stability had been restored, U.S. policy, a higher relative wage base, and larger investment costs combined to discourage foreign direct investment in the United States on a wide scale.

During the 1970s, however, that picture began to change. The United States found itself facing new inflationary pressures created by balance-of-payments deficits and aggravated by the continuing flow of investment capital away from its own shores, a major factor in the

---

[8] Calculated using the annual reports of the nine largest U.S. single-bank holding companies.

[9] IBCA Banking Analysis, Ltd., *Comparative Banking Profitability* (London; 1981), p. 21–22.

notable decline in American productivity. While these events stimulated policy moves to encourage foreign direct investment in America, it was only the breakdown of the Bretton Woods agreements in 1971— and subsequent depreciations of the dollar—combined with the oil crisis of 1973 that began to make investment in resource-rich America truly attractive and affordable to overseas corporations.

Between 1974 and 1981, the foreign direct investment position in the United States doubled from $31 billion to roughly $80 billion, a trend that can be expected to accelerate even more.[10] With recent Federal Reserve Board moves to tighten money supply growth and the recognition in Washington of the need to get hold of the federal budget, the dollar has strengthened dramatically, to the point where today it dominates international markets. More and more foreign companies are looking to invest in U.S. markets—and with them are coming their banks.

FOREIGN BANKS IN THE UNITED STATES

A report issued by Controller of the Currency in August of 1979 provides an interesting perspective on the growth of foreign banks in the United States. The report noted that, while the number of overseas branches of U.S. banks tripled from 240 to 730 between 1966 and 1974, the number of foreign bank branches in the United States *alone* tripled in a much shorter period, rising from 104 in November of 1972 to 330 near the end of 1979. Since that time, more branches have been added, and the figure now stands at above 400.[11] At the same time, foreign banks boosted their average annual lending growth rate in the United States from 17 percent a year in 1976 to 32 percent a year in 1979 before slowing to 12 percent in 1982. Recent estimates indicate that foreign banks now hold around 15 percent of the U.S. commercial and industrial loan market and account for 14 percent of U.S. bank assets.[12]

The meaning of this development is clear. The United States no longer serves simply as home base for major banks' international operations: it is fast becoming the focus of all international action, presenting new opportunities in capital and joint venture financing, credit and economic analysis, foreign exchange, and trade finance for American banks. And this trend is progressing even faster as American bankers, forced to evaluate where and how they can best afford to compete, look increasingly to domestic opportunities for international growth.

---

[10] Continental Bank, Economic Research and U.S. Department of Commerce statistics.

[11] Author's estimate, based on the American Banker's annual survey of International Banking.

[12] Continental Bank, Economic Research.

REGULATORY CHANGE IN THE UNITED STATES: OPTIONS MULTIPLY

Opportunities are being opened in large measure by the remarkable pace of regulatory change in the United States. For decades, American banks had the curious experience of being international organizations before being truly national. Located in the world's largest financial market, they found much of it closed to them by federal and state legislation and, as noted earlier, were driven to look overseas for growth opportunities.

Now, the regulatory web which has so long constricted banking activities in the United States is beginning to become unraveled. Major strides toward deregulating the banking industry have been made in the past three years, creating important new options for international banks.

THE INTERNATIONAL BANKING ACT

In 1978 the passage of the International Banking Act aimed at putting foreign and domestic banks operating in the United States on a more equal competitive footing. While the Act can be criticized for perpetuating the view of banking as an exclusive sector of the economy subject to peculiar regulations, on the whole, the Act was a strong step forward in recognizing evolving competitive realities in the United States. One of its most important aspects was the Federal Reserve Board revision of Regulation K, which significantly expanded the powers of Edge Act corporations. Among other things, the revised regulations broadened the financial operations of Edges, eased restrictions on the employment of funds, liberalized leverage limits, and, by allowing interstate branching by Edge corporations, indirectly increased their lending limits. The object of the revision was to allow U.S. banks to compete effectively and efficiently with similar foreign-owned institutions in the United States and abroad, and that objective has, to a large extent, been fulfilled. Since its implementation, Edge operations across the country have been expanded substantially.

THE OMNIBUS BANKING BILL

If the International Banking Act represented an initial attempt by U.S. regulators to recognize certain aspects of the evolving banking environment, evolution has since given way to almost revolutionary change. As inflation and interest rates have risen in recent years, consumers and corporate customers alike found that traditional bank-related methods of saving, investment, and financing have provided insufficient returns. A major cause of this development was restrictive government regulations that arbitrarily defined banks' markets for them, keeping them out of new markets despite unmet and growing demand for innovative financial services. It is no surprise, therefore, that other financial institutions, unrestrained by the regulations that have shackled banks—moved in to fill the void.

Money market funds, insurance companies, large retailers, security brokers and dealers not only stepped up their efforts in their own industries but also entered traditional banking markets. Corporations, once banks' best customers, have in many ways become their prime competitors, as shown by the dramatic growth of the commercial paper market. While banks were doing their best to innovate by moving into fields like corporate and commercial finance, a cumbersome regulatory apparatus continued to restrict the range of their activities in what was becoming an integrated, nationwide financial services marketplace.

Over time these restrictions gave rise to serious market distortions, which today are most evident in the mortgage market but cut across the entire American economy as well. Increasingly, the shock of inflation has made it clear that a regulatory system built up haphazardly to meet needs perceived 50 years ago no longer serves our economy well. The result has been encouraging moves to deregulate banking, and after years of effort, two particularly important steps were taken last year.

The Depository Institutions Deregulatory and Monetary Control Act of 1980 (the Omnibus Banking Bill), signed into law on March 31, reflected the efforts of many banks to achieve more equitable roles and let free market forces determine market share among financial institutions. The Act's most widely publicized provisions allow for the phase-out of interest-rate deposit ceilings, the nationwide establishment of NOW accounts, the setting of reserve requirements on transaction accounts for all deposit-taking institutions, and the removal of reserve requirements on personal savings accounts. Other provisions, however, while less publicized, may be more important in the long run, for the Act grants to the Depository Institutions Deregulatory Committee the powers to eliminate interest restrictions on deposits and to create new account types. In short, it promises to allow the creation of new financial instruments and new funding techniques that ultimately could make banks more competitive both at home and abroad.

No less important, a White House study made public on December 31, 1980, also recommended fundamental changes in the restrictive McFadden Act of 1934 and the Douglas Amendment to the Bank Holding Company Act of 1956, both of which have served artificially to limit bank activities to a single state. As these and other archaic barriers to competition fall, banks will at last be able to meet competitive realities head on and grasp the long-foreclosed opportunities that structural change will bring.

INTERNATIONAL IMPACT

These are significant measures in themselves and will open a new world of opportunities—and decisions—for U.S.-chartered banks; the need for banks to choose among expanded options is sure to have an impact on the allocation of resources to international operations. But these measures have been accompanied recently by other proposals whose impacts could be far more direct. Carrying further the process set in motion by the International Banking Act and the Omnibus Banking Act, in June of 1981 the Federal Reserve Board approved a plan to allow banks to establish International Banking Facilities (IBFs) in this country. Through these facilities, which can be tied in with existing Edge Act offices and branches as well as head offices, banks are able to accept deposits from and make loans to non-U.S. entities free from reserve requirements, interest-rate ceilings, and taxes, much as shell branches do today. The IBF bill has some significant drawbacks: further regulatory change at both the state and federal levels will be necessary if the bill is to live up to its full potential. The IBF bill, however, does suggest the direction and speed with which regulatory change affecting international operations is proceeding in the United States.

Finally, the heightened involvement of brokerage firms and insurance companies in traditional bank deposit-taking and lending activities is blurring the long-standing distinction between commercial and investment banking in the United States, established by the Glass-Stegall Act. While it is not likely that the Act will be revised suddenly or radically, the process of change is well underway, and it is possible that within the next decade U.S. banks will enjoy domestic funding and underwriting opportunities similar to those now provided by merchant banks overseas.

The United States, of course, is not the only country in which banking horizons are opening. In Spain, Australia, Great Britain, France, and Germany, financial systems are under intense review. Many developing countries, too, are recognizing the benefits internationalizing their systems of banking and finance could bring—and inviting American banks to participate in the process. These developments, along with changes in the United States, all point to a strong future international role for American banks.

THE CHANGING SHAPE OF BANKING: THE FINANCIAL SUPERMARKET

If regulatory change in America and elsewhere is helping U.S. bankers answer the question of *where* they will compete, it is influencing *how* they will compete as well. Increasingly, bankers no longer think of their business purely as banking. There continue, of course, to be opportunities for growth in traditional banking areas like trade finance and medium-term lending. But profit requirements increasingly demand an ability to market and deliver a wider, more complex range of services worldwide. To compete effectively and profitably both at home and abroad, U.S. banks are gradually transforming themselves into global financial supermarkets, able to bring to relationships an array of credit and noncredit services that go far beyond attractively priced funds. Banks are developing new and innovative fee services, both to support their core lending business and to enhance income without adding assets to their balance sheets. Increasingly, the areas of strongest growth in international banking are financial services, including international bond operations, foreign exchange trading and advisory services, and financial consulting, international investment management, leasing, and global cash management. In the future traditional commercial bank deposit and lending services may be only two out of many important financial activities.

CHANGING APPROACHES

This transformation, however, is not taking place haphazardly. At the same time that they are expanding their international services, banks are refining the organizational frameworks from which those sevices are offered.

Perhaps the most notable organizational change at major American banks has been the consolidation of responsibility for interest-rate sensitivity, liquidity, capital, and risk management into a corporate treasury function. The scope of major banks' international operations and the magnitude of their involvement in money markets worldwide have placed a high priority on coordinating interest rate, liquidity, and other risks at every level of every organization.

With this integration of responsibility, changes in the ways in which banks approach their overseas markets already have begun to appear. Previously, major banks took something of a scatter-gun approach to expansion. Now networks are being consolidated as technology lessens dependence on physical facilities and as the awareness grows that it is not the number of locations an institution maintains but the profitability of those locations that matters.

Many banks have, for example, begun to unwind investments in affiliates and consortia. The motivations differ from institution to institution: they range from disinterest in supporting a competitor bank to lack of operational control to the desire to avoid contingent liabilities. All, however, stem from the fundamental recognition that international operations today must be closely coordinated with one another and with domestic operations as well.

Another, similar trend is the redeployment of resources to those areas that carry the greatest profit potential. In some European and developing country markets particularly, competitive loan pricing has been too intense to allow what most banks would consider a reasonable return. As a result, branches are being scaled down to representative offices. A few banks are leaving areas entirely, and manpower, technological, and capital resources are being shifted into more fertile territories, notably the Far East, Latin America, and Canada.

Hand-in-hand with this redeployment of resources goes a growing deemphasis of market share. Market share remains, of course, an important aspect of long-term profitability, but with the slowdown in global economic growth, it is becoming increasingly difficult to turn share increases into earnings increases. Given capital constraints, bankers are increasingly reluctant to write loans at any cost simply to gain— or retain—a customer. Today, the dominant attitude is that deals must be structured to fit a bank's own books not those of its competitors.

In place of an across-the-board emphasis on market share, banks are turning more and more to the strategy of delivering specialized services to specific markets, downplaying "generic" services. This is particularly noticeable in lending. There has been a marked decline in the willingness of many banks to participate in syndicated credits, except as lead manager where returns are highest. Instead, banks are turning to specialized forms of lending where they are able to bring more to a relationship than just attractively priced funds. For example, project lending demands a high degree of technical as well as financial expertise and sophistication, and banks that can combine those skills can command a premium in the marketplace. Similarly, local currency financing—another growth area as customers increasingly seek to minimize translation risk—demands highly developed skills and in-depth market knowledge. Banks with the required expertise and experience will be able to generate increased business. Other forms of lending, like trade finance, are attractive not only on their own merits but because they lend themselves easily to pass-through arrangements, in which banks originate and package credits which are then passed on through secondary markets to ultimate asset holders, generating fee income without adding assets to the balance sheet.

There also has been a noticeable shift in the markets to which banks are trying to appeal. Traditionally, major banks have concentrated on major American or foreign-based multinational companies. Increasingly, however, such customers are able to demand lower-priced loans than their banks are able to offer prudently. Banks, therefore, have begun to turn elsewhere. The primary target market, abroad as in the United States, has become the medium-sized corporation, where wider spreads typically are available.

Some banks also have begun to emphasize the overseas retail market, but their performance to date has been somewhat disappointing. While

American banks have a clear technological edge over foreign banks that, in theory, should ease entry into retail banking, expanding in the consumer market often has proven more difficult than originally expected. With the exception of Great Britain, most overseas consumers have established banking relationships; bankers are discovering that abroad, as in the United States, it is extremely difficult to get customers to transfer their accounts at all much less to a foreign bank.

PETRODOLLAR RECYCLING: A CHANGING ISSUE

The trends and the opportunities described above—the increasing integration of international with domestic operations and the increasing importance of the United States in international finance—all stem essentially from deregulation of the financial marketplace in America and overseas. There is, however, one area—petrodollar recycling—in which it is greater, not less, participation by government officials that is helping banks make the most of new opportunities.

As noted above, the dramatic growth in banking's scope and volume over the past two decades created an increasing dependence on the private banking system rather than official facilities to handle global capital flows. American banks demonstrated an extraordinary resilience in adapting to the demands of this task. Operating through the Euromarkets, the private banking system has been able to handle the recycling of petrodollars from oil importers quickly and efficiently, even as the OPEC surplus rose to a staggering $115 billion in 1980.

In the wake of those successful efforts, a number of concerns have received an extensive publicity. As outlined earlier, many banks have reached internally and externally imposed country lending limits. The Euromarkets themselves have come under intense regulatory scrutiny and may soon be subject to supervisory control. And for some of the largest borrowers among developing countries, the cost of new borrowing, combined with the mounting cost of servicing existing debt, continues to raise serious questions for banks and government regulators alike.

It should be noted, however, that although recycling remains a serious issue, the importance of those concerns has started to diminish recently. In 1983 the OPEC surplus is expected to disappear and the current account will likely fall into a deficit.[13] At the same time that the dollar amounts are decreasing, official involvement in recycling is increasing. Not only have OPEC nations shown a greater willingness to participate directly in the recycling process than was previously the case, the International Monetary Fund (IMF) has developed a program for providing medium-term loans to help finance oil-induced

---

[13] Continental Bank, Economic Research.

balance-of-payments problems. The World Bank also is considering extending its policy of long-term development finance to include interim loans that would assist in the recycling of international liquidity.

While the amounts involved so far are relatively small, these are certainly positive steps, suggesting that the commercial bank share of petrodollar recycling will grow progressively smaller in the years ahead. In light of the trends in deregulation and changing competition outlined above, as that obstacle to the profitable growth of American banks diminishes, the development of U.S. banks as international financial supermarkets should strengthen apace.

51
International Banking: The Achievement and the Challenge

DAVID ROCKEFELLER
Chairman (Retired)
The Chase Manhattan Bank, N.A.

The explosion of international bank lending over the past 25 years is one of the truly remarkable achievements of the 20th century. In this period, the world's banking systems quietly engineered a global financial structure that has contributed enormously to the economic aspirations of people everywhere.

The key to human progress has always rested upon an innovative response to problems that otherwise might seem insoluble. In this case, the innovation of historic importance was the financial community's realization that barriers to the flow of international capital mobility had outlived their usefulness and, in fact, retarded the growth of all nations, rich and poor alike.

In the 1950s and 1960s this understanding mainly took the form of reducing barriers to capital movement between industrialized nations. The innovation of the past decade has been the development of free capital flows between the developed and developing world, barriers that previously had virtually *guaranteed* that scarce capital would not be employed where it was most productive.

The growth of international bank lending over the past decade is dramatic proof of the magnitude of this international financial revolution. At the end of 1973, international bank loans amounted to $320 billion. By year-end 1981, the total had grown to about $1.5 trillion. This is the *achievement* for which all of us can be duly proud as we create the opportunity for a more efficient and just distribution of new investment around a world sorely in need of scarce capital.

However, before we become too self congratulatory, we must ask ourselves how well the world economy has used this new opportunity and to what extent the international banking structure will be *chal-*

lenged by future world developments. To blindly assume that the past growth of international bank lending will continue along a straight line into the future world would be short-sighted indeed. A current global economic slowdown, combined with problems of continued inflation and rising tides of protectionist sentiment, will surely demand extreme caution and the best that is within us.

GLOBAL CONVALESCENCE

The key feature of the current global economic outlook is the disappointingly slow rate of growth forecast for the near future.

Europe is in recession, and recovery will likely be slow.

In Japan, the expected pickup in domestic demand has been delayed.

The U.S. economy continues on its stop-go path, confounding the forecasters and producing little in the way of real growth.

Growth prospects for the developing countries also are disappointing.

I believe there are three main reasons why the pace of recovery from the current global economic slowdown is likely to be relatively slow.

First is the magnitude of the shock inflicted by the second round of OPEC price increases. Although less in percentage terms than the 1973–74 increases, it was roughly comparable in terms of absolute magnitude. The volume of resources transferred from oil importers to oil exporters is very nearly equal.

Second, in most industrialized countries, policymakers are more intent to control the growth of monetary aggregates and limit the inflationary consequences of higher oil prices. Although a worthwhile goal, this delays economic recovery in the short term. For example, the commitment of our own Federal Reserve to stricter monetary control has produced unprecedented high interest rates that inevitably constrain the growth of the U.S. economy and have strong repercussions abroad. They have led to higher domestic interest rates and hence slower growth in the other industrialized countries and added to the international payments deficits of those countries who have been heavy borrowers in international capital markets.

The *third* drag on global economic recovery is the sharply reduced capability of many developing nations to sustain growth targets in the face of worsened balance-of-payments positions. The option of financing deficits is less viable now for many LDCs. The difficult alternative for these developing nations is to restrict imports even further.

The fortunes of these LDCs are tied closely to the prospects of our own nation—a fact that often gets lost in the dust of ideological dispute.

THE THIRD WORLD: FIRST IN TRADE

The developing nations now provide a larger export market for the United States than all the developed nations put together, excluding only Canada. Between 1973 and 1979, U.S. exports to developing countries grew at an average annual rate of 20 percent, compared with a rate of 15 percent to industrialized countries.

On the import side, the developing countries contribute significantly not only to supplies of oil and strategic raw materials but also to lower-priced consumer goods which help combat inflation in this country.

All of this underscores to me the tremendous importance of the developing nations to the self-interest of the United States. This importance, I regret, has not been reflected in our aid to these nations. For example, in 1978 U.S. official aid to LDCs amounted to less than what Americans spent on flowers and plants; $4.8 billion as opposed to $5 billion. And in the same year, we spent $18 billion on tobacco and $31 billion on alcoholic beverages!

However one evaluates or judges such facts, the relationship of the United States to the developing nations is not an issue which can be swept under the rug as it has been so often in the past. We must deal with it soon, and we must deal with it effectively.

What is needed, to my mind, is not the increasing of one form of aid or another but rather a much sharper focus on the measurement of requirements and successes. What works? What doesn't work? What is or is not in our own broadly defined self-interest? What can we afford to do in such a manner that both we and the recipients—our fellow nations—find acceptable?

The economics of foreign assistance has been studied over and over again—indeed, I have personally been a member of two presidential commissions on the subject. It is a difficult subject about which there have been some good approaches, though no panaceas, and politics make it virtually impossible to gain any easy victories. National pride, varying governmental structures, and extreme ideological differences springing from geopolitical conflicts all tend to create flies in almost any ointment.

Much of the rhetoric regarding what rather simplistically has been called the "Third World" or "North-South" dialogue, has focused on demands for the redistribution of the world's wealth. However, the real issue, it seems to me, is not the *redistribution* of wealth but rather the *generation* of wealth. That—to be successful—must be a cooperative undertaking. More rhetorical confrontations can only result in more hot air—one commodity in more than ample supply.

To say this is not to ignore the needs of people in Third World countries—or, indeed, in parts of our own nation—who suffer from a very low standard of living and whose prospects for improving their lot are abysmal without concerted assistance from the more fortunate. Some 800 million people worldwide now live in absolute poverty. In addition, some 850 million people have no access to education, and some 460 million people are now malnourished. Only one fourth of the people in developing nations have access to safe water. This cannot simply be an economic or political concern. It must be a human and moral concern.

FAITH IN TRADE

A second challenge for the international banking structure lies in the threat of rising protectionism brought about by industrialized nation's attempts to protect dwindling markets in this recessionary environment.

Creating alternatives to protectionism will require, above all, an abiding faith in the mutual benefits of trade.

We might begin by recognizing that Americans are not about to be driven in a Japanese car, fueled by OPEC oil, straight into a poorhouse built of German steel. At the same time, we must acknowledge that long gone are those idyllic days after World War II when the United States produced fully half of all the exports in the world. The reality, of course, is somewhere in between.

The full economic picture, however, has to encompass more than the exchange of goods across national boundaries. There is also an enormous and growing flow of services associated with such enterprises as insurance, construction and maintenance, shipping, and banking. And in these areas, the United States has done exceedingly well.

In fact, our export of services has grown to become a major component of our trade effort, and even though it is not counted in the balance of trade, it definitely figures in the balance of payments.

Not long ago it was necessary to defend American corporations against the charge that their overseas investments meant a loss of dollars and jobs for this country. The answer, of course, was that these investments would not only benefit recipient nations, but the return flow of profits would benefit America and American workers by sustaining and creating jobs in trade-related industries. Indeed, from this international seed, we can reap a bountiful repatriated harvest.

Recent figures show that U.S. manufacturing firms are continuing to increase their investments abroad so the way is still being paved for welcome dividends in the future. Meanwhile, foreign businesses have been stepping up their investments in this country. They are now led by the Netherlands followed by Great Britain, Canada, West Germany, and Japan.

This mounting flow of two-way investments, like the flow of two-way trade, is healthy—and the mutual interdependence it fosters should be conducive to mutual gain.

For much of the rest of this year, unfortunately, the world economy is expected to be sluggish. Many of our major trading partners are experiencing a pronounced slowdown, while the less developed countries that are largely dependent on imported oil are, for the most part, being severely battered by higher prices.

In this situation it is unlikely that U.S. exports will show any significant growth. At the same time, however, I don't think I'm being unduly optimistic when I say that we should at least be able to maintain our present strength.

In the United States, the recession and mounting unemployment in basic industries has added to the political pressure for trade restrictions. Yet even short-term protectionist measures can cause serious economic dislocations and often set a dangerous precedent. Controls are often imposed as a temporary measure—but like most bad habits become terribly difficult to kick.

So we should proceed with caution on this issue because protectionism all too often invites retaliation and becomes a form of mutual self-destruction. Over the longer term, trade and global capital investment stimulate competition, offer consumers more choice, and provide a powerful incentive for producers to increase their productivity.

There are appropriate ways to cushion against the rudest shocks of a changing marketplace without standing in the road and commanding change to halt. That's only a good way to get run over.

There will be difficult adjustments for some of our industries. We may have to anticipate an altered mix of economic activity that best suits our future needs. But these are things that the marketplace should largely decide.

I am absolutely convinced that any thrust toward protectionism will cost this nation more jobs, income, and production than it could ever hope to save.

Protectionist sentiment cannot be cast off by simple incantation. We must attack it at its roots—and it is rooted in the chronic ailments of the global economy. Obviously, no nation can maintain a vigorous export policy while its trading partners suffer from hyperinflation and an extreme debt burden.

A SURPLUS OF DEBT

Many of our best export markets are today suffering from massive debt accumulated in the scramble to pay for petroleum imports.

The middle- and upper-income LDCs borrowed extensively from commercial banks after the initial round of OPEC price hikes in 1973 and 1974.

These early loans have long been the subject of sufficient—perhaps even undue—attention. While today it is generally recognized that this money was, for the most part, prudently lent and productively utilized, doubts are again being raised about the present creditworthiness of LDCs, their renewed need to borrow, and the capacity of the financial community to serve them.

The common implication seems to be that today's deficits might prove too large to be financed. In fact, that concern is illogical. A deficit that cannot be funded cannot come into being. Rather, the appropriate questions to ask are:

> What are the constraints on LDC economic growth imposed by higher energy costs and tighter borrowing limits?

> Will LDCs adopt the prudent policies that recognize these limits, or will they rather postpone the necessary adjustments until forced to do so by the disruption of capital flows?

> Will disruptions in servicing of past loans be sufficiently widespread and sychronized to create serious difficulties for the smooth functioning of the international financial system?

> What will be the global political and economic cost of slower growth and thwarted national and individual expectations in the LDCs?

In order to gain some perspective as to why the high cost of petroleum imports will have such a significant effect in limiting LDC growth, a look to the past is in order.

The deep recession following the first major round of oil price hikes in 1973 was surmounted by most nonoil LDCs without drastic effects on their level of economic activity and long-run development plans. Indeed, these economies suffered far less than their industrialized counterparts.

This phenomenon was due to the fact that middle-income LDCs were able to borrow so extensively from commercial banks in the Euromarkets. The relatively unregulated nature of these markets enabled them to adapt quickly and effectively to this sudden surge of demand. These prompt and ample loans enabled the middle-income LDCs to sustain sharp increases in their current account deficits without having to cut import demand sharply by reducing economic growth.

The outlook facing these same nations in the days ahead, however, is markedly different. The present level and composition of the debt of nonoil-producing LDCs inhibits their ability to borrow more and hence causes them to be more severely affected by the cost of oil imports.

Some middle-income LDCs are showing more signs of excessive borrowing than they did in 1974. Fortunately, the number is still small, but already by 1978, the nonoil LDC debt service had exceeded its earlier peak reached in 1971. This has taken place despite an increase in export growth and a significant increase in the LDC share of world trade.

A few middle-income LDCs have tried to minimize the probability of a credit crunch by rolling over their debt before it matures. This restructuring has enabled them to increase average maturities and reduce interest-rate margins. Overall, however, average LDC debt maturities have declined substantially since 1973. On the other hand, the share of private debt—which is of shorter maturity than official debt—has increased substantially in the past five years.

Although these facts give rise to concern, there are at least a few positive trends mitigating the negative factors.

Reserve positions for the most part are strong.

Commercial loan maturities are spread out quite evenly.

World inflation has reduced amortization costs in real terms, particularly for countries exporting manufactured goods.

The quality of economic management in the middle- and upper-income LDCs has been improving.

The softening of world oil prices as a result of a worldwide oil glut at least temporarily has eased the pressure on many oil-importing LDCs.

Based on these circumstances, there is good reason to believe that most of the more advanced developing economies—those nations that have been the major borrowers from the private banking system—will take reasonably prompt steps to bring their payments deficits under a fair degree of control. There is already evidence that adjustment measures are being adopted, although more remains to be done.

In short, policymakers in most developing countries are well aware that foreign borrowing constraints are now much tighter than they have been in the past. But translating this recognition into policy action—and the reduced growth targets necessarily entailed in such actions—requires great political skill and courage.

While there are no easy solutions, the economic problems of adjustment can be minimized or at least reduced in a number of different ways.

One important step that can be taken is to strengthen the credit facilities of official agencies such as the World Bank, the various regional development banks, and the IMF. There is a particular need for larger subsidized credit facilities for the lower-income LDCs, many of whom do not have the ability to borrow from private markets or the economic strength to take the tough adjustment measures normally recommended by the IMF. The governments of the industrialized nations and those OPEC members with major payment surpluses could work cooperatively to meet this need. I hope they will do so.

For the middle- and upper-income developing nations there is a need for official credit at maturities longer than conventional IMF lending and not tied to particular investment projects—credits of the sort provided by the Supplementary Financing and Extended Fund Facilities of the IMF. As of the moment, the IMF"s holdings of usable currencies would appear to be adequate. Nonetheless, if borrowing from the IMF reaches the proportion I believe possible, an increase in the funding of the Supplementary Financing Facility will become necessary.

I have stressed the lending role of the IMF because I believe it extremely important that official credit be provided on a conditional basis wherever possible. If the leverage of the international agencies with the LDCs in securing agreement over policy adjustment is to be restored, two requirements must be met. There must be greater coordination in lending between the private banks and the international agencies, and the international institutions must be better funded.

Continued and even greater free trade also will alleviate the problems of many of the middle- and upper-income LDCs. On the other hand, a swing toward protectionism by the industrialized countries would undermine the healthy effects of the flow of petrodollars to those LDCs with a diversified export base.

POLITICAL QUARRELS, ECONOMIC NEEDS

A final challenge, and perhaps our most difficult, is the effect of global political considerations upon the free flow of capital. In today's politically charged environment, one may wonder how the channels of trade have managed to remain as open as indeed they have.

This question is hardly academic for a major international bank which may operate in roughly a hundred different nations—of vastly differing cultures and diverse and changing political systems; nations which may encompass traditional as well as contemporary enmities.

By doing business throughout the world, we have learned that ideologies and political systems change rapidly but economic needs are subject to more gradual and steady change. The necessary ingredients for economic development, such as capital and management talent, are the same under any type of economic or political system. There is no communist or capitalist way to build a dam or drill for oil. Since banks concentrate on these economic needs, we are prone to do business with nations encompassing a varied mosaic of cultures and ideologies. To some, this may appear to be an immoral compromise of principles. To others, it implies a willingness to compromise which can lead to a more peaceful and understanding world. Herein lies the debate, and international bankers must be able to clearly define their position.

This doesn't mean that banks can or should ignore the political and moral ramification of their lending decisions. For example, Chase Manhattan has an ethical standards policy on all lending, both domestic and international, which states: "Strict attention should be given to the legal, moral, and social implications of all loan and investment decisions on a global basis. We should seek to avoid business with identifiably harmful results and assure that we always carefully evaluate the long-term, as well as the short-term, meaning of our decisions." As a result of this policy, Chase makes no loans to South Africa which tend to support the apartheid policies of the South African government.

GOVERNMENT INTERVENTION

Another important development for corporations and financial institutions is the steadily increasing role of governments in business affairs. One could debate whether this development is fostering a better life for the masses of the people, but one cannot question the reality of the trend.

The widening role of governments around the world has more to do with using their power as a convenient tool for national determination than with the competing values of capitalist and socialist economic systems. The driving force for economic and social change in many of the world's nations today is government, not private industries or individuals. In a growing number of nations, one must often accept the fact that the government probably owns the principal commercial bank or the major manufacturing enterprise, or, at least, has a large share of their ownership.

A characteristic by-product of increased government intervention is the tendency toward subordination of economics, or economic rationality, to the achievement of political and social goals.

In today's highly interdependent world, economic sanctions to forward political ends have assumed an even greater and more far-reaching significance. These various policies, which David Hume rather derisively, yet aptly, called "jealousy of trade" are evident virtually everywhere—in both the East and the West and in developed as well as developing nations.

While it is not unusual for host nations to attempt to exert political pressure on the foreign business community, I have no doubt that, in the long term, the preeminent consideration of most nations in choosing a bank for business will be to select the one offering the best products, services, and terms. If a government were to disregard totally these basic business criteria, I would question whether it would be looked upon as a sound credit risk or a desirable long-term customer for any type of business.

Another thorny difficulty for foreign companies is doing business on a day-to-day basis with two or more nations which are politically hostile to each other. I recall one day several years ago when Chase was thrust into the middle of the Mideast conflict. One editorial broadcast that day alleged that Chase had bowed to the Arab boycott by refusing to open an office in Israel. On the same day a major newspaper in the same American city reported that Chase was facing boycott proceedings by the Arab League as a result of the business it was doing with Israel. In other words, no matter which way the situation was viewed, we couldn't win!

Our response, at the time—one which I believe remains immutable today—was to note that our decisions to serve virtually all the nations of the Middle East, and the world for that matter, are based on sound economic reasons and are not motivated by considerations that must be viewed as primarily political.

The activities of any foreign business must be predicated upon sound economic reasoning tempered by a strong ethical underpinning that provides an overall framework for action. Subject to these essential ethical guidelines, both at home and abroad, the best way for a business to do well is to do good by making solid contributions to customer needs.

International banking has grown rapidly over the past quarter century. The foundation remains firm. The structure stands tall. However, if the system is to continue to serve its primary function of providing capital where it is needed most, bankers must confront these challenges with innovation and steady persistence. The world's governments must also be encouraged to recognize the benefits of free trade and the value of free capital movement. Working together, we can lift the global economy out of its present doldrums into a future that is worthy of our highest aspirations.

Index

A

Abu Dhabi, foreign exchange market, 356
Acceptance house, 67, 68
Acceptances; *see* Bankers' acceptances
Accepting Houses Committee, 299
Account party, 239, 240
Accounting and internal control; *see also* Audits and examinations
  correspondent accounts
    cable remittance, 660
    dual currency subsidiary ledgers, 660
    foreign draft, 660
    mail remittance, 660
  definition, 659
  Foreign Corrupt Practices Act, 666–67
  foreign currency translation, 665–66
    definition of forward currency transactions, 665
    FASB Statement No. 52, 665
    forward exchange contracts, 665–66
  foreign environmental factors, 656, 657, 659
  foreign exchange trading, 663–65
  foreign facility system, 658
  income taxes
    accrual basis recording, 666
    cash basis recording, 666
    deduction/credit treatment, 666
  lending, 660–63
    bankers' acceptances, 661
    credit examination, 662
    credit review, 662
    formal policy, 661–62
    letters of credit, 661, 663
    other considerations, 662
  overseas accounting unit, 657
  reference lists for internal control evaluation, 659, 667–73
Administrator of the International Development Cooperation Agency, 441

Advising Bank, 242, 244, 245
Affiliate, definition, 581; *see also* Foreign affiliates and subsidiaries
Afghanistan
  foreign banking restrictions, 739, 744
  political instability, 91–92
African currencies, 339
African Development Bank (AfDB), 473
  activities, 526, 528
  history, 525–26
  members' voting power, 527
  membership, 526
  record of accomplishments, 528
  sources of funds, 526
  subscriptions to capital stock, 527
African Development Fund (AfDF)
  activities, 529–30
  history, 529
  members' voting power, 530
  membership, 529
  record of accomplishments, 530
  sources of funds, 529
  subscriptions to capital, 530
Agency
  defined, 788
  foreign banks in U.S., 792–93
Agreement corporation, 36, 42, 607–11
  regulation by Federal Reserve, 751, 755
Algeria
  restrictions on foreign bank entry, 740, 744
  U.S. bank claims, 744
All-African Peoples' Conference, 525
Amandry, Monique, 468 n
American Institute of Certified Public Accountants, statement on auditing standards, 658–59
Analysis of Current Operations of Foreign-Owned U.S. Banks, 790
Andean Group, 511

Anderson, Lester D., Jr., 183
Annual Report on Exchange Arrangements and
    Exchange Restrictions (IMF report), 350,
    351, 352–53
Antirecession cartels, 566
Arbitrage, 230
    defined, 235
    foreign exchange market, 228–29
Argentina
    restrictions on foreign bank entry, 744
    U.S. bank claims, 139
Argentine peso, 359, 361
Arnold, Jasper H., 257 n
Ashton, H. G., 299
Asian currencies, 357–59
Asian dollar, 17, 647
Asian Development Bank (ADB), 473
    activities, 524
    history, 522–23
    membership, 523
    record of accomplishments, 525
    sources of funds, 524
    subscribed capital resources of members, 523
    voting power of members, 523
Asset method of interest expense allocation,
    691–92
Audits and examinations, 710
    external
        outside auditors, 718–19
        regulatory examinations, 719
    internal
        compared to internal controls, 711
        credit review, 714–15
        definition, 711
        external auditors, 715
        independence, 711–12
        monitoring controls, 712
        organization and staffing, 713
        reporting, 712–13
        supervisory examinations by government,
            715–16
    international banking activities, 716
        automation, 718
        host country culture considerations, 717
        investment banking, 717
        regulation and accounting practices, 716–
            17
        scope of business, 716
    organization of overseas auditing, 718
Austin, Paul, 644
Australia
    project financing, 312
    restrictions on foreign bank entry, 742, 744
Australian dollar, 357, 358
Austria, restrictions on foreign bank entry, 744

Austrian schilling, 338, 351, 355
Autostrade, 206

B

Back, Leonard A., 270
Bahamas
    banking supervision, 780
    branches of U.S. banks, 788
    entrepot market, 5
    eurocenter, 18
    limited offshore banking facilities, 657–58
    restrictions on foreign bank entry, 744
Bahrain
    banking supervision, 780
    financial center, 5
    offshore banking, 356
    restrictions on foreign bank entry, 740, 742,
        744
Baker, James C., 788 n, 790 n
Balance of payments deficit financing, 562
Balance of payments financing, 81
Balance of payments trend analysis, 112
Banco Central do Brasil, 47, 48, 49
Banco Central de Venezuela, 70
Banco do Brasil, 48
Banco de Guayaquil, Ecuador, 121
Banco de los Trabajadores, 69
Banco Industrial de Venezuela, 70
Banco Nacional de Commercio Exterior, 62
Banco Nacional Mexicano, 61
Bangladesh, restrictions on foreign bank entry,
    741, 744
Bank Administration Institute (BAI), 711
Bank of America, 138
Bank-to-bank guarantee, 408
Bank-to-bank lending, 117–28
    assessing and managing risks
        analyzing individual banks, 121
        country analysis, 120
        financial statements, 122, 123
        knowledge of country's banking system,
            120–21
        marketplace reputation, 124
        office visits, 125
    credit facilities, 125–27
        extended to subsidiaries, 126
    Eurodollar market, 118–19
    Eximbank, 408
    risks and rewards, 127–28
Bank of Canada, 50
Bank checkings, 124–25
Bank of England, 68, 368
Bank examinations, 715–16
    overseas, 718–19
Bank Export Services Act, 754, 763

Bank holding companies, 766
  Federal Reserve regulations, 756
    foreign activities of U.S. bank organiza-
      tions, 757–59
    foreign banks and foreign holding compa-
      nies, 759–61
Bank Holding Company Act, 40, 756, 759–60,
  763, 793, 797
  Douglas amendment, 811
Bank for International Settlements (BIS), 76, 79,
  130
  Federal Reserve regulation of international
    banking, 763
  multilateral bank supervision, 778
Bank of Italy, 56
Bank of Tokyo, 56
Bank-transmittal collection letter, 282
Bankers' acceptances
  acceptance credit agreement, 258, 259
    clean acceptances, 259
    draft, 259
    purpose statement, 259–60
  accounting and internal control, 661
  advantages for borrowers
    cost of funds reduction, 256, 257
    extension of legal lending limit, 257
    Federal Reserve participation, 256–57
    no compensating balance requirement, 256
  bank benefits, 261
    commission, 256, 261–63
    interest cost of discounting draft, 256
    potential goodwill, 263
    profit, 261–63
  bank organization and marketing, 263–69
    allocation, 265–66
    availability of rates, 267
    discounting and rediscounting, 264, 265
    servicing, 266
    solicitation, 266
    structures of organization, 266–67
  correspondent banking, 549–50
  definition, 252
  disadvantages to borrowers, 258–61
    documentation, 259–60
    eligibility requirements, 260
    maximum term, 261
    prepayment, 261
  elements of cost for the borrower, 256
  eligibility and ineligibility for discount, 252–
    54, 256, 260
  Federal Reserve Act of 1913, 253, 255, 257
    Regulation A, 253
  Federal Reserve regulations, 253, 753–54
  import and export transactions, 254–55
  letters of credit, 254
  lines of credit, 125

Bankers' acceptances—Cont.
    transactions for dollar exchange, 255
    transactions involving goods in storage, 255
    transactions involving goods in transit, 255
    typical transaction illustrated, 267–69
Bankers' Association (London), 368
Bankers' Association for Foreign Trade, 607
Banking havens, 19–20
Banque Francais du Commerce Exterieure, 404
Barbados, restrictions on foreign bank entry,
  744
Bardepot scheme, 224
Bareboat charters, 173, 182, 188
Barrett, Anthony G., 103 n
Bates, P., 103 n
Baum, Warren C., 472
Behrens, Jack, 656
Belgian franc, 338, 348
Belgium
  Euromarkets, 5
  restrictions on foreign bank entry, 744
Belize, restrictions on foreign bank entry, 744
Bell, Carl T., 486 n, 499 n
Bench, Robert R., 764, 770 n
Beneficiary (letter of credit), 239, 240, 242, 243,
  244, 246, 247
Benin, restrictions on foreign banks entry, 739,
  746
Berglund, Milton E., Jr., 594
Bermuda
  limited offshore facilities, 657
  restrictions on foreign banks entry, 740, 742,
    744
Berne Union, 411
Bill of exchange, 271, 272
Bill of lading, 279–80
  air waybill, 280
  barge, 280
  negotiable form, 280
  ocean, 280
  railroad, 280
  straight assignment, 280
BLADEX (Latin American Export Bank), 514
Bodmer, David E., 331
Bolivia, restrictions on foreign banks entry, 744
Bond ratings, 215–16
Botswana, restrictions on foreign banks entry,
  740, 744
Branch banking; see Foreign branch banking
Brass plate banks, 20
Brazil
  external debt-service ratio, 114
  inflation indexing, 47
  inflation rate, 177
  interest rates, 48
  international banking, 47–49

Brazil—*Cont.*
  restrictions on foreign banks entry, 744
  ten largest banks, 48
  U.S. bank claims, 138
Brazilian Central Bank, 361
Brazilian cruzeiro, 359, 360–61
Bretton Woods agreement, 74, 82, 463, 464,
  465, 505
Brinckmann, Hans, 786
British pound, interest rate subsidies on exports,
  403
Broker, definition, 362; *see also* International
  money broker
Bulgaria, restrictions on foreign banks entry,
  739, 744
Bulk carriers, definition, 202
Bull dog bonds, 214
Burma, restrictions on foreign banks entry, 740,
  744
Burundi, restrictions on foreign banks entry,
  744

                          C

Caldwell, J. Alexander, 104 n, 111 n
Cameroon, restrictions on foreign banks entry,
  740, 744
Canada
  branch banking, 557
  chartered banks, 49
  Euromarket, 5
  export financing, 403
  Inter-American Development Bank, 507
  international banking, 49–50
  project financing, 312
  restrictions on foreign bank entry, 740, 741,
    744
Canadian dollar, 338, 348
Cape Verde, Republic of, restrictions on foreign
  bank entry, 744
Capital inflow, 6
Capital outflow, 6
Cargo liners, definition, 202
Cargo tonnage, definition, 202–3
Caribbean Development Bank, 511
Caribbean Economic Community, 511
Caribbean Group for Cooperation in Economic
  Development, 474
Caribbean region
  IFC aid, 498
  Secretariat for the Task Force on Private-Sec-
    tor Activities, 498
Carlisle, Miles, 486 n
Carlozzi, Nicholas, 46 n
Casey, John Patrick, 674
Cash flow lending, 161

Cash transaction in foreign exchange market,
  322–24
  black market, 323
  commercial banks, 323
  spot market, 323
Catalog of World Bank Publications, 481
Cayman Islands
  Eurocurrency market center, 18, 223
  offshore shell branches, 19, 20, 560, 657
  U.S. branch banking, 788
Center for Monetary Studies in Latin America,
  780
Central African Empire, restrictions on foreign
  bank entry, 742, 744
Central America, 511
Central American Bank for Economic Integra-
  tion, 511
Central banks, 751
Certificate of inspection, 246
Certificate of weight, 246
Certified information systems auditor (CISA),
  713
Certified internal auditor (CIA), 713
Certified public accountant (CPA), 713
Chad, restrictions on foreign bank entry, 744
Chalk, John M., 252
Chartered bank auditor (CBA), 713
Chase Manhattan Bank, 138
Chile
  IFC aid, 498
  restrictions on foreign bank entry, 744
China, People's Republic of, 438, 439
  ideology, 93–94
  national cohesion, 92
  political geography, 96–97
  political system collapse, 88
  restrictions on foreign banks entry, 738, 740,
    744
CHIPS (Clearing House International Payments
  Systems), 128
Citibank, 36, 138
Class of gross income, determination of, 688
Clearing Banks Association, 68
Clearing House International Payments Sys-
  tems (CHIPS), 128
Cline, William R., 103 n
COFACE, 404
Co-financing
  Inter-American Development Bank, 508, 514
  World Bank program, 475–80
    documentation, 480
    export credits, 476
    loan agreements, 480
    official sources, 475–76
    operations, 478–79

Co-financing—*Cont.*
  World Bank program—*Cont.*
    opportunity identification, 477, 480
    private investors, 476–80
Collection drafts, 272–76
  checks for collection, 273–74
  clean draft, 274, 275
  days after date, 273
  days after sight, 273
  documentary collection, 275, 276, 279
  sight or usance, 272
Collection terms; *see* International collections
Colleran, Joseph A., 239
Colombia, restrictions on foreign bank entry, 740, 744
Comecon; *see* Council for Mutual Economic Assistance
Commercial Bank Guarantee Program, 407, 408, 409
Commercial draft, 272
Commercial invoice, 279
Commercial letters of credit; *see* Letters of credit
Commercial sales contracts, 168, 169
Commercial take or pay contract, 169
Commerzbank, 52, 63
Commission of the European Communities, 473
Committee on Banking Regulations and Supervisory Practices of Bank for International Settlements, 778
Commodity foreign exchange transaction, 324–25
  option contracts, 324
Common Market; *see* European Economic Community
Comparative advantage, principle of, 111
The Competitive Balance Between Domestic Foreign Banks, 794
Comptroller of the Currency, bank supervision, 766, 767, 769, 770–72, 776
Comptroller of the Currency Staff Paper, 790
Comptroller's Handbook for National Bank Examiners, 667
Comptroller's Manual for National Banks, 667
Confirmed letter of credit, 244
Confirming bank, 244
Congo, Peoples Republic of, restrictions on foreign banks entry, 740, 741, 742, 744
Consortia banking, 42–43
Consultative Group on International Agricultural Research (CGIAR), 474
Container ships, definition, 202
Contracts of affreightment (COA), 188
Controlled foreign corporations (CFAs), 703–4
  disposition, 704
  taxation of operations, 703–4

Convertible-loan stock, 304–5
Cooperative Financing Facility, 400
Corporate transaction in foreign exchange markets, 326–27
Correspondent account, 659–60
Correspondent banking, 41, 118, 127
  acceptances, 549–50
  advantages, 547
  correspondent accounts, 659–60
  credit-related relationships, 549–50
  definition, 548
  letters of credit, 549, 550
  money market credits, 550
  noncredit services, 550–52
    clearings, 551
    collections, 551
    documentation of terms, 551–52
    foreign exchange services, 551
    payments, 551
  terms and conditions statement, 552–56
  trade development and business referrals, 552
Costa Rica, restrictions on foreign bank entry, 740, 741, 744
Council for Mutual Economic Assistance (COMECON)
  banks, 50–51
  country risk evaluation, 78
  foreign exchange transaction control, 51
  international banking, 50–51
  membership, 50
Country exposure management systems, 772–74
  quantification and disaggregation, 773
Country Limitation Schedule, 419
  default claims, 427
Country risk, 77–79, 129, 140–44
  categories of, 140–43
  economic risk analysis
    basic premises, 104
    exchange-rate risk, 103
    external financial position, 106–7, 112–15
    quality of management assessment, 106, 109–12
    repayment on timely basis, 102
    resource base assessment, 106, 107–9
    sectoral risks, 103
    techniques, 103–6
  evaluation, 77
  external factors, 96–99
    political geography, 96
    traditional relations, 98–99
  insurance programs, 142
  internal-external factors interaction, 99–101

Country risk—*Cont.*
  internal factors, 88–95
    external threat, 94–95
    leadership ability, 94–95
    national cohesion, 90–92
    political geography, 91–92
    political system, 88–90
    religion, 93
    traditional values, 93–94
  political stability, 77, 85–88
  rating systems, 142
  sovereign and quasi-sovereign risks, 140
  supervisory evaluation, 769–72
Covered-interest arbitrage, 230
Crawling-peg exchange-rate systems, 360
Credit allocation, 27
Credit examination, 662
Crédit mixte, 403
Credit review, 662
Cross-currency funding, 646–47
Cross-national risk, 76–80
  country risk; *see* County risk
  legal jurisdiction, 80
  regulatory control, 79–80
Cuba
  Eximbank loan, 399
  foreign bank entry restrictions, 739, 744
Currency basket, 380; *see also* Multicurrency
  reserve assets
Currency exchange markets; *see* Major foreign
  exchange markets *and* Minor currency and
  special exchange markets
Currency management, 313–15
  advisory groups, 314
  hedging, 314
  merchant banks, 314
Cyprus, restrictions on foreign banks entry, 742,
  744
Czechoslovakia, restrictions on foreign banks
  entry, 739, 744

D

Danish krone, 351, 354
Daylight overdrafts, 126, 128
Deadweight-DWT, definition, 202
Deferrable income, 700
Definitive bond, 211
Denmark, restrictions on foreign bank entry,
  742, 745
Deposit interest rates requirements, 27,
  560 n
  Edge Act Corporations, 606
  Eurobanks, 27, 560 n
Depository Institutions Deregulatory Commit-
  tee, 811

Depository Institutions Deregulation and Monetary Control Act of 1980, 811
  definition, 751 n
  regulation, 751–52
Deregulation of banking, 810–11
Deutsche Bank, 52, 63
Deutsche mark
  interest rate subsidies on exports, 403
  lead currency, 337–38
  volume in U.S. foreign exchange market, 348
Deutsche mark denominated Eurobond, 12–13,
  209
Devaluation risk, 590–91
Developing countries
  aid to, 819
  debt surplus, 821–24
  exchange markets, 349
  export market for U.S., 819
  imports, 819
  lower income, 823
  middle income, 821, 823
Development Assistance Council of the OECD,
  473
Development Bank of Singapore (DBS), 63
Development Forum Business Edition, 481
Direct Investment Fund, 455
Discount Loan Program (Eximbank), 409
Displacement, definition, 203
Djibouti, Republic of, restrictions on foreign
  bank entry, 745
Dollar, U.S.
  currency risk cover, 379–80
  foreign exchange trading, 337
  interest rate subsidies on exports, 403
Dollar-denominated Eurobond, 12–13
Domestic International Sales Corporations
  (DISCs), 433
  dividends treated as foreign source income,
  689
  Edge Act Corporations, 607
  foreign tax credits, 680
Dominican Republic, restrictions on foreign
  banks entry, 740, 742, 745
Draft, 271
Drapalik, J. Frank, 656
Dresdner Bank, 52, 63
Dual banking system, 791
Dun's Marketing Identifiers, 627
Duseberg, Horst, 223
Dutch guilder, 348

E

Economic infrastructure loans, 137
Economic management
  development strategy, 110–11
  economic stabilization policies, 111–12

Economic management—*Cont.*
  exchange rate policy, 112
  fiscal policy, 111
  monetary policy, 111–12
  principles of, 109
  technical competence, 110
Economic Recovery Tax Act of 1981, 693–94, 705, 708
Economic risk analysis
  assessing quality of management process, 106, 109–12
  assessment of resource base, 106, 107–9
  basic premises, 104
  exchange-rate risk, 103
  external financial position, 116–17, 112–15
  sectoral risk, 103
  structured approach, 104, 105
Ecuador, restrictions on foreign bank entry, 740, 742, 745
Edge, Walter E., 603
Edge Act, 36–37
  expansion abroad of U.S. banks, 785
Edge Act Corporations, 40, 42, 527, 581
  agreement corporations, 607–11
  branching, 604, 608, 726
  capital restrictions, 607–8
  correspondent banking, 605
  equity investments, 606
  Federal Reserve regulations, 751, 755–56, 757–59
  flight capital deposits, 605
  foreign-owned banks, 792
  future prospects, 609
  history of, 603–4
  legal constraints, 724, 726, 730
  location and total assets, 609–11
  Regulation K, 603, 605, 606–7, 726, 730, 757–59, 810
  Senate Committee Report, 795
  subsidiaries, 608–9
  supervision, 766, 767
Egypt
  IFC aid, 498
  restrictions on foreign bank entry, 742, 745
80/20 corporations, 683
Einzig, Paul, 320
Eisenhower, Dwight, 506
El Salvador, restriction on foreign bank entry, 740, 745
Energy costs as challenge to banks, 803–4
Ensor, Richard, 104 n, 140 n
Entrepot financial centers, 3, 5, 10, 53
Epstein, Jose D., 503

Ethiopia
  foreign bank restrictions, 739, 745
  political stability, 92
Euro/Asia currency operations, 578
Eurobank, 20
  transfer of Eurocurrency funds, 21–22
Eurobonds, 7, 10, 11, 12–13, 15
  characteristics of, 12
  convertible, 306
  currency, 208
  definition, 204
  distinguished from Eurocurrency, 17
  distribution, 211
  Euro-deutsche mark sector of market, 209
  form, 211
  growth of market, 207
  history of, 205
  lead managers of internationally syndicated issues, 213
  legal covenants, 214
  listing, 210–11
  marketplace, 210
  maturity, 209–10
  merchant banks, 305–6
  new issues, 14
  payments, 211
  secondary markets, 12, 211
  size of market, 13
  size and timing of bond issues in Eurodollar sector, 208–9
  straight, 306
  total issues and placements by currency of denomination, 209
  type of instrument, 210
Eurocenter, 17–18
Euro-commercial paper market, 10, 13, 210
Eurocredit market, 218
  distinguished from international bond market, 218
Eurocurrency, 17, 20
  destruction of, 33
  transfer, 21
Eurocurrency CDs, 16
Eurocurrency liabilities, 727–28
Eurocurrency loans, 204
Eurocurrency markets, 10–11, 16–33
  attraction to banks, 28
  attraction to borrower, 27–28
  certificates of deposit, 16
  deposit insurance, 21
  deposits, 23–25
  destruction of Eurocurrencies, 33
  dollar deposits, 208
  Eurobanks, 20–21
  Euro-investments, 28–33

Eurocurrency markers—*Cont.*
  foreign currency loans, 225–36
    agreement, 232
    funding, 226–29
    long term, 233
    prepayment, 232–33
  freedom from controls, 25–27
  informality, 20
  interest-rate structure, 224–26
  international banks access to, 648
  interrelationship with foreign exchange mar-
    kets, 225–26
  major market center, 223–24
  operations, 233
  origins, 223, 647
  size of, 23, 24, 25
  time deposits, 16–17, 40–41
  transfer of funds, 21–22
  uses of, 229–32
Eurodollar deposit, 17
Eurodollar market
  definition, 647
  deposit creation, 17
  loans, 727
  origin of, 647
  reason for existence, 560 n
  Regulations D and Q, 647
Euro-Dutch guilder bond issues, 211
Euro-equity market, 13
Euro-investments, 28–33
  currency of, 28–29
  lending rates, 32
  profitability of loans, 32–33
  roll-overs, 33
  types of, 29–32
    corporate and governmental loans, 31
    loans to affiliates, 31
    London interbank offer rate, 29, 31
    investment in negotiable securities, 32
Euroloans, 32–33
Euromarkets, 5, 9, 17
  growth, 11
  laissez-faire nature, 9–10
  lending to governments and state entities,
    129–60
European currency unit (ECU), 383–85
  composition, 384
  dollar value, 383–84
  laundering function, 385
  marketability, 386
  partial remonetizing of gold, 385
  performance, 386
European Development Fund (EDF)
  activities, 533–34
  history, 533

European Development Fund—*Cont.*
  membership, 533
  sources of funds, 533
European Economic Community (EEC), 40,
    533, 780
European Investment Bank (EIB), 473
  activities, 532–33
  capital structure, 531
  history, 531
  membership, 531
  record of accomplishments, 532–33
  sources of funds, 531–32
European Monetary Operation Fund (EMCF),
    384–85
European Monetary System, 337
  European currency unit, 383–85, 386
  secondary European currencies, 351
European unit of account (EUA), 383, 384
Eurorate, 226
Eurosterling deposit, 17
Eurosterling rate, 225, 226
Evitt, H. E., 321
Exchange rate
  defined, 235
  floating, 331
  risks, 103
Eximbank; *see* Export-Import Bank of the
    United States
Exotic currencies, 338–39
Expatriates, U.S., taxation, 705–6
Export Banking Group, 780
Export credit
  definition, 312
  Inter-American Development Bank, 514
  merchant banks, 312–13
  project financing, 313
Export Credits Guarantee Department (ECGD)
    (U.K.), 180, 404
  activities, 542
    export insurance, 542
    guarantees for supplier credit financing,
      543–44
  history, 542
  record of accomplishments, 544
  sources of funds, 542
Export Development Corporation (EDC) (Can-
    ada), 541–42
  activities
    export credits insurance, 541
    foreign investment guarantee, 541
    loans, 541
    surety insurance, 541
  history, 541
  record of accomplishments, 541–42
  sources of funds, 54

Export financing, 164
Export-Import Bank of the United States (Exim-
    bank), 37, 46, 393
  bank-to-bank guarantee, 408, 409
  capital stock, 394
  competition with counterparts, 402
    interest rate subsidies, 403
    procedures for providing subsidies, 403
  commercial bank participation, 400, 407–
    8
  congressional and public relations, 400–
    402
  constraints and directives, 394
  direct credits
    application form, 405
    financial guarantee, 405
    loan disbursements, 405
    preliminary commitment, 406
    repayment, 404–5
  discount loans, 409
  exposure, 396
  future prospects, 409
  history, 398
  interest rates, 396
  loan disbursements, 405
  medium-term guarantee program, 400, 407–
    8
  operating earnings, 396
  organization, 394
  purpose, 394
  sources of funding, 395–96
  supplier credit programs, 400, 406–7
  World Bank, 401
Export-Import Bank Act of 1945, 394
Export-Import Bank of Japan (EIBJ)
  activities
    direct loans to foreign governments, banks
      and corporations, 539–40
    loans to domestic borrowers, 539
    terms and conditions, 540
  history, 538–39
  record of accomplishments, 540
  sources of funds, 539
Export letters of credit, 242–45
  discrepancies in documents, 246–48
  foreign currence, 248–51
Export subsidies
  competition among nations, 402–3
  credit war, 403–4
  procedures for providing, 403–4
Export trading companies, 763
Export Trading Act of 1982, 255, 261
Expropriation, 169–70
  OPIC insurance, 446–49
External debt service, ratio, 113–15

External financial position indicators, 106–7,
    112–15
  balance of payments trend, 112–13
  external debt burden, 112, 113–14
  level of international reserves, 112, 114
Eyre, Stephen C., 710

F

FEBA London Limited, 372
Feder, G., 103 n
Federal Deposit Insurance Corporation (FDIC),
    766, 770–71
Federal Financing Bank, 395–6
Federal Financial Institutions Examination
    Council (FFIEC), 776–77
Federal Reserve Act, 729, 754, 785
Federal Reserve Bank
  Eurocurrency markets, 223, 224
  imposition of Regulations Q, D and A, 223,
    224, 253
  International Banking Facilities, 224
Federal Reserve Bank of New York (FRB-NY),
    771
Federal Reserve System
  bank supervision, 766, 767
  export trading companies, 763
  international bank regulation
    agreement corporations, 751, 755
    bank holding companies, 756–61
    bankers' acceptances, 753–54
    Edge corporations, 751, 755–56
    foreign branches of members, 751, 752–53
    investments in foreign banks, 754–55
    joint ventures, 758
    member banks, 751–55
  international banking facilities, 761–62
  money supply growth, 809
  Regulation D; see Regulation D of Federal
    Reserve
  Regulation K; see Regulation K of Federal
    Reserve
  Regulation Q; see Regulation Q of Federal
    Reserve
  Regulation U, 731–32
  Regulation X, 732
Federally chartered (national) banks, 766
Fields, David M., 436 n
Fiji, restrictions on foreign bank entry, 745
Finance and Development, 481
Financial Accounting Standards Board (FASB),
    Statement No. 52, 665
"Financial supermarkets," 800, 812–13
Financial transactions in foreign exchange mar-
    kets, 327–28
Finland, restrictions on foreign bank entry, 740,
    742, 745

Finnish markka, 351
Floating exchange rates, 331
Floating Rate Notes (FRNs), 210
Foreign affiliates and subsidiaries
  equity investment options, 585–87
    branch, 586
    joint ventures, 586, 587
    portfolio investment, 586
    subsidiary, 585–87
  equity vehicle choices, 580–81
  managing foreign investment vehicle, 588–93
    audit function, 592
    budgeting, 589
    credit policy, 589, 590
    financial planning, 589
    foreign exchange and devaluation risk, 590–91
    liability management, 589–90
    management information system, 588–89
    operations manager, 591–92
    public relations program, 592–93
    staff operation, 591
  pre-investment considerations
    feasibility study, 582–85
    foreign exchange risk evaluation, 583–84
    foreign investment laws, 584
    investment option study, 584–85
    marketing plan, 585
    political risk analysis, 583
    strategic planning, 581–82
  restrictions on entry by foreign countries, 740–41
Foreign assistance, 819
Foreign Assistance Act of 1961, 436, 438, 439, 440
Foreign bank, defined, 755
Foreign Bank Act of 1978, 792
Foreign banking market, 7, 9
Foreign banks in international banking
  Brazil, 47–49
  Canada, 49–50
  COMECON countries, 50–51
  Germany, 51–53
  Hong Kong, 53–54
  Italy, 54–56
  Japan, 56–57, 618
  Korea, 57–59
  Kuwait, 59–61
  Mexico, 61–62
  Singapore, 62–64
  Spain, 64–65
  Switzerland, 65–67
  United Kingdom, 67–69
  Venezuela, 69–70
  U.S.; *see* Foreign banks in U.S.

Foreign banks in U.S., 785–99, 809
  agency form, 788–89
  branches, 789, 793
  capital levels, 790–91
  combined assets of agencies, branches and subsidiaries, 788
  competitive advantage, 791, 794
  early history, 785–86
  future prospects, 794, 799
  International Banking Act, 792
  interstate banking, 792
  motivation, 786
  operations in U.S., 790–91
  postwar expansion, 786–88
  Report of Committee on Banking, Housing and Urban Affairs, 794–98
  representative offices, 780
  subsidiaries, 789–90, 793
    banking, 789
    securities affiliates, 789
    New York Investment Companies, 789–90
Foreign bonds
  definition, 204, 214
  issues, 214
  markets, 6–7, 214
  Yankee bond market, 214–18
Foreign branch banking, 36, 37, 39, 41–42, 557–79
  activities
    acceptance of deposits, 568–69, 573
    advising foreign companies, 570–71
    credit assessment, 565–68
    economic reporting, 571
    foreign exchange trading, 562–63
    import financing, 563
    interbank placements, 562
    international money management, 570
    international term lending, 561–62
    loan syndication management, 570
    local lending, 563–65
    securities analysis, 571
    short-term financing of international trade, 563
    social and cultural awareness, 566–68
    traditional bank services, 569
  contrasted with representative office, 595–96
  correspondent banks relationship, 575–76
  Federal Reserve regulation, 751–55
  foreign banks in U.S., 789
  future prospects, 576–79
  location of branches, 788
  problems, 572–76
    country exposure, 575
    exchange rate risk, 575
    foreign government restrictions, 572, 735, 740, 741

Foreign branch banking—*Cont.*
  problems—*Cont.*
    obtaining adequate local currency, 573–74
    staffing, 574
  reasons for establishing, 557–61
    access to overseas money markets, 559
    exemption from Federal Reserve require-
      ments, 559–60
    profit, 558–59, 578–79
    provision of commercial bank services, 560
    services to local business, 558
  supervision, 766
Foreign branch translation
  net worth (balance sheet) method, 702
  profit and loss method, 701
Foreign Credit Insurance Association (FCIA),
    142, 400
  assignments, 426
  benefits, 411
    to commercial banks, 413
    financing assets, 412
    insurance protection, 412
    marketing tool, 412–13
  claims, 427
  consignment coverage, 425–26
  cooperation with Eximbank, 410–11
  discount loan, 409
  discretionary credit limit, 426
  history and organization, 410–11
  multibuyer policies, 414–21
    agricultural commodity program, 419
    approval of limits procedure, 420
    buyer credits, 418–19
    master policy, 415–18
    premium, 420
    prequalified foreign banks, 420
    short-term comprehensive, 418
    supplier credits, 419
    services policy, 421
    small business policy, 420–21
  nonacceptance, 424–25
  political risk only policy, 424
  preshipment or contracts coverage, 425
  products covered, 413–14
  risks covered, 413
  single buyer policies, 414, 415, 416
    medium-term single sale, 415, 416, 421,
      422
    medium-term repetitive, 415, 416, 421,
      422–23
    short-term-medium term, 415, 416, 421,
      423–24
  uplift provision, 426
Foreign Credit Restraint Program (FCRP), 6,
    11, 32, 38

Foreign currency letters of credit, 248–51
  exchange risk, 251
Foreign currency loans, 81–83
  costs, 232
  Eurocurrency loan agreement, 232
  exchange risk, 231
  funding, 226–29
    matching, 228, 233
    unmatched, 229
  long term, 233
  multicurrency borrowing, 82
  prepayment, 232–33
  uses of Eurocurrency market, 229–32
Foreign currency transaction, definition, 665
Foreign currency translation, 665–66
Foreign Direct Investment Program (FDIP),
    38, 39
Foreign Direct Investment Regulations, 11,
    38
Foreign direct investment in U.S., 809
Foreign dollar bond market; *see* Yankee bond
  market
Foreign equity market, 7
Foreign exchange
  accounting functions of foreign trading oper-
    ation, 663–65
  cash transaction, 322–24
  as commodity, 322
  commodity transaction, 324–25
  corporate transaction, 326–27
  definition, 320
  financial transaction, 327–28
  import-export transaction, 325
  international money broking; *see* Interna-
    tional money broking
  major markets; *see* Major foreign exchange
    markets
  managing risk; *see* Foreign exchange risk
    management
  minor markets; *see* Minor currency and spe-
    cial exchange markets
  multicurrency reserve assets; *see* Multicur-
    rency reserve assets
  origins of markets, 319–20
  professional arbitrage transaction, 328–29
  speculative transaction, 329–30
  supervision, 776–77
  trading operations, sequence of, 663–65
Foreign Exchange and Currency Deposit Brokers Association, 362, 367, 368, 372
Foreign exchange risk management; *see also*
  Multicurrency reserve assets
  bankruptcy of counterparty, 377–78
  external errors, 377
  internal errors, 377

Foreign exchange risk management—*Cont.*
  procedures and controls, 375–77
    daily trading summary, 376
    decision-making process, 376
    hedging currency exposure, 377
    internal control, 376–77
  trading policies, 373–75
    claims against a bankrupt, 375
    credit risks, 374, 375
    fluctuation in value of currency, 374
    size of positions taken, 374
Foreign government treatment of U.S. banking
  organizations; *see* Legal and regulatory
  constraints within other countries
Foreign Public Sector Credit Review Committee of Comptroller of the Currency, 770
Foreign subsidiary and affiliate banks, 42
Forward cover, 379
Forward exchange contracts, 665–66
  hedging contracts, 666
  speculative contracts, 666
Forward exchange market, 322–23, 379
  Asian currencies, 358–59
  commodity transactions, 524
  cover for currency risk, 379
    forward cover, 379
    multicurrency baskets, 380
    universal currency, 379–80
  developing countries, 349
  Latin American currencies, 360–61
  Scandinavian currencies, 354
  tied to interest movements, 328
Forward rate, 225
France
  credit control on foreign banks, 749
  export subsidies, 402–4
  major financial markets, 5
  restrictions on foreign banks entry, 745
Frank, Charles R., Jr., 103 n
Free trade, 805
Freighter, definition, 202
Frieden, Jeff, 133 n
Full-payout finance lease, 179
Full service banking facility in foreign country,
  658–59; *see also* Foreign branch banking
Functional currency, 665
Funds transfer
  corporate cash management considerations,
    293–98
    cash inflow/outflow perspective, 293–94
    foreign exchange implications, 297
    instructions for transfers, 294–95
    security-of-payment, 295–96
    timing, 295
    value-dating, 297

Funds transfer—*Cont.*
  cross-border transfers, 290, 291–93
    airmail transfer, 293
    basic mechanism, 291
    cable transfer, 293, 294
    methods of execution, 293
    methods of request, 293
  definition, 290
  intracompany, 291
  intracountry, 290, 291

G

Gabon, restrictions on foreign banks entry, 745
The Gambia, restrictions on foreign banks entry, 740, 741, 742, 745
Gap
  accounting report, 664
  definition, 649
  interest rate management, 649–51, 652, 653–
    55
  liquidity risk management, 651–55
  negative, 650
  positive, 651
  risks associated with, 649
Garcia, J. C., 104 n
Gas and chemical carriers, definition, 202
Gaynor, R. L., 788 n
General Accounting Office, investigation of
  Eximbank, 401
German Democratic Republic, restrictions on
  foreign bank entry
Germany, Federal Republic of
  financial market, 5
  foreign bond market, 7
  foreign sector of domestic market, 6
  international banking, 51–53
  national banks, 52
  restrictions on foreign bank entry, 745
Ghana, restrictions on foreign bank entry, 740,
  745
Ghandi, Indira, 89
Glass-Steagall Act, 732, 756, 763, 791, 793, 797,
  812
Glidden, W. B., 764 n
Gold, 385
  as component in multicurrency baskets, 388
  partial remonetization by European mone-
    tary system, 385
Government borrowing in international financial market, 129–60
  credit availability, 147–49
    indications of creditworthiness, 148
    market conditions, 149
  debt servicing problems, 152–54
    commodity price problems, 152–53
    inappropriate borrowing strategies, 153

Government borrowing in international financial market—*Cont.*
  debt servicing problems—*Cont.*
    oil price rises, 153–54
    political unrest, 153
  default record, 149, 151–60
    historical experience, 151–52
  differentiating between government borrowers, 144–47
    decentralized agencies, 145
    sovereign authority, 147
  dimensions of, 130–31
  multilateral institutions, 160
  political considerations, 147
  protection, 156–60
    guarantees and collateral, 156–60
  purposes of, 130–37
    general-purpose, 133, 135–36
    private with government guarantees, 133, 137
    program-related, 133, 135–36
    project-related, 133, 136–37
  risks in lending, 139–47
    categories of, 140–42
    insurance programs and ratings, 142–43
  sovereign immunity, 147, 154–55
  U.S. bank claims, 137–39, 149–50
Government intervention in business affairs, 825–26
Greece, restrictions on foreign bank entry, 742, 745
Greek drachma, 351, 355
Greene, James R., 129
Greenfield projects, 312, 444
Gross tons, definition, 203
Group of Thirty, 780
Groupe d'Contact, 780
Guarantees in international borrowing, 156–60
Guatemala, restrictions on foreign bank entry, 740, 745
Guinea, restrictions on foreign bank entry, 739, 745
Guinea-Bissau, restrictions on foreign bank entry, 745
Guttentag, Jack, 46 n
Guyana, restrictions on foreign bank entry, 739, 745

H

Haiti, restrictions on foreign bank entry, 740, 745
Haley, John C., 35
Hamilton, Alexander, 73
Hamlet, William F., 252

Hard currency, 277
Harfield, Henry, 257
Harland, Aidan H. F., 624
Hedging
  currency management, 314
  defined, 235
  foreign exchange transactions, 326, 332, 377
  tax treatment of subsidiary hedging exposure, 708
Hell-or-high-water contract, 169
Herring, Richard, 46 n
Herstatt, I. D., 121, 128
Hertzberg, Daniel, 484
History of Foreign Exchange, 320
Hitler, Adolf, 98
Honduras, restrictions on foreign bank entry, 745
Hong Kong
  banks, 54
  entrepot, 53
  financial market, 5
  restrictions on foreign bank entry, 738, 745
  supervision of banking, 780
Hong Kong Association of Banks, 53
Hong Kong dollar, 338, 357, 358
Houpt, James V., 42 n
Human resources, 107
Hume, David, 825
Hungary, restrictions on foreign bank entry, 740, 745
Hurley, C. Keefe, Jr., 751
Hutton, Clark H., III, 723

I

IBA; *see* International Banking Act
IBFs; *see* International banking facilities
Iceland, restrictions on foreign bank entry, 740, 742, 745
IDA; *see* International Development Association
IFC; *see* International Finance Corporation
IFC/General Policy, 501
IFC Preliminary Project Information Required, 501
IMF; *see* International Monetary Fund
IMF special drawing rights (SDR), 350–51
Import-export transactions in foreign exchange market, 325
  open-account basis payment, 326
Import letters of credit, 240–42
  discrepancies in documents, 248
  foreign currency, 248–51
  lending controls, 662–63
"In lieu" foreign taxes, 679

Income taxes; *see also* U.S. taxation of international banking operations
  accrual or cash basis recording, 666
  credit/deduction treatment of foreign taxes,
    666
  domestic financial reporting, 666
Incremental capital output ratio (ICOR),
  111
India, restrictions on foreign bank entry, 740,
  745
Indian rupee, 357, 359
Indonesia
  debt-serving problems, 153
  restrictions on foreign bank entry, 740,
    745
  U.S. bank claims against, 138
Industrial Bank of Japan, 56
Industrial Reconstruction Institute (Italy), 54
Insurance certificate, 280–81
Inter-Agency Consultive Board, 473
Inter-American Conferences, 504
Interagency Country Exposure Review Committee (ICERC), 771–72
Inter-American Development Bank
  co-financing activities, 508
    complementary financing, 514–15
    export credit, 514
    joint financing, 514
    parallel financing, 514
  conciliating members' views in decision making, 510
  development role, 510–11
  institutional features, 510
  lending activities, 515–19
    achievements, 517–19
    agricultural and rural development, 517–
      18
    energy resource development, 517
    industrial and mining sector, 518
    procurement, 516–17
    project supervision, 516
    transportation and communications systems, 518
  levels of authority, 509–10
  membership, 503, 506–8
  origins, 504–6
  outlook for the 80s
    energy, 519
    food production, 520
    nonfuel minerals, 520
    social concerns, 520
  purpose and function, 507–8
  resources
    capital, 511
    Fund for Special Operations, 513
    Social Progress Trust Fund, 513

Inter-American Development Bank—*Cont.*
  resources—*Cont.*
    two-way benefits, 515
    Venezuelan Trust Fund, 513
  subscribed capital, 503
  World Bank cooperation, 473
Interbank credit, 117
Interbank exchange market, 338, 339
Interbank Euroloans, 29, 31
Interbank placement, 562
Interbank redepositing, 562
Interest Equalization Tax (IET), 6, 11, 38, 39,
  206
Interest income taxable by U.S.
  80/20 corporations, 683
  foreign corporations in business with U.S.,
    683–84
  International Finance Subsidiaries, 683
  residence of obligor, 681–82
  withholding tax, 682–83
Interest rate requirements
  Edge Act corporations rules, 606
  Eurobanks, 27, 560 n
  Regulation Q., 27
Interest spreads on international loans, 807
Internal control system; *see also* Accounting
    and internal control
  compared to internal auditing, 711
  definition, 658
Internal organization and personnel, 615
  bank-within-a-bank concept, 616
  choosing appropriate structure, 619
  functional integrated structure, 618–19
  staffing
    benefits, 621
    characteristics required for officers, 620
    nonofficer staff, 620–21
    offshore posting, 621
    rotation of personnel, 622
    training function, 622
Internal Revenue Code, taxation of international banking operations, 676–709
International Arrangement on Guidelines for
    Officially Supported Export Credits, 403
International Association of Foreign Exchange
    Traders, 334
International Bank of Economic Cooperation,
  50
International bank lending, growth of, 817
International bank regulation, 751–63
International Bank for Reconstruction and Development; *see* World Bank
International banker, 73
  risks, 74
  role, 73

International Banking
    foreign banks; *see* Foreign banks in international banking
    United State; *see* United States in international banking
International Banking Act of 1978, 734, 754, 756, 760, 788, 789, 792, 793, 794
    foreign and domestic bank competition in U.S., 810
International Banking Facilities (IBFs), 224, 724–25
    depository institutions operating, 752
    Federal Reserve regulation, 761–62
    full-service banking facility, 658
    legal constraints, 724–25, 726, 728, 730
    limited offshore facility, 657
    money market dispersal, 577–78
    Regulations D and Q, 724, 761
International bonds
    capital markets, 205
    definition, 204
    Eurobonds; *see* Eurobonds
    foreign bonds; *see* Foreign bonds
    issues by type or nationality of borrower, 207, 212
International Chamber of Commerce, 284
International collections
    collection drafts, 272–76
    collection instructions for the bank
        in case of dishonor, 276
        in case of need, 278–79
        discount or interest, 277
        hold for arrival of merchandise, 277
        legal action, 279
        payment of bank fees, 276
        principal/agent relationship, 279
        protest instructions, 277
        provisional deposit, 277
        remittance of proceeds, 276
    drafts for negotiation or purchase, 283–84
        uniform rules for collections, 284
    exporters' options for payment, 270–72
    process for exporters, 281–83
    process for importers, 284–85
    shipping documents
        bill of lading, 279–80
        commercial invoice, 279
        consular invoice, 281
        customs invoice, 281
        inspection certificate, 281
        insurance certification policy, 280–81
International Credit Insurance Association, 411
International Development Association (IDA), 462; *see also* World Bank
    Articles of Agreement, 466
    assets, 466

International Development Association—*Cont.*
    establishment, 466
    membership, 466
International Finance Corporation (IFC), 462
    Articles of Agreement, 467, 487
    authority, 491
    capital-markets programs, 498
    catalytic role, 496–97
    contacting IFC, 501–2
    distinctions between IFC and World Bank, 463–64
    diversifying into natural resources and service industries, 500
    establishment, 466–67
    financial resources, 488
    future trends, 499–501
    investment policies, 492–96
    loans to international banks, 486
    objectives, 487–88
    offices, 492
    organization, 490
    projects and investments, 489–90
    size of commercial banks involved with IFC, 499–500
    staff, 491–92
    syndications department, 50
    technical assistance and financial services, 497–99
International Finance Subsidiaries, 683
International financial market, 3
    foreign banking market, 7–8
    foreign bond market, 6–7
    foreign equity market, 7
    foreign sector of domestic markets, 5–6
    government borrowing in; *see* Government borrowing in international financial market
International Financial Statistics series, 481
International flow of funds, 644–46
International funding
    domestic and offshore currency markets, 647–48
    flow of funds, 644–46
    liquidity management; *see* Liquidity management
    multicurrency funding, 646–47
International Investment Bank (IIB), 50
International Labor Office (ILO), 473
International leasing
    accessing medium term financing, 177
    bank-affiliated companies, 175–76
        joint venture agreements, 176
        leasing subsidiaries, 175–76
        money-center banks, 175
    bareboat charters, 182
    competition, 182

International leasing—*Cont.*
  definition, 173
  evolution of industry, 174
  exchange rate variations, 178
  indexation methods, 177
  inflationary economies, 177
  lease-financing contract forms, 179–81
  linking lease financing to export subsidies,
    180
  participants, 174
  regulations, 176–77, 182
    tax and accounting, 177
  residual value insurance, 181
  size of individual transactions, 178–79
  training personnel, 178
  uses, 174
  variable (floating rate) lease agreement, 177–
    78
  vendor relationship, 181–82
International Monetary Fund (IMF), 76, 114,
    160, 462
  Annual Report on Exchange Arrangements
    and Exchange Restrictions, 350–51, 381–
    83
  Articles of Agreement, 350
  Central Banking Department, 780
  developing countries, 823–24
  establishment, 463
  petrodollar recycling, 815
  purpose of, 463
  special drawing rights, 350–51, 381–83
International Monetary Market (IMM), 332,
    335–36, 345
International money broking
  bank-to-bank dealing, 363–64
  bank dealer operations, 365–66
  broker, 362
    qualifications, 368
  central clearing houses, 372
  control and supervision in London, 368
  dealer and broker interaction, 365–66
  direct dealing, 371–72
  ethical practices, 371
  history, 362–63
  introducing new banks to international mar-
    ket, 370
  long-term prospects, 371
  offices, 364
    continental brokers, 369–70
    London, 368–69
    overseas, 369
  operations in foreign exchange and interna-
    tional currency markets, 363–64
  Reuters proposed system, 372
  settlement procedures for errors, 366–68
International Telecommunications Union, 473

International term lending, 561–62
Interstate banking by foreign banks, 792
Investment management, 308–10
  institutional ownership of equities, 309
  merchant bankers, 308–10
  offshore funds, 310
Iran
  political geography, 91–92
  restrictions on foreign bank entry, 745
Iraq, restrictions on foreign bank entry, 739,
    745
Ireland, restrictions on foreign bank entry,
    745
Irish pound, 351, 355–56
Irrevocable letter of credit (ILC), 419
Islamic Development Bank, 534–36
  activities, 534
  history, 534
  member countries' subscriptions, 535
  membership, 534
  record of accomplishments, 535
  sources of funds, 534
  voting power of member countries, 535
Israel, restrictions on foreign bank entry, 745
Issuing bank (letters of credit), 239, 240, 241,
    242, 243, 245
Issuing Houses Association, 299
Italian lira, 338, 348
Italy
  central bank, 56
  international banking, 54–56
  largest banks, 55
  restrictions on foreign bank entry, 745
  state ownership, 55
Ivory Coast, restrictions on foreign bank entry,
    745

J

Jacobsen, Daniel T., 710
Jamaica, restrictions on foreign bank entry, 745
Janssen, Richard F., 460 n, 480 n, 487 n
Japan, 5
  bank financial statements, 123–24
  banks listed, 57
  branch banking, 557
  foreign banks, 787
  foreign exchange control, 57
  history of banking, 56
  Samurai bonds, 214
Japanese yen, 337, 338, 348
  interest rate subsidies on exports, 403
Johnson, Earl I., 348
Johnson (Debt Default) Act, 732
Joint Standing Committee (London market),
    368

Joint ventures; *see also* Foreign affiliates and subsidiaries
contrasted with representative office, 596
definition, 580–81
investment option, 585–88
Jordan, Robert L., 436 n
Jordan, restrictions on foreign bank entry, 740, 745
Jordanian dinar, 356
Just, R., 103 n

K

Kammert, James L., 436, 462, 486, 502 n
Keenan, Robert, 410
Kennett, W. A., 779
Kenya, restrictions on foreign banks entry, 745
Khoury, Sarkis J., 36 n
King, Colbert L., 462
Korea, Republic of
banking system, 57–58
banks, listed, 58
foreign banks, 59
IFC aid, 498
lease financing, 181
resources, 107
restrictions on foreign banks entry, 740, 741, 742, 745
Korsvik, William J., 734
Korth, Christopher M., 3, 16, 38, 802 n
Kubaryah, Roger M., 348
Kubitschek, Juscelino, 506
Kuwait, 59–61
central bank, 60
history of modern banking system, 59
investment banks, 61
restrictions on foreign bank entry, 745
specialized banks, 60–61
Kuwait dinar, 338, 356, 357

L

Lange, John D., Jr., 402 n, 409 n
Laos, restrictions on foreign banks, 739, 745
Latin America
economic integration, 511–12
Inter-American Development Bank; *see* Inter-American Development Bank
OAS, 505
Latin American currencies, 339
Latin American Export Bank (BLADEX), 514
Latin American Free Trade Association, 511
Latin American Integration Association, 511
Latin dollar market, 7
LDCs; *see* Developing countries *and* Less developed countries
Lead currency, 337
Lead managing bank, 219–20

Leasing; *see* International leasing
Lebanon, restrictions on foreign bank entry, 745
Legal and regulatory constraints within other countries
congressional report, 734
entry restrictions, 735–41
branches, 735, 740, 741
defense of, 738
high capitalization requirements, 737
reciprocity, 737
representative offices, 735, 739, 740
operating restraints, 741–46, 748–50
asset/capital ratios, 748
credit controls, 748–49
differential advantages, 749–50
economic and balance of payments policy measures, 749
explicitly discriminatory regulations, 743, 748
limits on size of loans to individual borrowers, 748
purposes, 741–43
unintended differential effects, 748–49
Legal constraints on international banking within U.S., 723
affecting activities of bankers
acquisition of margin stock, 731
guarantees, 730–31
Johnson Act, 732
lending limits, 729–30
letters of credit, 731
Regulation U, 731
Regulation X, 732
affecting costs to banks
interest on deposits, 728–29
local taxes, 726
reserve requirements, 726–28
Section 23A of the Federal Reserve Act, 729
withholding taxes and foreign tax credits, 725–26
credit transaction enforcement difficulties, 723
Edge Act Corporations, 724, 726
International Banking Facilities, 724–25, 726, 728, 730
specifications of business conduct, 723
Legal covenants, 214
Lender of last resort, 765
Lesotho, restrictions on foreign bank entry, 745
Less-developed countries (LDCs); *see also* Developing countries
borrowing in international financial markets, 130–33
commodity-price problems, 152–53

Less-developed countries—*Cont.*
  creditworthiness indicators, 148
  loan risks, 143–44
  market conditions, 149
  U.S. bank claims, 131, 137–38, 149–50
Letters of credit
  acceptance financing, 254
  accounting and internal control, 661
  amendments, 245–46
  confirmed, 244
  correspondent banks, 549, 550
  discrepancies in documents, 246
  export, 242–45, 246–48, 248–51
  foreign currency, 248–51
  functions, 239–40
  import, 240–42, 248–51
  international collections, 271
  irrevocable, 419
  legal constraints on international banking, 731
  unconfirmed, 244
Leveraged lease, 180
Liberia, restrictions on foreign bank entry, 746
LIBOR; *see* London interbank offer rate
Libya, restrictions on foreign banks, 739, 746
Limited offshore facility, 657–57; *see also* Foreign branch banking
Line of credit, 125
Liners, defined, 201–2
Lipman, Charles F., 436 n, 437 n, 455 n
Lipson, Leonard A., 674
Liquidity management, 644
  definition, 648
  interest note management under gapping, 649–51, 652, 653–55
  liability management, 649
  managing liquidity risk under gapping, 651–55
  matching assets and liability maturities, 649–50, 651
  risks associated with gapping, 649
Loan stocks, 304–5
Loans classified by degree of risk
  National Bank Examiners rating
    current, 714
    doubtful, 714
    loss, 714
    OLEM (Other Loans Especially Mentioned), 714
    substandard, 714
Local currency financing, 814
London
  Eurocenter, 18
  financial market, 3–4
London Dollar Certificate of Deposit, 210
London Interbank Bid Rate (LIBID), 221

London interbank offer rate (LIBOR), 29, 31, 177, 210, 220, 221, 515, 727–28
London Stock Exchange, listing, 303–4
Long-Term Credit Bank of Japan, 56
Luxembourg
  entrepot market, 5
  restrictions on foreign bank entry, 746

M

McCormick, Linda W., 606 n
McFadden Act, 603, 609, 762, 791, 793, 797–98, 811
McNamara, Robert T., 403 n
Madagascar, restrictions on foreign banking, 739, 746
Major foreign exchange markets
  currencies traded, 337–39
  location, 339
  market participants
    banks, 332, 333–34
    brokers, 332
    central banks, 332, 335
    commercial customers, 332–33
    International Monetary Market, 332, 335–36
  mechanics of trading, 336–37
  operations
    European markets, 343–45
    Hong Kong markets, 341–43
    New York market, 345–47
    Singapore market, 341–43
    Tokyo market, 339–41
  timing, 339
Malawi, restrictions on foreign bank entry, 746
Malaysia, restrictions on foreign bank entry, 740, 742, 746
Malaysian ringitt, 357, 359
Mali, restrictions on foreign bank entry, 746
Malta, restrictions on foreign bank entry, 740, 742, 746
Management information systems (MIS), 588–89
Mandich, Donald R., 373
A Manual of Foreign Exchange, 321
Manufacturers Hanover Trust Company, 138
Mao Zedong, 93
Margin stock, 731
Market makers in Eurobonds, 211
Marketing international services, 624
  account plans, 629, 630–31
    account defined, 629
    coordination or sales meetings, 631–32
    form for writing, 630–31
  advertising, 637–38
  credit extension, 624, 625
  international departmental plans, 625

Marketing international services—*Cont.*
  marketing course for domestic officers, 632,
      639–42
  marketing plan, 625
    customer analysis, 626–27
    development, 626
    information, 627
    matrix approach, 628–29
    profitability, 628
    service analysis, 627
  sales training, 638–39
  selling techniques, personal level, 635–36
  territorial offices, 626, 627, 631
  trip organization, 633–34
    follow-up sheet, 634
    maintenance trip, 633
    overseas sales territory, 633
Maroni, Yves, 103 n
Marsh, Donald R., 557
Marshall, John, 154
Marshall Plan, 436, 437
Martin-Burns Letters, 761 n
Matched funding of foreign currency loans, 228
Matching assets and liability maturities, 649–50,
    651
Mathis, F. John, 36 n, 37 n
Maturity distribution of claims of U.S. banks,
    149–50
Mauritania, restrictions on foreign bank entry,
    746
Mauritius, restrictions on foreign bank entry,
    746
Mayo, Alice L., 103 n
Meehan, Arthur H., 319
Merchant banking
  acceptance market, 301–2
  advisory work, 313
  commercial banking, 300–302
    range and type of credit facilities, 300–301
    competition with international banks, 300–
        302
  corporate finance services, 302–8
    debt issues in U.K., 304–5
    equity issues in U.K., 303
    international capital markets, 305–6
    new issue business, 303–8
    obtaining listing on London Stock Ex-
        change, 303–4
  currency management, 313–15
  definition, 299
  export credit, 312–13
  future prospects, 315
  general financial advice, 308
  investment management, 308–10
  loan syndication management, 570
  mergers and aquisitions, 307–8

Merchant banking—*Cont.*
  origins, 299–300
  project finance, 310–13
    commercial, 310–11
    risk categories, 311
    syndication of funding, 302
  subsidiaries established in conjunction with
      branches, 560–61
Mergers and acquisitions
  merchant banks, 307–8
  regulations governing, 308
Mexican peso, 359, 360
Mexico
  debt restructuring, 102
  Euromarket borrowing, 133
  international banking, 61–62
  largest commercial banks, 61
Minor currencies and special exchange markets,
    348
  Asian currencies, 357–59
  characteristics of, 349
  convertibility, 349
  developing countries, 349
  European secondary currencies, 351, 354–56
  exchange rate arrangements and policies, 350
  Latin American currencies, 359–61
  Mideast and African currencies, 356–57
Miossi, Alfred F., 800
Monetary authority of Singapore (MAS), 64
Monetary Control Act of 1980, 751 n
Money
  definition, 321
  foreign exchanges, 321–22
Monitor visual-display information service, 372
Monthly Operational Summary (World Bank),
    481
Moody's bond ratings, 215
Moon, Phillip G., 117
Morgan Guaranty Bank, 138
Morocco, restrictions on foreign bank entry,
    740, 741, 742, 746
Mozambique, restrictions on foreign bank en-
    try, 746
Multicurrency baskets, 380, 388
Multicurrency borrowing, 82
Multicurrency reserve assets
  commodity components, 388
  currency risk cover
    forward cover, 379
    use of single universal currency, 379
  European currency unit, 383–85
  evolution of currency baskets, 380–81
  gold component, 388
  mechanics of multicurrency business, 387
  regional currency baskets, 388
  special drawing rights, 381–83

Multinational Banking Division of Comptroller
of the Currency, 767, 769
Multinational corporation, 326
foreign exchange transactions, 326
Muncie, Peter G., 462

N

Nacional Financiera, 62
Nalen, Craig A., 436 n
Nassau
Eurocurrency market center, 223
offshore shell branches, 19, 20, 560
National Advisory Council on International
Monetary and Financial Policies, 398
National Bank Examiner, 714
National Bank Surveillance System of Comp-
troller of the Currency, 776
National banks (federally chartered banks), 766
National Banking Act, 789
Nationalization of projects, 170
Naveja, Albert F., 547
Near banks, 49
Nee, Frank W., 428
Negative pledge covenant, 214
Nelson, M. C., 656
Nepal, restrictions on foreign banking, 739
Net tonnage, definition, 203
Net worth (balance sheet) method of foreign
bank translation, 702
Netherlands
domestic financial market, 5
restrictions on foreign bank entry, 742, 746
Netherlands Antilles, restrictions on foreign
bank entry, 739, 740, 746
New Community Instrument (NCI) for borrow-
ing and lending, 532
New York Banking Law, 730
New York Clearing House Interbank Payments
System (CHIPS), 297
New York foreign exchange market, 320
New York Investment Companies, 789–90,
792–93
New Zealand, restrictions on foreign bank en-
try, 740, 746
New Zealand dollar, 357, 359
Newman, Denis, 204
Nicaragua, restrictions on foreign bank entry,
746
Nippon Fudosan Bank, 56
Niger, restrictions on foreign bank entry, 740,
746
Nigeria
IFC aid, 498
restrictions on foreign bank entry, 740, 741,
742, 746
U.S. bank claims, 138

Norway, restrictions on foreign bank entry, 740,
746
Norwegian krone, 351, 354
Nostro account, 659

O

OAS; *see* Organization of American States
O'Brien, Richard, 129 n, 140 n
OBOs (ore/bulk/oil carriers), definition, 202
OECD; *see* Organization for Economic Cooper-
ation and Development
OECD countries, loan risks, 140–41, 143
Organization for Economic Cooperation and
Development, 402, 473, 480
Offshore financial center, 4
Offshore markets, 17
Offshore posting, 621
Offshore shell branch, 560
Oman, restrictions on foreign bank entry, 740,
742, 746
Omnibus Banking Bill, 810–12
OPEC; *see* Organization of Petroleum Export-
ing Countries
Open-account basis of payment, 326
Opening bank, 239
Operación Panamericana, 506
OPIC; *see* Overseas Private Investment Corpo-
ration
Opportunity loss, 142
Optimum intervention, principle of, 109
Ore/bulk/oil carriers (OBOs), definition, 202
Organization of American States (OAS), 504,
505, 507
Organization of Petroleum Exporting Coun-
tries (OPEC)
foreign exchange centers, 356
funds in international banking, 44–45
loaning in Euromarket, 130
oil embargo, 97
World Bank, 475
Orion Bank, 42
Orsich, A. D., 379
Outright rate, defined, 236
Overseas equity vehicle, 580; *see also* Foreign
affiliates and subsidiaries
Overseas Private Investment Corporation
(OPIC), 142, 170
application procedure, 454
basic insurance coverage
expropriation, 446–47
inconvertibility, 446
war, revolution, insurrection, 447–48
basic insurance definitions
co-insurance, 445
eligible investors, 443
investment form, 445

Overseas Private Investment Corporation—
  Cont.
  basic insurance definitions—Cont.
    less developed countries, 444
    nature of coverage, 445–46
    new investments, 444
    reinsurance, 445
  contacting OPIC, 459–60
  contractors' coverage, 450–51
  direct financing or loan guaranties, 437, 439
  finance programs, 455–59
    adequate financing plan, 456–57
    economic soundness, 455–56
    eligible enterprises, 456, 459
    local development contribution, 456
    OPIC guaranty, 459
    prohibited enterprises, 456
    project ownership, 455–59
    size of OPIC participation, 457
  foreign affiliates and subsidiaries, 583
  future trends, 460–61
  insurance against risks, 437, 439
  interference with operations (IWO) insur-
    ance, 453
  investment-mission tours, 461
  loss from currency inconvertibility, 437
  mineral projects, 451–52
  oil and gas projects, 452
  operations and resources, 438
  organization and policies, 440–42
  program costs, 448–50
  reserves in relation to outstandings, 440
  staff, 441–42

                         P

Page, Diane, 785 n
Pakistan, restrictions on foreign banks entry,
  741, 746
Panama
  banking supervision, 780
  restrictions on foreign bank entry, 746
Papua New Guinea, restrictions on foreign bank
  entry, 741, 746
Paraguay, restrictions on foreign bank entry,
  746
Parrish, Karl M., 173
Porter, J. Charles, 606
Pension funds
  merchant banks, 308–9
  United Kingdom, 308–10
People's Republic of China; see China, People's
  Republic of
Performance Analysis Reports of Comptroller
  of the Currency, 776
Personnel; see Internal organization and per-
  sonnel

Peru
  commodity price problems, 152–53
  restrictions on foreign bank entry, 740, 746
  U.S. bank claims against, 138
Petrodollar recycling, 815–16
Pflug, David L. Jr., 73
Philippines
  restrictions on foreign bank entry, 740, 742,
    746
  U.S. bank claims, 138
Pinsky, Neil, 36 n
Placing, 304
Poland
  restrictions on foreign bank entry, 740, 746
  restructuring of external debt obligations, 102
Political risk, 85–88
  forecasting instability, 85–87
  project financing, 169–70
Political risk insurance, 170
  Foreign Credit Insurance Association cover-
    age, 424
Portugal
  IFC financing for SPI, 498–99
  restrictions on foreign bank entry, 740, 746
Portuguese escudo, 351, 355
Porzencanski, Arturo P., 802 n, 803 n
Position sheet, 664
Position taking, 333
"Postoffice box" branch, 560
Prebisch, Raul, 505
Private Export Funding Corporation (PEFCO),
  400, 405
  borrower method of approach, 431
  commitment fee, 430
  deferred pricing, 430
    fixing dates, 430
  disbursement procedure, 431–32
  fixed interest rate, 430
  funding, 433
  general characteristics, 429–30
  lending operations, 429–32
  loan agreement, 431
  loan purchase programs, 432
  origin, 429
  purpose, 428
  relationship with Eximbank, 428, 429, 431,
    432, 433
  statement of financial condition, 434
  statement of income and retained earnings,
    435
Private Investment Company for Asia (PICA)
  activities, 537
  history, 536–37
  record of accomplishments, 537–38
  shareholders, 537
  sources of funds, 537

Privity, 404
Professional arbitrage transaction in foreign exchange market, 328
Profit and loss method of foreign branch translation, 70
Project advisor, 171–72
Project cycle, 470
Project financing
  advisor role, 171–72
  bank specialization, 814
  bank-sponsor relationship, 165
  definition, 161
  determination of translation rate, 162, 163
  estimation of future cash flow, 162, 163
  evaluation of project, 162–63
  export financing, 164, 312
  Greenfield projects, 312
  institutional debt placement, 165
  merchant banks, 310–13
  nature of project, 161–62
  risk analysis, 164–71
  supply
    completion risk, 164, 166–67, 168
    currency or foreign exchange risk, 170–71
    market risk, 168–69
    political risk, 169–70
    technology risk, 167–68
    supply risk, 164, 166–67
Protectionism, 820
Public Law 480, 38

Q–R

Quasi-sovereign borrowers, 140
Qatar, restrictions on foreign bank entry, 740, 742, 746
Readily marketable staple, 255
Reconstruction and economic development loans, 135–36
Reconstruction Finance Corporation, 399
Redistribution of wealth, 819
Refrigerated vessels, definition, 202
Regional Development Agencies, 522–44
  African Development Bank, 525–28
  African Development Fund, 529–30
  Asian Development Bank, 525–28
  European Development Fund, 533–34
  European Investment Bank, 531–33
  Export Credits Guarantee Department, 542–44
  Export Development Corporation, 541–42
  Export-Import Bank of Japan, 538–40
  Islamic Development Bank, 534–36
  Private Investment Company for Asia, 536–38
Regional representative office, 600
Regulation A of the Federal Reserve, 252

Regulation D of the Federal Reserve, 39–40, 223, 647, 726–27, 761
Regulation K of the Federal Reserve, 40
  Edge Act Corporation rules, 603, 605, 757–59, 810
  branches, 606, 726
  lending limits, 730
  organization, 606
  ownership, 606
  permissable activities in U.S., 606–7
  rate limitations, 606
  reserve requirements, 606
  export trading companies, 763
Regulation Q of Federal Reserve, 647, 728–29, 761
  deposit interest rates, 27, 223
  inducement to overseas banking, 39
Regulation U of Federal Reserve, 731–32
Regulation X of Federal Reserve, 732
Reimbursement banks, 548–49
Report of the Committee on Banking, Housing and Urban Affairs, United States Senate, 794–98
Report to Congress on Foreign Government Treatment of U.S. Commercial Banking Organizations, 734
Report of Examination (U.S. bank examiners), 769, 772, 773, 774
Representative office, 580
  activities and responsibilities, 600
  business development strategy, 599–600
  capital intensive, 598
  correspondent relations, 597
  conforming to strategy of parent bank, 596
  contrasted with full branch, 595–96
  credit policy issues, 596
  definition, 594
  foreign bank entry restrictions, 735, 739
  foreign banks in U.S., 790
  interpretive evaluation, 601–2
  joint ventures contrasted, 596
  level of business development activity, 597
  opportunity cost analysis of establishing price, 598–99
  reasons for choice as foreign investment vehicle, 594–95
  regional office, 600
  regulatory environment analysis, 596
  selection of personnel, 601
  subsidiaries contrasted, 596
Reserve requirements
  Eurocurrency deposits, 27, 560 n
  Regulation D, 726–27
Resident of the United States, definition, 681
Residual value insurance, 181
Resler, Don A., 290

Resource base of country, 107–9
 financial, 108
 human, 107–8
 natural, 107
Reuters Money Dealing Services, 336, 372
Riley, David H., 362
Robert Morris Associates, 122
Rockefeller, David, 817
Rolk, Th. Lundberg, 486 n
Roll-overs, 33
Romania, restrictions on foreign bank entry, 746
Rome Convention, 533
Roosevelt, Franklin D., 399, 504
Rotberg, Eugene H., 483 n
Rwanda, restrictions on foreign bank entry, 747

S

Saini, K., 103 n
Samurai bonds, 214
Saudi Arabia, restrictions on foreign bank entry, 740, 741, 747
Saudi Arabian Monetary Agency (SAMA), 356–57
Saudi Arabian real, 338, 356–57
Scandinavian currencies, 338, 351, 354
Schirano, Louis G., 161
Schooner Exchange v. McFadden, 154
Section 23A of Federal Reserve Act, 729
Sectoral risks, 103
Securities and Exchange Commission (SEC), 7
Securities affiliates, 789
Security underwriting; see Eurobonds, Foreign bonds and International bonds
Seligman, Barnard, 35
Senegal, restrictions on foreign bank entry, 747
Seychelles, restrictions on foreign bank entry, 747
Shell branches, 20, 762
Ship financing; see Tanker and Shipping loans
Ship loan documentation, 196–97, 200–201
Shipping industry; see also Tanker and shipping loans
 defined, 184
 development, 184–85
 size of ship, 185
 specialization, 184–85
Sierra Leone, restrictions on foreign bank entry, 747
Sight draft, 272
Silk, Leonard, 483 n
Singapore dollar, 338, 357, 358
Singapore
 banks, 63
 entrepot activities, 5, 63

Singapore—Cont.
 international banking, 62–64
 restrictions on foreign bank entry, 740, 742, 747
Singapore interbank offer rate (SIBOR), 31
Single investor tax lease, 179–80
Societe Financiere Europeinne, 42
Solomon Islands, restrictions on foreign bank entry, 740, 747
Somalia, restrictions on foreign bank entry, 739, 747
Sommers, James B., 785
Soss, Neal M., 785 n
Soussa, Antoine G., 290 n
South Africa, restrictions on foreign bank entry, 740, 742, 747
South African rand, 357
South Korea
 borrowing in international financial markets, 133
 U.S. bank claims, 138
Sovereign immunity, 147, 154–56
 waivers of, 156
Sovereign risks, 140
Soviet Union; see USSR
Spain
 international banking, 64–65
 major banks, 64–64
 restrictions on foreign bank entry, 747
Spanish peseta, 351, 354–55
Special drawing right (SDR), 350–51, 381–83
 certificate of deposit, 386–87
 IMF as significant borrower, 387
 marketability, 386–87
 performance, 385–86
 role in international monetary system, 382–83
Speculative transaction in foreign exchange market, 329–30
Spot exchange rate, 225, 226
 defined, 236
Spot foreign exchange market, 322–23
Sri Lanka, restrictions on foreign bank entry, 747
Standard & Poor's bond ratings, 215
Stand-by letter of credit, 731
State chartered banks, supervision, 766
Statement of Principle and Standards for Internal Auditing in the Banking Industry (Bank Administration Institute), 711–12
Sterling, British, 337, 348
Stone, E. C., 603
Straddle, 327
Straight consignment, 280
Straight-loan stock, 304
Stuhldreher, Thomas J., 788 n, 790 n

Subsidiaries
  credit facilities, 125–27
  definition, 580
  foreign banks in U.S., 789–90
Sudan, restrictions on foreign bank entry, 747
Superintendent of Banking, New York, 766
Supervision of international banking, 764–81
  bank dealing policies, 777
  coordination of supervisors, 778–80
  costs, 768
  country exposure management risk, 772–74
    legal lending limits, 774
  evaluating country risk, 769–72
  foreign exchange, 776–77
  funds management, 774–76
    asset/liability committee, 775
    forward planning, 775
    information system, 775
    liquidity, 775
  government policy support, 777–78
  interbank deposit activity, 776–77
  international supervisory agenda, 780–81
  internationalization of domestic supervision,
    766
  multilateral supervision, 777–81
  on-site inspections, 765, 766, 767–69, 775–76
  regional centers, 768
  remote examinations, 765, 767–69, 775–76
  Report of Examination, 769
  support for lenders of last resort, 765
  state-chartered banks, 766
Surinam, restrictions on foreign bank entry,
  739, 740, 741, 747
Sutin, S. E., 104 n, 580
Swap, 327, 328
Swap rate, 225, 230
  calculating interest rate, 234–35
  defined, 236
Swap transaction, defined, 236
Swaziland, restrictions on foreign bank entry,
  747
Sweden, restrictions on foreign bank entry, 740,
  747
Swedish krona, 351, 354
Swiss banking code of 1934, 66
Swiss franc, 337–38, 348
Swiss National Bank, 67
Switzerland
  banks, 66
  cash foreign exchange market, 323
  entrepot market, 5
  foreign bond market, 7
  foreign sector of domestic market, 6
  history as financial center, 65–66
  international banking, 66–67
  restrictions on foreign bank entry, 747

Syndicated Eurocurrency credits, 204, 218
  advantages, 221
  instruments, 219
    revolving-credit facility, 219
    term loan, 219
  loan management, 570
  market development, 218–19
  pricing, 220–21
    agents fee, 221
    commitment fees, 220–21
    front-end fees, 220–21
    interest computation on loan, 220
    prepayment penalty, 221
  profitability, 221
  syndication, 219–20
    covenants, 220
    default terms, 220
    lead bank, 219–20
    timetable, 220
Syndicated loans; *see* Syndicated Eurocurrency
  credits
Syria, restrictions on foreign bank entry, 740,
  747

T

Taiwan
  management of economy, 106
  restrictions on foreign bank entry, 747
Take-or-pay contract, 169
Takeovers, 307–8
Tanker, definition, 185, 202
Tanker market, 185–88
Tanker and shipping loans
  documentation, 196, 200–201
  loan analysis, 188–93
    company analysis, 189–92
    financial analysis, 192
    fleet analysis, 192
    introduction, 189
    project analysis, 192–93
    sources of repayment, 188–89
  outline of terms, 194–96, 197–200
    account, 200
    amortization, 194, 197
    amount, 194, 197
    assignment of insurance, 196
    assignment of proceeds, 195
    availability, 196, 200
    borrower, 194, 197
    commitment fee, 194, 197
    drawdown, 194, 197
    events of default, 196, 199–200
    expenses, 196, 200
    final maturity, 194–95, 197
    governing law, 196, 200
    guarantees of payment, 195–96